W9-ATY-421

The
Collapse
of the
Tokugawa
Bakufu
1862–1868

UNIVERSITY OF HAWAII

PRESS  HONOLULU

THE
COLLAPSE
OF THE
TOKUGAWA
BAKUFU
1862–1868

Conrad Totman

Printed in the United States of America

02   01   00   99   98   97   7   6   5   4   3

Publication of this book was supported in part by a grant
from the National Endowment for the Humanities.

Library of Congress Cataloging in Publication Data

Totman, Conrad D
  The collapse of the Tokugawa bakufu, 1862–1868.

  Bibliography: p.
  Includes index.
  1. Japan—History—Restoration, 1853–1870.
2. Japan—Politics and government—1600–1868. I. Title
DS881.3.T63   1980   952'.025   79–22094

ISBN 0–8248–0614–X

For HAROLD CARY
whose love and respect for history were inspiring

and SHANNON MCCUNE
whose enthusiasm for Asian studies was contagious

Contents

Maps

Acknowledgments

The goodwill and generous cooperation of many people underlie this book. Most especially it would have been quite impossible for me to carry out the necessary research without access to ''Dai Nihon ishin shiryō kōhon'' (Manuscript of historical materials on the restoration) at the Historiographical Institute of Tokyo University. I am grateful that the institute's governing officials approved my two requests to spend academic years doing research there despite the fact that during my visit in 1968–1969 the university was seriously disrupted by student unrest and during 1972–1973 the institute was dislocated by a basic remodeling and expansion of its facilities.

Of the many institute members whose cooperation enabled me to use the manuscript, I am particularly indebted to several people. Professor (emeritus) Konishi Shirō, former head of the Restoration Section of the institute, oversaw arrangements for both my visits. Professor Konishi and his successor Professor Yamaguchi Keiji and research staff members of the Restoration Section furnished study facilities and friendship during my second visit and helped in the laborious task of bringing hundreds of manuscript volumes out of storage for my perusal. Professor Kanai Madoka bore the troublesome burden of arranging both visits and was a constant source of kindly encouragement. Mr. Kawamura Shinichirō and his staff in the institute's Library Section graciously helped me obtain manuscript volumes and other materials during my first visit, and Mr. Kawamura transcribed materials for my later use. The staff of the Tokyo University Central Library also helped me greatly by providing a most pleasant study room and the substantial reference materials and books of the Library Collection.

In the United States I profited from books in the collections of the libraries of Chicago, Harvard, and Northwestern Universities. I thank my wife Michiko for typing the final manuscript, my children for bearing with their father's monomania all these years, and several relatives for tending the children while Michiko typed.

I was supported in Japan in 1968–1969 by a Fulbright-Hays research grant and a fellowship from the Social Science Research Council and in 1972–1973 by a Senior Fellowship from the National Endowment for the Humanities. Northwestern University readily granted me leaves of absence, and the university's Research Committee furnished research funds upon request.

All these and others I thank, but the shortcomings of the study are my own personal burden.

Introduction

Just after New Year's of 1868 the army of the Tokugawa bakufu was pounded to pieces in four days of hard fighting. With the defeat of that army, the bakufu fell, and the political system that had given Japan some two hundred fifty years of peace, the Great Peace as it was called, came to an end.

Let us state why directly. The regime fell because the imperialist intrusion of the mid-nineteenth century presented it with a set of political tasks that it could handle neither then nor at any time in its past.

This is not to deny the truism that this regime, like any regime, would have fallen eventually. But it is to say that the alternative paths to collapse were foreclosed by the imperialist intrusion. That was so because the foreign intrusion was many faceted and hit many critical points in the Tokugawa political order. Not only did it create unprecedented demands on the system, moreover, but it also created and sustained a politically unnatural coalition of anti-bakufu forces long enough for that coalition to devise a political strategy sufficient to its purpose of toppling the regime.

To assert that it was the foreign intrusion rather than some alternative difficulty which destroyed the regime in no way lessens the fundamental character of the 1860s crisis. Systems function within contexts. The disjunction between the Tokugawa system and the context of the 1860s was monumental. In consequence the crisis was as deep and wide-ranging as any regime is ever likely to face. The era was one of systemic crisis. The alternatives Japanese society faced were harsh: radical transformation, chaos, or colonial subordination.

To interpret the regime's collapse in this way is to say, moreover, that the regime did not collapse because various long-range socioeconomic trends undermined it. It is also to say, however, that it fell for reasons far more complicated than any failure to satisfy the demands of far-sighted patriots.

It is to say that the multidimensional political struggles of the sixties can be more fruitfully viewed as a bipolar contest between the bakufu and an unstable coalition of critics than as a triangular contest between conservatives, reformers, and radicals. That means, too, that it is more useful to observe the way hostile elements worked together against the regime than to focus on their own internal discord. And that means that the continuity during the sixties of the anti-bakufu movement, rather than a putative shift from radicalism to moderation during 1864 or so, is the more significant consideration.

And lastly, to emphasize the systemic character of the 1860s crisis is to say that in a final analysis the hostility between the bakufu and its critics must be seen in conjunction with a fundamental process of change. In that process key elements on both sides of the conflict moved from positions of basic support for the old order to abandonment of that order and a quest for a new unified and change-oriented system. This widely shared redefinition of purpose was important because it made possible the elite's regrouping once the political stalemate of the sixties had been broken.

In examining the relationship of the regime and its critics, we face a double task. We must explain both why the regime as a political structure collapsed and why its leaders did not successfully use their leading positions as a basis upon which to construct a reorganized polity. Even if one concedes at the outset that the old regime could not survive unchanged, it does not necessarily follow that the required changes could be made only by outsiders. In some ways established leaders should have found it relatively easier to make such changes, while in other ways their position was a distinct liability. To explain the failure of the regime both as a structure and as a political leadership requires examination of how the foreign threat of the 1860s related to both basic structural characteristics of the polity and changes the polity had undergone during the two preceding centuries. This examination is necessary because to deny that those changes destroyed the regime is not to say that they had no effect on the way it expired. Surely they did have an effect.

This formulation of the problem requires us to look carefully at the policies and performance of bakufu leaders and to examine with care a number of wider considerations: the process of diplomatic relations; the character of domestic opposition; the administrative condition of the regime; its financial situation; the condition of groups associated with the bakufu; and the situation of society at large. Casting the net thus widely is demanding. But it will prove worthwhile because it will make clear the breadth and depth of the 1860s crisis and help disabuse us of any tendency to treat the agonies of the age as trivial and the disagreements among men as merely expressions of incompetence, perverse stubbornness, or unreasonable ambition. A world was at stake, and those who realized it cared very much.

The Tokugawa political system, called by scholars the *bakuhan* (*bakufu* plus *han*) system, has been described at length elsewhere. It suffices here to recapitulate briefly the salient aspects. In the name of the emperor and his court in Kyoto the hereditary Tokugawa shogun at his great Chiyoda castle in Edo officially kept the peace. As part of his function he enforced from about 1640 until 1853 an established foreign policy of isolation, or *sakoku* as it came to be called. Domestically he was expected to keep the peace among those hereditary lords, the daimyo, whose 250 or so administratively autonomous baronial domains or *han* occupied some three-quarters of the country. The shogun claimed that his government, the bakufu, had the right to inspect their domains and enforce a few basic regulations among them. But his suzerain role found its main expression in the established hostage system, called *sankin kōtai*, which kept a daimyo's immediate family permanently at Edo and the daimyo himself there half the time. In addition to supervising the daimyo, the bakufu administered its own domain, which sprawled across central Japan and occupied about a fourth of the country.

To implement his national peacekeeping duties and to supervise his domain, the shogun maintained an elaborate, highly bureaucratized government. Normally the highest officials in it were the *rōjū* or senior councillors, of whom about five cooperated in handling affairs together, usually under the real leadership of one of their number, the *rōjū shuseki* or chief councillor. These senior councillors were usually selected from among the forty-odd men who constituted the middle stratum of *fudai* or vassal daimyo. The vassal daimyo were a group of modestly enfeoffed lords totaling some 150 families. Their formal identity as vassals of the Tokugawa house dated mostly from the late sixteenth century, before Ieyasu the Tokugawa founder established his claim to a national hegemonial role.

Subordinate to the senior council were a number of other officials also drawn from the ranks of vassal daimyo, most notably the Kyoto deputy (*shoshidai*), keeper of Osaka castle (*jōdai*), junior councillors (*wakadoshiyori*), and superintendents of shrines and temples (*jisha bugyō*).

Most administrative offices were staffed by lesser vassals of the shogun, the liege vassals (variously called *kikushi*, *jikisan*, or *hatamoto* and *gokenin*). These included the crucial administrators who served various inspectoral functions (as *ōmetsuke* and *metsuke*), who administered Edo and other cities (as *machi bugyō*), who handled financial affairs (as *kanjō bugyō*), and who administered (as *daikan* and *gundai*) the shogun's domains, the source of the regime's regular land-tax income. Then in the regime's last years it was mostly liege vassals who handled the details of foreign affairs (as *gaikoku bugyō* and magistrates of ports such as Kanagawa and Nagasaki) and commanded the regime's new military forces (as *rikugun bugyō*, *kaigun bugyō*, and so forth).

To identify political office only begins preparing one to explain political process. Much of process has to do with the interaction of those in office and those not. In the *bakuhan* system the greatest daimyo were not permitted to participate in bakufu decision-making—regardless of whether the great lord were himself a related *(shinpan)* daimyo, that is, head of a branch of the Tokugawa family itself, or an outside *(tozama)* daimyo, that is, an unrelated baron who because of his ancestry was not considered a true and loyal vassal of the shogun. This exclusion of major related and outside daimyo from bakufu office was preserved intact until 1862 despite the fact that the foreign intrusion gave them a new and most potent reason (and excuse) for seeking to influence the councils of national government. Indeed, one of several crucial themes in the politics of the regime's final years was the tension that existed between those lords seeking to influence affairs and established bakufu leaders seeking to keep the barons effectively under control.

The line of cleavage between established leaders and the great barons was a major expression of a general pattern of cleavage built into this hereditary system—the cleavage between those whose status gave them the right to institutional positions empowering them to confront the perceived problems of their lives and those whose status denied them such a right. This phenomenon is sometimes conceptualized as a class cleavage between ''upper'' and ''lower'' samurai. It was actually a much more complex and relativistic tension in which the identity of those above and those below depended on the problems at hand. Within the daimyo and Tokugawa domains themselves the most basic underlying tension was between those vassals who had and those who lacked access to politically significant administrative and advisory positions. Those who had such access could help decide policies dealing with problems of economic hardship, military unpreparedness, corruption, or abuse of power. Those without such access could do little more than observe, memorialize, or act outside the system.

At the national level the basic tension was between those who had and had not a legitimate means to address broad national issues such as foreign policy or general domestic policy. Whereas great daimyo and their advisors were nominally and functionally ''upper'' samurai in their own domains, they were at the national level functionally ''lower'' samurai even though these same great daimyo held some of the highest formal ranks in the national status hierarchy. Functionally their position was analogous to that of the richly heritaged imperial court nobles at Kyoto, whose high status failed to give them a legitimate role in real politics, and to that of the minor vassals and *rōnin*, or masterless samurai, whose exclusion from national affairs was even more complete.

What distinguished these three types from one another nationally was not so much the modest difference in their degree of ongoing influence in national affairs as the alternative means available to them for trying to gain access to power. Courtiers could use their high status for political leverage; daimyo, their high status and autonomous power; minor vassals and *rōnin*, their numbers and their capacity to plot and threaten in the relative safety of their obscurity. The interaction of these three groups as they sought to influence national affairs was another important theme in the politics of the regime's final years.

When major political problems came to be perceived as national in scope during the 1860s, this hereditary cleavage between ''ins'' and ''outs'' was one of great importance to the bakufu because it gave rise to an ad hoc coalition of ''outs'' that was formidable in its dimensions. Nevertheless during most of the Tokugawa period the basis of divisions in operational politics lay elsewhere. Operational divisions existed among the more restricted numbers of those whose rank enabled them to participate in the political process within the *han* or bakufu. Since there were always more people eligible for most offices than there were offices available, and electoral parties were not the mechanism by which access to office was regulated, some other means had to exist to determine who would get into office and thereby secure opportunity to make policy and enjoy perquisites. The operational political system was one of clique or factional interaction in which groups of eligible men worked together to secure office and govern or, when others were in office, to unseat those others. The specific content of factional politics at any moment depended upon a host of particular considerations such as the issues of the moment, the personalities involved, the traditions of the domain, and the larger contemporary political scene. But in any event three basic facts—of problems that required attention, of more eligible officeholders than significant offices, and of a great deal of contact between bakufu and *han* because of *sankin kōtai*—sustained a lively political system with a high degree of interplay between its parts. Another noteworthy theme of the

1860s was that habitual factional politics grew less and less workable as new issues, conditions, and groups confounded affairs, and that situation eventually drove power holders to seek new techniques of governance.

The *bakuhan* system was thus characterized by a complex set of factional, status, personal, and institutional tensions that had both local and national implications. Paralleling these were tensions, or contradictions if you will, at the level of political ideology. As scholars of Tokugawa political thought have pointed out,[1] by the nineteenth century the ideology of the samurai had come to embrace a number of ideals that could not always be mutually reconciled in a persuasive manner—respect for the hereditary status system and for meritorious performance of duty; for the Tokugawa political order and for the imperial institution; for an agrarian-based economy and for fiscal adequacy; for effective management of the barbarian and for preservation of the honor of Japan, however Japan was defined. During the 1860s these ideological tensions also emerged as important factors in the political process.

During the Tokugawa period these tensions of political structure, process, and value were kept under reasonable control by the institutional system, the resulting distribution of interests and balance of powers, the major ethical norms of the *bakuhan* system, and the exclusion of disequilibrating forces from abroad. As a result the polity did not break up and slip into civil turmoil. On the other hand these tensions did reinforce the institutional autonomy of the domains and· the pluralism of political thought, and hence inhibited those in control from willfully pursuing any policy of unification. Consequently the *bakuhan* system and the Great Peace endured from about 1600 until well into the nineteenth century despite profound socioeconomic changes in Tokugawa society. During the 1860s, however, all that changed, and central themes we shall encounter in this study of Tokugawa collapse are the tension between bakufu leaders and great lords, the interaction of lords, nobles, and politically active minor samurai, the malfunctioning of factional politics, and the internal tensions of political ideology.

These facets of political discord were supplemented in the years 1862–1868 by administrative difficulties—notably in terms of finances, military reform, and civil administrative efficiency. And beyond them, the whole process of political disruption during the sixties had broader and deeper ramifications directly affecting the elemental well-being of the public in general and the prospects for Japan as an independent society.

To give order to the chaotic politics of the 1860s and thus facilitate examination of these several analytical considerations, it will help to use a synthetic approach to the political process. We may postulate basic strategies by which bakufu leaders could address these several facets of political crisis as they manifested themselves. If one assumes a solidly unified system to be essential for handling the challenges of the decade, bakufu leaders could cope only by a monumental program of radical institutional and ideological reorganization. Such a task would have required the strongest sort of national political leadership, and in the *bakuhan* system there were essentially two possible ways for bakufu officials to create such a leadership.

One way would be for a bakufu leader to incorporate the greatest daimyo and their followers into bakufu ruling councils and gradually to shift their commitments from domain to central regime, thus inducing them to approve a policy erosive of local autonomy and lend their support to its implementation. The weaknesses in this ''inclusivistic'' policy would be that, first, the incorporation of great daimyo and their advisors in the central regime might invite resistance from those groups who thereby would lose their traditional functions and prerogatives in the bakufu. And second, the great daimyo thus incorporated in the regime might be unable to overcome the pressure from their own vassals to protect their domains. Moreover, as the process of unification generated disputes of one sort or another, the great lords might also find in retreat to domanial position a political lever of such great use as to thwart the basic centralizing trend.

The other way would be for a bakufu leader to found his enterprise on the land and manpower resources of the Tokugawa regime's traditional core groups: the populace of the Tokugawa domains, liege vassals and their subordinate forces, and the vassal and certain lesser related daimyo. A leader so empowered could then presumably use that force to destroy the autonomy of the great daimyo piecemeal or by abrupt dissolution of their domanial arrangements. Then with the rival power broken, he would move to integrate their manpower and land into his new political order. The difficulty in such an ''exclusivistic'' enterprise lay in two major considerations. First, unless those daimyo who would be expected to cooperate in the process of domanial dissolution could envision a future more attractive to themselves than that of a petty feudal baron, they might refuse to support the project. Indeed, under pressure from their own vassals and their own particularistic loyalty they might actively oppose it. This eventuality could leave a core utterly inadequate to its task. But even with all core elements cooperating, the central power so mobilized was not clearly greater than the excluded domanial force and might generate a countercoalition capable of thwarting such an enterprise or even destroying the regime.

In the fifteen years of crisis culminating in 1868 one can see both solutions being tried and both failing. In general terms one can say inclusivistic tendencies predominated in the decade before 1863. However, the exclusivistic strategy predominated in the later years as domestic tensions grew more acute and national reconciliation increasingly difficult. This study opens with an extended inquiry into the Bunkyū reform, the bakufu's last and greatest effort at inclusivistic governance. It then follows the bakufu through three agonizing years of confusion, uncertainty, and misguided strategy. The study closes with an extended examination of the content and collapse of the Keiō reform, the last and greatest Tokugawa effort at exclusivistic governance.

The Tokugawa *crise de régime* may be said to have begun with the arrival of Matthew C. Perry's fleet in 1853. It was not until 1862, however, that the domestic political situation entered a state of profound disorientation from which the bakufu never recovered. The preceding nine years can accordingly be summed up very quickly.

Abe Masahiro, chief councillor and bakufu leader during the Perry crisis, successfully avoided war by capitulating to the American demands. Following Perry's departure, Abe held his administration together by outmaneuvering critics of his foreign policy. It was the finest performance in a career marked by repeated displays of political skill, and it enabled Abe to launch the Ansei reform. That modest program focused on military strengthening, most notably the construction of a series of fortifications in Edo bay. The reform made some progress despite a host of obstacles but lost impetus after two years. The obstacles that thwarted reform also exhausted Abe, and before his untimely death in 1857 he had turned most affairs of government over to Hotta Masayoshi.

Hotta proved as politically inept as Abe had been astute. He faced greater problems than Abe because he had to confront new and more severe demands presented by the American Townsend Harris. Harris used threats of British force as liberally as Perry had used threats of American force to extort privileges of trade, travel, and consular residence in Japan. The privileges of travel and residence were sharply opposed by most political elements in Japan, and Hotta's acquiescence in them during 1857 led him into a domestic dispute that rapidly acquired major proportions.

An escalating sense of ethnic danger in face of the imperialist onslaught prompted important figures, notably key daimyo such as Tokugawa Nariaki of Mito, and also lesser samurai to lose whatever confidence they had in Hotta's government and to try to replace it with a stronger leadership in which their voices could be heard.[2] The opportunity for such a replacement arose when it became apparent the ailing shogun would beget no successor. By early 1858 a severe political contest had arisen over who was to be named shogunal heir, and Hotta thoroughly bungled the awkward problem of resolving the coincidental matters of Harris' treaty demands and the shogunal succession. In his effort to resolve matters Hotta tried and failed to secure court approval of his policy, and that failure badly discredited him within the bakufu. In consequence he fell from power when people close to the shogun deftly maneuvered to name Ii Naosuke *tairō* or great councillor.

Ii proved to be a very different sort of ruler from either Abe or Hotta. Abe had been a practitioner of integrative, consensual politics, skillfully securing the positive support of influential great lords, regular bakufu administrators, shogunal intimates, and advisory vassal daimyo. Hotta was Abe's picked successor, inherited his ruling group, and tried to govern in his manner. However, he failed. He lost the support of great daimyo, failed to retain the goodwill of shogunal intimates, discouraged the administrators, and alienated the advisory vassal daimyo.

Ii was a practitioner of exclusivistic rather than inclusivistic governance. He had no interest in consensual politics, believing instead in authoritarian rule by top bakufu leaders. He browbeat administrative subordinates into silence, alienated most vassal daimyo who tried to work with him, and drove great lords into resentful inactivity. He cowed the court, which Abe had cultivated and by which Hotta had been confounded. Ii devoted his greatest effort, however, to a long-drawn-out vendetta with Nariaki of Mito. It was a destructive, misguided feud and finally goaded Mito men into assassinating him in early 1860.

Some months before his death Ii had found in Andō Nobuyuki a talented assistant whom he promoted to the senior council, and after Ii's death Andō took charge of affairs. By then Ii's policy of authoritarian rule had moved, except in regard to Mito, beyond the early stages of punishment called the Ansei purge to a stage of bakufu-led reconciliation. Andō chose to adhere to a somewhat relaxed version of that conciliatory policy of Ii's later months. He continued cultivating the goodwill of the court, mainly through the plan to marry the new young shogun Iemochi to the imperial princess Kazunomiya. He tried to soften great daimyo antipathy toward the bakufu and attempted to rebuild Edo-Mito ties. Finally he attempted to pacify dissident samurai who resented Ii's diplomatic and foreign trade connections by taking a less permissive attitude toward the foreigners. The most impressive expression of his stronger foreign policy was a mission to Europe that persuaded the British and French governments to delay for a few years the opening to trade of four additional ports and cities.

For well over a year Andō's regime enjoyed relative tranquillity, largely because of the lingering influence of Ii's forceful rule. During the latter half of 1861, however, great daimyo began to return to the political arena from which Ii had so abruptly ejected them. The first initiative was taken by Chōshū, and Andō welcomed it. He saw in it an opportunity to strengthen bakufu ties with both court and Chōshū in a manner that would commit them to acceptance of bakufu supremacy and bakufu foreign policy.

Even as that encouraging development was taking place, however, other dissident samurai were carrying on a general campaign of terror, and one group developed a plot to assassinate Andō. In early 1862 the plot was implemented and Andō was severely wounded. He did not die, but he spent months recuperating, and so that attack removed from command another bakufu leader as effectively as Abe's death, Hotta's disgrace, or Ii's murder had done.

The loss of Andō's leadership coincided with the return to political activity of other great daimyo and court nobles. In the context of domestic violence these factors conjoined to precipitate the Bunkyū reform, a period of political change and disorganization unprecedented in Tokugawa history. It marked the end of customary bakufu leadership of the polity and the beginning of fundamental political crisis. And so it is the point of departure for this study.

The year 1862 can thus be seen as a watershed year in Japanese history. Until that year the bakufu was the primary polity in Japan, exercising in fact as well as in theory control over all major aspects of the Japanese political process. From 1862 until its fall in 1868, however, the bakufu was only a regional polity trying to recover control of politics in the whole country but actually controlling affairs in only the central part of Japan, sometimes even excluding Kyoto.

These years of crisis have been viewed in many ways by historians, but in English works the currently preferred approach is that outlined by Yoshio Sakata and John W. Hall in an article published in 1956 and more recently used by William Beasley in his study, *The Meiji Restoration*.[3] In that approach attention is focused upon the activities of dissident groups, and the years 1860–1864 are treated as a phase of extremist violence that failed to unhorse the regime and so gave way during 1865–1867 to a phase of organized *han*-based preparation for a coup d'état—a coup that came off successfully in 1868.

Because this present study focuses upon the bakufu, it uses a different chronology, and it concentrates upon some aspects and events that receive scant attention in other studies. Conversely it glosses over complexities in the politics of other groups by referring to "Satsuma policy," "court pressure," "dissident samurai," "angry commoners," "foreign diplomats," and so forth, and it reduces the heroes of other works to nameless men of Satsuma, Chōshū, the court, and so on. The overall rhythm of developments that emerges from a study thus focused can be outlined easily enough.

In terms of bakufu failure, the years 1862–1867 subdivide most usefully in this way. During the months from 62/5 to 63/3,[4] the months of the Bunkyū reform, the bakufu experienced a political crisis so traumatic it nearly collapsed entirely. It did not quite die, however, and from about 63/4 until 66/6, some three years, the regime pursued an ultimately unsuccessful effort at conservative reconstruction. During the first year and a half of that conservative effort the bakufu enjoyed rather surprising success in the face of dilemma after dilemma. But from about the end of 1864 through the middle of 1866 it steadily lost ground in a string of political reversals culminating in a disastrous military defeat at the hands of Chōshū.

That defeat in the fighting of the second expedition to punish Chōshū, or what I call the Summer War, discredited what remained of the conservative orientation and so made 1866 a second watershed year in the history of the sixties. Whereas 1862 marked the end of the bakufu as the primary polity in Japan, 1866 marked the end of the old regime more broadly conceived. Dreams of preserving the *bakuhan* system were abandoned. After that the political issue which remained to be settled in Japan was whether men from the bakufu or men from great domains or elsewhere would lead in the nation's attempt at unification and modernization.

From 66/8 to 67/10, then, a somewhat changed bakufu leadership pursuing a very different strategy undertook to reorganize the regime and restore it to primacy. By the latter half of 1867 the undertaking had acquired a profoundly radical character and was clearly intending to move Japan into that new era of national unification and modernization. But at year's end the western rivals rebelled, and the bakufu rapidly disintegrated in the face of that last great insurrection.

This outline of the years 1862–1868 also suggests the questions that need to be answered. Concerning the Bunkyū reform, the basic questions are these: What was it all about and why did it work out as it did? Concerning the conservative reaffirmation of the next three years, we wish to learn what was achieved and why it failed. About the Summer War of 1866, we seek to understand why it was so traumatic and its lessons so decisive. As for the final year of radical reorganization, we ask what was being attempted, what was achieved, and why the effort ultimately failed.

Then, answering those questions, we shall be in a better position to address the larger question of why the bakufu and its leaders fell as they did when they did and to consider, in closing, the general character of the Tokugawa *crise de régime*.

Part
ONE

THE LOSS OF PRIMACY

CHAPTER 1

The Bunkyū Reform I
Months of Achievement
1862/4–9

THE PRECIPITATION OF CHANGES: 62/3–6

POLITICAL REFORM: 62/7–INT. 8

ADMINISTRATIVE, FISCAL, AND MILITARY REFORM:
62/5–12
1. *Administrative and Fiscal Reform*
2. *Military Reform*
3. *Problems in Military Reform*

The Tokugawa bakufu's time of troubles began early in 1862. The regime came under pressure from the court, certain daimyo, and *shishi* or samurai activists to change policies and initiate reforms. That pressure surged upward as the year progressed, and by the autumn it had given rise to the Bunkyū reform, a renovation effort led by one of the most active daimyo, Matsudaira Shungaku of Fukui. Part of the reform was a series of political changes that within six months reduced the bakufu to a secondary role in national politics. Part of it, however, was a set of administrative, fiscal, and military changes which, if sustained long enough, would eventually permit a reversal of that political decline. The Bunkyū reform was thus at once a long step toward ultimate disaster for the regime and a short step toward avoidance of that disaster.

The reform had aspects strongly reminiscent of Abe Masahiro's Ansei reform, but it also had substantial differences. Whereas Abe's reform had been a direct response to foreign danger, the Bunkyū reform was mainly a response to severe domestic difficulties. Like the Ansei reform, it was inclusivistic in orientation, but it was more radical in content and embraced a number of seemingly contradictory elements. It was marked by far greater internal conflict and proceeded in an environment of much greater confusion, tension, and spreading demoralization. The most complex reforms involved administrative and military reorganization, but the critical reforms were the political ones dealing with bakufu-court and bakufu-daimyo relations. They were the critical ones because their outcome directly determined the outcome of the others.

It was the political reforms that most interested Shungaku. During the months 62/3–6 he worked his way into a leading role at Edo, and during the next three months he overcame internal opposition to his program. In consequence by 62/9 he had rammed through the bakufu most of the reforms and policy orientations he sought. By then, too, lesser officials were making substantial progress in carrying out administrative and military reforms.

During 62/9, however, political affairs deteriorated seriously, precipitating a new and more divisive period. When the divisions were seemingly healed by year's end, policy still appeared to serve Shungaku's purposes, but it actually had taken on a much more ambiguous character. By 63/3 developments had led to Shungaku's defeat, and that outcome in turn permitted other reforms to peter out. In consequence the Bunkyū reform came to an inglorious end, having done more to weaken both the bakufu and the larger polity than to strengthen either.

THE PRECIPITATION OF CHANGES: 62/3–6

Affairs at Edo were quiet during the weeks immediately after Andō Nobuyuki's injury on 62/1/15. Reports of great *han* and court maneuvering shortly began to reach bakufu leaders, however, and these initiated five months of escalating external pressure and bakufu accommodation, in which proliferating demands by court, daimyo, and *shishi* produced commensurately greater bakufu concessions and internal anguish.

Prior to the attack on Andō the attempt by Nagai Uta of Chōshū to mediate court-bakufu differences had stalled. Following the attack the senior council, led by Kuze Hirochika, hoped to appease critics of the regime, and thereby reduce the likelihood of further violence, by reviving the Nagai mediation. Before that maneuver achieved anything, however, the quiet was disrupted when the Chōshū daimyo, Mōri Yoshichika, met

Kuze on 3/15 and bluntly denounced the Ii and Andō regimes. He presented a series of policy recommendations and warned of the dangers to Edo if they were not followed.[1] Most notably he suggested that Matsudaira Shungaku and Tokugawa Nariaki's son, Yoshinobu of Hitotsubashi, both of whom had been punished by Ii, be named respectively great councillor *(tairō)* and shogunal regent *(hosa)*. He also urged that former officials punished by Ii be given responsible office. That, he asserted, was the only way to revive *(fukko)* the bakufu. Mōri's arguments reinforced similar requests earlier advanced by imperial delegates directly or through Nagai, and they intensified consideration of the matter within the bakufu.

Probably forewarned of Mōri's message, Edo leaders tried to strengthen themselves on the day they received it by naming to the senior council men whom the discontented might trust—namely, Itakura Katsukiyo and Mizuno Tadakiyo. Itakura was the forty-year-old grandson of Matsudaira Sadanobu, and Mizuno, ten years his junior, was the son of Tadakuni of Tenpō reform fame. Both men were understood to oppose foreign contacts, and Itakura had the added virtue of having been dismissed from office by Ii. Both were able officials, but the older Itakura proved the more influential.[2]

In succeeding weeks the external pressure for reform was intensified by reports of growing *shishi* activity in the Kyoto vicinity. Coming so soon after Mōri's blunt advice, these reports led to more conciliatory actions. On 4/11 Andō formally resigned office, and four days later Edo issued a portentous but characteristically pious announcement of intention to reform, to economize, and to revive martial spirit. The bakufu then learned, probably within a few days, that Shimazu Hisamitsu, father of the Satsuma daimyo, had recently reached the Osaka area with an uncommonly large military force. Both its size and its purpose were unclear. Reports of size ranged as high as three thousand men and a hundred cannon. Hisamitsu's purpose was rumored to be, among other things, to join *rōnin* in an assault on the Kyoto deputy's headquarters and other points of bakufu strength in the Kinai (Kyoto-Osaka) region.[3] Edo's earlier moves had obviously failed to satisfy critics, and confronted by the news of greater trials yet to come, on 4/24 the bakufu modified the terms of house arrest that Ii had imposed on Shungaku and two other vigorous daimyo, Tokugawa Yoshikatsu of Owari and Yamauchi Yōdō of Tosa.

Such gestures were hardly sufficient, however. By month's end bakufu leaders knew that both Hisamitsu and the court wanted Kuze to come to Kyoto to discuss matters. From the outset Kuze opposed the trip, evidently because he feared falling into a trap much as Hotta Masayoshi had done in 1858.[4] Even before he was forced to make a decision, however, a new and audacious *démarche* by Mōri on 5/2 complicated matters again. On that day he proposed to Kuze that the shogun himself go to Kyoto to consult daimyo and thereby unify the country and manage the foreigners.

No shogun had been to Kyoto in two centuries, and for a mere daimyo to propose such a trip was quite extraordinary. Predictably Mōri's message precipitated more disagreement, and again leaders tried to strengthen their hand by artful compromise. On the following day Matsudaira Katamori, the daimyo of Aizu, was instructed to participate in bakufu discussions. Aizu was a prestigious and traditionally cooperative related *han*. And Katamori at twenty-six was a young and amenable personality and therefore an attractive appointee to regular officials. At the same time his appointment would appeal to the regime's critics because, despite his former association with Ii Naosuke, he was lord of a great *han* and was considered by vassals of Shungaku to be a virtuous man.

After receiving instructions to participate, Katamori asked that Shungaku, age thirty-four, also be included, and on the seventh his request was accepted.[5] Bakufu leaders did not make that concession lightly, however. Although they invited Shungaku to sit in, they rejected suggestions that Yoshikatsu and Yoshinobu, the latter a year younger than Katamori, also be included. Moreover, two days later the sixteen-year-old shogun was declared to have come of age and unassertive Tokugawa Yoshiyori of Tayasu was with much fanfare dismissed as shogunal guardian *(kōken)*. The clear implication was that the shogun no longer needed a regent or guardian and hence there was no reason to appoint Yoshinobu to any such position.

This attempt by bakufu leaders to use related daimyo without accommodating their views was well rooted in customary practice, but this time it was not destined to succeed. Far from quieting the discontented, the admission of Shungaku only brought one of their most articulate spokesmen into the heart of affairs and generated more intense disagreements within the councils of government. Although Shungaku, Katamori, the senior councillors, and other officials were in agreement that the threat of political disorder was real, they disagreed on how best to address the danger. Consequently policy matters assumed extreme importance in their eyes and substantive disputes soon became very heated. Shungaku's presence also exacerbated matters because he held strong convictions, had a somewhat brittle temper, wanted quick action, and found it difficult to deal gracefully with the senior councillors on a give-and-take, consensual decision basis. Furthermore, there was no clearly delineated institutional relationship between Shungaku (or Katamori for that matter) and the councillors. His position was presumably consultative and advisory, like that of Tokugawa Nariaki in Abe's administration in 1853–1854, but Shungaku and his supporters desired his role to be a leading one in the manner of Ii.

Whereas Katamori and key Aizu vassals were fearful of the pitfalls of bakufu politics and young Katamori was discreet in his advice, Shungaku began to act from the outset as though his view ought to prevail. Thus from his second day of active participation (5/8) he argued with vigor and heat, contending in the face of senior council objections that the shogun should go to Kyoto, that major reform (referred to as *kaikaku* or *henkaku*) should be made, that Yoshinobu should be appointed, and by subtle implication that the *sankin kōtai* system should be modified. Two days later he and his vassals even inquired about naming Fukui men to bakufu office as attendants *(sobatōdori)*. On the eleventh, after four days of discussion had failed to persuade the councillors to accept his views, he announced that he had a headache and stayed home.[6] It was the first of repeated byocotts he would use in following weeks to extract concessions from officialdom.

As the month advanced, the pressure from Shungaku, Kyoto, and elsewhere had ever more impact. By the twenty-second bakufu leaders had agreed, despite internal opposition, to the idea of a major reform. It would be designed to strengthen bakufu military forces and reduce waste by returning to the austere, administratively simpler "pre-Kan'ei" system of Ieyasu's day.[7] The phrasing was important: most of the bakufu's nonmilitary offices had not existed in Ieyasu's day. The plan threatened an immense range of vested interests and generated commensurate resistance. Shungaku's pressure also led by 6/1 to a formal decision that the shogun would go to Kyoto—but very frugally—later in the year. With those decisions made, junior councillor Sakai Tadamasu was dismissed and several other officials were fired or demoted for reasons of obstructionism or corruption.

Sakai et al. were not the first casualties of the embryo Bunkyū reform. Shungaku's aggressive debut in affairs had already combined with the embarrassing matter of Kuze's aborted trip to Kyoto to make the latter's position intolerable. Those developments undermined his leading role in the bakufu, and his decline was reinforced by the proliferating rumors of imminent bakufu collapse. Some daimyo were reportedly preparing to abandon Edo. Some were reportedly preparing to take over bakufu functions in Kyoto. War and division were seen pending.[8] And Kuze could be blamed. After weeks of intense difficulty, the experienced and respected councillor submitted his resignation on 5/26, and a few days later it was accepted. Accompanying him in retirement was senior councillor Naitō Nobuchika, whose long tenure (since 1853) had made him nominal chief councillor. To replace them, 53-year-old Wakizaka Yasuori was recalled to office. He gave the senior council a nominal chief with good ties to Kyoto, years of service, and considerable prestige but little forcefulness.

Then Shungaku's position was strengthened greatly, if awkwardly, by the arrival at Edo on 6/7 of the elderly and urbane imperial delegate Ōhara Shigetomi, who was supported by Shimazu Hisamitsu and a heavily armed force of some eight hundred highly motivated Satsuma samurai.[9] The precise objectives of the Ōhara mission changed as time passed, but the basic goals of the court-daimyo offensive of mid-1862 were these: to bend bakufu foreign policy to fit the *jōi* predilection of the court (Hisamitsu's own view notwithstanding); to open the bakufu to sustained court–great daimyo influence; and to punish those associated with the regimes of Ii and Andō and rehabilitate those injured by them. The mission did not, of course, state its intention in any such manner. Formally Ōhara sought unity of court and bakufu, domestic solidarity, expulsion of the foreigner, and consolidation of the peace. To this end he wished, much as Mōri Yoshichika had proposed three months earlier, that the shogun name Shungaku and Yoshinobu to high office as great councillor and shogunal guardian.

Ōhara and Hisamitsu presumed evidently that through these men it would subsequently be possible to achieve their other larger objectives. They soon found, however, that even those modest initial goals were not easily attainable. Fukui men regarded the title of *tairō* or great councillor as demeaning: it was a mere vassal daimyo post and Fukui was an illustrious related *han*. In a few days they accepted the alternative formulation of *seiji sōsai* or supreme councillor, a sort of political high commissioner with authority analogous to that of great councillor. Officialdom, however, remained opposed, allegedly regarding Shungaku's appointment as a threat to their own control of affairs.[10] There was even stronger opposition to Yoshinobu. Those who advocated his appointment encountered utter intransigence from senior councillors, lesser officials, shogunal attendants, and even Aizu and Tayasu men. In part the opposition reflected Yoshinobu's role in the earlier bitter Ii-Nariaki feud, but some argued that he was too impractical for responsible office, and others reportedly opposed his appointment because acquiescence would symbolize bakufu capitulation to Satsuma.[11]

Meanwhile Shungaku kept encountering resistance to his internal reform proposals and began to consider resigning his advisory post. Angered and discouraged by the resistance, he denounced "bakufu selfishness" and on 6/14 began his third boycott of the castle. He resisted the many pleas that he return to duty and derived no visible comfort from the knowledge that his demands for both the shogunal trip and internal reform had been accepted in principle. Instead he kept everyone on edge for the rest of the month by openly toying with the idea of resigning.

Shungaku's long boycott left Wakizaka, Itakura, and Mizuno as the senior men facing the continual pressure from Shimazu and Ōhara. Then, on the twenty-seventh, the three councillors were rudely shaken by a warning that some Satsuma samurai intended to accost them and "discuss matters" when they left the castle that evening. Mindful of Andō and Ii's misfortunes and the many other recent acts of violence, the senior councillors reportedly delayed their departure until the danger was past. On the following day they agreed to name Yoshinobu guardian, even though that might subsequently lead to his being named shogun. Pressed thus by Shungaku, Ōhara, and militant Satsuma samurai, bakufu leaders capitulated. On the thirtieth they informed Shungaku that he was to be named supreme councillor and Yoshinobu shogunal guardian. [12]

Despite that notification, Shungaku still refused to participate in affairs. As another concession to him, inspector general Ōkubo Ichiō, who had been supporting many of his proposals, was transferred to the post of chamberlain *(sobashū)* with special authority close to the shogun (as *goyōtoritsugi*), thus strengthening Shungaku's influence on Iemochi. Then on 7/6 Yoshinobu was reappointed head of Hitotsubashi, and the next day the shogun formally designated him guardian, the announcement pointedly saying he had done so "due to imperial request." Those changes satisfied Shungaku. He agreed to return to duty, and on the ninth he was designated supreme councillor, also "due to imperial request." Some officials hoped his appointment would offset Yoshinobu's expected malign influence, but the phrasing clearly indicated that the shogun, or at least those who formulated his edicts, was not necessarily pleased with the appointments. The phrasing also acknowledged in principle, however, that the court's desires could determine crucial personnel matters of the Tokugawa house. [13]

After two months of hard struggle Shungaku had finally rammed his way into a position from which he could pursue his reform plans. In terms of political process the immediate purpose of Shungaku's maneuvers during 62/5–6 had been the routine formation of a new ruling group or clique strong enough to execute his policies. Like other men before him, he had cultivated support among lesser officials, such as inspectors general Ōkubo, Komai Chōon, and Okabe Nagatsune and inspector Asano Ujisuke, whose influence had risen in consequence of the deep divisions at higher levels. He had used their support in pursuit of his policies and, when that was insufficient, had boycotted affairs and threatened to resign. To strengthen his hand, he had badgered opposing high officials until they resigned and with charges of obstructionism and corruption had removed uncooperative lesser officials from positions of influence, replacing them with more acceptable men. He was unusual insofar as he was exceptionally outspoken in discussions and argued fiercely with others. And in particular he was different in the unprecedented extent to which he cultivated and used support from forces outside the bakufu, notably great daimyo and the court, to advance his policies regardless of the extent of internal opposition.

In terms of political content the developments of these two months had not been at all routine. The triple threat of imperial displeasure, daimyo maneuvering, and *shishi* intimidation had extracted an unprecedented concession from the regime: central bakufu offices could be modified at the behest of outsiders and despite broad-based opposition within the bakufu. That key concession made possible the Bunkyū reform, which Shungaku and his advisors, notably Yokoi Shōnan, had begun planning even before he had accepted the post of supreme councillor.

The importance of Shungaku's and Yoshinobu's appointments should not be underestimated. By 62/7 the bakufu had been profoundly shaken. The customary pattern of control by middle-ranking vassal daimyo with the title of senior councillor had been challenged and supplanted. The center of its power structure penetrated, the bakufu seemed open to almost any sort of change the outsiders might have in mind.

The erosion of bakufu strength was reflected in the quality of rumors circulating at the time. During Abe's era, there had been talk of foreign invaders and of corruption and incompetence, but only few and vague references to dynastic weakening of critical moment. The most explicit of those, moreover, came from supporters of the regime, rather than its enemies, from men who hoped by their warnings to prod the regime to renewed vigor. Hotta's failure in 1858 gave rise to more complicated rumors of the regime losing imperial favor and of daimyo taking affairs into their own hands. Ii's repression intensified the rhetoric of imperial loyalism, but instead of daimyo initiatives, the rumor world of 1859–1861 talked of angry samurai and avenging men of virtue who would punish the wicked. As 1862 passed, the climate deteriorated even further. Pundits referred more and more freely to dynastic change, war and confusion, and direct punishment of the corrupt by the righteous. Histori-

cal analogies were ever more readily drawn: the Ōnin war, the era of
Hideyoshi, the Jōkyū rebellion. A weak and indecisive or even disloyal
bakufu leadership was to blame for what was wrong and, the critics
argued, should be replaced by a cohesive national leadership under imperial auspices. Shungaku presumably was expected to accomplish that
task.

POLITICAL REFORM: 62/7–int. 8

Armed with his new title of supreme councillor, Shungaku tried to persuade bakufu officials to adopt his ideas on reform. Those ideas had been
developed, largely by Yokoi, beyond the particular policies Shungaku
had advocated in 62/5 into a much broader and coherent venture in inclusivistic politics. Accordingly the political aspects of the Bunkyū reform
were largely an expression of Fukui ideas.

In order to restore court-daimyo-*shishi* support of the bakufu, Shungaku wished to pursue several concessive policies. He wished, as did
Ōhara, to obtain pardons for those who had been convicted of plotting
assassinations or other crimes. As a corollary he wished to purge and
punish those responsible for Edo's ''selfish'' policy. He wished to carry
out a drastic modification of the *sankin kōtai* system, whose costs had
long been a severe burden to Fukui and other *han*.[14] He wished to adopt
a policy of ''respectfulness'' toward the court in order, as he argued it,
to blunt court-*shishi* criticism. As one aspect of that policy he would have
the shogun go to Kyoto as the court wished, provided the other reforms
had been previously initiated.

The granting of pardons was the first matter addressed by Shungaku
after his appointment as supreme councillor. It was fought out during the
first four days of his rule and set the tone for much of the Bunkyū reform.
Predictably officialdom was uniformly opposed to pardoning or rehabilitating the memory of those who would murder bakufu officials. Even
Ōkubo, Okabe, and Asano were opposed. Less expectedly and more
portentously, Yoshinobu was opposed.

Yoshinobu's father had been Ii's chief enemy, and his family fief of
Mito had been the primary target of Ii's purge. He himself had been
denied appointment as shogunal heir, stripped of his position as lord of
Hitotsubashi, and forced into confinement by Ii. And his recent appointment as guardian had been most strenuously opposed by those who had
worked with Ii and Andō. All that notwithstanding, Yoshinobu spoke
out sharply in opposition to the amnesty. He argued with passion that
those to be amnestied were in fact guilty as charged and there was no

ground for pardon. His opposition to the amnesty may have reflected a real anxiety about the erosion of bakufu authority. It may have been a calculated and rather successful attempt to build rapport with officialdom. Or it may have reflected a basic conservatism in his outlook. Certainly it foreshadowed the conservative position that became characteristic of Yoshinobu thereafter, and that made good sense in view of his obvious candidacy for a future shogunal succession.[15] Furthermore, the dispute with Shungaku foreshadowed a pattern of conflict between the two that was to reappear frequently in coming months. It would slow decision-making and confound attempts to devise a consistent policy supported by a consolidated bakufu.

Despite the protests of Yoshinobu and most officials, however, on 7/12 Shungaku put his authority as supreme councillor on the line. He argued forcefully that an amnesty was essential if the bakufu were to erase the stigma of selfishness and recover the goodwill of court and daimyo. His stubborn persistence was rewarded. The bakufu accepted the principle of amnesty for those punished by Ii and Andō. In following weeks Mito men were pardoned; ritual gestures rehabilitating Nariaki were made; and personnel changes were imposed upon Mito despite protests of the daimyo, Yoshiatsu.[16]

Disputes relating to the amnesty program raged on for about a month after the decision of the twelfth, and they became entwined with the related question of punishing those officials associated with the Ii-Andō regime. Shungaku pressed on, however, his position bolstered by added demands from the Ōhara-Shimazu mission. Moreover, alarming reports of growing anarchy, agitation, vigilante action, and social pamphleteering in and near Kyoto indicated that during 62/7 *shishi* in the city had launched a systematic program of terror directed mostly at those associated with Ii's regime.[17] Those reports added weight to the arguments for amnesty and retribution.

Under this growing assault the senior councillors finally agreed to carry out an expanded purge. On 8/16, amid widespread rumors of sweeping punishments,[18] the bakufu ordered both Kuze and Andō on formally unspecified grounds of malfeasance in office to retire to domiciliary confinement and to surrender lands they had received while in office. In succeeding days a few more office changes were made. They included the dismissal at Ōhara's insistence of the Kyoto deputy, Honjō Munehide, also associated with Ii. Honjō had only just been named deputy on 6/30, replacing another man whose ties to Ii had similarly provoked imperial disfavor and contributed to his dismissal.

Concurrently Edo pressed the Hikone *han* government to punish

Nagano Shuzen and other *han* vassals who had worked with Ii.[19] In consequence at Hikone a number of office changes and punishments were meted out. On 8/1 Nagano committed suicide in preference to execution like a common criminal, and Ii's other trusted retainer, Utsuki Rokunojō, was imprisoned and later executed. In succeeding weeks hundreds of other Hikone men were imprisoned or put under house arrest. Moreover, as the court wished and much to the dismay of Hikone, the *han* was deprived of its customary role as Kyoto protector *(shugo)*. Then, although the *han* was not fully relieved of its garrison costs in the city, Hikone was ordered to surrender sizable territories (40,000 to 60,000 *koku*) it had held for generations to support its role as protector. The *han* protested, and peasants on the territory erupted in violent opposition to the threatened transfer, but the surrender order stood.

At considerable cost to traditional supporters of the regime, Shungaku's policies of amnesty and purge thus made progress. Other aspects of his program, however, fared less well. Most immediately it was the issue of a shogunal trip to Kyoto that created serious complications. Although senior councillors had accepted the trip in principle, most officials were still opposed and obstructed its preparation. In delaying the trip, however, they were leaving Kyoto open to machinations of daimyo and *shishi*, and that prompted Edo leaders to seek some alternative means of strengthening the bakufu presence there.

As early as 62/4 officials had been aware of bakufu weakness at court. Efforts to induce prestigious Tokugawa supporters, notably Kuze, Yoshikatsu of Owari, and Shungaku himself, to go to Kyoto had all come to naught, however, and the situation there had deteriorated steadily. From late 62/5 Shungaku urged Katamori to accept a post at Kyoto. He felt Katamori's presence there would overcome the obvious weakness of the deputy and project the bakufu's new reformist image into the city. Probably he also hoped thereby to ease the pressure on himself to go. Despite Shungaku's urging, however, Katamori was no more eager than anyone else to bell the imperial cat.[20] His advisors were disturbed at the difficulty and costs of the task because Aizu was far from Kyoto and had other exhausting burdens. They were concerned about his relationship to the deputy, making it clear Aizu would not accept that title, which was for vassal daimyo. They also fretted about the prospect of conflict with great outside lords and about the political dangers inherent in serving the unstable leadership at Edo. In a phrase, for Aizu, as for Kuze and the others, the political risks involved in going to Kyoto seemed to outweigh by far the possible gains in prestige.

In this matter bakufu leaders backed Shungaku, and by the end of

62/7 the special title of Kyoto protector *(shugoshoku)* was settled upon. While there was some official concern at the creation of another position superior to established vassal daimyo offices, it was judged necessary in this case because vassal lords lacked the manpower necessary to counter the influence of great daimyo and *rōnin* in Kyoto. Aizu, moreover, with its tradition of stern warrior deportment and loyal service to Edo, was deemed especially appropriate to the task. Furthermore Katamori, a relatively simple, direct, and soldierly sort of young man with a reputation for gentle humility and integrity, seemed a very apt appointee. Despite agreement on the title of Kyoto protector, however, the issue remained unresolved. Aizu men continued stubbornly to resist duty in Kyoto, and Shungaku came under renewed pressure from both bakufu officials and Hisamitsu to proceed there himself as a representative of the shogun. The proposal alarmed Shungaku, not only because of the political dangers it would entail for Fukui, but also because it would remove him from Edo at a time when his whole reform program was on the brink of collapse. The plans for both reform of the *sankin kōtai* system and a shogunal pilgrimage to Kyoto were stalled, and Shungaku was about to lose the sometimes helpful support of Hisamitsu and Ōhara, who were themselves preparing to return to Kyoto. Should Shungaku leave too, reform at Edo would surely cease.

Then, however, on 8/21–24 the situation was dramatically changed by two developments that Shungaku turned to advantage. These developments were a characteristic case of the way in which foreign and domestic crises—*naiyū gaikan*, ''rebels at home, aggressors abroad''— would repeatedly combine in later years to force the bakufu into major concessions.

One development was precipitated by men of Satsuma. On 8/21 Hisamitsu and his retinue left Edo for Kyoto. As they passed through Namamugi near Yokohama, men in his train attacked a group of foreigners who refused to show Hisamitsu the respect deemed appropriate. In the process they killed an English merchant. Far from arresting the assailants and turning them over to the bakufu for punishment, Hisamitsu disclaimed any knowledge of the men involved and hurried on in defiance of bakufu instructions that he stop and act. The British were already up in arms over an incident of 5/29 in their consulate at Tōzenji near Shinagawa. There a vassal of Matsumoto *han*, who was assigned the hateful duty of protecting foreigners, had killed two British soldiers and then committed suicide. Coming so soon after that murder, this second incident unleashed a storm of foreign fury. On 8/22 Itakura, Mizuno, and bakufu diplomats found themselves confronted with the necessity of coercing a great domestic power or facing retribution by the foreigners, who already were launching a barrage of angry protests, demands, and threats of naval attack on Edo.[21]

The second development flowed from the arrival in Edo on the eighteenth of the young Chōshū heir, Mōri Sadahiro. He conveyed news of the court's most recent desires. The court, he reported, now wished the bakufu to increase Nariaki's court rank posthumously and honor other daimyo whom Ii had punished. It also wished Edo to rehabilitate more dissident samurai, including some recently slain by Hisamitsu's men in Kyoto, for which action the bakufu had just rewarded the Satsuma leader. Sadahiro and other Chōshū men also conveyed information on the Kyoto situation and on the court's displeasure that Edo had neither repudiated the treaties nor, despite the promises of late 62/5, made any real progress on the shogunal trip to Kyoto.

Shungaku skillfully turned these new complications to advantage. After learning that Hisamitsu had refused to cooperate in the Namamugi incident, he decided to avoid entanglement in the whole crisis. On 8/24 he stopped going to the castle, leaving regular officials to cope with the belligerent foreigners as best they could. Officials of course hoped to settle the diplomatic problem peacefully and accordingly wished to secure at least some cooperation from Hisamitsu. They regarded Shungaku's aid as essential to that effort and thus were particularly concerned to prevent his permanent alienation. Hence it was comparatively easy for him to secure concessions on domestic reform as a quid pro quo for cooperation on the Namamugi crisis.

Shungaku's task was made easier by the evidence of a worsening situation at Kyoto, which made it all the more imperative that Edo retain the goodwill of such high-ranking and well-regarded men as the Fukui lord. Shungaku was also helped by the fact that the crisis hit the bakufu at a moment of renewed weakness of leadership. Wakizaka, who had just returned to duty three months previously, had become discouraged with the general trend of events, particularly Edo's deepening subservience to Kyoto and, after Namamugi, the failure to make Satsuma obey bakufu orders. He also resented Shungaku's high position. From mid-62/8 he refused to cooperate with the other senior councillors, later asked to be relieved of his duties ''due to illness,'' and did not participate in affairs even when his resignation request was rejected. By default Itakura became the most influential senior councillor. He too was unhappy about the trend of affairs, but after thinking about resigning, he decided to stay on.[22] The upshot was a bakufu leadership unusually vulnerable to the pressures from Shungaku and others.

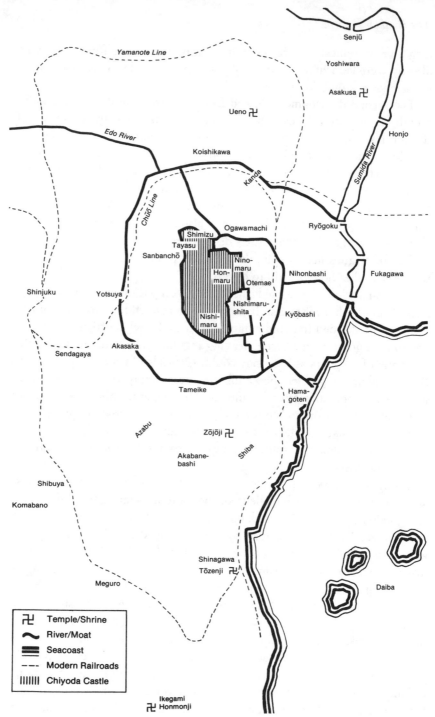

MAP 1. Edo. Adapted from map no.32, map volume, *Nihon rekishi daijiten* (Tokyo: Kawade shobō shinsha, 1961).

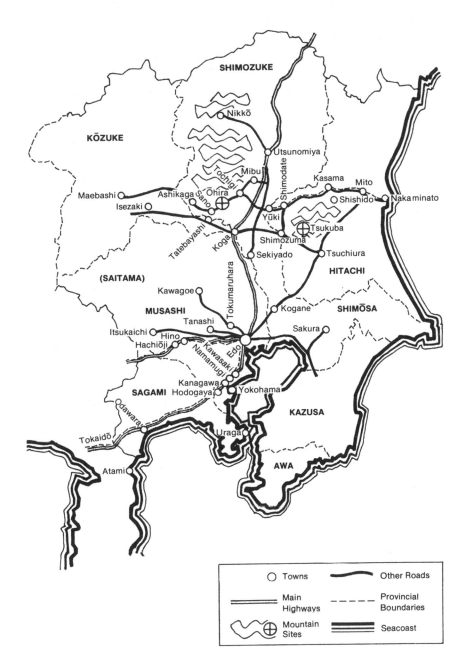

MAP 2. The Kantō. Adapted from map no. 33, map volume, *Nihon rekishi daijiten* (Tokyo: Kawade shobō shinsha, 1961).

After Shungaku had started his newest boycott, Okabe Nagatsune assumed the task of maintaining communication with him. On 8/27 Yokoi Shōnan explained to Okabe at great length the logic of the overall reform program, including most importantly implementation of the sho-gun's trip to Kyoto and abolition of the *sankin kōtai* system. He also advocated use of "able men," vigorous military strengthening, and ini-tiation of foreign trade as a joint bakufu-daimyo venture. Yokoi later re-peated his arguments to Itakura, Mizuno, Ōkubo Ichiō, and others. They were discussed at once by Yoshinobu and officials and reinforced the im-pact of Shungaku's boycott. By letter Shungaku also reiterated his de-nunciation of bakufu "selfishness" and his demand for major reform. Itakura had been particularly opposed to basic changes, but the pressures finally overwhelmed him, and action quickly followed. On int. 8/3 (third day of the intercalary eighth month) the bakufu formally appointed men to oversee the reform, having given the supreme councillor tacit as-surance that the *sankin kōtai* system would be modified. Three days later, after being urged by Okabe and after extracting more concessions on particular reforms, Shungaku returned to office. Another three days later, after more extensive discussions involving Shungaku, Yokoi, Yo-shinobu, Itakura, Mizuno, Okabe, Asano, the Confucian scholar Haya-shi Noboru, and others, the reform was agreed upon by bakufu leaders in council.

In succeeding days details of the reform were spelled out, and that pro-cess led to more multiway quarrels between Shungaku, Yoshinobu, and regular officials. Most notably Yoshinobu protested Shungaku's sugges-tion that the formal distinction between vassal and outside lords be abolished, seeing it fraught with dangerous implications for the future. Then he angered senior officials by demanding that they cease accepting sizable gifts from daimyo. They resisted the assault on valuable office perquisites, and in irritation Yoshinobu adopted Shungaku's technique. He began to boycott the castle on the fifteenth and threatened to resign two days later. In response Shungaku stopped pressing his point about daimyo distinctions, and finally senior officials capitulated on the matter of office perquisites.

With those issues resolved, and despite the continuing opposition of some junior councillors who were dismissed a few days later, on int. 8/22 the sweeping *sankin kōtai* reforms were announced.[23] The bakufu notified daimyo of a new attendance schedule that would have them spend a hundred days in Edo every three years. They were informed that wives and heirs could return home at will, and they were urged to economize on their trips and discontinue ritual gift exchanges.

Exploiting the crisis atmosphere of late 62/8, Shungaku had thus succeeded in eviscerating the institutional centerpiece of the bakufu's whole system for controlling great daimyo. He also had made progress on the issue of the shogunal trip. Itakura had long objected to the plan, apparently because he saw it as destructive of bakufu interests, which it was his obligation to protect.[24] Hayashi Noboru and other Confucian scholars also bitterly opposed it. But by the middle of the month Yokoi had persuaded most key officials, including Ōkubo, Okabe, and even Itakura, that the trip was necessary. On the twenty-second, the day other reforms were announced, the bakufu ordered a number of officials, including Mizuno Tadakiyo, Okabe, superintendents of finance Oguri Tadamasa and Kawakatsu Kōun, and inspector Jinbō Nagayo, to prepare the shogunal trip. Five days later inspectors Asano and Yamaguchi Naoki and some other officials were added to the group, making it just about the most formidable body of administrative talent the bakufu could muster. By 9/7 the planning committee had done its work and it was announced formally that the shogun would go to Kyoto in 63/2.

The conjunction of dilemmas in late 62/8 had thus induced officials to yield to Shungaku on both *sankin kōtai* and the shogunal trip. It also had prompted them to abandon their effort to send him to Kyoto. Instead they decided to make Katamori go. Despite the opposition of Aizu officials, the senior councillors on int. 8/1 finally summoned him to the castle and handed him orders to accept the title of Kyoto protector. His vassal advisors objected at once, but Katamori reportedly argued the importance of doing one's duty to the Tokugawa house and the court, and the order was not withdrawn. At twenty-six years of age, Katamori, lord of Aizu by adoption, son of the related daimyo of Takasu by birth, and brother of Yoshikatsu of Owari, of Mochinori the current daimyo of Owari, and of Matsudaira Sadaaki of Kuwana, had accepted the task of restoring Tokugawa honor and authority in the imperial capital.

Good soldier that he was, Katamori set advisors to work at once planning logistics of the operation. He sent others to Kyoto to investigate and make preparations there. His expeditious activities were disrupted a few weeks later, however, when he became embroiled in painful political wrangling at Edo. In consequence it was nearly year's end before he actually departed for Kyoto.

The severe pressures that had led to bakufu concessions were again followed by office changes. Most notably the senior councillors finally abandoned hope of retaining the cooperation of Wakizaka. On 9/6 his resignation request was reluctantly processed and he was dropped entirely from office. Five days later he was replaced by the promotion of Ogasawara Nagamichi to the title of acting senior councillor *(rōjū kaku)*. Because Nagamichi was to play an important and rather erratic role in future years, he deserves special comment.[25]

Nagamichi was heir to the daimyo of Karatsu and an impetuous man of ambition, vigor, and decisiveness. Born in 1822, he was at age forty still only an heir. In 62/6 he had represented the daimyo of Karatsu at an audience in which the shogun had formally announced his intention of going to Kyoto. Shortly thereafter Nagamichi had submitted to the bakufu an opinion supporting the trip and speaking in favor of the current verities of court-bakufu unity and frugality. He asserted the need for a greater effort than just a routine reform *(chūkō)*. He approved the trip to Kyoto and urged that it be economical. He stressed the importance of reward and punishment as foundation for any adequate reform, dwelt on the widespread public hardship, the inflation, the danger of upheaval, and hence his advocacy of return to the simple system of pre-Kan'ei years.

Perhaps that forthright assessment with its echoes of the Fukui position was well received. At any rate, on 7/21, a few days after Shungaku became supreme councillor, Nagamichi was appointed master of shogunal ceremony *(sōshaban)*. It was the first step in an extraordinarily rapid rise to high office. After less than a month as master he wrote a long memorandum spelling out the wasteful and useless character of the master's office, whose functions were mostly related to the *sankin kōtai* audiences, and the bakufu abolished the position when it reformed *sankin kōtai*. By then Nagamichi had come to the attention of high officials, and he had just been promoted directly to junior councillor, with certain customary duties in charge of bakufu medical facilities, perhaps as a way of utilizing his reputed skill as a literary and learned man.

Nagamichi's prior statements accorded well with Shungaku's view of affairs. And perhaps his character as a strong and able member of a middle-ranking vassal daimyo house made him attractive to regular officials. On 9/11 he was promoted directly to acting senior councillor, bypassing several superintendents of temples and shrines, the keeper of Osaka castle, and the Kyoto deputy, all of whom had seniority. The move was uncommon in itself and perhaps unprecedented insofar as he was an heir rather than daimyo.[26] In further evidence of his rapid rise, on 10/1 he was given duty handling foreign affairs, in which capacity he was to consult on matters with Itakura and Mizuno. With Nagamichi's appointment the senior council came to include a man with views that seemed very close to those of Shungaku. How well he could close the gap between Shungaku and officialdom, however, remained to be seen.

As of early 62/9, then, Shungaku had been able to exploit the external pressure of court, great daimyo, *shishi*, and foreigners to force bakufu officials, against the will of most of them, to agree to the most dramatic political changes in Japan since the seventeenth century. Not only had special offices been created enabling related daimyo to displace middle vassal daimyo rule, but a major reform had been initiated that destroyed the coercive value of the *sankin kōtai* system. Furthermore the bakufu had committed the shogun to a pilgrimage to Kyoto that signified a degree of shogunal subservience to the court never intended by the regime's founders. Where this remarkable venture would end could hardly be predicted.

ADMINISTRATIVE, FISCAL, AND MILITARY REFORM: 62/5-12

By 62/9 Shungaku's political reform seemed to be making extraordinary progress despite the extensive difficulty it had encountered. In the background structural aspects of reform were also moving ahead almost as rapidly. In terms of those changes—administrative, fiscal, and military—the Bunkyū reform was essentially a dramatic intensification of previous efforts such as Abe's Ansei reform. The basic lines of the reform had mostly been long established, but the Bunkyū reformers did realize some previously unattainable objectives.

The rationale of reform was simple: the foreign menace had to be withstood. The unstated corollary was equally straightforward: by enabling the regime to fulfill its political responsibilities, those who constituted the regime could save their favored position in life. Withstanding the foreign menace required that the regime's military capability be increased—and that was taken to mean essentially that samurai élan must be raised by altering habits of indolence and new military skills and technology must replace obsolete practices. This military reform, however, cost money and hence required economizing in other aspects of government since there were presumably no great untapped sources of income open to Edo. This economizing could be achieved in part by eliminating wasteful customary expenses and in part by eliminating a host of inessential offices. The latter undertaking would also enlarge the pool of available military manpower.

1. Administrative and Fiscal Reform

By late 62/5 bakufu leaders had prepared the way for extensive reform. On 5/22 an official shogunal notice to assembled vassal groups acknowledged that:

> Political affairs are drifting. Ostentation is condoned, samurai indolence increasing, and the élan of the Tokugawa house collapsing. Mindful of the

new foreign contacts, we must make military preparation and undertake reforms in accord with the time. The system must be simplified and a true samurai spirit revived [fukko itashi]. Because we wish the samurai spirit to gleam, you should be of strong resolve and present to us such suggestions as you may have.[27]

Other notices both before and after this one indicated specific projects and particular emphases of the reform, and during succeeding months these began to be implemented. One by one, case by case, in a prodigious feat of structural assessment, a host of travel regulations, work procedures, and dress requirements of bakufu officials and others in the castle were simplified. Many expensive gift-exchange customs were outlawed or curtailed. A large number of customary ceremonies that involved both daimyo and officials were eliminated or severely simplified.[28]

In several ways the personnel burden of the regime was slashed. Old and infirm officials were ordered to retire from office, and large numbers did so. Daimyo and lesser Tokugawa vassals were ordered to economize in all things and in particular to dismiss all but a minimal number of minor attendants. Several offices were abolished and their duties ended or assigned to others, thus reducing by scores the numbers of expensively stipended officials and by hundreds or perhaps thousands the numbers of menial attendant personnel whose families were directly sustained by the bakufu fisc. Then the reforms associated with the modification of *sankin kōtai* on int. 8/22 eliminated the attendant functions of thousands more.

Office procedures were altered to foster efficiency as well as economy. Several offices were reorganized to help utilize the new naval and army technology. Well-established practices of hereditary succession among lower bakufu positions, particularly within the military units, were modified and replaced, at least in theory, by specified mechanisms for appointing vassals primarily on the basis of demonstrated military commitment and ability. Commitment was to be shown by active participation in the training programs of the new bakufu military institutes; ability was to be shown in tests administered by competent specialists.[29]

Inevitably reforms of this magnitude hurt some people.[30] The Edo populace was injured by a rapid loss of income stemming from the reduction in bakufu employment and the concurrent exodus of daimyo families. By late 62/int. 8, a reported forty thousand Edo residents had been thrown out of menial attendant jobs, and poorhouses were set up to aid their families. This development came at a time when daily living costs were gradually escalating, with costs of daily necessities for Edo consum-

ers having nearly doubled from average levels of recent years. In response
to the worsening situation discontent grew. Rumors began to circulate
that some among those who had lost jobs as servants, merchants, artisans, foot soldiers, and day laborers were planning to assemble in the
Marunouchi district adjacent to the castle to protest their hardship.

Those rumors elicited several responses from the bakufu. Officials
decided for a while to return home during daylight hours and to increase
their security guards. Because Shungaku was popularly blamed for the
hardship and one report said he would be attacked, Fukui men on 9/1
convinced him of the prudence of staying indoors until the danger had
passed. Officials discussed the feasibility of enrolling the unemployed in
infantry units to give them firearms training and income and hence reduce
their discontent. And as a token gesture of concern, on 9/1 the bakufu
acknowledged the public hardship by instructing authorities everywhere
to help the unemployed return to their original villages and households
and assist them in taking up work as farmers and local laborers. This effort was to be made in appreciation of their years of service to the
Tokugawa family. In essence the bakufu had begun to cannibalize itself
in order to save itself, and predictably the weakest were the first to suffer. But as far as possible their suffering was to be ameliorated to avoid
further difficulty for the regime.

An observer from Hikone, writing on 10/21, described Edo in terms
suggestive of the changes. As he reported it, the city still appeared to be
thriving; at any rate brothels were doing a lively business. But familiar
faces were few and an air of parting farewell was about the town. The
thoughts of warriors had turned to their fiefs as the women left Edo.
Some commoners were not doing well; things were deteriorating before
one's eyes; and the surface bustle disguised an inner decay.[31] He might
fairly have added, however, that the situation could have been worse.
Many vassal daimyo who might have departed did not do so, and in consequence the exodus from Edo was less than complete.

2. Military Reform

The economizing that had precipitated public hardship was partially justified in the name of military strengthening, a rationale that was neither
new nor specious. Over the years the bakufu had spent huge sums directly and through the daimyo in constructing coastal fortifications, purchasing warships, and supporting men in the study of new technology.
Already by early 1861 these and other costs had, according to the senior
council, become enormous, far in excess of income, making frugality imperative.[32] In 1862 finances were no better, but the Edo government

was determined nevertheless to pursue its program of military strengthening.

One aspect of the military effort was invigoration of the naval development program that Abe had started and Ii had permitted to languish. In 62/6 bakufu military leaders completed an analysis indicating that Japan's primary military need was naval, due to the nation's long coastline. The study called for expansion of naval and coast defense facilities by using western technology but avoiding uncritical copying of European ways. In line with that study steps were taken to buy more warships, weapons, and support facilities, to send more men abroad for naval training and foreign study, to expand training facilities in Japan, and to erect a foundry for the construction of steam engines. Particular effort was made to strengthen defenses in the Kinai region.

All those projects consumed bakufu funds, and they were only the start of an enterprise whose political and fiscal implications were profound. Thus Takashima Shūhan, who had long advocated the use of modern firearms and who frequently gave Edo advice on military matters, argued in early 1862 that Japan required a fleet of some two hundred warships to defend itself from foreign attack. Since, as he argued, the bakufu obviously could not afford to buy or build even a fraction of those vessels, the daimyo should do so.[33] A few daimyo had already purchased or requested special permission to purchase warships, and on 7/4 the bakufu granted that permission freely to all, thus ending a prohibition that had stood for centuries. The need for naval development was thus fostering expansion of daimyo naval capacity and daimyo contact with foreign powers, with all the political consequences those trends might entail.

Allowing the daimyo to buy warships did not, however, really reduce the costs to Edo of naval strengthening. So much had to be done that even much-reduced plans could soak up all the revenues the bakufu might locate. Thus at the end of 1862 acting naval magistrate (*gunkan bugyō nami*) Katsu Kaishū surveyed the Kinai defense situation with Ogasawara Nagamichi and other officials. He then submitted to the senior council a report calling for much-expanded coastal artillery construction, deployment of more troops, and formation of a thirty-ship navy to secure the Kinai area, where he proposed to locate a new naval headquarters and shipyard.[34] That set of proposals was by itself well beyond Edo's fiscal capability, and in succeeding years Katsu and others repeatedly proposed even more expensive schemes of naval and coastal strengthening.

Bunkyū military reformers saw naval development as more important than army strengthening, but that judgment would soon be challenged by events. More important in the end for the survival of the regime was the contemporaneous attempt to create an effective new army, again revitalizing an Abe program that Ii had abandoned.

One reason army reform was needed so badly was that dramatic changes had recently begun to take place in western shoulder arms, and they were rapidly making the Japanese land forces' firearms ever more obsolete. Because the changes were still proceeding, they presented continual problems to bakufu military reformers, making new schemes obsolete even before they could be implemented. These technical changes affected three aspects of arms use: range and accuracy of fire, rate of fire, and reliability of fire. Rifling of barrels and the development of "Mini" bullets (shaped projectiles of smaller diameter that expanded on firing to fit the rifled barrel snugly, absorb more of the powder's energy, and so exit the muzzle spinning at a higher velocity) increased range and accuracy greatly. The combining of powder and projectile into a single unit, the paper cartridge, increased the rate of fire sharply by reducing to a single procedure the cumbrous process of muzzle-loading. The development of percussion caps using fulminic acid and the use of greased cartridges increased substantially the reliability of fire, especially in damp weather, by eliminating dependence on exposed powder and flint.

These three related developments made the midcentury muzzleloader a much superior tool of carnage, and during the 1840s major European armies switched to the new-style weapons, known generically as Mini rifles. Many old weapons were simply modified and kept in service, the British army's Mini rifle being a modified muzzle-loading version of the old smoothbore Enfield, for example. Westerners did have large numbers of old smoothbore flintlocks to dispose of, however, and these became available for sale to others, such as the Japanese, at modest prices.[35] By the 1850s, however, some military men in Japan were aware that they were being offered obsolete goods and newer weapons were available. Some of these were then imported, most notably by Saga *han* in Kyushu.

During the 1850s and 1860s the revolution in small arms continued, with the gradual development of better firing systems, metal cartridges of various sorts, the breech-loading rifle, the multishot pistol, and their eventual combination in the repeating rifle. In the 1850s bakufu military leaders acquired some revolver-type multishot pistols. Breechloaders and repeaters, however, were still rare even in the west, not becoming major weapons of war there until well into the 1860s and even later. The primary infantry weapon of the west was still the improved muzzleloader—the Mini rifle—and it was this type of weapon that bakufu reformers intended to acquire in 1862.

Bunkyū military reformers were concerned to obtain modern equipment, but as they saw it, the question of small-arms technology was only one aspect of a much broader and more basic problem of general military obsolescence. Another facet was the problem of organizing and training men for effective use of their weapons. Recognizing the inadequacy in this regard of prior bakufu efforts at reform, from early in the year they sought more general knowledge of European military training methods. They obtained a Dutch report dated 1851 that provided extensive information on the general content, organization, and extent of Dutch naval, regular army, and territorial militia training. The report also discussed the difficulties of assuring adequate training amid rapidly changing military technology. The reformers' summary of the report concluded with a series of concrete recommendations for abolishing bow-and-arrow training, for training of foot soldiers by landholding liege vassals, for weeding out incompetents at the military institute (kōbusho), for reforming its promotional criteria, and for sending men abroad for military training.[36]

As the year progressed, reforms in military training were initiated in line with those recommendations. Training facilities were expanded; personnel were added and shifted around; and a host of other changes were made. In 62/4 the bakufu ordered inspectors to encourage firearms practice among liege vassals and to form an infantry unit using those men. A month later it announced that firearms training was to follow western procedures. Liege vassals were to inform themselves on those matters, and they and their vassals were to go to the military institute or elsewhere for training. As recruiting efforts continued, officials also observed the weapons training, which evidently involved some two thousand men or more. On 5/21 inspectors were ordered to assemble the men, organize them into units, take them outside of Edo, and supervise them on an overnight training bivouac at Tokumaruhara in Musashi province—a training area where Takashima had tested new-style imported weapons in past years.[37]

Objections were raised to the training program because liege vassals had to arm and support themselves or any men they furnished, and few had monies available for such use. The problem was discussed by officials at the military institute, and the bakufu agreed to pay those who participated. During the summer and fall a stream of military orders fostered firearms training, expanded infantry forces, phased out the use of archers, and addressed countless petty obstructions and problems. For all the effort, however, training remained haphazard. Men came as interest and desire for pay dictated. Early reports indicated the program was not issuing in a well-trained, cohesive fighting force.[38] Even if all had gone well, however, the project constituted little more than a resurrection of Abe Masahiro's old military policy, and the persistent inadequacies of the effort prodded reformers to pursue more radical solutions.

The inadequacies of training were apparently regarded as part of over-all weakness in the military instructional program, and during 62/9 military leaders completed preparation of a proposal for its general reorganization. Reflecting the earlier report of the Dutch study, their proposal asserted that the army and navy were separate services, but since there was no essential difference in the basic training of army and navy officers, they should receive that training together. This consolidated training, the report went on, would require foreign advisors, so English, American, and other foreign military men should be hired to teach at an officer training school to be set up in Yokohama. In preparation for that undertaking, liege vassals and their kin should apply at the military institute, and those accepted would then receive financial support during their period of training. In two or three years, the report concluded, that should yield a useful officer corps for both the army and navy.[39]

Beyond this plan for revised training, the Bunkyū reformers worked out an elaborate program for fundamental reorganization of the bakufu's entire armed force.[40] By late 62/7 they had designed a wholly new structure and spelled out how existing manpower would be fitted into it. In following months the plan was reviewed and revised, and by 62/11 planning had clearly adopted an overall framework that conceptualized a dual service, navy and army, rather than the older variety of forces distinguished by weaponry and connection to the shogun. Elaborate tables of organization for both army and navy were developed to specify the officers' chain of command, designate their stipends, relate them to the existing command hierarchy, and correlate them to the western officer rank structure. In later months further measures fleshed out the military reorganization.

The new tables of organization reallocated manpower resources to form a triune army of infantry, artillery, and cavalry. About half the army would be recruited from and supported by landholding liege vassals; the other half would be supported by funds derived from lower-ranking stipended liege vassals. The plan envisaged an army of some 13,500 officers and men, over 8000 of them infantrymen. The infantry was to be of three basic types. Some 6300 men would form heavy infantry forces, mostly equipped with old-style firearms. Another 1000 men equipped with Mini rifles would constitute a light infantry. Another 850 with Mini rifles would form a force of marksmen close to the shogun. The cavalry would have two branches. About 900 mounted men armed with carbines and swords would be heavy cavalry and another 200 with short pikes would form light cavalry. The artillery also would have two branches. Some 350 men would form a light field artillery force firing forty-eight cannon of about 8-pound weight while another 450 firing fifty-two 16-pounders would form a heavy artillery force. Another 2000 men would provide additional manpower at artillery emplacements. This total triune army force would be commanded by about 1400 officers.

This radically reorganized army was to be manned by troops drawn from the traditional source of bakufu manpower, the liege vassals. On 11/28 a new and presumably realistic schedule of the liege vassal's duty obligations was announced.[41] It slashed in half the nominal obligations in force since 1649 and specified them in terms of men (furnished together with their weapons by fief holders) or money (mostly from holders of stipends). Fief-holding liege vassals were to select recruits from able men on their fiefs and send them to Edo for assignment to the infantry and training with firearms. A rationalized system of recruitment and service was promulgated. Only men between the ages of fifteen and forty-five were to serve. They were to serve for terms of five years, and if a man passed the age of forty-five during his period of service, he was to furnish an alternate to complete his obligation. Titles and honors were specified, and the men were to receive a modest level of support from their lords, but the bakufu would provide commissary services.

During 62/12 the bakufu began implementing this plan for a modernized army. On 12/1 Ōzeki Masuhiro, an experienced military reformer, was designated army commander *(rikugun bugyō)* and Oguri Tadamasa took the subordinate title of commander of infantry *(hohei bugyō)*. At the end of the month Misoguchi Shōnyo was also designated commander of infantry and a number of subordinate officer appointments were made, giving substance to the new officer chain of command. On 12/7 the bakufu hit directly at its customary forces by ordering its main vassal groups *(yoriai, okumuki, sanbantō)* to organize infantry and cavalry units and train at the military institute with appropriate weapons. In succeeding weeks further specific actions continued the process of reorganization.

Thus by the end of 1862 it was clear that bakufu military leaders had accepted the necessity of scrapping the hallowed system of Ieyasu, even as they attempted to legitimize the reform by asserting that they were returning to the ''pre-Kan'ei'' system of the great founder's day. In succeeding months, however, the momentum of this military reorganization was lost even more rapidly than it had developed. By 63/5 the firearms practice at Tokumaruhara was being phased out amid complaints of the costs involved and the hardships imposed on farmers in the area. Two months later, to the great frustration of those who had been implementing it, the reform appeared completely stalled.[42] More than a year was to pass before the effort would again get underway.

3. Problems in Military Reform

There were probably several reasons for the failure of this military reform. Most immediately changes in the political situation hurt it. The shogunal trip to Kyoto and the foreign crisis of early 1863, which we discuss in succeeding chapters, seem initially to have derailed it. The collapse of the Bunkyū political reform dealt it a severe blow.

Even without those external disruptions, however, the military reform had internal weaknesses that hobbled it. Based essentially on a Dutch book with the translated title of *Sanpei takuchiiki* or ''Tactics of the three combat arms,'' it attempted to follow the large pattern, building down from the top, setting up an infantry structure of battalions and regiments and a cavalry structure of platoons and squadrons without developing a system to assure that the basic building blocks of soldiers and tactical leadership were sound. To realize the grand design that had been worked out on paper and implemented by fiat, training was given by some men who had studied Dutch tactics at Nagasaki or by others who had received some instruction from foreigners living at Yokohama.[43] This did not constitute the sustained and coherent program that would furnish a cadre capable of sound tactical leadership.

The reformers recognized their need for a competent cadre. We have already noted the great attention they gave to questions of training and their continuing dissatisfaction with the results. In 63/1 Ōzeki wrote to officials in Kanagawa explaining that with actual training about to start, it was necessary to obtain both English and French studies of military matters and human assistance in the actual training.[44] The request was not followed up, however. Ōzeki got no reply until 63/4 and no assistance came then. So from the outset the system suffered from a lack of consistent well-trained cadre and did not evolve into a self-developing program that could displace the other archaic units. Rather, it resulted in the creation of a few new low-status firearms units totaling only some two thousand to four thousand troops.

For another thing the attempt to make firearms the main weapon of bakufu forces was confounded by the reluctance of men to drill like common foot soldiers and the failure of reformers to make that drill compulsory. Moreover the requirement that liege vassals arm the men they furnished created a cost they were reluctant and perhaps simply unable to assume. It also seems to have made it hard to assure a uniform weaponry of reliable modern firearms.

There is also another facet to the liege vassal problem. Bakufu plan-

ners may have miscalculated badly the real capacity of liege vassals to furnish men. Although they envisaged a force of some thirteen thousand
men sustained by liege vassal land production and stipend resources, the
manpower-money schedule of 11/28 slashed the total customary levy by
about 50 percent. Later in 1866 when military reformers reestimated the
manpower worth of that reduced schedule, they concluded it would have
yielded only about half of what the Bunkyū reformers had assumed.[45] If
the later calculation was more accurate, and bakufu experience in military
reform during 1866–1867 suggests that it was, then the Bunkyū reformers could have realized their aim only by squeezing liege vassals much
harder then they anticipated or by paying for their manpower in some
other way.

This last point brings us to another area of difficulty that hurt the
Bunkyū reform and was to plague the regime ever more disastrously in
following years. That was bakufu fiscal inadequacy. It had a direct impact on the Bunkyū reform in ways that foretold with great precision central problems of later years.

First, it forced the regime to place the main burden of army reform on
liege vassals, even though that policy undermined the quality of the new
forces. In later years this issue was to lie at the heart of bakufu military
reform difficulties and prove so intractable that eventually it drove bakufu
leaders to become institutional revolutionaries in their search for a solution to the problem.

Second, it prompted the regime to retrench harshly, even though doing so fostered hardship and discontent among the regime's supporters.
In later years this policy was to be pursued ever more forcefully until it
wrecked bakufu morale and finally drove some of the regime's supporters
into a state of semirevolt.

Finally, it encouraged the regime to continue fostering military development, army as well as naval, among the *han* even though the greatest
of them were clearly becoming a menace to Tokugawa supremacy. This
policy continued long enough after 1862 to contribute appreciably to the
remilitarizing of the entire archipelago. Some of the great *han* were pursuing programs of military strengthening quite independently of Edo's
urging, and later they were to do so in defiance of Edo's wishes. But in
the early 1860s the bakufu was fostering this strengthening and in the
process was helping to undermine the credibility of the Tokugawa civil
order and contributing to a severe shift in the balance of military capabilities that soon would prove very disadvantageous to Edo.

In several ways, then, the fiscal difficulties of 1862 were prophetic of
agonies and enterprises yet to come. For all that, however, the structural

reforms that generated those difficulties clearly lay on the path that must be followed if Tokugawa leaders were to contain the foreign threat and preserve their favored positions in Japan. The Bunkyū reformers were aiming at the transformation of the military system, the rationalization of the administrative structure, and the elimination of waste. Those changes caused suffering, at first to low-status people and later to high-status people, but the changes and consequent disruption were essential regardless of the regime's fiscal situation if it were to cope with the demands of the day. They were necessary prerequisites to those later stages of reform that also must follow if the regime were to survive.

These structural elements of the Bunkyū reform were thus of enduring importance to Edo, but they did not directly address the central political question of the day: Who would control national policy-making? The political facet of the Bunkyū reform addressed that crucial question, and the crisis of late 1862, to which we now must turn, was the result of the struggle then going on to determine its answer.

CHAPTER 2
The Bunkyū Reform II
Months of Disintegration
1862/9–1863/3

POLITICAL CONFLICT: 62/9–11

    1. *The Politics of Expulsion and Imperial Respect: 62/9–10*
    2. *The Depths of Abasement: Purge and Appeasement: 62/11*

INTENSIFIED POLICIES FOR CHANGED PURPOSES:
62/12–63/1

    1. *First Steps in Controlling Court and* Shishi
    2. *The Shogunal Pilgrimage*

THE END OF THE BUNKYŪ REFORM

    1. *Failure of the Bunkyū Political Reformers: Kyoto, 63/2–3*
    2. *The Bunkyū Reform in Review*

By the beginning of 62/9 Matsudaira Shungaku had achieved much of his program of political reform. And in the background bakufu officials were making progress in their program of structural reform, especially in terms of military modernization. In the half-year from 62/9, however, bakufu leaders found themselves engulfed by extreme and irreconcilable demands coming from court, great lords, *shishi*, and foreigners. Attempts to cope with those demands repeatedly dragged the bakufu into bitter internecine quarreling and paralysis and eventually into untenable policies. In consequence the whole Bunkyū reform fell apart and Shungaku fled to Fukui in defeat and disgrace.

POLITICAL CONFLICT: 62/9–11

During his first three months as supreme councillor Shungaku had been engaged in contests that essentially pitted proponents of particular domestic change against defenders of particular domestic customs and arrangements. The defenders had largely been routed, but they had accepted their defeats peacefully.

The intra-bakufu political conflict of the next two months, by contrast, grew initially out of bakufu efforts to reconcile colliding foreign and court-daimyo-*shishi* desires. As communicated to Edo in late 1862, the basic court-daimyo-*shishi* desires vis-à-vis foreigners were two: to restrict and eventually end those concessions which foreigners had secured by threats of violence and the resultant formality of treaties and to modify or end that Tokugawa hegemony in Japan which gave the foreigners their unjustified security. The foreigners, however, wished to extend their concessions and strengthen their security.

The two positions were irreconcilable, but neither side was prepared to yield gracefully. The foreigners, unlike the people of Edo or low-ranking Tokugawa vassals or even senior councillors, all of whose interests had been sacrificed in the initial reforms, were recognized by bakufu leaders as both willing and able to wage war to defend and advance their particular interests. And *shishi*, of course, were also willing to kill. The bakufu thus was caught between *jōi* anger and foreign firepower, and in consequence the political disputes at Edo were raised to a level of anguished intensity which matched that of Ii's Ansei purge and had consequences which boded far worse for the Tokugawa regime.

1. The Politics of Expulsion and Imperial Respect: 62/9–10

During the months 62/9–10 the political contest at Edo revolved about the conjoined issues of ''expelling the foreigners and respecting the court.'' On the one hand were demands for expulsion and respect that emanated from court, daimyo, and *shishi* and were supported by Katamori and men of Aizu. On the other were the threats of foreigners that helped sustain a pervasive official resistance to those very demands. In the expulsion matter Yoshinobu threw his weight onto the side of officialdom, and that left Shungaku nearly alone in the middle, where he stumbled between positions and finally came down, more or less, on the side of the court. By late 62/10 that choice had forced the Edo leadership into a formal commitment to policies of expulsion and imperial respect that were to haunt the regime for a long time thereafter.

This disorderly process of decision-making commenced in early 62/9. By then Edo was well aware that during the prior two months the court had gradually adopted, at the behest of radical samurai and courtiers, more extreme positions on the matters of imperial prerogatives and foreign affairs. Bakufu leaders were particularly fearful that before long the court might well call upon them to expel the barbarians promptly, and that fear lent urgency to the search for a solution to the Namamugi crisis. Then on about 9/14 news arrived that the court had indeed decided to demand the foreigners' expulsion, and on that day a more moderate formal notice from the court warned Edo that Hyōgo must not be opened despite stipulations to the contrary in the 1858 treaties. In response bakufu leaders decided to take the initiative by sending Yoshinobu west at once to persuade the court to ratify those very treaties, including the agreement to open Hyōgo at the end of 1867.[1] As soon as that decision was made and notice of it sent off to Kyoto, however, it was undone, and it was Katamori of Aizu who precipitated its undoing.

Katamori had earlier dispatched vassals to Kyoto to investigate the situation there because of his impending service as Kyoto protector. They apprised him of the depth of the court's and *shishi* commitment to expulsion, news that could only have reinforced the *jōi* sentiments already held by many Aizu men. The reports suggested that Yoshinobu's upcoming mission would only widen the Edo-Kyoto rift, and accordingly Katamori tried to forestall it.

On the seventeenth he submitted a memorandum arguing that bakufu officials had been wrong in making earlier treaties and should be punished for doing so. He acknowledged that benefits did derive from foreign commerce but asserted that all the concessions of the 1858 treaties, excepting the clauses opening Nagasaki, Hakodate, and Yokohama, should be repudiated as the court wished. By taking that action, he argued, and by then consulting the daimyo about affairs and by then going to Kyoto, the shogun would restore unity to the polity. Should that not be done, he added, his mission as protector would become impossible.[2] It appears from the mode of his argument that Katamori was attempting to build a foundation of goodwill for himself at Kyoto by demonstrating that he shared the court-*shishi* view of affairs. He also was attempting to temper it to accommodate the strong contrary view at Edo, but his memo opened the entire issue again, and Shungaku quickly emerged as the most eloquent proponent of a revised policy.

In earlier years, in line with the advice of Hashimoto Sanai and later Yokoi Shōnan, Shungaku had been a defender of the treaties. In 62/9, however, as he learned of the court's more assertive position and as he learned, too, that some dissidents were denouncing and threatening Yokoi, he became more receptive to the *jōi* arguments among his own vassals, arguments made with particular vigor after the decision of 9/16 to send Yoshinobu westward. In an effort to accommodate those sentiments, he proposed to the bakufu three days later a devious scheme by which it was to repudiate all its previous and immoral treaties, stimulate a vigorous resolve to accept any inevitable war, assemble the daimyo to have them discuss and settle policy, thereby unify the country, and then undertake a Japanese-originated policy of negotiating treaties with foreign countries.[3] His proposal was akin to positions advocated years earlier by Nariaki and others. By 1862, however, it was infinitely more difficult of realization because the foreigners were far more entrenched and the proponents of expulsion far more active than before.

The proposals of Katamori and Shungaku precipitated intense debate in which the senior councillors (notably Itakura and newly appointed Ogasawara Nagamichi) and other officials, including Okabe Nagatsune and Yamaguchi Naoki, opposed the two vigorously. Oguri Tadamasa criticized Shungaku for his fundamental argument that the bakufu should base its policy on respect for imperial wishes, contending that in accord with six hundred years of history the bakufu itself should manage affairs. Katamori supported Shungaku, but Yoshinobu tended to oppose him, gently at first and more insistently later. For days the debate raged on in great heat, with Chōshū men actively prodding Shungaku to maintain his position and urging the bakufu to revive the pugnacious 1830s policy of ''shell and repel'' *(ninen naku uchiharai)*.[4]

Seven days of argument yielded nothing, however. Officials refused to change bakufu policy, and Yoshinobu, who had become ever more obdurate, was planning to leave for Kyoto in a few days to defend the treaties. Accordingly on 9/27 Shungaku again ceased going to the castle and prepared for submission his resignation as supreme councillor. Ōkubo Ichiō undertook at once to mediate and expressed interest in Shungaku's argument that the daimyo should be assembled to discuss policy. Yoshinobu offered to delay his departure ''two or three days'' and prepared for Yokoi an eloquent defense of his view that the court must be won to the bakufu position. By 10/1 Shungaku had reversed himself and accepted Yoshinobu's formulation. On that day he returned to the castle, and as a conciliatory gesture the latter's departure was formally postponed until the ninth.[5]

At once, however, events conspired to disrupt this apparent reconciliation. On the same day a formal notice from Kyoto informed the bakufu that Yoshinobu's trip should be delayed until 62/11 or later because another imperial delegate was being sent to Edo. That was not welcome news to officialdom: one imperial delegate had done enough mischief; another could only do more. At stake, too, was the fundamental issue of whether Kyoto or Edo was in charge. Accordingly on the third Edo reaffirmed that despite the court's notice Yoshinobu would depart on the ninth.

That response did not please men of Fukui. They assumed that the coming imperial delegate would advocate closing the ports, and in line with the strategy of accommodating court wishes, they again urged Shungaku to oppose Yoshinobu's trip. The pressure led Shungaku to reverse himself a second time, to urge Yoshinobu's delay, and again to support Katamori's argument that court desires be accommodated and treaties repudiated. Yoshinobu's departure was delayed again, but he and officials continued to resist on the larger issues, and for several days bakufu debates dragged on indecisively. Shungaku denounced the indecisiveness, and the frustrated debaters considered warning Kyoto that Edo would ''restore authority to the court'' (seiken o henjō) if the latter rejected the treaty arrangements. No policy decisions were reached.[6]

Then on the eleventh young Katamori unintentionally raised the debate to a new level of acrimony. On that day he presented the senior council an imperial notice brought from Kyoto by one of his vassals. In it the bakufu was instructed to treat the coming imperial mission properly, by which was meant revising established procedures so as to show clearly bakufu subordination to the emissaries. Katamori's presentation of the notice, which should have come via the deputy, won him the censure of Ogasawara Nagamichi, who argued that his protector job did not involve matters of that sort, and that of Itakura, who criticized him for improperly receiving an imperial message (just as Mito had done in 1858). Itakura correctly saw the incident as another instance in the breakdown of established bakufu governing procedures. Shungaku equally correctly saw Itakura's outburst as evidence that key bakufu officials were not really willing to assent to imperial wishes, and in irritation he stayed away from the castle the next day. On the thirteenth he submitted his previously prepared resignation as supreme councillor together with an extraordinarily long statement that unhappily summarized recent discussions, especially the foreign policy debate. He reviewed his own opinions on policy and his complaints about bakufu indecisiveness and selfishness and then laid the blame for Japan's troubles at the feet of those officials who failed to show proper respect to the court.[7] At the highest bakufu levels the substantive issue of foreign policy had thus by 10/13 been subtly turned into an instrumental issue of national control cast in the rhetoric of respect for the imperial institution.

During the next several days the senior councillors were exposed to additional pressure from several sources. Yamauchi Yōdō, on whose behalf the court had been lobbying at Edo for some time, warned that bakufu insistence on keeping the ports open would lead to court repudiation of Edo and upheaval in the western provinces. Katamori threatened to resign his office if the court's position were not adopted. The Kyoto deputy warned from afar of the danger of not mollifying the rabid *jōi* sentiments in Kyoto. The pressure took its toll, and by 10/18 Okabe was able to inform Shungaku that Itakura and Ogasawara felt unable to oppose the *jōi* view any longer. The two were so distressed that they in effect hid behind their one supporting superior, Yoshinobu. In a letter they sent him the next day, they spelled out very clearly their conviction that the bakufu could not have it both ways as some (presumably including Shungaku) were arguing. Rather it must risk war by offending the foreigners or repudiation by offending the court. They asked Yoshinobu to decide which risk to take, but to do so sincerely, by which they seem to have meant deciding in terms of policy as a whole rather than particular interests or tactical considerations. [8]

This burden of lonely choice was more than Yoshinobu was ready to bear. He had been buffeted by Shungaku and Katamori. He knew that the imperial embassy, led by radical 25-year-old Sanjō Sanetomi and 23-year-old Anenokōji Kintomo, was already en route and upon arrival would demand a firm *jōi* policy as well as acknowledgment of Kyoto's primacy. When key supporting officials adopted an ambiguous position, he caved in, even though lesser officials still defended the treaties. On the twentieth he accepted a nominal compromise suggestion of Yōdō. In effect it accepted Shungaku's wish that imperial demands for more respectful procedures and *jōi* be accepted, but it hedged the latter by suggesting that the date for expulsion ''unavoidably'' must be unspecified. Yoshinobu then urged Shungaku to return to duty and, angry at the verbal *jōi* triumph and his own defeat, on the twenty-first or second he submitted his own resignation as shogunal guardian. [9]

Regular bakufu leaders found themselves in a terrible situation. Sanjō's imperial delegation had left Kyoto ten days earlier and was due to reach Edo a few days hence. By then policy decisions would have to be made and some semblance of a cohesive leadership reestablished. But Shungaku was refusing to serve and had asked to resign because the bakufu had not formally committed itself to accepting Sanjō's prior demands on ritual procedures and his anticipated demand for expulsion of the foreigners. Yoshinobu likewise was refusing to serve but for the opposite reasons: he had asked to resign because the bakufu had not formally committed itself to rejecting those very demands. The senior councillors still preferred Yoshinobu's original anti-*jōi* position. However, they and lesser officials found themselves pressed directly by Shungaku and indirectly by Yōdō and Mōri Sadahiro, by Katamori, by officials at Kyoto, and by their foreknowledge of Sanjō's purpose. Then on 10/23 Edo received from Kyoto a report that activists there regarded Ōkubo, Okabe, and Oguri as the three archenemies of *jōi* who must be murdered if they were not removed from office. That notice apparently proved to be the last straw. Ōkubo had ceased going to the castle the day before. After receipt of the Kyoto report, Okabe too decided to stay home, and the senior councillors concluded that they must accept Shungaku's demands. Again the conjoined pressure of court, daimyo, and *shishi* had prevailed.

This capitulation to Shungaku was the key to getting Edo's tattered leadership back together in time to meet Sanjō's embassy. As soon as Shungaku learned that his will had prevailed, he at once joined ongoing efforts by Mizuno, Itakura, Ogasawara, Ōkubo, Mito men, and others to persuade Yoshinobu to swallow his pride and return to duty. On 10/26 the efforts finally succeeded. That afternoon Shungaku and Yoshinobu returned to the castle discussions. On the following day court-daimyo pressure secured another victory when the shogun formally instructed Yōdō, as the court had long been urging, to sit in on bakufu deliberations in the castle.[10] An outside daimyo had joined three related lords in the inner councils once limited to vassal daimyo and liege vassals.

At the cost of agreeing to the principle of a *jōi* policy and making another concession on great daimyo political participation, bakufu leaders had at the very last minute reestablished their appearance of unity. On the following day Sanjō's mission entered Edo, escorted by the young Tosa lord, Yamauchi Toyonori, with a force of five hundred men as buoyant as those Hisamitsu had brought to town five months previously. The imperial delegates were welcomed by senior councillors and others in a properly respectful manner and were told the shogun had measles, was in isolation, and could not meet them. Undeterred, the delegates informed the bakufu they would wait, and in consequence they stayed in Edo for a month awaiting the shogunal audience that was to be held according to new deferential procedures worked out in the interim.[11]

The delay in the shogunal audience postponed formal bakufu commitment to the court's expulsion policy, but it did not materially alter the outcome. During 62/11 domestic politics again came to dominate the scene, but before addressing those matters, the outcome of the *jōi* issue can be summarized.

As previously agreed, the bakufu did accept on 11/2 the imperial message calling for a *jōi* policy, and the acceptance led to heated debate on the character of the bakufu reply. Despite the heat, defenders of the treaties were in fact already defeated, and as 62/11 progressed, the real topic as far as foreign policy was concerned was the instrumental one of how to implement any policy of repudiating the treaties. One line of thought, for example, postulated war and addressed itself to the question of defense, proposing that the primary task was to defend Kyoto and prepare provisional plans for withdrawing the imperial heir to a safer location should that be necessary. [12]

Finally the shogun met the imperial delegation. A few days later, on 12/4, Sanjō formally resubmitted to the shogun the imperial instructions that the bakufu resolve upon an expulsion policy, then consult the daimyo and settle upon a date, and inform the court of the decision by early spring or sooner (within a very few weeks, that is). On the next day the shogun replied that he had seen the imperial notice and was respectfully dutiful. Since he was responsible for policy, he went on, he would consult the daimyo, go to Kyoto, and report in detail then. That vague statement was then signed by the shogun in an extremely humble manner as "your retainer, Iemochi." [13] The court delegation had in effect traded off an explicit date for *jōi* in return for more evidence of shogunal subordination. Two days later Sanjō's mission departed Edo, its goals largely achieved.

2. *The Depths of Abasement: Purge and Appeasement: 62/11*

While Sanjō was awaiting his shogunal audience during 62/11, bakufu leaders implemented a new and extreme phase of the policy of respect for the court. It was all part of Shungaku's overall strategy, but it was implemented primarily by Ogasawara Nagamichi. As Nagamichi saw the situation, the essential sequence of measures was this: first, to punish all who had cooperated with Ii or later Andō, Kuze, and Naitō; concurrently to comfort the people and manage foreign affairs so as to avoid war; then to apologize to the court for the sins of Ii et al.; and thereby to achieve court-bakufu unity. [14]

After being rebuffed in some awkward first attempts to implement that strategy, [15] Nagamichi presented his memorial to the shogun on 11/5, following Iemochi's formal acceptance of the imperial letter on expulsion. In his memorial Nagamichi argued that Hikone and the three former

senior councillors must be punished in order to remove their stigma from
the bakufu so that a strong and wealthy nation (fukoku kyōhei) could be
achieved. It was impossible to avoid opening the country and hence the
treaties would have to be retained, he argued, and by punishing high officials and thus demonstrating bakufu contrition Edo would free the
treaties of the onus of disobedience to the imperial will. He was proposing in effect that the rituals of domestic obeisance be used to escape the
trap of jōi-foreigner conflict. Itakura and other officials found his frankly
protreaty formulation acceptable, and Nagamichi was given responsibility
for preparing the purge charges from information furnished by other officials.

Officials had acquiesced in the purge, probably seeing the strategy as
the least unacceptable choice, but none seemed interested in being associated with it. Thus on the ninth, as Ogasawara was assembling information on those to be punished, Itakura started to boycott the proceedings,
most likely because of displeasure with the general trend of affairs and
out of fear of assassination. The next day Yoshinobu also began to stay
home ''due to a cold'' and on the fifteenth resubmitted his resignation.
Lesser officials, whose morale was plummeting as rapidly as Ogasawara's purge list was growing, wished that Itakura in particular would
return to duty, perhaps in the belief he would temper Ogasawara's
charges. When they received reports of a shishi plot to murder Itakura,
they urged Yōdō to exert efforts to control the would-be assassins, but
Yōdō warned that the control of shishi could not be guaranteed unless
Itakura abandoned his tergiversation on the matters of imperial respect
and jōi. Itakura accordingly continued to stay in the safety of his mansion, but he did see Nagamichi's list of proposed guilty and suggested
lighter punishments for certain men. In line with his comments, charges
against several lesser officials were dropped, but most of the purge remained intact.

By 11/20, while Sanjō was still awaiting his shogunal audience and
Itakura and Yoshinobu were still boycotting affairs, Nagamichi was ready
to act, and the first verdicts were announced. It had been less than fifteen
days since the basic decision to punish people had been made.

The whole purge procedure was thus handled in an arbitrary and summary manner that made Ii's Ansei purge look like a model of judicial rectitude. Nor is that surprising. Ii was seeking to establish the degree of
offense against a clearly defined set of norms whereas Nagamichi was
blatantly scapegoating on the basis of vaguely defined criteria of error in
order to cast onto a hapless few the onus for policies of the past that had
come home to haunt present leaders. Thus the practice of bakufu self-

cannibalization, which had begun earlier as an attack on the privileges of menial servants and low-ranking vassals, had risen to include high-ranking men who differed from their assailants only in the fact that their term of office was done.

As finally promulgated on lists of 11/20 and 23, Hikone was ordered to surrender 100,000 *koku* of land or nearly one-third of the *han*'s remaining tax resources. Matsudaira Yoritane of Takamatsu, who had long been cooperative with Ii, was ordered into domiciliary confinement. Seven former senior councillors (Manabe Akikatsu, Andō, Kuze, Naitō, Hotta, Wakizaka, and Matsudaira Noriyasu) and a few other former high officials, as well as a long list of lesser officials that included Ōkubo, Asano Ujisuke, Komai Chōon, and two of Ii's closest supporters, lost land or were put into domiciliary confinement or dismissed from service or forced into retirement. These punishments were accompanied by a shuffling of officials that moved other offensive men into innocuous positions where their administrative talents could still be used. In sum Naga-michi's purge routed the Ii remnants, destroyed the core of the existing liege vassal leadership, and added vast new evidence that only a fool would take bakufu office. Or as Katsu Kaishū said upon learning of the purge: ''What with the recent reversals and upheavals of government, one cannot but fear for the land. Officials will panic and simply look after their own necks. Someone has certainly made a blunder.''[16]

The purge was supposed to demonstrate bakufu contrition for alleged former insults to the imperial dignity, and so on the twenty-third the shogun made an unprecedented statement of apology for the dismal state of affairs and asked the emperor to demote him by one court rank. Two days later Yoshiyori of Tayasu similarly confessed himself guilty of unsatisfactory work while shogunal guardian and surrendered his court rank. The court eventually rejected Iemochi's gesture but accepted that of Yoshiyori.

Just as the earlier purge of 62/8 was the negative side and the amnesty of 62/7 the positive side of a single policy of atonement, so the purge of 62/11 was matched by more amnesty actions. This expanded amnesty, which involved Mito men in particular, had been demanded by the court in the notice presented Edo by Mōri Sadahiro in late 62/8 and had been a subject of debate in following weeks, with Itakura objecting to it vigorously. By late 62/9 the bakufu had apparently agreed to the amnesty in principle but no implementive action had been taken. Concurrently with Sanjō's mission, however, Ikeda Yoshinori, the daimyo of Tottori and a son of Nariaki, had come to Edo at court behest to secure pardons for those Mito supporters of *sonnō jōi* whom Ii and Andō had punished.

Mito men themselves lobbied through both Sanjō and Ikeda, and the efforts ultimately bore fruit. On 11/21 and 28 the bakufu issued orders that finally pardoned, rehabilitated, and restored to *han* office some more Mito men and removed from power others of the currently ruling conservative faction. The latter order formally pardoned those men who had died or been punished for "patriotic" services, which included those who had murdered Ii Naosuke, tried to murder Andō, and attacked the British consulate at Tōzenji. [17]

As autumn hurried by, the bakufu thus found itself being forced to accept the principles of expulsion and subordination to Kyoto. The shogun was making abject apologies; officials were being punished for loyal service, and the regime's most savage enemies were being honored for their deeds. There were very few bitter dregs that Edo seemed unprepared to swallow.

The extent of bakufu decline was made all the more apparent by the gains its enemies were scoring. Bakufu officials were thoroughly familiar with the many facets and subtle expressions of Tokugawa supremacy and so were painfully aware by late 1862 of the magnitude of the court-daimyo-*shishi* accomplishment. Those achievements must be realized if the dimensions of the bakufu dilemma are to be appreciated.

The court's success was clearly symbolized in the revised procedures of the Sanjō mission and the treatment accorded it in Edo. While awaiting the shogun's recovery from measles, the delegates received respectful visits from the mighty, prompting one delighted attendant of Sanjō to note: "Here in Edo where the power of the bakufu is so great and [officials] bustle about so importantly . . . now top bakufu officials, the *sanke* and *sankyō* [principal related] daimyo, and lesser men all quake before the imperial authority and call upon the imperial delegates. The imperial restoration will soon be here. Oh joy. Oh joy." [18]

Then on 11/27 the new-style shogunal audience was held. The courtiers rode all the way to the audience building entry (*genkan*) rather than walking partway. There they were greeted in person by the shogun and top officials rather than by a master of shogunal ceremony. In previous years the master would have taken them to greet the senior councillors and then the shogun on his raised platform. This time the shogun led his visitors to an inner reception room, and there the courtiers took a seat above him and received homage from all the assembled officials and daimyo. Then the shogun stepped up to the courtiers' level to receive the imperial instructions calling upon the bakufu to discuss and settle upon a date for expelling the barbarian.

Many other developments seemed to justify the optimism of Sanjō's attendant. The court was successful in ending official bakufu constraints on the management of its own affairs. It also succeeded in telling Edo how to manage bakufu affairs in Kyoto and even in the Tokugawa *han* of Owari and Mito. Then, in anticipation of full political responsibility, on 12/9 the court designated twenty-nine court officials and nobles as *kokujigakari* with putative duties discussing national affairs at court. But the substance of the court's emergence was most clearly demonstrated in the plethora of orders it issued to great daimyo during 62/10–11 informing them of the expulsion order, instructing them to come to Kyoto to defend the city, or calling upon them to participate in political discussions.

Nearly as obvious as the court's success was the burgeoning independence of the daimyo. It was reflected in their various acts of defiance, overt displays of military power, and covert displays of intrigue. It was evident in their entry into political discussions and their success in having Edo respond to their wishes. Publicly it was most visible in the steady stream of great daimyo removing their families from Edo and sending their own forces to Kyoto, usually with formal bakufu approval because the bakufu recognized it could not stop the trend.

Perhaps the most frightening form of challenge was that presented by *shishi*, whose activities in Kyoto continued unabated and whose tactics of terror were again being applied in the Kantō as well as in Kyoto. The first sharp warning of renewed activism in the Kantō had been the 10/23 report of a plot against Ōkubo, Okabe, and Oguri. Then on 11/11 bakufu leaders learned of a plot by Satsuma men to kill Itakura for his alleged role in leading the anti-*jōi* forces and thus showing disrespect toward the emperor. Other reports even spoke of a plot hatched in Kyoto to poison Yoshinobu. The most ambitious *shishi* venture was attempted on the thirteenth when some Chōshū samurai implemented a plan to murder foreigners in Kanagawa. They were delayed by reinforced bakufu guard units and then stopped at the last minute by intervention of some *han* officials. A month later on 12/12 they tried again, that time successfully burning a new English legation that the bakufu was in process of constructing. Before the bakufu could take any punitive action toward the men, however, Chōshū officials dispersed them. Edo leaders were unwilling to order them turned over for punishment, having just failed to induce Satsuma to surrender men who had actually committed murder at Namamugi.

By 62/12, in short, the bakufu seemed on the brink of disintegration. Internally it was ravaged by retrenchment, reform, and Ogasawara's purge. Externally it had surrendered the symbols of authority, did not pretend to control the great lords, had agreed to an impossible foreign policy, and was unable to keep the peace even in the city of Edo. As matters were going, there seemed precious little reason to expect the regime to survive far into the New Year.

INTENSIFIED POLICIES FOR CHANGED PURPOSES: 62/12–63/1

The steep decline in bakufu fortunes and the bitter internecine fighting that had accompanied it seriously damaged Shungaku's fragile control of affairs and gave rise to a new strategy for bakufu recovery. The senior councillor Ogasawara Nagamichi seems to have been the prime initial exponent of that new strategy.

Stated simply, Nagamichi appears to have been proposing that Shungaku's devious strategy of *sonnō jōi* be adopted to secure the objectives of regular officials. The daimyo were recognized as beyond control by direct coercion, so bakufu efforts at revival were to be directed initially toward resecuring the court and pacifying *shishi* in hopes daimyo would then become less defiant. The rhetoric of *sonnō jōi* that daimyo and *shishi* had been using for their own complex purposes would be similarly used by Edo to recover court and *shishi* goodwill. The purge, apologies, and pardons, as damaging and humiliating as they had been, were to serve as first steps in this strategy, and the policy of respecting and protecting the court, particularly the upcoming shogunal trek, would be used to reestablish a massive bakufu presence in Kyoto. With court and *shishi* quieted, the daimyo could then be confronted. Divide and conquer was perhaps a workable strategy, and out of the ashes of Tokugawa defeat would thus be built a new era of Tokugawa hegemony and political tranquillity.

That was, of course, a very risky strategy. Whereas daimyo, *shishi*, and court need not accept primary responsibility for either *jōi* rhetoric or *jōi* convictions, the bakufu must. Bakufu officials had no illusions about their capacity to fight aggressive foreigners, and so in following weeks and months many officials, especially bakufu diplomats, never really subscribed to the notion of using *jōi* rhetoric, fearful that they might later be unable to repudiate any expulsionist promises they had made.

On the other hand, if the policy were either overtly rejected or openly described as an exercise in deception, it would only enrage the bakufu's critics all the more. In consequence even Nagamichi did not speak openly of any such overall strategy. As a result his purge had its harsh, demoralizing impact and the shogunal trek remained a topic of bitter dispute within the bakufu. But that such was his strategy seems suggested not only by his earlier-noted memorial of 11/5 but also by the precipitous manner in which the purge was handled, the limited resistance to it, the great publicity given it, the half-hearted enforcement of its punishments, and the speed with which ousted officials later returned to important positions. Whatever subtle intentions may have lain behind the purge, however, it was not until the very end of 62/11 that this new bakufu strategy for recovery began to take real shape. And then it did so in response to new reports of coincidental foreign and domestic difficulties.

1. First Steps in Controlling Court and Shishi

On about 11/24 or 25, bakufu leaders heard rumors that French warships were going to go to Osaka to thwart the court's *jōi* orders. On the twenty-fifth, apparently in response to those reports, Ogasawara and Itakura recommended the rapid deployment of major forces to the Kinai area. On the following day more alarming news was received from Kyoto. A report from Kyoto city magistrate Nagai Naomune indicated that the deputy and lesser officials had no influence at court, that outside daimyo influence was mushrooming, and that the court-Satsuma effort to name Shimazu Hisamitsu protector was a direct slap at Edo and Aizu. Accordingly, Nagai wrote, Yoshinobu, Shungaku, Katamori, and Yamauchi Yōdō in particular should all hasten there by steamer within ten days. He also expressed fear of an Ōnin-type war because of the activities of Satsuma and Chōshū in the Kyoto region.[19]

Under the stimulus of Nagai's report officials discussed the Ogasawara-Itakura proposal for deployment westward, and it seems to have evolved into a plan for a major reassertion of bakufu strength in the Kinai. As Yoshinobu outlined the plan to Shungaku on the twenty-eighth, he would lead a force of twenty thousand troops to Osaka to protect the court and guard the Kinai coastline. Then, with an overwhelming Tokugawa presence established, the shogun would hasten westward to assume nominal charge.[20]

That bold plan was discussed at once by Shungaku, the court nobles at Edo, men of Satsuma, and probably Yōdō of Tosa. Many of them doubtless sensed in it an attempt to reassert Tokugawa power in Kyoto, and Satsuma in particular could not have been keen on the proposal. Shungaku and Yōdō favored a joint Tokugawa-daimyo effort at restoring order in the city, and Shungaku moved quickly and adroitly to deflect the bakufu scheme. On the twenth-ninth he secured Itakura's support for a plan that called on Hisamitsu and his son the Satsuma lord to go to Kyoto to bolster court-bakufu unity *(kōbugattai)*, and on 12/1 he, Yōdō, Yoshinobu, and the senior councillors formally agreed to urge the Satsuma men to be present in Kyoto by 63/1/20, by which time Shungaku and Yōdō would also be there.[21]

There are several possible reasons for the bakufu's easy abandonment of the bold scheme. Perhaps it was dropped so quickly because of the opposition of Shungaku and others, or because Satsuma goodwill was still sought in conjunction with the pending Namamugi issue, or because the twenty thousand troops were found not to exist, or because military reformers warned that such a venture would totally disrupt their program of reorganization. Or perhaps it was dropped because the alternative scheme seemed nearly as useful and much less expensive. It would, after all, serve to pit Satsuma against Chōshū extremists, and that in turn would pit some nobles against others, and those divisions would leave Edo the stronger. At any rate the final arrangements blunted any effort to use the deployment as an overt means of restoring bakufu hegemony.

In other ways, however, bakufu leaders did begin to show some effective resistance to the court. Most importantly the persistent court effort to have Hisamitsu named protector continued to encounter fierce resistance at Edo, and because of the widespread hostility to it, the Satsuma scheme never was realized. In another matter, during prior weeks the court had sought authority to create an imperial defense force *(shinpei)* under its own command. Such a development clearly would have undermined the fundamental shogunal claim to a role as the appointed protector of the court. Accordingly, when the shogun on 12/5 formally responded to Sanjō's message, he quietly deflected the court's demand for its own army along with related changes in palace guard arrangements, promising instead that reinforcements for Kinai defense would be sent from Edo.

Then the bakufu began to implement a considerably reduced version of the late 62/11 proposal for Kinai defense. During the first days of 62/12 decisions on westward deployment were made, and a series of orders were issued to strengthen the bakufu's position at Kyoto prior to the shogun's entry. As soon as Sanjō left Edo on the seventh, officials and armed forces were dispatched under Katamori (12/9), Yoshinobu (12/15), Nagamichi (12/16), and subordinate military unit commanders. A dramatic Tokugawa revival was not about to occur, but at least the start of a difficult recovery would be attempted.

This first bakufu effort at militant domestic diplomacy proved strikingly ineffective. Undertaken for conflicting purposes and implemented without sufficient planning, the westward deployment proved an inadequate vehicle for any purpose at all. Of the three high officials who had led elements westward, only Nagamichi went by ship, and he stayed in the Osaka area until 63/1/11. The others went overland, and so it was well into 63/1 before the first bakufu delegations and military units were established in the imperial city. Upon arrival, moreover, they found that the court was indeed in the hands of perfervid expulsionists, just as earlier reported, and against their enthusiastic posture the men from Edo were pathetically uncoordinated and uncertain of themselves.

Meanwhile Hisamitsu had written from Kagoshima in late 62/12, urging on a variety of grounds that the shogun's trip be delayed. His letter reached Edo early in 63/1, and his position was quickly adopted by Shungaku. He and representatives of Satsuma lobbied to undo the plan for a shogunal trip, perhaps because they realized it was more likely to serve bakufu aims than their own *kōbugattai* goals. Fukui men were able to persuade Itakura and Mizuno Tadakiyo that the trip should be postponed because of the intensity of *jōi* opinion in Kyoto, and so bakufu leaders at Edo agreed to seek imperial approval of the delay. Spokesmen of Fukui and Satsuma were sent posthaste to Kyoto and lobbied for delay from about 1/16 to 1/21. The court refused to agree, however, and so bakufu leaders adhered to their plans for the trip.

While failing to change court wishes, the Fukui-Satsuma lobbying in Kyoto did succeed in alarming the newly arrived Edo delegates, notably Yoshinobu, Okabe, and Katamori. After arriving, Yoshinobu and Okabe had quickly concluded that if the bakufu hoped to retain or regain the court's goodwill, the shogunal trip would have to be made and even then it would take great pressure to change the court's devotion to *jōi*. This realization helped confirm their support for the trip and probably made Yoshinobu more receptive than before to the strategy of employing *jōi* rhetoric sans substance to Edo's advantage. Accordingly both he and Okabe opposed the Fukui-Satsuma effort, urging instead that the bakufu adhere to the shogunal trip and the verbal *jōi* policy.[22]

Katamori was even more upset by the Fukui-Satsuma effort. *Shishi* violence in the city had continued at a high pitch even after his arrival with hundreds of retainers, and on 1/28 he sent a message to Edo expressing his concern about reports that the trip might be delayed and in consequence the *jōi* decision unfulfilled. He feared such an outcome would frustrate his task of pacifying the city and lead instead to an eruption of great violence in the Kinai district.[23] To oversimplify a bit, Katamori was urging *jōi* as a means of restoring tranquillity and Tokugawa control at home whereas Yoshinobu and Okabe were urging *sonnō* as a way to avoid genuine *jōi* while still resecuring Tokugawa control at home.

In the outcome these first moves to strengthen the Tokugawa presence in Kyoto had had little effect on the city. They had, however, generated more pressure for the shogun's trip and so helped reaffirm bakufu commitment to the trek despite the growing opposition of Hisamitsu and Shungaku and the enduring skepticism of many at Edo.

These year-end moves to strengthen the Tokugawa presence in Kyoto were paralleled by efforts to resecure control of *rōnin* and other *shishi*.[24] After the ports were opened in 1859 the bakufu had been repeatedly embarrassed and its morale seriously damaged by the activity of such men, and during 1862 the numbers of *rōnin* increased rapidly, prompting some officials at Edo to seek ways to enlist them in support of the regime. At least one *rōnin* also envisaged bakufu-*rōnin* cooperation as a means to foster national unity against the barbarian. That was Kiyokawa Hachirō, an active *rōnin* originally from Shōnai *han* who had a record of antiforeign deeds, a vigorous commitment to imperial loyalism, and a considerable number of followers. In 62/11 Kiyokawa urged Shungaku to create a force of bakufu-led *rōnin*, arguing that the bakufu could never suppress the *shishi* and so should join them. He also offered to aid in the enterprise.

During late 1862 several strategies for using these men were proposed, but the plan to turn erstwhile critics of the regime into its defenders became possible only after the bakufu accepted a policy of *sonnō jōi*. Three days after the formal shogunal acceptance of the court's *jōi* policy on 12/5, bakufu leaders decided to use *rōnin* support. On the following day the bakufu ordered a military institute official to assemble them and supervise their training, and in succeeding days more officials were appointed to that duty. The respected Udono Chōei was given a commanding function in the *rōnin* force; details of pay and training were worked out, and by month's end perhaps as many as five hundred *rōnin* were participating, presumably because many of them were in dire need of income. During 63/1 they were sorted out, and some 250 were organized into seven companies *(kumi)*, each consisting of officers and 30 men.[25]

Later that month Kiyokawa indicated his intent to assemble an additional force of perhaps a hundred and proceed to Kyoto. Lest his plans lead to further *rōnin* trouble, Udono was put in charge of the *rōnin* going west, and on 2/8 he, Kiyokawa, and a force of some 230 set out for Kyoto under bakufu orders and at bakufu expense. Among the men was Kondō Isami, who later became leader of a part of the *rōnin* force.

Kiyokawa saw himself as working to bring tranquillity to the realm *(tenka)* and fostering loyalty to the emperor, and he preached *sonnō jōi* ideas to his followers. Doubtless the *rōnin* generally saw themselves as going to defend the emperor and expel the barbarian, but in bakufu eyes they were going to protect the shogun. As one observer later recalled: ''It being evident that the number of *rōnin* was multiplying and that *han* were changing the names of their vassals and sending them in the guise of *rōnin* to Kyoto to spy on affairs, the bakufu would use poison to control poison in order to ward off danger during the shogun's trip to Kyoto.''[26]

After the *rōnin* unit reached Kyoto, it provided a sometimes useful police force with extensive connections to the network of activist samurai. Its men were not always trustworthy, were guilty of some acts of savage violence, and quarreled among themselves and with other *shishi*. After 63/3 the group divided, the great majority, whose tribulations we note later, returning to Edo with Kiyokawa, where they were entitled the Shinchōgumi. Those few men who stayed in Kyoto, including Kondō, were assigned to patrol duty under Katamori and became known, in fame or notoriety, as the Shinsengumi.

These *rōnin* units were formed, then, as an adjunct to the shogunal trek, and like the deployment of Katamori and the others, their creation was seen as prelude to the great pilgrimage that would, it was hoped, restore Tokugawa control of the imperial institution.

2. The Shogunal Pilgrimage

The key element in the year-end strategy of Tokugawa revival was the shogunal trek to Kyoto, an event unprecedented in over two hundred years of the Great Peace. Originally conceived as a way of expressing the *kōbugattai* ideal of bakufu obedience to Kyoto, the purpose of the trip had subtly changed, and, as we noted earlier, by 63/1 Shungaku was trying to delay it. He found much support for his position within the bakufu itself because the trip had always been anathema to many and remained so despite the regenerative purpose it had come to embody for some officials. The grounds of this enduring opposition deserve attention.

Back on 62/9/7 the bakufu had announced that the shogun would go to Kyoto in 63/2. In the following months, amid the swirl and furor of political conflict, administrative preparations for the trip were made. The planning had been preceded and was accompanied by a series of disagreements, some within the bakufu, some between bakufu leaders and outsiders, as to the best way to handle the trip. And surrounding the whole matter was an aura of anticipation and speculation about its meaning.

In the world of speculation, some envisaged as early as mid-1862 that such a shogunal trip would lead the daimyo to shift their *sankin kōtai* residences from Edo to Kyoto and thus disrupt the entire polity. By 62/9 some were fretting that the trip would lead to conflict in Kyoto between the forces of the bakufu, Satsuma, and Chōshū. And one rumor said that the shogun would stay in Kyoto for ten years and name the daimyo of Kaga or Sendai as resident keeper of the castle (jōdai) at Edo. Later the rumor of a ten-year sojourn reappeared, and it was speculated that in the shogun's absence foreigners would attack Edo and settle there.[27] Insofar as these rumors suggest a general estimate of the trip's potential, it appears that few attached great promise to the scheme as a means of restoring Tokugawa preeminence.

Not surprisingly, therefore, one finds that within the bakufu profound distrust surrounded the whole venture, and opposition to it was never stilled. Opponents of the trip had from the outset argued against it on fiscal grounds. An official estimate of the cost presented on 7/20 by Kawakatsu Kōun and Oguri Tadamasa used precedents of the seventeenth century to put anticipated expenses at 1,500,000 ryō.[28] Another estimate was twice that figure. Even the lesser figure was more than the total regular annual income of the bakufu. Officials of the inspectorate (ōmetsuke and metsuke) argued that the funds should be used to buy the bakufu a modern naval armada. Travel by ship was proposed as a way to save money, but on 7/21 Shungaku, Yoshinobu, and the senior councillors rejected that plan, affirming that the shogun would go by land.[29]

From 62/8 planning for the trip focused on means of minimizing costs of overland travel.[30] Daimyo on the Tōkaidō, the route of the proposed procession, were said to be impoverished and still unrecovered from the disastrous earthquakes of 1854 and 1855. Accordingly the bakufu notified them that the shogun would not stay at their castles en route. Moreover those responsible for the temples, shrines, and inns at which the shogun would stay were admonished to exercise restraint in preparing for the occasion. In succeeding months a series of notices were issued whose intent was to minimize costs and economic dislocation. A 62/10 notice, for example, warned that the numbers of accompanying personnel must be minimal and expenses en route kept carefully under control in order to prevent inflation and resulting public hardship in Kyoto. To facilitate the order, a set of precise guidelines was spelled out, indicating exactly how many attendants were to be in the entourage.

Even with the most rigorous control, however, it was apparent that the cost of moving a vast number of men overland to Kyoto and back in a manner appropriate to a shogunal procession would be immense, and that knowledge prompted Katsu Kaishū and others to reiterate their advice that the shogun travel to Kyoto by ship. To do so would relieve all the intermediate daimyo and post-town operators of the immense costs of rebuilding highways and reconstructing and repairing their inns, resting

places, castles, and towns in order to make them presentable to the passing shogun. It would also shorten the trip by days and reduce the need
for a train whose numbers would be commensurate with the shogun's
status and precedents of the seventeenth century. Arguments that the
shogun would get seasick were dismissed; precedents for the sea trip
were unearthed; planning proceeded. By late 62/12 proponents of a sea
route had won.

Other costs remained, however. In 62/9, for example, the Kyoto
deputy ordered extensive repair work on Nijō castle, which had been
built two centuries before, and on areas of the imperial palace still showing scars from a fire in 1854. Also in mid-1862 individual daimyo began
to request permission to accompany the shogun; however he might
travel, they would mostly go overland, and someone would have to pay
those costs. Living costs in Kyoto would be considerable too, to say
nothing of the accompanying gifts and bribes, not the least of which
turned out to be the 63,000 *ryō* the shogun gave out to the Kyoto
townspeople and 60,000 *hyō* of added rice stipends granted to the nobility.

Quite apart from the monumental problem of costs, the trip continued
to be disturbing to bakufu leaders as an expression of their political weakness. Even after the trip was agreed to, they could not organize it as they
chose. On 9/9, for example, when announcing the duties of several officials and Tokugawa relatives, the bakufu instructed Yoshiatsu of Mito to
serve at Edo during the shogun's absence. Later, however, Edo received
a request from Kyoto that Yoshiatsu and members of the procourt faction
at Mito accompany the shogun, and in the outcome the bakufu yielded to
the request. In a notice to Yoshiatsu it informed him that although he had
earlier been instructed to stay at Edo during the shogun's absence, the
court wished him to come to Kyoto, and therefore he was to do so.

Preparation of the shogunal trip thus went ahead in a sea of doubts,
pessimism, and fiscal concern. By year's end, however, as Ogasawara,
Itakura, Yoshinobu, and other bakufu leaders came to view it as the cap-
stone in a program designed to restore bakufu control of the court, they
took steps to try to assure it would work out that way. Besides establishing a prior Tokugawa presence in Kyoto and enlisting *rōnin* support, they
attempted to have the shogun's accompanying military forces headed by
a very prestigious and staunchly pro-Tokugawa leader, Hachisuka
Narihiro of Tokushima.[31]

Narihiro had been born the twenty-second child of former shogun
Ienari and became daimyo of the outside *han* of Tokushima (257,900
koku) in 1843. He had been rather active in politics during the 1850s

and had acquired a reputation as a sensible advocate of Tokugawa supremacy tempered by an awareness of daimyo interests and court sensibilities. He framed his opinions in a sophisticated manner and couched them in the rhetoric of his day. Practically all bakufu leaders had sought his support over the years, and during 1862 he was repeatedly subjected to pressure to play an active role. He consistently rejected Edo's blandishments, however. In their greatest effort to get his cooperation, bakufu leaders on 12/18 designated him commandant of the army and navy (*rikugun sōsai* and *kaigun kata*) in charge of the forces that were to accompany the shogun to Kyoto. Presumably the new title would put him on a par with Shungaku and perhaps superior to Katamori during the shogun's visit to Kyoto. He was ordered to participate in governmental deliberations at once and was told that his two prior requests notwithstanding, he was not to return to his fief during the winter. Rather, because he was a close relative of the shogun, he was to proceed to Kyoto, returning to his fief in the spring only after the shogun's visit had ended. Even these new titles were not enough to snare Narihiro, however. On 63/1/7 he reiterated his wish to head for Tokushima later in the month, and on the twenty-second, when it was apparent he would not accept his duty orders, he was formally relieved of the new commandant title. Seven days later he departed for home. If the shogunal trek were going to achieve a Tokugawa revival, it would have to do so without Narihiro's aid.

While the effort to recruit Narihiro was in train, other preparations continued. Late in 62/12 the bakufu had announced that Iemochi would go to Kyoto by ship, and on 63/1/21 the sailing date was set for 2/21. On the following day, even as Narihiro was being released, Shungaku and a retinue of about eighty departed for Kyoto with Katsu on the *Jundōmaru*, reaching Osaka after a slow, stormy, seven-day trip and finally getting to the Fukui residence in Kyoto on 2/4. The *Jundōmaru* then headed back east because it was supposed to carry the shogun unless the recently purchased steamer *Lyman* (later *Taiheimaru*) returned in time from its maiden commercial run to Shanghai.

Meanwhile Edo hummed with preparations, contingent after contingent set out for Kyoto, and more and more orders for Edo castle duty were issued. The great shogunal progress was clearly going to take place, but its preparation only seemed to highlight the extent of bakufu weakness and unease. The malaise was reflected in two actions, one scarcely noticeable and one very noticeable but very unclear in its precise meaning.

The scarcely noticeable action occurred on 1/22, the day Shungaku left town. On that day the bakufu issued an order that in a sense confessed its dependence on the goodwill of the Edo populace, the very people who had been the primary bearers of the burden of retrenchment in the Bunkyū reform. In a notice to inspectorate officials the bakufu referred to recent reports that burglars were breaking in at night here and there in town and that armed and violent men were assaulting and robbing travelers on the streets. If that were so, they were to have the city magistrate and others instruct the townspeople to draw up neighborhood plans for self-defense. Should neighbors hear trouble, they were to hasten to the scene and apprehend the troublemakers. Should the latter be too numerous for capture, the townsmen were authorized to kill them. If the troublemakers were captured alive, they could be sued in the courts.[32] In short, the police being inadequate, organized vigilante action by townspeople would be approved.

The more noticeable action occurred on 2/9. On that day the bakufu abruptly announced that the shogun would go by land rather than by sea and would depart Edo on the thirteenth, eight days sooner than previously planned. The reason for this last-minute change is uncertain, but it likely was a product of two coinciding factors. The controversial plan to go by ship may have lost its appeal to many officials and shogunal attendants because the three runs between Edo and Osaka that Katsu made during 63/1 and 2 were so hectic due to high seas as to make the land route look safe, comfortable, and fast enough by comparison. There also reportedly was concern lest British vessels capture the shogun on the high seas en route to Kyoto. And the switch to land travel, whatever its cause, made an earlier departure date advisable if the time of arrival were to remain relatively unchanged.

This shift to travel by land was likely the main reason for the accelerated date of departure. Additionally, however, some officials may conceivably have urged it in an attempt to delay responding to British demands for satisfaction in the Namamugi and Tōzenji incidents, or perhaps in hope the diplomatic issue could somehow be used to aid bakufu maneuvers in Kyoto. At the time, the senior British representative in Japan, Colonel St. John Neale, was assembling naval forces at Yokohama prior to submitting his government's demands for reparations and other forms of satisfaction. By 2/2 Edo leaders knew the essential nature of Neale's intentions and were trying to decide how to respond. Their first thoughts inclined toward keeping the shogun at Edo until the issue had been resolved, but no decision was made at once. When they did decide on 2/9, it was a decision to leave earlier, but since the bakufu did not know when Neale would present his demands, it is not clear that the two matters of his presentation and the shogun's departure date were causally connected. In any case, on 2/11 Neale made it known that he would deliver his government's demands within a few days, and two days later the shogun departed Edo as scheduled, a few days before Neale was able to make his representation formally.[33]

Thus the shogun, symbol of 250 years of Tokugawa supremacy based on control of the great heartland of Japan and maintenance of an unquestioned capital city at Edo, departed his headquarters, journeying, as one commentator foresaw it, ''to the enemy camp.''[34] He had departed in seeming haste on a trip that was in almost all ways a subject of intense doubt and disagreement. And in the end the skeptics' fears were justified, even if their alternative schemes would have been equally disastrous.

THE END OF THE BUNKYŪ REFORM

In the course of 1862 Matsudaira Shungaku had worked his way into a leading role in the bakufu and had been able to start implementing most aspects of his Bunkyū reform. The high point of his effort had been reached in the reform decisions of 62/int. 8, and in following months his effectiveness was undercut by the greater radicalism of court-daimyo-*shishi* pressure on the one hand and the ongoing resistance of officialdom and gradual emergence of a new bakufu strategy of revival on the other. By early 1863 he found himself participating in a shogunal trip he did not really favor, and within weeks developments culminated in his downfall and collapse of the Bunkyū reform.

Shungaku's failure did not mean, however, that regular bakufu leaders had triumphed. They had not. The configuration of forces and events that wrecked Shungaku's enterprise was equally disastrous to their new strategy for revival. The weeks at Kyoto demonstrated what so many at Edo had suspected: that a bakufu policy of imperial loyalism and verbal *jōi* was untenable either as a way to restore Tokugawa leadership at home or to avoid a real collision abroad. But by the time of Shungaku's fall key bakufu leaders were *faute de mieux* so committed to the policy that it was not repudiated for another year and a half, during which time it gave rise to internal political quarrels of the most bitter and most damaging intensity.

1. Failure of the Bunkyū Political Reformers: Kyoto, 63/2–3

By the end of 63/1 Yoshinobu, Katamori, Yamauchi Yōdō, Ogasawara Nagamichi, and several lesser officials, including Okabe and inspector

Sawa Kanshichirō, had reached Kyoto with forces justified as defense against the foreigners and intended from Edo's viewpoint to strengthen the bakufu's position at court. Then on 2/4 supreme councillor Shungaku also entered town, hoping that with Satsuma support he could restore moderation to the court's foreign policy and press on with his *kōbugattai* scheme for a limited restructuring of the polity at home.

By then a large number of other daimyo also were in Kyoto, together with their attendant military forces. Moreover a host of adventurers had descended upon the city in hopes of finding excitement and political fulfillment in support of imperial honor. It had become painfully obvious to the Edo delegates how serious was *shishi* violence in the city, how weak bakufu control there, and how strong the Chōshū-supported radical influence at court.

In face of this situation the Edo delegates were deeply divided on how to cope with radical demands.[35] Sawa emerged as an outspoken and apparently sincere supporter of *sonnō jōi*, and Katamori, too, continued to urge that the bakufu act to repel foreign ships in order to resecure court-*shishi* support. Neither Nagamichi nor Yoshinobu favored actual expulsion, but they found the position difficult to oppose because of their desire to regain court-*shishi* goodwill. So they tried to finesse the matter with their policy of *sonnō* and verbal *jōi*. Thus divided and pitifully fearful of offending imperial sensibilities, the delegation from Edo was rapidly overwhelmed by the elegant men of Kyoto, who were themselves often responding to *shishi* threats or carried away or intimidated by *sonnō jōi* enthusiasm of lesser courtiers.

The extremist pressure yielded its most important fruit on 2/11 when the court instructed bakufu delegates to specify a date for expelling the foreigners. The delegates attempted to procrastinate, but Shungaku's arguments, Yoshinobu's stubborn resistance, and the intense displeasure of Okabe and other officials, who saw verbal *jōi* being displaced by the real thing, were all to no avail. On the fourteenth the Edo group yielded and gave the court formal assurance that the shogun's visit would be limited to ten days and that within twenty days after his return to Edo, or in mid-63/4, the expulsion policy would be implemented. Four days later the court formally announced this decision, thereby binding the bakufu publicly to its commitment.

Thus within ten days of his arrival Shungaku found one key element of his intended policy repudiated. His loss was not bakufu gain, however. Katamori and the others who hoped through a *jōi* policy to woo the court and *shishi* back to a pro-bakufu position found themselves, as many had feared, agreeing to wage unwinnable war without getting any domestic quid pro quo. And those such as Yoshinobu who hoped to regain court cooperation by outloyaling the imperial loyalists found themselves unable to stop the rush of events.

To the contrary, in succeeding days bakufu leaders saw more and more evidence of the inadequacy of their policies. To begin with, although quelling the extremists within the city was their chief ongoing concern during 63/2, efforts by the Tokugawa spokesmen to secure a court order to pacify *shishi* made no headway. Rather, they found radical pressure reducing their own group when late in the month Yōdō ceased active participation due to pressure from Tosa vassals. During the same weeks *shishi* violence grew worse, and Katamori was unable to stop it, in part because the court obstructed his activities, in part because many of the *shishi* lived in daimyo residences and were therefore beyond his jurisdiction as protector.

The whole trend of developments was alarming to the Tokugawa group, and in consequence on 2/19 Shungaku revived the plan to present the court with a choice: either formally assume the authority hitherto vested in the shogun or formally state that the shogun did have the governing authority customarily associated with his title. The bakufu representatives at Kyoto approved that proposal and it was presented. Most of the representatives likely had approved the statement in hopes it would force the court to acknowledge Tokugawa authority and so enable them to suppress the extremists in the city. Shungaku, however, may have hoped that the court would actually accept the restoration of authority.[36] Whatever lay behind the maneuver, the court very shrewdly accepted the proposal but sent no answer. The court's failure to reply may have stemmed from deep internal disagreements on how best to respond, but the upshot was that it had in its hands the very patent of Tokugawa authority, which it could keep for itself or restore to Edo as it saw fit.

While thus holding the bakufu's authority hostage, the court pressed on with its reassertion of primacy. Radical court officials spoke with unconcealed contempt of the Tokugawa position. The court made further organizational changes to facilitate its reassertion of active governing authority and on the twenty-third revived its request for an independent military force to be under imperial control and drawn from the domains. The great lords, who perhaps saw in that scheme a challenge to their own military independence, did not favor it. Bakufu officials were also opposed, and Katamori strongly protested it as an insult to his effectiveness as protector. However, court proponents of the imperial force could and did justify it by pointing to the impending date of expulsion and also, somewhat hypocritically, to the failure of the Edo delegates to quell the rampant lawlessness and overtly antishogunal plotting and activity of *shishi* in the city. During 63/2 the Edo delegates capitulated and approved imperial formation of a force of 1200 men to be drawn from the *han*.

At Kyoto matters were thus going abominably for the bakufu, and the news from Edo was no better. Early in 63/2 the senior councillors there had reported to Yoshinobu on the impending crisis over Namamugi, and on the sixteenth Kyoto heard from Edo that the British intended to secure an indemnity—by military attack if necessary. About seven days later they learned details of the severe demands and early deadline (reported as a fifteen-day limit and on 2/26 as a twenty-day limit expiring on 3/8) recently presented to Edo in Neale's ultimatum.

That information precipitated discussion among both Tokugawa representatives and court officials, but being far from the scene, they could do very little. After debating the virtue of resolving that everyone in the country be ready to die in resistance to the aggressor, they decided on the twenty-seventh to send daimyo home to prepare defenses. The bakufu representatives ordered Okabe and Sawa to return to Edo to participate in the negotiations with the British but rescinded the order shortly after. Other orders were issued for accelerated defense preparation near Osaka, and in succeeding days officials there initiated frenetic preparations for a war they expected to erupt shortly.

While affairs in both Kyoto and Edo were steadily deteriorating, young Iemochi was making his stately advance westward. From Edo he moved along the Tōkaidō, visiting Ieyasu's grave at Sunpu on 2/21, passing through the old Tokugawa homeland of Mikawa, stopping near Nagoya on 2/27, at Ōtsu on 3/3, and finally entering Kyoto on the following day.

Shungaku went to Ōtsu to meet the shogun and his accompanying officials, notably senior councillors Itakura and Mizuno. There the men from Edo first heard of the miserable state of affairs in the city. They learned of the proposal to return authority to the court and heard Shungaku recommend that the shogun submit to the court his resignation as shogun while he himself would resign as supreme councillor. The latter action had its origins late in 63/2 when Fukui men had become sufficiently upset by affairs to induce Shungaku to draft a new statement of resignation that would be submitted as soon as the shogun arrived. Shungaku followed the plan but linked his own resignation to that of the shogun, perhaps by way of encouraging the latter. Those newly arrived from Edo had no intention of quitting, however. Itakura in particular adopted a strong position in defense of shogunal dignity and was able to stiffen

the bakufu group sufficiently to get them to insist upon an imperial reply
to the proposal of the nineteenth.

On the shogun's first day in Kyoto Itakura, Mizuno, and Ogasawara
persuaded the court to allow Yoshinobu as Iemochi's spokesman to present the matter of shogunal authority directly to the emperor on the following afternoon. Yoshinobu did so and after a vicarious exercise in shogunal self-criticism obtained at last an imperial statement of shogunal
authority. The statement was explicit enough, but it also included instructions that the shogun expel the barbarians. Then on 3/7 the court
formally notified Iemochi of his duty, adding clauses stressing the importance of informing the daimyo on important national matters and of
respecting ''lord-vassal'' relations—that is, reasserting ultimate imperial
superiority and the importance of Edo behaving accordingly.37

The symbolic crisis had been survived, helped no doubt by imperial reluctance to accept responsibility for its own *jōi* rhetoric. The qualified
symbolic victory did not, however, conceal the bakufu's continuing substantive defeat. In succeeding weeks the court engaged in ritual pilgrim-
ages and other gestures that blatantly flaunted imperial pretensions and
shogunal inferiority both in terms of policy-making and the status hierarchy. Not since the Muromachi period had a shogun been given such a
patently empty title of authority.

The shogunal party had thus resecured elemental Tokugawa authority,
but that did not particularly cheer Shungaku. On the ninth he sent his
resignation to Itakura, Mizuno, and Ogasawara and ceased participating
in matters of state. The reason for that action is not entirely clear, but the
whole trend of affairs certainly must have encouraged it. Basically Shungaku's difficulties were the product of the changed character of political
conflict. In earlier months he had been successful because he had been
able to use the pressure of court, daimyo, *shishi*, and even foreigners to
bludgeon the bakufu into policy concessions. By early 1863, however,
the central political issue had changed. Political alignments had also
changed in a way that robbed him of his capacity to play one side against
the other.

To elaborate, in early 1863 the radical *sonnō jōi* advocates had successfully made the substantive issue of foreign policy rather than the instrumental issue of domestic power the focus of attention. But by then
bakufu officials in Kyoto had taken somewhat disorderly possession of
the verbal *jōi* strategy that Shungaku had advocated so stubbornly during
62/9 and 10, and he had switched to a strong anti-*jōi* posture. Consequently it was he rather than they who was left in the uncomfortable position of being anti–*sonnō jōi*. Instead of being able to play one side off

against the other, he found himself on the outside, in direct conflict with some of the court-*shishi*-daimyo elements he had previously depended upon in his struggles with officialdom. Furthermore bakufu officials were far from united on the character and purpose of their *sonnō jōi* posture. Even when the radical trend of court policy drove them and Shungaku together in common opposition to any genuine policy of expulsion, there were men such as Sawa and Katamori who opposed the anti-*jōi* effort. Their pressure effectively thwarted Shungaku's attempts to find a base of support in bakufu opposition to radicalism of any sort.

The man who could have helped Shungaku most was Hisamitsu, and he was out of town. But even if he had been in town, he might not have helped Shungaku because by then relations between the Tokugawa and Shimazu were thoroughly poisoned. By 63/2 Hisamitsu had managed to offend almost all those associated with the bakufu. His cavalier reaction to the Namamugi murder had embittered bakufu diplomats and regular leaders. His attempts to acquire special ranks and roles had angered conservatives. The lobbying to name him Kyoto protector had generated intense resentment at Aizu. Then his letter from Kagoshima that had reached Edo in early 63/1 aroused even more suspicion among officials. Although he had tried to delay the shogunal trip, to the satisfaction of many, he had also urged that the two outside lords Yōdō of Tosa and Ikeda Yoshinori of Tottori be given leading roles in the senior council and Shungaku and Yoshinobu greater influence on the shogun.[38] It was advice that could only deepen Edo leaders' distrust of Satsuma intentions.

Looking at the other side of the coin, we find that Hisamitsu too had reason for intense frustration. His attempts to secure a role at both Edo and Kyoto had been rebuffed; his foreign policy views had been rejected; and on the face of it bakufu leaders seemed determined to use the shogunal trip to restore Tokugawa hegemony rather than to facilitate the admission of great lords to a role in national decision-making. Then on 2/14 the bakufu delegates at Kyoto had agreed to set a date for expulsion—which could only have worsened the situation and reduced even further the likelihood that Hisamitsu would cooperate.

Thus the thorny question of expulsion with its entwined issue of Namamugi had altered political alignments and priorities in such a way as to deprive Shungaku of almost all the foundations of his political strength. In another more personal way too the foreign crisis probably was the crucial factor in prompting Shungaku to resign.[39] In convoluted debates at Kyoto on how to handle the conjoined expulsion and Namamugi issues, a recurrent proposal in 63/2 had been to have Shungaku or someone else go east in Iemochi's place to handle the British problem, the general program of expulsion, or both. For Shungaku, who already had been tarred with the anti-*jōi* brush, the prospect of being the one to appease the British could not have been pleasing, and his resignation may well have been designed to avoid that politically deadly task. If so, he acted just in time. On 3/11, two days after he submitted his resignation as supreme councillor, discussions at court eventuated in a formal order notifying Iemochi that he was to stay in Kyoto while either Yoshinobu or Shungaku was to go east to ''prepare defenses'' against the British at Edo. On the next day Ogasawara called upon Shungaku and pointed out that the *jōi* policy should not really be implemented anyway and that since Shungaku shared that view, he should return to duty and go east to mediate the Namamugi matter. Shungaku, however, knew a bear trap when he saw one and did not accept Ogasawara's suggestion. Nor did he yield two days later when the court asserted that it was he as supreme councillor who should go east. The court may have been discreetly trying to escape its own *jōi* dilemma, but Shungaku was not about to help it do so at such risk to himself and Fukui. He continued his boycott of discussions.

Bakufu officials and Yoshinobu, however, wished to have him remain in office, if only because they too wished mightily to avoid the duty he had been assigned. He was, moreover, their one best hope of winning Hisamitsu's cooperation for a pacific settlement with the British. With the Satsuma lord approaching Kyoto from the west, they assiduously tried to get Shungaku to return to duty. Their efforts were futile, however. Shungaku continued to boycott all conferences of state.

On 3/14 Hisamitsu entered Kyoto and, as reports had forewarned, promptly submitted a fourteen-point statement denouncing those officials, particularly Shungaku and Yoshinobu, who had yielded to irresponsible opinion and approved the impossible policy of expelling the foreigners. He went on to attack radical court leaders and demand that the bakufu punish radical samurai and *rōnin*, abolish the useless new imperial armed forces, and compel daimyo and vassals to return to their fiefs. He attacked the whole phenomenon of disobedience and asserted the fundamental importance of loyalty and warrior governance.[40] This ringing reassertion of the established social order utterly undercut what remained of Shungaku's *kōbugattai* policy of conciliation. Moreover, it paradoxically placed Hisamitsu in temporary league with the mainstream of regular bakufu official opinion, that body of opinion Shungaku had overwhelmed with such difficulty in 1862. Four days later Hisamitsu left the city again, heading for Satsuma to prepare for the confrontation with Britain that he had done so much to precipitate.

Shungaku's hope for a joint *kōbugattai* effort with Satsuma had ended in utter failure. Thoroughly dismayed at that disastrous outcome, he reiterated to Itakura his conviction that the shogun should resign. He blamed officialdom for the sad state of affairs and reaffirmed his intent to resign despite imperial instructions that he return to Edo to handle the closing of the ports. After repeated pleas had extracted neither bakufu nor imperial approval of his resignation, he departed abruptly for Fukui on the twenty-first. Four days later the Kyoto bakufu announced that Ogasawara would return to Edo to handle the British affair and Yoshiatsu to supervise the *jōi* program. And in an uncommonly acerbic formal notice, the bakufu stated on the following day that Shungaku had returned to his fief even though his request to resign the imperially sanctioned post of supreme councillor had been refused; the bakufu stated also that his men had been extremely rude to the court. He was therefore dismissed and ordered under house arrest.[41]

Shungaku's Bunkyū reform had ended a shambles. Far from forging any sort of national unity, he had merely led the bakufu to the brink of disaster and finally in frustration fled the field, leaving it to regular bakufu officials, Yoshinobu, and Katamori to devise some means of avoiding war with the foreigners and extricating the shogun from a court that still seemed to be thoroughly under radical *sonnō jōi* influence.

2. The Bunkyū Reform in Review

By 1863/3 the bakufu had been more sorely buffeted than ever in its past. Externally, shogunal authority had been effectively reduced to the point where the shogun could on his own authority do little beyond administering the Tokugawa domain. He (that is, his advisors) could not even determine his own top officials in Edo, much less Kyoto. He had surrendered his claim to authority over the court, the great daimyo, and the handling of foreign affairs. And, as soon would become evident, he was a hostage held captive in Kyoto.

Looking at the Bunkyū reform as a whole, one finds that many instructive points emerge. The administrative and especially the military reforms, as we noted earlier, did break out of the constraints of established structure. To really have enduring value, however, they would have to be pursued much further, and that could be done only if a strong reformist leadership retained power. The disastrous outcome of the political aspect of reform discredited progressive leaders at Edo, and structural reforms soon stagnated.

The crucial weakness in the political aspect of reform was that reform leaders were not agreed on its ultimate purposes. All agreed that it should

preserve the hegemony of the ruling elite in Japan, the political autonomy
of the daimyo in Japan, and the autonomy of Japan in the world. Even
those purposes were incompatible, but of more direct political consequence was the sharp disagreement on how political privilege was to be
distributed within the elite. Specifically, Shungaku wished to secure a
permanent leading role in national politics for some of the great daimyo
by opening top levels of bakufu officialdom to all daimyo and lower
levels to favored *han* vassals. Regular officials, especially senior and
junior councillors, wished to preserve the existing pattern of rule by men
selected from among ''true'' vassals of the Tokugawa family. They were
applying to the bakufu essentially the same criteria of personnel selection
that great lords such as Shungaku applied to their own *han*. The effect,
however, was to exclude from a legitimate role in determining national
policy men such as Shungaku, Hisamitsu, or Mōri Yoshichika and their
advisors. The reason for such a policy presumably was that if those great
lords acquired regularized political roles in the bakufu, they would
thoroughly overshadow lords of the much smaller vassal daimyo *han*.
Hence the disagreement on purpose and much of the political infighting
and paralysis.

In terms of substantive policies, the Bunkyū reform contributed nothing to bakufu resolution of its foreign problem. To the contrary, the verbal *jōi* policy turned into a millstone that was to burden the regime for
months. During the reform, moreover, the quality of foreign policy
debate was unchanged from prior years except insofar as a greater degree
of ambiguity and tortured logic was produced by the growing difficulty of
the dilemma. It is true that during those months foreigners made no great
new inroads on Japanese sovereignty, although the Namamugi incident
did prompt the British to enlarge their military forces garrisoned at the
imperialist beachhead of Yokohama. On the other hand, as the year ended, a flotilla of foreign vessels was assembling in the bay, and clearly a
crisis was building that might well issue in severe new encroachments on
Japanese independence.

It was in the realm of domestic politics that the implications of 1862
were most profound. It is not an exaggeration to say that in that year the
bakufu surrendered in both theory and practice its limited writ as the central government of Japan. The locus of power had broadened immensely
and become extremely diffuse, and in consequence the regime's cohesiveness had evaporated. As new forces intruded into the decision-making
process, the grounds of decision-making became more vague, and the interests involved more varied and in more open and fundamental conflict.
By early 1863 it was impossible to tell who had authority to decide any-

thing of political consequence, and because of the diversity of those enjoying influence, it was impossible to achieve a consensus. Unless that situation could be changed, the regime could not hope to save itself.

Other lessons may be gleaned from the political experience of 1862. We have seen that a crucial weakness in the political reform was its leaders' lack of agreement on their goals. That situation reflected Shungaku's failure to forge a unified leadership group. The customary way such a group emerged in the bakufu was for a new leader to purge uncooperative men, replacing them with others who would work with him. In his rise to power Shungaku attempted to do just that, but he never was able to get truly solid supporters into key positions. He failed to do so because he was an outsider, and almost none of those eligible for bakufu office really favored his ultimate goal of opening the bakufu permanently to more outsiders. In consequence even those officials, such as Ōkubo and Okabe, who most fully supported him broke ranks sooner or later, leaving him only tenuously in control of affairs. That outcome suggests that formerly effective techniques of governance might very well be inadequate in the face of the far more basic problems Edo was beginning to encounter.

The Ogasawara purge also deserves comment. In a way it reflected the bakufu's routine use of purges as an orderly means for changing policy and policymakers as I have discussed that process elsewhere.[42] But it was a very abnormal purge in two ways. First, it was precipitated by forces external to the bakufu and hence was not merely a transfer of power within the group of traditionally sanctioned power holders carried out by members of the group for purposes of their own. Second, it was grounded not in traditional canons of political morality but rather in the vague new ethic of disrespect toward Kyoto—a criterion that ultimately was controlled by people outside the bakufu. Because of these abnormal characteristics, Ogasawara's purge did not serve as a helpful device of government. On the contrary, it contributed to the demoralization of the regime. That it was partly a hypocritical gesture and that the punishments were not later rigorously enforced made it no less traumatic at the time for the men who served as Nagamichi's scapegoats.

The shogunal pilgrimage also was a disaster, proving as harmful as its opponents had feared. As a proposed action, it is true, the pilgrimage did have some value. One can argue, for example, that the decision to make a shogunal trip to Kyoto facilitated military reform. Some men were invited to train with the intention that those who showed the most progress would be able to accompany the shogun on his great expedition, and in all likelihood a short-range concern to protect the shogun and his prestige and to outgun Satsuma and Chōshū in Kyoto probably helped greatly to get radical military reform measures promulgated. One can also note that much of the other reform—the elimination of luxury, expensive customs, and superfluous offices—was justified as saving money to pay for the shogun's expedition, as well as for military development. As an actual event, however, the pilgrimage was a huge financial drain and a political disaster.

In the several measures of reform, purge, and leadership alteration that had occurred during 1862, one overall outcome is apparent. Defenders of the regime were in almost every instance injured and its critics benefited. The townsmen of Edo suffered; many low-ranking bakufu retainers had their interests seriously damaged; elite guardsmen were ordered to surrender privileges and dignities based on generations of familial loyalty. Higher officials found themselves being punished for active defense of Tokugawa interests. And the highest officials of vassal daimyo status found their classic position of leadership usurped by quarrelsome men not all of whom had any fundamental interest in Tokugawa well-being.

In return for this damage to its supporters the Tokugawa house itself made only ephemeral gains and experienced both real and ritual setbacks that were of enduring consequence. In the modification of the *sankin kōtai* system it lost its single most important mechanism for controlling the daimyo and freed them to use their wealth for military purposes and their time for political maneuvers. It retained some great daimyo cooperation only by accepting their political influence. The bakufu accepted humiliating changes in its relationship to Kyoto in order to avoid overt imperial denunciation and for the same reason acquiesced in a foreign policy that was openly recognized at Edo as being impossible of realization. That was the price, too, for regaining some degree of *shishi* cooperation. In cultivating *shishi*, moreover, the regime was offering funds and training to men who only recently had been actively attacking it in word and deed, and who would do so again as soon as Edo's policies changed.

Clearly 1862 had been a bad year for the bakufu. However, in considerable degree this massive erosion of the bakufu position was but the culmination of a process of decay that had been at work for years, especially since 1857. The year made manifest what had already become true: in the face of concerted opposition the bakufu in fact could no longer enforce its hegemony in Japan. In the spring of 1863, then, the Bunkyū reform leadership was discredited and the real position of the bakufu was established: it was one force in a field of political forces struggling to establish control over Japan's destiny.

Part
TWO

THE ATTEMPT AT RECOVERY

CHAPTER 3

The Start
of Conservative
Reaffirmation
1863/3–12

THE BAKUFU DIVIDED: 63/3–6

1. At Edo: Diplomatic Crisis
2. At Kyoto: The Shogun in Captivity
3. Ogasawara's Armed March on Kyoto

THE BAKUFU REUNIFIED: 63/6–12

1. Policy Deadlock and Domestic Deterioration: 63/6–8
2. Settling upon a Foreign Policy: 63/8–10
3. Preparation for a Second Shogunal Trip: 63/10–12

VIOLENCE IN AND NEAR EDO: 1863

The second year of the Bunkyū era, or 1862, had been a hectic one for the bakufu. By year's end Matsudaira Shungaku's attempt at inclusivistic reform was in serious trouble, and during early 1863 it foundered and the bakufu moved to the brink of ultimate disaster. At Kyoto the court nearly secured real governmental leadership, failing only when those great daimyo whose domanial power supported its pretensions abandoned the radical courtier-*shishi* program of restoration. Concurrently the foreigners at Yokohama nearly began their punitive war, being bought off only at the last instant in 63/5 and agreeing instead to a prolonged process of negotiation.

The debacle at Kyoto discredited leaders of reform, and after Edo survived the diplomatic crisis, a more conservative administration set about the task of reconstructing the bakufu position. The task was pursued for a year and a half. During 1863 it was repeatedly foiled by one difficulty after another, but during 1864 it weathered severe challenges and by year's end had attained a level of success, at least on the surface, that must have surprised even bakufu leaders themselves.

THE BAKUFU DIVIDED: 63/3–6

With Shungaku's fall regular officials reestablished their leading role in the bakufu, but that did not make their situation particularly enviable. Their group in Kyoto was still badly divided over the whole diffuse issue of *sonnō jōi* and so was unable to manage the surviving radical *shishi*-court alliance. Leaders at Edo meanwhile faced immediate and critical problems of war and peace, but their attempts to handle that issue expeditiously were hampered by the awkward situation of their colleagues in Kyoto. The tortuous path by which the divided bakufu dealt with these problems demonstrated again the serious inadequacies of the bakufu as a political form under existing conditions. It also illustrated how domestic problems prevented the regime from abandoning the untenable policy of verbal *jōi* recently settled upon.

1. At Edo: Diplomatic Crisis

When the shogun departed Edo on 2/13, he left behind officials responsible for administration of the castle, the city, Kantō and domanial affairs, and diplomatic matters. Most notably the Owari daimyo Tokugawa Mochinori was nominally in overall command at Edo, and senior councillors Matsudaira Nobuyoshi and Inoue Masanao were formally put in charge of diplomatic affairs. A host of lesser officials also received specific duty assignments during the shogun's absence, but of these various duties, it was the diplomatic responsibilities that proved most burdensome. Whereas the political actors at Kyoto enjoyed the luxury of engaging in quarrels whose implications were neither clear nor immediate, those left in charge at Edo had to make real decisions concerning the two distinct but inextricably conjoined issues of British demands springing from the Namamugi incident and Kyoto demands for expulsion of all foreigners.

On 2/19 the Edo leaders received the British ultimatum presented by Colonel Neale. He would launch an attack unless the bakufu within twenty days met his demands for apology and an indemnity for the Namamugi murders. Moreover, Edo was expected to help the British obtain from Satsuma a further indemnity and the guilty parties who were to be punished. The attempt to use Edo against Satsuma was itself thorny and raised problems concerning the limits of bakufu power and authority. And the indemnity was particularly severe: about $440,000 (Mexican silver), or roughly a third of the bakufu's regular annual income.

The ultimatum was made all the more unpleasant when Inoue and Matsudaira learned, probably on the following day, that the Kyoto delegates had agreed to an expulsion date of mid-63/4. In consequence they felt they could not on their own authority respond to Colonel Neale's demands and instead successfully sought delay in the deadline.[1] They used the time gained to two ends: to try to obtain support and guidance from the Kyoto delegation and to prepare for the war that appeared unavoidable, whether as a result of British or court demands.

From early 63/3 British belligerence made Inoue sufficiently concerned lest negotiations fail that he alerted daimyo in the Kantō to the prospect, instructing them to prepare for trouble.[2] In orders to the daimyo still in Edo, the senior councillors explained that they were trying to delay any British decisions until the shogun's return. If that were impossible, however, they had no choice but to drive the British away even though defense preparations were inadequate. Daimyo and liege vassals were assigned defense tasks in the Edo-Yokohama area, and their women and children were ordered evacuated from the city. As preparations were made, the general populace became panicky. A rash of hoarding abruptly pushed prices up, and some people began selling their possessions even at giveaway prices and fleeing the coastal areas of the bay. Alarmed by the spreading disorder, the bakufu called upon daimyo and officials to take measures to restore tranquillity. In anticipation of conflagration able-bodied men were ordered to organize more fire-fighting units. And lest the city be captured by the invaders, on 3/9 the Edo leaders worked out procedures for evacuating the shogun's ladies to the inland city of Kōfu. They also made plans for transporting the shogunal shrines of Ueno and Zōjōji out to the mountains. Four days later Inoue notified liege vassals that those with fiefs should send their families back to their fief residences. He observed that this move was in keeping with the reform of 1862 and was appropriately done now due to the crisis with Britain. And those vassals on stipends were to move their families outside the city to safety.

Meanwhile bakufu negotiators, including foreign magistrates (*gaikoku bugyō*) Takemoto Masaaki and Shibata Masanaka, obtained further delays from Neale despite the contradictory notices they were receiving

from Kyoto. And at Kyoto some negotiating time was gained when expulsion was rescheduled for 5/10. Accordingly until the latter part of
63/4 Edo waited in readiness. Although there were no further major defense moves, popular unrest and flight, sporadic denunciation of the negotiators, *rōnin* agitation, and scattered acts of violence did persist.

As noted in the preceding chapter, Ogasawara Nagamichi had finally
been ordered to go east from Kyoto to handle the British, and Yoshiatsu
of Mito had been ordered to return to supervise Edo defenses and the
overall program of expulsion. Nagamichi reached Edo on 4/6 and Yoshiatsu five days later. Upon his arrival Yoshiatsu was formally put in
charge of foreign policy but was ordered to consult with Mochinori and
the senior councillors. Whereas Kyoto had called in various formulations
for his overseeing the expulsion of foreigners, his task as restated at Edo
on 4/14 was to take charge of handling them with the outcome of the
enterprise unspecified.[3] Bakufu leaders thereby temporarily preserved
some maneuverability vis-à-vis final goals.

In succeeding days, however, Sawa Kanshichirō, who had returned
from Kyoto, been fired from his position as inspector, and then on 4/19
been promoted to foreign magistrate, vigorously argued in favor of expulsion and rejection of the British demands. And Nagamichi, who was
caught between his own convictions and his orders from Kyoto, adopted
an ambiguous posture, not openly agreeing that the British demands must
be accepted until 4/21.[4] His agreement on that day seemed to settle that
issue in principle, but the expulsion date of 5/10 was approaching.
Moreover, public malaise was persisting, so leaders at Edo ordered
daimyo to be alert in case of either war or panic among the people. They
ordered residents in the Shiba-Shinagawa coastal area to remove themselves inland, and a stretch of the Tōkaidō highway was also ordered re-
located to remove it further from the foreigners' beachhead at Yokohama.[5]

During those last days of 63/4 the discussions at Edo were confused
and acerbic. When debate shifted from the immediate issue of the British
demands to the larger issue of expulsion, lesser officials in general appear
to have become cautious despite their key role in the actual negotiations
and their strong commitment to the established diplomatic policy. Likely
they were mindful of *shishi* anger and the recent politics of purge and ap-
peasement. At any rate on 4/23 Nagamichi specifically wrote them that
they should present their opinions ''without fear of giving offense,'' an
assurance that most probably was given because it was needed.[6]

Four days later on the twenty-seventh Inoue and Matsudaira formally
notified the daimyo that the court wished the ports of Nagasaki, Hako-

date, and Yokohama closed and every last foreigner expelled within twenty days.[7] But on the same day Colonel Neale stated firmly to bakufu negotiators that the British would accept no further delay in the indemnity matter. The issues had been utterly joined, and something had to give. Accordingly on that day Ōta Sukeharu, who was sixty-four years old, deaf, and infirm, was recalled to office as senior councillor. He was joined on the next day by vigorous Sakai Tadamasu as junior councillor and forceful Matsumae Takahiro as superintendent of temples and shrines. All were associated with the infamous ''Ii-Andō regime'' and were by reputation committed to bakufu supremacy and peace with the foreigners.[8] Their presence shifted significantly the balance of pressure within the leadership and seems to have broken the policy deadlock. Despite the previous day's announcement that all foreigners were to be expelled, on 4/28 both the court and the foreigners were informed that the indemnity payment would be made.

Three days later, however, probably in the evening of 5/2, Edo leaders received a letter from Yoshinobu, who had recently left Kyoto with orders to take charge of expulsion at Edo. In his letter Yoshinobu advocated a resolute policy of expulsion to be commenced by negotiation at once, and he threatened to have executed any officials who did not cooperate. Whatever Yoshinobu's intent,[9] this note and the supporting arguments by its bearer revived the disputes at Edo. Nagamichi, Yoshiatsu, and Mochinori promptly tried to reopen the indemnity issue in hopes it could be used to help achieve the harbor closings. Lesser officials opposed the effort, arguing that the shogun should resign rather than pursue the expulsion order. Thoroughly dismayed by this dangerous reversal and renewed deadlock, Inoue and Matsudaira began to boycott affairs.[10] Much as they feared, on the next day, when bakufu negotiators requested a further delay from Colonel Neale, the colonel refused. Instead he ordered his ships to get up steam and start troop deployment, warning that further delay would result in bombardment at the end of three days. This information only intensified the crisis atmosphere.

On the next day, the fourth, with Inoue, Matsudaira, and many lesser officials refusing to participate in affairs and with Mochinori rushing to Kyoto to discuss the impending conflict, Nagamichi, Yoshiatsu, and some other officials and Mito vassals discussed the crisis. The only matters they could agree on were to wait for Yoshinobu's arrival and urge the daimyo and liege vassals to prepare for the worst. Waiting was hard, however, for men in such sharp disagreement and so close to disaster. On 5/7 Yoshiatsu wrote to Kyoto that the payment would not be made, a statement directly contradicting the bakufu letter of 4/28, which he had signed. That afternoon Ogasawara, armed only with sailing orders from Inoue and Matsudaira, abruptly prepared to leave by warship, presumably for Kyoto and presumably to convince leaders there to abandon their policy of expulsion. His ship left Edo the next day, putting in at Yokohama in the early afternoon. There it was met by a messenger sent overland from Edo by Yoshiatsu with instructions countermanding the senior council's sailing order. Ogasawara halted, but he agreed only to a day's delay.

During the course of his delay events moved quickly but confusedly. Colonel Neale's three-day ultimatum had expired and bakufu negotiators at Kanagawa had been notified on 5/7 that the colonel had ''turned matters over to Admiral Kuper'' for settlement of the indemnity. On 5/8, in an action reminiscent of the Perry crisis a decade earlier, two British ships approached Edo surveying the sea floor, presumably as preparation for inshore bombardment.

Late that day, a few hours after Ogasawara dropped anchor at Yokohama, Yoshinobu reached Kanagawa after an unhurried fifteen-day trip from Kyoto. He met Kanagawa magistrates Asano Ujisuke and Yamaguchi Naoki, who made clear the urgency of accepting the British demands. After that discussion and apparently without meeting Ogasawara, Yoshinobu went on to Edo by evening. What, if anything, he advised is not clear, but his conduct was apparently taken to signify tacit consent, or else his view was considered unacceptable, because after he left Kanagawa, Ogasawara had negotiators inform the British that he would pay on his own authority if necessary.[11] On the next day, as promised, Ogasawara arranged the payment. It was originally to be made in three installments, but the British insisted that it all be paid at once due to the recent procrastination. Accordingly it was delivered, coins valued at 440,000 silver dollars that filled over twenty chests and took three days to assay.

Along with the British demands, Edo leaders had been discussing the larger problem of expulsion. Even as Nagamichi was settling with the British at Yokohama, other bakufu officials, Yoshinobu, and Yoshiatsu were gathered at the castle in Edo debating hotly the court's order to expel all foreigners the following day. Most officials came down against expulsion of any sort, but they were opposed by Yoshinobu and Yoshiatsu and by anonymous threats to those associated with Ii, Andō, and ''disloyal government.'' Predictably the outcome was a compromise, and in content it reflected Yoshinobu's earlier letter and the general strategy of verbal jōi. It was agreed to begin on the morrow to discuss with the foreigners arrangements for closing all the ports. In accord with that compromise Ogasawara presented the British a note advising them that the court had decided to close the ports and expel them and that discussion of this enterprise was to begin at once. The British and other foreigners promptly rejected the note, warning of the calamities they would bring down upon Japan if the policy were enforced. In face of this response Edo ceased pressing the matter and it went into abeyance.

This chaotic resolution of the Namamugi incident and expulsion policy did not end their reverberations. Most obviously the bakufu had lost more of its means of buying warships or army supplies. Internally the capitulation led to more scapegoating as leaders tried to salvage the regime's honor by casting the blame on a few hapless officials. Moreover Edo's handling of both affairs, along with other developments of following weeks, gave rise to rumors of bakufu-foreign cooperation against the great *han*, notably Chōshū. The facts of capitulation to the British and sabotage of the expulsion scheme together with rumors of traitorous misconduct embittered true advocates of *jōi* and undercut the bakufu policy of pacifying court and *shishi*. On the other hand the bakufu had not repudiated its verbal *jōi* policy. In following months attempts to implement the policy were constantly to complicate both internal politics and foreign relations. The regime had avoided bombardment, war, and military defeat, however, and so had slipped less sharply into the colonial slough than it might well have done. Instead it had gained time in which to try to undo the mischief of court-daimyo-*shishi* attempts to manage an intractable foreign intruder.

2. At Kyoto: The Shogun in Captivity

While Edo was caught in the grip of foreign crisis, bakufu leaders at Kyoto were bogged down in court politics, able neither to control court behavior nor return the shogun to Edo. The effort to get the shogun out of Kyoto had begun even as Shungaku's leadership was disintegrating in mid-63/3, but it had soon stalled, largely because of the divisions among bakufu leaders in the city. The character of those divisions is worth noting because they not only delayed the shogun's departure for over two months but also were central to the bakufu's internal disputes for the next two years.

The situation as of mid-63/3 was as follows. The Kyoto representatives of the bakufu were thoroughly concerned about affairs at Edo, but none was eager to take charge of them. Shungaku was in process of resigning, determined to dissociate himself completely from affairs. Katamori was determined to stay in Kyoto to protect the court. Yoshiatsu had proceeded to Kyoto rather than returning to Edo as earlier instructed by the court, and that instruction had been retracted. Yoshinobu expected war to start, had protested the court's order that either he or Shungaku go east, and had gotten the court to stop insisting on his own return.

The senior councillors and other regular officials in Kyoto were the only high-ranking men who seemed willing to go face the British. They were by then thoroughly disillusioned with the whole scheme of using the shogun's presence to restore bakufu influence at Kyoto and were urging that he return east. Having gone from the frying pan into the fire, they wished to give the pan a second try. With their superiors all trying to avoid the British, they began lobbying to have the court permit the shogun's return, justifying it as essential not only for avoiding collision with the British at Edo but also to avoid a possible direct British approach in the Kinai. Yoshinobu joined this effort, urging the court to let Iemochi depart on 3/21.

By then Katamori and his men were thoroughly frustrated by the difficulty of keeping the peace at Kyoto, by the insulting prospect of an imperial army, and by the divisions among bakufu officials concerning the basic policies of imperial respect and expulsion of the foreigners. They had become firmly wedded to the policy of making the bakufu rather than radicals the vanguard of *jōi* and protector of the court in the national struggle against the foreigners. They saw the shogun's continued residence in Kyoto as crucial to their objectives. When on 3/19 preparation began for Iemochi's imminent departure, Katamori launched a major campaign to prevent it. He and his advisors lobbied vigorously, threatening to resign, arguing that Tokugawa prestige in Kyoto was at stake, and finally assembling hundreds of Aizu vassals at Nijō castle with the threat that they would die rather than see the shogun depart. This blunt Aizu challenge was supported by Yoshiatsu, Yoshikatsu, and others, and it succeeded in compelling the shogun, Yoshinobu, the senior councillors, and lesser officials to agree to a further ten-day delay in the shogun's departure.[12]

Ogasawara and Yoshiatsu, as noted earlier, were then dispatched to handle diplomatic affairs at Edo, and in the following days the court and advocates of *jōi* carried out a series of delaying maneuvers that kept the shogun at Kyoto for a month. On 4/21 he went to Osaka, staying around there and inspecting defenses both by land and by Katsu's ship until 5/10. During his trip rumors that he would return east and talk of antishogunal plots proliferated. Some of his vassals urged that he go on to Edo. However, Aizu men, court officials, Yoshikatsu, and others opposed on the grounds he should protect the court during the expulsion effort and so preserve the unity of court and bakufu and sustain Tokugawa influence in the realm. Aizu prevailed, and on 5/11 the shogun returned to Kyoto. Seven days later he gave the court a detailed report on his inspection.[13]

Thus for two months the entangled issues of foreign affairs and domestic politics had so sharply pitted individuals and groups against one another that no decisive action of any sort had been achieved. Finally, however, on 5/18 and 19, after the shogun's report had been accepted, the issue of his return to Edo was raised anew.[14] While it was being discussed, leaders in Kyoto learned that the British had in fact been appeased and the expulsion date had passed uneventfully at Edo. They learned, moreover, that Yoshinobu had submitted his resignation. Itakura, Mizuno, and others seized upon this news to urge that the shogun be sent back to Edo ''to punish bad officials'' and effect expulsion.

This new argument linking the shogun's departure to the *jōi* policy struck a sympathetic nerve at court. The message was then reinforced by news that Yoshiatsu and Mochinori had also resigned and withdrawn from affairs. These reports made it clear that all those in whom the court reposed any confidence had removed themselves from the Edo scene. By 5/24 the pressure from Itakura, Mizuno, and other bakufu officials had led the court to conclude informally that the shogun's departure must be permitted in order to reinvigorate the policy of expulsion. Yoshikatsu, who was serving as shogunal guardian while Yoshinobu was in Edo, fought back vigorously, as did Katamori, some *shishi*, and certain court nobles. But on 5/30 the court formally stated that the shogun would depart for the east on 6/3 in order to implement the imperial order for expulsion. Still opposing, Aizu men wrote Mizuno an eloquent protest. Katamori too wrote Mizuno, urging that the shogun remain at Kyoto on the several grounds that the court wished it, that Yoshikatsu wished it, and that it would aid pro-bakufu members of the court, offset outside daimyo influence, foster court-bakufu unity, quiet the *rōnin*, and reassert bakufu influence in the region. In previous weeks Aizu had been the key element keeping the shogun at Kyoto, and this new effort might well have reversed the court's order. Before the effect of the Aizu lobbying could be seen, however, a dramatic new factor was abruptly introduced into the situation by men from Edo. That factor nearly precipitated open hostilities between segments of the bakufu in the Kinai.

3. Ogasawara's Armed March on Kyoto

That new factor was Ogasawara Nagamichi's armed approach to the city.[15] This remarkable venture requires attention because it illustrates with particular clarity a host of problems besetting the bakufu. At one level it illustrates how the bakufu was being divided and pitted against itself by the elemental confrontation of imperialism and *sonnō jōi* ethnic sensibilities and by the domestic complications that confrontation was generating and sustaining. At another level it illustrates how the division of the bakufu into two parts, one at Kyoto and one at Edo, sustained differences in priorities and disrupted the processes of decision-making and policy implementation. At yet another level it epitomizes the general trend toward remilitarization of politics, a process that undermined both the ethos and the institutions of Tokugawa hegemony.

The precise origins of Ogasawara's effort are obscure. It appears, however, that two lines of thought came together and issued in his expedition. The first line involved the use of foreign support against perceived domestic enemies in order to repudiate the expulsion policy; the second involved the use of force to extract the shogun from Kyoto. Concerning the first, while awaiting the shogun's return from Kyoto during 63/3, French and British diplomats had offered to make their firepower available to "help" the bakufu overwhelm the advocates of *jōi*. The offer was refused, but it likely appealed to some officials nonetheless for reasons of domestic power quite apart from foreign policy or the foreigners' intentions. At some point, moreover, Ogasawara may well have argued, as it is reported, that it was Satsuma and Chōshū who were sustaining the court's *jōi* position and accordingly that it was appropriate to seek foreign aid in punitive expeditions against the two *han* as steps leading to a change in court policy.[16]

The theme of extracting the shogun from Kyoto reflected the intense displeasure with which bakufu officialdom and many vassal daimyo had regarded the whole shogunal trek from its inception. At Edo opposition to the trip had never been stilled. As soon as the shogun had left the city, people had begun urging his return, and on 4/5 daimyo and officials at Edo formally expressed their wish to that effect. Sixteen days later vassal daimyo in the hall of geese *(gannoma)* submitted a formal group petition that he be returned to Edo. And at some point in mid-63/4 officials at the bakufu's army headquarters *(rikugunsho)* apparently proposed that enough new-style troops (infantry, artillery, and cavalry) be sent to Kyoto to secure his release.[17]

During the indemnity-expulsion crisis of the next fortnight the issue went into abeyance, but after that crisis had passed, these two strands of thought were picked up again. One of the Kanagawa magistrates apparently asked the French to transport troops to Osaka. And on 5/17 junior councillor Sakai Tadamasu reportedly met British and French delegates secretly at Yokohama and discussed sending troops to Kyoto to recover the shogun, secure imperial approval of the treaties, or both.[18] By then rumors of bakufu-foreign cooperation against the great *han* were beginning to spread, which suggests that the matter had already been discussed at some length within the bakufu. By the next day a chief line of argument called for Ogasawara to go to Kyoto as he had abortively set out to do on 5/8 during the indemnity crisis. No implementive decision appears to have been made, however, perhaps because Ogasawara became ill and missed a planning session that evening.[19]

On yet the next day, Yoshinobu, who was himself trying to resign, urged Ogasawara to sail to Kyoto with certain able officials to "explain" the diplomatic situation. The following afternoon Ogasawara boarded the bakufu steamer *Lyman*, which had recently returned from a commercial run to Shanghai, and he and subordinate officials (notably city magistrate Inoue Kiyonao, inspectors Tsuchiya Masanao and Mukōyama Eigorō, and Mizuno Tadanori, who had recently retired after years of diplomatic service) sailed in the rain down to Yokohama. There they discussed affairs with Kanagawa magistrate Asano Ujisuke and others. Discussions that evening and the next day included conversations with British officials concerning the rental of vessels for transporting troops to Osaka.

Ogasawara's moves during the next few days are uncertain. He probably spent most of the time in the Yokohama vicinity, mostly on board the *Lyman* and at bakufu offices in the port. But one reliable report indicates that late on 5/21 he returned by horse to Edo, where he discussed matters with officials there at the residences of senior councillor Matsudaira Nobuyoshi and junior councillor Suwa Tadamasa. In those sessions he probably discussed his venture with other officials, including military unit commanders and Oguri Tadamasa, who was momentarily out of office. By then Yoshinobu seems to have become alarmed at the militant character the venture had acquired, and he began to oppose it. He proposed to go himself instead of Ogasawara, but the suggestion was turned aside, probably because of fear he would not stand fast against the court's expulsion policy. In any event out of the turmoil and secret maneuvering a decision finally emerged. On 5/24 and 25 Ogasawara began to assemble units of the bakufu's newly trained western-style army and dispatch them from Yokohama by ship. By one account these forces included some 150 cavalry and 1300 infantrymen who were being transferred to Osaka for "coastal defense."[20]

That evening Ogasawara left for Osaka on a bakufu warship, accompanied by Mizuno, Inoue, Mukōyama, Tsuchiya, probably Asano, and many lesser officials. On 5/27 and 28 more of the assembled infantrymen were loaded on two rented British ships flying bakufu flags. Those ships hauled the troops to the coast of Kii. There they were transferred to two other bakufu vessels for the final leg to Osaka lest the use of British ships be discovered and invite charges of bakufu collaboration with foreigners against other Japanese. Other forces numbering over six hundred were dispatched overland on 5/29.

On 6/1 Ogasawara, his accompanying officials, and lead elements of his troops, including cavalry, were disembarked at Osaka. They promptly headed for Kyoto, halting their march for the night at Hirakata midway between the cities. Clearly ''coastal defense'' was not their purpose. Ogasawara's accompanying officials were a group whose predominant specialty was foreign affairs, and they were sharply opposed to the expulsion policy. The character of this group suggests quite strongly that their major objective was to persuade the court to abandon its *jōi* policy, and the troop strength was to provide coercive reinforcement sufficient to overawe extremist opposition—by force if necessary. A corollary purpose was to return the shogun to Edo, even though bakufu leaders in the city seemed on the verge of achieving that goal anyway.

The city that Ogasawara was approaching was extremely vulnerable because by 6/1 the position there of both the *kōbugattai* and the *sonnō jōi* advocates had been sharply eroded. Shimazu Hisamitsu of Satsuma had long since left the city in a huff and a hurry, taking most of his troops with him. Most other *han* forces had also long since departed as daimyo had prepared their fiefs for foreign war. The independent imperial army had never materialized. As for those related lords who favored some sort of *kōbugattai* arrangement, Shungaku and Mochiaki of Echizen had both returned to their castle in disgrace; Mochinori of Owari was at his, and Yoshikatsu was trying to resign and go home. Yoshiatsu's resignation had been accepted on the day before, and a vassal of Yoshinobu had just arrived in town to lobby for his. As a consequence of these several developments the city was in the hands of a rather small number of radical *shishi*, the heterogeneous people of the court, a smattering of *han* forces, and the internally divided leadership of the bakufu group there, most notably Matsudaira Katamori and senior councillors Itakura and Mizuno. The councillors wished to get the shogun back to Edo, and while Katamori opposed the idea, he did often show a willingness to be persuaded by the reasoned arguments of others.

Under these circumstances Ogasawara's objectives seemed easily attainable, and his effort should have been helped by the rumors and reports that preceded him. During the course of the day on 6/1 the court learned to its consternation that on the highway from Osaka Ogasawara was approaching with an army reportedly composed of a thousand infantrymen, eight pieces of artillery, and a cavalry force of a hundred. This report lent substance to prior rumors that if Ogasawara's demands were not met, he and an army of a thousand men would control the nobles, behead some if necessary, demand a policy of open ports (*kaikoku*), take the shogun back east if the court rejected the demand, burn the palace if the court refused Edo's orders, and send an armada against Satsuma and Chōshū.[21] Compared to these rumors, which may very well have reflected his innermost desires, Ogasawara's actual objectives were quite modest and reasonable: release of the shogun and repudiation of *jōi*.

These objectives were not both attained, however, and the men who thwarted Ogasawara were his own colleagues in Kyoto. Whereas Ogasawara had linked the shogun's departure to the formal repudiation of *jōi*, Itakura and Mizuno had linked it to the implementation of a policy of verbal *jōi*, and the court's statement of 5/30 had made the linkage between expulsion and shogunal trip formal imperial policy. Accordingly when bakufu leaders in Kyoto heard of Ogasawara's approach, they viewed it as a disastrous turn of events. It not only threatened to jeopardize the shogun's prospects of departure but to destroy entirely their chance of leaving Kyoto without incurring further imperial animosity and thereby aiding anti-bakufu elements. Hence the leaders in Kyoto promptly sent junior councillor Inaba Masami and some subordinates to Hirakata to stop Ogasawara's advance. Later reports indicated that he had pushed north to Yodo, however, with Kyoto as his obvious next stop. Moreover intense lobbying by Tsuchiya and Mukōyama, who had gone on ahead to Kyoto, had demonstrated beyond a shadow of doubt the depth of Ogasawara's resolve. Accordingly senior councillor Mizuno Tadakiyo and others, including representatives of Aizu and Owari, went south to deter him on 6/4.

The meeting between the Edo and Kyoto groups on 6/4 was difficult. The issue of expulsion quickly came to a head. The delegates from Kyoto argued that if the bakufu truly committed itself to expelling the foreigners, the task could certainly be achieved. The men from Edo rejected that assertion, and the issue remained deadlocked. Ogasawara himself apparently refused to meet Mizuno or his colleagues, insisting instead that he would speak only directly with the shogun because only thus could he be sure the latter was not being misinformed. What Ogasawara meant, presumably, was that only by direct argument could he be sure that the shogun would sanction his own recent settlement with the British and Edo's sabotage of the expulsion policy.[22] However, the operational implication of Ogasawara's position was that either he must be admitted to Kyoto or else the shogun should be allowed to depart so that the two could meet. The exchange of views had revealed the distance separating the two sides on the *jōi* question, but in the end Ogasawara did agree to halt his advance elements at Fushimi. Moreover his argument reinforced the earlier attempts by bakufu officials in Kyoto to negotiate the shogun's release.

Even after these negotiations ended, matters remained tense. Ogasawara stubbornly sat at Yodo for the next few days, debating the wisdom of pushing on to Kyoto regardless and refusing to withdraw his army despite continuing criticism from both the bakufu and the court groups in the city. In the city the bakufu group had prepared Kyoto defenses— probably some three thousand bakufu troops, of whom a thousand or more had modern rifles, plus forces of Aizu, the Kyoto deputy, Mito, and other *han*—to repel his feared attack and offset the military preparations of *shishi*. The real possibility existed, bizarre as it may seem, that the first major domestic military conflict in two centuries of Japanese history would be fought not by the bakufu and its enemies but by contending forces of the bakufu, both of whom were seeking the same larger purposes of Tokugawa peace and prosperity.

While the two sides stood poised, bakufu leaders in Kyoto proceeded with their own policy for gaining the shogun's release. Although the shogun did not leave on 6/3 as the imperial statement had specified, a formal farewell audience was held at court that day, with bakufu officials and vassal daimyo in attendance, and the shogun's departure was then set for the ninth or tenth. With the court committed to a departure date, the shogun sent Ogasawara a personal note that was conciliatory in tone but explicit in ordering him to stay out of Kyoto. On the sixth the court ordered the bakufu to punish Ogasawara severely, but bakufu leaders at Kyoto procrastinated until the shogun had left Nijō castle as planned on the ninth. Then as the shogun departed the city and the danger of an intra-bakufu battle passed, leaders formally ordered Ogasawara and his accompanying officials, some of whom were still at Fushimi, all dismissed from office, censured for misgovernment, and ordered into confinement under the keeper of Osaka castle pending final punishment.[23]

At Osaka the next day the shogun ordered Ogasawara to prepare a statement justifying his payment of the indemnity and "his march upon Kyoto to reverse the imperial policy of expulsion."[24] In his statement Ogasawara reviewed the agonizing discussions leading first to the indemnity payment and subsequently to his own trip. That trip, he argued, was intended to explain Yoshinobu's resignation and the indemnity payment. As for *jōi*, he argued that while it was not incorrect in principle, depending upon the circumstances it could be counterproductive. But be that as it may, after eloquently protesting his own honorable intentions, he asserted that he certainly had not been scheming to reverse the imperial order for expulsion. If his argument was a bit disingenuous, it was about as much as could have been expected under the circumstances. On the following day he went under house arrest in Osaka.

Perhaps because bakufu leaders were uncertain of their next move, the shogun ''inspected coastal defenses'' for a few days at Osaka. Then despite Katamori's protests, when reports of renewed British belligerence were received his retinue hurriedly headed east in a flotilla of four warships. They reached Edo castle on 6/16, ending at last the most harrowing and disastrous shogunal venture in the history of the Tokugawa family.

In the outcome an intra-bakufu armed clash had been avoided, and profound disagreements and profoundly contrary policies within the bakufu had been clumsily compromised. Ogasawara et al. had avoided war at Edo and then had led an expedition that may well have been the decisive factor in finally securing the shogun's departure. On the other hand he had failed miserably at reversing the court's diplomatic orientation, and he and his supporters had been fired for their trouble. The Kyoto group too had helped secure the shogun's departure, and it had salvaged at least the rhetoric of a policy of cooperation with the court against foreigners and had with some reluctance punished those who had defied it. But in the end the bakufu still was obligated to expel the barbarians, so it was still trapped in the elemental conflict between Japanese ethnicity and imperialism.

The Bakufu Reunified: 63/6–12

Tokugawa officialdom was glad enough to be done with Kyoto, but the shogun's return to his great Chiyoda castle was still not a time for rejoicing. For one thing fire had again laid part of it waste during his absence. On 6/3 a conflagration had broken out in Iikura south of the castle, swept through Azabu, and spread northwest over into Akasaka and north up Nishikubo street to the castle, where it penetrated the western enceinte and burned it completely. It was hardly an auspicious beginning for a Tokugawa revival, adding one more expense to the huge costs of the Namamugi indemnity, the Kyoto trip, the coastal defense measures, and Ogasawara's military expedition.

For another thing bakufu leaders found themselves bitterly divided on fundamental policy issues. The division had been harshly crystallized in the military confrontation between Ogasawara and the bakufu leaders in Kyoto, and it was laid bare in the continuing disputes at Edo. The ''Kyoto group,'' with Yoshinobu and Yoshiatsu as their most prestigious spokesmen, argued in following weeks that bakufu policy must take into account the court's commitment to expelling the foreigners. They were sustained in that position by ongoing pressure from Kyoto and elsewhere in the country. The ''Edo group'' argued with equal vigor that bakufu policy must take into account the foreigners' commitment to preserving their treaty privileges. They were equally sustained in their position by the presence and military activities of the foreigners. The irreconcilable implications of these positions produced months of anguished paralysis that was only overcome by slow and clumsy implementation of dubious compromise policies, most notably plans to negotiate the closing of Yokohama and to make a second shogunal trip to Kyoto.

1. Policy Deadlock and Domestic Deterioration: 63/6–8

During the first two months after the shogun's return the storm of political conflict at Edo centered on the question of expelling the foreigners. At stake in the debate was not the question of expulsion by force: everyone of consequence at Edo rejected that even though the court was still ordering bakufu and *han* to carry it out. The issue, rather, was whether and how the bakufu would proceed in attempts to get the foreigners to abandon the three trading ports. Lesser disputes also arose over the questions of how the bakufu should respond to the impending English-Satsuma confrontation, the several foreign collisions with Chōshū, and the persistent rumors of bakufu-foreign cooperation against the *han*.

It is unnecessary to follow the details of this conflict.[25] Its character was essentially the same as in previous months: heated arguments, boycotts, resignation efforts, abortive appointments, abruptly canceled orders, embittered dismissals. Most notably, Itakura and Yoshinobu repeatedly tried to resign. Katamori nearly went east from Kyoto to coerce the bakufu to expel the foreigners. A plan to send Yoshinobu to Kyoto fell through. Sakai Tadashige of Himeji was named senior councillor and was almost designated great councillor. And such vigorous men as Sakai Tadamasu, Asano Ujisuke, Oguri Tadamasa, Matsumae Takahiro, Mukōyama Eigorō, and Inoue Kiyonao were dismissed or resigned. Finally, however, by early 63/8 a futile compromise position was reached in which it was agreed that an attempt would be made by the end of the month to close only Yokohama. On 8/10 and 12 the shogun formally announced that negotiations to close that port would begin shortly, that they might break down, and that accordingly all should prepare for war.

The policy of expulsion by force, which had earlier been redefined into expulsion by negotiation, had thus been redefined again to negotiation about only the one primary trading port. As a countergesture, probably for domestic consumption, the bakufu again made moves designed to strengthen coastal defenses in preparation for the war that still might result should negotiation ultimately fail. New titles were created, and Itakura, who had been very displeased with Edo's newest redefinition of expulsion, was on 8/15 put in overall charge of national defense, given authority over a newly organized defense command, and instructed to tighten up defense coordination, particularly in the Edo and Kinai regions. The bakufu was about back to Abe Masahiro's position of 1854: negotiate until defenses were sufficient for expulsion. It remained to be seen whether the foreigners would agree to abandon Yokohama.

These foreign policy disputes were so intense because the issue had such severe domestic implications. Yoshinobu, Itakura, and others had fought vigorously for a policy of negotiating the port-closing not because they had an intrinsic personal commitment to the policy but because they saw it as the bare minimum essential to the recovery of imperial goodwill, which was in turn deemed essential to resecuring daimyo-*shishi* confidence and obedience.

During these weeks of political discord the domestic problems also made themselves felt at Edo in other more direct ways. The nub of the issue was *sonnō jōi* activism, and to Edo its most alarming expression was in Matsudaira Katamori's continuing difficulty in controlling the city of Kyoto. On 6/22 Katamori dispatched a vassal to Edo with a set of insistent requests designed to increase his power in the Kyoto region. He warned that if his requests were not approved, he would have to quit his post. The bakufu had earlier lost the support of Shungaku and then that of Yoshikatsu, who had just left Kyoto for Nagoya. It dared not now lose its last major supporter in the city. In response to Katamori's requests and to continuing evidence of radical influence at court, Edo agreed in succeeding weeks to provide him with subordinate inspectors, finance officials, and clerks; to excuse him from handling much of the bargaining with the court; to keep in close and prompt communication; and to furnish him with more patrol forces (*yoriki* and *dōshin*). In actions that gave him unprecedented authority, Edo granted him full powers to handle all disruptions in and around Kyoto. He was given a greater role in the selection, promotion, rewarding, and punishing of the other major resident bakufu officials in that city; authority to deploy them; and, in the event of crisis, authority to command nearby daimyo and bakufu officials in Osaka, Nara, Fushimi, and elsewhere in the Kinai.[26] Only the keeper in the great castle at Osaka was not put under his command. Not since Ieyasu's day had the regime delegated such power of independent action to an official in the Kinai region. As long as Katamori was loyal, Edo was the stronger for it, but should he grow restless, Edo would be the loser.

Despite this immense grant of authority Katamori was unable to pacify the city. As the summer passed, Kyoto continued to be disturbed by persistent anti-bakufu, anti-foreign-trading-merchant, and pro-*jōi* agitation, as well as by repeated assassinations and other forms of violence. Extremist samurai, many from Chōshū, also continued to influence court policy. They promoted schemes for manipulating the court or bakufu or for ousting Aizu and thus the bakufu from Kyoto. They hoped thereby to realize the *jōi* foreign policy and radical restoration that had slipped through their fingers earlier in the year.

Reports reaching Edo from elsewhere made the news from Kyoto all the more worrisome because they suggested that Chōshū itself was nearly in a state of insurrection. Chōshū was in fact defying Edo on foreign policy by repeatedly firing on foreign ships, thus pursuing an expulsion program that it knew very well was not Tokugawa policy, regardless of the earlier statements of bakufu delegates in Kyoto. Equally worrisome, Chōshū seemed on the verge of acquiring a hegemonial role vis-à-vis neighboring *han*. To elaborate, because Chōshū had assumed a leadership role in implementing the court's expulsion order, on 6/13 the court instructed five adjoining *han*, including the two vassal *han* of Kokura and Nakatsu, to cooperate with Chōshū in the undertaking. Kokura resisted court and Chōshū pressure on the grounds that it could not act without orders from Edo. But in responding thusly, Kokura was inviting assault by Chōshū on grounds of disobedience to the court. On 7/4 Kokura informed Edo of its neighbor's warlike activities and of its unauthorized intrusions into Kokura territory in preparation for attack on foreign shipping. Later in the month Chōshū groups began pressing the court for authority to punish Kokura for failing to obey the expulsion order. Information on this situation flowed steadily into Edo, a report of 8/21 indicating that Chōshū was preparing for domestic war.[27] The implication was disturbing: Chōshū, it appeared, was ready to expand.

Even more direct Chōshū defiance was in store, however. In instructions of 7/8 bakufu leaders had ordered Chōshū to desist from attacking foreigners. A few days later they instructed a courier *(tsukaiban)* and a small group of assistants to proceed by bakufu ship to Chōshū to deliver the order personally. In Chōshū the courier was assaulted and abused, his message rejected, his ship seized, and he and one attendant finally murdered as he was leaving the *han* on 8/21.

In short, as of mid-63/8 the domestic situation suggested that only forceful action at home and a dramatic success in foreign policy could restore bakufu prestige enough to make Edo's voice again persuasive. The feeble compromise plan to negotiate Yokohama's closing seemed hardly sufficient, and yet even it was almost surely impossible of realization.

2. Settling upon a Foreign Policy: 63/8–10

The frustrations and worries of the summer were finally eased when new developments at Kyoto and Yokohama opened up to bakufu leaders new opportunities for political maneuver. It was not easy to agree upon the meaning of these opportunities, however, given the basic differences of priority that continued to divide men at Edo. Consequently policy decisions emerged only with difficulty and were implemented with great hesitation and amid much backing and filling.

As of mid-63/8 the bakufu's one outstanding policy of the moment was to negotiate the closing of Yokohama by month's end. Relentlessly, however, men's minds were forced back to their domestic problems by worsening reports from the west that culminated with two alarming notices received on 8/21. One of them indicated that Chōshū seemed bent on war, as mentioned earlier, and the other reported that the court had ordered certain major *han*, notably Tottori, Okayama, Tokushima, and Yonezawa, to lead an imperial expedition to punish the bakufu should it fail to expel the barbarians.[28] The deadly alliance of court, great daimyo, and *shishi* seemed to have revived.

The following night, however, Edo received a long and very different kind of report from Katamori and the new deputy Inaba Masakuni. It said that at Kyoto men of Aizu, cooperating with forces of Satsuma, the deputy, and others, had on 8/18 carried out a coup that ousted Chōshū men and radical nobles from their positions of influence at court. The reviving alliance had evidently been snuffed out at the onset.

This report precipitated heated debate. All next day bakufu officials discussed its implications, but once again their councils bogged down in disagreement over the stubborn question of how to deal with court and foreigners. Those like Yoshinobu who adhered to the view that somehow a policy of verbal *jōi* must be pursued argued that the 8/18 coup provided an opportunity to recover court goodwill by adopting two policies: pushing on with the closing of Yokohama and then sending the shogun again to Kyoto. Others opposed both proposals. Some diplomats in particular argued that it was a precious opportunity to repudiate the absurd dream of closing Yokohama. Other men argued vigorously against another shogunal trip. Itakura's inclination still lay with Yoshinobu, but he had to acknowledge that the bakufu was unable to fight. The other senior councillors apparently were neutral, caught between the impossibilities of both alternatives.[29]

As so often happened in those years of crisis, the disputes set off at Edo by the 8/18 coup were bitter: officials resigned, boycotted affairs, or were fired while others were appointed. Despite all the agony, however, the policy that emerged was only another cautious attempt to meet all views. On the matter of closing Yokohama, it was decided within a few days to delay the official closing date. In the interim the new senior councillor Sakai Tadashige, who supposedly had good connections at court, would proceed to Kyoto to ''explain'' the matter and get a clearer picture of the situation there. As for a second shogunal trip, just before Sakai departed on Katsu's ship on 9/2, he was instructed to report to court that the shogun had expressed a wish to go to Kyoto ''before long.''[30] And as another interim measure three daimyo (of Oshi, Shirakawa, and Shinjō of Uzen) were ordered to proceed as rapidly as possible to Kyoto to provide more bakufu guard forces at court.

Thus the 8/18 coup at Kyoto wrought no dramatic changes in bakufu policy. Rather, it prompted the regime to play out the ineffectual policies already settled upon. One reason for this outcome was that the coup had also wrought no change in Kyoto's commitment to *jōi*. Rather, men in that city feared that the coup would encourage Edo to backslide on the expulsion policy. Accordingly in following days and weeks groups there barraged Edo with demands that the policy be implemented and discussed various strategies for forcing the bakufu to do so.

The court's posture was revealed not only in the notices sent eastward but also in its response to Sakai's mission. He had proceeded to Kyoto with inspector Togawa Hanzaburō and others, hoping no doubt to modify the court's *jōi* posture. Upon arriving in the city, however, he discovered that the court had already ordered a courtier to go east, as in 1862, for purposes of compelling Edo to close Yokohama. To forestall that trip, Sakai joined Katamori and others in a lobbying campaign. The court responded by seizing the initiative yet again, abruptly ordering him to return eastward with an imperial reprimand censuring the bakufu for its failure to expel the barbarians. Sakai unhappily accepted the order. In subsequent communications that were complicated by his precipitous departure, he was only able to inform the court through Katamori of the difficulties of negotiating, of the need to avoid war, and of Edo's sincerity.[31] It had been a most unsuccessful trip.

While Sakai was thus being overwhelmed by the court, Edo leaders were attempting to close Yokohama. During 63/9 they finally undertook to negotiate the matter with the foreigners. As many had warned, however, the efforts were rebuffed. On 9/14, the new official date for closing Yokohama, a major negotiating team that included Mizuno, Itakura, and Inoue, junior councillors Inaba Masami and Tanuma Okitaka, newly appointed foreign magistrate Ikeda Chōhatsu, and other officials tried to persuade the foreigners to begin negotiating the matter. They argued among other things that without such a development there might occur a revolution in Japan and that would hurt trade. This and other efforts failed, however, and by the end of the month the bakufu's attempts had been utterly frustrated. The French and British ministers would not even discuss the matter, and the Americans and Dutch argued that they would have to consult their home governments before they could discuss it. Bakufu officials, who recalled that the recent mission to Europe had won a delay in opening certain ports, were encouraged by this latter response to hope that a solution to their dilemma might lie in another mission to the home governments.

Even as the diplomatic effort was foundering, however, and within days of Sakai's return on 9/29, developments in both Edo and Kyoto began to neutralize the diplomatic issue that was pitting the two political centers against one another.[32] In the early days of 63/10 leaders in Edo decided that their best strategy was, after all, to send another mission abroad to negotiate the closing of Yokohama. On the eighth the senior councillors sent Katamori a notice of that decision with instructions to emphasize at court that the bakufu's previous indecisiveness had been overcome and the emperor could be confident of Edo's new resolve to close Yokohama.

Just a few days before that, in reply to Sakai's report of his trip and the imperial censure of Edo's tergiversation, Mizuno had sent a long letter to Katamori summing up the progress, or lack of it, in the negotiations. He warned of the risk of war and explained that the foreigners felt they must consult with their home governments before any decision could be made. By the time Katamori presented that notice to court, Shimazu Hisamitsu had reached Kyoto from Kagoshima, which had just been bombarded by the British as revenge for the Namamugi incident. Under the influence of Shimazu and leaders of other moderate great *han* the court had begun to adopt a new and more accommodating strategy for dealing with Edo and the foreigners. Mizuno's report on the difficulties of negotiation reinforced the great *han* pressures, and on 10/7 the court finally agreed to ''delay'' the courtier's trip east. Five days later, in a last verbal fling, the court again called for expulsion. But it also said that responsibility for it lay with the bakufu and that no one was to challenge Edo's implementation of the policy. A few days later Kyoto learned that Edo had already decided to handle the task by sending a mission to Europe.

As a result of these concurrent developments in the two cities, the diplomatic issue, which had been central to politics for nearly a year, was temporarily removed from the political scene. In succeeding weeks the mission to Europe was organized, and in 63/12 bakufu diplomats at Yokohama were given the papers authorizing them to carry their negotiations to completion. There was some discussion of the precise authority to be given the negotiators. One draft instructed the diplomats to discuss and settle the closing of Kanagawa and other matters. Ikeda Chōhatsu, who finally was put in charge of the mission, proposed that the group be instructed to preserve the national polity *(kokutai)* and secure peace and to negotiate unwaveringly for those objectives. The advocates of port-closing finally secured much of the rhetoric they wanted, however. As finally formulated, the shogun ordered his diplomats to negotiate the closing of Kanagawa as well as other matters and to cherish the national polity.[33] It was left to Ikeda and his colleagues to figure out how to do those things simultaneously.

3. Preparation for a Second Shogunal Trip: 63/10-12

The court's disengagement from foreign policy matters was one result of an overall effort by Shungaku, Hisamitsu, and others to revive the *kōbu-gattai* effort that had aborted earlier in the year.[34] In line with that grand strategy, when the court on 10/7 postponed the courtier's planned trip to Edo, it ordered Katamori to send eastward at once instructions that Yoshinobu should come to Kyoto "to report details of the closing of Yokohama." Four days later the court handed Katamori a formal order that the shogun also was to come.[35] For the rest of 1863 the dominant issue at Edo was the problem of that proposed trip.

From soon after the 8/18 coup men representing the court and great *han* had been urging the shogun to go west, but the bakufu response had been hesitant, to say the least. Nearly two months passed with no real action beyond the vague promise that Sakai had conveyed of a shogunal visit "before long." Two developments of 63/10 reduced the level of Edo's opposition, however. The apparent reconciliation on foreign policy removed one major hurdle by suggesting that the bakufu would not again be nailed to the cross of expulsion. Then the appointment on 10/11 of Matsudaira Naokatsu of Kawagoe to Shungaku's former title of supreme councillor *(seiji sōsai)* seemed to give bakufu leadership the exceptional solidarity it would need for a successful sortie to Kyoto. Naokatsu was a relative of recently promoted senior councillor Arima Michisumi, had

been involved in the debates of preceding weeks, and had opinions that
certainly carried weight. His appointment did not mean that he was in
charge of affairs as Shungaku had been, however. Rather it seems to
have meant that Yoshinobu, the senior councillors, and others of influence had filled a key leadership position with a man acceptable to
themselves—before any outsider could fill it for them.

The outsider they surely had uppermost in mind was the former
supreme councillor himself. Back in 63/5 the bakufu had pardoned Shungaku for his unauthorized flight to Fukui, but it had pointedly ignored
him when it repeatedly ordered the Fukui daimyo Mochiaki to come to
Edo. Nor did the court forgive him for his disobedience. During the summer, however, after the indemnity-expulsion crisis was safely past,
Shungaku and his Fukui advisors debated the merit of returning to political activity. Shungaku also maintained active contacts with a few great
lords and from 63/9 began to correspond with such bakufu officials as
Katsu Kaishū, Ōkubo Ichiō, Nagai Naomune, and Katamori. Then on
10/6, following a widespread campaign by his supporters, the court also
pardoned him, and in a few days he left for Kyoto and a revived political
life. With painfully fresh memories of the catastrophic outcome of the
Bunkyū reform, many at Edo could not but fear the consequences of
Shungaku's return to activity. By appointing Naokatsu supreme councillor, the Edo leaders closed the post to him, and that increased the likelihood that a second shogunal pilgrimage would not be turned into another
exercise in bakufu self-flagellation.

Still, opposition to the trip remained high. In their reply to the imperial order that the shogun proceed to Kyoto, Naokatsu and the senior
councillors stalled for time. They stated on 10/17 that because of the
continuing negotiations on Yokohama the shogun's proposed trip should
be delayed and Yoshinobu should go in his place.[36] A few days later,
after some procrastination and despite considerable misgivings, Yoshinobu did depart for Kyoto in accord with the earlier imperial order.

When they sent the official statement of 10/17, the senior councillors
spelled out some of the obstacles to the trip in a private note to Katamori.
They mentioned that many officials opposed the trip, that the costs of a
full pilgrimage were worrisome, that there were insurgents to be pacified
in the Kantō, and that impoverished people near the post stations might
engage in uphcavals (*ikki*) if burdened by a shogunal trek. Therefore,
they reported, when it occurred, the trip would likely be made by ship.
Moreover, due to the plan to send an embassy abroad to negotiate the
closing of Yokohama, it would not be possible for the shogun to leave at
once.[37]

The pressure from court, daimyo, Katamori, and others took its toll, however, and within a fortnight the senior councillors resigned themselves to the trip.[38] After undergoing one last round of badgering by men sent from Kyoto, they announced on 11/5 that the shogun would depart "as soon as possible" in accord with imperial wishes and despite the difficulties such a trip would entail due to the ongoing negotiations about Yokohama. In a separate note to Katamori they instructed him to assure the court that the trip would indeed be made "as soon as possible," but since it would take time to arrange the appropriate shipping, early 63/12 was the estimated date of departure. On 11/5 the bakufu also made a series of major decisions as to what domains would provide ships and who would accompany Iemochi and who would stay at Edo during his absence.

Despite these actions the great bulk of lesser officials and bakufu people, including men in the military institute, remained opposed to the trip on a variety of grounds, notably fiscal. Against them were high officials, especially the supreme and senior councillors, who believed it to be unavoidable. All sorts of objections and alternative schemes were raised. Most of those who had been ordered to accompany the shogun objected to the duty and resisted by the usual tactics of boycotting affairs and getting "sick." In consequence few measures beyond the issuance of orders to leading officials seem to have been taken until 11/15. On that day Yoshiatsu of Mito was very ceremoniously instructed to serve as the shogun's stand-in at Edo during the trip.

Then within hours of Yoshiatsu's appointment a fire of suspicious origins broke out and burned both the main and second enceintes of Chiyoda castle, raising the question of whether the trip should be delayed because of the added reconstruction duties at Edo. Naokatsu argued that the trip should be carried out to foster kōbugattai and to help in dealing with the western daimyo. The senior councillors tended to agree, but many lesser officials vigorously opposed, their position clearly strengthened by the disaster.

While the bakufu was trying to cope with that disaster, news of it was speeding westward, reaching Kyoto within five days. There the news generated rumors that it was perhaps the work of Chōshū radicals who hoped by burning the castle to stop or delay the shogun's trip and hence thwart the kōbugattai effort. Fearful that the fire would have just this effect, daimyo, court leaders, and bakufu officials in the city decided to renew their calls for the shogunal trip and dispatched spokesmen at once by bakufu warship. On 11/26 Kyoto city magistrate Nagai Naomune reached Edo, where he argued for the shogunal trip and was assured by

Naokatsu that it would take place despite the objections of lesser officials. Representatives of Katamori reached Edo at the same time and conveyed his emphatic support for it. Others from Kyoto also lobbied to assure the trip. The pressure was sufficient and a merely token delay was agreed upon. The senior councillors wrote Katamori on the same day that the shogun would leave for Kyoto on or about 12/18 or 19.

Meanwhile Yoshinobu was slowly making his way toward Kyoto while a force of some two hundred or more troops, mostly from the military institute, plus others from Mito, went by land with the intention of entering Kyoto at the same time as he. He had been sent in response to imperial instructions, and some at Edo had opposed his going lest it upstage the shogun or otherwise hurt Tokugawa interests. More, however, tended to favor it, some doubtless seeing it as an alternative to the shogun's going while others saw it as a preparatory action. In either case, it was viewed as part of a major effort to strengthen the bakufu's role in Kyoto.

On 11/26 Yoshinobu finally reached the city, but once there he did not really help Edo. Rather, the months back east evidently had been so difficult for him that he at once began speaking unfavorably, though probably correctly, of those he recently had left. He reported that officials were still wedded to obsolete notions and that both the new supreme councillor and the new junior councillor Ogyū Noritaka were committed to restoring the old bakufu position. He reported that in recent months there had been schemes to oust Itakura, rumors of a plot to poison the shogun, and efforts to secure his own dismissal.[39] By explaining Edo's politics in terms of personal vendettas rather than vexatious problems, he was certainly not serving Edo's purposes. Rather, until unplanned complications arose in 64/2, he cooperated with Shungaku and other lords in the renewed *kōbugattai* effort.

Yoshinobu's conduct seemed to bear out the concern of those officials who opposed the shogunal trip. Despite the assurances Naokatsu had given Nagai on 11/26, some officials at Edo continued to try to prevent the trip. Some argued that more bakufu forces should be deployed to Kyoto before the shogun again went there. Some inspectors continued to boycott all affairs, arguing that with so much unrest in the country the trip should be postponed until the next spring. Others warned of the danger that the shogun might again become captive at Kyoto and that for the shogun to abandon the home of his supporters was to abandon his power. Preparation went ahead, however, amid the protests.

As the month progressed, the entourage was assembled, travel regulations were issued, and orders for the handling of affairs at Edo were promulgated. On 12/13 Arima Michisumi left Shinagawa by ship with an advance party that included Nagai and an artillery force. Four days later the departure date for the shogun was reset at 12/27 because of the continuing objections to the trip. When that day arrived, Iemochi, Naokatsu, senior councillors Sakai and Mizuno, and a following of nearly four hundred at last boarded a bakufu steamer at Shinagawa for the second shogunal trip to Kyoto. Despite the fearfulness of accompanying officials who urged Katsu to transfer them all to land because of the high seas, they steamed on and reached Osaka on 64/1/11. Four days later they entered Kyoto.

For the second time in a year the bakufu was bifurcated. The shogun and certain key officials were at Kyoto while other men and the heart of administration were at Edo. For the latter the necessary regulations and patents of authority had been given before the shogun's departure. Under the titular supervision of Yoshiatsu of Mito, Itakura, Inoue, and Makino Tadayuki were the three responsible senior councillors, with Makino also in charge of diplomatic affairs. The main focus of Edo's concern, however, was not diplomacy, as it had been during the first bifurcation. Rather, the chief concern was preventing any harm, especially by fire, to the Tayasu and Shimizu mansions, the sole surviving residential structures in the once-glorious castle. Considerable attention was also given to keeping the peace and security of the city. That these were the primary concerns for those remaining in Edo bespeaks the magnitude of unrest that had developed during the preceding months. That unrest was to swell in succeeding months until it became an insurrection posing a greater threat to the regime than had the court-daimyo-*shishi* assault of 1862.

VIOLENCE IN AND NEAR EDO: 1863

Violence had begun to mark the Edo vicinity from the time trade began at Yokohama in 1859. After intensifying in 1862, it had subsided at year's end when the bakufu officially adopted its policy of obedience to court and expulsion of foreigners. With the apparent abandonment of that policy in early 1863, however, violence in and near the city began to revive.

One reason the unrest had declined was that some of the troublemakers had enrolled in the bakufu's *rōnin* force, as we noted before, and then gone to Kyoto. While there, however, members of the group had quarreled with one another and with others. During 63/3 as the indemnity crisis was developing, the court instructed the *rōnin* force to return to

Edo in case war were to start with England. Accordingly the group divided, with permission of its leader Udono Chōei, and about 250 men under Kiyokawa Hachirō returned east with the intention of helping drive the foreigners from Yokohama. They reached the city on 3/28, were put under command of the military institute, and were housed in the city at Honjo and elsewhere.

From about the time Kiyokawa's men reached Edo, the city began to experience agitation again: placarding, threats to burn Edo and Yokohama, rumor-mongering, and sporadic acts of violence.[40] Some of this agitation was due to the disillusionment of these men and others as they discovered that Edo leaders did not share Kyoto's newly announced commitment to expulsion. The placards, of which only a fraction can likely be attributed to Kiyokawa's men, denounced bakufu officials who opposed expulsion, linked them with the regimes of Ii and Andō, and complained of various other abuses and criminal policies. Rumors of a *jōi*-inspired insurrectionary plot appeared, and Kiyokawa was implicated in the seditious activity. On 4/13, just before the plot was to unfold, he was murdered at age thirty-four, cut down at night on a street at Akabanebashi, just south of the castle. It was probably done at the order of someone within the bakufu. The bakufu used the occasion of his murder to try to improve its control of the *rōnin* force. Within hours it had rounded up and imprisoned *rōnin* suspected of involvement in the plot, increased guard patrols near their barracks, changed their officials, and punished some for malfeasance. The next day some 227 surviving *rōnin* were entitled Shinchōgumi, given increased stipends, and transferred to the command of Sakai Tadasumi of Shōnai, who had special duties keeping the peace in Edo.

When the indemnity crisis reached its peak, the bakufu on 5/7 ordered Sakai to deploy the Shinchōgumi to the Shiba coastal strip, where the foreign attack would come if negotiations failed. The unit then listed 267 men, of whom 53 were from Mito and many others were originally from Shōnai or were former bakufu retainers. Despite their deployment, however, the men never had a chance to prove their worth. War was avoided and they were returned to their billets, safe, sound, and unsung. And there they learned of the bakufu's capitulation and failure even to attempt to expel the barbarians by force. The basis for their cooperation with the regime had been utterly destroyed. Only the need for a stipend kept them enrolled. The consequences of this crisis of purpose, which they shared with other *rōnin*, gradually became apparent.

As the summer passed, the Shinchōgumi became more rowdy, and other activists in the city also became more aggressive. Some were embittered by the betrayal of *jōi;* others were critical of the presumably harmful domestic impact of foreign trade. By 63/9 the bakufu felt compelled to take new measures to quiet the city. On 9/19 city guard patrols were intensified, and in succeeding days bakufu vassals were prohibited from hiring unidentified people and *han* vassals were forbidden to sleep outside their lords' mansions.[41] These moves were obviously designed to isolate and make vulnerable those samurai who were no longer under effective domanial control.

While the bakufu was thus trying to improve its control of the city, the character of discontent was also slowly changing. During 63/10, as we noted before, the diplomatic issue dropped out of the political scene, and a parallel trend was evident in the placarding activity in Edo. With the coming of cold weather, the literary agitation reached a peak, and by 63/11 its content was heavily economic. Back in 1862, according to a city magistrate's report, inflation in the city had raised the commoners' cost of living by some 50 percent above ''normal,'' as measured primarily in terms of white rice and other comestibles. Through the next several months to the middle of 1863 prices changed little, but in the last months of the year a modest two-year decline in the price of rice ended with the price still well above the pre-1858 level. And the price of soy sauce and salt, two basic necessities, went up rapidly.[42] Earlier in the year the bakufu had tried to help its lesser retainers by assuring them loan funds, but that did not help commoners directly, and by late 1863 the renewed inflation was apparently disrupting the lives of commoners and lesser samurai alike.

From 63/9 placards reflected the deteriorating situation, ever more frequently decrying inflation and consequent public hardship. They blamed it on wholesale merchants such as Mitsui and Daimaru and the foreign trade. And they warned that the evil ones would be punished for injuring the people and the land of the gods. Nor were the threats empty. During 63/10 some twenty people were murdered in the city, and uncounted others were attacked and threatened. Among the dead were one man engaged in foreign trade administration and one vassal of Yoshinobu. Other attacks were aimed at Edo merchants, Yokohama merchants, and men associated with the long-dead Ii Naosuke. One worrisome aspect of the situation was the extent to which the keepers of the peace were becoming the breakers of the peace. Men of the Shinchōgumi continued to be implicated in some of the violence. By then too members of the new bakufu infantry units were suffering from demoralization, and some of them also became engaged in brawls and abuse of city folk.[43]

This growing turbulence in Edo led to new bakufu orders for the deployment of vassal *han* forces around the city and elsewhere. Thus in a long explanatory order of 63/10 to the daimyo of Tanakura the senior councillors pleaded for help in keeping the peace in Edo. In brief summary they frankly acknowledged that the *rōnin* trouble in the city had created a critical and unpredictable situation, that men calling themselves "patriots of the realm" *(tenka yūshi)* were stirring up the people, and that matters had to be quieted before the city reached the boiling point and affairs got completely out of control.[44]

In response to these pleas more patrols took to the streets, but the city was still in for more trouble.[45] The world of popular rumor perceived the merchants as making massive profits, and some stores were plundered. Placards denounced high interest rates and threatened to stop business activities and distribute the merchants' wealth to the masses. Other placarders of 63/10 threatened to start fires around the castle, and in fact several fires of suspicious origin were put out before they caused great damage.

Then in the late afternoon of 11/15 (which was a brisk clear day and Christmas for the foreigners), a fire of unexplained origin erupted inside a room near the Hirakawa gate of Edo castle, not far from the shogunal ladies' private offices and residence area. The fire rapidly spread into a raging monster. It consumed the entire main enceinte, leapt across an immense battlement and moat to the east, and destroyed the second enceinte. Although the fire was rumored to have been the work of Chōshū radicals trying to stop the shogun's trip westward, it could as well have been the work of a distraught shogunal retainer trying to stop the trip. Or it could have been an accident attributable, perhaps, to the general state of malaise affecting the whole regime. In any case, by the time the embers had cooled on the morning of 11/16, the seat of shogunal government had been utterly destroyed. The western enceinte was still in ruins from the earlier fire and now the rest of the castle was gone. The whole apparatus of government was stopped.

Within a few days procedures were worked out for handling various governmental duties in officials' residences. Procedures for donating gifts of clothing, utensils, and so on to the shogun and his homeless household were established, and the necessary and predictable orders for frugality were given.

The holocaust not only disrupted government and revived opposition to the shogunal trip but also led to more stringent police measures in the city. Five days after the castle burned, or about as soon as officials got matters back into motion, new orders were issued to control unauthorized people in the city and to prohibit people from walking around at night

without lights that would disclose their movements. Two days later the
bakufu completely abolished the Shinchōgumi by dissolving its leadership
structure and assigning its members to officers directly under the command of Sakai Tadasumi. The force then numbered some three hundred,
who were still hard to control, restless about delays in their pay, and unreliable on patrol. It was hoped that Sakai would be able to reorganize
and discipline the men, thereby turning them into a surer asset of the
regime.

The next day, 11/23, was a dry, windy, wintry day, the kind when
all Edo feared fire. And on that day another fire of suspicious origin
erupted in the Mitsui store at Nihonbashi, blossomed into a minor conflagration driven by the wind, and consumed some hundred dwellings
before it was controlled. Apart from the castle fire it was the worst of
several, including one at Daimaru, that had erupted during the month.
When the Mitsui store burned, a thousand people reportedly went there
in hopes of receiving distributed largesse, which suggests that the pam-
phleteers' message was reaching a considerable audience.

In response to these troubles and the consequent orders for tightened
security, patrols of gendarmes seem to have begun something akin to a
reign of police terror in the rough area of Yoshiwara and Asakusa, not far
from Honjo, in order to bring the city back under control. At least the
city patrols began to report many arrests and killings night after night in
that vicinity. Troublemakers from the defunct Shinchōgumi and elsewhere were thrown into jail. During 63/12 the effort paid off in an
abrupt drop in the level of placarding and some decline in violence and incendiarism in the city.

Thus by the time of the shogun's second departure for Kyoto, Edo had
been partially quieted again. It was a small victory, however. The unrest
there was only the nearest part of nationwide turbulence, reports of
which had been flowing into the castle ever since 63/8.

From the Kinai came constant news of violence in and near Kyoto.
Two well-known incidents elicited particularly sharp responses in Edo.
The first was the Yamato rising of 63/8, the second the Ikuno incident
of 63/10.[46] Both were minor eruptions led by radicals who had been active in Kyoto, and they were worrisome primarily because they were not
simply plots designed for immediate limited purposes but rather appeared
to be first instances of a sustained insurrectionary effort with clear ambitions of national magnitude. They seemed to give substance to the radical
rhetoric of the past year and hence were alarming to Edo.

The Yamato rising was worrisome for other reasons. Although it was
actually a minor incident involving perhaps 35 *rōnin* and 150 or so lesser

followers, save for a brief period of probably larger numbers, reports reaching Edo spoke of up to 2000 insurgents. Nervous leaders there and in Kyoto were prompted to make a heavy-handed and costly response. The pacification forces that were deployed involved, by one summation, some 4000 troops of Tsu, 1700 of Hikone, 1800 of Kōriyama, 200 to 300 of Koizumi, several thousands of Kii, and others of Shibamura, Yanagimoto, and Takatori. Even granting great exaggeration in these figures, it was a costly uprising to suppress. By contrast the Ikuno incident some 90 kilometers west of Kyoto was not costly: it collapsed even before *han* forces were deployed. More importantly the risings demonstrated the vulnerability of the bakufu fisc. In both instances small bands of armed men were able to overrun bakufu intendancy offices, the administrative foundation of regular bakufu tax income. In response to the Yamato rising the bakufu ordered four intendancies guarded by certain daimyo. Later, after receiving more extensive information on the earlier rising and some reports on the recent Ikuno incident, Edo ordered seven more daimyo to deploy forces to seven other intendancies in central Japan.[47] The implication was clear: in the face of insurrectionary efforts, the bakufu fiscal base was dependent upon protection of nearby daimyo. Should enough of those daimyo and their advisors decide not to support the bakufu, it could not long survive.

These developments far to the west had been disturbing to Edo, but even more portentous events were occurring nearer at hand. From as early as 63/9 there had begun to appear reports of unrest in the Kantō provinces. Men styling themselves Tenchūgumi, Shinchōgumi, or Mito *rōnin* claimed to be preparing to expel the barbarians. Using their borrowed authority and prestige, they were reportedly extorting from the wealthy and enrolling the poor in their marauding bands. By 63/11 the problem was severe enough to make Mito and Hitotsubashi officials keenly fearful that Mito's political fabric was unraveling again. On 12/11 Itakura dispatched an order to daimyo and liege vassals in the Kantō to report all incidents of lawlessness and tighten up controls at barrier points. Disturbing reports continued to come in, and on the twenty-seventh, the day the shogun left for Kyoto, the first topic that the remaining leaders addressed was pacification of the Kantō.[48]

One result of the intensifying rural turmoil was that it finally led to the piecemeal implementation from late 1863 of long-standing proposals by Egawa Tarōzaemon and others for the formation of peasant constabulary units in bakufu lands to keep the peace and resist outside troublemakers, including foreigners. The peasants were organized in small units *(kumi* or *shōtai),* armed primarily with firearms and pikes, paid modestly, and

commanded by local leaders under the authority of bakufu domanial administrative offices. In the Kantō they were located at several places
around Edo such as Hino, Tanashi, Itsukaichi, and Hachiōji. In more distant bakufu lands their headquarters were the local administrative offices
(jin'ya or daikansho). On several occasions they were to prove useful in
succeeding years in suppressing local riots and upheavals. In some cases,
however, attempts to enroll hard-pressed peasants into the militia only
created more discontent, particularly in areas administered by unpopular
intendants (daikan or gundai), and this outcome could lead to abandoning of the militia locally or to increasing the potential for local
upheaval.[49]

Whatever the particular outcome of these efforts at forming militia
units, however, they did little to reassure Edo leaders in late 1863.
Rather, leaders were by then keenly aware of widespread shishi activity
in Edo, throughout the Kantō, and to the west. They had begun to try to
deal with it by employing ruthless police tactics, by deploying ever more
military forces, and by creating new peasant militia units. These efforts
had some positive effect, but by their nature they could only be temporary measures. And they did little to improve the morale of Tokugawa
supporters in the city. Instead, the trouble in and around Edo only
reassured those bakufu retainers who believed that the regime could
restore its prestige and recover imperial goodwill only by expelling the
barbarians, thereby demonstrating Tokugawa loyalty to court and Japan.
As two retainers wrote to the senior councillors during 63/12, the
shogun should expel the foreigners and then present himself honorably to
the emperor—the hearts of the four classes of people being uneasy, indecisiveness would only lead to disruption and civil war.[50] Even as the
shogun and his advisors were hoping to restore bakufu prestige at court
and in the west, it was rapidly eroding in the east, in the Tokugawa
home territory, among the Tokugawa people, commoners and retainers
alike.

The bakufu's performance during 1863 had not been exemplary. It is
true that the regime was in a less parlous state at year's end than it had
been in late 1862. It is also true that the regime's leaders had settled the
Namamugi crisis without war, had escaped the imperial trap, and had
gradually eviscerated the court's expulsion policy. These were considerable achievements in themselves. But in the course of doing these things,
the bakufu had proved itself unable to resolve the intractable conflict of
imperialism and Japanese ethnicity. Instead it found its own counsels so
bitterly divided by this larger conflict that it was unable to formulate ef-

fective policy. Even the cobbled-up compromises it did settle upon added to the regime's woes, angering foreigners and *shishi* and allowing court and daimyo to reactivate their role in affairs.

The fateful alliance of court, great daimyo, and *shishi*, which had proved so disastrous until it splintered in early 1863, had been further disrupted by the 8/18 coup at Kyoto. But by year's end it was acquiring momentum again, this time as two basically separate movements. One was a conservative *kōbugattai* movement at Kyoto that was dominated by Satsuma and Fukui; the other, an insurrectionary *shishi* activism that had roots throughout the country but was most active and threatening to Edo in the unrest of the Kantō area. Whether the conservative leaders of the bakufu would be able to manage these parallel threats remained to be seen as the year came to an end.

CHAPTER **4**

The Apex
of Conservative
Reaffirmation
1864

THE BAKUFU AT KYOTO: 64/1–5

THE KANTŌ INSURRECTION: 1864

1. *Disaster Approaches: 64/1–8*
2. *Disaster Recedes: 64/8–12*
3. *A Summing Up*

INSURGENTS, FOREIGNERS, COURT, AND CHŌSHŪ:
64/6–12

1. *Policy Paralysis and Resolution: 64/6*
2. *Chōshū, Court, and Foreigner: 64/7–9*
3. *Managing Chōshū and Kyoto: 64/10–12*

REACTIONARY REVIVAL: 1863–1864

1. *Revival of* Sankin Kōtai *and Other Practices*
2. *Who Advocated Reactionary Revival and Why?*
3. *The Suppression of* Shishi *Activism*

The year 1864 began with the shogun on board ship en route to Kyoto.
He and his advisors were going west in response to intense pressures
from the court, certain great lords, and bakufu delegates in Kyoto. They
were going not with the intention of accommodating the *kōbugattai* wish
to end Tokugawa hegemony but in hopes somehow of turning the situa-

tion to bakufu advantage—it was apparent that the advocates of *kōbugattai* could not simply be ignored.

As matters worked out, bakufu leaders scored a startling victory at Kyoto within four months. They hardly had time to savor that triumph, however, before they found themselves confronting an insurrection of unprecedented magnitude in the Kantō. That upheaval, which can be viewed as a *sonnō jōi* challenge by their low-status rivals, dominated their attention during most of the rest of the year, finally being overcome only at terrible cost to everyone involved.

In the meantime the *kōbugattai* collapse at Kyoto had tempted radical *sonnō jōi* activists from Chōshū to try to revive their restoration venture of early 1863. This second attempt was thwarted on 7/19, again by the combined military forces of Aizu, Satsuma, and others, but this time the conflict involved a major battle, not a palace coup, and it ravaged the city of Kyoto. That outcome infuriated the court and led to a fierce demand from almost all elements in Kyoto for the severe punishment of Chōshū. Edo leaders accepted nominal responsibility for this court-sponsored punitive expedition, seeing in it an opportunity to cultivate imperial goodwill while playing some enemies off against others. In conjunction with that venture the bakufu was able to obtain court acquiescence in bakufu foreign policy and to direct daimyo energies away from Edo, against both Chōshū and activists within their own domains.

Insofar as time, resources, and distractions allowed, bakufu leaders were also pressing on with other aspects of a general attempt at conservative revival, and by year's end the regime seemed to be in remarkably good shape. A variety of old procedures had been restored to some degree. The Kantō insurrection had been overcome. The court had accepted Edo's general leadership in affairs. The daimyo had obeyed orders to deploy against Chōshū. Chōshū had submitted. And across the land *shishi* had been or were being subjected to severe repression by *han* leaders. From the vantage point of Edo it appeared that the fateful alliance of court, great daimyo, and *shishi* had been broken. The bakufu, it seemed, might yet outlive the imperialist-ethnic confrontation.

THE BAKUFU AT KYOTO: 64/1-5

Well before the shogun reached Kyoto on 64/1/15, the substantive issues that were supposed to occupy the Kyoto political assembly had been identified by the *kōbugattai* leadership. They were to be those of diplomacy, which had so vexed Edo prior to 63/10 and which Edo hoped it had sidetracked, and Chōshū, which had elicited little attention at Edo despite the alarums of summer. After the shogun arrived, how-

ever, the instrumental issue of who would control the bakufu and the political process rapidly and relentlessly emerged as the issue on which all
else finally turned.

After their arrival the shogun's senior advisors, notably Matsudaira
Naokatsu, Arima Michisumi, Mizuno Tadakiyo, and Sakai Tadashige,
agreed to the general plan for Chōshū's punishment that *kōbugattai*
leaders in Kyoto had previously formulated. Both they and Yoshinobu
were alarmed, however, when Shimazu Hisamitsu, Matsudaira Shungaku, and Date Munenari began pressing the bakufu to repudiate its position on the closing of Yokohama. They feared such a repudiation would
wreck the delicate agreement on foreign policy that court and bakufu had
reached in 63/10 and lead again to domestic embarrassment for Edo.

The group from Edo was also upset by the efforts of Hisamitsu, Shungaku, and other daimyo to obtain access to regular senior council sessions. On 2/15 and 16, as I have reported elsewhere, the coincidental
issues of foreign affairs and political participation precipitated a bitter
clash between Yoshinobu on the one hand and Hisamitsu, Shungaku, and
Munenari on the other.[1] The clash was so harsh that it had the result,
whatever may have been its origin and intention, of stopping both the
great lords' attempt to alter bakufu foreign policy and their attempt to sit
in on senior council sessions.

On 2/19 the shogun stated clearly to the court the bakufu intent to
close Yokohama. The statement sustained the policy of 63/10, and the
court approved it. In a long announcement to assembled daimyo the next
day, the shogun reviewed recent discussion of the expulsion issue, announced his resolve to close Yokohama, and exhorted men to improve
their military capabilities and pursue coastal defense work in the Kinai
region. In clearer terms than ever before, and in line with pressure ema-
nating from Mito, Tottori, Okayama, and elsewhere, the bakufu had
claimed the rhetoric of *sonnō jōi* as its own.

Behind this rhetoric of expulsion the bakufu intention, as explained by
a vassal of Yoshinobu to men of Fukui two months later, was quite
straightforward. The court having as of old granted the bakufu full authority to govern, the bakufu would order the embassy in Europe to pursue its negotiations. If that embassy upon return the following winter indicated that the port-closing had been arranged, Yokohama would be
closed. If not, then new political discussions would have to be undertaken to decide policy. And if ''thoughtless expulsion'' were demanded,
the bakufu would have to refuse to pursue it and return authority to the
court.[2] In short, the rhetoric of *jōi* was not to be confused with the reality
of confrontation. Yoshinobu had attained the essence of the policy of ver-

bal *jōi* that Shungaku had advocated more than a year earlier. It remained to be seen what benefits Edo would derive therefrom.

The bitter clash of 2/16 threw the entire political situation in Kyoto into confusion, and more than a month of indecision and unproductive maneuver passed before matters began to clarify in a different and momentarily stable political configuration. When they did clarify, they did so in a way very satisfying to Edo. One by one the great lords gave up hope for their *kōbugattai* effort. Amid much talk, maneuver, regret, and rumor they withdrew from matters, surrendered their formal positions as imperial advisors, resigned their nominal roles in bakufu councils, and unhappily left for home. This trend was welcome enough to the delegates from Edo. They made that clear on 3/20 when they ordered Arima Michisumi to return to Edo. He had acquired a reputation as a sympathizer of Hisamitsu and had encountered friction and frustration as the *kōbugattai* effort fell apart. His departure from the Kinai seven days later deprived the great lords of a receptive man within the bakufu. In his place officials at both Edo and Kyoto were beginning to suggest the reappointment of Ogasawara Nagamichi, who was not known as a friend of great daimyo.[3]

During Arima's last days at Kyoto complex, obscure maneuvers were excluding both Shungaku and Hisamitsu from any role as military protectors of the court and paving the way for their smooth departure from the city. What excluded them was Yoshinobu's appointment on 3/25 as *kinri shuei sōtoku* or supreme commander of imperial defense with control over defenses in the Kinai region. With his appointment a key element in the emerging political configuration had been put in place, and shortly afterward both Shungaku and Hisamitsu left town.

Yoshinobu's preemptive appointment enhanced the titular Tokugawa military presence in the Kinai area, but the daimyo departures reduced the actual defense capabilities there just when a new foreign armada and invasion force were assembling at Yokohama. Given the determination of bakufu leaders in Kyoto to appear more loyal than the loyalists, this situation was worrisome to them. It was worrisome, too, because they knew well enough that Tokugawa primacy depended on more than just appearances. Aizu troops, who previously had had a key defense role in the city and had thereby sustained the Tokugawa presence, had been relieved of that duty and put in the vanguard of the incipient Chōshū expedition. After it aborted with the *kōbugattai* collapse, bakufu leaders hoped to reassign Aizu troops to their old duty. However, when the bakufu ordered Katamori on 4/7 to return to his old post of Kyoto protector, he refused. The matter was of great concern to bakufu leaders, and its handling illustrates well the tortuous nature of *bakuhan* politics and its severe limitations as a technique of national governance.[4]

Unquestionably one aspect of young Katamori's problem was his health. The nature of his sickness is not clear, but the symptoms suggest a stress-related condition such as a bad case of ulcers or possibly alcoholism. At any rate during 64/1 he had become gravely ill, starting a long-drawn-out medical siege that nearly killed him in early 64/3. Thereafter for the rest of the year and well into 1865 he suffered periodic relapses, spending most of his time at home, much of it in bed, often begging off duty as a result or performing his tasks despite his weakness.

There were also major political aspects to Katamori's difficulties. The whole pattern of conflict during 64/2, the foreign policy and Chōshū issues and the contest for control of affairs, was distressing to him and his men because Aizu was a model *happō bijin*, a "universal beauty" enjoying the goodwill of almost everyone. As the months passed, Aizu men in Kyoto found themselves caught in the middle of these quarrels with commitments leading to all groups involved.

To elaborate, from the latter part of 1862 Katamori had revealed himself to be a champion of bakufu respect toward Kyoto and resistance to the foreigners. In his position as protector that posture had paid great dividends. It had surely helped him retain the devoted support of his vassals despite the ruinous fiscal burden of maintaining a defense establishment in Kyoto. It also had enabled him to maintain good relations with key men in the court, with the Shinsengumi and some other *rōnin*, and with men from such important *sonnō jōi*–oriented *han* as Mito, Tottori, Okayama, and Owari.

The *sonnō jōi* inclination of Aizu was tempered, however, by circumstances past and present. It was qualified by the strong *han* sense of loyalty to the Tokugawa family and by the fact that Edo was doing much to pay for Aizu's costs in Kyoto. Moreover, from early in 1863 radical Chōshū activists in the city had repeatedly embarrassed Katamori and gradually driven Aizu into a position of hostility toward them despite their shared rhetoric of *sonnō jōi*. His role in the 8/18 coup had embittered radicals more widely even as it repaired his somewhat shaky image at Edo. Then he had become a vigorous proponent of a firm punitive policy toward Chōshū, a posture that confirmed radical hatred for Aizu but improved his relationship with such great daimyo as Shimazu and Yamauchi of Tosa. The Aizu-Chōshū quarrel had not, it appears, reduced the *sonnō jōi* zeal of Aizu men—indeed it was in a sense an expression of it—and so Aizu seems to have retained considerable goodwill among such *han* as Mito, Tottori, and Okayama.

Because of his good soldierly characteristics of vigor, commitment, and loyalty, because of the widespread confidence he enjoyed—and because everyone else was reluctant to grasp the nettle—in 64/2 Katamori had been chosen by leaders in Kyoto to command whatever military measures might be needed to chastise Chōshū properly. Nominally he was subordinate to the lord of Kii, but actually he was to be the source of real military muscle and the symbol of imperial commitment to the project. After receiving lavish gestures of praise and regard from both shogun and emperor, on 2/11 he had been ordered to surrender his title of Kyoto protector and take that of commandant of the armed forces (*rikugun sōsai*, retitled *gunji sōsai* two days later) with duties in the disciplining of Chōshū.

Some Aizu men and probably Katamori himself were unhappy about the new job, however. They argued skillfully that Aizu's leading role would only make Chōshū more stubborn and less likely to accept a settlement, so Katamori should not be involved in the expedition. Doubtless there was more to their concern than that. For one thing marching against Chōshū would likely cost even more than maintaining a presence in Kyoto, and the quid pro quo was not commensurate. As protector, Katamori had gradually assumed responsibility for law and order throughout the Kinai region and had acquired considerable goodwill at court. Much that had been gloriously successful was being exchanged for the grimy political hazards of attacking those whose chief fault was an excess of goodness—a surfeit of *sonnō jōi* zeal that many men of Aizu shared. Katamori and his advisors were most unwilling to undertake a task that could so easily split the *han* or throw it out of the company of angels and into the company of devils. Aizu's resistance led court and bakufu to reissue orders for him to accept his new post, and he finally did. Aizu men remained very worried, however, painfully aware that an unsuccessful military effort would be as much a disaster for Aizu as for Edo.

Consequently late in the traumatic day of 2/16, as the prospects of daimyo cooperation were falling apart, Aizu men revived efforts to have the appointment reconsidered. The next day, amid the wreckage of the *kōbugattai* movement, Katamori sought clarification of his command. With the basis of an allied force gone, he had no intention of ending up *le général sans armée*. In response to his inquiry, the senior councillors informed him that he had in fact command over all bakufu forces, both the traditional brigades of the regime and the modern units newly formed in the military institute. He also received explicit but imprecise authority over the navy.[5] In their efforts to induce Katamori to accept his thankless task, bakufu leaders had granted him more military authority than any man outside the senior council or the shogun himself in over two centuries. Aizu leaders knew full well, however, that authority was not power. To rebuff Chōshū, Katamori would need more soldiers than the bakufu alone could provide, and in late 64/2 he had no reason to expect them to materialize.

The deterioration of Katamori's expeditionary resources was soon matched by deterioration in his health. By month's end he was formally reported sick; by 3/5 rumors were circulating that he had died. Some said he had committed suicide, others that he was merely dead, others that he was not dead at all but just fatally ill. And both court and bakufu repeatedly sent emissaries to inquire and comfort him.[6]

Court and bakufu concern for Katamori's health did not spring from human compassion alone. With the *kōbugattai* movement in tatters and Yoshinobu under severe criticism by the daimyo, Katamori was the one man who retained both great political respect and the military power to back it up. His illness was a matter of severe political concern. Barring other dramatic developments, until he was ready there would be no Chōshū expedition, regardless of how contemporary disputes over the handling of Chōshū delegates were resolved. If he died, even the defense of Kyoto itself might become immensely more complicated.

As of early 64/3, then, the bakufu seemed in danger of losing the keystone to its position in Kyoto. Nor were those bakufu leaders in Kyoto the only ones concerned. When senior councillors Itakura, Inoue, and Makino at Edo learned of Katamori's reassignment to the Chōshū command, they fired off to their colleagues in Kyoto a letter protesting it. They asserted that Katamori had been the pillar of the bakufu in Kyoto and that without his loyal presence there it would be hard to keep the city under control. They warned, moreover, that with his reassignment it would be very difficult later to induce him to reaccept his onerous duties in the city. Therefore it was important to transfer him back to his former post at once.

On 4/7, as we noted a bit earlier, the Kyoto bakufu had formally ordered Katamori to reaccept his old position. As the senior councillors at Edo had feared, however, Aizu was not eager to reassume old burdens. Though Katamori was actually feeling better, he declined to accept on the grounds of continuing illness. In succeeding days bakufu officials negotiated vigorously with Aizu men, applying great pressure and, more important perhaps, offering substantial rewards. Finally on 4/22 Katamori stated that despite his illness he had no choice but to accept the duties of protector. He was still a good soldier and not a half-bad bargainer. In the Aizu-bakufu maneuvering of 64/1–4, Aizu had been given in perpetuity 50,000 *koku* of land earlier allotted as office land and had received from

Edo additional gifts of 40,000 *ryō* in gold and a loan of 10,000 *hyō* of rice. The bakufu was paying dearly for Aizu's support, but at least it had been retained and Tokugawa military preeminence in Kyoto had been assured. Another sturdy piece of the desired political configuration was in place.

The appointment of Yoshinobu as *kinri shuei sōtoku* and the reappointment of Katamori as Kyoto protector were two important items in the bakufu's reassertion of authority. The bakufu's triumph of early 1864 had many other facets.[7] Thus on 3/23, the day the court was formally notified of Yoshinobu's coming appointment and as rumors were circulating of the shogun's imminent departure for Edo, or at least Osaka, the bakufu ordered the armed forces of daimyo, both vassal and outside, to discontinue guarding the city of Kyoto. In their place the forces of the protector, deputy, city magistrate, and Shinsengumi were to take charge of city police. The appointment of Matsudaira Sadaaki of Kuwana, who was Katamori's brother, as deputy and the reappointment of Katamori as protector gave substance to these orders. Later Yoshinobu was given more troops for his duty as *kinri shuei sōtoku*, and two minor vassal lords were added to Kyoto guard duty. For the first time in two years the bakufu had reassumed sole responsibility for preserving the emperor's tranquillity. More pieces of the emerging configuration were falling into place.

Other evidences of the bakufu triumph continued to appear. On 4/7 the bakufu notified the court that Edo was reassuming the maintenance of an imperial shrine near Utsunomiya which the court had taken over during the months of radical restoration activity. Ten days later the Kyoto bakufu announced that it would loan warships to the daimyo to facilitate their *sankin kōtai* journeys. This mock-magnanimous gesture foreshadowed a bakufu effort to revive the *sankin kōtai* system of old. Accompanying these actions were a series of shogunal audiences with the emperor that demonstrated the new intimacy of the two and reiterated the policy decisions previously agreed upon. This benign trend was nearly undone when news of growing trouble in the Kantō and renewed activist pressure for a policy of expulsion revived efforts at court to get all three ports closed. Yoshinobu and bakufu officials were able to stop that, however, and a few days later the shogun triumphantly departed Kyoto. Traveling by sea, he reached Edo late in the day on 5/20, to find that reconstruction of the western enceinte had been commenced during his absence.

In late 1863, as in 1862, many in the bakufu had feared and resisted the trip to Kyoto. But whereas the first trip had proved as baneful as its detractors had feared, the second had turned into a success more complete than its strongest proponents could have hoped for. The rhetoric of *sonnō jōi* had been turned to Edo's advantage, and *kōbugattai* in the sense of court-bakufu unity had displaced the *kōbugattai* of court-daimyo unity.

Nor was it merely a triumph of terminology. The radical restorationists were thoroughly, if momentarily, in eclipse. The great lords too had been stymied and had retreated to their domains in docility and disarray. The court was left utterly open to the bakufu. While various ceremonial concessions had been made, the Edo leaders had moved vigorously to reassert the old constraints and to assure that enough military forces and enough major leaders remained in the city to sustain those constraints. Even Yoshinobu, who had survived the first trip with his influence intact, had been removed from his former post as shogunal guardian and skillfully tied down in Kyoto, shut away from the decision-making process and committed, like Katamori, to serving Edo's purposes. The situation of the regular bakufu leadership seemed more satisfactory than at any time since the resignation of Kuze Hirochika two years before.

THE KANTŌ INSURRECTION: 1864

The men who returned to Edo with the shogun on 5/20 had much reason to be pleased with the way things had worked out in Kyoto. They had no reason, however, to be pleased with the situation in the Kantō. During their absence the reviving *shishi* activism and broader public discontent that had begun to manifest themselves in late 1863 had continued to grow. By the end of 64/5 the regime had a serious insurrection on its hands, one whose magnitude, duration, and future potential dwarfed the Yamato and Ikuno incidents of 1863. As the year progressed, that potential was realized, and by the middle of 64/8 the insurrection had acquired enough momentum to threaten the very survival of the regime.[8] For three months war was waged in deadly earnest until by the end of 64/10 the insurgency was broken. Remnants then made a harried two-month march to the Kinai where they finally surrendered, only to pay a terrible price for their effort.[9]

1. Disaster Approaches: 64/1–8

Activist agitation in the Kantō had appeared in late 1863. During the winter it continued, with more and more samurai and commoners participating. From 64/1 the bakufu began to press Yoshiatsu and his advisors to get Mito men back under control. It also ordered daimyo forces deployed here and there to suppress the troublemakers. Nevertheless, small dissident bands kept operating, most notably a group whose leaders included Tamaru Naonobu and Fujita Koshirō, both of Mito.

These men had been embittered by the factional conflicts in Mito during Ii Naosuke's rule. And then they had been disillusioned in 1863 when the bakufu capitulated to foreigners on both the indemnity and expulsion issues. In succeeding months they discussed the possibilities of joint action with men of Okayama, Tottori, and Chōshū, and in their travels they invoked *sonnō jōi* rhetoric to recruit followers and justify their constant demands for sustenance.

In 64/2 the political possibilities of this activity were sharply improved when court and bakufu leaders in Kyoto formally agreed to close Yokohama. On 3/6 leaders at Edo informed daimyo and officials that the shogun and emperor had resolved to close the port, and news of the Kyoto decision probably reached the Kantō activists about the same time or shortly after. The closing of only one port was not sufficient to satisfy them, but it did provide a rationale for initial measures designed to prod the bakufu into a total expulsion policy.

Twenty-one days later, on 3/27, Tamaru, Fujita, and some sixty-three followers set out for an assembly at Mt. Tsukuba, the highest peak in a mountainous ridge rising out of the Kantō plain between Mito and Edo. Soon other groups joined them, and their number rose into the hundreds. In search of a concrete purpose, they finally decided to travel to the shrines at Nikkō by way of Utsunomiya. There they would assert the honor of Nariaki, proclaim their loyal intentions to both the imperial and Tokugawa ancestors, and issue a call for a policy of *sonnō jōi*. They proposed to proceed from there to Yokohama where, in obedience to the imperial order announced by Edo, they would help the bakufu expel the foreigners.

The group that assembled for that trip in the early days of 64/4 were variously estimated at a few score to four hundred people equipped with a few horses, a few dozen firearms, and other simpler weaponry. Probably about 130 actually reached Utsunomiya on 4/5. There they were given 1000 *ryō* by the daimyo and permitted to rest in his castle grounds. Then as they traveled northwest from Utsunomiya toward the Tokugawa mausolea at Nikkō, their numbers reportedly grew to between 150 and 250. Against them the Nikkō magistrate (*bugyō*) could mobilize some 500 assorted men. A clash seemed in store, but when the men reached Nikkō, a diplomatic means was found to permit their honoring Nariaki. Then they departed peacefully toward Ōhira mountain near Tochigi town to the south. They did not push on from there toward

Yokohama as planned, but that outcome was not very reassuring to Edo leaders because they heard that at Ōhira the insurgent band was continuing to grow.

This new eruption of Mito activism opened old and deep cleavages within that *han* and quickly led to political complications within the bakufu. Those complications involved relations with court and foreigners as well as with Mito proper. With the shogun still at Kyoto, Yoshiatsu was nominally in charge at Edo. His principal advisors there were *han* officials at his Koishikawa residence, and they included Takeda Kōunsai and others sympathetic to the Tsukuba group. These men strongly urged Yoshiatsu to proceed with the closing of Yokohama as a way to forestall the rapidly escalating unrest in the *han*. In response during 64/4 he wrote leaders in Kyoto a number of letters advocating a firm policy of expulsion. In reaction to that communication, the senior councillors at Edo wrote several letters opposing such a policy. The lobbying for a firmer policy at Kyoto was thwarted there by bakufu leaders, as we noted previously, but at Edo Mito men continued to urge officials to close the ports.

Besides creating political problems, the Mito unrest was reviving concern about social control in and near Edo. The bakufu deployed both its own and vassal daimyo forces to protect Nikkō and on 4/12 ordered the outside lord of Toyama (100,000 *koku*) to dispatch his best troops to the shogunal shrines at Ueno lest *rōnin* endanger them. And it ordered four other *han* to work with the Kanagawa magistrates in defending Yokohama against the bands assembling northeast of the city.

At Ōhira the number of dissidents gradually rose to several hundred by late 64/5. They busied themselves constructing three small cannon and other weaponry, strengthening the defenses of their mountain bastion, and extorting funds, horses, weapons, and other supplies from vulnerable folk within range. Sometimes they did so by posing as *han* or bakufu officials, sometimes by winning local supporters to their *sonnō jōi* cause, and sometimes less delicately by threats of arson and murder. Their range of activity grew in proportion to their numbers. By late 64/5 people as far away as Isezaki, 45 kilometers west of Ōhira, and others in the northern districts of Shimōsa province some 90 kilometers to the southeast were being subjected to organized extortion. [10]

The Ōhira group rejected efforts of Mito emissaries to induce them to go home, but on 5/30 they did abandon Ōhira and return to their original nest at Mt. Tsukuba. In the course of that move they began to harass nearby vassal *han*, notably Shimodate and Mibu. Then on 6/6 a force of two or three hundred of the men approached the town of Tochigi, which was administered by Toda of Ashikaga, and demanded some 20,000 or 30,000 *ryō*. When refused, they attacked Toda's forces with firearms and burned the town, withdrawing only when the defenders received reinforcements a couple of days later. Driven from there, they went on, one group threatening to burn Yūki, others extorting funds elsewhere and adding followers as best they could. Predictably these activities generated great concern among bakufu intendants, landholding liege vassals, and minor vassal lords in the area. They quickly began informing Edo of developments and seeking bakufu assistance and protection.

Even by itself this intensified turbulence of early 64/6 was sufficiently worrisome to the recently reunified bakufu. In addition, however, Edo had begun receiving reports of minor trouble elsewhere. Then it learned that at Kyoto on 6/5 a Shinsengumi force of some thirty men had crushed a small group of about twenty *shishi* plotters, including Chōshū men, in the Ikeda-ya, an inn in the city. The Aizu report of this matter was mild in tone but could only have served to reinforce Edo's concern about a possible Mito-Chōshū connection. After all, if one group had been found, how many more were still undiscovered? And other evidence of *rōnin* scheming and of frictions springing from police troubles in Kyoto only served to heighten the sense of potential danger to the west. *In toto* the information suggested the real possibility of a linkup between the Kantō insurgents and Chōshū men. To prevent such a dire development, the bakufu on 6/9 ordered fourteen daimyo and some lesser vassals to mobilize forces sufficient to suppress the Mito men, pacify the region, protect intendancies, control all barrier points, and prevent the ingress of *shishi* from Chōshū.

These developments of early 64/6 ushered in a month of the most confused and frenetic activity. During that month the insurgents continued to rove about, extorting supplies where they could, with one group attacking forces of Tsuchiura and burning a village in the process. Some tried again to win Yūki to their cause, acquiring substantial sympathy there, while others added recruits from local troublemakers and ordinary commoners. In their most daring exploit a band of one hundred reached Sendagaya in west Edo, where they broke into a bakufu gunpowder warehouse and made off with considerable stores of ammunition.[11] This raid led to an elaborate investigation and belatedly to strengthened guards at armories in Edo, but for the insurgents it was a welcome replenishment of depleted munitions.

The Tsukuba problem was thus quite enough all by itself, but during 64/6 the whole Kantō situation was severely exacerbated when Mito's *han* government was ravaged by internal convulsions. In effect *han* leaders played a game of musical chairs, in which Takeda Kōunsai and the pro-Tsukuba elements at Koishikawa were ousted by Ichikawa Hirosane and some five hundred men who had marched in battle array from Mito to Edo to induce Yoshiatsu to denounce the Tsukuba men. Ichikawa succeeded. But after his force had left Mito town, a coalition of *han* officials secured control there, adopted a conciliatory policy toward the Tsukuba group, and led a force of seven or eight hundred men to Kogane, just northeast of Edo, where they met Takeda and some of his followers. The purpose of the Kogane group was to change Yoshiatsu's policy yet again, and, in the view of some of them at least, to restore the *jōi* policy that the bakufu, as we note later, had just repudiated a few days before. [12]

Within the bakufu itself the political situation was even more chaotic, as we also note later on, but despite the political paralysis at Edo, administrative leaders pressed on with the pacification effort. A steady flow of military orders appeared, and on 6/17 a pacification force departed for Tsukuba. It consisted of some seven hundred Mito men led by Ichikawa and armed with three to five cannon and at least two hundred firearms and a bakufu force of some three thousand with several cannon and over six hundred firearms. This force marched slowly north despite the objections of some officials such as Matsudaira Naokatsu, who argued that the insurgents should be pacified by implementation of the court-ordered policy on Yokohama. Other officials also protested, and the troops themselves were lethargic. Leaders of vassal *han* were hesitant about cooperating, and pundits in Edo freely expressed fears and pessimism about developments. [13]

Despite the widespread problems of morale that all this resistance implied, by early 64/7 the pacification army was finally deployed for battle, having been augmented with thousands of troops from several nearby vassal *han*. Most of those had taken up defensive positions at selected spots ringing the insurgent headquarters at Tsukuba. The attack force itself consisted of 2500 men, including infantry, cavalry, and artillery commanded by officers such as Kawakatsu Kōun and Misoguchi Shōnyo. On 7/7 the battle erupted, and the attack force routed the insurgents. Two days later, however, units of the latter attacked at daybreak, burned the bakufu army's headquarters, and put the expedition's commander and staff to flight. That blow obliged the bakufu army to withdraw to Yūki and caused Shimozuma troops to fire their own *han* headquarters and flee for Edo. When news of that insurgent victory got around, volunteers began to pour in, making matters worse than ever for the regime.

This humiliating reverse was followed by several discouraging days for Edo leaders. In the city rumors of war were rampant. Mito men kept pressing Yoshiatsu to be more sympathetic to the insurgents, and large groups finally memorialized him to return to Mito, take the lead in a policy of *jōi*, and so pacify the rebels and preserve the *han*. Just to the northeast at Kogane the large assembly of Mito men remained. A bakufu order to Yoshiatsu secured the withdrawal of only about half, or some four hundred of them. Takeda and certain other sympathizers of the Tsukuba group stayed put and others went to an encampment in Nakaminato, a small port town southeast of Mito. Further to the north in the Tsukuba area the insurgents continued their activity, in the process dealing reverses to *han* forces in a number of minor skirmishes. Encouraged by developments, Fujita, Tamaru, and their colleagues began reviving plans for an assault on Yokohama. And from Kyoto came reports of a renewed Chōshū challenge to bakufu control of the city, including a report by Katamori in mid-64/7 that a fight with the assembled Chōshū forces would be a major problem.

Against this fretful background the bakufu slowly pushed on with its mobilization. It put junior councillor Tanuma Okitaka in charge as general commander of the Kantō pacification army. With its new battalions already in the field and other large units at Kyoto, the bakufu turned to its traditional elite forces only to discover that when available units were assembled, they only added up to some six hundred men with two cannon and eighty firearms.[14] Already, it was clear, the bakufu was scraping the bottom of its manpower barrel. Its dependence on daimyo support was painfully apparent. Accordingly various orders were issued to tighten control in the Kantō and identify all daimyo forces available for use in the city. Special couriers were hurriedly dispatched to persuade the Tōhoku lords at Morioka, Akita, and Sendai to send forces to aid in the Kantō. New efforts were made to mobilize peasant militia units.[15] A more complex command structure was set up under Tanuma. And more detailed logistical arrangements were started as it became evident that the regime was facing a rebellion whose magnitude might yet surpass that of Shimabara.

It was in this period of bleakness that bakufu leaders once again received greatly encouraging news from Kyoto. Probably late on 7/23 or 7/24 Edo learned that a Chōshū attempt to seize Kyoto by force had been repulsed and the attackers thrown into full retreat. This good news was followed almost at once by news that Ichikawa's force had proceeded from Tsukuba to Mito castle, arriving there on 7/23 and establishing in the castle a solidly pro-bakufu presence. And two days later the force repulsed an assault by a force of some five hundred insurgents.

The good news on both fronts elicited a vigorous response. By then the bakufu's paralytic crisis of 64/6 was past and a major leadership change had been made. In contrast to the usual fumbling efforts of prior years, this time Edo seized the opportunity to regain the political initiative in dealing with both Chōshū and the Kantō insurgents. The new confidence vis-à-vis the insurgents was evident in a forceful order of 7/26. That order denounced them for misconstruing the court's intention on expulsion and for engaging in turbulent behavior that hurt the good name of Mito, inconvenienced the bakufu, worked hardship on the common people, and made a mockery of the ideal of imperial loyalism. The order called for the quick crushing of the Mito insurgents and was followed at once by Tanuma's prompt departure for Tsukuba.[16]

This newfound resolve among bakufu leaders did little to improve the real character of the military situation, however. Instead, Kantō affairs steadily worsened. Despite Tanuma's brisk departure, weeks passed before he got his various forces satisfactorily coordinated and felt ready to engage the enemy in major fighting. During those weeks the insurgency continued to flourish. The situation in Mito grew ever more chaotic, and the rebels began to achieve ominous success in swaying the allegiance of important men.

The most serious threat to Edo came from the defection of Matsudaira Yorinori, a second cousin of Nariaki and the daimyo of Shishido, a branch of the Mito house. His unintended and unnecessary defection illustrates how fragile was the bakufu position, how situational pressures shaped behavior, and how costly were political mistakes. Late in 64/7, as Mito was teetering on the brink of chaos, the bakufu approved Yoshiatsu's request that Yorinori be designated his representative at Mito castle. On 7/30 he received orders to go there and restore peace to the *han*.

Yorinori was a bad choice.[17] Previously he had gone on record as a cautious advocate of closing Yokohama. And just four days earlier he had betrayed his own inclination by writing to Yoshiatsu's brother Ikeda Mochimasa of Okayama, urging him to participate actively in national affairs in accord with Nariaki's wishes. Mochimasa was a vigorous man who had been a leader in the attempt to mediate the Chōshū problem. He also had expressed repeatedly his strong approval of the *sonnō jōi* motivation of the Tsukuba insurgents and his belief that the well-being of Japan was intimately tied to the triumph of the ''virtuous faction'' at Mito. Yorinori probably shared this sentiment, and such a predisposition made him an unlikely champion of Edo's cause.

On 8/4 Yorinori left Edo to assume command at Mito. As his entourage wended northward, it picked up thousands of followers, particularly those assembled at Kogane, and including Takeda Kōunsai. Consequently, as he approached Mito castle, he was viewed by Ichikawa's men not as a cooperating pro-bakufu force but rather as the leader of a pro-Tsukuba internal faction. Accordingly Ichikawa's group did its best to obstruct Yorinori's advance and mobilized general popular opposition to him—with success due apparently to the deep bitterness that the Tsukuba group's plundering and violence had generated among many Mito commoners. Attempts to mediate the Ichikawa-Yorinori dispute failed. By 8/10 the two groups that Edo hoped would cooperate were ready to do battle.

During the next few days Yorinori's supporters fought sporadically both with Ichikawa's men in the castle and with some of his supporters stationed near Nakaminato. In the process they cooperated actively with some units of the Tsukuba insurgents themselves. By 8/17 Yorinori had captured Nakaminato. A few days later he headed back to Mito, intending to gain control of the castle—by negotiation if possible, by force if not. Whatever his original purpose may have been, Yorinori had in fact been drawn into cooperation with the insurgents, and Shishido men hurried off to assist him. A Tokugawa-branch *han* was in rebellion.

Other daimyo were also wavering. On 8/6 former keeper of Osaka castle Tsuchiya Tomonao of Tsuchiura wrote Edo an earnest entreaty on the matter. In rough paraphrase, he argued that although the *rōnin* had to be quelled, it was the foreign intrusion which had generated their discontent. Tanuma, he wrote, had been sent to pacify them, and he Tsuchiya had been ordered to assist as well. Countless tens of thousands shared the insurgents' *sonnō jōi* view, however, including many in Edo, Kyoto, and Osaka. Given their fight-to-the-death commitment to *jōi*, it would be hard, he feared, to suppress them. If, however, prominent men were to summon the insurgents and discuss matters with magnanimity and reason, they could be managed if one understood their *sonnō jōi* convictions. If one established clearly that Yokohama was going to be closed, people everywhere would feel reassured. Merely to announce the intention to achieve *jōi* and the port's closing, however, would not be enough. Procedures to do so would have to be established because the feelings of anger had been building for ten years.[18]

Tsuchiura, just south of Tsukuba, was one of the largest *han* (95,000 *koku*) in the Kantō. If it were lost, even just to neutrality, the other Kantō *han* might also be lost, and it was clear that without daimyo support the bakufu could not prevail. Even more ominously, there was uncertainty about the great outside fiefs of Okayama and Tottori. Their lords were sympathetic to those against whom Edo was fighting. They had for weeks been actively solicited by the insurgents. They had spoken repeatedly in their behalf. And they were at that very time openly expressing opposition to Edo's concurrent policy toward Chōshū.

The bakufu was in a very dangerous situation. Further insurgent successes might encourage Chōshū to try again at Kyoto, and that attempt might prompt Okayama and Tottori also to move. Moreover additional bakufu reverses might discourage its defenders one by one until a mass defection developed and its defenders became its assailants, the more so when news of the impending diplomatic humiliation became known. It is perhaps understandable why Itakura Katsukiyo, who had recently opposed Naokatsu very strongly on matters and had been removed from office in the turmoil, was just at that time preparing to leave the city for his own fief near Okayama and rejecting entreaties that he stay around awaiting reappointment as a senior councillor.[19] A prudent lord might wisely have concluded that it was time to be at his own castle, among his own men.

2. Disaster Recedes: 64/8–12

As things worked out, the middle of the eighth month was the nadir of bakufu fortunes in the Kantō. A crucial battle late in the month stopped the immediate danger, and victories during 64/9 turned the tide decisively. More reverses during 64/10 seemed to belie Edo's triumph, however, and it was not until the last two months of the year that bakufu leaders at last considered the Kantō sufficiently pacified that they could devote their attention to other matters.

During 64/8 pacification commander Tanuma had slowly deployed his forces around Tsukuba. On 8/22, however, he learned that the mountain was empty and the insurgents were headed for Mito castle, where Yorinori's forces were starting their attack. The implication was obvious: if they overwhelmed Ichikawa and secured the castle, they would gain an immense propaganda victory and a substantial tactical advantage. Accordingly Tanuma promptly dispatched a picked force toward Mito. By 8/24 the lead elements of that force were at the edge of town, and an artillery exchange made it clear to the townsfolk that the war had come to them in earnest. Merchants closed and locked their shops. Women and children fled to the villages, and the armies marched into town.[20]

On the next day more forces reached Mito, and Tanuma set up his headquarters at Kasama, some 15 kilometers to the west. Different sources give different figures, but the general magnitude of the warring armies seems clear. The bakufu, according to one report, sent to Mito a picked force of six hundred troops that was supplemented by three hundred from Nihonmatsu and eight hundred from Mibu. Within the castle were Ichikawa's several hundred men. Against this force was Yorinori's following, conservatively reported at some eight hundred, and one day away were several hundred more insurgents hurrying to reinforce him.

For days it had been raining, and on 8/25, as the skies lowered ominously, the armies with their firearms and cannon met in combat that might in the outcome decide the fate of the Tokugawa dynasty. The fighting was fierce and went on for three days. The losses sustained by both sides were great, but finally Yorinori's troops were forced to retreat toward Nakaminato, losing some cannon and firearms in the process. As they fell back, they started burning the town, but the repeated torrential downpours doused most fires, soaked the armies, and saved the town. The castle had been relieved; the regime survived.

During 64/8 Tanuma's army had been plagued with colds and sickness brought on by the unseasonal rains. But the outcome of the battle for Mito castle cheered men up, and Tanuma at last was able to take the initiative. From 9/1 he began to deploy his units vigorously, pursuing scattered bands and slowly surrounding and trapping the main rebel force at Nakaminato. There Fujita and Tamaru were awkwardly allied with Takeda and the hapless Yorinori. They were fielding a total force of some two thousand or more troops, of whom the majority probably were politicized commoners, mostly peasants, and a minority Mito samurai.[21]

In most of the scattered contests the numbers of insurgents were few, and the pacification army enjoyed massive numerical superiority. At Nakaminato, too, it had a decisive advantage. Again the figures are frequently contradictory, but at the height of the struggle in 64/9 the bakufu, it appears, was able to set against the insurgents' two thousand men or so some five thousand bakufu troops. About three thousand of them were carrying shoulder arms. Offshore it had three steamships patrolling to prevent any escape by sea. Ichikawa's Mito forces numbered in the high hundreds, probably, and the ten to twenty *han* that had been ordered to assist likely contributed six thousand troops, many with firearms. At any given moment, of course, portions of this force were in reserve and other large portions were stationed at various defense points. But Tanuma probably did have upward of five thousand men available as a striking force at any one time.

Despite their numbers the pacifiers sustained some reverses. And when, as usual, they won their engagements, they found that the rebels would retreat only to regroup and continue their struggle. Gradually, mercilessly, during 64/9 the noose was tightened about Yorinori's forces. In costly savage fighting that went on day after day men were killed by the score, dying in battle, being executed by their captors, committing suicide. Weapons were seized, stores destroyed, villages and homes burned, but still the war ground on.

By 64/10 Tanuma had moved his headquarters into Mito, and the entire situation seemed much better. It was apparent that the vassal daimyo had been able to keep control of their forces and were gradually getting the required contingents deployed. The danger of mass defections was past, and full pacification seemed only a matter of time. On 9/16 Yorinori, who had never felt comfortable in his unexpected role of insurgent leader, had at last agreed to surrender with a handful of close retainers. Ten days later he was sentenced to death by suicide. Some men, including at least one liege vassal, protested his death sentence, but to no avail. On the night of his sentencing he committed suicide. He was thirty-five years old. A number of his retainers also committed suicide, and twenty other Shishido men were beheaded like common criminals.

The insurgency had been dealt a severe reverse, and others at Nakaminato hoped a settlement would soon follow. But it did not. The bakufu had committed itself too deeply to accept a compromise, and the struggle raged on. By 10/10 the main bakufu force had increased its numbers yet more, had tightened the encirclement at Nakaminato, and was bombarding the insurgents from both land and sea. On that day, another rainy day, the pacification army attacked and a fierce battle ensued. Despite its artillery bombardment and assault, however, the bakufu force was dealt a stunning defeat. The encounter was of major proportions. The participating bakufu force, including detachments from Fukushima, Mibu, Mito, Utsunomiya, and Shibata, numbered some 6700 men plus perhaps 500 peasant militia personnel. The insurgents were some 2000. The bakufu casualties were around 80 dead, nearly 200 wonded or missing, and seven cannon and uncounted other equipment lost to the enemy. The insurgents only reported six dead.[22]

Seven days later, after regrouping and engaging in a series of indecisive encounters, the bakufu forces again launched an all-out attack and again were routed. This time they fled in disarray, abandoning heavy cannon and other equipment on the field. Another assault the following day, 10/18, also ended in rout, and with these reverses Tanuma became the butt of ridicule.[23] What was being forgotten by his critics, however, was that three months previously the insurgents had been operating freely throughout the Kantō. Now they were bottled up, cut off from food supplies, exposed to naval bombardment, and in an unwinnable position.

Despite these dramatic victories, the rebel situation had become extremely dangerous. The conflict had been at least as corrosive to their élan as it had been to that of the bakufu. Whereas the pacification force had continued to grow in size, probably numbering by late 64/10 well over 10,000 men and perhaps 1500 peasant militiamen, the insurgent force could only shrink. In the face of such overwhelming odds, many among the rebels began seeking diplomatic means of breaking the impasse. And after the recent setbacks, some within the bakufu force also urged negotiation. Secret contacts between the two camps were established, and when on 10/23 Tanuma launched another coordinated attack, the leaders of some 1100 of the insurgents surrendered as per agreement. The others, whose leaders included Takeda, Tamaru, and Fujita, broke out to the northwest and began a long tortuous trek into the mountains.

The surviving insurgent force numbered about a thousand. They had managed to take their twenty to thirty small cannon and equipment with them as they fled, and after a fighting retreat they found time to regroup, establish a new command organization, and settle upon a strategy. They proposed to travel to Kyoto and there appeal to the emperor and Yoshinobu for understanding and support. As the force moved westward, it pleaded its *sonnō jōi* case where necessary to avoid conflict, hoping to reach Kyoto intact. During 64/11 it passed through the foothills of the western Kantō and into the mountains of Shinano, escaping most pursuers, fighting rarely, plundering only as necessary to survive, and descending into the Mino foothills north of Nagoya by month's end.

By 64/12 the Kantō had again become quiet, and the insurgents came under the jurisdiction of Yoshinobu, the supreme commander of imperial defense *(kinri shuei sōtoku)*. The reports reaching him in 64/11–12 told of a *rōnin* force whose numbers were variously estimated at 600 to 2500, but most commonly 700 to 1000 men or so, with 150 to 200 horses for mounts and packhorse service. In response to these reports, bakufu, *han*, and peasant militia forces on the insurgents' route of march were put on guard and Kyoto city defenses again were mobilized. On 12/3, after receiving imperial approval, Yoshinobu moved up to Ōtsu and ordered troops eastward to intercept the approaching force, which had already turned northward toward Echizen. His own force numbered over 1300 men, of whom about 800 were infantrymen of one sort or another and 170 were artillerymen. In succeeding days a vast number of daimyo, mostly vassal lords from the Kinai area, also dispatched battalions of troops to positions north and east of Kyoto. By the middle of the month the forces under Yoshinobu totaled at least ten thousand.[24]

Stymied by unfriendly forces, barred from Kyoto, and unable to obtain the political support they sought, the insurgents again turned to petitions and mediation, but without success. With the hope of triumph at Kyoto blasted, their cohesion collapsed, and within a few days the mediation led to a surrender. That capitulation in turn led to disbandment of the army of suppression just a few days before the New Year. With the internment of those last 823 men, including Takeda, Tamaru, and Fujita, the most far-reaching, potentially disastrous, sanguinary, and costly insurgency faced by Edo since 1638 sputtered and died.

3. A Summing Up

The insurrection had been survived, but the bakufu paid a considerable price in terms of morale, manpower, and finances.

Forced into the position of opposing sonnō jōi, the regime had been torn by bitter divisions that reached from highest officials to lowest vassals. The divisions had been revealed not only in political paralysis and a rapid turnover of officeholders, but in scattered acts of insubordination, threats of defiance, acts of violence, and the feckless performance of the pacification army.

The Kantō insurrection was also costly in manpower. An appreciable number of men died or sustained debilitating wounds. The regime's armies were tied down completely for four months and partially for a whole year. Thousands of han troops also were immobilized guarding Edo, Yokohama, intendancies, barrier points, Nikkō, and other symbolic places. On 10/9, for example, the vassal daimyo of Ueda han notified Edo of the forces he would commit to the Chōshū expedition and acknowledged that the figures were below those of the seventeenth-century regulations he was supposed to follow. However, he explained, he had prisoners to guard, had to be prepared for trouble nearby, and had to have men ready to defend bakufu intendancies in the region.[25] Even months after the insurgency had collapsed, large numbers of men were still tied down guarding the nearly two thousand prisoners, whose presence was a source of continuing worry to their captors.

In other ways too the insurrection hurt Edo in terms of manpower. The brutal attack on sonnō jōi proponents deprived the regime of all hope of recruiting to its standard rōnin such as those who had originally formed the Shinsengumi and Shinchōgumi. And the Kantō insurgents themselves were mostly from Mito. Had history gone differently, they might have been among the regime's most avid supporters. As it was, 1302 of them were dead. Hundreds died in battle; scores of others committed suicide; and tragically large numbers were executed for their crimes or died in captivity. Of those who surrendered in the Kinai, the terrible number of 353 died at the executioner's hand during early 1865. Of those who surrendered in the Kantō, over a hundred reportedly died in captivity. Hundreds more were exiled. And the families of some of those involved in the upheaval also were punished, Takeda's family most brutally perhaps. And Mito itself, quite apart from the insurgents, was lost to Edo as an effective source of support, its finances wrecked, its leadership torn to pieces, its territory ravaged, its manpower decimated, its very soul destroyed by the tragedy it had known.[26]

The regime also received in the insurrection solid proof that all the years of rhetoric about the flabbiness of its military forces were warranted. Poorly motivated, lacking commanders as well as troops experienced in combat, hastily mobilized, and only partially coordinated, the armies made a lamentable showing. Even their immense manpower superiority—two to one at the worst, usually three to one or better—was not enough to prevent humiliating routs and reverses. And when routed, the troops were prone to flee the field, scattering in all directions, putting all possible distance between themselves and their tormentors, on occasion even going home.[27] Their inept performance prompted army commander *(rikugun bugyō)* Takenaka Shigemoto and the infantry commanders *(hohei bugyō)* to call in 64/12 for the development of a practical program of military training that would include geography, surveying, mathematics, and fortifications.[28] And other military leaders were contemporaneously pursuing other efforts to expand the training in modern warfare.

The one moderately bright spot in the picture was the performance of the bakufu's new-style forces that had received training in unit tactics. Unlike the *han* forces, it was reported, when the drilled troops suffered battlefield reverses, they did not scatter, but rather retained their essential formations and regrouped as soon as possible.[29] It was hardly a cause for rejoicing, however. Officials in the bakufu had been trying to create that modern army for ten years, and when it did prove its superiority to the old forces on the field of battle, it did so in a situation of too little and too late. It was a moderately able vanguard force of maybe three thousand men whose performance was repeatedly undercut by the poor showing of the thousands of archaic, ineffective samurai with whom it was combined.

Another more obvious cost to the bakufu was the fiscal drain. Quite apart from the costs of replacing stolen munitions and expended matériel and rebuilding ravaged towns and villages, there were major costs in fielding the armies. Total costs are hard to find, but there are a few suggestive figures. All the direct vassals of the bakufu were given added stipends in accordance with their positions, and already by 64/7, before the crisis had peaked, Tanuma reported that he had paid out sums totaling 80,000 *ryō*. This figure does not appear to have included troop costs for later months or the sums allotted to daimyo to defray their expenses. And it clearly did not include the costs of maintaining fleet strength off- shore, strengthening the defenses at Nikkō, barrier points, and inten- dancies, or interning and disposing of the thousands of captives. Sugges- tive of these costs were ''loans'' of 5000 *ryō* each to a senior and junior councillor dispatched to Nikkō on defense duty on 11/9 and a report by Katsu Kaishū in 65/1 that the interning of men in the Kinai was costing ''2000 in gold,'' presumably *ryō*, per day.[30] Likely the insurrection cost Edo far more than the Namamugi indemnity, which had amounted to some 330,000 *ryō*.

INSURGENTS, FOREIGNERS, COURT, AND CHŌSHŪ: 64/6-12

The Kantō insurrection was the dominating issue at Edo in 1864, but it was far from the only matter of concern. While the struggle raged on, ac- tivities of the foreigners and developments in Kyoto were independently presenting new problems and new opportunities for the leaders of bakufu resurgence.

After the bakufu was reunified at Edo in 64/5, interacting foreign and domestic problems quickly led to a severe policy paralysis that was not overcome for nearly a month. Then a few weeks after it was overcome, news of the Chōshū defeat at Kyoto on 7/19 and of the successful defense of Mito castle a few days later precipitated a burst of energetic bakufu action designed to deal vigorously with Chōshū, foreigners, and Kantō insurgents. That action soon bogged down, however, and months of complex and indecisive maneuver followed before matters gradually clarified during 64/10–12. Even then the major element in that clarified situation, the Chōshū expedition of 1864, ended as it had begun: as a policy of Kyoto. Its primary exponents were the court, certain great daimyo, and bakufu representatives in that city while Edo's role in it was both minimal and ambiguous.

Nevertheless by year's end the Kantō insurgency had been quelled, Chōshū appeared pacified, the foreigners were quiet, and the court had formally accepted Edo's foreign policy. Not surprisingly, therefore, ex- cept for some nagging suspicions concerning their own high-powered spokesmen in Kyoto, Edo leaders found considerable reason for satisfac- tion with the way the year had worked out. Things looked far, far better than they had on either of the two preceding New Years.

1. Policy Paralysis and Resolution: 64/6

The Kantō insurgency was only one of the troubles besetting Edo leaders in 64/5. During the shogun's visit to Kyoto, the foreigners had gradual-

ly assembled an invasion force for use against Chōshū. Under the aggressive leadership of British minister Rutherford Alcock the foreigners had
demanded that the bakufu punish Chōshū for its attacks of 1863 on
foreign shipping and had landed some 1500 troops at Yokohama to consolidate their beachhead and underline the demand. Edo leaders had
already heard of Chōshū's determination to resist any such punishment,
however, and had prudently postponed a response until the shogun's
return. By way of further complication, the shogunal group returning
from Kyoto was newly committed to closing Yokohama, but the trucu-
lence of both Alcock and the new French minister Léon Roches made the
honoring of that commitment seem extremely problematic.

In the weeks after the shogun's return to Edo the three matters of
Kantō insurgency, Yokohama, and the Chōshū-foreign confrontation
became intertwined and created a political crisis even more bitter and
complex than that of the previous summer.[31] The crisis was so bitter
because the Kantō issue was perceived as one of immediate life-or-death
importance to the regime. It was so complex because it involved a number of independent variables, most notably the unstable factional groups
within Mito and groups within the bakufu as well as the three separate
key issues. Instrumentally, however, the process of dispute had the usual
characteristics of policy paralysis, boycotting, pressuring, threatening,
hiring, firing, and punishing. The lines of cleavage within the bakufu
were similar to those of the previous year. The arguments stressed the in-
terconnectedness of problems; and the resolution, as always, involved a
capitulation to the foreigners dictated by bakufu weakness.

The foreign demand for punishment of Chōshū was the first matter to
be addressed. On 5/27 the reunified bakufu notified the foreigners that
Edo was not able to punish Chōshū at that time. Moreover, the
foreigners were told, only the closing of Yokohama could quiet the
domestic unrest and so make possible the punishment of Chōshū at a later
time. As many officials expected, however, the foreigners rejected the
proposal on Yokohama and proceeded with their own plan of attack, having made it clear that Edo would end up paying the costs anyway.[32]

The failure of this first attempt to solve the diplomatic problem led to a
shift in priorities. The Chōshū matter receded, and policy disputes at Edo
came to focus on Yokohama. This time it was Matsudaira Naokatsu and
Yoshiatsu of Mito who were formally in charge of closing the port, and
so it was they who insisted on doing so, arguing that only thus could the
Mito dissidents be pacified. They were supported by Sawa Kanshichirō,
who was briefly reappointed foreign magistrate, by some other lesser officials, and by the considerable lobbying effort of Mito men, the lords of
Okayama and Tottori, and others. They were opposed by almost all

other bakufu officials of consequence, who argued, among other things, that expulsion would require unity of the country and so the dissidents must be brought under control before any attempt be made to close the port.

Until almost the end of 64/6 that dispute nearly paralyzed the regime. One cause of this paralysis was Naokatsu's attempt to bludgeon the bakufu into accepting his opinion, which so angered officials that all senior councillors, most junior councillors, and many lesser officials boycotted affairs for much of the period. During the crisis a few key administrators attended to essential matters, going to the mansions of senior officials to obtain the necessary orders on major actions, most notably measures to counter the accelerating Kantō insurgency.

It was a ghastly situation. In the castle affairs were paralyzed as people struggled quixotically to decide whether or not to throw the barbarians out. Just out of town in Edo bay a foreign armada was assembled with an invasion beachhead already secured. The leaders of that force were waiting for the bakufu to punish Chōshū or to do the punishing themselves—in effect they were daring the bakufu to try and shut Yokohama down. Out of town in the other direction at the same time a serious insurrectionary threat was developing, and it would only get worse if the bakufu either acted against Chōshū or failed to close Yokohama. Mito was torn asunder and unable to control its own men, and reports from Kyoto told of *rōnin* schemes and then of a suddenly renewed Chōshū threat there. The possibility existed—and was clearly seen to exist by those at Edo—of a major insurrectionary east-west alliance.[33]

Not surprisingly then, given the complexity of the issues and the gravity of their implications, the political maneuvering was intense and confused. In brief summation, by 6/18 senior councillors Itakura and Sakai Tadashige, former senior councillor Ōta Sukeharu who had temporarily returned again to advisory duty, junior councillors Ogyū Noritaka and Suwa Tadamasa, and several lesser officials had all been removed from office. All had opposed the plan to close Yokohama,[34] and their departures suggested that Naokatsu and Yoshiatsu were winning the day, even though they too were not in full accord on matters.

On 6/19, however, the foreigners stated unequivocally that they would not tolerate closing of the port. They threatened to repudiate earlier agreements postponing the opening of other ports and cities and delivered an ultimatum warning that if the bakufu did not start to deal with Chōshū in twenty days, they would do so themselves.

That menacing action seems to have reversed the political trend within the bakufu.[35] Naokatsu continued to argue that Yokohama had to be closed to appease the Mito men and Chōshū. However, more key magistrates and other officials threatened to resign if the plan to close the port were not dropped. The young shogun was thus faced with the prospect of his few active central administrators resigning. Moreover he probably was disturbed by rumors among his ladies concerning schemes of Yoshinobu at Kyoto, who was assumed to be supporting Naokatsu's view. In the event, he agreed to dismiss his supreme councillor, although that meant in effect abandoning the policy of expulsion that he had committed himself to at Kyoto only a few weeks before.

On 6/22–23 the forceful and heavy-handed Naokatsu was dismissed. Sawa and another lesser man who had shared his view were fired and ordered into confinement. And anti-*jōi* foreign magistrate Takemoto Masaaki was given special advisory duties close to the shogun. In succeeding days several major appointments were made. Most notably Abe Masatō, a former liege vassal with considerable diplomatic experience, was abruptly promoted to senior councillor. Suwa, who had just been fired, was designated acting senior councillor, and Ogyū was reappointed junior councillor. Itakura was not reappointed, and so the new senior bakufu leadership was clearly more opposed to any policy of *jōi* and also domestically more conservative and less inclined to tolerate court or daimyo challenges than it had been before. As further evidence that conservative anti-*jōi* elements were ascendant, on 7/7 Matsumae Takahiro, who had served briefly as superintendent of temples and shrines during the Namamugi crisis, was appointed acting senior councillor and given a special title commanding military forces *(kairikugun sōbugyō)*. Then ten days later Sakai Tadamasu was reappointed junior councillor. And at lower levels such vigorous officials as Kyōgoku Takaaki, Yamaguchi Naoki, Komai Chōon, Kikuchi Takayoshi, and Kurimoto Kon were recalled to service or given more important duties.

With these appointments made, the internal political crisis passed. In the outcome it had led to an appreciable change in bakufu leadership. In terms of policy, that change entailed a decision not to appease the Kantō insurgents and to abandon in all but name the policy of closing Yokohama. The question of the foreigners' demands vis-à-vis Chōshū was left unresolved, but no decision at all was a decision of sorts given the strategy adopted by the foreigners.

2. *Chōshū, Court, and Foreigner: 64/7–9*

The resolution of political conflict in late 64/6 left the bakufu with a leadership more unified than at any time since early 1862. In consequence the regime was able to respond with unaccustomed speed to new developments. That was particularly evident after Edo learned of Chōshū's defeat at Kyoto on 7/19. However, because unity of leadership neither eliminated the causes of bakufu difficulty nor assured Edo a clearer grasp of its predicament, rapid response was not necessarily either effective or sustained response. Thus, although Edo's policy toward Chōshū was soon cast in bold terms, the larger scheme quickly proved impractical, and the Kantō insurrection, diplomatic problems, and internal resistance all conspired to prevent Edo from moving against Chōshū before 64/10. And then other considerations arose that in the end led Edo to play no effective role in the *han*'s suppression.

By 64/6 militant elements had acquired control of Chōshū, and a force of several hundred Chōshū men plus some *rōnin* traveled to the Kinai region to denounce the bakufu, proclaim their support for the Mito insurgents, protest their own virtue, preserve the expulsion policy, and restore Chōshū influence at court.[36] Their presence just outside the city exacerbated conditions of unrest already troubling the court, and among bakufu representatives there it generated disputes concerning a proper response. Yoshinobu and senior councillor Inaba Masakuni counseled moderation while Katamori and his brother Sadaaki the deputy urged prompt action. For nearly a month indecisive negotiations progressed, and the war of nerves between Chōshū and the city defenders provoked considerable fear and a plethora of rumors. Thus by mid-64/7 rumors said that Nijō castle would be burned, that the Chōshū mansion in the city would burn, that the mansion of Maeda of Kaga would be plundered for firearms, that angry townsmen would burn the city, and that Osaka castle would burn.[37]

By 7/18 pressure from Katamori, other bakufu officials in the Kinai, a few daimyo, and some court officials had elicited a court order for suppression of the Chōshū forces. In response Chōshū attacked on the following morning. The battle was about on the scale of the 7/7 battle at Tsukuba but was much more destructive because it was fought in the city. Fires ignited during the fighting and driven by brisk north winds raged for two days, the glow being visible at Osaka some 50 kilometers away. The holocaust reportedly burned some 28,000 or more dwellings and other buildings, including several mansions of the nobility and daimyo, temples, government offices, and bridges, with consequent suffering for the townsfolk and relief costs for the bakufu. Reality had proved as bad as rumor.

The court was understandably incensed at this destruction and came down strongly on Katamori's side. On 7/23, after it was clear that the fighting was done, the court issued Yoshinobu an imperial order to punish Chōshū for its assault upon the imperial dignity. The Chōshū extremists were more clearly than ever identified as the "enemies of the court," and their sympathizers there were stripped of office and power. The possibility for a united crusade against Chōshū, which had evaporated earlier in the year with the collapse of the *kōbugattai* movement, had been reborn. In accord with court-daimyo sentiments, on the same day bakufu spokesmen at Kyoto issued over Inaba Masakuni's name formal bakufu orders to the daimyo to mobilize forces for punishing Chōshū.

During these weeks leaders at Edo had been aware that Chōshū men were again disturbing Kyoto, but they had seen the issue essentially in terms of its relationship to the Kantō insurrection. Thus on 7/2, after learning of the Chōshū forces' arrival in the Kinai, Edo sent orders to a total of forty-six *han* along the highways between Edo and Kyoto instructing them to stop any eastward movement of the Mōri men. Simultaneously bakufu couriers were ordered to inspect all barrier points at once to assure that a Chōshū-Mito linkup could be prevented.[38]

Then on the twenty-fourth, when Edo leaders first heard of the battle at Kyoto, they ordered public mourning for the violence there, dispatched officials westward to get more information, and sent a notice to Yoshikatsu of Owari to go to the stricken city. And perhaps because fears of the east-west linkage were uppermost in their minds, during the following two days they seized the massive Chōshū residence in Edo, confined its 130 to 200 residents, took charge of its thousands of menial employees, and confiscated its considerable resources.[39]

Almost at once the Chōshū matter became entangled with other considerations of bakufu-court relations, foreign policy, and internal factional matters, and several days passed before a policy began to take shape. When it did take shape, however, it was conceived in broad terms as one part of an overall process of Tokugawa reassertion.[40]

To elaborate, on 7/20 Katamori had dispatched a vassal for Edo posthaste to lobby for vigorous bakufu leadership in the coming punitive expedition. The Aizu vassal met senior councillors Mizuno and Matsumae, probably on the twenty-seventh. He urged them to have the shogun proceed at once to Kyoto to lead affairs and to appoint "able officials," most particularly Itakura and Naokatsu. The councillors were not very cooperative. Katamori's message had raised in an unwelcome manner issues of a factional character that revived indirectly the whole issue of Yokohama. Furthermore it entangled the question of a shogun-led expedition against Chōshū with the question of another shogunal progress to Kyoto. Even if these other issues had not been injected, moreover, the bakufu was just then trying to find manpower enough to suppress the Kantō insurgency. Accordingly it is not surprising that in his reply Matsumae said Katamori was asking for too much in calling for another shogunal trip to Kyoto. Jointly the two councillors took a rather ambiguous position, suggesting that the shogunal trip should perhaps occur after the fighting had been ended. Several senior officials also argued emphatically that the cost of traveling and the burden it placed on the people at the way stations en route would make the trip unwise.[41]

This negative response dismayed Katamori's delegate, who argued with some heat that if the shogun did not go, he should resign his title. Despite the intensity of these presentations, however, bakufu leaders stood firm. They favored the punishment of Chōshū in principle; they did not favor another shogunal trip under existing circumstances.

Even as the senior councillors were objecting to Katamori's formulation, however, diplomatic developments were conspiring to cast the issue in a different light. Ikeda Chōhatsu, who had been sent to Europe in late 1863 to negotiate the closing of Yokohama, had failed to do so and had returned on 7/22, much sooner than expected. The earlier court-bakufu accord on foreign policy had been premised on that mission's eventual success, and the court kept badgering Edo to close Yokohama. Ikeda's return threatened to raise the whole vexatious issue to a higher level of discomfort. Something would have to be done about it before bakufu enemies at court could turn it to advantage, but the first frantic efforts to nullify Ikeda's presence by dispatching another mission to Europe bore no fruit. Concurrently the foreigners, as noted earlier, were threatening to punish Chōshū themselves if the bakufu did not do so. On 7/27 and 28 their seventeen-ship armada set sail for that purpose despite repeated bakufu requests that action be delayed while Edo settled the matter. Even after the fleet sailed, some officials hoped to prevent the attack, but others doubtless saw in a foreign trouncing of Chōshū an opportunity for further bakufu recovery.

After a few more days of discussion and indecision, Edo leaders settled upon an overall policy for coping with their several problems. Most importantly they decided to accept the imperial order to punish Chōshū. The shogun would go to Osaka to lead the expedition and by doing so persuade the foreigners not to bombard Chōshū. The bakufu would thus demonstrate both shogunal authority and opposition to foreign belligerence. Such an expedition would also satisfy Kyoto's demands for a shogunal visitation while not suggesting, as would a simple trip to that city, that the shogun was at the beck and call of the court. Moreover, there would not likely be a better chance of getting broad daimyo cooperation against Chōshū. And as cynics within the bakufu surely suspected, since the foreign assault on Shimonoseki was almost certain to take place anyway, it was a particularly opportune moment to deal with that *han* militarily.

On 7/30 the senior councillors at Edo reissued the daimyo mobilization orders that Inaba had forwarded from Kyoto. On 8/2 the shogun assembled lords and officials in Edo and notified them of the imperial order to chastise Chōshū. On the following day a duty assignment notice was issued. It made clear that the shogun was going to Osaka to handle the Chōshū expedition, not to make a trip ''up to Kyoto.''[42] This was to be an expedition of shogun, leader of armies, not shogun, obedient servant of the court. Not surprisingly it was the stronger advocates of Tokugawa supremacy, senior councillors Abe, Suwa, and Matsumae, and junior councillors Ogyū, Inaba Masami, and Tachibana Taneyuki, who were to lead the shogun's entourage. For internal planning purposes the tentative date of departure was set at 8/30.

This shogunal trip was only part of the whole program for dealing in a comprehensive way with the elemental problem of *naiyū gaikan*— ''rebels at home, aggressors abroad.'' On the same day, 8/3, Edo sent one delegation westward hurriedly to try to mediate the Chōshū-foreign dispute. It also ordered inspector Tsukahara Masayoshi to lead another delegation to Europe to reopen the Yokohama issue that Ikeda had failed to handle acceptably. And two days later it notified the foreign representatives at Yokohama that it wished the Chōshū bombardment delayed while the issues again were negotiated.[43] This burst of diplomatic initiatives bore no fruit, however. The first delegation was too late; the second never left; and the foreigners refused to delay. So much for the new leadership's coordinated program. The flurry of orders had served only to reveal Edo's overall strategy.

Out of the whole package only the expedition against Chōshū made progress, and that haltingly. On 8/7 Edo leaders designated Yoshikatsu of Owari commander of the expedition and Mochiaki of Fukui vice-commander. Then Edo addressed the critical issues of funds and fodder. It ordered fourteen wealthy merchants in the Kyoto-Osaka region to make contributions to defray the costs of two shogunal trips to Kyoto, the reconstruction of Edo castle, and gifts to the imperial court. The posted contribution schedules demanded a total of 710,000 *ryō* and said that levies on others would be announced later.[44] During the month orders were also issued for the nationwide collection of rice and other necessities. On 8/13 the bakufu announced more campaign duties, ordered Yoshikatsu and Mochiaki to commence organizing the expedition, and issued tactical orders to daimyo and lesser bakufu military commanders. Initial campaign plans of early 64/8 had envisaged the deployment in the lead units (which were destined for Yamaguchi by way of Iwakuni) of a main force of liege vassals led directly by the commander. But in the revised battle plan of the thirteenth this liege vassal force was replaced by troops of several *han*. In the outcome the expedition consisted almost entirely of domanial forces from western Japan, although Edo ordered some ninety-two liege vassals, mostly men with official positions, to mobilize their own retainers and proceed in assigned formations to participate. As the month advanced, the bakufu posted more orders concerning the trip, and on the twenty-third it reset to 9/10 the date by which units should be fully prepared for departure.[45]

Despite this appearance of expeditious preparation the enterprise was from the first bogged down in dispute and uncertainty. The court, bakufu leaders in Kyoto, and Edo failed to coordinate their actions, thereby creating confusion and irritation among recipients of contradictory orders. Moreover these were the worst weeks of the Kantō insurrection, and the sharply scaled-down role of liege vassals likely reflected the discouraging impact of that problem. Furthermore, almost certainly there continued to be hot opposition to a third shogunal trip among lesser officials, particularly those responsible for financial affairs. That opposition was suggested not only by the demands made on merchants but also by the constant emphasis on frugality in the military orders that kept appearing. The question of finances also helped revive debate about whether the shogun should go by land or by sea.[46]

Then in the latter part of 64/8 unresolved foreign problems again complicated affairs, presenting Edo with both greater political hazards and a new political opportunity. This time the foreign complication sprang from the bombardment of Shimonoseki, which the bakufu had been unable to delay. The four-power assault against Chōshū in early 64/8 had been savagely effective, and by month's end the foreign representatives were back in Yokohama and ready to obtain satisfaction from the bakufu as well. Led by Alcock, they demanded an astounding indemnity of 3 million Mexican dollars. The extortionate nature of the demand was obvious, and the foreigners, particularly the British, were making it on the assumption that it was unpayable. They offered to waive it in return for the creation of another trading port, preferably Shimonoseki or one on the Inland Sea. Roches warned the bakufu negotiators that if they failed to acquiesce, the foreign powers might negotiate directly with the court in the Kinai and secure direct imperial approval of the treaties.[47] Threatened thus with a complete denial of bakufu authority, the negotiators capitulated and finally on 9/22 formally accepted the indemnity-or-port demand.

The bakufu had again settled with the foreigners by the usual and un-avoidable policy of capitulation. Having done so, it faced the task of making that settlement acceptable to Kyoto, even though it represented, at least by implication, a complete abandonment of the earlier agreed-upon policy of negotiating the closing of Yokohama. While Edo leaders had doubtlessly abandoned in fact any real hope of closing the port, they were still determined to maintain the facade of intent, as the orders of 8/3 for another embassy to Europe had indicated. And they most cer-tainly did not want the matter again to become a subject of acrimonious Edo-Kyoto discussion.

As early as 8/24, when bakufu leaders knew what the victorious foreigners were demanding and what the outcome must be, they had decided to take a vigorous stand vis-à-vis the court. They proposed to combine their arguments on foreign policy with information on the Kantō situation and statements about both the Chōshū expedition and the planned revival of *sankin kōtai*. The total argument, it was hoped, would persuade Kyoto that satisfaction of its desire to see Chōshū punished depended upon its acceptance of bakufu foreign policy.

On the twenty-ninth senior councillor Abe Masatō left Edo by steamer together with foreign affairs experts Kikuchi and Kurimoto to arrange im-perial acceptance of Edo's policy before the shogun himself proceeded west to chastise Chōshū.[48] Abe's task, so reminiscent of Sakai Tada-shige's charge a year earlier, was to assure that the bakufu would not, as during both previous shogunal trips, be put on the political rack at Kyoto because of its foreign policy. Abe spent several days at Osaka and then at Kyoto discussing matters before he, together with Yoshinobu, had a for-mal audience with the emperor on 9/24. Abe explained to the court that the shogun had been delayed in his westward advance by the Kantō in-surgency, which, he reported, had involved a thousand men who were being pacified only with difficulty. He also reported the foreigners' warn-ing that if the bakufu did not accept their indemnity demands by 10/5, they would sail to the Osaka area to negotiate directly with the emperor. He argued that with the Kantō insurrection still raging, the shogun would not be able to fight the foreigners effectively, and hence would feel com-pelled to resign if ordered to do so. Similarly, he argued, the shogun could not fight both Chōshū and the foreigners simultaneously.

Abe's report gave the court something to ponder. Apparently the most disturbing prospect was that of a foreign assault on the Kinai shore. Ac-cordingly when he and Yoshinobu again attended the emperor on 10/1, they learned that the court would acquiesce implicitly in the Yokohama situation and that Abe was to return east at once and prevail upon the shogun to depart promptly as the Court had ordered. Four days later the emperor stated formally that he realized how difficult it would be to deal jointly with Chōshū and the foreigners, so the Chōshū suppression should be handled at present—he would refrain, he said, for the time being, from commenting on the foreign matter. Despite the niggardly formal wording, the statement came much closer to constituting a de facto court abandonment of its insistence on the closing of Yokohama than had the imperial notice of a year earlier.

Thus before the end of 64/10 the foreign problem per se had been dealt with and the danger of diplomatic embarrassment at Kyoto appreciably reduced. Moreover the Kantō insurrection was rapidly collapsing, and so the major obstacles to a shogunal trek to Osaka had been overcome. By then, however, other factors were beginning to encourage further procrastination at Edo.

3. Managing Chōshū and Kyoto: 64/10–12

The Chōshū expedition of 1864 is usually pictured as a creature of the bakufu.[49] Our evidence indicates that this was not the case. Bakufu leaders had reasserted their supremacy at Kyoto before the shogun departed for Edo in 64/5, but when the Chōshū threat arose in following weeks, bakufu representatives in Kyoto neutralized one another, leaving policy initiative in the hands of court officials and others in the city. Then the destruction caused by the battle of 7/19 seems to have driven all elements in Kyoto together in a hard-line posture that was adopted and implemented in its first stages entirely without reference to or participation by Edo.

Before 7/19 leaders in Edo had been so fully occupied with their own problems that they had played no role in shaping policy toward Chōshū, and when they learned of the battle in Kyoto, they interpreted it in terms of their own more immediate problems. After making some indecisive gestures, they responded with big overarching plans that really amounted, in terms of punishing Chōshū, to little more than passive cooperation and moral support for Kyoto's policy. It was a pattern they adhered to with good reason during 64/8 and 9 despite intense pressure from Kyoto to play an active role in punishing the *han*.

From late 64/10 bakufu leaders could have changed that pattern of passive support had they really been eager to pummel Chōshū, but they did not do so. To the contrary, during 64/10, even as Edo overcame the major real obstacles to active participation in Chōshū's punishment, de-

velopments encouraged the belief that such participation would be unnecessary. It would be unnecessary because the expedition against
Chōshū was occurring anyway, despite the widespread lack of enthusiasm for it that had become evident. Moreover, concurrent developments led Edo leaders to begin shifting their attention away from Chōshū
to their own representatives in Kyoto, whose behavior, notably their intense lobbying at Edo, was generating great distrust and resentment
among senior officials.

The lack of enthusiasm for the Chōshū expedition, even apart from
Edo, cannot be ignored. From first to last Shungaku refused requests
from both Kyoto and Edo that he participate. Yoshinobu, despite his verbal support for it, kept a clear distance from the expedition after it was
actually initiated in 64/8. The commander, Yoshikatsu, also resisted his
orders during 64/8 and 9 and only agreed to take command after receiving considerable pressure from both Edo and Kyoto. Many other daimyo,
too, did not really welcome the campaign. Wakizaka Yasuaya, for example, son of former senior councillor Yasuori, had been courted by men of
Chōshū, seemed to have sympathies of a *sonnō jōi* nature, and expressed
his position by objecting to the great burden the expedition would put on
small *han* such as his own Tatsuno (51,084 *koku*) near Himeji.[50]
Daimyo of several other larger *han* with ties to the Tokugawa family,
notably Tokushima, Okayama, and Tottori, displayed their disapproval
of the enterprise. Some critics argued that until expulsion had been
achieved, domestic peace should be maintained. Whatever the form of
the argument, the point was that support for the expedition was limited
mostly to the court itself, Satsuma and the few other major *han* active in
Kyoto, the bakufu representatives there, and, in principle, the bakufu
leadership in Edo.

Nevertheless, despite the extensive opposition, despite Edo's procrastination, and despite the arguments of Yoshinobu, Katamori, vice-
commander Mochiaki, and others that the expedition must wait until Edo
take the lead, the court reiterated its insistence that it not be delayed.
Under this pressure Yoshikatsu grudgingly left Nagoya for Kyoto and
shortly began organizing his expedition. By 10/15 he had his staff and
program sufficiently together to move down to Osaka. There amid considerable confusion he completed preparations. On 11/1 he left for Hiroshima, site of the expedition's advance headquarters. At about the same
time Inaba Masakuni, inspector general Nagai Naomune, inspector
Togawa Hanzaburō, and other bakufu officials from Kyoto also departed
for the advance headquarters. And Mochiaki headed by ship from Osaka
to Kokura to command the front there. As 64/10 progressed, the

Chōshū expedition thus seemed to be developing acceptably, and this trend encouraged Edo leaders to sit tight.

This progress in the Chōshū expedition was all the more welcome because the Shimonoseki indemnity agreement had made the costs of a shogunal trip even more unacceptable. Orders issued during 64/10–12 revealed this continuing intense concern with finances. Thus on 11/4, when more mobilizing orders were issued, the bakufu called to everyone's attention the fact that manpower requirements had been trimmed and that excess personnel and baggage should be eliminated. To achieve that objective Edo issued precise regulations limiting travel costs. In the same vein when replying to those at Kyoto who kept calling for a shogunal advance, Edo leaders pointed out impatiently that they at Kyoto could accept the court's wish for such an advance because they were unaware of the fiscal problems involved.[51]

The combined weight of fiscal objections to a shogunal trip of any sort and political objections to any trip that smacked of shogunal subordination to the court was immense. It enabled the senior councillors week after week to resist the intensive lobbying directed at them, at lesser officials, and at ladies near the shogun by representatives of court, daimyo, and bakufu delegates at Kyoto. In consequence the expedition was carried out and the year came to an end with Iemochi still snug in his redoubt by the bay.

The constant lobbying by Edo's representatives at Kyoto thus failed to turn the Kyoto-sponsored Chōshū expedition into an enterprise truly of Edo's making. Rather, that lobbying gradually led bakufu leaders to grow very suspicious of their representatives and to redirect their attention from Chōshū itself to those men, most notably Katamori and Yoshinobu.

The Edo-Kyoto conflict of views that was generating this suspicion was not new of course. It had repeatedly evinced itself during 1862–1863, notably in Ogasawara Nagamichi's armed approach to Kyoto, and it would do so again and again in future. But during the summer and autumn of 1864 it grew particularly acute. One elemental dimension of the problem doubtless was its power-struggle aspect. Katamori and Yoshinobu believed they should be able to play key roles in policy-making, but the senior councillors wished to preserve their own classic monopoly of authority. The leadership changes of 64/6 exacerbated the tension by placing in charge at Edo a group particularly committed to this reactionary vision.

Another reason for the growing estrangement was that the leadership changes of 64/6 put in charge men whose foreign policy view was quite at odds with the Kyoto belief that Yokohama should and could be closed to trade by negotiation. The Edo position was particularly worrisome to Aizu men because they had strong conscious fears that the Tokugawa house was collapsing. They believed that only by resisting the foreigners could it regain the imperial support and *shishi* confidence necessary to its survival.[52]

Yet another reason for the estrangement was that the Kantō insurrection dominated the attention of Edo leaders, reducing problems of west Japan to a secondary position. For men at Kyoto, however, the Kantō insurrection was distant and trivial while the Chōshū question seemed to demand immediate attention. This new Edo-Kyoto divergence in domestic priorities was to cause problems that would outlast the insurrection itself, persisting into 1865 and doing considerable harm to the bakufu.

A final reason for the growing mistrust, one could suggest, was that Katamori and Yoshinobu tended to confuse the ''how'' of decision-making, which was factional politics, with the ''why'' of the particular decision on Yokohama, which had to do with the basic *jōi*-imperialist conflict and its entangled domestic considerations. This tendency led men in Kyoto to deal unwisely with those in Edo, and that helped poison relations between the two. Thus during 64/6 when the Edo leaders had been locked in conflict over the Yokohama issue, Yoshinobu and Katamori had perceived that conflict as essentially a continuation of a presumably enduring struggle between an Ii-Andō prowestern faction and rivals who opposed a cooperative accommodation of the foreigners. Katamori's subsequent efforts to influence Edo reflected that frame of reference, and in consequence his advice thoroughly entangled the issues of faction, foreign policy, and court-bakufu relations and produced only heated disagreement.[53] By the late summer of 1864 the bakufu's representatives at Kyoto were deeply suspicious of the moral caliber and political judgment of the Edo leadership. However, their efforts to guide Edo back to what they considered sound policy had only served to foster at Edo a strong skepticism about their loyalties.

As autumn progressed, the focus of the Edo-Kyoto discord shifted from the Yokohama issue to that of the shogunal trek. Katamori was a most persistent gadfly, and Yoshinobu and others also were unrelenting in their attempts to badger the leaders at Edo into taking the shogun westward. On 9/17, for example, Katamori and Mochiaki both wrote Edo to urge the shogun's advance. Mochiaki recounted the sorry record of the bakufu's inability to get any related daimyo to lead the expedition. He warned that delay was not only hurting court-bakufu relations but also encouraging more daimyo to dissociate themselves from the venture.

Katamori argued in a similar vein that the opportunity to galvanize a united effort against Chōshū must not be missed lest the whole scheme of political revitalization be lost—with consequences disastrous for Japan.[54]

The relentlessness and cogency of the lobbying made it hard to resist. As a grudging concession, on 10/5 Edo leaders notified Kyoto that the shogun might after all make a trip there. They stated that the expedition was designed to quell Chōshū, that there was no plan for the shogun to visit Kyoto, but that the appropriate men should be prepared just in case he did decide to call upon the emperor.[55] Doubtless such a grudging concession only increased Edo's irritation at the constant badgering. And gradually the senior councillors began to focus their attention on what seemed to be evidence of persistent insubordination by Katamori and Yoshinobu, both of whom knew full well that Edo opposed any shogunal trip to Kyoto but both of whom continued nonetheless to demand just such a trip.

At first, it appears, Edo tried to coerce the two by using economic sanctions. Katamori was the most influential man in Kyoto and the most insistent advocate of a shogunal trek, in part because of constant pressure he too received from court and great *han* vassals. He was therefore the clearest rival to the bakufu leaders and apparently the first to come under pressure. From 64/9 Edo reportedly tried to control him by withholding a newly promised monthly stipend of 10,000 *ryō* and 2000 *hyō*. Then beginning in 64/11 Yoshinobu also found himself unable to draw from the Osaka treasury the monthly support he had been authorized.[56] These efforts did not silence the two, however. Katamori's men were still firm advocates of a shogunal trip, and they, Katamori himself, Yoshinobu, Matsudaira Sadaaki, and others continued to lobby for it.[57]

While Edo was thus retaliating ineffectively against Katamori and Yoshinobu for their continual lobbying, it also was apparently learning that Yoshikatsu, the expedition commander, was implementing without approval from Edo an unexpectedly lenient policy toward Chōshū. Saigō Takamori of Satsuma, who was serving as an aide to Yoshikatsu, is usually credited with inducing him to compromise with moderate elements in Chōshū. However, Yoshikatsu's inclination to compromise antedated Saigō's influence and reflected the widespread daimyo sentiment earlier mentioned. But whatever the source of Yoshikatsu's decision, Edo suspected that Yoshinobu was playing the key role in encouraging a conciliatory court opinion that presumably was then becoming Yoshikatsu's policy.[58]

This suspicion seems to have convinced Edo leaders that they must exercise firmer leadership in the west. The collapse of the Kantō insurrection had at last made such a role seem possible, and perhaps because of the success of Abe's recent trip, it was decided to use another mission by a senior councillor as the means of exercising that leadership. The gradual shift of the bakufu's concern from Chōshū to Kyoto was reflected in the evolution of that mission.

To elaborate, on or shortly after 11/10 Matsumae Takahiro, who was known for his stubborn resoluteness, his support of a firm Edo leadership, and his suspicion of Katamori, received cryptic orders to go west to supervise the Chōshū matter.[59] In succeeding days details of the trip were worked out, and as of the nineteenth the bakufu plan also called for junior councillor Tachibana Taneyuki to go to Chōshū by ship.[60] About four days later Matsumae left by land with a thousand infantrymen and five or six hundred other accompanying persons, including inspector general Komai Nobuoki and inspectors Yamaguchi Naoki and Mukōyama Eigorō.

Within days of Matsumae's departure the shifting focus of the bakufu's interest began to appear. On 12/7 Tachibana was ordered to go to Kyoto rather than Chōshū, accompanied by inspector general Jinbō Nagayo and inspector Tsukahara Masayoshi. Three days later the men left, along with inspector general Ōkubo Tadanori. Ōkubo was instructed to meet Yamaguchi at Kyoto and proceed with him to Yoshikatsu's headquarters at Hiroshima with a set of guidelines for the latter's dealing with Chōshū. All the others, evidently, were to stay at Kyoto. Meanwhile Matsumae was moving west with his battalions, and by early 64/12 it was rumored that his purpose was to compel Yoshinobu to return east. On 12/13 when he was at Ōtsu, and two days before entering Kyoto, he notified the court by letter that he had several purposes. Most notably he was to instruct Yoshinobu to go east after the Mito insurgents had been quelled and was to provide sufficient military forces in Kyoto to keep the peace after Yoshinobu's departure. He also notified the court that Tachibana too was coming, and on the twenty-second the latter arrived.

During his stay, Matsumae talked at length with court officials. He came under attack because of Edo's procrastination on the shogunal trip and in turn bluntly criticized the court for alleged softness toward Chōshū. He and Tachibana both urged the court to allow Yoshinobu (who was out of town at the time handling the Kantō insurgents) to go east, but the court refused to do so. In the outcome the court assured Matsumae that it was not adopting a softer posture toward Chōshū, and he thereupon sent a notice to Yoshikatsu instructing him not to be too lenient. On the other hand, both he and Tachibana concluded that the court's insistence on a shogunal visit could not prudently be refused. Both soon headed back east to advocate that policy, Matsumae leaving on about 12/25 and Tachibana two days later.

The Matsumae-Tachibana mission had utterly failed to reassert Edo's control over its representatives in Kyoto. Nor did its original task of managing the Chōshū expedition work out any better. While the mission's effort to manipulate the court was foundering, Yoshikatsu was at Hiroshima completing his own settlement with Chōshū. In negotiations carried on between Hiroshima and Hagi during 64/11 and 12, Chōshū leaders had agreed to punish those blamed for the radical activity of the *han*, to suppress radical elements within the *han*, to return the nobles who had fled Kyoto in 1863, and to make other gestures of subordination to court and bakufu. That outcome made it possible for the expeditionary headquarters at Hiroshima to send out on 12/27 a notice to all daimyo permitting most of them to recall their forces. The following day Yoshikatsu dispatched a note to Kyoto reporting that Chōshū had been subdued as the court had ordered.

Meanwhile Ōkubo and Yamaguchi were heading westward from Kyoto with guidelines for Yoshikatsu. His terms of settlement (which were approved by Inaba, Nagai, and Togawa) were more lenient than those being communicated by the two men from Edo. The latter's stipulations included the requirement that Mōri father and son and the nobles who had fled Kyoto come to Edo and that the armies not be withdrawn until these requirements be implemented. Yoshikatsu, however, had already signed his terms, authorized the army's disbandment, left Hiroshima, and started east before the two officials reached him on 65/1/5. Understandably he refused to accept their instructions.[61]

Thus as the year 1865 began, Edo seemed to be facing two problems to the west: to get Yoshikatsu to make minor modifications in his Chōshū settlement and to bring the court and bakufu delegates at Kyoto more fully into line. Despite the failure of the Matsumae-Tachibana effort these seemed rather simple problems in view of all that had been accomplished in the year past. A series of major immediate political and military problems had been surmounted, and in the background the long-range program of reactionary revival had finally in the latter part of 1864 begun to take fuller shape.

REACTIONARY REVIVAL: 1863–1864

By its nature a narrative political history focuses on the most visible aspects of the political process. Accompanying the visible drama, however, are background trends and developments that in themselves may constitute central themes of the overall process. During the years 1863–1864 the longer-term bakufu political process involved a basic attempt at reactionary revival designed to undo the damage presumably done by the Bunkyū reform, especially in its political aspects. This attempt was pursued doggedly for two years despite repeated reverses, imbroglios, crises, confusion, and contradictions, and by the latter part of 1864 the limits of its promise seemed apparent.

1. Revival of Sankin Kōtai and Other Practices

The central element in this larger policy of revival was the reestablishment of the *sankin kōtai* system. The first move had been taken almost as soon as Shungaku's reform effort had collapsed in early 1863. On the day the shogun returned to Edo from his first Kyoto trip, the bakufu ordered great daimyo of the northeast, including those outside lords who were considered most friendly to the Tokugawa family, to return to Edo "to discuss matters." The greater lords begged off, several on grounds of illness, and repeated calls during 63/8 failed to dislodge them. Several lesser lords did agree to come and arrived later in the summer. The bakufu was able to halt further exodus by ordering those daimyo and *kōtai yoriai* (landholding liege vassals with alternate attendance obligations) who were still in the city to stay there, despite prior requests and arrangements to depart.[62] Still and all, it was an inauspicious beginning.

This discouraging response, together with other problems of the moment, seems temporarily to have stalled any further moves to restore the pre-1862 order. The underlying intent was revealed, however, in conversations officials subsequently had with Katsu Kaishū and in the rather unobtrusive appointment in late 63/10 of several minor vassal daimyo to the office of master of shogunal ceremony (*sōshaban*).[63] These appointments constituted reestablishment of the masters office, which had been abolished a year earlier and which had existed primarily to handle the routine monthly shogunal audiences of daimyo at Edo on *sankin kōtai*. Then a few days later the bakufu ordered revival of ceremonial clothing requirements that had been drastically simplified during the Bunkyū reform. The notice explained that deterioration in the realm (*tenka*) was due fundamentally to the fact that ancestral laws had been changed. The order to restore old clothing regulations, it was stated, was simply a measure to clarify this ancestral law. Rectifying first such matters as that, it would then be possible to handle more difficult tasks.[64]

These pallid gestures were submerged by the eruption of violence in Edo in the final months of 1863, and then matters lay dormant during the awkward first months of the shogun's second visit to Kyoto. With the collapse of the *kōbugattai* assembly, however, bakufu leaders returned to the question of *sankin kōtai*. On 64/4/17, as noted earlier, those in Kyoto informed daimyo that they would be permitted to borrow shogunal ships for their journeys to Edo. That arrangement presumably would deprive them of any reason to complain about the costs of the journey. Then on 5/26, six days after the shogun's return to Edo, daimyo in the hall of geese *(gannoma)*, almost all vassal lords, petitioned the bakufu to revise the *sankin kōtai* system so as to have three-year cycles that included one full year at Edo, rather than the three-month visit established in 1862.[65]

Within days the bakufu again bogged down in conflict over the Yokohama issue, and then its energies were consumed by the Kantō insurrection. By the last days of 64/8, however, developments had begun again to coalesce in a manner that revived hopes of Tokugawa recovery. By then the bakufu had consolidated its leadership group, had decided to accept the foreign terms on Shimonoseki and let the Yokohama issue lie dormant, and had already dispatched Abe Masatō westward to obtain imperial agreement to this diplomatic settlement. Moreover, Chōshū had again been routed at Kyoto and an imperial order of chastisement had been given. The bakufu had instructed daimyo to deploy in accordance with the imperial order, and preparations were underway for a forceful shogunal advance to Osaka. In the Kantō the siege of Mito castle had been lifted, and it appeared that Tanuma's forces would soon overwhelm the insurgents.

Within this context prospects looked very good for a reassertion of Tokugawa authority, and on 9/1 the big move was made. The bakufu went beyond the hall of geese proposal and ordered the daimyo to return to the pre-1862 *sankin kōtai* regulations. The notice elicited a number of protests from daimyo who warned that the order would disrupt the Chōshū expedition and hurt the bakufu. But senior councillor Matsumae Takahiro, who as an outside daimyo was a major conduit of protest, determinedly urged the daimyo to obey the regulations.[66]

During the next few weeks Edo again became bogged down in the Kantō upheaval, where its armies encountered unexpected reverses. But by late 64/10 the situation was much improved. Aware by then of daimyo dissatisfaction with the previously announced *sankin kōtai* revival, the bakufu adopted a somewhat different tack. On 10/25 an ''earnest'' shogunal request was made to vassal lords to send wives and children to Edo at once. It was pointed out that the shogun would soon depart for the west, that a prompt response was therefore appropriate, and that neither snow nor illness were to be deterrents. Ii of Hikone and the antechamber *(tamarinoma)* lords in particular were urged to respond as an example for lesser daimyo. There was no immediate reply, however, and the year ended with the issue still unsettled.[67]

Related measures to restore the regime's posture were also taken.[68] On 64/10/17 the bakufu ordered all ships passing Uraga to report to officials there all persons on board ship, as had been the practice before 1862. Two months later leaders reintroduced the old, elaborate regulations for inspecting all retinues leaving Edo to ascertain that they contained no women.

Other moves were made to restore the old order of things in the city itself. Following their exodus from Edo in 1862–1863 some daimyo and lesser warriors had evidently rented their mansions or houses to commoners, perhaps as an income-producing or protective measure. The practice was contrary to established regulations, and in 64/11 a minor daimyo's secondary mansion was confiscated when the bakufu found townsmen living in it. A few days later the bakufu warned its liege vassals that the rental of residences, barracks, or other buildings for commoners' use was prohibited, that various violations had been reported, and that within a month all such practices must cease. That order presumably would serve two purposes: it would help restore the separation of samurai and commoners that had seemed to be eroding, and it would deprive liege vassals of a means to make a profit out of staying away from Edo. By implication it was a policy that would be applied to daimyo as soon as the bakufu felt it could do so.

Within the administration itself efforts were made to restore the orderly command structure that Ii Naosuke had symbolized and that had been modified by the Bunkyū reform or weakened during the several later political crises.[69] One aspect of the problem was addressed by an order of 63/10 that repudiated an 1862 measure allowing key subordinate magistrates (the *jisha, machi,* and *kanjō bugyō*) freely to enter the senior council office *(yōbeya)*. Then early in 1864 a broader aspect of the problem was confronted. Senior councillor Makino Tadayuki sent higher liege vassals *(hatamoto)* a notice in which he observed that during the past year they had been in the habit of going to the residences of senior councillors to present petitions on affairs in the morning hours before the latter went to castle for duty. He warned that the practice was bad and should be stopped. Instead such petitions should be sent upward via unit commanders. The order evidently was not very effective, and shortly after the 64/6 crisis the bakufu again forbade such men to enter the private residences of senior officials to present petitions on national affairs—due to the existence of great national problems, the bakufu explained, men had been doing so recently and it was troublesome. Henceforth those who had petitions to present should take them to the tribunal office *(hyō-jōsho)*, and those with commanders or supervisors *(kashira* or *shihai)* should transmit their petitions through them. Whether or not the order had any effect is not clear, but it may have contributed modestly to the rather more orderly political process of the following months.

In toto the regime had had only marginal success in restoring old practices. The old *sankin kōtai* regulations had been reissued, the exodus from Edo had been stopped, and during early 1865 a number of lesser lords were to return to the city. A number of other older regulations had been reestablished, but their political significance was minor. The institutional accomplishments of reactionary revival were unimpressive.

2. *Who Advocated Reactionary Revival and Why?*

The main objectives of bakufu policy during 1863–1864 were to survive and, if possible, restore the older pattern of Tokugawa preeminence. It is certainly safe to say that practically all bakufu personnel supported the notion of Tokugawa primacy. However, it is very difficult to identify with precision the forces giving this revival its strongly reactionary character—practically no records exist to indicate who argued which way on many of the less dramatic issues.

At the middle level of officialdom, most importantly the inspectorate and various magistracies, it is impossible to locate any distinctly reactionary orientation. For one thing, officials moved in and out of office with dizzying frequency for a great variety of reasons, many of which had little to do with large-scale policy goals. Hence office changes were often not a guide to policy tendencies. Moreover this very insecurity of office seems to have fostered among middle-level officials a reticence about matters outside their area of official responsibility and competence, and so their views on many matters are unknown and often, perhaps, unimportant. Within their areas of competence, however, these men were at the cutting edge of administrative problems, notably diplomatic, military, and financial. They were constantly under pressure to devise real solutions to real problems, and this pressure tended to make them pragmatically innovative and reform-oriented rather than reactionary in their advice. Consequently, insofar as these men were influential in shaping bakufu policy, their cumulative impact on administration was more likely progressive than reactionary.

It is possible to observe that in the years of reactionary revival Ōkubo Ichiō and Okabe Nagatsune, who had worked with Shungaku, stormy

Sawa Kanshichirō, who had distinct *sonnō jōi* inclinations, and Katsu Kaishū, who had been unduly favorable to daimyo participation in affairs and not very deferential to senior councillors, left office and lacked influence. And vigorous supporters of bakufu leadership—such as Yamaguchi Naoki, Komai Nobuoki, and Mukōyama Eigorō with foreign knowledge and contacts; Komai Chōon, Jinbō Nagayo, Misoguchi Shōnyo, and Tsukahara Masayoshi with training in the modern army units; and Kyōgoku Takaaki with both diplomatic and military knowledge—were increasingly at the center of affairs by the latter part of 1864. But all this did not necessarily constitute a reactionary trend. To the contrary, most of the middle-level officials who came to play stronger roles in later 1864 were subsequently to participate actively in the radical reform of 1867. Among the liege vassals, then, one finds much impetus for the policy of forceful bakufu leadership, but not much evident impetus for a reactionary strategy to that end.

At the lowest levels of officialdom there likely was a reactionary inclination because most developments of the preceding few years—notably the Bunkyū reform, the perceived impact of foreign trade, domestic turbulence, and inflation—would likely have encouraged people at that level to view the future as worse than the past. The menial servants, minor attendants, and low-ranking guardsmen of the bakufu could and in various ways did obstruct policy implementation by refusing to cooperate. But they had no effective means of influencing overall policy-making and cannot reasonably be identified as an important source of reactionary revival.

It may well be that the reactionary impulse derived in part from a body of historically obscure persons close to the shogun, such as the bakufu's Confucian scholars, shogunal attendants, and perhaps ladies of the shogunal household. Scattered bits of evidence suggest that this was so. By themselves, however, these people could not make policy. They could only aid and support one or another official or group of officials.

It appears from the performance, composition, and reputations of the top level of officialdom, namely junior and senior councillors, that they constituted a major locus of the conservative orientation. Certainly those outsiders such as Shungaku and Hisamitsu who resented the bakufu reassertion of 1863–1864 blamed it on selfish, reactionary bakufu leaders who were seeking to protect their own perquisites at the expense of "able daimyo," the court, enlightened figures, and even the well-being of Japan itself. The hall of geese petition and other hints of vassal daimyo behavior that I have discussed elsewhere[70] suggest that the reactionary thrust may have derived primarily from a conservatism among the vassal lords who had seen the whole Bunkyū reform as an unwarranted intrusion of outsiders into a properly structured political order and who viewed a stubborn defense of the status quo as the best defense of their own interests and responsibilities.

That these vassal lords may have been the mainspring of reactionary revival is not too surprising. At the time the alternatives facing them appeared to be the maintenance of bakufu primacy or the formation of a court-sponsored regime dominated by great lords and working through the bakufu administrative structure. In this context reaction meant forcing court and great lords back out of their newly active role in the national political process, thereby preserving vassal daimyo primacy in that process. Reaction was thus basically one expression of an exclusivistic approach to governance. It was instrumental in character and political in motivation, but it could align with the philosophical reaction of a Confucian scholar, as it seems to have done in 1863–1864. Alternatively, however, it could also align with administrative reformers if that seemed in the interests of vassal daimyo primacy. Hence it could rather easily evolve into other forms of exclusivism, and in 1865 it began to do so.

Reaction also meant, of course, preservation of the established pattern of vassal *han* feudal autonomy. As of 1863–1864, however, it seems unlikely that that was a significant consideration in vassal daimyo thinking because there existed no real threat to that autonomy in any case. None of the anti-bakufu movements purported to be attacks on daimyo autonomy. And within the bakufu only a few lesser officials, notably some of those who were becoming more active in late 1864, were beginning to discuss the notion of centralization of power and abolition of feudal domains. In following years as this antifeudal notion steadily gained prominence, it did so in a manner that promised to assure vassal daimyo primacy in the polity. And bakufu officials of vassal daimyo rank responded to the idea about as favorably as did lesser officials. The implication of all this is that vassal daimyo support for conservative reaffirmation can be explained as bakufu or official or bureaucratic exclusivism or privatism, but it cannot be explained as feudal decentralization or *han* privatism.[71]

3. *The Suppression of* Shishi *Activism*

The political reverses Edo suffered during 1862–1864 were administered by the sometimes coordinated forces of great *han*, court, *shishi*, and foreigners. We have seen how during 1864 the bakufu attempted to dispose of the foreign problem, overcame the challenge from court, and addressed itself to the problem of the *han*. The suppression of the Kantō insurgents can be viewed as a major move to suppress *shishi* activism, as can the suppression of Chōshū. These, however, were only the greatest instances of a nationwide movement to discipline the *shishi*. Most of this program was conducted by *han*, not by the bakufu, and so the details lie beyond the scope of this study. However, the trend fitted into the larger pattern of conservative reaffirmation and so must be noted briefly.

During 1864 and continuing into 1865 daimyo, bakufu, and court cracked down on their lesser samurai and courtiers very sharply, demonstrating with brutal clarity that without high-ranking acquiescence minor men could not prevail.[72] In the east not only were the Kantō insurgents executed in great numbers, but men at Utsunomiya who had sympathized with them were also punished. Shirakawa *han* to the north of Utsunomiya also punished those vassals who had refused to resist the insurgents.

Elsewhere, too, high-ranking warriors whipped their vassals into line. Hisamitsu of Satsuma had all along shown a solid commitment to the status hierarchy and kept Satsuma men severely in line. In Tosa Yōdō had initiated a policy of conservative reaffirmation from mid-1863, and reaction at court and elsewhere enabled him to press on his antiradical campaign so that by the end of 1864 radical forces there had been nearly exterminated. In Himeji in 64/12 the daimyo, former senior councillor Sakai Tadashige, ordered the execution of several vassals. According to the charges, they had vigorously advocated *sonnō jōi* sentiments, had resolved to persuade their lord not to support the bakufu but rather to attack bakufu forces in Kyoto, and had begun accordingly to plan joint action with vassals of other domains. And during 1865 Zeze, Shimabara, and Fukuoka *han*—and probably many others—also jailed, executed, or otherwise punished dissident vassals. From early 1865 reports of *rōnin* or *shishi* activities became minimal. The placarding at Edo and Kyoto that had been so common in preceding months nearly ceased. Even by the end of 1864 the trend suggested that the bakufu need not fear again that fateful alliance of court, daimyo, and *shishi* which had disrupted affairs in recent years.

The suppression of *shishi* activism seemed to constitute a nationwide contribution to the bakufu's policy of conservative reaffirmation. We have treated the years 1863 and 1864 as years in which that reaffirmation gradually overcame obstacles and made considerable apparent progress. At the same time, however, when one studies those two years one is struck by a startling paradox: they look so alike on the surface as to appear repeats of a single model. It looks as though Edo leaders had regarded 1863 as such a bad year that they decided to dismiss it as a mere rehearsal and run through it again to see what improvements could be made. Let us examine some sequential highlights.

Item	1863	1864
Bakufu decides to send the shogun to Kyoto	late 1862	late 1863
Shogun goes to Kyoto	63/2	64/1
Foreigners demand satisfaction for past slights	63/2	64/4
Kyoto assembly collapses	63/3	64/3
Crisis in foreign policy peaks	63/5	64/6
Shogun returns to Edo	63/6	64/5
Foreigners attack a great western *han*	63/7	64/8
Aizu et al. oust Chōshū from Kyoto	63/8	64/7
A senior councillor goes to Kyoto	63/9	64/9
Bakufu ''settles'' its foreign policy	63/10	64/9
Bakufu considers a shogunal trip again	63/10	64/8

The second time through the slightly altered sequence went much better. In 1864 the shogunal trip was much more successful and the foreign crisis much less severe. Chōshū's ouster from Kyoto was much more decisive. The senior councillor's trip was more successful. And Edo was much less a prisoner of Kyoto or great daimyo in planning its policy in the later months of the year. It was the cumulative effect of these improvements in discrete but comparable situations together with the pacification of the Kantō, disciplining of *shishi*, and marginal gains in restoring *sankin kōtai* and other older practices that underlay the bakufu's sense of accomplishment as 1864 gave way to 1865. It was these which sustained the hope that the court-daimyo-*shishi* alliance had been broken and the regime might yet outlive the imperialist-ethnic confrontation.

The hope did not seem so unreasonable. Consider all that had been accomplished in the year just past. Early in the year daimyo influence at Kyoto had been displaced by bakufu influence. Subsequently breaches in bakufu leadership had been healed. Then the court had acquiesced in Edo's accommodationist foreign policy and adopted a posture toward Chōshū that Edo welcomed. Moreover, the outstanding foreign problems themselves had been resolved. The daimyo had responded to orders to punish Chōshū. The called-for related daimyo leadership had, however reluctantly, materialized. And the costs of a shogunal trip had been avoided. The last of the Kantō insurgents had just been interned. Bakufu officials were even then at work near Kyoto determining their final disposition. And throughout the country extremists were being whipped into line.

At year's end Edo leaders seemed to be facing only two immediate problems: to stiffen Yoshikatsu's settlement with Chōshū and to bring the court and bakufu representatives at Kyoto under firmer control. In view of all that had been achieved, surely those two little tasks would soon enough be disposed of. And with those immediate tasks achieved, then the larger program of reaffirmation would surely make progress. In the outcome 1864 had been a good year, superior to 1863, which in turn had been preferable to 1862. Eighteen sixty-five might be even better.

CHAPTER **5**

The Failure
of Conservative
Reaffirmation
1865–1866/5

Eighteen sixty-four had turned out to be a relatively successful year for the Tokugawa bakufu. It was only if one knew more about far western Japan than did Edo or if one examined larger and less visible trends that the weaknesses of conservative reaffirmation became apparent. The weaknesses were there, however, and during 1865 the achievements of the preceding year rapidly came undone as developments far to the west began to bear on the political center and as the cumulative implications of the less apparent trends began to make themselves felt at the political surface. This calamitous process, once started, did not stop until the accomplishments of the previous months had been utterly undone, the leaders of conservative revival discredited, and basic weaknesses of the regime fully exposed.

The central political issue confronting the bakufu during the eighteen months starting in 65/1 was the problem of Chōshū. It went through three stages, culminating in political changes in 65/4, 65/10, and the final resort to war in 66/6. Both the changes of 65/4 and the final resort to war were products directly of the Chōshū problem. The political changes of 65/10, on the other hand, were primarily a consequence of the severe diplomatic crisis of 65/9–10, during which the foreigners finally implemented their long-standing threat to go straight to the Kinai and, if necessary, bypass the bakufu and negotiate directly with the court. Their *démarche* threatened to destroy Tokugawa pretensions to national authority. By intense maneuvering, however, the bakufu preserved its claim to such authority vis-à-vis the foreigners. That success was attained at a very high price in terms of morale, careers, and diplomatic concessions. And even as the price was being paid, the Chōshū issue returned to center stage, where it remained until the desperate resort to arms was undertaken.

THE CHŌSHŪ ALBATROSS: 65/1–9

Near the end of 1864, when the resolution of other matters had finally allowed bakufu leaders to concentrate their attention on Chōshū, the management of that *han* had quite suddenly become a venture of immense significance to Edo. Most immediately it was of intrinsic importance because the court-ordered chastisement of Chōshū was the only major short-run political issue that remained unresolved. For the bakufu to survive, Chōshū extremism and defiance had to be dealt with and the house of Mōri again made an obedient part of the established order. Beyond that the Chōshū issue had in Edo's eyes become entangled with the problem of managing obstreperous related lords, notably Katamori, Yoshinobu, and Yoshikatsu. Its resolution also was to be the symbol and example of bakufu mastery of great lords in general. Success in that larger endeavor would then combine with the restoration of *sankin kōtai*, the reestablishment of Tokugawa preeminence in Kyoto, and other aspects of reactionary revival to demonstrate that the old order had been restored, the interests of the Tokugawa house secured, and civilization itself preserved.

After two years of intermittent impact, Chōshū had thus by 1865 become the dominant issue facing the bakufu, an albatross that was to hang about the neck of Edo leaders for the next eighteen months, its weight finally pulling them from power and discrediting their whole effort at conservative reaffirmation.

1. Failure of the First Policy: 65/1–4

In the very early days of 1865 leaders in Edo learned that their policies toward Kyoto and Chōshū were in deep trouble. Reports indicated that at Kyoto the court was unwilling to let Yoshinobu go east, and that to the west an open dispute concerning Chōshū existed between Yoshikatsu and those sent from Edo. Bakufu leaders also heard reports of continuing dissidence in Chōshū, and when Matsumae Takahiro returned to Edo on 1/8, he came into bitter conflict with his colleagues. These alarums and collisions marked the beginning of bitter internecine conflict that ravaged the highest levels of bakufu leadership for months but failed to produce a successful policy for dealing with Chōshū.

At Edo Matsumae recommended that the shogun leave for Kyoto soon, reporting that he had in effect given the court assurances the shogun would do so. Junior councillor Tachibana Taneyuki, who reached Edo the next day, also advocated the trip. Edo leaders were appalled that the two had not only failed to accomplish their mission but had even adopted positions that were thoroughly unacceptable. Their advice was sharply rejected, and they began boycotting affairs.[1] A few days later Edo learned of Yoshikatsu's settlement and of his blunt refusal to accept the instructions carried by Yamaguchi and Ōkubo. Faced with more evidence that their whole program of reconstruction was coming apart at the seams, the Edo leaders resolved to apply more pressure. On 1/15 they notified court, daimyo, and liege vassals that the shogun's trip west was being canceled because further dealing with Chōshū would be done in Edo. As a sop, however, the announcement said that when the time was right, the trip would be made.

Bakufu leaders still saw Yoshinobu and Katamori as main sources of their trouble and resolved to try again to establish direct senior council control over Kyoto. On 1/19 senior councillors Honjō Munehide and Abe Masatō were formally ordered to proceed to Kyoto at once with armed forces. Their task was to achieve what Matsumae and Tachibana had failed to do.[2] In several ways, however, their prospects of success were even less promising. Externally, for one thing, the Chōshū matter was more than ever a *fait accompli*. Most of their disadvantages, however, were internal. Specifically, the emissaries themselves were less forceful individuals and commanded less respect at Kyoto. Moreover the court not only knew their purpose beforehand but also knew that senior councillors Matsumae and Inaba opposed the Honjō-Abe venture and wanted to see it thwarted. Other problems plagued the effort too, and in the outcome the court and bakufu representatives in Kyoto stubbornly rejected all the instructions they received from the two councillors. In consequence, despite modest efforts at intimidation, by the end of 65/2 the venture had ended with Honjō in Osaka awaiting the court's wishes and Abe en route back to Edo bearing informal imperial instructions to the shogun to come west.

The miserable failure of the Honjō-Abe effort was accompanied by an upsurge of pressures that soon forced leaders at Edo to alter their policies toward both Chōshū and court. With Abe and Honjō headed for Kyoto and Matsumae and Inaba refusing to cooperate, the remaining senior councillors (Makino Tadayuki, Suwa Tadamasa, Mizuno Tadakiyo, and Honda Tadamoto) tried to strengthen their positions. On 2/1 they gave former councillor Sakai Tadashige of Himeji, a staunch supporter of the punitive Chōshū policy, the title of great councillor *(tairō)*. This gesture, however, proved of no value in the face of the internal and external obstacles that soon confounded their general strategy.

As for the internal obstacles, the Chōshū imbroglio created severe disputes among lesser officials. Some men, of course, had vigorously urged the first expedition and in early 1865 urged direct bakufu leadership of a second one as a demonstration of power essential to the preservation of bakufu authority.[3] More, however, had opposed the first expedition because of other problems such as *rōnin*, foreigners, the Kantō insurrection, or the fiscal strain. And proposals to revive the expedition revived their opposition. Some officials, such as Nagai Naomune and Togawa Hanzaburō, who had recently returned to Edo from Hiroshima, tried to resign or refused to serve in any capacity at all. Others balked at specific assignments. On 2/5 the Edo leaders ordered Komai Chōon and an inspector to go to Chōshū with troops from Owari and escort the Mōri lord and heir to Edo. Komai refused the order, arguing that it would be hard to enforce and disastrous if unsuccessful. The other inspectors general agreed with him. Six days after Komai's refusal, the senior councillors ordered Jinbō Sōtoku to replace him and appointed him inspector general. Jinbō promptly refused the order on grounds of illness, and so inspector Tsukahara Masayoshi was promoted to inspector general in return for accepting the task. Shortly afterward Jinbō was fired and Komai was fired and ordered into confinement. And Tsukahara proceeded very, very cautiously, managing to get only as far as Osaka by 3/22.[4]

The external resistance was equally stubborn. Yoshikatsu repeatedly scuttled orders from Edo. He refused to stop his army's disbandment. He refused to return to Edo as commanded. He proposed to Yoshinobu that the great daimyo assemble to discuss the Chōshū matter. And later he rejected as impossible another bakufu order that he reassemble forces to bring the Chōshū leaders to Edo. Meanwhile the court's own hard line on Chōshū was being modified by Satsuma activity, and on 3/2 it bluntly instructed the bakufu to cancel the order that the Mōri lord and heir and five nobles proceed to Edo. Katamori protested that instruction, seeing in it evidence of excessive Satsuma influence at court. He, Yoshinobu, and Sadaaki tried to soften the court's order and apparently kept it from being transmitted formally to Edo. In the end, however, the senior councillors still knew that the court's posture had changed.[5] Within a few days Edo also received advice from the daimyo of Tsu, Tatsuno, and Hiroshima that the orders to Mōri would be very hard to enforce.

From every side the senior councillors thus found their Chōshū policy under fire. They also were finding that their efforts to avoid a shogunal progress to Kyoto were under sharp attack. As in the past Katamori was one of the most persistent lobbyists in the cause of a shogunal visit. He feared that the great daimyo or court or both might take matters into their own hands if the shogun were absent and thus undo the restored Tokugawa authority of 1864. He therefore lobbied actively and effectively for the trip.[6] The court, for somewhat different reasons, also used every means it could find to put pressure on Edo. It finally ordered Abe east on 2/24 with informal news of its desires and three days later sent the bakufu a formal order that the shogun was to come west. On 3/8 Abe reached Edo, where he reported on the Kyoto situation and advised that the shogun's trip be carried out. Matsumae, who had finally returned to duty, supported this view, and despite the strong opposition of Makino and Suwa, Edo leaders began to alter policy. Officials again debated at length the relative merits of going to Osaka as planned back in 1864 or directly to Kyoto as Katamori was urging. Some men apparently advocated compromise policies that would satisfy those at Kyoto, but most officials agreed that the regime was at stake and that forceful, decisive action was necessary. The debate was doubtless fueled by reports of radical victories in the civil war then convulsing Chōshū. These reports had reached Kyoto by 3/7, probably reached Edo by about the middle of the month at latest, and substantiated in detail earlier rumors of insurgent success in the *han*.[7]

In the outcome the bakufu fell back on the "leader of armies" strategy of 64/8. On 3/17 Sakai, Honda, Mizuno, Makino, and Abe notified the court that "in regard to pacifying Chōshū," the shogun would proceed to Osaka as the court had ordered. There would be some delay, however, because there were other matters to attend to first. In an added note to Katamori, the leaders showed clearly their discontent with the decision. They reported widespread opposition to it and indicated that the shogun would go to Osaka, deal with Chōshū, and then, if it seemed proper, go to Kyoto.[8] The decision was reaffirmed twelve days later in a notice to the daimyo. It informed them that reports indicated Chōshū was again defiant. If the *han* refused to respond properly to Tsukahara's mission, then it would have to be dealt with quickly. The shogun had announced plans to go to Osaka, and accordingly the lords were being instructed to prepare for an expedition.[9] If the trip had to be made, it would be an expedition by the shogun, military leader, not shogun, imperial servant.

Some bakufu leaders, most notably Sakai and Suwa, continued for a while to try to delay the trip. Katamori, however, kept up his lobbying effort, and the court put pressure on the two obdurate councillors by ordering them to come to Kyoto because the shogun's trip was being delayed. After the experiences of Matsumae, Tachibana, Abe, and Honjō the two were not at all interested in going and begged off on 4/11. By early 64/4, then, the bakufu had accepted the trip as unavoidable, and both Suwa and Makino resigned from office. Inaba Masakuni, who had been severely compromised by the revival of Chōshū resistance and the conflicts at Edo, also resigned, and Matsui Yasunao took his place.[10] Sakai remained in office as great councillor, but his influence was minimal.

On 4/19 the bakufu abandoned the last vestige of its earlier policy by ordering Tsukahara to discontinue his attempt to bring the Mōri men to Edo. It announced that the shogun would leave Edo for Osaka and Himeji on 5/16, the day memorial services celebrating the 250th anniversary of Ieyasu were to be completed. One strategy for sustaining bakufu preeminence had failed; another was about to be tried.

2. Another Strategy Is Implemented: 65/5–9

The plan to compel Chōshū's submission without moving the shogun from his bastion in the east had come to nought, but bakufu leaders had not therefore abandoned their basic aim of reestablishing control over that *han*. Rather, they had adopted a scheme in which the shogun would bypass Kyoto, proceed directly to Osaka and then Himeji, and there serve as nominal leader of another subjugation expedition. Then with Chōshū defeated, the shogun would proceed in triumph to Kyoto and reassert Tokugawa primacy there. Thus two birds would be killed with one, albeit expensive, stone.

This new plan encountered opposition, however, before it was even put into operation. The court, upon learning of Edo's plan, quickly denied that it had summoned the shogun in order to carry out a Chōshū expedition, as the Edo announcement claimed. And Katamori, from the moment in late 65/3 when he recognized the nature of the projected trip, urged that the shogun go to Kyoto before proceeding with the subjugation. He argued that the recent changes in Chōshū would make its suppression very difficult and ran the risk of wrecking the whole plan to visit Kyoto.[11] Moreover he hoped that his proposed change of priorities would quiet imperial antagonism toward the bakufu plan. Still committed to imperial loyalism as an integral part of the bakufu-led status order he championed, Katamori believed imperial support was a prerequisite for daimyo cooperation in the enterprise and their cooperation necessary to its success.

Other Tokugawa relatives were even less cooperative.[12] Yoshikatsu tried to have the bakufu reverse its decision. Mochinori of Owari refused to lead the advance forces when asked, and Mochitsugu of Kii agreed to take his place only with the greatest reluctance. The real desire of Edo leaders—to have Yoshikatsu lead the expedition—was not even seriously pursued.[13] Mochiaki and Shungaku of Fukui also opposed the Edo decision. They protested it in writing and sent men to lobby against it. Other daimyo also weighed in with objections of one sort or another. Nevertheless Sakai and the senior councillors pressed on with their undertaking despite this external opposition to a militant expedition and the equally widespread concern among bakufu officials and shogunal vassals about the dangers of again getting caught in the imperial trap.

During 65/4 and 5 the bakufu issued the plethora of orders, regulations, and instructions on economizing that had become normal for shogunal expeditions. Honjō, Abe, and Matsumae were ordered to go with the shogun; Mizuno, Honda, and Sakai were ordered to stay at Edo during the shogun's absence. Troops were trained, forces were juggled about, vassal *han* forces were assigned duties, and additional men were mobilized. Funds were disbursed and frantic efforts were made to scrape up money to pay for the venture as well as the concurrent $500,000 foreign indemnity payment.

On 65/5/16 the shogun and his entourage left Edo by land for their third trip to the Kinai. As stated, they were marching to punish Chōshū in accordance with the court's request. In evidence of this, the shogun was surrounded by his troops. Several of the units were equipped with firearms, and cannon were slung on horses. The travelers did not know it, of course, but it was to be the last shogunal trip, and nineteen-year-old Iemochi was never again to see his family's castle, his mother, or his wife.

The shogun's trip was a leisurely one, and as the cortege advanced, bakufu leaders made conciliatory token concessions to Katamori. On the day of departure Aizu was granted the monthly stipend promised back in 64/9 and then withheld.[14] Then, as the shogun was en route, the objections of some inspectors and other officials were partially overridden, and Katamori and the court were informed that the shogun would stop at Kyoto before settling in Osaka, but only for a formal call on the emperor. After more than a month of traveling, the shogun on int. 5/22 entered the city and had his imperial audience. With Katamori's support matters went as the bakufu intended. Chōshū's wrongs were specified: its continued defiance, its illegal foreign trading, and its vigorous purchases of foreign arms in preparation for insurrection. Then the court blandly instructed bakufu leaders to prepare policy carefully. After two nights there the shogun hurried on to Osaka.

Honjō Munehide had reached Kyoto a fortnight previously, and from that date periodic policy discussions had begun between court officials, Yoshinobu, Katamori, and Honjō. They were joined later by Abe and other officials of the shogun's suite. The men from Edo, whose intentions had been so seriously upset by Chōshū, advocated a somewhat harsher punishment of the insurgent *han* than did Katamori or Yoshinobu.[15] For weeks officials scurried back and forth between Osaka and Kyoto, trying to resolve their differences, and by 6/17 that was done. The Osaka bakufu and its Kyoto representatives were able to inform the court that their plan was to summon certain high-ranking Mōri men to Osaka for interrogation and, depending on the outcome of the questioning, to take further steps as seemed appropriate.

That flaccid compromise could not have been very satisfactory to the Osaka leaders. It is true they were not eager for war because it was alien to their political style and because they were not at all sure how it would work out. They had pressing reasons, however, to settle the whole matter as quickly as possible. They were troubled by the massive expenses of the trip, which was costing about 175,000 *ryō* per month,[16] and those outlays could be stopped only when the trip had ended. Moreover, the leaders at Osaka faced severe problems of morale and order among their forces. Despite its great expenditures the bakufu was paying its troops very meagerly, and in consequence some of the peasant conscripts began foraging in neighboring villages.[17] While it seems unlikely that the brigandage was common, even a very few instances would be counterproductive for the regime and would reinforce the leaders' desire to terminate the expedition as soon as possible.

Yoshinobu, too, and perhaps others wished to press on with the campaign and get it over because certain unspecified troublemakers reportedly were trying to disrupt affairs in the Kinai, and delay only seemed to invite more such trouble.[18] However, the bakufu's Kyoto representatives were under severe counterpressure from the court and certain daimyo who urged that the expedition be canceled, or at least delayed until daimyo could assemble to determine policy. Spokesmen of some *han* warned that as things stood their own *han* and many others might not cooperate in an attack on Chōshū. The situation was developing much as Katamori had feared: by intent of some and the condition of others the punitive expedition was being undermined even before it began. And this was happening even as the expedition's target, Mōri Yoshichika, was ordering people of Chōshū to prepare to resist by war the encircling bakufu army.

Meanwhile the initial decision of 6/17 was being implemented. The daimyo of Hiroshima had been ordered to convey the summons to Chōshū on 6/23, and that order had begun a process of talk-write-wait-talk-write-wait that was to continue for months while bakufu orders were reluctantly transmitted, rejected, reformulated, retransmitted, and again rejected. The first bakufu order to Chōshū had elicited a response whose essence was known in Osaka by mid-65/8: the designated men were ''sick'' and could not come to Osaka as ordered. When the bakufu on 8/18 ordered alternates to appear at Osaka by 9/27, they too were reported to be ''sick.'' By 9/15 the Osaka leaders knew that Chōshū was not yielding. More pressure was evidently necessary. In accord with the wishes of their Kyoto representatives, who argued that the court must approve any military effort, on that day the shogun left Osaka for Kyoto to obtain an imperial order for the suppression of Chōshū.

At Kyoto some court nobles and representatives of Tsu, Satsuma, Owari, and Echizen opposed the bakufu's request. However, skillful and sometimes aggressive counterarguments by Abe, Katamori, Yoshinobu, and Sadaaki prevailed. On 9/21 the court formally accepted the bakufu contention that because of Chōshū's failure to respond to the earlier instructions, the expedition could not be stopped. Two days later the shogun departed for Osaka. Thus the strategy adopted in 65/4 seemed, slowly and at great expense, to be working out.

The court's approval did not lead at once to bakufu action, however, because it was obtained just as the Osaka leaders were being engulfed in the worst diplomatic crisis since 1863.

THE DIPLOMATIC CRISIS OF 1865

Back in 64/9 the bakufu had accepted the foreigners' demand for a $3 million indemnity or another open port. The foreigners had believed the bill to be so outrageously high that Edo would have to open the port.

Edo, however, was not prepared to open Shimonoseki, which would only serve to enrich Chōshū through trade and increase Chōshū's ties to the foreigners. The alternative port was Hyōgo, but efforts to get court agreement to the opening of Hyōgo had failed. Accordingly on 65/3/10 the foreigners were informed that domestic conditions made it difficult to open a port on the Inland Sea and so the indemnity would be paid. The bakufu proposed to pay the first installment in 65/6 but asked that because of the Chōshū difficulty the second be delayed nine months until 66/6, after which date payments would be made at the scheduled three-month intervals. The foreigners' reply to that request was delayed pending advice from home governments.[19]

The foreigners in Yokohama had long since made known to bakufu negotiators their interest in getting more concessions—namely, more open ports, imperial approval of the treaties, tariff adjustments, and other advantages. And some favored sending a fleet to Hyōgo to extract the desired concessions by a direct threat to the imperial court. Reliable news of these matters soon reached Osaka along with rumors of a foreign intent to proceed there to open Hyōgo. Accordingly on 7/6 Honjō was ordered back to Edo to prevent the foreigners from doing so. During the next two months, then, as the leaders at Osaka pressed on with their Chōshū venture, they did so in the shadow of this growing diplomatic crisis—another instance of interacting "rebels at home, aggressors abroad"—whose magnitude and precise character they could guess at only vaguely.[20]

In the Kantō, meanwhile, matters were moving ahead.[21] On 8/17 Harry Parkes, the arrogant and ill-tempered British minister who had recently replaced Rutherford Alcock, received his government's instructions concerning the indemnity delay. In line with them he proposed that the bakufu open Hyōgo and Osaka on January 1, 1866 (65/11/15), get imperial approval of the treaties, and revise downward the tariff schedule. In return for these concessions the foreigners would cancel two-thirds of the Shimonoseki indemnity. The 1864 demand for a port or money had escalated to ports plus monies plus other concessions.

The foreign representatives jointly presented their newest demands to bakufu diplomats, but because the shogun and several key councillors were already at Osaka, officials at Edo were unwilling to accept them. Parkes, however, was unwilling to wait for the shogun's return. He proposed instead to proceed directly to Osaka with sufficient military force to carry out his instructions regardless of the obstacles. During the next few days he overcame French objections, won the approval of the other foreign representatives, and prevailed upon or ignored the skeptical foreign merchants at Yokohama. The foreign diplomats then presented their plan of action to bakufu officials at the port. Lengthy discussions ensued, eventually involving councillors Mizuno Tadakiyo and Sakai Tadamasu as well as Kikuchi Takayoshi, Kurimoto Kon, and other diplomats. Despite vigorous efforts these officials were unable to dissuade the foreigners from their newest enterprise. Accordingly on 9/13 the nine assembled ships left Yokohama, a bit more than a year after the assault on Shimonoseki and two years after the assault on Kagoshima. The foreigners, it appeared, had developed a new annual holiday sport, but this time their primary victim was to be the bakufu, not an outside *han*.

1. Crisis at Osaka: 65/9–10

Leaders in Edo tried to keep their colleagues at Osaka posted on this ominous development. On 9/5, after the foreigners' overall plan was known at Edo, Yamaguchi Naoki and an inspector were promptly ordered west. They reached Osaka on the evening of the thirteenth and reported immediately on the course of negotiations at Yokohama and on the foreigners' plan to extract directly from the court an agreement to open the ports should the shogun refuse that demand. The two delegates also may have argued that imperial approval of the treaties should be obtained; at least Yamaguchi was convinced that the court's refusal would invite foreign retaliation. Honjō Munehide and other officials were also sent west three days after Yamaguchi to notify the Osaka leaders of the coming crisis, apparently with the expectation that the demand for Hyōgo's opening would be accepted.[22]

On 9/14 leaders in Osaka decided that despite Yamaguchi's report the Chōshū venture must go ahead. On the next day the shogun, with Abe, Matsui, and other officials, departed for Kyoto. Two days later Osaka officials learned that the foreign armada had reached Hyōgo bay the night before and intended to proceed to the Osaka shoreline.[23] The crisis had come, and the prior warning was of little value because the difficulty of choice was not lessened thereby nor the degree of maneuverability more clearly identified. On the one hand war had to be avoided. On the other hand the court could not be alienated lest it refuse to support the bakufu's Chōshū policy and so destroy any hope of securing daimyo cooperation in the expedition—or in any other bakufu effort, for that matter. Because of the unacceptable nature of the choices available, the armada's presence precipitated three weeks of confusion, frenetic bargaining, and policy reversals reminiscent of, but worse than, the Namamugi crisis. Only the main points can be dealt with here.

During the first few days Inoue Yoshifumi and the other Osaka city magistrate handled most of the discussions with the foreigners while senior councillors Ogasawara, Matsumae, and Honjō (who had just returned from Edo) stayed in the background at Osaka. On 9/23 Abe (who had just hurried back from Kyoto) and the other bakufu negotiators were warned by Parkes in an uncommonly bludgeoning speech that if the emperor did not agree to the treaties and the bakufu to the opening of Hyōgo by the twenty-sixth, the foreign forces would commence an invasion and march on Kyoto. Predictably this ultimatum prompted intense debate at Osaka and equally intense anguish at Kyoto when reported there.[24]

Abe knew full well that the foreigners were both able and willing to wage war to gain their objectives, and he was also freshly acquainted with the samurai mood in Kyoto. Accordingly he strongly urged the bakufu to approve the demand on Hyōgo, warning that if the foreigners were to land, they might collide with Aizu men and other samurai eager to defend the imperial dignity. Matsumae supported Abe. The shogun, however, who reached Osaka on 9/24, evidently found this prospective decision distasteful and promptly asked that Yoshinobu and Katamori be summoned to discuss the matter. The councillors agreed to this proposal —reluctantly, one suspects—and it was rushed to Kyoto. At the court's request Katamori stayed on duty, but Yoshinobu was permitted to go, and early on the twenty-sixth he arrived from Kyoto alone.

While awaiting Yoshinobu's arrival, the Osaka leaders had concluded that in view of the foreigners' intransigence and abrupt deadline, they could only accept the demands as Abe and Matsumae advised. After hearing a summary of developments, however, Yoshinobu strongly opposed this decision. He warned that it would reopen the court-bakufu split of the Ii-Andō years and urged that the shogun get imperial consent before a decision was made. This proposal, coming as it did from a man whom several councillors and many others close to the shogun still did not really trust, led to heated debate. Finally, however, it was agreed to try to get the foreigners to delay a few days while imperial consent was obtained. Contrary to the expectations of Abe and Matsumae, the foreigners agreed to the ten-day request, which was made with great dramatic appeal by Inoue Yoshifumi. After some fast messenger activity straightened out the confusion, early on 9/27 Yoshinobu returned to Kyoto where he and Katamori lobbied for court approval of the treaties in anticipation of the shogun's imminent arrival.

During the next two days the shogun did not travel up to Kyoto as Yoshinobu had led the court to expect.[25] The court, which was influenced by Satsuma agitation, was thoroughly incensed at both the for-

eigners' demands and bakufu concessiveness and doubtless viewed the
shogun's failure to appear as evidence of bakufu arrogance. On the
twenty-ninth the court proposed ordering Abe and Matsumae to commit
suicide and Sakai Tadashige and Mizuno Tadakiyo in Edo to surrender
half their domains and accept dismissal and confinement. Aizu men
shared the court's anger at bakufu conciliatoriness, but Katamori restrained them. At the urging of Yoshinobu, Katamori, and Sadaaki, the
court also restrained itself, merely ordering Abe and Matsumae to be
stripped of office and confined to their fiefs.[26]

The reason the shogun had not gone to Kyoto as Yoshinobu had expected was that after the latter's departure on 9/27, leaders at Osaka
had begun to fret about sending the shogun to get imperial approval of
the treaties. They knew all too well how persuasive the court could be on
its own home ground, and officials began debating the advantages of the
shogun's going to Edo instead.[27] Then on the twenty-ninth the Osaka
group heard of the court's intention to punish Abe and Matsumae severely, and on the next day, 10/1, they received the official order for dismissal and confinement. News of this development evoked intense anger at
Osaka. There the two men were already awaiting a preemptive bakufu-
ordered punishment,[28] and the court's action was seen as an intolerable
intrusion into the private authority of the Tokugawa lord over his own
vassals. The order deepened officials' suspicions of Yoshinobu and precipitated a major discussion involving Mochinori of Owari, Mochitsugu
of Kii, the junior and senior councillors, and lesser officials. Among the
many proposals advanced was an argument by Yamaguchi Naoki and
Mukōyama Eigorō for a shogunal resignation and return to Edo.[29] Finally
a proposal along this line was worked out: the bakufu would request imperial approval of the treaties, the opening of Hyōgo, the replacement of
Iemochi with Yoshinobu, and Iemochi's prompt return to Edo.

The disconsolate Abe and Matsumae served as the necessary sacrifices.
They were dismissed by the bakufu and ordered home in a notice clearly
stating that this was the will of the court, not the shogun. Concurrently
Mochinori and Ogasawara were sent up to Kyoto to deliver in a sealed
envelope the shogun's elegant resignation of his titles. In it he explained
that he was too young and incompetent and had failed to secure the national well-being. On the evening of 10/2 this resignation note,
together with an unhappy review of problems since 1853 and a strong
appeal for approval of the treaties,[30] was delivered to Kyoto. The bakufu
also announced that the shogun would start back east on the following
day, leaving Yoshinobu to take over his military functions and Mochitsugu to take charge of Osaka castle.

As promised, on the third the shogun departed Osaka, heading inland away from the foreign armada. The prospect of the bakufu in effect leaving the court to deal directly with the foreigners precipitated great dismay and a sharp reaction in Kyoto among both courtiers and bakufu representatives. In a flurry of confused actions the court sent an order to Iemochi to come to Nijō instead of going to Edo. Yoshinobu, Katamori, and Sadaaki all went to meet him at Fushimi that evening to induce him to proceed to Nijō and there obtain imperial approval of the treaties. This newest proposed reversal of policy was finally accepted despite widespread official objections.[31] On the following day Iemochi entered Nijō castle. There Yoshinobu, Katamori, Sadaaki, Ogasawara, and lesser officials lobbied vigorously to persuade the court to approve the treaties despite Satsuma's advice to the contrary. When a court-sponsored assembly of samurai also argued the necessity of treaty approval, the court at last consented on the evening of the fifth. It agreed to accept the treaties but reserved the right to ask for specific revisions in them. It rejected the petition to open Hyōgo.

On 10/7 Honjō and Yamaguchi notified the foreigners that the emperor had agreed to the treaties but opposed the early opening of Hyōgo, and so the bakufu would pay the rest of the indemnity. Tariff rates, however, could be discussed at Edo. This notice had accommodated some belligerent last-minute protests by Parkes, and with its receipt the foreigners left the area and returned to Yokohama. The crisis had ended, but its reverberations would continue for some time.

2. The Attempt to Keep Hyōgo Closed: 65/10–12

The foreigners' departure from the Kinai ended the immediate crisis. It did not solve the problem of Hyōgo, however, because imperial approval of the treaties on 10/5 had carried a rather vague stipulation that the port would not be opened.[32] In the course of lobbying for court approval of the treaties, Yoshinobu had apparently indicated that the foreign request for Hyōgo's opening would be rejected. He likely meant rejection of the diplomats' new request for a Hyōgo opening date of late 1865 and not rejection of the earlier agreement to open the port at the end of 1867. Bakufu negotiators chose to interpret the court's notice to the foreigners in that way on the seventh, and by the tenth bakufu leaders in the Kinai were agreed among themselves that the treaty provision for opening Hyogo at the end of 1867 still held.

Ambiguity remained, however. The court's intent was certainly to keep Hyōgo closed indefinitely, and in hopes of avoiding more domestic trouble over the issue, on 10/27 Mizuno Tadakiyo and Honda Tadamoto in Edo discussed the matter with Léon Roches. The French diplomat suggested that if Hyōgo were unacceptable, some other port might be opened instead. It was an unwelcome suggestion. Because Kagoshima was assumed to be the alternative port that would be sought, such a solution would only strengthen Satsuma-British political ties. It would also enrich the Shimazu and conversely, as Oguri Tadamasa pointed out, reduce tariff income at Yokohama, a loss that would be serious cause for worry.[33] When Parkes was asked about the possibility of keeping Hyōgo closed, he was even more obdurate, insisting that it must be opened as per treaty.

The Hyōgo issue was complicated, moreover, by the fact that another $500,000 indemnity payment was due within a few weeks and the funds to pay it were not so easily obtained. Finance officials at Edo argued that Hyōgo should be opened in exchange for canceling the remaining indemnity installments, as the foreigners had proposed. Their point was underlined on 11/12 when bakufu diplomats, after urging the foreigners to agree to a delay in the next installment, were told that if they wished a delay, they should agree to open Hyōgo at once.[34] Thus at Edo the indemnity problem was generating continued pressure for the immediate opening of Hyōgo, but at Osaka those officials trying to improve bakufu-court relations were under pressure to try to keep the port closed indefinitely.

By then Kinai leaders had heard that Parkes had rejected the request to keep Hyōgo closed, and the rumor world even reported that the foreigners in near future would again sail westward to demand the port's opening. In an attempt to satisfy the court and also preclude another foreign visit to Osaka, Ogasawara, Katamori, Yoshinobu, and newly reappointed Itakura Katsukiyo skeptically ordered Honjō Munehide east to negotiate an agreement to keep Hyōgo closed. Accordingly on 11/20 Honjō and his assistants sailed for Kanagawa. Shortly before sailing, Honjō optimistically described his mission in this way: he was to go east to arrange peaceful foreign relations, secure the basis of court-bakufu unity, strengthen the legal basis of trade, keep Hyōgo closed without opening an alternative port, prevent the residence of foreign diplomats in the Kinai area, and stop foreign contacts with Chōshū.[35]

After Honjō reached Kanagawa, instead of consulting with Mizuno and other officials at Edo, he went directly to urge Roches to agree to keep Hyōgo closed. Roches disclaimed any authority to change the treaty in that way, and on the following day Parkes rejected the proposal as summarily as he had done earlier. Honjō's one-man diplomacy had not worked a miracle. When he did belatedly meet Mizuno, at the latter's request, he was warned that refusal to open Hyōgo as per treaty would only bring another foreign fleet to the Kinai. That view was then communicated to the Osaka leaders. In response, Itakura and Ogasawara sent instructions that while the Chōshū matter remained unsettled, such a crisis must be avoided and discussions should therefore focus on the possibilities of delaying indemnity payments and on the choices for an alternative port.

Those instructions were followed. The question of closing Hyōgo was dropped. A brief three-month delay in the indemnity payment was agreed upon, and discussions concentrated on the politically safer issues of recoinage, trade, and tariff reform.[36] The Hyōgo issue thus went into abeyance. However, it never entirely left the political scene because of the almost total court opposition to the presence of foreigners, which anti-bakufu forces continued to exploit for their own advantage.[37]

PERSONNEL CHANGE AND POLICY FAILURE: 65/10–66/5

In early 1865 bakufu leaders had attempted to apply hard-line policies toward Chōshū and the court. External pressure and internal sabotage had thwarted the attempt and forced Edo to fall back on the slow and expensive strategy of a shogunal trek westward. That strategy seemed gradually to be making progress, but then it was severely disrupted by the renewed foreign harassment. The Hyōgo crisis halted action vis-à-vis Chōshū, precipitated an alarming offer of shogunal resignation, and accelerated greatly a process of leadership change that had begun early in the year with the failure of the hard-line policy.

By the end of 1865 this process yielded a nearly complete repudiation of the leaders who had emerged during the conservative reaffirmation. The process of personnel change also revealed that the political stress of 1865 had stripped away most of the conservative vision of the 1864 leadership, reducing it to a barebones concern for the preservation of Tokugawa primacy. In this deteriorating context, as reactionary means to that end lost their plausibility, radical means to that end began to look attractive and to gain adherents among some of those bakufu leaders most closely associated with the policies of 1864. The men who displaced them in late 1865 were not really more progressive than they, and so the leadership change is best seen not as one in which progressive leaders replaced conservatives but rather as one in which proponents of an attenuated inclusivistic vision displaced exclusivists.

The new leadership of late 1865 made great effort to heal the court-bakufu breach caused by the Hyōgo crisis and to revive the *kōbugattai* tone of 64/4. They did succeed in restoring the forms and tone of court-bakufu unity, but beyond that their successes were minimal. Internally they failed to forge a leadership with the cohesiveness of the late 1864 group, and instead they quarreled persistently over policy. Externally they were unable to devise a new strategy for dealing with Chōshū, and the drift to war continued. That outcome suggests that the deterioration of Edo-Chōshū relations had proceeded beyond the point where any sort of peaceful reconciliation could have been achieved. The issue had become one of supremacy in Japan and had to be settled on the battle-field.[38]

1. Personnel Change: 65/10–12

The resignations of Suwa and Makino in 65/4 had been the first ruptures in the conservative leadership forged during 1864. Then with the shogun's arrival in the Kinai two months later, bakufu representatives there, notably Yoshinobu and Katamori, acquired more influence in per-sonnel matters. They agitated for more extensive changes, notably the reappointment of Itakura, Ogasawara, and Matsudaira Naokatsu.

During the summer only Ogasawara was seriously and successfully pursued, perhaps because while he had earlier cooperated with Shunga-ku, he had also displayed a readiness to act decisively in defense of bakufu interests. Ogasawara was also attractive because his occasional letters to the senior councillors in the two years after his confinement in 1863 had revealed opinions quite in line with bakufu policy as it devel-oped from about mid-1865. Thus back in 64/10 he had urged that the shogun go west in order to assure Chōshū's submission. He had also argued that Katamori was loyal to the Tokugawa even though Edo lead-ers at the time deeply distrusted the Aizu lord. That judgment had subse-quently been proved correct. He also dwelt at length, as he had in earlier essays, on fiscal problems, warning that inflation had to be controlled and a sound currency was essential to that end. It was a view finance of-ficials could only agree with as the fiscal situation grew steadily more chaotic. And in 1865 he had even begun to familiarize himself with the vocabulary and substance of modern western weaponry, an effort that fit-ted well current thinking within the bakufu.[39]

Ogasawara was thus a man whose status, vigor, and ideas made him an attractive candidate to bakufu leaders. Accordingly, to make a long story short, during the summer the Osaka leaders recalled him to duty, the Edo leaders brought him up to date on the diplomatic situation and on 8/30 he reached Osaka. Four days later he met the shogun and was for-mally designated acting senior councillor.[40]

The other two men did not return to duty. Itakura was apparently invited to come to Osaka in 65/7 but did not respond to the call. The matter of Naokatsu gave rise to long, tortuous, and ultimately unproductive negotiations that dragged on for a year or so with a noticeable lack of enthusiasm on either side. At a lower level of officialdom there also were personnel changes. In early 65/9 Nagai Naomune and Togawa Hanzaburō were summoned to Osaka, and rumors at the time indicated that Nagai and Ōkubo Ichiō, both friends of Shungaku, might soon be recalled to duty.[41] Before any such moves took place, the Hyōgo crisis erupted, but it was already clear that the tide was running hard against the leadership orientation of late 1864.

Inevitably the Hyōgo crisis discredited more men. It also enabled critics of the existing leadership to attack those whom they resented. Akitsuki Taneki, heir to an outside *han*, gifted and respected man, active scholar, correspondent of Shungaku and sometime bakufu official, made no bones about whom he would blame.[42] In 65/10 he repeated charges denouncing Matsumae for proposing to ''rely on the foreigners, abolish the emperor and the daimyo, establish a prefectural *(gunken)* system, make the shogun presiding executive *(daitōryō)* of the realm *(tenka)* and base government office on talent.'' He reported that many in the bakufu shared this view and asserted in this regard that Abe Masatō, Sakai Tadamasu, Oguri Tadamasa, and Takemoto Masaaki specifically ought to be jailed. It is worth noting that Akitsuki considered them guilty not of being reactionary, conservative, or uncreative, but rather of collaborating with foreigners, obstructing *kōbugattai*, and threatening domanial autonomy. He seemed to want, at least when writing Shungaku, a bakufu leadership more sensitive to great *han* interests.

From the Hyōgo crisis to year's end a large number of influential men left office, including four senior councillors and four of the five officials mentioned by Akitsuki. In the outcome the leadership of 1864 was sharply altered.[43] At Osaka the change strengthened substantially the hand of bakufu representatives in Kyoto and of men associated with the inclusivistic orientation. Specifically, during 65/10 Nagai and Togawa were recalled to office; Katamori received special instructions to participate in bakufu discussions; his brother Sadaaki received similar instructions; and Itakura was recalled to office. Abe and Matsumae had already been cashiered, and a number of lesser but influential officials were also dismissed. Four of them (Takemoto, Mukōyama, who had proposed Iemochi's resignation, Komai Nobuoki, who had supported him, and Ōkubo Tadanori) were also ordered into confinement. These actions at Osaka were followed during 65/11 by similar developments in Edo.

There Sakai Tadashige and Sakai Tadamasu were both fired, and Honda Tadamoto refused to serve and was later dismissed ''due to illness.'' Finally, a large number of lesser officials were shuffled from office to office.

In sum these personnel changes, the greatest since the crisis of 64/6, altered bakufu leadership sharply. They also had a symbolic function. Much like Ogasawara's purge of 62/11, they were the internal expression of a great effort by Osaka leaders during 65/10 to repudiate the recent nastiness and demonstrate that the post-Hyōgo bakufu was a revitalized regime dedicated to serving the imperial interest. The effort succeeded in forestalling attempts by men of Satsuma and other *han* to use the Hyōgo crisis as an excuse for revitalizing the court-daimyo assembly policy of late 1863. Schemes to strip Iemochi of his authority were turned back, and on 10/25 the shogun summoned his officials and the daimyo to a ceremonial meeting at Nijō castle. There he admonished them to be diligent, strengthen defenses, and so put the emperor at ease. Newly reappointed Itakura informed officials of the bakufu's commitment to imperial loyalism and called upon them to work faithfully together. Two days later the shogun attended court for an audience in which he formally accepted the imperial order to get well and withdraw his resignation request. In formal reply the emperor called upon him to reinvigorate his government, prepare defenses, and ward off the foreigners. The bakufu then notified the *han* of imperial approval of the treaties, and on 11/3 the shogun finally returned to Osaka castle. The harsh breach between Kyoto and Osaka had been covered over again. The spirit of 64/4 appeared to be alive and well.

In this climate of renewed amity it was Yoshinobu who seemed to have emerged as the most influential individual, just as in early 1864. Once again, however, his triumph was more apparent than real. The matter is worth noting in some detail because it illustrates how the political demands of the 1860s were generating new stresses within the regime.

The long-standing distrust that many in the bakufu felt toward Yoshinobu had been reinforced during 1864–1865 by his vigorous effort to develop what amounted to a private modern army under his own command.[44] That military effort had begun legitimately enough in early 1864 as an attempt to give himself real leverage in his new position as *kinri shuei sōtoku*. In 64/4 Sakuma Shōzan had advised him to adopt a western military system using healthy young conscripts, and Yoshinobu had then asked Edo to furnish him just such infantrymen for use in

Kyoto. Edo agreed to do so, and the men began to arrive. By 64/8 he was making the reorganization and assigning men western-style firearms and uniforms despite the protests of many who argued that these reforms betrayed the spirit of Nariaki and the land of the gods. Despite this discontent, Yoshinobu pressed on, his effort sustained by the Chōshū threat, by the possibility of a foreign *démarche* in the Kinai during the summer and fall, and then by the Kantō insurgency. As time passed, he accelerated his schedule of live-ammunition practice. By year's end he was able to field a force of some 1300 men, of whom about 300 were regular infantry, 170 were cannoneers, and 500 were armed with a variety of shoulder arms.

During 1865 Yoshinobu continued to train and expand his force, and by the latter part of the year he was reportedly training a thousand men in the use of firearms. They were identified as peasants organized in two battalions, armed with Mini rifles, and commanded by Hitotsubashi samurai carrying Enfields. They drilled and practiced their firing quite regularly near Kyoto. By late 1865 this modernized infantry force probably was more effective than the unreformed forces of Katamori.

By the time of the Hyōgo crisis, then, Yoshinobu was, potentially at least, a man who would have to be taken seriously in a military sense. All he needed was a private domain to support his private army. Then his stature was greatly enhanced by the outcome of the Hyōgo crisis because of his role in stopping unilateral action by Osaka and then securing court acquiescence to the treaties. Indeed his performance in 65/9 transformed him temporarily from ineffectual outsider to avidly courted, if not avidly heeded, pivotal figure. Osaka and Kyoto competed to shower kindnesses on him. In the most extreme instance, when the court was discussing special promotion and duty for him after Iemochi's resignation, it suggested to the bakufu that Yoshinobu be awarded the tax income from the three provinces of Settsu, Kawachi, and Izumi, where he was handling coastal defense work. In effect the court wished to give him the private domain to support his private army. Yoshinobu, however, who doubtless saw himself as a future shogun rather than a future daimyo, prudently rejected that court proposal, with its clear implication that the court was authorized to carve up the Tokugawa domain. Therefore, on 10/20, the court simply informed him that henceforth he was to have the special privilege of coming to imperial audiences in a wheeled vehicle. Yoshinobu did not really benefit from this show of extraordinary imperial solicitude, however. It only served to exacerbate bakufu distrust of him, even as it forced Osaka to outbid the court for his goodwill.

In the wake of the Hyōgo crisis Yoshinobu was thus a military figure able to play one side off against the other in terms of gestures of respect. He rapidly discovered, however, that he had very little success in using his position to shape real policy. That situation was first revealed in the area of his special authority: Kinai defense. Despite his occasional urging, the bakufu had not made great efforts to fortify the Kinai coast, and even after the Hyōgo crisis that state of affairs did not change. The reason, of course, was that the bakufu was by then badly overcommitted in its Chō-shū venture and had no resources for coastal defense. In any case, Yoshi-nobu's calls for a greater effort went unheeded. Perhaps in frustration at his own ineffectiveness, perhaps in an effort to prod Osaka into action, or perhaps in hopes of avoiding blame for the next diplomatic crisis of which rumor spoke at the time, during 65/11 he notified the court and bakufu that he wished to resign his titles because no real defense prepara-tions had been made. The court rejected his request, assuring him that no one else could fill his shoes, and on 12/12 the bakufu concurred.[45] Yo-shinobu was indispensable, perhaps, but he also might be dangerous. He was not trusted by a good many bakufu officials, and so he was ineffec-tive.

The personnel changes of late 1865 had displaced the remnants of the relatively united leadership of late 1864 with a considerably less cohesive group dominated by Itakura, Ogasawara, Katamori, and Yoshinobu. Of the four, Yoshinobu appeared the most influential. However, having ac-quired military forces and prestige that made him more suspect than ever, he found himself repeatedly clashing with others over policy matters. Although the four shared a general inclusivistic orientation that enabled them to paper over the Osaka-Kyoto breach, beyond that they were able to do little. They were unable to solve the Hyōgo problem. They were unable to devise and agree upon an effective policy for handling Chōshū, as we note below. In consequence in following months the bakufu con-tinued stumbling into war with a leadership as badly divided and demor-alized as that which had inherited the wreckage of Shungaku's Bunkyū reform.

2. The Drift to War: 65/10–66/5

Even as the reverberations of the Hyōgo crisis echoed through the bakufu, its leaders old and new turned their attention again to the domes-tic albatross about their collective neck. On 10/7, after the diplomatic crisis had passed its peak, bakufu leaders in the Kinai notified the court that Chōshū had not obeyed their most recent order summoning *han* rep-resentatives to Osaka. In response the court promptly instructed the shogun to assemble the daimyo to discuss affairs and settle Chōshū policy. Bakufu leaders objected immediately, fearful that the daimyo in assembly, following Satsuma leadership, might strip the shogun of authority. Their objections were sufficient. On the tenth they obtained court agreement to delay that call to assembly and pressed on with their own Chōshū policy.[46]

Bakufu leaders were aware of their military weakness and hopeful that the recent and ongoing changes in Tokugawa leadership might induce Chōshū to negotiate a settlement. Accordingly on 10/18 they instructed Katamori, Sadaaki, and Ogasawara to obtain imperial approval of a plan to dispatch an inspector general westward to interrogate the Chōshū lord and heir at Hiroshima. The court approved this plan, which not only moved development away from war and back to talk but also constituted another concession to Chōshū sympathizers in that it moved the talk westward to relatively neutral territory. Whereas in 64/12 Mōri and son had been ordered to go to Edo and in 65/4 their representatives had been asked to go to Osaka, in 65/10 they were being required only to go to Hiroshima.

This decision of 10/18 restarted the slow process of travel-talk-travel. On 11/16 Nagai and Togawa, who were known to have opposed the former hard line toward Chōshū, reached Hiroshima together with another inspector and a small train of subordinates. There they interrogated representatives of the Chōshū leaders and encountered dissembling and tergiversation. On 12/12 they decided to leave Hiroshima, reached Osaka five days later, and reported Chōshū's blatantly uncooperative attitude and its determination to fight.[47]

After Nagai and Togawa returned, the expanded bakufu leadership of Itakura, Ogasawara, Yoshinobu, Katamori, and Sadaaki debated the distressing situation at length, both among themselves and with lesser officials. They discussed a proposal by Yoshinobu to send Ogasawara and others to Hiroshima to interrogate the Chōshū men yet again in hopes of finding evidence of contrition that would enable the bakufu to adopt a policy of leniency. That suggestion was opposed by the senior councillors and was soon abandoned on the ground that more information would not change matters. Instead the debate continued as leaders searched for ways to salvage their regime. By the end of the year they saw the issue in stark terms of the preservation or loss of bakufu authority. Inevitably they disagreed among themselves because their purpose—to present demands sufficiently harsh to prove Edo's supremacy but sufficiently lenient to be accepted peacefully by Chōshū—was impossible of realization given the Chōshū attitude.[48]

In their desperate late 65/12 quest for a solution, bakufu leaders turned to some of the staunchest advocates of the inclusivistic tradition of Abe Masahiro and Matsudaira Shungaku. They listened at length to the advice of Nakane Yukie of Fukui, and they called both Ōkubo Ichiō and Mizuno Tadanori down from Edo and elicited their opinions.

Ōkubo was forthright and outspoken. He argued that the bakufu was erring by concentrating on superficial aspects of authority and neglecting long-range considerations. He said the bakufu should move to settle the Chōshū affair promptly and leniently and concentrate on basic reform. To this end it should summon the lords to a general congress that would deliberate and initiate widespread political reforms. He criticized the leaders for past indecisiveness and angered Itakura by his insistence on the importance of consulting the daimyo. He expressed opposition to the attempt to restore the *sankin kōtai* system and other old practices. When the senior councillors asked him what punishment should be given Chōshū, he replied that that question should be submitted to the daimyo assembly, but he did make several suggestions on alternative specific requirements.[49] His suggestions were not especially lenient, but his overall advice proved unwelcome anyway because it touched in an unacceptable way on the fundamental issue of authority that had become embedded in the Chōshū problem.

Just as Ōkubo's suggestions revealed the limits of Itakura's adaptability, concurrent attempts at mediation by Nakane had disclosed the growing distance between the views of Ogasawara and those of Shungaku, who was again giving *kōbugattai* advice from afar. Neither Itakura nor Ogasawara was enthusiastic about existing policy. They could only have been discouraged by contemporary rumors of a Satsuma-Chōshū accord, and they agreed with Nagai Naomune's argument that a "lenient" policy must be pursued because war would likely result in defeat.[50] But leniency was one thing, surrender quite something else, and Chōshū's intransigence made it extremely difficult to achieve the one without encompassing the other.

Itakura and Ogasawara were thus unable to accept the most concessive advice they received, but in the year-end policy debates the sharpest disputes did not arise between the councillors and these lesser advisors. Rather, they arose between Itakura and Ogasawara on the one hand and Yoshinobu on the other because it was Yoshinobu who proved to be the proponent of the harshest policy. He contended with much good reason that unless the Mōri showed true remorse, they must be severely disciplined; and the councillors replied, with equally good reason, that that would be impossible to do. The basic correctness of both positions gave the disagreement a bitterness that was all out of proportion to its magnitude. In the outcome, however, Katamori and Sadaaki finally managed to reconcile the men. By 1/22 bakufu leaders had agreed on a compromise policy that dropped most of Yoshinobu's more extreme positions and was rather like one of those originally advanced by Ōkubo. In the final plan, which the court accepted on the twenty-third after some final debate and modifications, Mōri was no longer to be labeled an enemy of the court. Rather, he would retire, his heir would succeed, the *han* would lose 100,000 *koku*, and the families of three formerly punished *han* elders (*karō*) would be abolished.[51]

A few days later Mizuno was thanked for coming down to Osaka, Nakane went home in discouragement, and Ōkubo was thanked, relieved of his advisory tasks, and ordered back to Edo to treat a recurrence of beriberi.

After the policy decisions of 1/22, Ogasawara, the bakufu's man for hard tasks, was given full authority to handle the Chōshū matter. He was ordered to proceed to Hiroshima to present the *han* with notice of the clarified punishment and to obtain its peaceful submission. Despite the profound doubts of his own vassals,[52] on 2/4 he left in a Kii warship and reached Hiroshima three days later. He was soon joined by Nagai and other officials and forces of artillery and infantry numbering some 1500 men.[53] A fortnight later he instructed Hiroshima to send a man to summon Chōshū representatives. By then, however, some Hiroshima leaders were strongly opposed to the bakufu effort and balked at their task. In the face of resistance from both Hiroshima and Chōshū, Ogasawara became embroiled in a long struggle just to get his order sent to Chōshū. Convinced, however, that the bakufu was unprepared for war, he tenaciously kept on talking.

Not until 66/5/1 was he finally able to meet Chōshū representatives and inform them of the decision of 1/22. But then they in turn refused to carry the message to their *han*, and after more maneuvering Ogasawara's final deadline for a reply, 5/29, passed with no response. Accordingly he announced that he would proceed to Kyushu to lead the assault.

Meanwhile back at Osaka conditions were no better. As we note later, both the morale and the finances of the bakufu army were bad and deteriorating rapidly. From early in 1866 the situation had prodded certain lesser officials to favor some sort of conciliatory policy that would avoid war. When 66/5 arrived, the situation was worse. Even the shogun and senior councillors, as well as lesser officials, were said to be desperately eager to go back east. Amid the plethora of rumors that rushed about the Kinai and Kantō, one said that as soon as Chōshū's statement accepting the bakufu order was received, the shogun would promptly sail back to Edo. The rumor, with its implied disregard for court and *kōbugattai*, was

sufficiently common that Itakura felt the need to write Shungaku expressly to deny it.[54]

By 66/5 the bakufu was well aware that almost no great *han* would
support its attack on Chōshū. For months analyses of specific *han* had
revealed the steady erosion of support for the venture.[55] Nevertheless,
despite the evidence of great daimyo animosity, despite the rumors of insurgent plots in the Kinai itself, despite the evidence of disarray in their
own official ranks, despite the evidence that their own forces were reluctant to fight, and despite the regime's bankruptcy, bakufu leaders
adhered to their plan, convinced that only by bringing Chōshū to heel
could the regime survive. Thus in 66/3–4 when it was proposed to call
Katsu Kaishū back to duty to handle the Chōshū matter in the hope he
could obtain a peaceful settlement, Ogasawara advised against it on the
grounds that Katsu, like Ōkubo Ichiō, had advocated leniency and such a
position would be preposterous in the existing situation.[56]

During 66/4 those bakufu officials attached to the several armies to
coordinate affairs and assure obedience departed Osaka for their posts.
On 5/20, as news of Ogasawara's stalled efforts reached Osaka, the
bakufu sent a mobilization alert to its armies of suppression. Five days
later, after Osaka had learned of Ogasawara's 5/29 deadline, Mochitsugu of Kii was named head of the advance party (*seichō senpō sōtoku*) and
ordered to proceed to Hiroshima. He had displayed an increasingly strong
commitment to the venture and personally advocated a firm policy as essential to bakufu survival. He, his assisting senior councillor, Honjō Munehide, and others left shortly for their headquarters. Honjō arrived on
5/28 and Mochitsugu on 6/5. In succeeding days the last operational
orders were issued, and by 6/7 suitable statements had been submitted
to the court and dispatched to Chōshū.[57] Amid doubts and fears the War
of the Second Expedition to Subjugate Chōshū, or more simply the Summer War, began.

Eighteen months of peaceful coercion had proved fruitless; the Chōshū
albatross had not been shaken off. By 66/6 it should have been clear to
Ogasawara and other bakufu leaders that their whole year of trying to
talk Chōshū into submission had been misdirected. That strategy had
assumed either that Chōshū leaders accepted the legitimacy of the Tokugawa regime or that threats could precipitate a change of leadership as in
late 1864 or as in Mito in 1859. But clearly the Edo regime had lost its
legitimacy in the eyes of a Chōshū leadership that was both securely in
power and prepared to put the issue of supremacy to trial of arms. Indeed, for more than a year that leadership had been preparing single-
mindedly for the war that it regarded as preferable to the existing peace.

Part
THREE

THE SUBSTANCE
OF CRISIS

CHAPTER 6

The Foundations
of Military Defeat
1863–1866

PROBLEMS OF ADMINISTRATION AND PERSONNEL

MILITARY STRENGTHENING

   1. Military Reform: Edo
   2. Preparation for War: Osaka

FINANCIAL CRISIS

   1. Expenses: The Demon Uncontrolled
   2. Crisis Financing: The Techniques of Self-Destruction

DAIMYO DEFIANCE AND DEFICIENCIES

The preceding three chapters have recounted how the bakufu leaders of conservative reaffirmation emerged in the wake of the Bunkyū reform's collapse and made painfully slow progress at reconstructing the old order. They attained a high point of success late in 1864, only to place themselves in an untenably overextended position vis-à-vis Chōshū. Committed to an enterprise they lacked the resources to carry to completion, during 1865 they saw their gains frittered away. They dropped out of office as reverse followed reverse, until by early 1866 almost the entire senior bakufu leadership had been replaced.

Looking beyond this change in political actors, one can see that the political process itself experienced a basic change in character during the years of conservative reaffirmation. From 1862 until late in 1864 the political process had been extraordinarily complex, with the independent variables of foreigners, daimyo, court, and *shishi* all interacting in highly unstable but consistently disruptive patterns. During 1865–1866, however, the political conflicts dominating the attention of bakufu leaders became immensely more simple. *Shishi* became quiet, the Kantō was pacified, the court grew docile, and Edo's representatives at Kyoto began actively, if awkwardly, working directly with the senior councillors. Political issues had been simplified to a naked power struggle between the bakufu and Chōshū, but it was a struggle that bakufu leaders failed to win by their preferred strategy of verbal coercion. Instead they were forced to fight, and for that, as they knew very well, they were ill-prepared.

The task of this chapter is to explain how the bakufu came to be so unprepared for a war that it brought upon itself at such leisure. To that end it examines problems of bakufu administration, military capability, finances, and allied and vassal forces.

PROBLEMS OF ADMINISTRATION AND PERSONNEL

In an effective regime the interests of the regime itself and of the functionaries who staff it are in general harmony. During the Edo period that had been true of the bakufu, but during the 1860s it became less and less the case. The repeated political deadlocks and imbroglios, the spasms of reform, and the weakness of the exchequer all served to damage the interests of officials and make bakufu office a most unappealing career prospect.

The conflict of interests between officials and their regime appears to have been particularly acute from mid-1862 to mid-1864 when the administration was ravaged by a seemingly endless series of purges, policy reversals, and personnel shakeups. The picture that had emerged by the summer of 1864 was of an administrative machine overworked, demoralized, and beset by problems that were not only beyond its capacity to handle but increasingly perceived in that way.

Taking these three characteristics of overwork, demoralization, and insoluble problems in order, it appears that much of the overwork was created by splitting the bakufu between two cities, with the halves duplicating much of one another's work. Much overwork also stemmed from difficulty in finding competent men willing to run the risks of office-holding, which led to overloading those officials who were competent. Much stemmed, too, from the process of internal administrative reform and the confronting of new tasks. Thus on 64/8/28 an Aizu man in Edo lobbying for the shogunal trip to Kyoto was told it would be difficult for the shogun to leave soon. When he urged it upon Oguri Tadamasa, he was told that the bakufu was having difficulty finding people to fill positions vacated by those who resigned. The senior councillors were so busy, said Oguri, that they had no time even to discuss affairs, much less alter policies. He said he had heard it was difficult even to meet members of the inspectorate, and in consequence aggrieved men were seething with anger.[1] Doubtless Oguri's argument was partially designed to turn the Aizu emissary aside, but it also suggested a high degree of administrative trouble in the bakufu.

The demoralization stemmed in part from the existence of conflicting symbols of virtue, notably loyalty to the bakufu, which appeared to be in conflict with loyalty to the court, and the honest pursuit of a realistic but unwelcome foreign policy as against pursuit of the alluring *jōi* dream. But the demoralization also stemmed from the constant shifts of policy and the repeated demonstrations of policy failure. And the sense of failure was compounded by the awareness that service was dangerous. At the very least one was almost sure sooner or later to be denounced, discredited, dismissed, and even put in detention for some period. At the very most one might be hacked to pieces by self-appointed men of virtue.

As for the insoluble problems, the aggressive foreigners, ambitious nobles and daimyo, and angry and energized *shishi* were always visible. The inadequacy of every solution hitherto proposed was brutally clear by mid-1864: one need only read the reports streaming in from both the Kantō and Kinai to know that. And this inadequacy was driven home with ruthless clarity by the foreigners. It was little wonder that the bakufu by then seemed to be drifting into a make-believe world of reaction in which by fiat and decree the crises of a decade would be erased and the old order made whole again.

One can identify many specific developments contributing to the growing administrative crisis. One source of difficulty already alluded to was the repeated division of the bakufu into Edo and Kyoto branches. It generated political disputes, duplication of effort, and mechanical difficulties of coordination that Katsu Kaishū's sometimes rapid naval transport did not fully solve. One example must suffice. As soon as the court had ordered the punishment of Chōshū on 64/7/23, bakufu leaders in Kyoto instructed daimyo to prepare forces for deployment. Those instructions, sent out over Inaba Masakuni's name, were reissued a few days later by the senior councillors at Edo. Specific duty assignments in the two sets of instructions were not the same, however, and generated some confusion. The confusion was then compounded by other orders issued by the keeper of Osaka castle to daimyo in that region. Thus the vassal daimyo of Amagasaki in Settsu, just across the Yodo river from Osaka, wrote an unhappy note to Mizuno Tadakiyo at Edo protesting that he had received different orders from three bakufu headquarters (Edo, Kyoto, Osaka), that they ordered him to do different things, but that he lacked the troops necessary to obey them all. He wrote that his preference was to go to Kyoto as Yoshinobu had ordered him to do, but still he wished Mizuno to clarify his duty.[2] In the meantime he—and others—waited.

There were many other immediate causes of administrative malfunctions and attempts to deal with them. The paralysis of 64/6 at Edo, for example, when senior councillors and others were boycotting affairs, created particularly acute administrative problems. Because of the Kantō insurrection and foreign demands, matters had to be handled despite the paralysis, and so on 6/10 senior councillor Inoue Masanao posted a notice altering office procedures and authorizing officials to move freely to and from the offices of inspectors and finance officials, thus enabling these men to keep matters moving despite the paralysis at the decision-making level.[3] Each such ad hoc modification eased a specific problem, but cumulatively they undermined the orderliness necessary to effective routinized administration. The leaders of conservative reaffirmation tried to reverse the trend, as we noted earlier, but their attempts seemed to bear little fruit.

Among the liege vassal officials there was by 1864 considerable evidence of accelerating institutional instability and dysfunction. For one thing personnel movement was very rapid, with regular and irregular promotions and dismissals occurring with dizzying frequency. Moreover in an apparent effort to find enough competent personnel, the bakufu seemed to be overloading able men, giving them multiple titles and assignments and pulling into office more and more men with rather unusual backgrounds. These trends suggest that the regime was chewing up its regular manpower sources faster than they naturally replaced themselves. Also the regime kept churning up, trying, and abandoning new titles and duty assignments, evidently seeking some new internal administrative configuration that would energize itself with a minimum of real change or accommodation of outside interests.

In a phrase, during 1863 and 1864 good people who could be trusted were getting harder to find. And when they were found, they had ever more difficulty getting the machinery of government to do what had to be done.

During 1865–1866 the administrative difficulties seem to have eased. After the political crisis of 64/6 the rate of personnel change slowed down, and then as political struggle evolved into a simpler bakufu-Chōshū conflict, official life became much less hectic and unpredictable. The personnel changes following the Hyōgo crisis constituted the single major spasm in the two years after 64/6. Intervening changes were relatively steady, relatively nonpunitive, and relatively consistent in thrust. Advocates of conservative reassertion gradually gave way to men holding other views, politically more concessive at the top, more ready to pursue military and institutional reform below.

This improvement of the bureaucratic climate did not, it appears, overcome the problem of manpower recruitment that Oguri had mentioned in 64/8. The problem continued to be implicit in the frequent assigning of multiple offices to liege vassals, presumably men of unusual ability such as Oguri himself. It was implicit, too, in the difficulty bakufu leaders periodically encountered in getting men to accept unwelcome duty assignments. There was also probably a direct connection between the bakufu's difficulty in getting men to accept responsible office and the growing evidence that corrupt motives lay behind the acceptance of office by some high officials. Vassal daimyo had long used high bakufu office to promote their private affairs. There is some evidence, however, quite apart from the accusations made by Katsu during moments of anger, that there was more than the usual level of self-serving involved in the acceptance or handling of high office by Matsudaira Naokatsu, Matsumae Takahiro, Makino Tadayuki, Sakai Tadamasu, and Mizuno Tadakiyo as well as a few others.[4]

After the shogun went to Osaka in 65/6, Edo became a sort of political backwater, which probably contributed to the improved bureaucratic climate. The substance of politics at Edo became diplomatic affairs, contacts with Léon Roches, infantry training, concern with Mito, and other Kantō matters. Edo became the place to which officials were dispatched when they were in disgrace. Senior councillors and lesser officials were sent there after being fired. Shungaku's friends Ōkubo Ichiō and Katsu Kaishū, for example, whiled away their hours at Edo, the latter busily writing about his trip to San Francisco and about military matters.[5] The tone of official Edo life was reflected in a letter Katsu wrote Shungaku in 66/5, less than a month before the Summer War began. He reported that at Edo there was little news about the impending Chōshū expedition. High officials were rather inactive, he wrote, although there had been some talk during the spring about political reform and about reducing the number of officials and investigating their financial problems. On 6/23, after the Summer War had erupted and he had been recalled to duty, Katsu informed Itakura at Osaka that men at Edo were discussing the idea of national unification *(gunken no sei)*. He suggested that it was a sensible idea in principle but asserted that they had no plans on how the bakufu was to whittle down daimyo power.[6] Except for administrative processes such as military expansion, then, it appears that national politics was for men at Edo a rather distant and abstract thing.

Most of the political tension was at Osaka, where the futility of the bakufu's Chōshū policy was fully apparent and served to maximize demoralization. However, except during the weeks of the Hyōgo crisis and its aftermath, the basic continuity of policy served to minimize conflict. Perhaps administrators there were just too overwhelmed by their dilemma to engage in politics. The regime slid almost quietly into disaster, carried along, it appears, on a consensus of discouraged helplessness.

MILITARY STRENGTHENING

The political disorder that bred administrative stress and malfunctioning also fostered an interest in military strengthening. It did so because it encouraged officials to look to the use of force as a means of solving their problems. This was particularly so from late 1864, after the Kantō insurrection had demonstrated beyond doubt the regime's military weakness, and after politics had begun to take on the simplified form of a straight-out domestic power struggle between Edo and Chōshū.

In the year and a half before the Summer War of 1866 bakufu leaders at Edo did their best to revive the military strengthening program that had petered out in early 1863. While those at Edo pursued that program of basic strengthening, the leaders who were at Osaka after mid-1865 set about deploying their forces for the actual contest with Chōshū. Both efforts made visible progress, and yet both encountered severe difficulties and ultimately proved inadequate.

1. Military Reform: Edo

The collapse of the Bunkyū reform had ended one attempt to modernize the bakufu's armed forces, and after the shogun's return to Edo, military policy took on an older cast. The decision to close the ports refocused the bakufu's attention on coastal defense work, as in the 1850s. Throughout 1863 and well into 1864 military debate swirled about choices and problems related to that work: cannon emplacements versus warships; casting cannon in existing arsenals versus purchasing new arsenals versus importing weapons. And through the debates ran a constant concern with the costs involved and the time consumed in forming the necessary arsenals and shipyards.[7] This naval strengthening effort made some progress despite innumerable obstacles, and it consumed immense funds.[8] It proved to be misdirected, however, insofar as it did little to strengthen the bakufu against its domestic adversaries.

The control of domestic adversaries required stronger land forces, and during 1863–1864 some debates focused on the question of using commoners in the military, whether as peasant militia or as conscripts in regular infantry units. In these debates the Kantō insurrection and other evidence of insurgency tended to create a conservative alliance of convenience. That alliance embraced those who opposed in principle the development of infantry or the modification of the old restrictions on the import, sale, possession, and use of firearms and those reform-oriented officials, such as Misoguchi Shōnyo and Oguri Tadamasa, who wished to prevent the uncontrolled spread of firearms to potential enemies of the regime. The net effect of this alliance was to inhibit any army reform at all.

In late 1864, however, as the Kantō grew quiet, as the lessons of that conflict were digested, and as the Chōshū problem came into focus, military reformers such as Misoguchi, Oguri, Takenaka Shigemoto, Asano Ujisuke, Kawakatsu Kōun, and Kyōgoku Takaaki began to implement constructive aspects of reform. They shut down obsolete installations, acquired modern rifles and cannon, and made plans for the establishment of better arsenals and shipyards.[9] Then as 1865 progressed, with the port-closing policy abandoned in fact, emphasis shifted to the creation of a large army of infantry. That shift revealed a new belief at Edo that domestic rather than foreign enemies were the real threat to the regime.

The military dimensions of the domestic threat were suggested by a report prepared in late 1863, perhaps as part of the bakufu's attempted leadership at closing the ports. This report indicated the numbers of modern units (infantry, cavalry, artillery) that most outside daimyo, excepting Chōshū significantly enough, were supposed to be able to mobilize. *In toto* the lords were expected to field 116 infantry battalions of some 54,400 men at 400 men per battalion, 12 cavalry troops totaling 1224 men, and 50 artillery batteries manned by 3200 men. Among the major *han*, for example, Kaga was to have ten battalions, one troop, and five batteries; Satsuma, eight, one, and four; Hiroshima, five, one, and two.[10]

At the time, these data seemed to elicit no expression of bakufu concern, probably because the daimyo had nowhere near such numbers. But a year later, when bakufu policy was different, these calculations likely took on new meaning to Edo. By late 1864 bakufu leaders were interested in arming and training sufficient forces to keep abreast of this potential *han* military capability. As with naval development, however, reform leaders encountered great problems in trying to improve both the weaponry and the training of their land forces.

Edo military leaders were aware of the ongoing revolution in western small arms noted in an earlier chapter, but turning that awareness to the bakufu's advantage was not easy. Quantities of arms were available, but most were not the best, and the best were expensive. It has been estimated that by 1864 some ten thousand weapons had been imported at Yokohama at a cost of some 100,000 *ryō*.[11] These, however, were almost all muzzleloaders of varying types, and military reformers recognized that they were already becoming obsolete. For example, there were by early 1864 samples of a sixteen-shot repeating rifle at Edo, but the bakufu was unable to obtain the smaller-caliber metal cartridges they required.[12] As the year progressed, the reformers learned more. In 65/2, after receiving from the Dutch a report on various breech-loading carbines that were being manufactured for sale, they advised their superiors to obtain samples for examination. At about the same time they learned of new American developments in firing mechanisms, notably Edward Maynard's priming techniques, which were making percussion caps obsolete. They also learned more about the repeaters that were being produced in quantity. Learning of the diversity of new weapons, the rapidity of change, and the massive weapons production of Europe and Civil War America (the latter improbably reported at fifty thousand pieces per day), military reformers lost some of their enthusiasm for developing cannon and rifle arsenals and began again to favor direct purchases abroad. Although the prices of the newer weapons were appreciably higher, the reformers recognized their superiority and began purchasing such rifles and cannon as they became available at Yokohama. And they placed orders for more.[13]

Without trained personnel the weapons would be useless, however, and in the latter half of 1864 military leaders addressed again the question of training that had been central to the Bunkyū military reform.[14] In 64/9 acting army commander *(rikugun bugyō nami)* Misoguchi asked the senior councillors to instruct him to send men to Holland for two years to study the rapidly changing army and navy technology and techniques. Matsumae replied that the men should learn instead from the British military forces stationed at Yokohama. That would be cheaper and faster—both considerations of some consequence at a time when the Kantō insurrection, another shogunal trek westward, the punishment of Chōshū, and payment of another large indemnity were the central political concerns of bakufu leaders. Misoguchi promptly investigated that suggestion and prepared a report on its implementation, focusing his attention on the assembling and organizing of men to be trained as officers and the arranging of the foreign instruction.

As matters worked out, the assembling of men was successful, but the arranging of training was not, and so in the end no real progress resulted. To elaborate, as Misoguchi wished, in 64/10 Komai Chōon and Tsukahara Masayoshi began assembling the men. Orders were issued for relatives of liege vassals to be selected and sent to Yokohama for training in infantry, artillery, and cavalry tactics. As the men were located and began to gather, fuller tables of organization were developed. By 65/1 the new plan envisaged the eventual formation of six batteries of artillery manned by a total of 1380 men, two cavalry battalions (*daitai*) of 264 men, and twelve infantry battalions of 9600 men. In succeeding months more regulations were developed, supervisory roles were articulated, and pay scales were set up in such a way as to accommodate differences in family stipend levels.

A fundamental problem in this whole undertaking was revealed in regulations of 65/7. They spelled out the numbers of conscripts, horses, and other goods that each officer and man would have to furnish, the obligations being reduced from those of prior years. What that meant, quite simply, was that the bakufu lacked funds to staff and equip its modern force. Accordingly the basic idea that liege vassals would equip their own men remained intact, despite the recognized inadequacy and difficulties of that arrangement.

Meanwhile the British instructors were being sought. Officials asked Rutherford Alcock in 64/11 to help arrange the hire of advisors and language instructors. Alcock agreed to do so but shortly after was ordered home to London. Then in 1865 both Harry Parkes at Yokohama and officials in London reportedly rebuffed or neglected bakufu attempts to secure adequate British aid in army training. As a result the men who had been assembled at Yokohama received only a smattering of training from some locally hired French and British officers. As a corollary result, the unhelpful British response and Léon Roches's contemporary aggressive courting prompted bakufu military officials later in 1865 to turn more fully to France for the needed aid.[15]

The foreign training was difficult to arrange, but that in no way lessened the bakufu's need for a stronger army. Rather, the decision of 65/4 to have the shogun lead an expedition against Chōshū made the rapid expansion of effective forces imperative, and so Edo military leaders undertook to enlarge and modernize their forces themselves. To this end, during early 65/5 the bakufu ordered more relatives of officials to drill at the established military institute *(kōbusho)* in Edo. Then, in a move to create more infantry forces for immediate use, it abolished the large patrol force attached to the Kanagawa magistrate's office. It formed 538 higher-ranking men from this force into a western-uniformed legation guard *(bette gumi)* and formed a thousand lower-ranking men into two battalions of regular infantry *(hohei gumi)*.[16]

Circumstantial evidence suggests very strongly that it was the shogun's trip which necessitated this abrupt creation of two new infantry battalions. Detailed military regulations that Honjō Munehide sent to Yoshinobu on 5/17, the day before he himself left for the Kinai, indicated that the units going westward with the shogun were later to be replaced by others sent from Edo at six-month intervals. Honjō also reported that the infantry force being sent westward at that time numbered 2400 troops. To replace them in six months would thus require another 2400 or a total force of 4800, half in Edo and half in Osaka. While the total number of infantry available at that time is not clear, detailed barracks regulations of 65/11 specified that the four permanent infantry barracks adjacent to Edo castle (at Ogawamachi, Nishimarushita, Ōtemae, and Sanbanchō) were each supposed to house 22 companies *(shōtai)* of 50 men per company, which yields 4400 infantrymen in all.[17] Assuming then that as of 65/6 the bakufu had 4400 or fewer infantrymen but needed 4800, the extra 1000 in the two new battalions would provide the needed additional 400 or more men plus reserves. And there would be no billeting problem as long as the shogun held 2400 of them at Osaka.

These barracks regulations of 65/11 were issued by army commanders Takenaka, Misoguchi, Ogyū Noritaka, and subordinate infantry commanders. They probably were based on similar regulations of 1862 and reveal many aspects of the infantry program. Among the forty-one clauses, for example, it was stipulated that men aged eighteen to forty-five were to be recruited throughout bakufu domains and liege vassal lands for five-year terms of service. Although liege vassals and their relatives might form the officer corps, the troops would thus be drawn primarily from the peasantry. The infantry command structure was spelled out, duties were specified, training requirements were adumbrated, and security measures were listed. The severity of the disciplinary clauses hinted at what earlier and future experience clearly revealed: that simply keeping these rugged country soldiers under control was at least as much of a problem as getting them trained.

This conscript infantry force was the single most important element in the bakufu's military system. Because the training program was not progressing at Yokohama, however, it was not becoming the fully western-drilled force that reformers wanted. Concurrent with this program of force expansion, therefore, military leaders were making renewed efforts to secure foreign advisors, and after Alcock's departure, that meant mostly seeking French assistance. In 65/3 Kurimoto Kon, reportedly at the urging of Oguri and Asano, asked Roches to arrange the hiring of French military advisors. Roches responded favorably to Kurimoto's request. Accordingly the senior councillors formally asked him to help form the twelve battalions of drilled infantry that were supposed to grow out of the training at Yokohama. As the prospect of British assistance faded later in the year, Asano and Ogyū Noritaka concluded that they must rely more fully on French aid. In 65/10 they made a request to Paris for a group of fifty-one advisors of specified types.[18]

While waiting for a response from Paris, the military leaders launched a new recruiting campaign and started preparing training facilities at Yokohama. They periodically urged subordinates to submit the names of able persons and in 65/12 instructed members of various groups of lesser liege vassals and others aged seventeen to forty-five to go to Yokohama for military training in the new-style *sanpei* (three combat arms: infantry, artillery, cavalry) techniques. Of those who drilled, the best were to be admitted into the modern army organization. If things worked out as the planners hoped, an army of some ten thousand men would eventually receive French training at a permanent camp to be opened somewhere between Kawasaki and Hodogaya.[19]

Meanwhile the request to Paris had been lost in missed connections. Accordingly on 65/12/21 Mizuno Tadakiyo wrote Roches asking him to help obtain the French military advisors. In 66/1 Roches wrote to Paris requesting some thirty-five advisors to train a proposed 1000 infantrymen, 650 cannoneers, and 350 cavalrymen—a much smaller force than Edo had in mind. Then, perhaps because bakufu funding was insufficient, Paris trimmed the shrunken request even further to about seventeen advisors, and the matter was handled so slowly that no action was taken until after the Summer War had begun.[20] French aid thus proved no more useful than that of the English. Nevertheless, in the months before war military leaders did start training men as best they could in the incompleted facilities. The enterprise did not achieve its overall objectives, but it did train a few more infantry battalions, and it helped lay the foundation for later more drastic military reform.

Thus due in great part to lack of effective foreign cooperation and despite persistent effort by military leaders at Edo (who were approved by leaders at Osaka),[21] the year and a half of army reform had only a very limited success.

2. Preparation for War: Osaka

While Edo pursued long-range projects and tried to expand its modern army, at Osaka the forces for use against Chōshū were assembled, drilled, and sent to the front. Compared to the effort at Edo, that at Osaka was more successful in the sense that leaders there did field their army. It was not successful in the sense of fielding an army adequate to its task. The character and certain crucial weaknesses of that army were revealed well before fighting erupted.

On 65/11/7, the day Nagai Naomune's mission was ordered westward to negotiate with Chōshū, the bakufu issued assignments for the military expedition, should it prove necessary. The orders revealed both the bakufu's dependence on great daimyo support and its concern to assure that support. Thus the force that was to approach from Hiroshima (the Aki front) included Hiroshima, whose commitment was already unclear, Okayama, which openly sympathized with Chōshū, and Tatsuno, a vassal *han* that also opposed the expedition. Hikone and Takata, two propunishment *han*, were assigned to the task as well as Tsuyama and Akashi, related *han* that perhaps could be counted on in the end, although their association with Fukui made even that uncertain. On the Japan Sea approach (the Iwami front) were Fukuyama, Hamada, and Kii, who would cooperate, Matsue who might, and Tottori and Tsuwano, who opposed the project. The three other approaches from Shikoku and Kyushu were much weaker, with only Kokura strongly in favor of the venture and all the great *han* assigned there ranging from cool to strongly opposed. To help assure their cooperation, the bakufu attached supervisory officials *(gun bugyō)* and tried to intermix reliable and unreliable forces, and later it dispatched a sizable headquarters force to Kyushu to oversee the effort there. Despite these measures, however, the fundamental unreliability of much of the army was unmistakable.

During the fall detachments of direct shogunal forces and *han* forces of expedition commanders, notably from Kii, Hikone, and Takata, trained at Osaka and departed for the advance headquarters at Hiroshima or for duty stations elsewhere. The shogun himself also began to acquire some military training, trying his hand at horseback riding and firing rifles. And he continued the constant observation of bakufu army practice that he had begun after reaching Osaka in the summer.

Bakufu leaders had maintained an active program of training from the time of their arrival. There were displays of individual skills, practice in small unit tactics *(shōtai undō)*, and parades by assembled mass forces. It appears that, as at Tokumaruhara in 1862, the unit training was not fully compulsory, at least among units formed of regular samurai, and men volunteered to train with their groups. This voluntarism likely undermined the effectiveness of such units but was, perhaps, an unavoidable concession to samurai pride. For infantrymen, who were mostly peasants or other commoners, drill was compulsory and clearly specified in their service contracts.[22]

The size and character of these shogunal forces at Osaka can be roughly estimated.[23] In 65/11 they were formally organized in column formation for advance westward. Their column consisted of sixteen brigades *(ban)* of varied sizes, mostly consisting of two regular units apiece. For example, the large 1st brigade consisted of one battery of field artillery (eight fieldpieces), two infantry battalions *(hohei daitai)*, and three infantry companies *(shōtai)* plus nine commanding officers and attached inspectors. The smaller 6th brigade consisted of two companies of *sakite* (vanguard riflemen) and two of *shoinban* (elite swordsmen), with ten commanders and inspectors. The 9th brigade was the shogun's entourage and included most of the civilian officials, a large variety of military companies *(kumi)*, accompanying vassal daimyo forces, and much equipment. The 15th brigade was the men and equipment of the finance office.

The available information fails to indicate weapon types, numbers of men, or their battlefield formations. The numbers of various types of units can be determined, however, and using other sources it is then possible to estimate the numbers of troops of varying types and to suggest their battleworthiness.[24] In sum it appears that the bakufu had an army of nearly eight thousand troops in all at Osaka, not counting senior officers, civil officials and attendants, vassal daimyo forces, other rear vassals, and the carriers of palanquins, baggage, and equipment.

It was a sizable force, and about six thousand of the men used firearms of one sort or another. Probably about two-thirds of the total could be described as an effective fighting instrument (battalions of foot soldiers, artillery, and artillery guard units). Still and all, this war envisaged encirclement on widely separated fronts of an enemy who had the immense advantage of direct internal communication. Moreover it was reported that Chōshū had thirty-six modern battalions,[25] which at 400 men per battalion amounts to 14,400 soldiers. Against such an enemy the direct bakufu forces were utterly inadequate, a symbol hoisted to the sky in hopes it would frighten the foe into submission.

As in the past the brunt of the fighting was supposed to fall on daimyo forces, and so their capabilities were a crucial consideration. On the Aki front, for example, Hiroshima's refusal to cooperate ultimately left the forces of Ii of Hikone and Sakakibara of Takata as the lead forces in the war. As of 65/11 Hikone reported forces totaling 1800 fighting men.[26] Of these, over half were regular samurai or pikemen, less than a third had firearms, and of these latter only a handful were reported to have new-style weapons. Moreover the whole Hikone force was organized on traditional company lines unchanged since the 64/7/18 battle at Kyoto, and the men with firearms were interspersed among the troops of mounted samurai. Sakakibara appears to have had just about a thousand fighting men. At best only about a third of them were equipped with firearms, and they too were organized in traditional small units.[27]

These forces plus troops from Kii, which replaced Hiroshima, were to be the heart of the main striking force on the Aki front. On 65/7/29 Kii, which was much larger than Hikone or Takata, reportedly amassed fifteen thousand men for a review at Osaka castle.[28] The figure may be greatly exaggerated, but even if it is not, it seems probable that well over half the number were porters and other menial support personnel. One Kii battalion numbered 507 men, for example, but that force consisted of 65 samurai swordsmen, a cannon battery, 104 men with firearms, and 302 porters and other attendant personnel.[29]

During 65/11 elements of this army headed west to encampments near Hiroshima. Specifically on 11/15 and 16 some two thousand bakufu troops headed west. They consisted of three new-style 400-man infantry battalions; a 35-man cavalry troop with western-style horse-gear; a 400-man battalion of artillery guards; a battery of eight or ten field cannon on carriages pulled by wagon horses with western-style harness; a company of 50 engineers (*sakujikata*); and headquarters and supervisory staff. During the next ten days the forces of Ii and Sakakibara departed (as did another reported thousand infantrymen) and sizable units from Kii, to make a reported total of some five thousand men, presumably in addition to the two thousand of 11/15–16.[30] Their advance would, it was hoped, put pressure on Chōshū and facilitate Nagai and Togawa's negotiating at Hiroshima.

During succeeding months the young shogun, whom Katsu in a moment of good humor had described as ''wise in spite of his youth,''[31] continued to show growing interest in affairs of state. He believed that Tokugawa survival depended on bringing Chōshū to heel,[32] and he continued to review his forces at Osaka, assiduously inspecting them day after day. Most of the best forces were already gone by early 1866,

however, and those being reviewed in the spring were decidedly less effective ones. Bakufu leaders even had difficulty making them adhere to
basic regulations concerning use of uniforms and weapons.[33] The shogun
reviewed his own attendants and old-style guard units as well as those
new-style units still at Osaka or arriving from Edo, where training was
going on apace. The forces on display included swordsmen, pikemen,
and even specialists in jousting as well as cannoneers and infantrymen.[34]

Most of these forces apparently remained at Osaka, however, except
for the 1500 who, as noted earlier, went with Ogasawara to Hiroshima
in 66/2. As of 66/6/1 there were about 4400 bakufu troops, mostly in
infantry battalions, near Hiroshima.[35] Ogasawara had another four hundred or so at Kokura, and except for headquarters units, almost all the
rest of the bakufu army of suppression consisted of troops from those few
daimyo domains that agreed to participate.

The departure of troops in 65/11 had relieved the pressure of numbers on Osaka, but it provided no other advantages to the bakufu.
Although it put the best forces Edo could muster on the very border of
Chōshū, their deployment did not intimidate the *han* and secure its capitulation. Rather, it meant the men had to spend more weeks and months
in the dull routine of camp life far from their homes and families and far,
too, from the diversions of the big city. Those diversions had at least
given them the choice of being bored or being broke. Near Hiroshima,
thanks to the continuing wild inflation, they were both bored and broke.

By 1866 the fiscal condition of the bakufu forces at both Osaka and
Hiroshima was becoming critical, and one important reason is not hard to
find. Back in 65/8, reported one observer, liege vassals received daily
travel funds of 4 *gō* or 0.72 liter of hulled rice and 400 *zeni*, a sum that
was insufficient to cover their expenses. The infantrymen were paid only
4 *gō* of hulled rice with no money supplement for expenses. According to
the observer their condition was bad, and worst off were those from the
countryside, peasants, who had no other family income. These latter
were said to band together on occasion in groups of twenty or thirty and
go into neighboring villages, weapons in hand, to extort money from the
local folk. Confronted by these marauding soldiers, the local peoples furnished the funds.[36] Then in 65/11 even this stipend was cut by 10 percent. Moreover, as troops left for Hiroshima, it was announced that their
travel allowance would be reduced from 4 to 2 *go* of rice per day. For
lower-ranking men a compensatory supplement was issued, but since
most of the payment was actually in money, in the face of continuing inflation their condition remained precarious. Thus men of Hikone found
that rice prices were beyond their reach, and they had some nasty dis-

putes with rice dealers near Hiroshima, with consequent ill-will and difficulty. Also, during 66/5, eighty-odd men in one bakufu artillery unit
wrote to leaders at Osaka appealing for financial relief.[37]

Due in part, then, to this financial situation, problems of morale were
severe. But there were other causes of discouragement too. During 65/6
the Kinai (as well as the Kantō) had received unusually heavy rain, and in
the following month a heat wave hit Osaka, helping spread sickness and
death among the crowded men and even prompting rumors that the shogun had died. The men, moreover, were impatient to get on with it, to
fight or go home, and in their impatience and boredom they caroused,
wasted their money, and got into frequent scuffles. By year's end the
problems of morale were showing up in the advance encampments near
Hiroshima. During 65/12 Shinsengumi leader Kondō Isami, who had
gone to Hiroshima with Nagai and Togawa, returned to the Kinai and
reported to his superiors under Katamori that Chōshū men were resolved
to fight regardless of what *han* leaders might do. He also reported that,
by contrast, the *han* troops sent to Hiroshima, particularly by Ii and Sakakibara, and bakufu troops too were dispirited and wished only to
return east. He said that even if there were fighting, the bakufu could not
win and hence it could only be lenient.[38]

This bleak assessment of the situation was shared by a retainer of Yoshinobu. He reported that the liege vassals at Osaka had become so demoralized by the indecisiveness of bakufu leaders that ''if now an order
were sent down instructing those who wish to go west to do so and those
who wish to go east to do so, not a soul would start westward.''[39] Using their military force, as was normal, for purposes of peaceful political
coercion, bakufu leaders seemed to be losing most of its real military
value. It was a situation ill-designed to inspire optimism.

FINANCIAL CRISIS

The Chōshū imbroglio thus led the bakufu to pursue a major attempt at
military strengthening, but as of 66/5 the enlarged army was only semi-
reformed, and it was ravaged by pervasive demoralization. That demoralization was attributable in part to the fiscal crisis engulfing the regime.
And because that crisis affected much more than just the army, its character requires closer scrutiny.

For two centuries the bakufu had managed its finances in an awkwardly adequate manner. Its regular annual tax income had rather consistently
fallen somewhat short of regular expenditures, with a consequent gradual
accumulation of institutional indebtedness. Periodically this debt was

reduced or erased by using the occasion of extraordinary expenses, such as those incurred in recovery from a major fire or natural disaster, to raise extraordinary funds by making special levies on merchants and others, by recoining, and by requiring exercises in belt-tightening.

From the 1840s onward this general pattern had been strained by a gradual rise in the costs of coastal defense, and after 1853 the trend accelerated sharply. According to finance officials the annual deficit in the years 1853–1858 averaged some 738,000 *ryō* of gold and 13,900 *koku* of rice.[40] Ii Naosuke tried to deal with the problem by reducing defense expenditures, but from 1861 they began to grow again. It was in 1863, however, that the bakufu began to incur a whole host of immense new costs, just at a time when its regular income was beginning to decline seriously. Hence the real fiscal crisis of the regime dated from 1863, and it was a crisis of monumental, utterly unprecedented, and ultimately disastrous proportions.

The character of this fiscal crisis and the means Edo took to deal with it can be seen by examining bakufu expenditures and income, insofar as data permit, during the years 1863–1866.

1. Expenses: The Demon Uncontrolled

The years 1863–1866 were disastrous for the bakufu fisc. Unexpected costs piled up one on top of another: three expensive trips to the Kinai; two major indemnities; the costs of new castle buildings and urban reconstruction following fires; the costs of suppressing the Kantō insurrection and fielding an army against Chōshū; and finally the costs of modernizing and expanding the bakufu military establishment. A total figure is impossible to reach. However, some major entries are available, suggestive costs of other matters can be found, and an overall picture emerges of a regime whose income was only a small fraction of its current expenses.

The single most crippling set of costs was that incurred in trying to sustain the policy of court-bakufu unity. The exact cost of the first shogunal trip is unknown, but comparable figures for the third are available and suggest that the first stay in Kyoto during 63/2–6 may have cost close to 1 million *ryō*.[41] The second trip reportedly cost about the same amount, despite the fact that the shogun went by ship. Fuller details exist on the third trip. To justify a *goyōkin* levy made in Osaka in 66/4, the finance office reported that trip-related costs for the period 64/9 to 66/5 had totaled 3,157,446 *ryō*. The report also estimated that in the coming six months until 66/12 the shogun's stay in Osaka would cost an additional 1,219,650 *ryō*, a figure that presumably assumed no outbreak of hostilities.[42]

Quite apart from the shogunal trips, controlling Kyoto proved to be an immense burden. To cite a few examples, Ogasawara's armed progress to Kyoto in 63/5 was expensive (about 20,000 *ryō* just for foreign ship rental), and every subsequent trip by high officials cost additional thousands of *ryō*. The deputy cost money: 10,000 *ryō* for Inaba Masakuni in 63/10 and another 10,000 for Matsudaira Sadaaki in 64/7. Yoshinobu also became a burden to the regime. In 63/9 he was awarded an annual stipend of 10,000 *hyō* to defray costs of his duties as shogunal guardian, and later, when he traded that title for *kinri shuei sōtoku*, he was granted 7500 *hyō* per month to cover his expanded costs. Katamori, however, was by far the biggest burden on Edo. To sum up the costs of the year from 63/5 to 64/5, for example, Aizu received from Edo loans of 30,000 *ryō* of gold and 10,000 *hyō* of rice and grants of 80,000 *ryō* of gold, 50,000 *koku* of land, and an annual stipend of 20,000 *hyō* of rice.[43] Despite this largesse, Katamori's job was still bankrupting his *han*.

Even before Iemochi's third trip to the Kinai began in 65/5, costs of the bakufu presence there were a major problem for the regime. That was revealed in a long set of instructions the senior councillors sent to Sadaaki three months earlier. The instructions were essentially an order that he and the keeper of Osaka castle not disburse funds without prior authorization from the councillors. At a political level the order was part of the overall attempt by Edo leaders in early 1865 to avoid another shogunal trip and to bring the prestigious Tokugawa representatives in the Kinai back under control. One aspect of the problem of control, however, was that the growing political activity to the west had shifted an immense amount of fiscal decision-making responsibility to bakufu officials there, and the finance office at Edo evidently had failed to develop accounting procedures that enabled councillors to keep close tabs on those decisions. In their attempt to deal with the political problem, the councillors produced a document that also shed light on the bakufu's financial condition.

The instructions to Sadaaki discussed how greatly fiscal responsibilities in the Kinai had grown. They referred to the annual stipend increases of 150,000 *hyō* given the court in 1864, to the *goyōkin* levies that brought monies in, to the expenses of the two prior shogunal trips, and to the costs of maintaining Yoshinobu and others in Kyoto. The councillors mentioned that over the past year funds totaling 851,500 *ryō* of gold and 8300 *kanme* of silver (about 140,000 *ryō*) had been shipped to the Kinai, and they expressed concern over how the funds had been used. They reported that the regime's total monetary income was 1,186,500 *ryō* and 8300 *kanme* and worried at length about the unspecified gap be-

tween that income and the various expenses of the regime. They acknowledged that the finance office should handle all these matters, but
regrettably the tasks had devolved upon the deputy, and so he should be
careful and report fully.[44]

By the start of 1865, then, the regime's Kinai expenses were consuming most of its monetary income and had outstripped its administrative
capabilities. Bakufu leaders recognized clearly that the repeated shogunal
trips were an intolerable cost and a significant cause of inflation. They
also could see that the trips had another serious impact: they constituted a
drain on the country's total rice resources. Partly because the trip necessitated the transshipment of rice, in which quantities were lost and
diverted, and partly because human bodies in motion simply consume
more calories than the same bodies at rest, there was a direct relationship
between the numbers who traveled and the quantities of goods consumed. Thus Katsu Kaishū was told early in 1865 that in the year past
the bakufu had disbursed 1,600,000 *hyō* of rice *(kirimai)* in all and that
persons accompanying the shogun had by themselves consumed 140,000
hyō in their spring and summer allotments alone.[45] What these figures
seem to mean is that nearly 10 percent of the rice that was supposed to
sustain about twenty thousand liege vassal families for a year had been
consumed by some five hundred families during a half-year trip. Furthermore the total rice disbursal in the course of the year had been substantially more than what the regime had received in tax rice, as we note later
on, and that meant it had to buy more on the market—a practice that
would only drive the price up and, worse yet, enhance the prospect of
general scarcity should the rice crop fall significantly short.

The regime's foreign-related expenses were comparably catastrophic.
Most immediately foreign in origin were the two major indemnities. The
Namamugi indemnity of 63/6 was about 330,000 *ryō* plus 70,000 *ryō*
later "loaned" to Satsuma to cover related costs. This sum was then
dwarfed by the absurd Shimonoseki indemnity of some 2,250,000 *ryō*,
which was a constant millstone about the bakufu's neck. Thus during the
early days of 65/7 officials at Edo secretly transported to Yokohama
some 30,000 to 40,000 *ryō* per day for delivery to the foreigners as
another $500,000 payment on the indemnity. Informed sources reported
that while the payment had been made on schedule, further payments
would be extremely difficult.[46]

One reason the bakufu would have difficulty meeting its next installment was that it was spending monies abroad for other reasons. During
late 1865, for example, copper coins worth 150,000 *ryō* were transferred from Edo to Yokohama for shipment to France, probably to help pay

for purchases being made in conjunction with the Yokohama and Yokosuka shipyards and other matters. That the coins were copper rather than
gold or silver was itself evidence of empty warehouses, but even that
sum was insufficient, and the Yokohama work was delayed for want of
funds, much to the irritation of Katsu. By 66/4 M. Fleury-Herard, the
bakufu agent in Paris, was asking for more money; and on 6/19, after
receiving his request from Paris, Oguri and Shibata Masanaka wrote,
even as the Summer War raged on, that they would promptly ship the
needed 300,000 francs (about $55,000) via a Mr. Westwood of the
Oriental Bank.[47] The regime's exchequer seemed to be smashing to
pieces on both Scylla and Charybdis.

These costs hinted at the other major dimension of the bakufu fiscal
crisis: military expenses. Initially these had been incurred in the
expulsion-related attempt to strengthen coastal defense. Thus in 1863,
for example, military leaders reexamined Abe Masahiro's Shinagawa for-
tification project. They worked out extensive plans for construction of the
fourth offshore battery and adjacent shore batteries and arrived at an estimated cost of 109,728 ryō. Other coastal work was done at Osaka, and
in the latter part of 1864 funds were disbursed in increasingly large
amounts for rifles, cannon, related equipment and facilities, and the construction of foundries, arsenals, and shipyards.[48]

To suggest the magnitude of these expenses, the Osaka city magistrate reported in 64/4 that he required thirty-five cannon for proper
coastal defense of the city. A less inhibited Satsuma vassal suggested that
Kinai defense called for the emplacement of some 810 cannon costing
about 1000 ryō apiece. Other Osaka officials presented other estimates
of weapons needs, including a 64/12 recommendation for 110 cannon
and carriages at a total cost of about 500,000 ryō (31,850 kan of
silver). The regime obviously could not afford to buy such cannon
abroad, and the bakufu had already decided to purchase a foundry instead. In 64/3 it sent 100,000 ryō to Yokohama to buy foundry equipment from Americans, but that arrangement apparently fell through. By
late 64/8 discussions with the Dutch had advanced far enough that they
quoted a price for a modest establishment: it was 156,000 Mexican
dollars or about 120,000 ryō.[49]

Besides land facilities and installations, a potential military expense
was the naval development plan that Katsu Kaishū had been vigorously
advocating for some time. During 1863–1864 large sums were expended, and various plans and proposals called for the spending of additional immense quantities on warships. As 1864 gave way to 1865,
however, the shift in priorities to army expansion was reflected in
defense spending and planning.

The general magnitude of army expansion costs was suggested by an extraordinarily detailed finance office statement of 65/1 estimating military expenses for the coming year. The meaning of the figures is not always clear, but it appears that total anticipated costs relating to the planned *sanpei* (three combat arms) force of some eleven thousand men would be over 2 million *ryō*. Of that sum 200,000 would be for weapons, powder, and other equipment, another 250,000 for a planned gunpowder factory, another 230,000 for cannon, and 1,300,000 for the triune force's manpower and officer corps. Because such an outlay was utterly beyond Edo's capacity, military reformers, as we noted when discussing this reform, reluctantly tried to have the bulk of the manpower cost absorbed by the liege vassals themselves through reliance on traditional conscript-horse-matériel levies. Despite this economizing measure, however, and despite both the very limited progress of the reform effort and the failure to build any gunpowder plant at all, at the end of 1865 Katsu heard that all 300,000 or more *ryō* in the Tameike treasury at Edo had been allocated for military expenses, and still those costs were hard to meet.[50]

Quite apart from the costs of shogunal trips, foreign demands, or military reform, in one way or another the court, Chōshū, the Kantō insurrection, and other problems cost the bakufu additional large sums. Many of those costs were in the form of assistance to daimyo, who were encountering intensifying hardships.[51] In 64/11, for example, the vassal daimyo Toda of Ōgaki requested a loan of 25,000 *ryō* from Edo. In explaining the request, he enumerated the recent extra burdens he had had to assume: defending the Fushimi-Uji district, guarding palace gates, participating in the 63/8/18 incident, and dispatching troops for the 64/7/19 incident and for preparatory and mopping-up operations. Also, he added, there were the costs of the Chōshū expedition: his castle would have to serve as a billeting area, and repairs were needed because fiscal shortages had forced him to let the castle become dilapidated. Furthermore, he reported, he had brought his family home from Edo just the year before, and with *sankin kōtai* being revived, he would have to arrange to return them, which would be very expensive.[52] The many requests of this sort that Edo received were doubtless justified, but equally obviously their accommodation hurt the bakufu exchequer.

Offsetting these costs were gifts by daimyo, mostly vassal lords, to help defray the costs of the Chōshū venture, but these probably totaled only a few thousand *ryō* and were gestures of goodwill more than substance.[53]

The bakufu leaders handling finances did not, however, agree to accept all the extra costs of the day. They refused many requests for aid, requests that probably would have been routinely honored in former years. The bakufu's reluctance to pay sufficiently may also have been at the base of some men's refusal to accept high office.[54]

The regime also tried to cut its costs at the expense of its more vulnerable lesser vassals, as it had during the Bunkyū reform. We have already noted the meager salaries of its troops, but the men almost lost even that level of income. In about 65/5 finance officials discussed the feasibility of converting the allowances (fuchi) of minor vassals and many troops from rice to money. The rate they considered applying would have amounted to an immediate cut of about one-third in the real income of these men and, with inflation continuing, a steady further erosion of their position.[55] The proposal evidently was not implemented, but that the plan could even be discussed at all just when the men were about to be sent westward to fight Chōshū suggests the straitened financial situation.

In many other ways, too, the bakufu tried to cut the costs of its manpower. It continued to admonish men on the virtues of frugality. In 66/1 it ordered that all nonmilitary construction be halted: not even leaky roofs were to be repaired. It tried to limit the numbers of liege vassal retainers and slashed liege vassal stipends in 65/11, as we noted before. Due to inflation, however, it was forced on 66/5/21 to increase the stipends of those lower vassals who were at Osaka with the shogun.[56]

As this last comment suggests, one other important factor wrecking the bakufu fisc was inflation, which began to get out of hand in late 1863, adding directly and indirectly to government costs. Thus when the emperor restored the shogun's authority in 64/4, he specifically called for measures to halt the rise in prices, and the shogun promptly ordered his officials to prepare a strategy for doing so. Those good intentions quickly collapsed, however, because with the eruption of the Kantō insurrection rice prices rose dizzily in Edo.[57] In 1865 and 1866 the inflation accelerated, evolving from a trend debilitating to the exchequer into a trend undermining the whole regime and fostering general samurai hardship and an insurrectionary mood among the populace. We examine that trend in the next chapter when considering those larger problems.

In sum, the bakufu fiscal crisis was primarily a result of the deluge of new expenses incurred from 1863 onward. They drove annual deficits wildly beyond the levels of the 1850s, and by the beginning of 1866 complete fiscal collapse was recognized as imminent. Ōkubo Ichiō considered money and supplies for the Chōshū venture inadequate. By 66/3 even Yoshinobu at Kyoto had apparently accumulated a debt of some 350,000 ryō and was unable to pay his troops enough to meet such simple costs as their monthly rent.[58] By the time fighting erupted in 66/6, the bakufu was thus hard pressed to cover its most elemental day-to-day costs.

2. *Crisis Financing: The Techniques of Self-Destruction*

If the regime could not stem its financial hemorrhaging, it would have to expand greatly its sources of regular tax income, find other massive sources of money, or collapse. In terms of meeting its bills, what particularly marked these years as a new stage of institutional disintegration was the extent of bakufu reliance on self-destructive forms of fund-raising.

This self-destructive trend was fostered by the regime's inability to expand its regular land-tax income. Adequate figures are not available, but scattered data suggest that during these years land-tax income actually dropped precipitously. During most of its history the bakufu had received annual tax income averaging about 800,000 *ryō* of money and 600,000 *koku* of produce. In 1863 the bakufu estimated the tax value of its lands at about 1,240,000 *ryō* of money, 750,000 *koku* of produce, and other miscellaneous income. How much of that actually was received is not clear. But in 1864, the year of the Kantō insurrection, when its estimates called for 1,440,000 *ryō* and 865,000 *koku*, it actually received only 466,000 *ryō* and 380,000 *koku*, or about one-third its expected regular income. The regime was trying to squeeze much more out of its land than in the past but was in fact getting much less.[59] The shortfall was immense.

There seem to be no records of actual land-tax income for the years after 1864, but there is evidence suggesting continued decline in the yield. First, the harvests in both 1865 and 1866 were poor in central Japan, and much bakufu land was in that area. Second, during the year and a half before the Summer War the bakufu gradually distributed land to others, with more than 110,000 *koku* being lost in that way, mostly to vassal daimyo. Efforts to replace this with land reclaimed from others proved futile.[60] Third, some income figures for 1867 suggest that by then the land-tax income pattern had deteriorated much further than in 1864. Likely the levels of the two intervening years were part of a general trend.

With its regular income declining and expenses skyrocketing, the bakufu sought its monies elsewhere. One new type of income that was both stable and substantial was tariff income from foreign trade. Tariff income figures do not appear to exist, but a statement by finance officials in 1867 suggests that by about 1863 the foreign trade at Yokohama may have generated income of about 1 million *ryō*.[61] If so, it was one powerful reason for officials to oppose both the closing of Yokohama and the sharing of trade with other domains such as Satsuma or Chōshū, even though that posture guaranteed more domestic trouble for the regime.

The promising character of tariff income prompted officials to pursue ways of maximizing their gain. The most notable strategy was an effort, begun almost as soon as trade started, to try to channel it through Edo merchants who could be controlled and taxed quite easily and thoroughly. The effort was only partially successful, however, and by 1864 the greater part of the Yokohama silk trade was being carried on by non-Edo merchants.[62] In a renewed effort to gain control of the trade, at the beginning of that year the bakufu reissued an earlier order prohibiting direct silk sales to Yokohama, and in following months there was a dramatic decline in the volume of Yokohama silk exports. The decline may have been caused primarily by the Kantō insurrection and other unrest of 1864 rather than merchant resistance to the order. But whatever the cause, late in the year, as the bakufu restored order in the Kantō, it also lifted the restriction on direct exports. With some assistance from Léon Roches trade volume then rose rapidly. As it did, bakufu officials and Roches began exploring bakufu-French monopoly trading arrangements that would benefit the regime by enabling it to pay for the massive military purchases then being made and planned.[63] The talks dragged on inconclusively year after year, however, and in the meantime the regime had to turn elsewhere for money.

There were other sources of immediate income, and these were exploited ever more frequently after 1863. Specifically, whereas the bakufu had recoined to its advantage at rates averaging about 200,000 *ryō* per year during the 1850s, in 1863 its recoinage profit was reported at 3,642,333 *ryō*.[64] Then in 64/8, as we noted earlier, the bakufu called upon major Kinai merchants to furnish 710,000 *ryō* in *goyōkin*. As the conservative reaffirmation disintegrated during 1865–1866, dependence on irregular income intensified and the search for funds grew more frenetic. Most especially the reluctant decisions of 65/3 and 4 to pay the Shimonoseki indemnity and send the shogun westward precipitated a desperate search for funds. Thus a few weeks after making those political decisions, the bakufu ordered the Sado magistrate to mine more gold from the old and long-exhausted mines of Sado island. Five days after issuing that unpromising order, it initiated a recoinage of several issues of coins, and early the following month it ordered the recoinage of several more issues.

More ambitiously, during 65/4–5 the finance office developed plans for another major *goyōkin* levy. On 5/3 a public notice reminded the populace of the immense expenses generated by the foreign intrusion, the

two shogunal trips to Kyoto, the spate of castle fires, and the coming expedition against Chōshū. Although townsmen had been solicited before,
the notice pointed out, they had enjoyed long security thanks to Tokugawa rule and should therefore contribute the funds requested in this time
of crisis.[65] To assure that funds would be forthcoming, long lists of dues
were prepared. In the case of Edo, for example, the city was subdivided
into twenty-three tax districts of varying exploitability. In each district
lists of families were drawn up and their obligations specified. As a whole
the city was to yield 627,340 *ryō*, of which 194 families in the 1000 to
10,000 *ryō* range were to contribute 397,750 while 1116 families in
the 100 to 1000 *ryō* range were to contribute 229,590. The contributors were instructed to make their payments by the end of the year, and
they were assured that the loans would be repaid in ten to fifteen years.[66]
Doubtless the assurances were unconvincing. In following weeks the Edo
merchant community was sunk in gloom and dismay, a gloom only partially relieved by members' success in evading the burden by bribing the
collectors.[67]

Comparable levies were imposed on Osaka and on intendants of bakufu domains, holders of *azukaridokoro*, and administrators of outlying districts and towns. Heads of even the smallest temples and shrines were all
called upon to prepare orderly contributions proportional to the wealth of
the contributors, many being dunned for only 1 or 2 *ryō* apiece.[68] During
following months funds gradually came in. In 65/10, for example, the
vassal lord of Kōriyama turned over 3000 *ryō* that he had collected.
Some other daimyo turned over similarly modest sums. Then at the end
of the year the regime renewed collection pressure. In a rush to clear outstanding debts, some twenty-six merchants in Edo and Osaka came forth
with a total of 308,000 *ryō* in contributions ranging from 2000 to
33,000 *ryō*.[69] It was welcome, but it was still only a small portion of
what the regime had hoped to get.

Following the decisions to meet indemnity payments and mount a shogunal expedition, other efforts to raise monies also were made. Late in
65/6 the townsmen of Fushimi were specifically ordered to contribute to
help defray the costs of the Chōshū venture. Again the levy was justified
on grounds of the foreign danger, castle fires, the shogun's trips, and the
obligations of all for generations of Tokugawa peace. A few days later
the regime devalued more coins and simplified regulations in order to expedite recoinage.[70]

Despite everything, however, income was insufficient. The regime
could not pay its way: it could not meet payments on the Yokohama
foundry; it was forced to slash its troop stipends; it failed to cover Yoshi-

nobu's expenses; and it still had empty warehouses. During 65/12 and 66/4 it paid in two stages another installment of the foreigners' Shimonoseki indemnity, and with that it ran out of money.[71]

It was in this context of economic disintegration just before the Summer War's outbreak that rumors of a major foreign loan appeared. There had been such rumors a year earlier in 65/5 as the bakufu had frantically recoined and sought *goyōkin* to pay an indemnity bill and send the shogun westward. Those earlier rumors indicated that the bakufu had requested, and unspecified foreigners had agreed to, a loan of 1,150,000 *ryō*. The report was probably unfounded and the rumors died down. But in 66/4 they reappeared, and that time the source of funds was specified as France. Ōkubo Ichiō assured Shungaku in a letter late that month that although Oguri had said the bakufu would need more funds before the Chōshū effort was completed, such funds would be obtained from below, not from abroad.[72] The rumor persisted, however, and with better reason than Ōkubo may have realized, as we note in examining the Summer War.

Ōkubo's assertion seemed to be substantiated, however, when in a last gallant gesture the bakufu tried again in 66/4 to obtain the *goyōkin* funds it had been unable to get the previous year.[73] In notices reiterating the causes of fiscal difficulty and reminding the Osaka wealthy that they were well off and owed their well-being to the Tokugawa house, the bakufu instructed men to make loans that would be repaid over a period of thirty years, starting in 1867. Some twenty firms were called upon to loan the government the handsome total of 2,525,000 *ryō* in sums ranging from 55,000 to 110,000 apiece. The sum was elegant but somewhat misleading. When the levy was imposed, the bakufu canceled unpaid portions of the 1865 obligation. Moreover, individual levies consisted not only of monies to be advanced anew but any sums paid toward the prior year's *goyōkin* plus any earlier outstanding debts. The levy, therefore, even if fully paid, would have yielded considerably less income than the figures suggested. The sums were also far below those mentioned in rumor and recommendation. In what was perhaps a softening up statement, the bakufu first notified the Osaka populace in 66/4 that the city magistrate had indicated the town could provide 7 million *ryō* in loans ranging from 300 to 200,000 apiece. However, the bakufu stated, such a levy would be unfair, and instead funds would be solicited from the entire country and Osaka dunned less heavily. Rumor spoke of a total levy on Osaka of 3 to 3½ million *ryō* in a collection that would even hit small "rear street" shops for 5 to 7 *ryō* apiece.

The actual levy was thus much less ambitious than it might have been or purported to be, but it immediately met resistance just the same. Unresponsive merchants were summoned to the city magistrate's offices and urged to pay. The sums did not immediately materialize, however, and in 66/7, as the regime was engulfed in war and upheaval, the levies were increased in an attempt to make up the difference. In the end most of the monies may have been obtained, but they came too late to help in the war.[74]

The destructive character of much of this monetary manipulation betrays the extent of the regime's dilemma. The men handling these policies were not blind fools. They knew that massive recoinage and borrowing were wrecking their monetary system. They were convinced, however, that the alternative, which was capitulation, was even worse, and so they struggled on. Yet even had these desperate efforts succeeded, they would have been pathetically inadequate in the face of mushrooming expenses. And they also contributed to more basic economic ills that alienated and injured daimyo and generated a new level of public unrest.

Daimyo Defiance and Deficiencies

As immediately ominous for the bakufu as the fiscal crisis was the mushrooming evidence that the daimyo were shifting en masse away from a posture of support for the regime. The defections of Chōshū and then Satsuma were the crucial ones, and they are well enough known, but they were only the most dramatic and extreme cases.

By 66/6, to suggest the range of attitudes, the daimyo may be thought of as falling into four general categories. There were a few great outside daimyo and their minor relatives (such as Chōshū, Satsuma, Uwajima) who were hoping for or actively working for the collapse of the Tokugawa regime. There were a large number of daimyo, mostly outside lords (such as great Tōhoku lords, Tokushima), who had become functionally neutral. Unwilling for one reason or another to engage in national politics, they would give no support to the regime, but they also would not actively oppose it. There were a rather large number of *han*, including many important ones (such as Okayama, Tottori, Fukui, Owari, Mito, Hikone), which were so severely torn by factions and embittered by recent experience that they tended to neutrality but could and sometimes did move quite easily and unpredictably between pro-bakufu and anti-bakufu positions. Then lastly there were a large number of daimyo, mostly vassal lords (such as Fukushima, Kokura, Obama, Takata, Ueda, Matsumoto), who would give the regime what support they could but who were financially strapped, short of manpower, and internally divided on questions of how to cope with current problems and hence unable to act effectively if at all. There were very few *han*, therefore, that could and would act vigorously in defense of Tokugawa interests.

The most wide-ranging daimyo defiance of the bakufu was in response to Edo's attempts to restore the *sankin kōtai* system and obtain cooperation against Chōshū. Some daimyo in all four categories, but more in the first categories than in the last one, participated in the defiance on both matters.

Looking first at the question of *sankin kōtai*, following the order of 64/9 that restored pre-1862 regulations, there had been no extensive written response from daimyo. But on 65/1/25 Edo again reminded them that they must come at the appointed time. That reminder elicited responses, and several major lords refused to comply. During the next few weeks, moreover, Satsuma men urged the court to oppose the *sankin kōtai* order, and their lobbying bore fruit on 3/2 when the court ordered Edo to revert to the reformed system of 1862. Katamori also opposed attempts to revive *sankin kōtai* on the ground it would be destructive of bakufu relations with both court and daimyo. Bakufu leaders, however, did not acquiesce at once. One reason probably was that their attempt to restore the system had been partially successful. A good many lords already were at Edo. Many others, mostly lesser daimyo and especially vassal lords, had returned or were returning to the city.[75] It may well have seemed that barring other complications the few die-hard recalcitrants could in time be brought into line. However, complications did arise due to the Chōshū problem. After the bakufu in 65/4 decided to send the shogun westward, it issued duty orders to the daimyo. In the orders of 4/15 those who had most strenuously objected to *sankin kōtai* —namely, the great lords from Kyushu, Shikoku, and western Honshu —were formally excused from their 1865 duty because of their tasks in suppressing Chōshū. Those orders constituted a de facto bakufu defeat, at least for the time being. A year later in early 1866 the Chōshū crisis again confounded bakufu hopes to restore the system. The year's delay for western daimyo was expiring, but they made no move to return to Edo, their defiance made safe by the bakufu's preoccupation with Chōshū. Then with the eruption of the Summer War the whole issue fell into abeyance. *Sankin kōtai* had not been revived.

Turning to the matter of Chōshū itself, during the first months after Edo's decision of 65/4 to mount a new expedition against the insurgent *han*, many lords, especially vassal daimyo, responded cooperatively. The great lords, however, did not cooperate as they received duty orders in the latter part of the year. During early 1866, as the prospect of war really began to materialize, the bakufu renewed its efforts to win the support of great lords, but those efforts too proved woefully unsuccessful.[76] To the extent that daimyo or their advisors could exercise volition, the available evidence suggests that as of mid-1866 few great outside *han*, and few great related *han* for that matter, were prepared to follow Edo's lead. Vassal *han* still seemed to be mostly supportive of the regime, but they were not free agents by any means. There is considerable evidence that even before the war with Chōshū began, their condition was precarious and hence their ability to support Edo limited.

One problem of the *han* was that of paralyzing divisions within them. In some the 1864–1865 crackdown on radicalism eased or erased the divisions, but in others they persisted. In Shimabara *han* in Kyushu, for example, the daimyo was a brother of Yoshinobu, and the *han* was deeply divided. Factions were bitterly at odds on the national questions that had ravaged Mito—imperial loyalism, reform, Chōshū policy, and so forth. This division led to savage struggle, to murder, and to punishment during 65/8–9 and contributed to the *han*'s decision not to act in the Summer War of 1866.[77]

Moreover, vassal *han* were in a fiscal bind. The first Chōshū expedition had generated complaints of *han* impoverishment,[78] and between 65/1 and 66/6 the bakufu received petitions from a number of vassal lords reporting bankruptcy or other extreme hardship and seeking assistance.[79] Those lords also made other efforts to deal with their monetary difficulties—ordering extra frugality, seeking permission to mint their own coins, trying to raise special taxes, reducing their staffs at Edo, and dipping into reserve food supplies.[80] Even more widespread were manpower difficulties, which were probably covert expressions of fiscal limitations since vassal daimyo forces had gradually been trimmed over the decades, probably as a response to fiscal pressures. Traditionally the bakufu had ordered *han* to deploy forces in a great variety of functions, and during the *bakumatsu* period such duties had multiplied. Guards had been increased in the cities, at intendancies, and at barrier points, and they had been assigned to the new treaty ports and consulates. Moreover forces had been deployed to quell *rōnin*, Kantō insurgents, Chōshū, and erupting commoners. Between 65/1 and 66/6 the bakufu received an unprecedented number of protests and requests from vassal daimyo for release from various obligations.[81] Even if these requests did not, as they well may have done, betray a growing reluctance to aid the regime, they did betray a shrinking capacity to do so.

In sum the daimyo were less obedient than ever before and less capable or less willing to support the *bakuhan* system than ever in the past.

The functional upshot was that by mid-1866 the bakufu was nearly alone in its contest with Chōshū. But by itself it could not preserve the old order.

To recapitulate this chapter, we have seen several factors that left Edo ill-prepared to defeat Chōshū in war. At the level of administration and leadership, the regime was overwhelmed by a sense of doom. Its leaders were deeply fearful that their policy of crushing Chōshū would fail, but they were unable to see any acceptable alternative policy. The sense of doom was well founded. Nearly two years of work at military strengthening had achieved only modest results, and the army that the bakufu deployed was only partially modernized, wretchedly paid, and painfully demoralized. By itself the bakufu's own army was not large enough or effective enough to defeat Chōshū, and so the regime had to depend on daimyo support. But almost all the great daimyo refused to cooperate, and most of the lesser daimyo who did cooperate were unable to furnish significant numbers of effective troops. The weakness of both daimyo and bakufu forces was partially attributable to the economic difficulties of the regime. And in the case of the bakufu those difficulties were direct expressions of the disastrous fiscal experience of the preceding three years. The years 1863–1866, the years of conservative reaffirmation, had thus undermined the bakufu, prepared it for military defeat, and moved it far toward ultimate failure.

CHAPTER 7

The Foundations of Social Disaster

1863–1866

THE IMPERIALIST MENACE
1. *Karafuto and Other Intrusions*
2. *The Anglo-French Rivalry: Growing Complications for Japan*
3. *A Summing Up*

GENERAL DOMESTIC DETERIORATION
1. *Popular Unrest*
2. *Upheaval: 66/4–6*

CONSERVATIVE REAFFIRMATION IN RETROSPECT

At the level of visible political action the years 1863–1866 constituted for the bakufu an attempt at conservative reassertion that reached a peak of success in late 1864, only to disintegrate in the face of Chōshū intransigence. In the background during those same years the bakufu was encountering difficulties of administration, pursuing with no great success efforts at coastal defense and later army strengthening, plunging precipitously toward fiscal disaster, and losing daimyo goodwill. These trends all contributed to the military defeat that befell the regime during the summer of 1866.

In addition two other major background trends of the years of conservative reaffirmation also boded ill for the regime, regardless of how the war turned out. The foreigners were developing a presence in Japan that threatened to drag the nation willy-nilly into a state of colonial subjugation. Domestically the general public was beginning to experience a degree of hardship that was driving it to the point of general insurrection. Unless stopped, either of those trends would eventually destroy the Tokugawa order.

THE IMPERIALIST MENACE

During 1863–1864 foreign complications were at the heart of politics, but after about 64/10 they intruded blatantly only in the Hyōgo crisis a year later. In a less obtrusive way, however, the foreign problem was by 1865 developing dimensions that were much more menacing than in prior years. They threatened Japan as an independent society, doing so even more in 1865–1866 when the Chōshū issue dominated politics than in the earlier months when the foreign danger had been more apparent and commanded more attention.

One objective of the Tokugawa policy of isolation had been to preserve Japanese sovereignty, meaning Japanese control of Japanese territory and societal processes. Imperialist encroachments on that sovereignty during the decade or so after 1853 had involved incursions into both territory and processes. During 1865–1866 there was new escalation of the territorial encroachment, more intrusion into societal processes, and the adoption by the foreigners of new strategies designed to break down what remained of Japanese resistance to foreign wishes.

1. Karafuto and Other Intrusions

Before 1865 the territorial encroachment had been mostly in the form of treaty ports, halfhearted claims of convenience to such outlying areas as the Ogasawara islands and Tsushima, and an off-and-on Russo-Japanese debate over Karafuto, the southern half of the island of Sakhalin. In the final years of the regime it was the encroachment via Karafuto that proved to be the most menacing territorial form of the foreign danger. The matter has been well studied already,[1] and only aspects pertinent to the bakufu disintegration need to be touched upon here.

The Russian approach to Japan became a political problem at Edo early in the nineteenth century. At that time reports of the Russian march across Siberia and into the waters around Japan generated severe concern among officials. Renewed Russian activity in and around Japan in the 1850s revived that concern. Japanese attempts in 1858 and 1862 to reach an amicable settlement by dividing the island of Sakhalin in half at the fiftieth parallel came to naught, however, because of Russian intentions to extend their sway over the entire island if possible.[2]

In 1865 the bakufu's concern about the Russian advance from the north was revived. According to reports dispatched to the Hakodate magistrate by Japanese officials in Karafuto, in 65/7 a Russian warship reached Kusunae (presumably Kushunnai at the forty-eighth parallel) and deposited over one hundred settlers on the island in an overt attempt to secure by immigration and settlement an area claimed by both countries. The people living in the area reportedly fled for safety, and rumors began to circulate about more ships coming with more settlers and military supplies. The report called upon the magistrate to have Edo deal with the matter before the next spring thaw permitted the transfer of more settlers from the Asian mainland.[3]

The news of intensified Russian migratory pressure dismayed the magistrate, and he promptly sent his own report on it to Edo in early 65/9. News of the problem thus reached Edo just when the Hyōgo crisis was raging. Leaders there were not eager to tackle more foreign adversaries, but specialists on foreign affairs warned that inaction might lead to loss of the whole island. Accordingly Mizuno Tadakiyo wrote the Russian foreign minister to report the development. He recapitulated the prior attempts at a negotiated settlement and requested a definitive agreement on the boundary.[4]

While Mizuno's communication was in transit, the Karafuto matter continued to concern bakufu leaders. Then in early 1866 the situation there worsened. Edo learned that during 66/2 some Russians had attacked and temporarily detained a traveling bakufu investigator and his six subordinates near the southern end of the island.[5] This last evidence that at least some Russians intended to seize the entire island without regard to Japanese claims prompted more agitation by the Hakodate magistrate and led the bakufu in 66/6 to order the preparation of a mission to Russia in the coming year. Thus by the time of the Summer War it appeared to Edo that a Russian advance through the northern frontier of Japan had already begun.[6]

This migratory encroachment from the north was probably the most dangerous territorial problem during 1865–1866, but the constant badgering by foreign diplomats in regard to the treaty ports was a much more tiresome and equally open-ended form of the problem. During those years officials weathered an unending stream of requests and demands, especially from American and British delegates, for new consulates and port facilities and more land for residences, warehouses, hospitals, and recreation areas.[7] Officials also found themselves embroiled in frequent negotiations about alleged restraints on trade. The accusations, most commonly leveled by Harry Parkes, were sometimes justified, sometimes not.[8] Officials also devoted considerable time to the ramifications of their expanding diplomatic relations: embassies traveling abroad, permanent posts in foreign countries, passports, study abroad, the establishing of foreign-language programs in Japan, and the acquisition of materials on international law and procedure.[9]

Bakufu diplomats also found that as domestic affairs drifted toward war, the foreigners were becoming more active in hawking their military wares. The activity was also intensified because Japan was a market previously dominated by the Dutch but recently opened up to aggressive competition from others, notably the French, British, and Americans. Bakufu diplomats were repeatedly pressured, most feverishly perhaps by the Dutch whose privileged position was disappearing, to buy these guns, those ships, some other cannon, and so on.[10] British and other merchants also ignored the treaty clause prohibiting foreigners from selling weapons to *han* and sold munitions directly to them. The accelerating gunrunning not only damaged bakufu and domanial finances but, as we note in more detail below, also fostered mutual suspicion and helped enmesh them in the rivalries of the imperialist powers.

The Hyōgo crisis constituted in itself a dangerous new escalation of foreign assertiveness. In it the foreigners finally acted upon their long-standing threat to deal directly with the court if the regime with which they had established formal diplomatic relations did not respond satisfactorily to their desires.

Then during early 1866 tariff matters were arranged. By their nature they presented no great immediate political problems, but the Tariff Convention of 1866, which was largely the work of Parkes, constituted a major extension of imperialist privilege into Japan. It overcame a variety of bakufu mechanisms to regulate trade and contained a revised tariff that favored the foreigners. In Grace Fox's words it ''meant a great reduction in the revenues from their customs'' that the bakufu received, and it ''prevented the enactment [by the Japanese] of appropriate measures to protect the development of their own industry against the competition of foreign products.''[11] It was a solid foundation upon which to construct a massive and enduring imperial commercial establishment in Japan.

2. The Anglo-French Rivalry: Growing Complications for Japan

Until 1862 the Japanese-foreign relationship had been a relatively simple one of undisguised bipolar conflict in which foreigners used their superior power to bludgeon the Japanese into acquiescence. From the time of the Bunkyū reform, however, as the bakufu lost control of the polity and as foreign establishments in Japan grew more involved, the simple bipolar conflict gave way to a complex web of connections, alignments, and antagonisms. The first notable evidence of this trend appeared during the diplomatic crisis of early 1863 when foreign diplomats, even as they prepared to assault Edo, urged bakufu officials to cooperate with them against the opponents of the treaties. Officials refused to do so, and that foreign effort to pit Japanese against Japanese failed. In succeeding years, however, the mesh of connections grew more complicated, with the French, British, bakufu, and great daimyo of the southwest playing the key roles.

At one level the original bipolar conflict always survived, with the imperialists consistently closing ranks to secure the overriding objective of economic advantage. At another level, however, different nuances of advantage perceived by each of the four major parties led to a secondary pattern of Franco-bakufu versus British-daimyo alignment. The matter has been sufficiently studied that it only merits cursory review here in terms of its effect on bakufu survival. [12]

The French-bakufu connection began to develop during 1864 as a result of two separate initiatives: one in France during the visit of Ikeda Chōhatsu's mission, the other in Japan after the arrival of Léon Roches.

Ikeda, as we noted earlier, had been sent to Europe in late 1863 to arrange the closing of Yokohama and other matters. In Paris, however, French negotiators insisted on every concession previously won and sought several more besides. In the process they warned, in Medzini's words, ''that Yokohama would remain open either with the bakufu's consent or through the use of force by the foreign powers.''[13] Ikeda soon realized the futility of his mission and instead agreed to draft a treaty dealing with other matters. While doing so, he discovered that the French were willing to sell the bakufu some obsolete warships and other weapons. Reaching Edo in 64/7 he presented his revised draft treaty and a final report in which he mentioned a French offer of weapons and cooperation against domestic enemies. [14] At the time the bakufu was awash in a sea of problems, and its newly forged leadership was in no mood for more concessions or ties with foreigners. Consequently it repudiated his effort and promptly cashiered and confined him. For the time being that closed one avenue of French involvement in bakufu affairs.

Roches reached Japan in 64/3 while Ikeda was still in Europe. For several months after arriving he achieved very little. Like Ikeda he found bakufu leaders uninterested in forging political ties with France for use against the great lords. It was not until the latter part of 1864 that officials who would welcome foreign cooperation, notably Kurimoto Kon and Oguri Tadamasa, acquired or regained significant influence in affairs.

Nor was Roches himself eager at first to develop a special relationship. Rather, he adhered to the older policy of cooperating with the British against the Japanese. It was not until late in the year, as Alcock his diplomatic senior was leaving for home, that he began to pursue a tentatively independent policy. When he did, however, he found some officials ready to cooperate, and in those circumstances he was able to start moving into a role of particular intimacy with officialdom.

As the Chōshū problem intensified during late 1864–1865, officials such as councillors Abe Masatō and Sakai Tadamasu, as well as Oguri, Takemoto Masaaki, Yamaguchi Naoki, Shibata Masanaka, and Hirayama Keichū, became more receptive to Roches's argument that the bakufu should deal forcefully with Chōshū. That trend was reflected in the military reform discussed earlier. It was also evident in a larger program of Franco-bakufu economic cooperation that also developed in the prewar months. At the level of overt Franco-bakufu political cooperation against Chōshū, however, Roches was unable to make much headway.

To elaborate the last point, by mid-1865 the Franco-bakufu political relationship was becoming visible. Thus on 6/21, shortly after the shogun's move to Osaka, Roches at his own request met Kurimoto and Yamaguchi at Atami (where he was "taking the waters") and received information on the Chōshū situation. According to Kurimoto's report to the Osaka councillors on 7/9, Roches had offered naval assistance against Chōshū if it were needed, and the senior councillors at Edo had expressed interest in pursuing that possibility. When Abe and Matsumae wrote Roches on 8/27, however, they were more cautious, being content with a statement of appreciation for his goodwill and asking only his good offices in their attempts to stop illicit foreign ship activities at Shimonoseki.[15]

At the same time Roches apparently was trying to use Parkes' belligerence to aid French interests at British expense. As Yamaguchi explained matters to Ogasawara Nagamichi in 65/8 in a session preparing Ogasawara for his return to duty, Britain held extensive possessions in East Asia and so did not fear Russia and hoped to acquire territory in Japan. France, by contrast, did fear Russia and so supported a strong Japan.[16] The analysis was almost surely that of Roches, likely given at Atami, and it was not particularly sound. But it did suggest the complexity of his strategy and at least identified friend and foe clearly enough for any who chose to believe him. In following months he continued to cultivate the bakufu, but he failed to induce leaders to seek direct French support against Chōshū. The reason, perhaps, was that the Hyōgo crisis had removed from office several who might have welcomed his aid, notably

Sakai Tadamasu and Takemoto Masaaki. The modified bakufu leadership of the post-65/10 months was far too sensitive to opinion in Kyoto to accept overt French cooperation.[17]

In a less obvious way, however, Franco-bakufu economic cooperation did continue to grow during the next few months. That growth was achieved primarily by a mission that left Japan prior to the Hyōgo crisis and pursued its negotiations in France, far from the turmoil wracking the bakufu. When its accomplishments were in due course reported to Tokugawa leaders, they were welcomed in a manner contrasting sharply with the response to Ikeda's earlier effort.

To summarize the matter briefly, a decision in early 1865 to build a major shipyard at Yokosuka led to the dispatch of a mission to France to implement both that decision and others. The experienced diplomat Shibata Masanaka, who had already been on one mission to Europe and who got on well with Roches, headed the delegation. In 65/int. 5, even as the shogun was traveling toward Kyoto, his group departed for Europe with instructions to complete several assigned tasks. Shibata was to hire a Frenchman to serve as permanent representative of the bakufu in Paris. He was to help arrange purchase of a European coin-minting machine. He was to work out the details for purchasing shipyard equipment. He was to arrange the training of people in western technology, particularly mining and construction. Finally, he was to start preparations for Japanese participation in the scheduled Paris Exposition. Shibata made some progress on all these matters, notably locating a banker, Paul Fleury-Herard, to serve as the bakufu's representative in Paris.[18]

Meanwhile in Japan during 1865 some other officials, notably Oguri, were developing a larger vision of Franco-bakufu cooperation. In this plan an officially sponsored trading company would cooperate to carry on trade, presumably in a monopoly manner and primarily in raw silk thread (*kiito*). Its purpose was to generate funds with which the bakufu could pay for French military equipment and advisors and the other costs of technical development.[19] A joint Dutch-British protest against such a monopoly was turned aside, and discussions continued. The Shibata and Oguri efforts converged in 65/8 when Oguri and a fellow superintendent of finance wrote Fleury-Herard after learning of his interest in Shibata's proposal. They formally asked him to represent the bakufu in Paris and to facilitate the purchase of foundry equipment and a coin mint. They also asked him to set up the French end of the trading company and to help in setting up the Japanese end.[20]

Fleury-Herard accepted this formal offer and proceeded to work on his assignments. The French portion of the company was soon established, eventually being capitalized at about $1 million (60 million francs). During 66/4 he was able to write from Paris that French arrangements for the trading company had been made and that A. M. Coullet had just departed for Japan to implement the agreement. Then Fleury-Herard proceeded to urge that the bakufu move quickly to set up electric generators and railroads because they would permit rapid deployment of troops in war and development of trade in peace. To pay for such facilities he recommended taxing transportation, trade, and industrial production. And, he added, François Verny, who had previously been hired to supervise the Yokosuka shipyard construction, would shortly return to Yokohama and could furnish details about arranging the purchase of equipment for the shipyard.[21]

Thus due to the Shibata mission and the supplementary instructions from Oguri, the bakufu had by the time of the Summer War been able to develop the French end of an elaborate fiscal-military relationship that was designed to help the regime reform and strengthen itself and might be used as the gateway to industrial development.

The deepening French association with the bakufu was offset by a gradual shift in the British posture. The shift was toward a diplomatic and military sympathy and eventual support, partly tacit, partly active, for those great *han* pursuing an anti-bakufu policy.[22] That development was a threat to Edo in several ways. It was intrinsically damaging insofar as it increased the actual strength of the great *han*. It was debilitating because it reinforced bakufu suspicions that the great *han* were a sinister force that had to be crushed. And it enabled Roches to pursue more effectively his game of exploiting Edo's fears to secure greater advantages for France and more influence for himself. That process in turn exacerbated daimyo distrust of the bakufu and compromised more and more bakufu independence of France.

Probably the most important dimension of the British-daimyo connection lay in the area of weaponry. The very lucrative business of illegal British (and American) gunrunning to the great lords began with Satsuma and was mostly carried on by merchants at Nagasaki, notably T. B. Glover of the Jardine Matheson firm. Starting with a Satsuma request for three thousand Mini-style rifles in 64/4 and another request of 65/6 for an additional hundred of them, the Glover-Satsuma connection grew apace.[23]

In the context of the Edo-Chōshū rivalry, however, it was not Satsuma but Chōshū's military strengthening that particularly alarmed Edo. The Chōshū civil war of 64/12–65/2 apparently provided fertile soil for gunrunning, and in the latter month Edo received reports of extensive illicit foreign trade at Shimonoseki. The reports were confirmed by Roches a month later in a message that explained how actively Chōshū was acquiring western military technology. Then on 4/14 Katsu Kaishū heard that Chōshū was employing a ''disreputable American'' military man to train troops.[24]

Alarmed by the news that Chōshū was being supplied by ship, the bakufu in 65/5 sought and obtained from a Kokura official additional information on the maritime activity. During the next few months the bakufu's concern with the illicit trade was repeatedly evinced, and reports kept Edo informed. The most overt violations were stopped by the deployment of bakufu ships to the west after mid-1865, but then the trade, especially that in weaponry, simply went underground, so to speak, being handled at night and through middlemen, notably Satsuma. The most striking instance occurred in 65/8 when Chōshū arranged the purchase from Glover of a warship and some 7300 rifles, of which 4300 were Mini-style.[25] In following months the trade continued to flourish.

The gunrunning certainly was not a British monopoly; Americans did very well by it. Edo saw it as primarily a British matter, however, and that view was reinforced by the tacit approval British diplomats gave the illicit trade. Thus when newly assigned to Japan from China in 65/int. 5, and even before presenting his credentials to the bakufu, Parkes visited Chōshū officials at Shimonoseki to check coastal defenses and sound out their views on matters. While there he heard the Chōshū version of domestic affairs, saw Mini-armed units, and was told the *han* needed two thousand rifles. He did not say the weapons would be supplied. However, even though the treaty he was supposed to adhere to and enforce expressly prohibited sale of munitions to anyone except the bakufu, he also did not say that British firms could not and would not supply the weapons without bakufu approval.[26] Nor did he in following months make any real effort to discourage the illegal traffic. His function, after all, was not to obstruct trade profitable to England.

Parkes' own dubious conduct was only part of what Edo perceived, with considerable justification, as a broader pattern of unfriendly British–great daimyo interaction.[27] The instances of Satsuma and British activity that most worried bakufu leaders were these. In late 1865 the bakufu learned of a daimyo mission to Europe, apparently an arms mission, and later Edo determined that it was from Satsuma. By early 1866 that mission was indeed in London actively seeking political support as well as arms. And its pleas elicited a favorable response, even to include ''a very large loan.'' In the latter part of 1865 bakufu officials, who correctly believed one of Satsuma's great goals to be direct access to foreign trading activity, saw the malevolent hand of Satsuma in the court's opposition to opening Hyōgo and even in subsequent proposals by Roches that another port—presumably Kagoshima—be opened instead. Then in early 1866 Ernest Satow, a politically active functionary in the British legation, wrote and had translated into Japanese a series of articles. In them he urged that foreigners no longer treat Japan as a single polity headed by the bakufu but rather as a cluster of daimyo principalities, which he doubtless recognized would be less capable of resisting foreign economic inroads. At about the same time British diplomats and Glover played an instrumental role in facilitating the Satsuma-Chōshū rapprochement that was to prove so disastrous to the bakufu a few months later.

The upshot of all these developments was that by early 1866 Japanese political leaders were thoroughly enmeshed in the Anglo-French imperialist rivalry. By then daimyo and bakufu suspicions of one another were feeding upon and fostering ever more cooperation with foreigners against one another. The interaction of foreign ties and domestic suspicions was neither immediate nor fully rational, however. Thus it was the Shibata mission that really advanced Franco-bakufu ties and should have been at the root of Satsuma distrust of the bakufu in 1866. But in the end it apparently was a report explaining the earlier Ikeda mission, which Satsuma received during the Summer War, that seemed to reveal the bakufu effort against Chōshū as part of a larger scheme to destroy the *han* in general. To explain the alleged purpose of the contemporary Shibata mission, the report asserted that Ikeda had urged the establishment of close ties between the shogun and France. He supposedly had urged construction of an arsenal at Yokohama, with funds borrowed from France and repaid at the rate of 250,000 (*ryō*?) per year over five years. He reportedly had proposed bringing French military advisors to Yokohama to train bakufu troops and convert the English-Dutch style forces to French. Using that power base, Ikeda reportedly had argued, the bakufu should weaken the daimyo and unify the country.[28]

The report to Satsuma may in fact have been close to what Ikeda had argued, but of course he had been repudiated and put into confinement for a rather long time. By the time of the Summer War, however, the orientation of bakufu leadership had changed considerably, and the Ikeda view was in process of becoming bakufu policy. The report was thus a somewhat better guide to current bakufu-French relations than the history of the Ikeda mission itself would have suggested. It helped confirm Satsuma distrust of Edo at about the same time that reports of Satsuma-British contacts were convincing bakufu leaders that that *han* was working to destroy the Tokugawa regime.

3. A Summing Up

During the three years before the Summer War the bakufu found itself slipping at an accelerating rate into the colonial slough. It had to confront a territorial threat to its northern frontier and allowed steady inroads at the treaty ports. It watched almost helplessly as foreign arms poured into the country and foreigners established ties with its incipient domestic enemies. Its finances grew more chaotic, and it was on the verge of going seriously into debt to foreigners. It was accepting foreign advisors, in the process yielding up some degree of authority to them, needing their advice on domestic affairs, and beginning the long-range process of remodeling Japanese society in some degree to the foreigners' specifications.

The Franco-British rivalry helped Edo insofar as it secured the bakufu's access to French assistance. But as we have seen, that assistance was niggardly, slow in coming, and sacrificed when necessary to advance the overriding interests of elemental Franco-British cooperation. The limited value of Roches's goodwill was most apparent in the matter of treaties and treaty ports, where his commitment to French interest was most compelling. Thus in the 65/9 crisis Roches and Parkes and the others all insisted on imperial approval of the treaties. Roches put his own posture in a favorable light, but he accepted most of Parkes's objectives and cooperated in attaining them. Only at the end did he, in adherence to his government's instructions, apparently help persuade Parkes not to insist on the immediate opening of Hyōgo and to accept bakufu treasure instead. When the bakufu sought to delay indemnity payments, the foreigners closed ranks. When treaty port concessions were to be made, they were as one.[29]

The imperialist rivalry hurt Edo insofar as it facilitated daimyo self-strengthening. It hurt too insofar as it exacerbated domestic political suspicions. Satsuma and Chōshū men had found it easy to believe that the earlier assaults on Shimonoseki and Kagoshima had enjoyed some degree of bakufu sponsorship or approval. By mid-1865 Mori Arinori of Satsuma suspected that Shibata's mission was intended to secure French support for bakufu policy against the great *han*. He also felt it reflected bakufu suspicions that Satsuma would in future be an increasing menace.[30] His fear of Franco-bakufu ties was shared by others. Thus Takasugi Shinsaku of Chōshū evidently regarded the shogunal expedition of 1865 as a joint Franco-bakufu attack on Chōshū.[31] Then after the British shifted to a policy of associating with the great *han*, the suspicions of foreign complicity became mutual and contributed appreciably to the steady erosion of bakufu-*han* goodwill. On balance one must conclude that the advantages to Edo of French cooperation were more than offset by the disadvantages of the resultant diplomatic complications.

In sum then, the diplomatic problems of 1863–1866 were exacerbations of former problems in terms of administrative bothers, political embarrassments, treaty port concessions, and expenses. But the problems were new in terms of encroachment by permanent settlers, foreigner-great *han* cooperation, and a visible Japanese dependence on foreigners for military training and technology. The years to 66/6 had seen the bakufu move well along the route to a colonial abasement that could be ruinous for bakufu and Japan alike.

GENERAL DOMESTIC DETERIORATION

The escalation in the imperialist menace was matched by escalation in the domestic crisis. There is massive evidence that by 1866 the old order was coming apart at the seams. We have seen evidence relating to the rulers, but among the general public too it is apparent that the political crisis of the 1860s was beginning to hurt much broader segments of the populace than ever before. Although the *shishi* had been quieted, there was appearing extensive popular unrest stemming from basic personal hardships and conflicts of interest. Even before the Edo-Chōshū quarrel was put to the test of steel, the ravaged public erupted in massive turmoil.

1. Popular Unrest

The elite's crackdown on *shishi* in 1864–1865 eliminated much of the visible discontent. Plotters, placards, and assassins disappeared from view. Even as they did so, however, hardships affecting both urban and rural people were beginning to appear. In the cities prices were rising very rapidly as government fiscal policies grew more reckless, as resources were diverted to swelling armies, and as the samurai population shifted from Edo to Osaka, Kyoto, and *han* castle towns. In Kyoto growing demand helped push prices up. In Edo food prices rose as daimyo reduced the volume of rice they sent to the city and as bakufu forces stored it for the coming campaign.

Bakufu leaders were well aware that inflation boded ill for the regime and that its control depended on sufficient production of goods and their effective distribution. Thus an order of 64/4 prohibited the shift of land use from rice and dry field foods to mulberry development. The order was needed, most likely, because profitable foreign sales of silk had fostered such mulberry production at the expense of foodstuffs. A year later in 65/3 a senior council order to lesser officials pointed out that prices had risen recently despite prior orders forbidding it, and the rise was causing severe hardship for the people. Moreover, the order continued, although the eruption in Kyoto and *rōnin* trouble of the previous autumn had been quelled, still productivity in the provinces needed to be increased and appropriate officials were to attend to that. They were also to facilitate the shipment of rice, prevent hoarding by villagers, and investigate all instances of such problems.[32] Concern about the urban grain supply persisted, however, and three months later the bakufu ordered more grain brought to Edo. A month after that, when the shogun was in Osaka, the city magistrate there ordered daimyo to bring grain to that city. According to that notice, rice reserves in the city had been depleted despite orders of 1864 to increase them. Due to flood losses in various places and the large numbers of troops in Osaka, the notice continued, inflation and public hardship were particularly severe, and therefore certain major daimyo were to bring more rice into the city.[33]

Governmental efforts to keep the urban peace evidently were sufficient for the time being, but malign trends continued to be evident. In Edo during the year there were the usual fires, including one in the Asakusa district that killed some thirty people. There were problems of burglars and occasional acts of individual violence. By the end of 1865 the city had become dangerous by night. Indeed prison records of Edo indicate that after a modest decline in the rate of commoner and minor samurai jailings in the city during 1864, there was a sharp increase in such jailings the following year.[34] That increase seems to suggest that beneath the surface the trend of developments was not good and only force majeure was preserving the peace. Katsu Kaishū reported that by the end of 1865 the combined pressure of devaluations, forced levies, inflation, and coin forgery had severely disrupted the urban economy.[35] After the shogun's arrival in Osaka public criticism and mocking of the bakufu was evident there.[36] Still and all, the urban turmoil was minimal considering the number of troops assembled in the cities and the extent of economic dislocation.

In the cities, then, the peace still held but there was evidence of growing hardship and explosive potential. In the countryside, too, evidence of increasing hardship was available. There was grumbling along the Tōkaidō because the shogunal progress of 1865 diverted large quantities of men, horses, and boats during the planting season.[37] Quite apart from the immediate cause, the grumbling was also one expression of a rural problem of much greater magnitude.

To elaborate, the highway system with its heavy use of porters, coolies, and pack animals depended upon the imposition of manpower levies on surrounding villages. Bakufu regulations fixed both the service obligations of villages and the rates charged to users of the service. These service obligations had always been heavy, and for years bakufu orders had repeatedly modified them to ease the burden. However, the inflation of the 1860s combined with the vast increase in road traffic to intensify village distress as able-bodied men spent more and more time at corvée work for fees that were becoming less and less adequate. The inflation and turmoil of 1864 wrought particular havoc. By the following year two shogunal trips, the Kantō insurrection, and the Chōshū expedition had created such hardships that daimyo with lands on the highways found their tax sources drying up and their burden of relief to impoverished villagers growing. In consequence some began petitioning the bakufu to excuse villages from corvée duty.[38] Thus in one early instance of the petitions, in 64/12 former supreme councillor Matsudaira Naokatsu of Kawagoe asked Edo to exempt from duty his villages in Musashi province and Saitama district. He explained that in that area crops had failed recently and there had been forest fires. Moreover there had been special defense assignments due to the Kantō insurgency, the defense of Nikkō, and the manning of coastal cannon emplacements. Furthermore, because of much intensified highway traffic in recent years villages had also had unusually heavy post-station duties. He requested therefore that the added corvée duties for the shogun's trip be waived.[39] Requests of that sort, which Edo received again and again in following months, were hard to refuse, but the manpower was needed. As a compromise gesture the bakufu raised the user rates at some places, although that meant increasing its own travel costs.

Hardship along the highways reflected a conflict of interests between the rural people and the rulers. A stream of complaints and protests reaching Edo from silk-producing areas burdened by silk-related taxes reflected another ruler–ruled conflict.[40] Other problems, however, caught the rulers in conflicts of interest between sectors of the public. Two instances were revealed by efforts of bakufu administrators in Osaka in 1864–1865 to hold down prices in two key commodities of daily use, cotton wadding and rapeseed oil. In 64/2 the Osaka city magistrate's office attempted to regulate the cotton wadding market by prohibiting all but authorized merchants from dealing in the material. The effort reflected a long-time dispute over control of the Kinai cotton trade. And more immediately it probably was a response to price rises following a great fire that destroyed some 14,500 houses in Osaka in 63/11,[41] although it may have been designed to anticipate demand by the army that was supposed to punish Chōshū before long. Whatever the reason for the order, it was resisted by a vigorously led producer organization in adjacent provinces. Within a few months the resistance obliged city officials to give up their effort, even though the great fire in Kyoto in 64/7 and then the assembling of an army to suppress Chōshū surely pushed prices even higher. Similarly, in early 1865 efforts by the same office to regulate the sale of rapeseed oil in Osaka elicited a broad-based and energetic resistance by producer organizations. By 66/3 the office again yielded to the demand for unregulated sales, despite the accelerating inflationary pressures of crop failure and impending war. Capitulation eased the open criticism by producers, but failure to curb inflation invited further criticism from the court and enhanced the risk of urban riot.[42]

In several ways, then, economic problems that directly involved the general public were bedeviling the regime more than in the past and creating discontent in both city and village. Yet the year 1865 proved reasonably tranquil. The only major disturbance was in 65/5 when some 1500 people in Iida town and nearby villages in central Japan went on a smashing spree due to high rice prices. They attacked grain shops and were temporarily successful in forcing the price down again. Prompt action by local *han* forces quieted the area by month's end, and there was no similar eruption again in Japan for nearly a year.[43]

The year 1866 was to prove very different. There is considerable evidence that the 1865 harvest was bad, just when marching armies were consuming rice in great quantities.[44] In the Kantō the rainy season dragged on into the sixth month (end of July), thus making for a short ripening season. In Uwajima heavy rains damaged the crop severely. In Echizen the autumn yield was off an estimated 20 percent. In Tsu *han* losses of nearly 150,000 *koku* were reported in the crop. It would thus appear that in a large part of central Japan rice production was down, and by spring of 1866 food supplies were growing short and an explosive inflation was beginning to rack the country.

By 66/4 matters had deteriorated so badly that the price of rice rapidly doubled and in places quadrupled. This change in rice price was paralleled by changes in other basic commodity prices, as the accompanying tables show.[45] The situation reportedly drove some of the indigent in Kyoto to commit suicide and prompted the court in that month to order Katamori to reduce prices in the city. The wild inflation was not limited to the cities, however, as the price schedule from Kariya, southeast of Nagoya, indicates.[46] The bakufu tried to restrain prices by various edicts and measures, including a severe crackdown on rice dealers, most of whom were overcharging.[47] It was unable to stop the inflation, however, and its lack of success was soon reflected in mass outbreaks of extraordinary severity.

Osaka Rice Prices (in silver monme per koku)

Year	Spring	Summer	Winter
1862	141.0	152.0	142.8
1863	157.3	140.0	150.0
1864	154.4	149.8	210.5
1865	248.3	299.5	447.9
1866	467.4	782.0	1373.6
1867	1388.8	856.1	722.0

Edo Consumer Prices

Year	Bean Paste (monme/kan)	Salt	Soy Sauce (monme/koku)	Sake (monme/koku)	Lamp Oil (monme/sho)	Cotton Cloth (monme/tan)
1862	3.1	45.0	146.0	326.0	6.2	8.8
1863	3.0	48.0	159.0	338.0	6.2	14.1
1864	3.0	62.0	190.0	341.0	8.8	26.5
1865	4.5	95.0	240.0	534.0	9.5	23.6
1866	6.8	113.0	256.0	767.0	9.7	37.5
1867	8.5	114.0	285.0	905.0	11.2	48.4

Edo Consumer Price Indices

Year	Method I*	Method II†
1862	190.0	191.5
1863	194.5	250.1
1864	223.4	398.6
1865	309.7	416.0
1866	397.8	602.1
1867	462.0	743.1

*Method I: bean paste, salt, soy sauce, sake, lamp oil.
†Method II: bean paste, salt, soy sauce, sake, lamp oil,
cotton cloth.

Kariya Rice Prices

Date	Mon/Shō	Date	Mon/Shō	Date	Mon/Shō
1865/1	178	1865/8	272	1866/5	585
2	178	9	290	6	542
3	182	10	328	7	564
4	200	11	334	8	572
5	214	12	348	9	612
Int. 5	244	1866/1	360	10	650
6	280	2	380	11	688
7	284	3	420	12	688
		4	558		

2. Upheaval: 66/4–6

Public order first dissolved in the Kantō. Reports spoke of public discontent, scattered agitation, groups of ''troublemakers'' assembling and moving about here and there, and village defense forces deploying against outsiders. In mid-66/4 people from thirty-eight villages in Hitachi assembled and launched an assault on rice merchants, attacking and destroying their houses. A month later peasants in two villages in Shimōsa province also erupted, attacking rice storage facilities. The same weeks saw outbursts in other rural areas in Kai, Kawachi, Bitchū, and other provinces.

While explosive discontent was thus beginning to vent itself in the countryside, the cities also were starting to erupt. These latter upheavals were much more visible to bakufu leaders and hence more alarming. As war neared in early 66/5, the Osaka-Hyōgo area was the site of widespread unrest.[48] The reason was not hard to find. Hulled rice that should have been selling for about 200 *mon* per *shō* was selling at prices ranging from 400 to 800, a level that most commoners could hardly afford. From 5/3 commoners in Nishinomiya began demanding that merchants reduce rice prices. The demands spread, and in Hyōgo, on the eighth, one or two thousand people armed with sticks and bamboo spears started moving about in groups of hundreds, smashing and looting. In response local commanders of various vassal *han* forces deployed troops. Some of the troops fired blank shot at the rioters, but that had no effect and so patrol forces charged with pikes and in some places used lethal shot and possibly cannon. For a few days the trouble continued, a number were killed. many more were wounded, and the upheaval spread.

The numbers grew to three thousand, perhaps ten thousand, and involved poor villagers from nearby areas. By 5/14 the Osaka populace itself was emboldened to join the fray despite a chilly pouring rain and the presence of thousands of troops. Crowds assembled and went to the shops of pawnbrokers and dealers in oil, sake, and rice. They extorted when they could and smashed when they could not. Some 192 rice shops were reported sacked and 2144 *koku* (about 10,000 bushels) of rice stolen. A few rioters were killed and hundreds were arrested, but rice prices in the city dropped rapidly in following days.

For the Kinai the worst was over, but during 66/6 the Kyoto area continued to be disturbed by gangs, and inflation spawned popular protests. These prompted the court to instruct several great daimyo to bring more rice to the city and the bakufu to release more stored rice for popular consumption. Many daimyo refused to furnish the rice, however, probably because they lacked reserves. Consequently the basis of hardship remained.[49]

At Edo too there was trouble.[50] During 66/4 in the Ryōgoku section of town some people had been placarding and agitating. They were demanding reduced rice prices and warned of a popular protest, but it did not materialize. Probably in reaction to the Kantō and Kinai turmoil and in fear of its involving Edo, the bakufu reportedly released some 20,000 *hyō* of rice for sale in mid-66/5. Perhaps it was this act that caused the retail price of rice to drop temporarily from some 370 *ryō* per 100 *hyō* to 200 *ryō*, which was still well above pre-1865 levels. The measure had little effect outside of town, however, and from about 5/20 in adjoining villages north and south of the city group agitation began to accelerate. It was fostered partly, no doubt, by the long-standing hardship of the highway stations.

On 5/28 at Shinagawa station just south of Edo a mob assembled and attacked some forty-one shops in the vicinity. On the next day mobs in the Shiba district of Edo sacked some eighty-six rice, sake, oil, and loan shops. In the next few days smashing occurred in the adjoining Azabu, Akasaka, and Yotsuya areas. The rioters were fewer than in Osaka: some 100 to 300 reported at Shinagawa and 700 to 800 in Shiba, and many were reported as young people fifteen to eighteen years old. In succeeding days the trouble continued. On 6/1–3 districts adjacent to the castle, particularly Kanda, were thrown into confusion as mobs smashed buildings. Then rival police patrols sent to quiet them ran amok and fought among themselves. All in all, it was a most inauspicious moment to launch a war against Chōshū.

The riots, the police violence, and later troubles in the city led to the sacking of the Edo city magistrate and the issuance of various regulations tightening up control there. It is apparent from these orders that with most of their army off to the west and other elements out restoring order in the Kantō, Edo authorities were scraping the bottom of the barrel in their search for guard forces. They had to settle for only a few men, two, three, or four, from each daimyo or liege vassal of stature.[51]

This upheaval within the city troubled Edo leaders, but it was primarily turmoil in the hinterland that occupied the daimyo of eastern Japan. During early 66/6 the rural unrest that had begun to appear in preceding weeks escalated to large-scale lawlessness. Musashi province, and particularly areas administered by Kawagoe *han*, became agitated. People gathered at meetings in Kawagoe town from about 6/7 to demand that rice prices be reduced. With similar agitation by groups elsewhere the clamor rapidly swelled and spread, involving thousands and thousands of people who surged about in many interacting movements large and small in scores of villages in four districts (*gun*) of Musashi. Not until the eighteenth was the upheaval quelled by forces of local *han* using rifles and cannon and supported by peasant militia units and hundreds of troops sent out by the hard-pressed leaders in Edo. In the upheaval the desperate protesters extorted supplies when possible, and otherwise sacked and burned the houses of the wealthy. In the lands of Kawagoe *han* alone, the daimyo report said, 94 houses were wrecked, 134 warehouses in 25 locations were sacked, 118 people were captured alive, and 2 had died. Elsewhere, too, hundreds were captured and others were killed and wounded.[52]

Almost at the same time a great upheaval occurred in Mutsu far to the north. There peasants in two districts erupted in violent protest of silk-related taxes, inflation, and other complaints. Starting on 6/15 purposeful rioters attacked the wealthy, seized supplies, and continued rampaging in village after village by the hundreds and thousands until about the twenty-fourth. By then most *han* in the region had deployed forces, many armed with firearms, and slowly but with difficulty they subdued the rioters and restored order.[53]

Just as the turbulence in Edo revealed the weakness of forces of control there, so the contemporary outburst in the Kantō hinterland laid bare the regime's weakness in that region. In Kawagoe the turmoil prompted *han* officials in 66/7 to mobilize a *han*-controlled peasant militia. Villagers in the northern part of the *han* acquiesced, but some eighteen villages in the southern part nearer Edo protested, fearful that the men would be sent off to fight Chōshū and that the order would create added burdens for the villages. During 66/8–10 they sent *han* leaders a series of written appeals, delegations, and organized assemblages of protesters. *Han* leaders feared the matter might lead again to new outbursts and took care to handle the protesters delicately. By 66/11 they had succeeded in persuading the villagers to accept the new order.[54] In short the *han* had found itself dependent on peasant support to keep law and order and had finally obtained that support, but only after much trouble.

Thus even before the Chōshū fighting erupted, economic dislocations had generated widespread unrest that climaxed in 66/6. It did quiet down for a while from 66/7, but a grim future had already been accurately foreshadowed on the night of 5/14 when a major storm smashed across central Japan and heavy rains and flooding wracked the provinces of Yamashiro, Tanba, and Echizen. It was the first in a rash of natural disasters that would fuel even worse popular trouble later in the year.[55]

The appearance of public hardship and unrest was troublesome to the bakufu for at least a couple of reasons. Coming as it did just when the regime was embarking on a major war, it raised the specters of total upheaval and collapse and demonstrated the thinness of the regime's police capacity. It also was blunt evidence that the economy had been stretched to the limit. There were no remaining reserves of food or wealth to commandeer. There were no easily exploitable resources of manpower that could be mobilized and sustained in political service. Moreover the unrest constituted additional proof, if it were needed, that the bakufu was not doing what court and samurai morality expected it to do—namely, unify the nation psychologically and put the emperor at ease by securing the well-being of his people. And while one could fairly point out that the insurrectionary behavior of courtier and samurai was a principal cause of the crisis, that is no adequate response because the burden of keeping the peace fell upon those who claimed the right to govern.

CONSERVATIVE REAFFIRMATION IN RETROSPECT

Between the Bunkyū reform of 1862 and the Summer War of 1866 bakufu leaders made a determined effort to reconstruct the good old days. After two years of agonizingly slow progress their whole effort fell apart in a string of reverses that culminated in disastrous military defeat.

We have seen how bakufu leaders struggled to rebuild their position after Shungaku's failure and the ways in which they appeared to be succeeding by late 1864. Chapter 4 suggested that the most impressive aspect of the conservative revival was the regime's apparent success in beating back the repeated court-daimyo-*shishi* assaults on its prerogatives. That success, however, was less a product of Tokugawa strength than of the inherent structural weakness of any movement that depended upon the combined power of those three institutionally unintegrated segments of society. Unfortunately for Edo the weakness of the whole did not mean that all the parts were weak. Most obviously, although the court-daimyo-*kōbugattai* coalition collapsed in both 1863 and 1864, the daimyo domains that were basic to it were individually beyond Edo's reach because of the regime's military inadequacy, an inadequacy demonstrated during the Kantō insurrection. Bakufu leaders may have congratulated themselves in the belief that the restoration of peace in the Kantō and then Chōshū's capitulation reflected the effectiveness of a Tokugawa will to prevail, but the greatest daimyo felt secure enough that many cavalierly spurned Edo's repeated attempts to restore the *sankin kōtai* system.

Nor could Edo properly claim all the credit for throttling the wave of *shishi* restorationism that had blossomed in 1862 and been suppressed during 1864–1865 in blood and blasted visions. In the east, it is true, the Kantō insurgency had been quelled, its instigators cruelly punished, and the vassal forces of Kantō *han* brought into line. And that was primarily bakufu handiwork. In the Kinai, however, where radical courtiers had been chastised and driven from positions of influence, and elsewhere in the country where *han* vassals were forced back into line, it was really the work of court and *han* leaders. And in the far west where the Chōshū radicals had been temporarily repudiated, some of their leaders executed, and their fief humiliated by foreign attack and domestic intimidation, it was really a transitory court triumph based on daimyo power. The bakufu's role in it was almost nil.

The apparent defeat of restorationism was thus not a victory attributable simply to the bakufu's conservative reaffirmation. Rather it was a temporary victory of high-ranking over lower-ranking members of the samurai and noble status groups. The fact that the bakufu as an institution benefited from the suppression of restorationism was almost incidental. That situation, however, seems to have been lost upon those at Edo who saw themselves as restoring an essentially worthy social order. In gradually triumphing over court and daimyo during 1864, those men alienated many who in fact were their allies of convenience in the contemporary repression of *shishi*. In consequence *shishi* activism was able to revive later, combining again with court-daimyo elements in new, more disciplined threats to the regime.

By the end of 1864 Edo had attained a level of triumph not so very unlike that earlier achieved by Ii Naosuke. It was about as successful as a conservative reaffirmation could be, benefiting from the weaknesses of its challengers and maximizing the value of its own residual prestige and powers. But it was success of a flawed variety, for it would have restored a political order fundamentally inadequate to the world of *bakumatsu* Japan. Consequently it could not endure, and in early 1865 its next crisis was foretold in the outcome of the Chōshū civil war. That war forged a new and superior form of daimyo-*shishi* alliance, one that had the potential later to become part of a fully revitalized court-daimyo-*shishi* coalition.

The narrative political history of the eighteen months leading to the Summer War is essentially the history of a tortuous and futile effort by the bakufu to intimidate peacefully men who would yield only to force. At a deeper level the history of those months also reveals much to explain why in 1866 Edo was unable to assemble sufficient force to compel Chōshū's capitulation. It reveals the limited success of military strengthening, the dubious value of foreign cooperation, the alienation of some daimyo, the immobilization of others, the disintegration of the bakufu fisc, and the erosion of Tokugawa morale. The forces that could support the regime would not and those that would, could not. The vulnerability of the bakufu was evident as never before.

At yet a deeper level it was becoming apparent during those eighteen months that Japan was slipping rapidly into the colonial slough. It was also becoming evident that the fiscal problems were not merely problems of the bakufu but of the entire system. They were affecting the entire samurai class, the supporters of the regime, most acutely. And they were fast becoming more basic economic problems. The political superstructure was evidently consuming the production of society faster than society could replace the food, fodder, and matériel consumed. Consequently the turmoil of the decade was at last beginning to affect the general populace widely and seriously. Revolutionary activity by lower members of the elite had been momentarily thwarted, except in Chōshū, but conditions favorable to either western imperialist conquest or more broadly based domestic revolution seemed to be developing.

Even before fighting erupted on 66/6/7 the prospects for the bakufu, for the samurai class, and for Japan as a whole were very bleak indeed. In following weeks the situation went from bleak to disastrous.

CHAPTER **8**

The Summer War of 1866

1866/6–8

The Summer War of 1866 was a decisive event in Japanese history. It marked the end of the old era, the start of the new. It marked it in several ways.

Bakufu defeat dealt a major blow to the residual fiction of Tokugawa supremacy, making it brutally clear to lesser *han* leaders all over Japan that they must fend for themselves, stripped of that protection from over-weening neighbors which Tokugawa hegemony had long given them.

Conversely Tokugawa defeat demonstrated that a great *han* constituted an effective instrument of political action, a lesson learned and thereafter acted upon by those in a position to do so. Although it did not become apparent until later, the Summer War had in fact determined the character of Japan's future leadership.

Moreover, military defeat destroyed the influence within the bakufu of those who had labored to preserve the old order and shifted policy sharply away from the conservative reassertion of 1864. At first the shift was back toward the inclusivistic *kōbugattai* strategy of Shungaku's Bunkyū reform. But within weeks the intrinsic futility of that approach demonstrated itself again. Thereafter the postwar bakufu was a semicoordinated instrument of revolutionary change pursuing policies as radical as those of its enemies. In the outcome bakufu leaders settled upon a strategy embodying both the exclusivistic characteristics of late 1864 and the progressive institutional reform characteristics of 1862. Like Shungaku's political reform, it was a strategy that would destroy the existing system. But whereas Shungaku's reform proposed no really functional alternative, the leaders of the postwar strategy that I call the Keiō reform attempted to create sinews of power that would eventually sustain a central government controlling all Japan and pursuing a range of ''modernizing'' enterprises.

Lastly the war demonstrated in a decisive manner that the old military system was obsolete. It thereby discredited defenders of the elite samurai military order and destroyed the ultimate rationale of samurai leadership in society. Examination of the fighting on the Aki (Hiroshima) front will make that military lesson quite clear and may suggest some sobering implications of the lesson.

All this probably would not have happened, at least not at that time, had Chōshū been defeated and the policies of conservative reassertion seemingly vindicated after their year and a half of setbacks.

THE SUMMER WAR: AN OVERVIEW

Bakufu armies were habitually miracles of disorganization. They assembled slowly and unpredictably and fought sporadically. At Osaka in 1614, at Shimabara in 1638, and, after the Great Peace had ended, in the Kantō in 1864 bakufu armies had grown slowly, undergone reverses, and only after surviving painful first efforts eventually acquired mass and momentum sufficient to overwhelm the opposition.

In 66/6 the bakufu began to run through the same pattern.[1] Fighting began on 6/7 with a naval bombardment of Ōshima, the principal island off the coast of Chōshū south of Iwakuni. Seven days later it began on the Aki front north of Iwakuni and two days after that on the Japan Sea coast in Iwami province. A day later fighting began at Kokura across the strait from Shimonoseki. This ill-coordinated commencement of war was surpassed by the dismal outcome of battle. It is true that the first sally at Ōshima by a joint force of bakufu and Matsuyama (Iyo) troops was successful. The Chōshū forces there were driven away and the island captured. But on 6/15 the enemy reappeared, attacked, and within three days had driven the invaders off the island. Elsewhere things went worse.

At the Aki front, as we note in more detail later on, advance units of Hikone and Takata attacked on land at the Ose river. They were defeated immediately and retreated several kilometers into Hiroshima territory. In Iwami the initial efforts of Hamada and Fukuyama troops were fruitless. They were outmaneuvered and driven into a defensive corner. Given no assistance and lacking firearms, they charged in desperation with swords and lances, only to be repulsed by Chōshū rifles and cannon. After a costly escape, they retreated. The next day at Kokura hard fighting erupted when Chōshū forces in five ships invaded Moji. The fighting was fierce, its intensity betraying the deep hatred Kokura felt toward its arrogant and overweening neighbor. In the outcome, however, the forces of Kurume refused to assist, and the men of Kokura and its related fiefs were forced to retreat until reinforcements from Kumamoto entered the battle, stabilized the front, and let the fighting end. The intended attack near Hagi never even began: Satsuma was to have been the main force there and it had refused to send troops.

On the battlefield everything seemed to be going wrong. The trend was worrisome, but it was not necessarily disastrous since it was the customary beginning to war by the peace-oriented Tokugawa regime. It also was not surprising that the first reverses were followed by quiescent periods on the several fronts. At the Ōshima front activity had ceased by 6/19. In Iwami the reverses of 6/16–23 were followed by a long quiet period as Hamada waited futilely for reinforcements. At Kokura bakufu officials wrote hurriedly to Osaka, reporting Chōshū's immense firepower advantage, the unreliability of daimyo allies, and their own need for more firearms. Ogasawara Nagamichi tried to prevent further rout by restraining Kokura until it was adequately reinforced, and Kokura commanders supported him by demanding in vain that their tired troops be replaced.

While those fronts were quiet, the lumbering machine of war began to experience improvements on the main battlefield in Aki. There the routed Hikone-Takata forces were replaced by bakufu infantry *(hohei)* under infantry commander Takenaka Shigemoto and units of Shingū *han* under

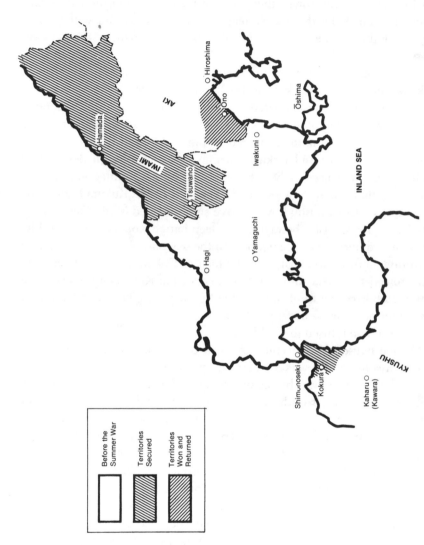

MAP 3. Chōshū Gains in 1866. Adapted from map no.35, *Shōwa Nihon chizu* (Tokyo: Tokyo Kaiseikan, 1941).

their daimyo Mizuno Tadamoto, who also was an attached elder *(tsuki karō)* of Kii. These forces were trained in western firearms tactics and upon commitment to battle repelled a Chōshū attack on 6/19. On the following day combined bakufu legation guards *(bette gumi)* and Miyazu *han* forces of Honjō Munehide also stopped an attack by Chōshū on another part of the Aki front. Five days later Chōshū forces launched another attack, overextended themselves, and were again driven back in hard fighting with combined forces of Ōgaki, Shingū, Kii, and the bakufu.

These efforts stabilized the Aki front near the town of Ōno and suggested that in classic fashion the tide was beginning to turn. The classic pattern was not followed in succeeding weeks, however, mostly because of the unprecedented extent to which *han* declined to participate. A few of those *han* had troops deployed as ordered in reserve or second-wave positions. But most had refused on one ground or another to commit forces or had managed to deploy them belatedly or only as far as their own borders. The massive daimyo betrayal compelled the bakufu to fall back on other vassal lords and on its own forces. Hurriedly orders were sent out to other *han*, but events outraced them and the war ended with few of those *han* participating actively in the fighting.[2]

The damage done by *han* abstention was compounded by poor political coordination among bakufu staff leaders. Mochitsugu of Kii at Hiroshima was forward commander of all front-line forces, meaning all forces actually attacking Chōshū. At Kokura Ogasawara was in charge of the Kyushu front. At Hiroshima Honjō, who was designated vice-commander under Mochitsugu, was coordinating efforts at the Aki front. Other officials were assigned to Iwami and the defunct Ōshima front. At all headquarters political leadership seems to have been unsatisfactory, but the most damaging political malfeasance occurred at Hiroshima and had its impact most directly on the Aki front.

The fighting of 6/19–25 stabilized that front, and forces there rested and replenished themselves. Encouraged by their growing capacity to outfight Chōshū, allied commanders of the Kii-Shingū-Hikone-Takata-Ōgaki-bakufu forces prepared plans for a coordinated offensive to commence on 6/29 and designed to drive the Chōshū troops back into their own land. Two days of rain delayed the assault, and then it was halted by confusion arising from extraordinary developments at the Hiroshima headquarters. Those developments laid bare the inadequacies of army leadership.

Whereas the battles of 6/19, 20, and 25 had raised the morale of field commanders at the Aki front, the more general reverses apparently had convinced Honjō—whose own poorly armed troops were already in combat—that the bakufu had no choice but to find a nonmilitary solution to its Chōshū dilemma.[3] Accordingly, in a most remarkable maneuver on 6/21 and 22 he talked secretly with the Chōshū delegates being held captive at Hiroshima. They apparently advised him that if he released them and canceled the order for Chōshū men to come to Hiroshima, Chōshū in its gratitude would accept the imperial order for submission. Honjō was persuaded. Acting completely on his own, on 6/25 he ordered Hiroshima officials to release and repatriate the men as the first step in a political settlement. Later, in explaining his action to Itakura Katsukiyo and Inaba Masakuni, Honjō wrote that he had been worried about rumors of Satsuma and England aiding Chōshū and troubled by the inadequacies of bakufu men and money. He also had been distressed by the obsolescence of the bakufu side's firearms in the face of Chōshū's modern forces, dismayed by the disastrous overall trend, and fearful that things could only get worse.

However sound Honjō's reasoning may have been, his handling of the problem was not. Releasing the men had no impact on Chōshū policy, but it did precipitate a first-rate crisis at Hiroshima. Mochitsugu learned of it on about 7/2 in a letter from Chōshū men explaining the secret negotiations. He was outraged at Honjō's insubordination and sabotage of policy, which he interpreted incorrectly as an act of official bakufu policy carried out behind his back. On 7/4 he sent Osaka his angry resignation as forward commander. On the following day he notified the armies of his action, told them Honjō was in charge, and withdrew Kii and Shingū forces from the Aki front. That body blow to the allied force at Aki added mightily to the demoralization growing out of the generally poor military experience.

The impact of the whole mess was not notably eased by Osaka's response. The ailing shogun immediately repudiated Honjō and rejected Mochitsugu's resignation. On 7/10 Osaka leaders ordered Honjō to return to the city to explain himself. On the next day Itakura sent the armies letters of reassurance in which the bakufu disclaimed any responsibility for Honjō's action and said affairs were to be pursued as before.

Meanwhile at Hiroshima acting forward commander Honjō made one last gesture in pursuit of his chosen policy. On 7/11 he ordered the remaining bakufu and *han* forces near Ōno to withdraw and be replaced by Hiroshima forces who would act as a buffer to prevent further fighting. That order was implemented, but four days later Honjō learned that he had been repudiated. He received orders to return to Osaka, and on the next day he departed.

This political failure at the main front undid the bakufu's modest military successes there and contributed to military disaster in Iwami. Hamada's pleas for support had yielded no appreciable results, and on 7/13, with the pressure in Aki lifted, Chōshū forces reopened their offensive in Iwami. In succeeding days they defeated the opposing forces of Hamada, Fukuyama, Kii, and Matsue. By 7/18 the Chōshū drive had reached Hamada castle, an advance of over 60 kilometers. The castle's defenders put it to the torch and retreated to Matsue. The next day Fukuyama forces called it quits and started for home. Matsue troops withdrew to guard their castle while awaiting reinforcements that again never came, and the front grew quiet for a second time. Hamada *han* and all the bakufu lands in Iwami had been lost to Chōshū.[4]

Meanwhile Mochitsugu had reluctantly reaccepted his post, but only after obtaining promises of reinforcements and written bakufu reassurances of commitment to the project. His reluctance was understandable. He was commanding an army that had been defeated at Ōshima and Iwami, that had been neutralized at Ōno, that had never existed at Hagi, and that had never really gotten organized at Kokura because so few agreed to come to the affair. He knew that most key daimyo had refused to cooperate and that others were withdrawing. He knew that at Osaka the shogun had become seriously ill and died. He knew that there was agitation to end the war and that the armies still in the field had lost heart for the ill-starred venture. Accordingly he wrote the several commanders of accompanying daimyo forces on 7/23 asking what plans of action they would suggest. He declared that in pursuit of the objectives of court and bakufu, there had been unintended mistakes, the Iwami front had not held, there had been a great sad event at Osaka, and there was distress and fear among the troops. Therefore, he inquired, what was to be done? If there were a withdrawal, it would be impossible to protect the realm *(tenka)* and so views on how to crush Chōshū were being sought.[5]

Mochitsugu's letter revealed his resolve to press on, and in succeeding days he moved his reorganized forces back to the front near Ōno. In the renewed fighting there both sides scored some locally impressive gains and losses, but then on 8/7 the bakufu position was wrecked. While that major reverse was being discussed at Hiroshima, policy changes were being made at Osaka and communicated westward. In the outcome on 8/10 Hiroshima troops were again sent in to neutralize the front.[6] With that the war in Aki ended.

While Mochitsugu was trying to salvage matters at Hiroshima, Ogasawara at Kokura was demonstrating again that vigor and intellect alone did not make a successful leader. His situation too was unenviable.[7] Fukuoka and Saga had refused to send troops beyond their own borders, and Kurume and Yanagawa had only provided token forces of three or four hundred men apiece. Apart from the brave but tired forces of Kokura, he had only the bakufu's *sennin gumi* of 250 men, some 150 legation guards, perhaps 700 men of his own Karatsu *han* who were his headquarters force, and two large battalions from Kumamoto. In effect the Kumamoto battalions were the core of his striking force.

In contrast to Honjō, who had come to doubt the wisdom of the whole enterprise, Ogasawara wanted revenge for the years of contempt the Mōri had shown the Ogasawara of Kokura and the months of contemptuous disregard they had shown his efforts to settle the conflict peacefully. He wanted to smash Chōshū. The Kumamoto leader at Kokura, however, had no intention of attacking, and on 7/23 he refused an order from Ogasawara to do so. The two men engaged in heated argument. The Kumamoto commander ridiculed Ogasawara, and the latter threatened to go back to Osaka and "discuss matters" there if Kyushu lords refused to cooperate. That quarrel poisoned the already strained atmosphere, led the man from Kumamoto to conclude that he might as well go home, and within a few days culminated in disaster.

On the night of 7/26 some 1500 Chōshū men equipped with rifles and cannon assembled and crossed the strait by ship, arriving with the dawn on the twenty-seventh.[8] They promptly commenced an attack on forces of Kumamoto and Kokura. What followed is not entirely clear, but an inspector reported that two bakufu warships in the area then opened fire on Chōshū's Shimonoseki batteries, causing the attackers to hesitate. Kumamoto men seized the opportunity to counterattack and drove the Chōshū invaders back. Adhering to bakufu practice, however, Ogasawara kept his own forces in reserve despite a Kumamoto request for aid, much to the anger of the latter. About then the sweltering heat gave way to rain, and troop morale collapsed along with the leaders' relationships. News of the shogun's death had just reached Kyushu, and that provided the angry Kumamoto leader with an excuse to stop fighting. Accordingly, after Chōshū had been repulsed he packed up and took his troops home on 7/30. Upon hearing of that, Yanagawa and Kurume troops also promptly left for home.

There are conflicting accounts of the matter, but Ogasawara reportedly received from the senior councillors at Osaka notice of the shogun's death and instructions to return home. On the night of 7/30, most probably after the *han* forces had left, he also left by bakufu ship for Nagasaki, allegedly as advised by inspector Hirayama Keichū. That same night, after learning of developments, leaders of the abandoned Kokura forces discussed their plight with Hirayama and the other remaining bakufu inspector and decided to put their castle to the torch and retreat into the hills. On 8/2 the abandoned *sennin gumi* also fled in retreat.

With the abrupt collapse at Kokura and the neutralization at Ōno, the last serious threats to Chōshū had ended. In succeeding weeks the bakufu continued to deploy bits and pieces of forces here and there in indecisive efforts to salvage the war. The only real fighting, however, was near Kokura where the private vendetta between men of Mōri and Ogasawara led to repeated encounters until late in 66/10.[9]

The military venture had sputtered out in confusion and disarray. Based on false hopes about daimyo behavior and pursued indecisively and without proper coordination, it ended up a political failure. Concerning the war as a military experience, Shibusawa Eiichi has summed it up succinctly in this way:

> Except at Ōshima, Chōshū forces everywhere were prepared first and took the offensive. Furthermore the Chōshū troops having lightweight equipment stressed firearms and generally followed western tactics. The [opposing] *han* forces used swords, pikes, and old-style armor and the conch shell [for battle calls], and the bakufu army never flourished.[10]

The *han* forces in general did poorly, but the performance of the bakufu's own units requires more attention. Their strengths and weaknesses are best seen by focusing upon the Aki front.

THE AKI FRONT

The Aki front was the only one on which the bakufu's own forces were in sustained combat. It is on that front, therefore, that one can most clearly see the relative roles of old- and new-style forces and the several military lessons that flowed from the war.

The Aki front was mainly a coastal area marked by narrow shallow valleys running between low, convoluted, scrub-forested hills. The Chōshū forces attacked from two principal points: northward near the coast from the Osegawa (Ose river) in the Wagi-Kino area, and eastward along the inland valley roads running from Asahara through Tsuda to Akashi and Hara villages and on to Hatsukaichi town.

Chōshū was opposed by an allied force composed of bakufu, Kii, Shingū, Hikone, Takata, Ōgaki, and a few Akashi and Miyazu troops. Initially their vanguard elements attacked southward from Ōtake on the Osegawa, but when that assault failed, they spent the rest of the campaign deploying their main battalions along the coastal strip between Ha-

MAP 4. The Aki Front in 1866. Adapted from map no. NI-53–33, "Hiroshima" (Tokyo: Kokudo chirin, 1970).

tsukaichi and Kuba with other forces guarding the flank on the roads leading toward Tsuda town. The allied armies were supported by two or three warships that on occasion bombarded the enemy forces on the narrow coastal plain running from Ōtake to Ōno.

The war on the Aki front had two phases: a first series of battles between 6/14 and 25 and a second series between 7/27 and 8/7. During the interim both sides replenished supplies, rested their forces, and did their best to strengthen themselves for the next encounter.

1. The Battles of 6/14, 6/19, and 6/25

By 6/13 Chōshū had about three battalions deployed on the border north of Iwakuni.[11] The allied forces were deployed in a series of camps scattered along the coast southwest of Hiroshima as far as Okata village. On that day advance forces of Hikone and Takata moved southward to Ōtake. By the following morning three Hikone units of some 450 vanguard *(sakite)* mounted samurai and one Takata vanguard unit of about 150 men were preparing to attack across the Osegawa into Chōshū.[12] In the meantime several companies of alert Chōshū men had crossed the river at Kino and then deployed into the hills above Ōtake. Iwakuni forces were deployed in a defensive line on the south bank of the river.

As the Hikone horsemen waded into the river, they encountered a withering random rifle and cannon fire from across the stream. And to their rear rifle and hand-mortar fire poured down upon them ''like rain'' from the hills. As the fighting progressed, the town of Ōtake began to burn, the roaring flames panicked the horses, and the Hikone-Takata forces retreated out of the burning town, only to find themselves again harassed on both flanks by Chōshū riflemen in the hills. Caught, as Ii's report said, in ''a field of death,''[13] Hikone units lost their cohesion and men fled in all directions, dropping their weapons, abandoning their horses, jumping into boats where they found them on the shore, running northward in terror, or hiding to avoid capture or death.

In their flight the defeated vanguard forces reached a larger Takata camp and the main Hikone encampment. The pursuing Chōshū units maintained their hilltop positions, routed the unprepared men, and overran the hastily abandoned camps. The main Takata force to the rear wished to attack, but as the magnitude of rout became apparent, the idea was abandoned. By nightfall Hikone had been smashed, portions of Takata had been badly mauled, and Chōshū troops had advanced about 6 kilometers to the village of Kuba, which they sacked and burned as the defeated armies withdrew. Then, as the hour grew late, the Chōshū-Iwakuni forces halted.

For the allies it had been a disastrous day. Ii reported that he lost powder for 16,500 rifle bullets, metal and hardware, and all his rice and gold supplies. Accordingly he asked for a bakufu loan of 30,000 ryō. [14] He also lost a number of horses, and ten or twelve cannon, two of them American-made. Sakakibara asked replacement of eight cannon with 300 rounds per piece and 200 rifles with 600 rounds per weapon.

Despite the magnitude of the defeat and the quantities of goods lost, the battle was not nearly so sanguinary as reports made it sound or as enthusiastic Chōshū and Tottori reports suggested. [15] Hikone listed eleven dead, thirteen wounded, one captured, one unknown. Takata had nine killed and four wounded. Chōshū had one dead and four wounded. The casualty rate was so moderate precisely because the rout was so complete. Had Hikone-Takata men stood their ground, they probably could have saved their equipment, but only at the cost of both taking and inflicting more casualties.

The defeat was due to several immediate factors. In the initial firefight at Ōtake the Chōshū forces were numerically equal to or superior to their opponents. Their arms were vastly superior and much more effectively deployed. Their use of a harassing fire from the high ground proved very effective against the mounted vanguard, and they benefited directly from the destruction of the thousand or so houses in Ōtake. The Chōshū men recognized at once the value of those tactics and adhered to them thereafter, constantly moving through the hills and burning houses as they advanced. Later in the day the Chōshū forces were outnumbered by perhaps 1500 to 1000. However, they benefited sufficiently from the initial successes, effective tactics, and the advantage of surprise to effect the abrupt collapse of the main Hikone camp and a major Takata encampment.

The incendiarism of the first day was valuable on the battlefield, but strategically it was troublesome for Chōshū. When the Chōshū commander reported the day's events to his superiors, he blamed forces of Iwakuni for the burning and sacking of Kuba and was sharply critical of their conduct. (The initial burning of Ōtake likely was accidental.) Hiroshima observers blamed Chōshū for the incendiarism and started relief efforts at once. Hiroshima protested the tactics of arson, but in later battles Chōshū troops still used them, even though Iwakuni men were reported to be behaving properly. [16] The issue became a source of substantial tension between the two *han*, leading to repeated rumors of Hiroshima joining the allies. That in turn prompted an intense Chōshū diplomatic campaign to preserve the big neighbor's neutrality. And later the issue helped thwart Chōshū efforts to induce Hiroshima to allow their forces free advance during Honjō's truce. [17]

Following the 6/14 rout, Hikone-Takata forces headed for the rear, and allied leaders sent replacements to the front. They consisted of Mini-rifle units of Shingū led by their daimyo, Mizuno Tadamoto, two battalions of Mini-armed bakufu infantry led by Takenaka Shigemoto, one battery of cannon with three companies of artillery guards, substantial forces from Kii, and a few from Ōgaki *han.* These were moved up to the vicinity of Ōno some 12 kilometers northeast of the border. Chōshū forces were deployed to the south in the Ōtake-Okata district, with advance units sent into the undulating ridge area called Shijūhassaka that paralleled the coast road from southwest of Ōno to northeast of Nakayama.[18]

On the eighteenth bakufu leaders at Ōno were ordered, much to their dismay, to send back to the rear half of their newly received cannon battery and one company of artillery guards. These were being redeployed to the collapsing front on Ōshima island.[19] Perhaps Chōshū forces learned of this redeployment; in any case that night they moved into battle positions in the hills overlooking the road to Ōno town. Their intention was to repeat their triumph of the first day, but the outcome of battle was quite different.[20]

As the morning lightened, Chōshū forces from above the allied encampments at Ōno commenced firing and shooting fire arrows down upon the units in town. In reply Mizuno had his cannoneers fire a few rounds back at the hills to elicit artillery replies that would enable the allies to pinpoint the Chōshū artillery emplacements. Then the Chōshū forces rushed down in coordinated attack from several points in the hills. Mizuno's riflemen, supported by Kii vanguard forces and bakufu artillery, and inspired by Mizuno's own personal bravery, stood their ground, returned the fire, and beat the attackers back.

The Chōshū men withdrew toward Okata, regrouped, and moved back up the road toward Ōno. While they had been regrouping, however, allied units had deployed for advance. They attacked the Chōshū artillery points and forced the cannoneers to withdraw. Then they advanced. A battalion of bakufu infantry moved down the main road toward Kuba while a second battalion was held in reserve. Ōgaki riflemen circled out by Matsugahara, and Shingū-Kii forces, which had carried the brunt of the initial Chōshū assault, provided cover in the rear.

The allied leaders too had learned quickly, and as they advanced, they swept the hills on both sides of the road. When the main infantry force met the regrouped Chōshū troops moving north on the road, it was the bakufu that held the high ground. In the ensuing firefight, the Chōshū troops were defeated, fell back, and then came under flanking fire from Ōgaki men moving down from Matsugahara toward Kuba. Accordingly the Chōshū forces retreated further to Okata. By then the day was spent and the allied commander, Takenaka, ordered the advance to halt.

In the fighting casualties again were moderate. Reports from Chōshū spoke of about six dead and perhaps fifteen to twenty wounded. Kii reportedly had ten dead, eighteen wounded; Shingū had six dead and sixteen wounded; the bakufu had two dead, about ten wounded; Ōgaki had perhaps four wounded.

The allied success was due to the quality and quantity of their forces and the orderly and effective leadership they received. The bakufu units engaged at any moment numbered about 400 infantrymen plus perhaps 120 men with the artillery, but the bakufu at the front had total forces of about twice that number and so fresh troops could be introduced easily. There also was probably a third infantry battalion in the rear at Itsuka-ichi, which could rotate on a longer basis. Toda of Ōgaki had perhaps 200 riflemen, and Mizuno of Shingū had about 300. The size of the Kii vanguard is not clear, but it was probably a *chūtai*—that is, a half- battalion, or about 200 troops.[21] Chōshū probably had over 800 men in the area, but the number actually committed to battle may have been appreciably less; at least in the fighting on the Ōno road, the figure 300 appears most frequently.

Chōshū's defeat prompted the local commander to write his government suggesting a few days' rest and asking for reinforcements. On the following day, however, other Chōshū forces that had entered Hiroshima territory at Asahara fought some 250 to 300 troops of Miyazu and a small bakufu legation guard force in western-type uniforms. The fighting appears to have been a standoff with substantial close-quarter fighting with pikes and swords. At day's end both sides withdrew, threw up barricades, and waited for reinforcements. Miyazu reported one dead and nine wounded; Chōshū, ten dead and three wounded; the legation guard may have had four or five killed; and thirty-five Chōshū men were reportedly captured.[22]

Following the setback of 6/19 Chōshū regrouped and obtained reinforcements consisting of two companies (*shōtai*) of perhaps a hundred or more men from Tokuyama and others from Iwakuni. With these they resolved to revive the attempt to drive northward to allied headquarters in Hiroshima city,[23] or at least to capture Ōno town. However, the allied success of the nineteenth had been extremely gratifying to their leaders, and the men who faced Chōshū were considerably less fearful than they had been a few days before.

On the night of 6/24 both sides deployed for action. Three companies of bakufu infantry with two or three cannon moved south of Ōno on the road to Kuba.[24] In the morning they encountered Chōshū forces approaching in battle formation and successfully turned their coastal flank, exposing them to fire from that side. Troops of Shingū and Kii were in the hills on the other flank, and in the ensuing firefight those holding the high ground again prevailed. Chōshū had to pull back to escape the trap between hill and sea, and as the men retreated, they dispersed into the hills. Other Chōshū troops rushed up on the road from Matsugahara, but they came under fire from Ōgaki and Shingū men deployed in the hills and encountered barricades on the road just west of Ōno. Their advance was stopped, and they too moved up into the hills. They then pushed through the brush to overlook Ōno from the west, and from there they and some Shingū-Kii forces exchanged indecisive fire until about 2 PM, when the Chōshū units broke off contact.

Meanwhile on the main road south of Ōno, the Chōshū men who had retreated and then deployed in the hills continued to come under attack from elements of Shungū, Kii, Ōgaki, and bakufu infantry forces. Some of these, fresh troops brought in on a rotation basis, went into the hills and chased the Chōshū men back. As the main Chōshū force stood dispersed and on the defensive, it came under naval bombardment from warships standing offshore The bombardment apparently hurt no one, but hitting troops already scattered and tired from several hours of severe pressure, it succeeded in panicking them. They fled further into the hills away from the coast and back to the rear south of Kuba to the Okata area, being followed by the ships' guns as they went. This situation prompted some of the terrified and disorganized men to argue that it was necessary to pull back at once to the Osegawa frontier.

With day's end and their inland flank at Ōno still exposed, the allies halted their southward advance after the retreating Chōshū men had broken off contact. Chōshū units inland also pulled back. On the following day a combined force of some four hundred bakufu infantrymen and Shingū troops went on an extended patrol in force as far as Matsugahara. They found no enemy there. The Chōshū men had taken what food supplies they could find, burned the houses in order to deny the enemy shelter, and retreated.

Again allied success was a product of quality and quantity. Chōshū had committed perhaps 700 to 1000 men to the fighting.[25] The allied forces were essentially those of the 6/19 engagement, probably over 1500 engaged at any given time. Battle casualties for the day are not very clear, but for Chōshū they were about seven dead and twenty wounded. Kii had one dead and nine wounded. Ōgaki had five or six casualties, the bakufu three. Shingū losses are not indicated.

2. The Interregnum: 6/26–7/27

By 6/26 the allied situation on the Aki front seemed to be improving. The allies outnumbered and outgunned their opponents. The latter's early advantages in experience, initiative, and élan appeared to be gone. Their major remaining advantage lay in the geography of the front. With a long exposed flank of rough, brushy terrain, allied leaders were reluctant to extend themselves far down the coast lest their forces be hit from behind, trapped, and decimated. Instead they repeatedly withdrew from salients secured in battle and hence scored no permanent territorial gains despite combat victories. Overcoming that problem, however, seemed only a matter of time. Once it was surmounted, they could expect to turn their strengths to more decisive advantage.

By contrast it is clear that following the 6/25 battle the Chōshū forces in Aki were in a precarious position. Aware that they were being defeated in the field, local commanders hurriedly started combining units in order to overcome their numerical weakness. They were worried about the impact of the naval bombardment and wished for offshore support. They also complained that the numbers of wounded exceeded the capacity of medical crews to handle them. Later in the war they complained of difficulty in supplying their forces and bringing in enough reinforcements and replacements. This problem of provisioning may have underlain the plunder activities.

Chōshū officers also were puzzled by allied tactics, which were having consequences of which allied commanders probably were unaware. On one or two occasions Chōshū attackers had intentionally withdrawn and set up ambushes, expecting the enemy to advance and get caught. But the enemy had not done so. Rather, as one Chōshū report described it, they had stayed behind their barricades, let Chōshū attack, and then stood fast, causing the Chōshū men to consume ammunition and build up so much residue in their weapons they had to retreat to clean them. Then, when the Chōshū riflemen were immobilized, the enemy attacked.[26] It seems less likely that allied leaders were suddenly so battle-wise than that they were cautious and lucky, but the effect on Chōshū was all the same.

Another Chōshū battle report threw light on another aspect of the war. It indicated that the rate of fire was about twice as great in the 6/25 battle as in the preceding engagements.[27] The increase was a cause for worry because munitions were limited and resupply difficult. The increased firing, which apparently was fouling the pieces of some men, did not result in increased allied casualties, however, and did not increase

Chōshū success. Rather, on 6/25 one sees somewhat more reliance by allied leaders on defensive tactics that Chōshū failed to overcome.

As of 6/25 local allied commanders thus had rather good reason to feel encouraged by developments on the field. And that night another infantry battalion and a half-battery of artillery set out from Hiroshima for the front at Ōno. During the next few days allied commanders at Ōno mapped strategy for a major frontal assault to drive the Chōshū invaders back across the Osegawa. It was scheduled for 6/29, but it rained on that day and again on 7/1, and that reportedly caused a delay in the planned attack. Then before it materialized, leaders learned of Honjō's actions at Hiroshima, and in the resulting confusion the plan was canceled.

During the ensuing weeks of quiet, Chōshū rotated its troops and moved new forces to the front, raising its Aki complement to about five reinforced battalions. It replenished supplies and tried to overcome bottlenecks in its transport system. Local commanders strengthened their battle lines on the Tsuda front by advancing to Toge, building defense works there, and then setting up a forward outpost at Akashi. They also deployed other units to Kushima to the northeast, a total uncontested advance of more than 20 kilometers. Chōshū commanders worked out routinized patrol duties in the captured Hiroshima lands and tried unsuccessfully to persuade forces of that *han* to retreat and let them occupy even more territory.[28]

On the allied side matters went less smoothly. As Honjō ordered, bakufu infantry battalions were pulled back to near Hiroshima on 7/13–14 and Hiroshima troops replaced them at Ōno. Kii and Shingū forces had pulled back earlier, and Ōgaki men did so on 7/13.[29] A few days later, however, Honjō was repudiated and Mochitsugu started to reopen the front.

Mochitsugu had learned well the tactical military value of the new weaponry. During the interregnum he ordered all Kii men to convert to rifles and on 7/17 took delivery at Hiroshima of five hundred Mini rifles for them. The troops were organized as battalions *(daitai)* composed of companies *(shōtai)*. They lost their historic battle streamers because those had simply proved to be splendid points of aim for enemy artillerymen zeroing in on their targets. Besides reforming his own troops, Mochitsugu sought a massive infusion of additional bakufu forces. When accepting the shogun's refusal of his resignation, he asked for thirty thousand picked troops organized as infantry, cavalry, and artillery. And as evidence of bakufu sincerity, he asked that Osaka send him immediately the two or three thousand troops held in the city plus five warships located there. He wanted other *han* troops issued firearms and wanted bakufu units put at the center of his assault battalions.[30] Very little of his request was honored, but he undertook nonetheless to make the best of a bad situation.

On 7/25 and 26 both sides began deploying again, preparing for renewal of hostilities.[31] On 7/25 the enlarged forces of Chōshū began moving forward. A battalion or more moved into the hills overlooking Miyauchi. They were backed up by two artillery batteries and protected by barricades of felled trees and brush. Smaller Chōshū units were widely deployed, some along the road leading from Kushima to Hatsukaichi, others near Nakayama, to the south and west of Ōno, near Matsugahara, and in the vicinity of Kuba. The allies' inland flank, which had been a cause for concern earlier in the war, was by 7/26 much longer, much more exposed, and threatened by much larger and better deployed Chōshū forces.

On 7/26–27 allied units moved into position. By road and ship they moved from Itsukaichi and points east down to camps from Hatsukaichi to Ōno. On 7/27 a company of Shingū men together with a company of Kii vanguard forces moved out from camp at Miyauchi to probe their perimeter. Moving through the hills toward Akashi they made contact with the Chōshū forward outpost there. The latter being outnumbered fought briefly and withdrew. Then, as two Chōshū companies advanced, the allied patrol returned to camp and contact was broken. The stage had been set for renewed warfare.

3. The Battles of 7/28, 8/2, and 8/7

On 7/28 the struggle between the enlarged armies began in earnest.[32] The allies set out to strengthen their flank by driving back the Chōshū forces threatening Miyauchi. They intended to clear Shijūhassaka south to Ōno and drive back the main Chōshū forces encamped southwest of there. Mizuno Tadamoto's force, enlarged to two battalions totaling some eight hundred men, moved toward Akashi, with flanking companies sweeping the hills until they made contact with the enemy. The reinforced battalions of Chōshū opened fire with rifles and cannon, but after wavering briefly, the men of Shingū pushed on, forcing the Chōshū units to retreat. Mizuno's men failed to score a breakthrough, however, and at day's end they broke off contact and pulled back to an encampment at Jigozen. Casualties are unclear, and allied reports of many Chōshū dead are not to be credited.

The main fighting took place to the south. There allied forces fought Chōshū units in the hills from Nakayama to Ōno and southward. The allied forces consisted of companies from two battalions of Kii infantry and from three battalions of bakufu infantry augmented by rehabilitated units of Hikone men. They were supported by artillery pieces guarded by three companies of artillery guards. The total force probably consisted of about two thousand troops who operated on a rotating basis so that perhaps half that number were engaged at any moment.

Their opponents were only a small portion of the total Chōshū force: seven companies, some 350 men, who were deployed in the hills along with some artillery. In the fighting, in which bakufu infantry and Hikone men were in the vanguard, the Chōshū units were steadily driven back out of the Nakayama area to the west. Those south of Ōno came under naval bombardment in the Kuba-Okata area and retreated to Matsugahara. Then with the day gone, with large Chōshū forces still uncommitted, and with others known to be deployed to the northwest, the allies broke off contact and returned to camps in the vicinity of Miyauchi.

Again the allies had demonstrated the superiority of their main force. They had not, however, overcome the problem of an exposed flank and so were unable to convert their strength into an effective weapon for subduing Chōshū. Nor had they improved their accuracy in reporting enemy casualties. Chōshū had about four dead and seventeen wounded, but allied reports spoke of forty to eighty Chōshū dead in the engagement. Kii reported it had no casualties; the bakufu infantry commander reported his losses at three dead and five wounded. Hikone men were credited with fighting well, but their casualties, if any, are unknown.

Two days later on 7/30 the allies' exposed flank was again the site of conflict. Hikone men discovered some Chōshū troops in the hills west of the Miyauchi-Ōno road and engaged them. Quickly the battle escalated to involve a reinforced Chōshū battalion on one side and parts of a Shingū battalion and some Hikone and Kii companies on the other. The fighting was indecisive. It was a rainy day, and as the rain grew more intense and the day neared its end, the allied forces broke off contact and returned to camp. Later, in the dark, about a battalion of Chōshū men advanced to attack the camp. Their assault coincided with a fierce downpour, however, and in the mud and darkness they made no headway and withdrew. Hikone reported seven wounded, Takata and Chōshū reportedly had no casualties that day, and Shingū and Kii made no casualty reports, perhaps because they had none.[33]

During 7/29—8/1 the bulk of the allied force was preparing a new drive to push the Chōshū invaders back.[34] On 8/1 units moved out to attack positions. What followed was a battle fought on three fronts: on the coast from Ōno to Okata; along the road from Ōno to Matsugahara; and north of Miyauchi in the area between Hara and Hera.

On the coast road a bakufu infantry battalion with attached Hikone troops, some artillery, and half the men in three artillery guard companies had no difficulty pushing Chōshū forces back south of Ōno. One reason was that Chōshū men evidently had laid land mines armed with trip wires at some points northeast of Kuba and then pulled back, hoping thus to surprise and halt their superior enemy. To their chagrin bakufu troops recognized the wires, cut them, and moved safely and rapidly ahead, driving some Chōshū men up into the hills to the west and pushing others back through Kuba to Okata. As their main force advanced, the allies launched a new maneuver of their own. Three warships sailed in close to shore, bombarded the Chōshū units, and then sent in landing parties of Kii forces to trap the Chōshū troops in a vise. The amphibious operation failed, however, because the landing was made too far from the combat zone and Chōshū men easily evaded the trap by withdrawing.

By day's end the allies were in control of Kuba, but apparently because they were in unfamiliar territory and because of developments on the other fronts, they pulled back to Ōno. That night Chōshū men burned what remained of Kuba village to assure that the enemy would not camp there in future.

The advance toward Matsugahara was handled by a battalion of Shingū riflemen and a force of Kii vanguard riflemen. They followed the established practice of sweeping the hills on both sides of the road as they advanced. The hills were precipitous, however, the Chōshū men knew the area well, and the Shingū-Kii men found it a tedious struggle driving them back. Starting at about 10 AM and fighting continuously for about four hours, Mizuno's men made only limited progress. The allied units took a number of casualties and the Shingū-Kii advance stalled about 2 kilometers east of Matsugahara. As the Kii forces began to fall back, Chōshū concentrated fire on Mizuno's men, who also were then forced to withdraw despite the arrival of reinforcements. Dispirited, they returned to Ōno.

The third front developed when forces of Hikone and Takata moved into the hills north of Miyauchi and made contact with Chōshū men advancing from Hara. The forces may have been about evenly matched numerically, but as the day progressed, Chōshū concentrated its fire on the Takata troops and turned their northeast flank near Hera village. Allied reinforcements consisting of a company of legation guards, Akashi troops, and some Ōgaki men were hurriedly sent in, but the Chōshū troops held their ground, burned Hera, and then withdrew, having demonstrated again their superiority over Hikone and Takata.

In sum, then, allied successes on the shore road were offset by stalemate at Matsugahara and defeat at Hera. That defeat raised the long-standing problem of the allied flank to an immediately serious level, a situation that Chōshū leaders seem to have recognized at once.

There is only one rate-of-fire report for the day, but the quantity of firing seemed to be continuing to escalate. And the trend was beginning to be reflected in heavier casualty figures: Hikone with two dead and sixteen wounded at Kuba; Takata with one dead and three wounded near Hera; Chōshū with five dead and thirty wounded at Kuba and Matsugahara; Kii and Shingū with twelve dead and eight wounded; and the bakufu with four dead and eighteen wounded, probably on all fronts. It was the most sanguinary battle to date.

On the next day, 8/3, a bakufu patrol in force advanced to Kuba. There it encountered enemy forces and returned to camp, having discovered that Chōshū had erected defenses west of the burned-out village. Warships were sent to break them up by cannon fire but with no appreciable success.

Chōshū field commanders were much encouraged by their success at Hera. Consequently on the following day they started developing tactical plans for a major flanking assault to smash the allied force once and for all.[35] By the night of 8/6 they were ready for an assault intended to "make a clean sweep of the enemy foundation."[36] They concentrated well over two battalions in position to attack the allied flank at its vulnerable Miyauchi point. Other units were grouped in two striking forces that would make a pincer thrust at Ōno via the coast road and the Matsugahara approach.

It was a rainy, windy night as a huge typhoon lashed the entire central portion of Japan. The men of Mōri moved through the sodden underbrush toward the Ōno encampments of bakufu infantry and artillery units, some Hikone units, and Shingū and Kii rifle, mortar, and howitzer units. At 7 AM firing commenced, Chōshū rifle and cannon fire raining down on the defenders. The attackers rushed down from the hills and along the road only to encounter solid defense works backed up by artillery pieces firing grapeshot. The assault was repulsed, renewed assaults were repulsed, allied shot "fell like rain," and the Chōshū troops pulled back. As the winds roared and the deluge continued, allied infantry went over their barricades, swarmed up rain-soaked hills, and sent the Chōshū forces reeling back.

Then bakufu infantry advanced along the coast road with caution, lest enemy units get behind them and overrun their base camp. As a result of the caution Chōshū cannoneers were able to withdraw their pieces successfully. Bakufu-Hikone units fanned out into the hills and dispersed the enemy scattered there, firing enough to keep ammunition carriers unusually busy, and capturing some supplies and men. Finally at 10 AM after counterattacks by Chōshū reinforcements had been beaten back and Chōshū had broken contact, the bakufu-Hikone men evacuated their newly erected breastworks and returned to base at Ōno, probably after learning of developments to the rear.

On the Matsugahara approach forces of Mizuno Tadamoto and Kii went into the hills, cut the Chōshū forces off from those on the coast road, and then drove them back through Matsugahara to Kuba, capturing two cannon in their advance. Mizuno distinguished himself again, standing fearlessly and rallying his men to advance. He finally halted them at Matsugahara, put up breastworks, and then returned to Ōno.

The day's fighting clearly constituted an allied victory on the Ōno front. But in the rear at Miyauchi the outcome was entirely different. Chōshū forces moving down from Akashi and nearby hills launched their assault at 6 AM, attacking Hikone and Takata forces holding that flank. Chōshū may have had a numerical advantage and clearly had a great psychological advantage due to success there five days earlier. The Hikone units fought well and held their ground, but the Takata troops grew disorganized. They discovered too late that in the downpour some of their powder had become soaked and useless. They were forced to use swords and as a result were overrun by Chōshū riflemen who surged into their midst, firing at close range, causing the terrified Takata men to drop their useless weapons and surrender or flee.

With their flank turned, Hikone men pulled back, and with their ammunition exhausted, they refused to counterattack when ordered. The victorious Chōshū forces surged ahead, overrunning silent artillery emplacements, killing the cannoneers, and chasing the routed forces out of the Miyauchi area, back through Kushido, and northeast along the coast road to fortified areas at Hatsukaichi. The Chōshū attackers then halted, collected their prizes of war—cannon, firearms, rice, other supplies, equipment, and a goodly number of heads—and pulled back.

The battle of 8/7 was the biggest of the war in Aki. That was apparent in the heavy casualty figures:

Shingū:	12 dead; 16 wounded
Hikone:	11 dead; 15 wounded
Kii:	4 dead; 35 wounded
Takata:	29 dead; 39 wounded
Chōshū:	3 dead; 16 wounded
Akashi:	1 dead; 2 wounded
Bakufu:	not reported

The allies' worst fear had been realized. Their flank had been utterly smashed, their link to the rear temporarily severed. When the magnitude of that disaster was recognized by leaders at Ōno and back at Hiroshima, it was decided, despite Mizuno's arguments to the contrary, that the entire force must pull back. The new barricades erected at Matsugahara and south of Ōno were destroyed. On 8/9 supplies were put on ship and sent back to Itsukaichi, and the troops marched back via the coast road.

At Hiroshima allied commanders began discussing how best to proceed. Takenaka Shigemoto and inspector general Nagai Naomune argued the importance of reopening the front promptly. But Hiroshima spokesmen lobbied against the proposal. As the debate progressed, on 8/10 a horseman reportedly arrived from Kyoto with instructions from "the shogun" advising against any more attacks at that time.[37] Accordingly the allied units were ordered withdrawn to their base camp at Kusatsu near Hiroshima city. Forces of Hiroshima *han* moved forward to neutralize the front again. The war in Aki had ended.

4. A Summing Up

A number of conclusions seem to emerge from this narrative. Chōshū made good use of its limited resources. It displayed good command control, reliable, well-armed forces, and effective if brutal fighting tactics. The bakufu infantry was competently led and proved to be a rock that Chōshū could not move. It was deployed conservatively and deliberately avoided dangerously exposed situations. But the infantrymen fought and in fact were usually in the thick of combat. By 66/7 their task was relatively easy because Chōshū commanders evidently had learned they should not waste resources on bakufu infantry but should concentrate instead on allied weaknesses. Indeed other allied forces at times complained about the relatively easy situation of the infantry.

Concerning these other forces, Mizuno Tadamoto distinguished himself as the allies' boldest and best commander. His Mini-armed riflemen were brave and effective, and although they, unlike bakufu infantry, were on occasion prime targets of Chōshū attack, they were always able to win or at least fight the enemy to a draw. The reformed Kii forces appear to have fought well, but they operated in the shadow of Mizuno's troops and bakufu infantry. Hikone troops after their first humiliation fought well and earned grudging praise from Chōshū, particularly those units operating with bakufu infantry. Takata, the weakest allied element, became the prime target of Chōshū attack, and Takata's collapse led to Hikone's defeat, which destroyed the allied front at Aki.

To sum up the direct human cost of the power struggle, in the six battles military casualties probably totaled 150 to 200 dead and 350 to 450 wounded—rather high figures considering the modest size of the combatant forces and the limited duration of hostile contact. Civilian damage in the area does not appear to have been calculated.

There are more general observations that also suggest themselves. In view of the outcome of the battle of 6/25, it is very tempting to argue that, on the Aki front at least, Honjō's maneuver drew defeat from the jaws of victory. It appears that a bold thrust on 6/25–26 could have thrown Chōshū back across the Osegawa. The ramifications of such a development are hard to predict, although the situation on the other fronts suggests that more than likely the outcome would have been little different.

Lest Honjō be left bearing an unwarranted historical burden, it must also be observed that the allies never displayed much of a bold thrust mentality. Their total available manpower at the Aki front was much greater than that of Chōshū, and their best units were as well armed, as well trained, and as well commanded. These best were, however, severely compromised by their association with obsolete units, and that factor may have contributed to poor coordination of command, so that some sections of the front, notably the inland flank, were left exposed while others probably had a surfeit of manpower. It also appears that by and large both commanders and troops were less willing than the enemy to take risks in order to advance. They did not test their own endurance as severely as did the Chōshū men. They appear to have lacked the intense visceral motivation necessary to carry the day, a condition that only became exacerbated during the latter weeks of war. Probably the enervating effect of months of tedium and difficulty could have been overcome only by exhilarating victories. When those did not materialize and casualties kept increasing, morale only continued to deteriorate.

At a higher level of generalization, when one traces the course of combat through 8/7 even less sanguine—but more sanguinary—conclusions suggest themselves. There seemed to be a steady growth in the forces of inertia, of defense. The barricades grew bigger and more common. There was commensurate growth in the ability of both sides to thwart the other's advance, the reluctance of either side to push beyond limited gains, and the willingness of both sides to abandon ground gained in order to protect base camps. These considerations all suggest that the longer the war dragged on, the less likely was the chance of decisive victory one way or the other. The rate of firing was going up, casualties were becoming heavier, but military gains were not commensurate. Indeed, to say it in exaggerated terms, the first battles remind one of Ichi-

notani and Sekigahara; the last battles hint of Sebastopol, Fredericks-
burg, Mukden, and Verdun. The rifle and all its accoutrements in the
hands of one side was a great weapon of conquest; in the hands of both it
was a costly, bloody weapon of little tactical advantage.

The rifle was doing nothing to make war more lovable or exhilarating.
But the dissimilar experiences of Takata-Hikone and bakufu infantry illustrate how the rifle, as used at the Aki front, was having a social level-
ing effect and a bureaucratic stratifying effect by demonstrating that commoners armed, organized, and trained properly were militarily superior to
inadequately armed samurai. And once the samurai's putative superiority
in war had been opened to question, his whole claim to social leadership
became open to doubt. At that level the Summer War proved to be a very
antifeudal experience.

THE HOME FRONT

Developments on the war front were the decisive factor shaping bakufu
policy during and after the Summer War, but several home front developments were also contributory. One matter that intensified worry, especially in the Kantō, was the massive popular unrest discussed previously.
Another source of distress was the expanding British involvement with
the greater western *han* in general and Chōshū in particular. Accompanying this aspect of the imperialist intrusion was deepening bakufu involvement with France. During the weeks of war the home front also witnessed renewed bakufu attempts to mount a successful war effort. These
attempts did not influence the outcome of the war, but they did contribute directly to the postwar situation.

1. Imperialist Complications

The war enabled foreigners to intrude significantly further into Japanese
affairs. The intrusion was both a general imperialist advance and a further
extension of the Franco-British rivalry into Japan. During the last year
and a half of the Tokugawa era the diplomatic roles of the two powers
were to reflect that extension.

Just before war began, the bakufu learned of mysterious British activities at Nagasaki and strongly suspected Parkes of helping Chōshū.
Leaders asked Roches to check the situation, and on 6/11 he sailed to
Nagasaki, arriving on the seventeenth. At the time Parkes was talking
with Satsuma leaders during a several-day visit to Kagoshima. Roches
met him when he returned to Nagasaki a few days later, and then the
two went to the Shimonoseki vicinity. In their travels they seem to have

done little more with the daimyo than gather information and express
opinions. Thus Roches argued that Satsuma had no reason to aid Chōshū
and urged the latter to settle peacefully. Parkes talked rather freely about
the desirability of restoring authority to the emperor and reducing the Tokugawa house to daimyo status in a daimyo-assembly type of government.[38]

Parkes also visited Uwajima privately, where, as at Kagoshima, he
cultivated goodwill and displayed British military techniques and hardware. The latter activity surely did no harm to the Nagasaki gunrunning
business. Weapons were a topic of great interest to Date Munenari, as he
had shown in earlier communications with Shungaku in which he sought
information on Enfield and Sharps rifles and Armstrong cannon.[39] Apart
from this marginal contribution to the British munitions industry, however, it appears that Parkes was mostly just cultivating the goodwill of
those who might, depending on the outcome of war, emerge shortly as
key Japanese leaders. His actions did show where his sympathies lay, but
Chōshū military success spared the *han* greater dependence on foreigners.
Consequently Parkes does not appear to have aided Chōshū as directly as
bakufu leaders feared.

The bakufu's concern about Parkes' activities was perhaps exaggerated. Nevertheless his secret trips, his belligerent refusal to respect the
bakufu's declared blockade of Chōshū, his other minor actions beneficial
to that *han*, and subsequent boasting at Yokohama about his influence
among anti-bakufu *han* all served to sustain the fear that British military
cooperation with Chōshū and the possibility of another British naval
démarche at Hyōgo were major dangers. Thus when Itakura talked with
Roches on 7/2, after the latter's return to Osaka, the dominating issue
was Parkes. Nor did Roches do anything to calm the fears. To the contrary, he willingly painted a picture of Parkes' evil intentions, reinforced
Itakura's distrust of the great western daimyo, whose British connections
he discussed, and continued presenting France as the compensatory
ally.[40]

The bakufu's concern about English-daimyo cooperation was not
limited to advocates of a firm policy toward Chōshū. Katsu Kaishū also
shared it. During 66/6 he reported, perhaps incorrectly, that Chōshū
was receiving 300,000 (*ryō* presumably) in gold from England and that
the English naval commander (Admiral King probably) was becoming
very involved with Satsuma. His worry about English involvement
prompted him to describe England as a ''famished tiger.'' At the same
time, however, he warned Inaba Masakuni that the bakufu should not
borrow money or warships from France, as reports suggested it might.

Katsu was concerned not only because such action would add to *han* distrust of the bakufu, but also because France was ''a hungry wolf'' that might well eat it up.[41] The problem of ''rebels at home, aggressors abroad'' was more complex and worrisome than ever.

Katsu's fears about Franco-bakufu ties were very well placed. The reverses of the Summer War provided a potent stimulus to both military reformers and their French sympathizers at Yokohama. On 6/2 Roches had sent a telegram to Paris warning that the moment was critical and urging his confreres to hurry with the military mission and other assistance he had earlier requested. Eight days later, as the war was beginning, he sent a hurried request for additional advisors. Then while checking up on Parkes' activity in western Japan, he visited the beleaguered Ogasawara Nagamichi at Kokura on 6/25 and responded favorably to his desperate request for warships, cannon, and a loan to pay for them.[42]

Returning to Osaka, Roches talked with Itakura, who had already heard, probably from Tsukahara Masayoshi, the gist of the discussion at Kokura. When conversation shifted away from the Parkes problem, Itakura urged him to discuss the matters of cannon, rifles, and warships with Edo officials. The possibility of a loan was of particular interest because the bakufu was bankrupt or very nearly so. When Itakura brought up the matter, Roches told him that the partially arranged Franco-bakufu trading company could pay for military and other purchases and do so without actually requiring gold or copper coins. Itakura mentioned that although Iemochi did not desire direct French military assistance in the war, he would welcome military instructors and equipment and wished establishment of the company so that their acquisition could be made speedily. Roches assured him that he would discuss the matter with Oguri Tadamasa upon returning to the Kantō.[43]

At Yokohama two days later, Roches moved briskly to act upon the senior councillors' request for aid. He also urged Kantō officials to pursue the war forcefully and again offered material assistance. By then A. M. Coullet, who had made the trading company arrangement in Paris, had reached Japan and joined finance officials and others in related discussions. On 8/4, a month after Roches's return and as the bakufu was preparing a reinvigorated war, the negotiations in Edo and Yokohama were successfully concluded. They resulted in overall agreement between Oguri and Coullet on a loan of 6 million Mexican dollars. It was to be used primarily for army reform, warships, and the Yokohama shipyard.[44] Whereas the earlier agreement on a trading company had created a mechanism for long-range government financing, the loan would provide funds for immediate use. On the following day Roches wrote Ogasawara. He reported he had met the senior councillors at Edo and they had decided to dispatch military forces to Kokura. He said he had promised them a French loan and then made the necessary arrangements with the superintendents of finance and the French trading company. He asserted, too, that if the bakufu cooperated with him and pursued military strengthening with vigor, in three years or so it would be powerful and the daimyo would submit.[45]

The salutary effect of the loan arrangement was immediately reflected in a major bakufu request for warships. To sum up the matter briefly, during 66/7 officials at Edo tried to purchase a few ships from the French or Dutch but were able to secure only one second-hand vessel, which they hoped to pay for with funds still held by some Americans. On 8/6, however, as plans went ahead for revitalized war and just two days after the loan had been arranged and funding possibilities seemed so immensely improved, Inoue, Matsui, and Ogyū, the senior councillors at Edo, wrote the American minister Van Valkenburgh. Knowing that Americans had vast military stores for sale because their civil war had ended, the three formally inquired if the U.S. Navy might have about eight warships it would sell to the bakufu quickly, and if so would he help arrange it.[46] Confronted by the prospect of military defeat and suddenly gaining access to funds, bakufu leaders had acquired a dangerous willingness to mortgage their regime to foreigners for a chance at victory. Civil strife was posing an ever-greater threat to Japanese independence.

2. The War Effort at Home

The worrisome factors of massive popular unrest and meddlesome foreigners added to the dismay caused by the disastrous course of war. Developments on the battlefront still were the prime determinant of policy, however. Military reverses precipitated renewed efforts at both Osaka and Edo. At Osaka the reverses led to fundamental reorganization of the Tokugawa military system and at Edo to formation of more infantry battalions.

Two officials reached Osaka on 6/22 with reports of the defeats to the west. Their reports precipitated frenetic activity. Within days a long proposal for basic military reorganization had been agreed upon by a combined group of officials (kaigun and rikugun bugyō, ōmetsuke, metsuke, kanjō bugyō, and kanjō ginmiyaku) and submitted to higher officials for review. With small modifications, mostly in the direction of more radical change, the proposal was accepted. In sum it called for scrapping the entire old-style military system and transforming it into an all-firearms triune force of infantry, artillery, and cavalry. The vision of

1862 had acquired a new validity in the crucible of defeat. The vassal-based army of an estimated eight thousand was to be expanded to some twelve thousand in thirty battalions of infantry or their equivalent in naval and artillery personnel.[47]

Several points emerge clearly from this proposal and the comments and modifications that followed. First, it was defeat in battle and the demonstrated superiority of modern weaponry that prompted and justified radical change. Second, the reformers were thoroughly disgusted that liege vassals with income of some 2,900,000 *koku* could furnish only four or five thousand men, and overcoming that gross inefficiency was a chief goal of the reform. Third, a total conversion to a modern military system was what the reformers wanted. But, fourth, status considerations were a major obstacle to free change. In the initial proposal, later modifications, and the final implementation arrangements, status distinctions were the primary determinant of unit composition, character, salary level, and organization. The child would thus acknowledge its parentage; but for all that, this military reorganization, like the defeat at Aki, was undermining the very basis of samurai rule. If carried to completion, it would work a revolution.

At Osaka, then, news of defeat in battle had led to plans for drastic military reform. At Edo news of defeat and of the Osaka response led in turn to an invigorated war effort. One of the two officials who had informed Osaka of developments to the west had subsequently gone on to Edo, arriving there late in the month with the same news and probably with information on the Osaka reaction. His reports precipitated the issuance on 7/4 of announcements recruiting another thousand infantrymen, enough for two more battalions. Conscription orders sent throughout the Kantō instructed village leaders to furnish one recruit per hundred populace, and the orders reportedly were obeyed with minimal resistance. Men from a host of menial professions were accepted in the army, their admission justified on the ground that ''with military reform underway, men from all places will be accepted as foot soldiers (*heisotsu*).''[48]

Two more battalions might help, but bad news kept arriving from the west. By about 7/8 at the latest Edo officials knew the seriousness of Iemochi's illness. They began discussing reform of the bakufu and policy toward daimyo along with matters of personnel selection and advancement.[49] While awaiting outcome of the illness, they pressed on with the war effort, thereby maintaining essential unity with Osaka.

On 8/1, doubtless after learning of Iemochi's death and probably after learning that Osaka intended to reinvigorate the war, the senior councillors at Edo issued a statement putting matters about as bluntly as possible. Mōri, they pointed out, had rejected the lenient terms offered. In the war that had resulted, however, Chōshū troops had rifles and had been successful. About half the bakufu's troops were in the war and had rifles, but reserves were inadequate, and in consequence success was difficult. On 7/18 Hamada castle had fallen. At Kokura Chōshū had invaded, established control over both coasts of the Shimonoseki straits, and closed it to ships. At the Aki front Ii and Sakakibara had been defeated, and bakufu and Kii forces were holding the line, but they lacked reinforcements. Consequently two inspectors were hurrying there with additional rifle units. That, however, would make it difficult to guard Edo, so men should come forth to repay their obligations by serving in the struggle. Military reforms would be made and no one was to be disgruntled at them.[50] Then, as an earnest of that final warning, Edo leaders abolished the title *kobushin*, or unemployed liege vassal of under 3000 *koku* stipend. Of the 2500 men in that category, half were abruptly assigned to the army and half to the navy.[51] The bakufu had suddenly acquired two more battalions of troops, but they were troops of the most dubious quality.

3. New Leader, Old Goal

Reverses at the front had thus precipitated efforts at both Osaka and Edo to salvage the war, but from mid-66/7 those efforts were displaced by developments at Osaka. Early in the month young Iemochi became painfully ill.[52] Then on 7/11, two days after leaders had learned of Honjō's debacle, the shogun's condition turned sharply worse and quickly brought to center stage the issue of shogunal succession.[53]

The Osaka situation at that juncture deserves recapitulation. From the background came pouring in a steady stream of disastrous reports from the battlefield. And amid the battle reports appeared evidence of divisions and rancor among the expedition's leaders. Also in the background were reports of popular uprisings in the northeast that must have reminded men of the turmoil just past in Osaka and Edo. Within Kyoto public discontent and incidents had led a worried court in late 66/6 to have Yoshinobu and Katamori strengthen their forces in and around the palace. At court vigorous lobbying by Satsuma men and their court supporters, particularly efforts to give the *han* a major role as protector of the court, had by 7/23 so intensified ill will between Aizu and Satsuma as to spark new rumors of a coming clash between the two.[54] Concern with the Satsuma problem was reinforced by reports and rumors of Anglo-Satsuma contacts and cooperation. All in all, the situation was ghastly. And at center was the young shogun, painfully ill for nearly a month, expiring at last on 7/20. With his dying the war issue was temporarily set aside and energies at Osaka were devoted to persuading Yoshinobu to succeed him.

Yoshinobu, lord of Hitotsubashi and *kinri shuei sōtoku*, was very well aware that it was a wretched time to try to govern. He knew strong forces were working for an imperial restoration and destruction of Tokugawa primacy. He knew too that he had many enemies within the bakufu and that his opinions did not necessarily carry weight. Thus he had complained to Shungaku on 7/1 that when he said things no one listened and that a shake-up of officialdom was in order.[55] Faced with these disadvantages, he was understandably reluctant to try to salvage a regime about which he had severe doubts in any case.[56] He was subjected to massive pressure, however, from many sources—Nagai Naomune, Kawakatsu Kōun, Katamori, Matsudaira Sadaaki, Shungaku, court officials, and most persistently and most persuasively Itakura. With the active mediation of Hara Ichinoshin, a Hitotsubashi vassal, a compromise was reached by 7/27 in which Yoshinobu agreed to accept the headship of the Tokugawa house but not to be named shogun, at least not until Tokugawa power had been demonstrated against Chōshū.[57]

Settling the succession was well and good, but it did not settle policy. Yoshinobu recognized the weaknesses of the several alternatives he faced. He just possibly may have considered ending the shogunate forthwith, and he may well have intended to pursue major reform. But on the matter of Chōshū, on which he had long been a hard-liner, he was inflexible. He still wished to give that *han* a sound thrashing and wished the court fully committed to the venture. Like so many leaders, he had no intention of presiding over his government's defeat, and so he resolved to fight on, at least until Chōshū forces had been driven back into their own territory, and preferably much further. He told a senior court official on the night of 7/26 that he wished to settle the matter promptly by driving to Yamaguchi within thirty days.[58]

Itakura supported Yoshinobu, and on the twenty-eighth the Osaka bakufu officially accepted his view. On that day the deceased Iemochi, whose death had been kept an official secret, was caused to announce that he was very ill and that Yoshinobu was to be his successor and was to proceed to the front as his representative and lead the Chōshū expedition. In his own statement Yoshinobu proposed to go to Osaka on about 8/10 and then take his army to Hiroshima, reaching there ten days later. On 7/29 the court accepted that plan, and on the next day Yoshinobu formally accepted arrangements for his succession to headship of the Tokugawa house.[59]

Katamori, too, wished to sustain the war effort and get into action himself. He argued that all forces at Osaka should be issued rifles, which would give the bakufu a large army of fifty thousand effective troops quickly.[60] That optimistic estimate was less sound, perhaps, than his fear that Chōshū might drive eastward and link up with Satsuma forces in Kyoto. To prevent that dire development, he proposed placing Kyoto defenses in the combined hands of his brother Sadaaki, Shungaku, and Yamauchi Yōdō. Then he would lead Aizu forces through Iwami while Yoshinobu would strike through Hiroshima in a pincer thrust at Yamaguchi. However, those court officials supporting Yoshinobu did not wish to lose both major protectors, particularly since there were several hundred Satsuma men in town to be kept under control. As they wished, Yoshinobu rejected Katamori's repeated requests for combat duty and planned instead to have Mochitsugu lead the Iwami column while he himself led the Aki drive.[61]

The new Tokugawa head thus appeared resolved to carry on the venture already begun. During the first few days of 66/8 leaders at Osaka proceeded with the plan to have him lead a reinvigorated war. The decision to persevere made it necessary to implement the military reform plan earlier worked out on paper. With the great lords refusing to cooperate and minor lords unable to help much, Osaka leaders had no choice but to abandon customary practice and wage their war with their own troops. Most of the modernized forces were already at the Aki front, however, and they were insufficient. The war had already demonstrated the obsolescence of the old-style units left at Osaka, so implementation of radical reform was essential if Yoshinobu were to lead an army westward.

Osaka leaders realized that a major obstacle to both radical reform and effective prosecution of the war was the low morale of liege vassals in the city. And they feared the problem had been complicated by Yoshinobu's succession because distrust of him was so widespread among those vassals that they might well refuse to accept his leadership. Officials proposed to attack those problems head-on. Vassals would be given a choice between going east and going west: those who wished could return to Edo with Iemochi's ashes; the others would go with Yoshinobu. On 8/1 Yoshinobu gave a stem-winding speech to the men, inviting all who had the courage to join him in a drive all the way to Yamaguchi castle. The response was reportedly enthusiastic.[62] Men who had been held at Osaka while the fighting went poorly at last seemed to see a prospect for glory. At long last they had, perhaps, a leader worthy of following.

With the men thus encouraged to sacrifice, on the next day the bakufu formed five new assault battalions called *yūgekitai*.[63] They staffed them at once by abolishing a variety of small units and recruiting rear vassals and unemployed samurai, arming them with rifles, and giving them hurried training. Orders of 8/3 required all liege vassals without exception to be enrolled in rifle units. And inspectors general were told to have daimyo form their troops into rifle units. Aware that problems of dignity arose when lower and higher-ranking liege vassals were integrated, the orders of 8/3 instructed the latter *(bankata* and *kumi yoriki)* to form several companies in the *yūgekitai* while the lower-ranking *dōshin* and men in other lower-ranking units were to enroll in artillery-related units. *Yūgekitai* members were to be paid in accord with their prior rank stipends and were required to attend drill. By these moves the reformers hoped to minimize discontent and maximize unit competence.

In line with the policy of total conversion to firearms, on 8/8 Osaka officials instructed those at Edo to halt all practice with swords and pikes and switch instead to firearms. They advised rather tartly that those men who failed to do so might just as well commit suicide. And shortly after that leaders ordered all those accompanying Yoshinobu to provide their own retainers with rifles and warned that men otherwise armed would receive no pay from the bakufu.

Out of this crash program of military reorganization Yoshinobu hoped to field immediate reinforcements consisting of some 1350 Hitotsubashi troops (the force he had previously created at Kyoto) plus some 5000 or 6000 bakufu troops organized in about thirteen battalions.

The problem of finances remained. The French loan would not provide monies for use in Japan, and the bakufu was bankrupt or nearly so. Its precise condition is not clear and perhaps was not clear even to finance officials. In 66/7, for example, Yoshinobu told Shungaku that the proposed shogunal advance would cost 1,300,000 *ryō* but that when officials surveyed their resources, they found all bakufu departments unable to muster a grand total of even 20,000 *ryō*. A month later Katsu Kaishū reported a somewhat more encouraging situation, saying that a forced loan in the Kinai had reportedly raised 300,000 *ryō*, that there was perhaps as much as 400,000 *ryō* on hand, and that another 500,000 could be obtained from the Honganji. Of this sum 400,000 would be allotted for Yoshinobu's venture.[64]

In any case the enterprise would be strapped for funds. Yoshinobu personally intended to do his part in the best samurai tradition by being the model of hardy frugality. He would travel simply, with only three backpacks: one containing a blanket; one a change of clothes; and one a timepiece and other personal items.

The objective of this great effort was somewhat obscure. For domestic

consumption it was described as a drive to Yamaguchi, but to most outsiders, such as Shungaku, both Itakura and Yoshinobu implied that they
only intended to drive Chōshū forces out of Iwami and Aki.[65] In fact, of
course, when the campaign began, its objectives would grow or shrink as
the tide of battle dictated.

During the first days of 66/8, then, the bakufu's home front situation
belied the disasters just then befalling it at Kokura and Aki. The apparent
arrangement at Edo of a massive foreign loan had opened up a great new
chance to buy the weapons with which to wage a bigger and better war.
And leaders had moved at once to seize the chance. At Osaka Yoshinobu's accession to headship of the Tokugawa house had given the regime
a leader apparently committed to a revitalized campaign. And to this end,
he had approved a fundamental reorganization of the regime's military
system. Within days, however, the picture was to change dramatically.

ENDING THE WAR

From the time men of Hikone waded into the Ose river, actions of men at
war became the dynamo of Japanese political history. That dynamo generated enough energy to thrust Japan appreciably further into the colonial
slough and to break the centuries-old pattern of bakufu military organization. The process of preparing for war that had set the dynamo in motion
contributed appreciably to unleashing public anger and violence all over
central and eastern Japan, and the havoc wrought by war later helped
spread it to western Japan. The dynamo had not, however, generated
enough power to break the political stalemate between the Tokugawa
house and its enemies. Rather, the struggle exhausted the combatants
and forced them back into a renewed political dialogue.

1. Preliminary Maneuvers

There had, of course, been opposition to the bakufu war effort even
before it began, and the disastrous course of events during 66/6–7 gave
renewed vigor to the antiwar movement. After learning of the first
bakufu reverses, a number of people began to advise disengagement.
They included Yoshikatsu of Owari and the daimyo and spokesmen of
several other han. They also included Katsu Kaishū, who had been recalled to duty just before the outbreak of war in the vain hope he could
persuade Satsuma to cooperate in the venture.[66]

It was, however, Shungaku of Fukui who emerged as the most vigorous advocate of disengagement, and so his position requires fuller consideration.[67] To backtrack briefly, after the collapse of his Bunkyū reform in
early 1863, Shungaku had fled to Echizen. Then he reappeared in Kyoto

later in the year for a second brief and thoroughly ineffective effort at shaping affairs. In 64/4 he again went home and stayed at Fukui for the next year, refusing to participate in the first Chōshū expedition. He kept himself informed, however, and observed with frank disapproval bakufu policy toward Chōshū, court, and *sankin kōtai*. After Edo made policy changes in 65/4, he was urged by Katamori and others to play a role in affairs. He still refused, however, on the ground that policy remained too reactionary. Rather, he began to correspond more vigorously and directly with officials and friends, supporting the reappointment of Ogasawara and Itakura, opposing the revived Chōshū expedition, and writing endlessly about *kōbugattai*.

In early 65/9 Shungaku was still resisting those who urged his going to the Kinai. When he learned of the Hyōgo crisis and the court's approval of bakufu plans to punish Chōshū, however, he decided on 9/25 to sally forth and set matters right. Two days later he was urged by a Satsuma vassal to go to Kyoto and join other daimyo in opposing the Chōshū expedition. With his decision thus reinforced, on 10/1 he left Fukui despite last-minute reconsiderations and concern about stepping into a chaotic situation. En route to Kyoto, however, he received more information from Fukui vassals about the utter confusion in the Kinai. In consultation with them he changed his mind and decided not to get involved. In a letter to Yoshinobu, sent on the day he returned to Fukui, he explained somewhat lamely that if he appeared in Kyoto at that time, the bakufu would probably see it as a Fukui-Satsuma maneuver, and so he had returned home.

After that abortive venture Shungaku continued to stay informed through his correspondence with Akitsuki Taneki, various other daimyo, Yoshinobu, Katsu Kaishū, Ōkubo Ichiō, and his loyal friends at court. By the end of the month he was feeling quite optimistic about affairs. He was cheered by the return to office of Ogasawara and Itakura, the apparent effectiveness of Yoshinobu, imperial approval of the treaties, foreign withdrawal from Hyōgo, and the decision to negotiate further with Chōshū. That improved outlook notwithstanding, he refused invitations to sally forth again. When Itakura and Ogasawara informed Fukui of Satsuma's hostile attitude toward the bakufu, however, he did agree to dispatch vassals to mediate the disagreement. They had no success. The spring of 1866 passed, time ran out, and hopes for peace died. Finally on 66/5/28 Itakura ordered Shungaku to come to Osaka to serve while the shogun led the march westward.[68] Shungaku opposed the whole plan, however, and refused to move. When war engulfed the regime, he was still in the safety of his castle town.

On 6/25 Shungaku finally left Fukui for the Kinai. However, he was going with the intention of thwarting that very westward movement which his presence was supposed to facilitate. Four days later he reached Kyoto, intensely distrustful of bakufu leadership and fully aware of his own delicate position and the difficulties of mediation. He stopped at Kyoto rather than Osaka to make it clear he would not serve as Itakura intended during the shogun's planned absence. In succeeding days he discussed matters with Yoshinobu, Katamori, Katsu, Aizu vassals, Satsuma men, and others. He talked about the campaign, Honjō's release of the Chōshū captives, the activities of Parkes and Roches, the shogun's illness, and other aspects of the situation. He made his own view known from the outset, summing it up for Yoshinobu at their first meeting on 7/1 in this way: "If it were as in former days, with military equipment, money, and foodstuffs prepared and the *han* fully obedient, then the suppression should go ahead. But today when the situation is not like that, it is a reckless venture."[69]

Shungaku thus arrived on the scene intending to stop the war. He found that the battlefield situation and other developments favored the effort, and during 66/7 agitation for disengagement continued. Shungaku lobbied discreetly for an end to the fighting, and other great daimyo continued to call for an end to the misadventure. Katsu fired off one after another ill-humored letter critical of officials, advocating conciliation, and trying in his inept manner to end the war. Most officials were in a difficult position to oppose the war openly, even if they did so in their hearts. But a few, such as Nagai Naomune, acknowledged that policy had failed and some change was necessary.

As we have seen, however, at both Edo and Osaka the early war reverses had mostly just elicited renewed attempts to secure a military victory. The hard-line position was advocated most vigorously by Yoshinobu, Katamori, the latter's vassals, and some lesser officials who hoped to salvage the effort by having Yoshinobu go to the front. Against those obstacles the early attempts to stop the carnage achieved nothing.

2. Of Words and Deeds and Ending Wars

As of late 66/7 the antiwar effort had borne no fruit. Then, as Yoshinobu's succession was settled, Osaka leaders resolved to renew the war effort. Even as they turned their energies to military reform and war preparation, however, Shungaku launched a remarkable counteroffensive designed to dissuade them from the planned expedition.[70]

When Yoshinobu agreed to succeed Iemochi on 7/27, he made it clear to Shungaku that he wanted to administer Chōshū a first-class trouncing. He also adopted a rather ambiguous attitude toward the latter's proposal that the great lords again be summoned to discuss affairs. His comments dismayed Shungaku and prompted him to talk dispiritedly of going home again. Then on 7/30 Shungaku received full details of the bakufu war plan together with acknowledgment that the problem of financing was acute. When he urged Itakura to assemble the lords to discuss matters, he was turned aside with the argument that because Chōshū was seizing lands in Iwami and Aki, there was no time to assemble them. Yoshinobu took the same line, and by day's end Shungaku had decided he would indeed go home to Fukui. On the next day, however, Itakura rejected his formal request to depart.

It was at this point that Shungaku and his vassals decided among themselves to make one last great effort to prevent the madness of another campaign. With that decision made, they launched one of the most intensive lobbying exercises of the entire *bakumatsu* period. For four days Shungaku and four or five of his vassals talked ceaselessly to Itakura, Yoshinobu, Sadaaki, court officials, lesser bakufu officials, Hitotsubashi vassals, and Aizu vassals. From early morning until late at night Shungaku was calling on people or writing letters. The arguments grew shopworn, and by the end they were being repeated over and over with more and more impatience and bitterness. The lords must be assembled. No, there isn't time. The war is lost and must be abandoned. No, Chōshū must be driven back. Without daimyo support the effort cannot succeed. But if Chōshū is not brought to heel, other daimyo will not become obedient. There is no money. It is being sought. The court has not really approved the expedition. Yes, it has. The second expedition never was really justified. Perhaps not, but one mustn't change horses in midstream. The exchanges ground on and on, but Fukui's arguments did not meet bakufu needs and so they achieved nothing.

By 8/5 the great Fukui effort was over, with little or nothing accomplished. Yoshinobu had formally stated at court that the bakufu's goal was only to drive Chōshū back to its own land, but he was still going to advance on schedule, with departure set for 8/11 or 12. The daimyo, he reiterated, would be assembled after the Chōshū situation had been rectified. Fukui was utterly impotent.

Others joined the Fukui effort. Officials at court argued fiercely about whether to support or oppose Yoshinobu's venture, and Satsuma lobbyists tried to prevent it. But it was all to no avail; the decision was irreversible. On 8/8, as a typhoon lashed the Kinai and the Yodo river flooded and cut all communication between Kyoto and Osaka, Yoshinobu, the shogun's surrogate, met the emperor in farewell audience prior to departure for Hiroshima four days later.[71]

At that juncture men far from the scene of political combat achieved by deeds what the articulate few at Kyoto had failed to achieve by words.

On 8/7 a messenger had arrived at Osaka just ahead of the typhoon. He brought news of the collapse at Kokura. At the time Itakura was at Osaka castle, and he and other bakufu officials, probably including such vigorous bakufu defenders as Inaba Masami, Tsukahara Masayoshi, Inoue Yoshifumi, and Takikawa Tomoshige, took immediate steps to cope with the development. They dispatched messengers east to alert Edo to the crisis and the need to prepare for battle. The statement the messengers carried recited the series of disasters to date, called the situation one of unparalleled danger, and asserted that prompt military reform was utterly necessary and must be made regardless of the difficulties. It might well work great hardships on lower-ranking people, but in this crisis liege vassals must make preparations to serve in battle and resolve to repay in death the generations of gratitude they owed.[72] Such was Osaka's response to the news from Kokura.

While messengers were carrying that statement eastward, the typhoon was passing on to the north. On 8/10 Itakura headed for Kyoto with inspector general Takikawa and others, arriving with the news of Kokura the following day. Yoshinobu thus learned of the collapse three days after taking formal leave of the court and the day before he was scheduled to start west on his great expedition to suppress Chōshū. At Osaka the news had elicited redoubled effort, but at Kyoto, where dubious reports of six or seven hundred casualties also circulated, the news from Kokura evidently shattered the new leader's vision of the future.[73] Or, a cynic might argue, it gave him an excuse to avoid a task for which he had no stomach in any case.

In a day of hectic discussions the senior councillors and inspectorate members reportedly still urged a quick military counterattack.[74] After learning of the Kokura disaster, representatives of Kii, Hikone, and Kurume also urged that Yoshinobu march west. Yoshinobu, however, evidently argued that the loss of Kyushu daimyo support was the critical factor. Somewhat surprisingly, the deputy Sadaaki rather quickly agreed, despite the angry objections of some of his vassals. The arguments of the two men suggest they did not really believe unaided bakufu strength was sufficient to defeat Chōshū, which suggests in turn that the Fukui effort had perhaps not been entirely in vain.

Katamori, however, was pressed by his men and opposed any delay in the planned attack. His men still feared an alliance of advancing Chōshū forces and Satsuma men in Kyoto and wished to march forth and salvage the situation themselves. The loyal Katamori thus became an opponent of

Yoshinobu's new plans. His view was reflected in a strong letter of that day in which he sharply criticized Yoshinobu's request to postpone the expedition, warning that such a decision would be dangerous to court and bakufu and fraught with disastrous implications.

Yoshinobu did not willingly lose Aizu support and tried to persuade Katamori of the wisdom of his new policy. Earlier he had rebutted Shungaku by insisting he would summon the daimyo only after quelling Chō-shū. This time when Katamori argued for a continued campaign, Yoshinobu rebutted him by arguing à la Fukui that he should first summon the daimyo and get their views, and then advance toward Chōshū if they advised it. Yoshinobu could not be accused of blind consistency, but he was doing his best, given the crooked path he had chosen to travel.

On the same day the new Tokugawa leader obtained court approval of a delay in his departure. On the thirteenth he started inquiries about securing not just a delay but a full armistice, and on the following day he finally met Shungaku to discuss affairs.[75] By skillful argument the emperor's objections to this abrupt change of direction were overcome despite the displeasure of some senior court officials and nobles. By 8/16 the court had informally decided to accept Yoshinobu's plan to announce the shogun's death and use that event as pretext for negotiating an armistice.[76] As matters worked out, these decisions were adhered to, the new expedition was abandoned, and the Summer War came to an end.

The Summer War had begun because the men of Mōri would not submit peacefully to the men of Tokugawa. It ended because the men of Mōri had persuaded the Tokugawa leader that they could not be forced to submit, not at once anyway.

The verbal antiwar effort was not very important in ending hostilities. Shungaku's lobbying may have helped marginally, but the other antiwar agitation seems to have had no effect. Yoshinobu's succession was a factor but not in a simple causal way. What it did was give the bakufu a leader who could make a decision, whereas Iemochi might not have been able to do so. But Yoshinobu's decision had been to fight on, until news of the collapse at Kokura undermined his resolve, leading him to do that abrupt—and courageous—*volte face* that led in following weeks to the disengagement of forces.

The battlefield experience did much more than merely bring the war to an end, however. It furnished decisive military lessons, as we noted earlier in assessing the Aki front. Furthermore defeat discredited conservative forces in the bakufu and enabled military reformers to effect basic changes in bakufu army organization. The reformers' efforts also bound them more closely to France, however, and both the military reform and French ties exacerbated great *han* distrust of the bakufu. This exacerbated distrust plus the realization that renewed civil war was very likely and military force had become the real arbiter of politics accelerated daimyo participation in the illegal arms trade. The resulting arms race only contributed to the certain disintegration of the Great Peace. The whole trend served, also, to force minor *han* to become much more cautious lest they end up on the wrong side and suffer the fate of Hamada and Kokura.

Yoshinobu thus assumed control of Tokugawa destinies and pretensions to national leadership just when the interest alignments and ground rules of the old *bakuhan* political order had been discredited. How well he would handle his responsibilities in an uncharted future remained to be seen.

Part
FOUR

THE ATTEMPT AT RENOVATION

CHAPTER 9
Recovery from War
1866/8–1867/1

The ill-starred Summer War having ended, bakufu leaders undertook to salvage what remained of their regime. In the immediate aftermath of defeat they adopted a conciliatory *kōbugattai* policy inspired primarily by Shungaku of Fukui.

Within a few weeks, however, the *kōbugattai* effort was discredited and a more forthright policy of revival was adopted. That policy, the Keiō reform, was adhered to through the next summer. It survived a severe test in 67/4–5 and seemed to be achieving considerable success by 67/9. It was only abandoned near year's end when new challenges were presented by domestic anti-bakufu forces.[1]

The Keiō reform was a political revival involving a major reorganization of the bakufu military and administrative structures.[2] Initially it followed the general lines of the Bunkyū structural reforms. However, it went well beyond them during 1867, ultimately acquiring a revolutionary antifeudal character that would lead, if the reform were to succeed, to unification of the polity and transformation of society. As that statement implies, the political ideal underlying the Keiō reform was vastly more radical than the Bunkyū reform's *kōbugattai* ideal of a feudal coalition under sponsorship of the imperial court. And as that statement suggests, by its nature the Keiō reform could only elicit the hostility of great daimyo. This situation, together with internal problems of the reform, ultimately confounded it. However, its failure does not reduce its significance as an indication of what had happened to the bakufu or, more broadly, as a measure of the extraordinary regenerative and adaptive capabilities of *bakumatsu* Japan.

The Keiō reform developed within a context of relative quiescence. There were several reasons for the quiescence. Once the bakufu gave up its war effort, Chōshū became quiet as it replenished its strength and readied itself for the future. The bakufu also was spent and devoted its energies to recuperation and preparation. The daimyo in general were exhausted, too skeptical to support the regime but too uncertain of their own position and capabilities to pursue active programs. Rather, the political elite returned to the older, safer, less demanding game of struggling for control of the symbols of authority. In that enterprise political efforts were again largely channeled through proxies at court. As a consequence the court again became the stage for political struggle. It tended, however, to become paralyzed because it reflected the larger national stalemate, and only gradually did it accept bakufu leadership again as the regime regained its footing near year's end. Hence the court, like bakufu and lords, was unable to play a decisive role in affairs. *Shishi* too were relatively quiet, no longer, it appears, believing in independent action and therefore tied to the passive postures of domanial leaders. And lastly the foreigners were quiescent, attempting to assess the implications of bakufu defeat and content to badger the regime on lesser issues while awaiting the opening of Hyōgo, scheduled for the end of 1867.

Commoners, however, were not quiet. To the contrary the postwar months were a period of unparalleled social difficulty. The consequent unrest was clearly worrisome to the rulers and surely encouraged their own cautious conduct. It was perhaps not by chance that the great lords remained politically inactive until after the public had become quiet again. In any case, the popular turmoil was contained by early 1867, and after that the Keiō reformers were able to press on with their program until *shishi*-sponsored great *han* activism thwarted them late in the year.

KŌBUGATTAI: THE WOULD-BE PHOENIX: 66/8–9

At long last in the autumn of 1866, nine years after the dream first stirred men to action, Yoshinobu was lord of the main Tokugawa house and apparently heeding Shungaku, long the champion of a court-centered, daimyo-manned *kōbugattai* regime. The *kōbugattai* scheme, tried twice early in 1863 and 1864, had twice come to nought. Yet it was rising again, the phoenix from the ashes of Tokugawa defeat.[3]

Shungaku's vision was still essentially that of his Bunkyū reform. He wanted a government under imperial auspices in which daimyo, or at least great daimyo, decided matters in consultation. In that regime the head of the Tokugawa house would merely be one of the daimyo, unless they allowed him the title of shogun. For purposes of administration able *han* vassals would be employed in a broadened bakufu, holding positions comparable to those of the inspectorate. That coalition regime could then determine and implement a unified national policy, thereby preserving Japanese independence.

On 66/8/12 when Shungaku realized that Yoshinobu was about to abandon the Summer War, he drafted a seven-point statement of tasks he believed Yoshinobu should pursue.[4] It suggests rather well what his policy involved. He advised Yoshinobu to:

1. Announce the shogun's death at once.
2. Succeed as head of the main Tokugawa house.
3. Have the court decide whether bakufu leaders should return to Edo or stay in the Kinai.
4. Change the existing Tokugawa family system and stop giving orders to daimyo such as Kii and Owari.
5. Have the court decide whether or not to abolish the posts of Kyoto protector, deputy, and city magistrate.
6. Restore to the court authority in such matters as foreign policy, the opening of Hyōgo, daimyo control, and coinage.
7. If the assembly of daimyo and nobles *(tenka shūgi)* decides to leave the shogunal office intact, then accept the post, but in any case reform other old practices such as giving orders to daimyo.

Shungaku's venture depended upon the cooperation of court, bakufu, and great lords. As things worked out, however, none of them agreed to cooperate. In the wake of the Summer War, moreover, the venture assumed that Chōshū would respond favorably to a conciliatory peace settlement. That assumption, too, proved wrong. The obstacles to the Fukui effort and hence its outcome can best be seen by observing how Chōshū, great lords, bakufu, and court responded to it.

1. The Response of Chōshū and Great Lords

Shungaku had long urged that Katsu Kaishū be called upon to mediate the Edo-Chōshū conflict. Then after the Kokura debacle led Yoshinobu to seek peace, Itakura advised the new Tokugawa leader to name Katsu emissary to Chōshū. Katsu and Yoshinobu had a considerable dislike for one another,[5] but Itakura overcame the latter's objections, and on the night of 8/14 Katsu, who was at Osaka, received an order to hasten to Kyoto. He reached the city a day later, discussed matters, and was told the shogun's death would be used to justify a cease-fire that he was to arrange. He learned that negotiations were supposed to achieve a Chōshū withdrawal in return for bakufu withdrawal, acknowledgment that the expedition had been unwarranted, and assurances that a *kōbugattai* policy would be pursued. Having received his instructions, Katsu left Kyoto and reached Hiroshima on the twenty-first. There he met Mochitsugu, talked extensively with him and others on the scene, and then proceeded to meet Chōshū representatives at Miyajima.

Meanwhile back at Kyoto on 8/21 the court issued a formal order for a cease-fire and military disengagement based on withdrawal of Chōshū forces to their own territory. The order was sent westward and reached Katsu at Miyajima nine days later as he was establishing communication with Chōshū. He recognized at once that the order sounded less conciliatory than his original guidelines and that Chōshū would find it utterly unacceptable. However, he was unable to get Mochitsugu and his subordinates to approve any tampering with it. His talks with Chōshū men began the next day and promptly foundered on their refusal to withdraw. The talks remained foundered despite his attempt to follow the original guidelines by promising bakufu reform of a *kōbugattai* sort.

Victorious in the field, Chōshū had no reason whatsoever to make concessions at the conference table. It refused to withdraw from lands conquered in Iwami, Buzen, and Aki provinces until after the bakufu had retreated and ''reformed'' the governmental system, by which Chōshū meant accept a political order dominated by great daimyo. That stance made not only the court's order of 8/21 but also Katsu's original instructions of 8/17 unworkable. Unable to find a middle ground, Katsu returned to Hiroshima and then went east, reaching Kyoto on 9/10. Three days later he resigned his task, claiming he lacked ability to carry it out.

The problem, of course, lay in the task, not the emissary, but whatever the reason for Katsu's failure, a key premise of Shungaku's plan had been confounded.

It was an outcome Itakura and Yoshinobu had feared, but one Shungaku apparently had not really expected. He had badly misread the larger situation and so misunderstood the Chōshū temper. To elaborate, back on 7/27 he had urged bakufu leaders to summon the daimyo, and Itakura had expressed concern about Satsuma's likely response. In reply Shungaku had advised him to have Katsu approach Satsuma—if that were done, ''Satsuma would willingly agree.''[6] Then on 8/13, when the proposal to have Katsu contact Chōshū gained pertinence, Itakura expressed fear that Chōshū would refuse to withdraw, and on the twentieth a senior court official also expressed fear that Chōshū might reject the peace offer. Shungaku, presumably with Katsu's instructions of 8/17 in mind, replied: ''Thus far Chōshū has fought vigorously because the bakufu expedition was not just, and the bakufu suffered reverses because the *han* disapproved and would not aid it. But now with the court order to stop the fighting, should Chōshū refuse to obey, then the justness of suppression would be clear and the lords of the realm would agree to cooperate.''[7]

That view was shared by Katsu who on the seventeenth told a Fukui vassal that ''should Chōshū refuse to withdraw, suppression would be justified.'' Clearly neither man favored further fighting and the phrase was used for purposes of persuasion, but it betrayed the inadequacy of their perception. They expected Chōshū to compromise, but there was no good reason why it should.

Shungaku's vision assumed, in addition to quick settlement of the Chōshū conflict, the willingness of great lords to assemble at Kyoto to deliberate on matters and formulate policy. Twice before the lords had been summoned, and twice they had assembled, leaving only after it had become apparent they were unable to govern. In 1866 the project was undertaken yet a third time, but on this occasion it did not even get started.

One difficulty was obtaining a proper call for a daimyo assembly. As soon as Yoshinobu had agreed to succeed Iemochi, Shungaku had begun to press for the assembly, arguing over and over that it was the most important order of business and the action upon which all else hinged. In succeeding weeks he repeatedly urged it, arguing furthermore that the lords must be assembled by the court, not by Yoshinobu. As those weeks passed, however, a host of petty disputes emerged to plague the project. The disputes were all expressions of a fundamental disagreement: Shungaku intended the lords to govern; Yoshinobu and other bakufu leaders hoped to use the assembly for other purposes—to gain time, to win some goodwill, to get daimyo support for Yoshinobu's appointment as shogun, or as an expression of bakufu supremacy.[8] In a compromise that satisfied no one, the court finally did issue the summons on 9/7, but stated that although it had issued the call, Yoshinobu had requested it.

Shungaku feared that formulation would only discourage the lords. However, daimyo behavior in general suggests they would have responded favorably to no sort of formulation. Shungaku had already done his best to induce them to come. Long before the court order finally went out, he had industriously written and written, urged and argued, trying to get Yoshikatsu of Owari, Munenari of Uwajima, Hisamitsu of Satsuma, and Yōdō of Tosa to come. But they refused. Yoshinobu also wrote letters and dispatched vassals to urge them, but still they refused. From the very outset the daimyo response to solicitation was different from previous years. They simply would not come. Then the court order of 9/7 went out, and when formal replies came in, they only confirmed the prior situation: almost no lords agreed to come.[9] Nor is there any reason to think they would have come even if the court order had been sent precisely in the manner urged by Shungaku. They evidently no longer shared his vision, and so the daimyo assembly never materialized.

2. The Response of Bakufu and Court

Chōshū and other *han* had thus done nothing to help Shungaku. The bakufu proved equally obstructionist. In the course of advocating their policy, Shungaku and his vassals revealed the extent to which their objectives threatened the interests of bakufu officials, and in consequence Fukui lost whatever official cooperation it might have hoped for.

Most obviously Shungaku hoped to prevent Yoshinobu from becoming shogun, and that purpose repeatedly put him at odds with bakufu leaders. He had strongly approved Yoshinobu's decision of late 66/7 to refuse the shogunal title, and in succeeding weeks he worked to prevent that decision's being undone, lest its undoing discourage the daimyo from assembling. Thus in both his seven points of 8/12 and a letter to Yoshinobu the next morning he argued that daimyo should decide whether there was to be a shogun. Itakura saw at once the risk that scheme entailed, and he mentioned to Shungaku the next day his fear they might not approve the shogunal appointment. Shungaku replied that the risk had to be taken: if the bakufu really reformed itself, things would work out all right. It was hardly a reassuring answer.

In opposition to that posture, Yoshinobu's supporters at court were prepared at least as early as 8/3 to treat him like a shogun, which seems to have been what Itakura and probably others wanted. Then when Yo-shinobu was designated head of the Tokugawa house on the twentieth, the bakufu issued a general notice that he was to be addressed in the cus-tomary manner as *uesama*. Shungaku rightly saw that as a step toward de facto shogun status and protested it. In defending the action, Itakura pointed out, probably correctly if somewhat disingenuously,[10] that the court previously had said it would treat him like a shogun in ceremonial matters. And he added that if Yoshinobu were treated like a daimyo, it would later cause complications.

The contemporaneous dispute over who would assemble the daimyo was another expression of the conflict over the shogunal title. Shungaku protested the compromise arrangement of 9/7, and after that he objected to plans for an imperial audience for Yoshinobu. He saw in that scheme, which Itakura, Hara Ichinoshin, and others were actively promoting, yet another step toward making him shogun without waiting for daimyo opinion. The symbolic issue of Yoshinobu's title thus became a central focus of bakufu resistance to Shungaku's effort. His plans also threatened other bakufu members, however, and generated other less visible opposi-tion to the *kōbugattai* scheme.

To elaborate, on 8/13 when bakufu leaders were formulating a post-war program and searching for policy alternatives, Itakura asked a Fukui vassal to summarize Shungaku's thoughts. The summary was mostly a restatement of the latter's long-standing interests, but as his final point the vassal spoke of opening high office to great daimyo. That point dis-turbed Itakura, who made a rather gruff but vague comment about how when ruin is imminent, things must be changed and reinvigoration is necessary.[11] That evening Itakura notified Fukui officials that the bakufu accepted Shungaku's ideas, specifically as formulated in a letter that morning—a letter that did not mention appointing great daimyo to high office, as did the vassal's presentation that afternoon. Shungaku did not subsequently press the point, but it doubtless had reminded Itakura and others that if the Fukui view prevailed, they were likely to lose much.

Then on 9/10, after the court had at last ordered the great lords to assemble, Shungaku tried to prod the bakufu into making some real prep-aration for a daimyo-assembly type of government. He had one of his men point out to Itakura that in many instances *han* vassals were more talented than their lords. He wanted to know how the bakufu planned to utilize that talent and suggested that such men should be specially ap-pointed to serve in inspectorlike positions *(daishō kansatsu)*. Four days later when he met Yoshinobu, he reiterated the advice, and in another conference on the twenty-second he asked what was being done about it. He was told that nothing was being done because no *han* vassals had appeared from whom to choose. Then Yoshinobu began to discuss the situation of various candidates among regular officials, which was not at all what Shungaku had in mind. Even in his farewell visit to Yoshinobu seven days later Shungaku's parting admonition was a reiteration of the point.

Shungaku's plans thus endangered a host of vested interests, and they generated defensive reactions among officials. Those reactions in turn provoked rumors, fueled conflicts at court, heightened daimyo distrust of the bakufu, and contributed to the general ruin of the Fukui enterprise.

Thus the actions of both daimyo and bakufu served to sabotage Shungaku's venture. Much of the sabotage was expressed in conflict and paralysis at court, but central to Shungaku's vision was a court that functioned constructively as focus of a joint noble-daimyo governing effort. The court's inability to fulfill that leading role was evident in many ways. Within the city of Kyoto bakufu defeat prompted a new rash of radical placarding and shishi agitation denouncing not only Aizu, Kuwana, and Hitotsubashi but also pro-bakufu court nobles.[12] Within the court itself the defeat encouraged Satsuma-supported, anti-bakufu restorationist elements to try again to control affairs. The conflict at court erupted at the end of 66/7 and thereafter complicated almost every political action requiring court approval, most notably the decision to end the war and then the plan to summon daimyo. Subsequently, the court quarrels continued, focusing in succeeding weeks on Yoshinobu's proposed imperial audience. Those delays and disputes thoroughly discouraged Shungaku, and well before that last matter was settled, the kōbugattai effort had collapsed.[13]

Confronted by late 66/9 with mountainous evidence that his project had failed again, on 9/25 Shungaku decided to go home. Perhaps to his surprise, when he sounded out bakufu leaders on the matter, neither Itakura nor Yoshinobu raised any particular objections. The next day he formally requested permission to go to Fukui for a vacation and to cope with fiscal problems and reform plans there. He promised to return when the daimyo were assembled. It was a safe enough promise. After making final farewell visits, he left on 10/1, reaching home five days later. With his departure the key force for kōbugattai had left. The phoenix had not risen.

The Bakufu's Postwar Reconstruction

The collapse of Shungaku's effort did not leave the bakufu stranded—it had served officialdom in effect as a conciliatory political front while they drew back from the brink of disaster. It gave them time to resolve some internal personnel matters, make policy decisions and reform plans, and begin processes of political fence-mending and self-strengthening. Yoshinobu indicated the general dimensions of those policies on 9/2 in an eight-point reform statement he submitted to the senior councillors: [14]

1. Govern with the object of Confucian benevolence: in particular, have affection for the people.
2. Select able men.
3. Reward and punish vigorously: in particular, rectify the criminal law.
4. Eliminate useless offices.
5. Slash unnecessary expenses.
6. Energize the army and navy.
7. Keep the faith in international contacts: in particular, make just commercial laws.
8. Maintain an honest coinage.

It was for the most part a hallowed rhetoric, quite acceptable to Shungaku and so monumentally bland as to reassure anyone who might distrust the new Tokugawa leader. Beyond that innocuous statement, however, detailed plans were being drawn up and concrete actions carried out. In their totality they would eventually constitute a degree of intentional change unprecedented in 250 years of Japanese history. An innocuous hallowed rhetoric was shortly to embody the main lines of massive reform.

Nor did the will to reform spring only from a few men at Osaka. During the Summer War, as we noted, the most dramatic military reforms had occurred there, but a similar if more implemental reform orientation also had been evident at Edo. After the war, too, the reform orientation was found in both cities. Thus one summary of topics being discussed by major officials at Edo, probably during late 66/8 or early 66/9, listed these items: [15]

On reforms
On ending the Chōshū war
On reducing the numbers of ladies in waiting
On matters concerning Kazunomiya
On the matter of twenty-four warships
On sending merchant vessels to foreign countries
On defending the Hitotsubashi residence
On detailed architectural plans for the main and western enceintes

On construction work for troop units in Edo

On presenting the secret letter from Yoshinobu to Roches, which must be handled without mistake

On investigating foreign political writings

On having Oguri go to Kyoto about matters of reform

The list suggests that officials there were addressing matters of substance as rapidly as men at Osaka. This basic harmony between the Edo and Kinai portions of the bakufu was of great importance to the postwar recovery and Keiō reform.

1. Strengthening Leadership

For years the bakufu had suffered badly from a divided and unstable leadership. Perhaps its single most important postwar achievement was in forming a leadership that was cohesive and stable. The achievement had several aspects, ranging from reacquisition of the shogunal title to extensive changes among lesser officials.

Before claiming the title of shogun, Yoshinobu had to establish himself as real head of the Tokugawa house. He worked at that task from his early days as Tokugawa leader. Many men close to the deceased Iemochi did not trust him, and they were speedily removed from the scene. On 8/21, the day after Yoshinobu's designation as *uesama*, all of Iemochi's close attendants "without exception" (*sobashū, koshō,* and *konando*) were summarily ordered back to Edo. On the same day Hara Ichinoshin and another of Yoshinobu's closest personal advisors were designated inspectors, and on the next day new men were appointed shogunal attendants. Then in 66/9 another of Yoshinobu's vassals, Umezawa Ryō, was named inspector, and more of Iemochi's intimates were removed from the scene when they were sent in stately and solemn progress back to Edo with the remains of their deceased leader.[16] Their return and the return of various military units had the corollary consequence of transferring most of the bakufu from Osaka back to Edo. That left Yoshinobu and his chosen followers at Kyoto as the center of the regime's Kinai branch.

While Yoshinobu was securing his Tokugawa position against internal critics, he also was addressing the external opponents of his claims to the shogunal title. During 66/9 the contest centered on the proposed audience that would signalize imperial willingness to treat him like a shogun. By 10/16 the opposition at court had been overcome, due largely to the lobbying of Hara.[17] Despite persistent objections, Yoshinobu had his audience, and the bakufu then moved quickly to solidify its victory. Five days later Itakura and junior councillor Ōkōchi Masatada were assigned permanently to Kyoto, becoming living evidence of bakufu supremacy there. Six days after that the court punished twenty-two nobles who had engaged in both the general anti-Yoshinobu campaign and a bitter protest to court in late 66/8. It ordered them confined and put their residences under bakufu guard. Those actions broke the back of the anti-bakufu group at court and paved the way for Yoshinobu to be named shogun. Hara helped there, too, vigorously encouraging *han* vassals to have their lords lobby for the appointment. In response men from Owari, Kii, Aizu, Kuwana, Matsuyama (Iyo), Kaga, and elsewhere did so. The pressure was sufficient, and by late 66/11 the court was prepared to approve. On 12/5 the formal ceremony took place and Yoshinobu received his full string of titles. [18]

After securing the shogunal title, Yoshinobu and Itakura also solidified those family lines nearest the shogunal office. To pacify Kii *han*, it was agreed that a child from there eventually would be adopted and designated successor to Yoshinobu. To reinforce the succession, on 12/27 Tokugawa Mochinori, formerly of Owari, was designated lord of Hitotsubashi. He had cooperated with bakufu leaders during the Hyōgo crisis and later during the Summer War. He had been rewarded with an appointment as Shimizu lord and was then moved to Hitotsubashi because of its greater role in the succession. Then on the following day Tokugawa Akitake, a younger brother of Yoshinobu and previously heir to Katamori, was designated head of Shimizu, a title to be held during his coming extended stay in France. Another brother of Yoshinobu replaced him as heir at Aizu. [19] These several moves stabilized the positions closest to the center of Tokugawa authority, filling them with people likely to support the new shogun.

The establishment of European-style foreign relations also required that the bakufu be acknowledged internationally as the government of Japan and Yoshinobu as head of state. That need was especially acute in late 1866 because of the defeat in war, the evidence that Satsuma men in Europe were trying to sabotage the regime, and the evidence that at least some British representatives on the scene also wished to see bakufu authority ended. Two undertakings were initiated to strengthen that international recognition.

The first undertaking was establishment of permanent Japanese missions abroad. For months bakufu diplomats had been preparing a Japanese delegation and exhibition for the Paris Exposition of 1867. After the war that venture was combined with the dispatch of permanent representatives to France and England. On 9/27 army commander Asano Ujisuke was designated foreign magistrate and ordered to make preparations for service as resident minister in Paris. Another experienced official was ordered to London in a similar capacity. Then on 11/28 Akitake was designated special emissary to France and head of delegation to the Paris Exposition. In following weeks the mission completed preparations, taking shape as a 25-man group with a high-powered negotiating team led by Mukōyama Eigorō. He had orders to negotiate some important fiscal, military, and technical matters, the uncompleted $6 million loan high on his list. On 67/1/11 the mission left Yokohama for Europe, reaching Paris two months later.[20]

The second undertaking was the arranging of a formal shogunal reception for the foreign representatives in Japan. By late 66/11 it was clear that Yoshinobu would be named shogun. It was equally clear, in view of apparent British antipathy toward the regime, that bakufu pretensions required the new leader to receive foreign diplomats formally. Accordingly on 12/1 and 2 the senior councillors at Edo informed them that because Yoshinobu was unable to return east they would shortly be invited to meet him at Osaka. The reception was then delayed by the death of Emperor Kōmei and then, it appears, by objections of courtiers and others who suspected it would lead to the opening of Hyōgo.[21] Finally, however, late in 67/3 the reception was held and the new shogunal reign seemed properly begun.

By the end of 1866 Yoshinobu's position in the rejuvenated bakufu was well established, and that was only the most obvious aspect of a much broader consolidation of leadership. Throughout the last months of the year Itakura worked assiduously to draw the best leaders into a habit of close Edo-Kinai cooperation in policy planning and implementation. The most able were summoned to Kyoto to discuss policy and make plans for reviving the regime.[22] To mention some main instances, in mid-66/9 Oguri Tadamasa and Tsukahara Masayoshi, who both had close contacts with Roches, were ordered west and on the twenty-fourth reached Kyoto, where they engaged in active discussions. On 10/20 Oguri headed back east, probably to implement decisions agreed upon. In the meantime acting senior councillor Ogyū Noritaka had been ordered west and reached Kyoto on 10/24. He had been promoted during the war, was known as a talented man, and had considerable military experience. Two days later Hirayama Keichū was ordered to proceed westward quickly. He departed shortly but was delayed by a visit to Roches at Atami and did not reach Kyoto until 11/20. While he was traveling, acting junior councillor Inaba Masami, also experienced in military matters as a former army commander (*rikugun bugyō*), was also ordered to come west, arriving on 12/11. Five days later the experienced senior councillor Inaba Masakuni, who had been recalled to duty shortly before the war, was also ordered west. During those same weeks an extensive transfer of other officials took place with many able and respected men being drawn into positions important to the administrative and military reforms then getting underway.

Ogasawara Nagamichi was not one of those summoned to Kyoto.[23] After the collapse at Kokura, he had gone to Nagasaki. He left there by ship on 8/6 and reached Osaka no later than the twenty-first. When he met Itakura at the castle that day, he was advised to stay out of sight because men were busily blaming him for the expedition's failure. Itakura, who had considerable respect for his talents, reportedly told him that when the dust had settled, he would seek his reappointment. Subsequently Ogasawara was dismissed and confined in Edo, evidently to pacify a revived court irritation toward him. To the surprise of many, however, on 11/9 he was reappointed senior councillor, reassigned his 30,000 *hyō* office stipend, and ordered back to active duty. He was still out of favor at court and so stayed in the east for the time being, but there he soon assumed the major fiscal and diplomatic duty titles of *katte gakari* and *gaikoku gakari*.

With Ogasawara's reappointment and the subsequent promotion of Inaba Masami to the senior council in late 66/12, bakufu leadership acquired most of the personnel it would retain to the end. It was likely the best group of leaders the regime had had in a decade at least, with Itakura providing a stabilizing, coordinating influence and perhaps a wisdom in policy-making that surpassed anything the bakufu had known since the death of Abe Masahiro.

This reinvigoration of bakufu leadership had one more dimension— that of reconciliation between Yoshinobu and former vassal daimyo officials. On 11/20, after months of slow maneuver, the bakufu finally ended the confinement of hapless former senior councillor Andō Nobumasa. Then former councillors Naitō Nobuchika, Abe Masatō, and Mizuno Tadakiyo (who had been ousted during the war) were allowed to attend Edo castle again.[24] And sometime afterward Matsumae *han* succeeded in rehabilitating the name of Matsumae Takahiro.[25] These gestures did not assure the bakufu of vassal daimyo support, but they did remove some grounds for complaint and may have improved the regime's chances of inducing such men to serve in high office.

In sum, then, the postwar bakufu had reasserted its customary claim to a suzerain role at home, and it was laying the foundation for an assertion of sovereign ruling authority that was really unprecedented in the *bakuhan* tradition. The regime had secured Yoshinobu's position as shogun and family head, had strengthened the cohesiveness of its central administration, and had tried to mend fences with those families who customarily had been pillars of bakufu supremacy.

2. Modernizing the Army

Yoshinobu's appointment as shogun preserved the Tokugawa claim to a suzerain role vis-à-vis the great lords. However, the leaders of recovery realized that enduring control of symbols was much more a result than a cause of political supremacy. They knew that such supremacy depended on real governing capability and that that in turn required a major expansion of the regime's military power.

To accomplish that expansion, bakufu leaders implemented fundamental changes in their military system, struggling to overcome two centuries of neglect and forge anew the most powerful army in Japan. Their reforms grew directly from the plans prepared during the Summer War. To assure a sufficient manpower base, on 8/26 the bakufu issued a new schedule of vassal military obligations based on the 66/7 reform plan. The new schedule presumably would yield over twelve thousand troops and constituted an increase over the requirements of 1862. It weighed most heavily on more wealthy vassals and required money rather than men from lesser vassals. It exempted the most minor bakufu retainers from any burden beyond their own military service but specified that henceforth that would have to be given without the customary supplemental salary.[26]

In succeeding weeks a prodigious series of orders and regulations was formulated and issued by Inaba Masami, Oguri Tadamasa, Takenaka Shigemoto, Misoguchi Shōnyo, Asano Ujisuke, Komai Chōon, and others. They eliminated most of the old units of swordsmen and pikemen, reorganized old-style firearms forces, and transferred units between Edo and Osaka to facilitate the changes. By year's end, and after much trial and error, the shape of the new system had emerged in considerable clarity.[27]

Several problems had to be addressed. One was to get men to accept training. Another was to minimize status conflicts. A third was to reduce military costs. In all these matters the bakufu had some success; in none was success complete.

To get men to train, two tactics were employed. One was to abolish other posts and give the dismissed men a choice between hunger and soldiering for pay. The other was to employ low-status men, mostly commoners from Edo and peasants from bakufu and liege vassal lands, who were more amenable to regulation and command.

To avoid status conflicts, broad status categories were adhered to in reassigning men. Although in fact there were several reorganization schemes proposed and a plethora of orders made and revised, the basic lines of the 66/7 plan survived. The essence of the matter was as follows.[28] Many *yoriai*, meaning unemployed liege vassals with family incomes of 3000 *koku* or more, were put in charge of their own retainers, their forces being titled *kumiai jūtai*. To assure that these small units of some twenty-five to seventy-five men acquired military competence and coalesced as coherent larger units, on 9/15 they were ordered to combine with one another and serve with infantry battalions. Later they were expanded to form independent battalions. Other high-status liege vassals were assigned to units entitled *okuzume jūtai*. Men of intermediate rank were assigned to units designated *yūgekitai*. Others, notably *yoriki*, were assigned to units simply designated *jūtai*. Lower-ranking vassals, mostly *dōshin*, were assigned to *sappei*, or artillery and artillery guard units. Just below this last level were the *hohei*, or regular infantry units. They had been formed before, during, and after the Summer War, had trained at the military institute, and were composed of peasants, commoners, and former menial servants of bakufu, daimyo, and others in Edo. In gross numbers most of this new army was in the *sappei* and *hohei*, and considerations of military efficiency made it highly desirable that the two be integrated. Hence, as the reform progressed, attempts were made to merge them in accord with orders issued during the war. The effort apparently failed, however, and dissatisfaction with *sappei-hohei* relations persisted far into 1867.

The matter of paying the new forces presented thorny choices. To rationalize and reduce costs, the bakufu established standardized stipend levels. They proved to be below current salary levels of many men being reassigned,[29] however, and that led them to resist transfer. Then on 11/15 the bakufu exacerbated the situation by "temporarily" shifting all salary supplements (*fuchi*) from rice to money, whose value was being steadily eroded by the wildly accelerating inflation.[30] The conversion rate was much more generous than the one considered back in mid-1865, but in the meantime rice prices had more than doubled. Hence the shift still constituted a net loss to the troops and evidently gave rise to sharp objections and further complicated recruiting.

The impact of salary arrangements upon recruiting was suggested by contemporary personnel maneuvers. On 10/28 men in a very long list of positions, including the elite guard forces (*ōban, koshōgumi, shoinban*), were instructed to switch to firearms and volunteer for training at the military institute. There was a considerable response, and during several days of recruiting in mid-66/11 several hundred men were examined for service. Only a small number of those candidates were higher-ranking men, however. Then on 11/26 a salary concession allowed those moving into the new units to retain their old stipends. After that, reformers felt emboldened to proceed, and on 12/2–4 most elite guard units were summarily abolished and men were reassigned to appropriate new units with no noticeable outcry.[31]

While addressing these problems of reorganization, the reformers also had to create satisfactory uniforms and duties for their growing army.[32] Successive sets of orders during 66/9–11 designated proper uniforms, rank, insignia, and apparel usage. The uniforms were so designed as to distinguish clearly between officers and enlisted ranks and between civilian and military offices. On 9/26 officers were "permitted" to wear their new uniforms, but the order as reissued on 10/3 made their use mandatory for officers on duty at the castle. A month later specified civil officials were required to wear dress distinct from that of military officers. For the first time in a millennium the military-civil distinction was being drawn in functional rather than hereditary terms.

As new units were formed and trained, they steadily took over guard tasks of old-style forces. In some cases changes were titular at first, with the same men at the same posts bearing new weapons and unit designations. But as the weeks passed, units were moved about and the old system was really and permanently changed. It appears that in much guard duty reorganization a key consideration was cost: units of lower-status men replaced those of higher status, thereby reducing actual costs of routine guard duty.

The ultimate success of this reorganized army depended in part on the quality of its equipment and training. Reformers addressed those matters too. As noted earlier, they were well aware of trends in western military technology and sought the best weapons available. To this end, on 9/12 officials wrote the Swiss consul general Bremwald asking for samples of new weapons they had heard about. In response he provided information on Colt, Spencer, Snider, Joslyn, Remington, and other breechloaders and repeaters, the latter ranging from six to forty-seven shots in capacity.[33] Knowledge of the weapons did not make them immediately available, but it did lead reformers later to begin shifting from the Mini-style weapons that had seemed so modern in 1862 to the newer breechloaders.

The reformers also tried to assure that training was effective. On 10/5 reform leaders in Edo, notably Inaba Masakuni, Inaba Masami, Tachibana Taneyuki, Hirayama Keichū, Kawakatsu Hiromichi, and Inoue Yoshifumi, went to Yokohama for two days of careful inspection of cavalry and artillery units there as well as observation of a British warship, the consulates, and the language school and customs office.[34] They also continued preparing for the French military mission that was then being assembled in France prior to departure for Japan.

During those months too, reformers gradually clarified the military hierarchy.[35] Battalion commanders and ship's captains were designated *kashira* with stipends of about 1000 to 2000 *koku* depending on the unit commanded. Above them were regimental commanders and vice-commanders of infantry, artillery, and cavalry designated *bugyō* and *bugyō nami* with suitably higher stipends. And above them in turn were army and navy commanders and vice-commanders, the *rikugun* and *kaigun bugyō* and *bugyō nami* with stipends of about 5000 *koku*. Whereas in the old system some military commanders had been under the junior council's control and others under the senior council, in the reorganized system all were subject to the latter. The chain of command was completed on 12/27 when acting senior councillor Ogyū Noritaka was designated *rikugun sōsai* (army minister) and acting senior councillor Inaba Masami was named *kaigun sōsai* (navy minister). Thus the newly created separate military hierarchies were at their top clearly subordinated to civil officials technically subordinate to the shogun and in practice responsible to the overall supervision of Itakura.

By the end of 1866 the bakufu thus had torn down its old military system and completed basic steps in forming a new one of infantry forces supported by modern artillery.

This massive military reform had been a response directly to the Summer War. During the same months rural turbulence led to formation of more extensive peasant militia. Initially the effort was prompted by the Kantō-Tōhoku upheavals of mid-1866 and by the demonstrated value of existing militia in quieting the region. In bakufu lands in Dewa the size of militia units was increased and the scale of their officer corps expanded. In the Kantō and to the west in Shinano the pattern of militia organization was modified in various ways to increase its capacity and reliability. At post stations, where special hardships generated greater discontent, new units were formed and loaned firearms and put under local command for training and deployment.[36]

Then late in the year, as we note further on, the area west of Osaka experienced widespread rioting. It may have been this trouble (or perhaps the impending opening of Osaka to foreigners) that led Misoguchi Shōnyo to advocate formation of peasant forces from the Kinai for assignment guarding Osaka. In 67/1 he and his colleagues, notably Takenaka, Komai, and Yamaguchi Naoki, prepared a survey of bakufu lands in four

provinces adjacent to Osaka. They calculated the lands could furnish 983
conscripts who could be put into an infantry force of 883 and an artillery
battery of 100. The plan spelled out at length the command structure
such a force would require and procedures for obtaining personnel for
command positions. It discussed problems of supporting the force at
Osaka, particularly the commissary problems caused by inflation.It
specified the need to assure that intendants *(daikan)* would provide the
necessary support, observing that local commercial production should not
be overlooked in fixing local rates for troop maintenance. And it stipulated that recruits should be between the ages of seventeen and thirty-
five and should be competent. The proposal was then forwarded to Edo
for consideration, but there it apparently was abandoned, perhaps
because the rural turbulence had passed or because other projects seemed
to make that one superfluous.[37]

Despite the outcome of this last matter, the military reforms of late
1866 were cumulatively the most extensive changes the Japanese military system had experienced in centuries. Together with the revitalizing
of bakufu leadership, they constituted a remarkable recovery from the
nadir of defeat and laid the foundation for even more basic changes in the
following year.

PROBLEMS OF THE POSTWAR MONTHS

The bakufu made visible progress in reconstructing itself after the defeat
of 1866, but it also encountered problems. Mostly they were just contin-
uations, often intensified, of problems earlier visible. Some were basically political in character; others were basically economic but had political
implications. Specifically the de facto disengagement with Chōshū was
not actually a settlement, and attempts to gain a pacific settlement not
only failed but complicated Aizu-bakufu relations. Evidence of daimyo
alienation continued to accumulate, and it was Tokugawa related houses
that most concerned the new leadership. The daimyo problem was partly
economic in character, and the bakufu's own overall financial situation
remained poor despite painful economizing. The economic ills of the
regime contributed to the deterioration of Edo, which was showing more
signs of decay. The decay in Edo was in turn part of the larger pattern of
popular suffering and unrest that had led to upheaval at midyear and continued at a high level until year's end.

1. Chōshū and Its Effect on Aizu-Bakufu Relations

After military defeat the bakufu tried again to settle peacefully its quarrel
with Chōshū. The first attempt by Katsu Kaishū failed, and so the bakufu

delegation at Hiroshima sent the court's armistice note on to Chōshū. The *han* refused to accept it, seeing in it another bakufu trick, but the refusal did not mean that war resumed. It could not really resume because so little remained of the army of subjugation. Daimyo forces had been heading homeward ever since the first reverses, and then Yoshinobu ordered further withdrawals after canceling his own planned expedition. By 66/9 most troops had left the front.

Then on 9/19 Itakura sent out instructions vaguely identified as coming ''from Kyoto'' that ordered remaining bakufu and *han* troops in Iwami and Aki to withdraw unilaterally. Careful schedules for withdrawal were issued. Regulations were sent out to assure that all outstanding bills for troop billeting were paid up, and during 66/10 this orderly withdrawal was completed.[38] On 10/18 Kaharu (the former Kokura) *han* and Chōshū agreed to end their war, and despite later reports of continued clashes and further Chōshū expansion into Kokura lands, by year's end that war had been formally concluded with Chōshū retaining for itself the northernmost district (Kiku *gun*) in Buzen province.[39] The war had ended, but in an unofficial détente, not an agreed upon settlement, and that was not satisfactory to bakufu leaders.

Almost certainly Yoshinobu's real wish still was to beat Chōshū into submission. But in the closing months of the year several major daimyo reaffirmed their determination not to cooperate in any war against that *han*.[40] Reminded thus that he would be alone if he chose to fight again, the new shogun had little choice but to find some other way to cut Tokugawa losses vis-à-vis the house of Mōri. At year's end he perceived just such an opportunity. It was presented by the sudden death of Emperor Kōmei after twenty-one years as an energetic, cantankerous young emperor. On 12/25 he died of smallpox at the age of thirty-five. Within a few days his death was announced, and on 67/1/9 succession of the fourteen-year-old Meiji emperor was formalized.[41] Yoshinobu had the court instruct Chōshū to withdraw to its own borders as part of a formal end to the expedition that would be arranged out of respect for the deceased emperor. Again, however, Chōshū refused to cooperate. In a move to strengthen Hiroshima *han*'s goodwill, Chōshū leaders did agree to surrender the small area seized in Aki, but they kept the much greater and economically valuable territories seized in Iwami and Buzen provinces.[42] In 67/2 *han* leaders notified Kyoto of their refusal to withdraw and pressed on with preparation for more war. The Chōshū problem thus persisted and was to plague Yoshinobu in following months.

Yoshinobu's attempt to end peacefully the state of war with Chōshū not only failed of its main purpose but also revived the discontent of Katamori and Aizu men. In the outcome Katamori did remain at Kyoto, but the whole episode revealed how basic and bitter the inter-*han* tensions had become and how difficult it would be for Yoshinobu to retain the goodwill of even the most well-disposed among the powerful *han*.

To elaborate, back in 66/8 when Katamori's advice had been repudiated, the war effort abandoned, and a daimyo assembly decided upon, the bitterness of Aizu men had been profound. They knew Aizu had paid dearly for its long vigil and saw all its effort being squandered.[43] Aizu had been the rock of the bakufu at Kyoto for four years, but repeatedly bakufu leaders had had to rediscover that. Yoshinobu's actions suggested that even he had not understood. During 66/8 and 9, Aizu leaders at Edo and Kyoto discussed the situation at length, worried about the planned daimyo assembly, and concluded, it appears, that the future for Aizu was grim. They called upon colleagues back at Wakamatsu to strengthen *han* military forces by switching to western-style rifle organization and to overcome *han* fiscal difficulties. *Han* vassals were sharply divided about the best Aizu strategy. Some asserted that Katamori should return to Wakamatsu at once and prepare for the worst. Others argued he should stay at Kyoto and work to revive the policies of crushing Chōshū and preventing the daimyo assembly. Still others argued that even if all other *han* withdrew their forces from the field, Aizu should go forth alone to crush Chōshū.[44]

During 66/10 as the *kōbugattai* effort foundered, the Aizu debate subsided. On 10/17, the day after Yoshinobu's shogun-like imperial audience, Katamori tested the situation. He notified the bakufu that Yoshinobu as head of the Tokugawa house should assume direct responsibility for guarding Kyoto and that Katamori should be permitted to resign. He urged in effect that the bakufu relocate itself to Kyoto and appoint major officials to handle affairs elsewhere. In token response leaders reassigned Itakura and Ōkōchi to Kyoto but rejected Katamori's resignation. Instead Itakura said his presence was needed because Chōshū was still unsubdued.[45] Perhaps the hint that one day Chōshū would be dealt with properly, taken together with the evidence implicit in the concurrent military reform, was enough to satisfy Katamori. At any rate he stayed on, and in following weeks Aizu ire abated.

Then, however, Yoshinobu's attempt to settle the Chōshū matter peacefully revived Aizu anger.[46] On 67/1/15 Yoshinobu instructed Katamori and his brother Sadaaki to deliver to court the request for a formal end to the expedition. Katamori bluntly refused to do so. Instead he urged Itakura to prevent the move, arguing vigorously that it was a betrayal of the court and a threat to the polity. He asserted that the request should be refused, adequate preparation made, and the war of subjugation resumed. Disregarding that advice, Itakura went to the court with Sadaaki and made the request himself. Katamori's direct protests to Yoshinobu also were to no avail, and that outcome led him again to discuss matters with his vassals. They angrily agreed that Yoshinobu was acting in an unacceptably arbitrary manner, in disregard of his advisors, with indifference to the interests of Kokura and other *han*, and disrespectfully toward the court.

On the next day Itakura wrote Katamori, reprimanding his vassals' agitation and defending the decision to end the state of hostilities. He pointed out that daimyo were advising it, but that if necessary the war could always be resumed at an opportune time. That rather devious reasoning did not satisfy Katamori, who replied that once troops had been disbanded, reviving the war would not be such an easy matter. In closing he observed that he was supposed to go to the castle, but somehow he had a cold and did not feel up to it. As an Aizu compiler later put it: "From that day on, Katamori had almost no connection with decisions of state."[47]

On the following day, 1/17, Katamori decided to resign as protector and in the classic manner began a boycott of Nijō castle.[48] His decision precipitated a war of nerves between Aizu and bakufu leaders that was to continue for weeks and poison the relationship of the two for months to come.[49] In the end, however, a combination of divided opinion in Aizu, Katamori's own abiding sense of loyalty, and pressure from both bakufu and court served to keep Aizu at Kyoto despite its enduring discontent with both bakufu policy in general and its own situation in particular.

2. Daimyo Alienation and Difficulty

The bakufu's difficulties with Aizu and Chōshū were in a sense particular expressions of the much more general phenomena of daimyo alienation and hardship.[50] There were several manifestations of those conditions, and cumulatively they constituted growth of centrifugal and decay of centripetal forces in the polity.

One manifestation of growing centrifugal force was daimyo "regionalism." Such regionalism was not new; indeed, it probably was as old as the *bakuhan* system itself, but it seems to have acquired new prevalence in the system's final years. On 65/10/6, for example, during the Hyōgo crisis, high officials of Maruoka, Sabae, Ōno, and Katsuyama *han*, all in Echizen province, gathered at Fukui to discuss the national situation with Fukui leaders.[51] The Summer War drove *han* together more than ever before. The Satsuma-Chōshū rapprochement is the famous instance, but the practice was much more general. The lords west of Tottori tended to turn to that great *han* for guidance and support in the face of Chōshū expansionism. Tōhoku daimyo expanded their mutual contacts and cooperation. Lords of the branch houses of Fukui tended to look to the parent house for political guidance. Lords on both Shikoku and Kyushu kept in contact with one another and coordinated their activities. For most *han* it almost certainly was not the bakufu they feared, but the bakufu's passing.

There were two other manifestations of the centrifugal trend. With war's end many vassal daimyo had, at least temporarily, gone home rather than back to Edo or Osaka. The bakufu itself ordered many to do so. Others requested permission to go, often on grounds of *han* impoverishment, and bakufu leaders were uncommonly responsive to the requests. This diaspora of the vassal lords was probably a fair indicator of both their domanial exhaustion and their growing uncertainty about bakufu prospects and their own futures. The other manifestation of the trend was widespread daimyo attempts to switch their armies to firearms. What is notable is that the effort was being made not merely by great *han* but also by many lesser ones, particularly vassal *han*. The bakufu instructed vassal lords to adopt firearms, it is true, but the bakufu had been doing that for years. It was the war that made the advice persuasive. In the end, though, the effort had only modest success, due probably to *han* poverty and a general lack of samurai cooperation. In consequence many of the petty fiefdoms had little choice but to put their faith in Edo, for whatever that was worth, or in big neighbors or neutralism.

The decay of centripetal forces was evinced in the inability of either bakufu or court to make daimyo respond to instructions. It would be misleading to assume the bakufu simply stopped trying to regulate daimyo after the Summer War. It did not. Thus on 66/11/20 it ordered them to present their scheduled dates for *sankin kōtai* trips to Edo and back to the *han* and for attending the castle. Seven days later it sought information on the numbers of people each *han* had at Edo, and in 66/12 it inquired about their imports of ships. Then in 67/1 and 2 it sought information on their troop strength and stipends in Edo, mansion sizes and locations in the city, and the names of all vassals with stipends of 10,000 *koku* or over. In early 1867 a few major daimyo begged off *sankin kōtai* or guard duty assignments,[52] but most apparently did not even bother responding to the various bakufu inquiries. That was itself evidence of a higher level of daimyo indifference to bakufu sensibilities. The regime was at least sustaining its formal claim to authority over the lords, however, and by early 1867 a good many vassal daimyo appear to have returned to Edo.

Heightened defiance of the bakufu was not particularly surprising, but readiness to disobey imperial orders also was far more widespread than ever before. The formal daimyo response to the court order of 9/7 to assemble in Kyoto was remarkable. Yōdō was ill. Mochitsugu was ill. The lord of Tsu was ill. The Tokushima lord was ill. So were the lords of Fukuoka and Kurume. The lords and ex-lords of Tottori, Okayama, Tokushima, Hiroshima, Tosa, Kumamoto, and Uwajima stayed at home, content to correspond extensively about whether or not to go. Finally on 10/12 Mochimasa of Okayama reached Kyoto. The Tsu heir and Matsue lord arrived six days later, and the Tokushima heir showed up on the next day. On 10/26 the court again ordered daimyo to come. On 10/28 the emperor met and thanked the five men who had bothered to make the trip (the daimyo of Kaga, Okayama, and Matsue; the heirs of Tokushima and Tsu), and two days later he again ordered some daimyo to come. On 11/1 the Fukuoka heir arrived, and on the eighteenth he asked to go home again. The lords of Matsue, Okayama, and Kaga also left, as did the heirs of Yonezawa, Fukuoka, and Tsu. By the end of the year the few who had come had gone home again. The message was discouraging: Yoshinobu's symbolic triumph notwithstanding, there was no longer in Japan an authority symbol capable of moving the feudal lords. There was no national polity; the *bakuhan* system no longer existed.

Daimyo alienation was certainly to some degree a result of the unprecedented fiscal difficulty they were experiencing. Before the Summer War *han* fiscal problems seem to have been particularly crises of lesser domains, especially vassal *han*. During the postwar months, however, large *han* too were driven to crisis measures. The months 66/7–12 were months of unprecedented domanial difficulty—reports of poverty, local disasters, requests for aid, and petitions for emergency fiscal authority flowed into the bakufu.[53] After the New Year the evidence of crisis diminished sharply, along with gestures of bakufu authority and expressions of overt daimyo defiance. Between bakufu and most daimyo a modus vivendi of mutual disregard appears to have been reached that was to last through most of 1867. The arrangement was perhaps better for the bakufu than most real alternatives, but it seemed to confirm the absence of any sort of national polity.

Bakufu leaders made some effort to cultivate the goodwill of vassal *han*, as we noted earlier, but attitudes among the great related domains were a more serious cause for concern. After Aizu, Mito caused the most worry and received the most attention. To make a long and pathetic story short,[54] the outbreak of war in 1866 revived agitation in Mito against the harsh rule of those in power since the Kantō insurrection. Both Kyoto and Osaka as well as Edo again became embroiled in the disputes, and during 66/9 bakufu leaders tried to quiet matters by making new leadership changes in the *han*. The effort generated counterdemonstrations, threats of violence, and absconding. After two months the bakufu abandoned its attempt to manipulate Mito. In 1867 the regime made a few more feeble attempts to manage the *han*, but its ineffectiveness, when compared to that of Abe Masahiro in the 1840s and Ii Naosuke in 1858–1859, betrayed the magnitude of bakufu decline. And the fact that the Mito leaders attacked in this last feeble attempt were those who had cooperated with Edo in 1864 indicated how fully the regime had alienated every segment of the *han* by the time of its collapse.

Fukui, Owari, and Kii were also of concern to Itakura and Yoshinobu, but they received much less attention. Shungaku, of course, had been embittered by the most recent failure of his *kōbugattai* venture and had gone home in 66/9. In late 66/10–11 Itakura urged him to return to Kyoto, explaining that daimyo were refusing to come on the ground his departure demonstrated the uselessness of doing so. Shungaku refused to move, however, and in the middle of 66/11 Itakura abandoned his lingering hope that the Fukui lord might support the regime.[55]

Owari had even earlier become thoroughly alienated. Yoshikatsu's embitterment had been growing for years, but the harsh dispute between him and bakufu leaders at the end of the first Chōshū expedition almost brought to a dead halt cooperation between Owari and the main Tokugawa house. Mochinori did later cooperate during the Hyōgo crisis and served loyally as guardian at Edo castle during the Summer War, and his reward was appointment to the Hitotsubashi title. Some Owari men also lobbied for Yoshinobu's shogunal appointment, but the *han* as a whole proved of no use to the bakufu, and leaders wasted little energy cultivating Nagoya.

Kii, by contrast, had been particularly close to the bakufu after Iemochi's accession in 1858. However, the handling of the Summer War generated much bitterness in the *han* because Kii had given so fully and in the end had been betrayed by so many: by Honjō, by Ogasawara, and even by Yoshinobu. Within Kii there had been even before the war a strong current of anti-Yoshinobu sentiment, and his succession added to Kii's alienation. During 66/9 Mochitsugu disengaged himself from the Summer War, returned to the Kinai, and resigned his office as forward commander on 9/14. Some Kii men and Mochitsugu himself supported Yoshinobu's shogunal appointment (perhaps in return for promises about the heir's position); but others, it appears, hoped to see Mochitsugu succeed. He did not and on 10/3 went home to Wakayama, later refusing to return to Kyoto when summoned. Instead Kii went its own way. In

66/12 it began a major program of *han* reform and military strengthening.[56]

As the last full year of the Tokugawa bakufu got underway, then, bakufu-daimyo relations had become generally quiescent. Outside lords were quite beyond bakufu control. Vassal lords cooperated passively with the regime. All the great related lords except Aizu were in some degree of alienated dissociation from the bakufu leadership. And Aizu itself was badly split, its leaders under substantial internal pressure to dissociate from the government of the last shogun.

3. Bakufu Fiscal Problems

The daimyo were not alone in experiencing fiscal hardships. The war dealt the bakufu severe economic setbacks. The war effort itself pretty much exhausted immediate resources and piled up a huge domestic debt. Moreover, it reduced the bakufu's base of tax land even as it created a series of new lingering costs. These developments forced the regime to pursue a number of policies designed to generate income and reduce expenses.

The war led directly to loss of land in Iwami and indirectly to loss of land in Kyushu. In Kyushu the war was followed by severe public hardship and upheaval. Accordingly, during 67/1 inspectors were sent there to study the situation carefully, and leaders accepted their proposal to assign the regime's lands to relatively trustworthy *han*. The *han* selected were Kumamoto, Kurume, Nobeoka, and Shimabara, and in 67/2 they received as *azukaridokoro* a total of about 50,000 *koku*. Later in the year other Kyushu lands were assigned to Kizuki and Takanabe *han*.[57] Those actions relieved the bakufu of an awkward task of administration and perhaps helped restore the balance of power in Kyushu. There, it was rumored, some *han* were sending hostages to Chōshū, presumably in deference to its emergence as the new hegemon.[58] But the price was still a loss of income for the regime.

The most striking new fiscal burden the war imposed upon the bakufu was supporting Hamada and Kokura *han*. By spring of 1867 those two *han* alone had cost the regime some 4000 *ryō* of money and 56,000 *hyō* of rice in grants and 3500 *ryō* in loans.[59]

Other costs unrelated to the war also kept appearing. Edo was hit, as we note below, with a spate of troubles that all cost the bakufu in one way or another. On 66/10/20, moreover, a major fire destroyed most of Yokohama, burning four wards *(machi)* of the new town, the foreign quarter, and all bakufu offices, including those of customs and the magistrate. The fire's overall cost was roughly estimated at a million *ryō*, and the bakufu would have to help in the reconstruction.[60] Edo also had to furnish French merchants with another $55,000 (300,000 francs) in order to retain their cooperation in financing the Yokohama foundry. It was unable, however, to meet its next half-million-dollar indemnity payment, despite foreign complaints about the matter.[61]

To cope with these fiscal demands, the bakufu did several things, few of them very successfully. The most dramatic move was the arranging in 66/8 of the $6 million foreign line of credit. Unfortunately for the regime, that great triumph proved dismally short-lived. The loan was to be arranged through the British Oriental Bank, which had a branch at Yokohama, but on 8/20 the local bank representative notified Oguri Tadamasa that he could cover only $1 million of the loan and the remainder would have to be arranged jointly through the main office of the bank and the Société Générale in France. Why the bank took that position is not clear, but the notice set in motion a long process of negotiation that continued well into 1867 before collapsing. In the meantime Oguri had to confront far more routine problems of meeting bills for foreign purchases by export of coins and short-term loan arrangements of a modest magnitude.[62]

While pursuing the foreign loan, attempts were also being made to increase agricultural production in central Japan. The disastrous typhoons of summer and autumn had caused severe river damage and necessitated extensive riparian repair. These exceptional demands, together with rampant inflation, made the customary riparian allocations totally inadequate. Accordingly on 9/21 the bakufu notified all daimyo, landed liege vassals, and intendants in Echigo, Dewa, and the Kantō and Tōkai regions that their usual allocations of 30 *monme* of silver per 100 *koku* of productivity were insufficient for all that had to be done. Therefore, the notice stated, officials were to go ahead and identify all needed riparian repairs. When estimates of total cost had been calculated, new allotment rates for the region would be established in the spring. Two months later the same notice was sent to landholders in Shinano province. At year's end finance officials were appointed to supervise spring river repair work in the Kantō-Tōkai and Shinano-Kai areas. On 11/22, moreover, it was announced that Oguri Masayasu, who was jointly Kantō intendant and superintendent of finances, would lead an investigating team through villages and uncultivated areas in the Kantō to encourage development of more crop land. The announcement admonished subordinate officials to make local arrangements prior to the visit in order to assure its success.[63]

Even if the foreign loan had been made, it would only have helped in foreign purchases, and the expansion of agricultural production was a long-range measure. In the interim domestic costs remained a major problem and forced the bakufu to other more familiar funding maneuvers. In 66/9 the regime may possibly have called again for nearly 700,000 *ryō* of *goyōkin* from the Osaka wealthy, likely those who had failed to respond to earlier calls. And on 10/15 it revised the value of some more old gold coins.[64]

Those gestures were in no way sufficient, and accordingly leaders dismissed more personnel and slashed perquisites of those not fired. It was mostly a story of numerous minor administrative actions, but a few dramatic instances of cost-cutting did occur. To mention one, it will be recalled that Iemochi's attendants had been sent back to Edo in 66/9. On 10/26 in thanks for their help they were generously given gifts totaling over 14,000 *ryō* in value, but a few days later about two hundred of them were abruptly fired. By the end of the year a host of inessential offices had been eliminated and hundreds of other men fired or retired from office. Many of those dismissed were directly reassigned to new military units, and others eventually enlisted. But many, including those *yoriki* whose positions were not hereditary, were simply dropped from the payroll.[65]

Those still on the payroll found it losing much attractiveness. For one thing, leaders exploited decisively the effect of inflation. On 10/11 the bakufu announced that retirement incomes, previously paid in both rice and money, would henceforth be paid entirely in money. And on 11/15, as noted earlier, reformers announced an exploitative ''temporary'' shift to money salaries for all lesser vassals receiving rice as salary supplements *(yaku fuchi* and *teate fuchi)*. Moreover the reformers slashed away at fringe benefits: expense accounts and office supply accounts for officials traveling or stationed outside Edo were repeatedly trimmed. And finally, although inflation at the post stations forced the bakufu to increase per diem allowances for men traveling on assignment, it tried to offset that increase by reducing their authorized retinues.[66]

With its Bunkyū antecedents this type of economizing was certainly not new, but the magnitude of its application appears to have been unprecedented. Cumulatively it accomplished much of what the Bunkyū reform had sought to do in restoring the ''pre-Kan'ei'' system of Ieyasu. The old civil government that had kept the peace for two centuries was gradually being reconverted into a lean and mean instrument of war. Inevitably that process created hardship and discontent among those who bore the loss, and in the end the savings realized were still insufficient to close the gap between income and outgo. Much more would have to be done if the bakufu were to become a solvent regime.

4. Problems in Edo City

After Iemochi left Edo back in 65/6, the city gradually slipped into a state of political somnolence. The absence of political action did not mean the old city enjoyed tranquillity, however. Rather, it was affected by both the economic troubles of the time and the discontent and difficulties engendered by war, defeat, and military reform. In consequence it had a worse winter in 1866 than in 1863.

For officialdom life in Edo had become rather quiet and comfortable. But minor people in the bakufu experienced most of the woes besetting their colleagues elsewhere. In the months before the Summer War troops at Edo found themselves hard pressed by inflation, and some complained about it to superiors. Others saw in the repeated conjunction of foreign and domestic crises evidence the Tokugawa house was in jeopardy. They expressed their dismay and advocated one or another strategy for survival.[67] Then during the war they rode out upheaval and unrest in Edo and the Kantō, learned of disasters to the west, and experienced in some degree the hurried military reorganization initiated at Osaka. After the war activity picked up. The main body of bakufu officialdom and military forces returned, and reform began to affect the lives of more and more people in the city.

At the popular level the city and its hinterland were even more agitated. The upheaval of 66/5-6 passed, but during the postwar months the city was wracked by a combination of public difficulties, soldiers' rampages, and mysterious fires.

The popular protests sprang directly from hardship. During 66/9 rice inflation spurted ahead. It led to more public demonstrations and even precipitated some minor abuse of foreigners, who were considered the cause of the trouble.[68] On 9/18 the American minister Van Valkenburgh blundered into the midst of a riot, from which he was extricated by the legation guard accompanying him. As he explained the turmoil, it was ''like the flour and bread riots of more civilized countries.''[69] As weeks passed, the numbers of impoverished increased, and foreigners complained of being beset by beggars, a rare phenomenon in Japan. According to Van Valkenburgh, ''foreign rice can be imported from China and sold at half the cost of Japanese rice as it now sells in market''—the latter having risen ''from one cent per pound to about five and a half cents per pound.''[70]

That situation, with its promise of profitable trade, led foreign diplomats to advocate the import of rice. In line with that advice, as winter approached, the regime announced on 10/13 that due to poor harvests and consequent inflation, the poor were suffering severely and so it would import rice from abroad. Moreover, it announced that to assure abundance of supplies, others should not hesitate to purchase such rice from foreign merchants and sell it freely. A fortnight later it was reported that 50,000 *hyō* of foreign rice had been brought into the city.[71]

The imports seem to have had little or no effect on prices. The inflation was apparently exacerbated by price gouging: rice that reportedly sold at warehouse for 70 *ryō* per 100 *hyō* was being retailed for 300. The situation was so bad that city poor by the hundreds were driven into bakufu relief hostels in the Kanda district and into certain temples that maintained relief facilities.[72] Soon the city and temple facilities were overrun. As city magistrate Inoue Kiyonao put it in mid-66/11: ''There are many impoverished in the city who have applied for admission to the hostels but have not been admitted.'' However, bakufu attempts during the month to limit the use of the hostels to fifty-day periods were not very effective. Where, after all, in the middle of winter, were the wretched to go? To discourage extended habitation, the bakufu offered a direct payment of over 45 liters of rice to each person who voluntarily left. It also offered to enroll the able-bodied in the army. To keep order in the crowded hostels, it issued strict regulations requiring all inhabitants to be in the compound by 6 PM, forbidding the introduction of sake, repeating the fifty-day limit, and issuing inhabitants rations enough for only thirty days at a time.

The situation was so explosive that Inoue took to patrolling the city daily to keep his eye on affairs. He maintained his coercive capacity at a visibly high level by deploying a total force of some seven hundred men, consisting of about two hundred infantrymen, fifty legation guard troops, and other *yoriki* and *dōshin*, as well as local guard units organized by ward officials. Matters were sufficiently worrisome that one commoner living in the Koishikawa district, probably a local man of consequence, wrote to Inoue during 66/11. He said his family had lived there for generations and owed much gratitude to the bakufu. He therefore proposed to help organize town patrols to be manned by some three thousand carefully chosen young men and deployed on full-time duty. Such a system, he argued, would be economical, convenient, and easy to implement. The proposal was not acted upon, but it did suggest the extent of the problem and the readiness of some commoners to participate in affairs.

In addition to popular suffering the city was beset by soldiers' unrest and rioting. Some of the turbulent men were perhaps simply rowdy souls hurriedly put into the new forces. Others may have been frustrated by the tedium and tensions of garrison duty after life at the front. But all had in common the economic problem of small, fixed salaries in a period of wild inflation. The situation was inherently dangerous and finally exploded. On the morning of 10/15 some two hundred bakufu troops rampaged in Yoshiwara, smashing a brothel and injuring several people. The eruption followed the arrest the previous night of twenty-eight men out of a group of fifty or sixty troops who had gone to a usurer's place and smashed it up, doubtless in some dispute over a loan sought or overdue. In following days other minor incidents occurred, and on 11/14 the bakufu warned soldiers about getting drunk and causing trouble. It complained that undisciplined infantrymen (hohei and heisotsu) were going into restaurants and teahouses, eating and drinking and refusing to pay, acting lawlessly, and bothering townspeople. Consequently, said the notice, men involved in such affairs were to be turned over to the city magistrate's office, where official complaints against them could be filed. The notice was to be read to the troops and posted for townsfolk. Seven days later Inoue's office notified ward leaders that if the troops caused trouble, they were promptly to summon the patrolling infantry (hoheigumi).[73] Evidently it required patrols armed with rifles to keep the peace.

On 11/15, the day following the bakufu's warning, Ōkubo Ichiō wrote a letter to Shungaku that shed more light on the problem. He wrote that in the city yoriki and drafted troops had abruptly been put together as infantry and were discontent. He spoke of reports that some of their wives and children were going mad or having abortions, measures seeming to reflect panic about present self-respect or future prospects. He acknowledged the merit of the intent in putting yoriki, dōshin, and draftees together, but observed that changing things around so much, even to the footgear men wear, and putting samurai together with people who wore no swords was generating much friction. He wondered whether it was better to be lenient, by which he meant not enforcing the reforms, or to have a large army of unhappy troops.[74] Ōkubo's report presumably referred to attempts to combine sappei and hohei, and it showed how military reform was playing a role in creating malaise and trouble.

There were no further indications of soldiers' riots during the winter, but worse troubles soon beset the city.[75] On 66/11/4 the Kakegawa han mansion burned and a fire broke out in the Fukagawa area. These conflagrations introduced a whole spate of fires. Five days later a major fire broke out in the Kanda area and, driven by northwest winds, roared down to Kyōbashi, burning some 130 administrative districts (chō or machi) adjacent to the castle proper before dying down a day later. A day after that disaster a portion of the Yoshiwara was incinerated, and the displaced ladies were moved to temporary quarters in Fukagawa and Asakusa. Two days later a fire started in an Inari shrine in the main Tosa *han* mansion, burning barracks, gates, and the main residence as well as part of the adjacent Tokushima mansion. Four days later a barracks in the Hikone *han* mansion burned. The fires evidently started a rise in the cost of construction materials, for on 11/30 the bakufu forbade increases in the price of lumber and related items. Then during the night of 67/1/2 the Okayama *han* mansion burned completely. That was the last in the spate of fires, which, if one includes the earlier Komoro and Fukuyama mansion fires of 66/4, involved seven daimyo mansions.

At last the bakufu was prompted to investigate, but no evidence of arson was uncovered. That finding was not necessarily comforting to city officials, however, because the most common explanation of the time was that with most people back at the *han*, mansions had become inhabited by a motley collection of *rōnin* and other people who by implication were careless, irresponsible, or worse. It is likely too that the impoverished were taking shelter wherever they could, and that out of this situation of urban decay and social disintegration fires arose, produced by carelessness of the socially disoriented.

5. The Apogee of Popular Unrest

The turbulence in Edo was only the tip of an iceberg whose contours already had been revealed in the upheavals of 66/5–6. During the latter part of the year much of the nation suffered a rash of natural disasters and resultant crop failures that combined with the malign consequences of war to produce widespread hardship and even more turmoil.[76] A first phase of the turmoil occurred in the last weeks of war and a second, much more severe phase during the winter. During those months there was perhaps a slight increase in the incidence of placarding and, immediately after the war, renewed reports of *rōnin* activities, but it was the public at large, not the activist few, who bore the brunt of the year's disasters.

The severe storms that lashed Yamashiro, Tanba, and Echizen on 66/5/14 were followed on 7/1 by major storms, flooding, and wind damage in Suruga, Tōtōmi, and Mikawa. The great disasters, however, occurred on the days of 8/5–8 and 8/15–16 when immense typhoons lashed much of central Japan. The first helped encompass bakufu defeat at Aki and then gave Yoshinobu an excuse for not starting west to attack Chōshū: the weather, he said, made it very difficult to transport military supplies.[77] Jointly the two typhoons ravaged Hyōgo and flooded Kyoto, tearing out bridges across the Kamo river, sweeping away scores of grain and freight boats of 30-*koku* capacity on the Yodo river, wrecking fields, toppling and washing away hundreds of buildings, felling trees, and killing scores of people and uncounted livestock. Then they roared up across Japan, leaving death and devastation in their wake. In some areas relief expeditions were formed, a number of them going from Obama to Tsuruga to help people dig out from the wreckage. According to Yokoi Shōnan they were the worst storms to hit the region in over two hundred years. Others called the 8/7 storm the worst in thirty or even two hundred years. One newspaper report guessed that in all perhaps ten thousand people had died.[78] During the next few months daimyo from all over central and eastern Japan submitted reports on storm damage: Morioka, Shōnai, Utsunomiya, Nakamura, Komoro, Takashima, Kaga, Ōgaki, Owari, Tottori, Akashi, and Okayama.

Then parts of central Japan were hit by early frosts caused, it appears, by continental cold weather sucked into Japan by the passing typhoon. The frosts ruined yet more of the harvest. As Makino of Komoro in Shinano reported on 11/12, summer weather had been bad and the crop had grown poorly. Then the rains and winds early in 66/8 had done great damage. On the morning of 8/9 white frost had covered the ground, and thereafter repeated frosts ruined the rest of the crop. According to reports handed him just that morning, he wrote, the *han* had lost some 25,250 *koku*.[79] And since Komoro's official productive capacity (*omotedaka*) was only 15,000 *koku*, that quite simply meant the entire crop had been destroyed.

In central Japan the bakufu tried to cope insofar as its writ still ran. On 6/14 it ordered an exceptionally sharp reduction in the use of rice for sake production. From time to time thereafter it released reserves for public consumption. It permitted the import of rice and instructed daimyo to bring it to the cities. On 10/4 it also ordered distribution of more warehouse rice to impoverished commoners on liege vassal lands.[80]

The measures were insufficient. After the typhoons of 66/8 ripped across Japan, peasants in Shinano grew restless and erupted at the Imaichi and Kiso stations of the Nakasendō. The winter—and the worst—were still to come. In Osaka itself there was visible discontent over inflation, and the bakufu saw serious insurrectionary potential in it. On 12/10 it ordered shrines and temples to extend assistance to the people. According to the notice there was suffering due to inflation and some people were getting ''bad ideas.'' Therefore temples were instructed to use their ''quiet teachings'' to pacify turbulent spirits and assist any needy who might enter their gates.[81]

In the outcome Osaka, like Edo, remained quiet, and the worst trouble occurred in the countryside to the west of there. During 66/11 peasants on Tsuyama lands in Mimasaka erupted, protesting rice shortages and daimyo tyranny.[82] According to the necessarily antiseptic report of the Tsuyama lord, on the night of 11/24 farmers in one district rioted. On the following morning farmers in an adjacent district also erupted and carried a complaint to the castle town. Officials were sent to reason with them, but some people behaved lawlessly, and so troops were dispatched. By early morning of 11/26 the farmers had returned to their villages. Unavoidably five people had been killed.

Other reports presented a rather fuller account of the upheaval. They blamed it on the bad weather, particularly the 66/8 typhoon, which destroyed half the rice crop and caused widespread hardship. Apparently the rioters at Tsuyama went directly to the daimyo's mansion on 11/25, beat down the gate, surged in and wrecked his residence, and then continued smashing all around the castle town. Others erupted to the south and went to the bakufu intendancy at Kurashiki where some five hundred people smashed rice, sake, and other shops, thereby generating heated arguments among warehouse officials as to the best means of pacification. Elsewhere, too, in the vicinity of Kawahara an estimated four or five thousand rioters smashed and protested during 11/25–27. They complained bitterly about their taxes, *goyōkin* (18,000 *ryō* allegedly levied by the daimyo in 1865 and 10,000 in 1866), and other fiscal burdens. They were shortly quieted by some officials supported by troops, but in the process a few were killed.

By 12/1 the unrest in Tsuyama had been quieted temporarily, but some of the more vigorous dissidents carried their protests elsewhere. On 11/30 some farmers crossed out of Tsuyama lands to the southeast into villages administered by Akō *han*, and there they protested and rioted out of control. The *han* deployed some troops, but on 12/2 more dissidents arrived from the Kawahara area, and the reinforced insurgents smashed and burned houses. In response more *han* troops were deployed the next day. However, the insurgents were reported to be pressing on the castle town, and so the *han* sent a hurried letter to Edo asking permission to recall troops stationed there. The bakufu approved, but before they arrived the unrest had quieted down. Contemporaneously some migratory people also entered adjoining lands of Amagasaki *han*. They went to lodge a protest at a village office, but local people failed to support them and so they threatened to burn down the houses of any who refused to cooperate. The threats sufficed and the assembled crowd pushed on to a nearby village assigned to Tatsuno *han*, where they smashed a rice dealer's shop. Officials from the local *han* intendant's office managed to quiet the group temporarily, but that night they smashed and burned more houses of the well-to-do. Some men armed with farm tools also attacked and burned guard barracks at the intendant's office, and the latter quieted the crowd only with great difficulty.

The numbers involved in this turmoil are not at all clear. Reports speak variously of 70,000, 30,000, 7000, 5000, 4000. In any event it was a major protest and revived a few weeks later. On 67/1/1 rural people (*hyakushō*) in Tsuyama again erupted briefly, and in succeeding days *han* officials sent out investigating teams to try to pacify them.

One of these later eruptions occurred on Shōdoshima, a large island in the Inland Sea west of Awaji and administered by Tsuyama.[83] People there had been subjected to exceptional tax burdens since 1862 and to special service burdens related to the Summer War. Combined with the general commodity inflation and crop failure in that area, these factors created an explosive situation. News of the turmoil on shore reached the island, and last-minute attempts by Tsuyama officials to ease the islanders' condition were pathetically inadequate. Agitation and petitioning began on 12/22 and a fortnight later gave way to attacks by the poorer and more vulnerable on property of the local wealthy. The attacks spread across the island in the next few days as organized groups of hundreds surged about assaulting merchants and property owners until 1/15 when the upheaval ended, having pretty well hit all the objects of local resentment. Three days later Tsuyama troops arrived, investigated, and punished some leaders, and later *han* authorities again made modest gestures of assistance. After about two months of turmoil, quiet had finally returned to the Tsuyama area.

As a phase of the 1860s political crisis the war had contributed indirectly to the suffering of Tsuyama by forcing the daimyo to be more ruthless in his exactions from the people. Farther west the war's impact was more direct. In parts of Kyushu, where there also was bad weather and hence a poor harvest, the troubles were compounded by the war because it disrupted life directly and then for a long period interrupted movement of rice and other goods at Shimonoseki. The upshot was exceptional suffering in western Japan, especially in the Hamada and Kokura areas. That in turn led to a rash of upheavals comparable to those in the Tōhoku, Kantō, and Tsuyama areas.

To summarize these matters very briefly, after Chōshū invaded bakufu lands in Iwami and destroyed the intendancy, peasants nearby erupted in apparent protest at the resulting economic disorder. Matsue troops in the vicinity were unable to quiet them, but advancing Chōshū troops did so later. During 66/8 there was more trouble in the Hamada area, and Chōshū troops quieted that too. At about the same time peasants in

Kokura started an incendiary rampage, and the bakufu intendant at Hita in western Bungo had to obtain assistance from Kumamoto to pacify them. Then later in the year, even as Tsuyama was in upheaval, the poor in Kizuki town in northern Bungo gathered. Eruptions soon spread in all directions through the *han*, and before the unhappy people could be quieted, troops from Kizuki, Kumamoto, Mori, and Hiji *han* as well as peasant troops from the Hita intendancy had been deployed. The intendancy itself was attacked on 12/5 by a band of robbers who killed some people, burned both the main and branch office, and fled with 10,000 *ryō*. And later in the month peasants in Usuki *han* in southeast Bungo also erupted due to hardship stemming from crop failure. On 67/1/26 the bakufu was notified by Kumamoto that in Kaharu *han* some ten thousand were homeless. Kumamoto being unable to help, it was asking the bakufu to aid the unfortunate.[84] Whether or not aid was forthcoming is unclear, but as matters worked out, the turmoil seems to have passed. In Kyushu, as in Tsuyama, quiet returned early in the new year.

In sum it was the worst winter in decades, perhaps in centuries. In the latter half of 1866 crop failure, political disorder and war, misgovernment, and the inflation and shortages spawned by these troubles had led to massive turmoil from one end of Japan to the other.

With the coming of spring, however, matters quieted down considerably. In Mutsu in early 1867 discontent over economic matters was limited to verbal protests and attempts at litigation. Inflation still caused restlessness in the Kantō, and that prompted the bakufu in 67/4 to issue orders against hoarding and to facilitate the distribution of rice.[85] But just as the visible evidence of daimyo difficulty faded in the spring, so the evidence of fundamental economic crisis receded, not to be renewed until a recurrence of war and upheaval in early 1868.

A Summation

Bakufu defeat in the Summer War destroyed what remained of the conservative restorative orientation in bakufu policy. Drastic military reforms were initiated during the war, and after it they were pursued much further. After Shungaku's *kōbugattai* effort ran its course, leaders reestablished the formal grounds of Tokugawa authority, consolidated the new shogun's position, and revitalized their leadership. They attempted to deal with the manifold problems they faced, notably the unresolved Chōshū conflict, the discontent of related lords, the hardship of various daimyo, the fiscal problems of the bakufu itself, and widespread public unrest.

The new year of 1867 found Yoshinobu's regime in a position considerably improved over that of the grim days of defeat. The problems of a disorganized leadership had largely been overcome. Major military reforms had been made, and the consequent dislocations had been survived. In the country at large the turmoil of the postwar months was passing. Popular unrest had peaked before year's end, and during early 1867 the country grew quiet again. In Edo matters improved and the spate of fires became a thing of the past. There was a sharp drop-off in reports of domanial distress, and so the overall social situation seemed to be on the mend.

As the year 1867 began, the foreigners were still relatively quiescent, and the daimyo too were quiet, if uncooperative. This new pattern of bakufu-daimyo relations did not seem very promising, but, as we note in the next chapter, it was one that leaders may have found understandable, inevitable, and acceptable for the moment. It was, after all, preferable to the more likely alternatives. The Chōshū albatross still hung heavily, but by ignoring it the regime was able to concentrate on other matters. Fiscal inadequacy continued to be a problem, but long-range remedial measures were being pursued, and in time the problem might be overcome.

In view of the disastrous year past, these enduring evidences of difficulty seemed modest compared to the signs of bakufu recovery. Yoshinobu, the new shogun, whose name was formally designated Yoshihisa by the bakufu on 67/2/21,[86] had some reason to feel he was not doing badly. On 3/15 daimyo and officials in Edo were all instructed to come to the castle to congratulate their new lord *in absentia*, and during succeeding days they did so. The third year of Keiō seemed to have begun auspiciously. Perhaps the naming of a new emperor on 67/1/9 had been a good omen.

CHAPTER 10

Domestic Politics and Diplomatic Perturbations 1867/1–9

THE POLITICAL PROCESS: 67/1–9

THE IMPERIALIST MENACE

1867: POLITICS AND DIPLOMACY IN RETROSPECT

During spring and summer of 1867 bakufu leaders continued to build on their achievements of the postwar months. Those in Kyoto succeeded in keeping control of the imperial symbol despite a major daimyo effort to wrest it from them. The regime's leaders also dealt with a series of newly menacing and complicating aspects of the imperialist intrusion. Those successes kept both the great lords and foreigners at bay while Tokugawa leaders pressed on with their Keiō reform.

THE POLITICAL PROCESS: 67/1–9

By 66/11 Yoshinobu and Itakura had reestablished bakufu control of the court. After the death of Emperor Kōmei, however, radical agitators quickly challenged them. Court leaders, with support from Yoshinobu and others, were able to resist demands that would have shifted radically the balance of power in Kyoto, but during 67/1 they did pardon most nobles punished in the suppression of radicalism in 1863–1864. The degree to which bakufu influence at court declined seems actually to have been minor. However, the trend was such that by early 67/2 at the latest Satsuma men in Kyoto had decided the time was opportune for Hisamitsu to reenter the political scene "to advise the youthful emperor."[1] Within a few weeks that opinion helped precipitate decisions by Hisamitsu, Date Munenari of Uwajima, Yamauchi Yōdō of Tosa, and finally Shungaku of Fukui to return to Kyoto.

The issue that seemed to offer leverage was the pending question of opening "the two ports and the two cities"—namely Hyōgo, Niigata (until the foreigners lost interest in it), Osaka, and Edo. By treaty they were to open on 67/12/7 (January 1, 1868), and before that date preparatory measures would have to be undertaken. Opposition to admitting foreigners to the Kinai area remained strong at court and among samurai of many sorts, and the great lords and their advisors hoped to advance their interests by squeezing the bakufu between foreign demands and domestic opposition. They intended to champion the cause of sonnō jōi at bakufu expense much as Yoshinobu had done at their expense three years previously.

1. The Hyōgo Issue Develops

The bakufu had failed in late 1865 to persuade foreigners to abandon their demand for Hyōgo. From time to time after that Shungaku had advised leaders to get court approval of the opening so as to avoid a repetition of the Hyōgo crisis. However, they had procrastinated because they knew all too well the depth of court feelings on the matter and were also aware that influential daimyo opinion was still divided and ambiguous.[2] To justify the avoidance, Yoshinobu had repeatedly turned Shungaku aside during 1866 with the argument that he would first settle the Chōshū matter and then deal with Hyōgo.

Bakufu attempts to manage Chōshū had not worked, however, and time was running out on Hyōgo.[3] During 67/2 the new shogun came under intensified pressure to take action. Four foreign magistrates, including Tsukahara Masayoshi, Inoue Yoshifumi, and Shibata Masanaka, wrote a memorandum reminding him that the opening date was near. They said preparations must be started to overcome in time whatever obstacles might arise. They reported that Harry Parkes kept raising the issue and argued that action was essential to avoid another major international crisis.[4] Parkes' badgering was worrisome because he had recently been cultivating the goodwill of major daimyo. It was reasonable to expect on the basis of past experience that in the event of difficulties over Hyōgo, Anglo-daimyo pressure would be severely embarrassing to the regime.

Yoshinobu was also coming under direct foreign pressure. In late 66/12 Roches had complained about the lack of preparation, and Yoshinobu had agreed to talk matters over with him. When the two did meet at Osaka on 2/6, Roches urged him to start making necessary arrangements promptly. He also warned that if the bakufu failed to abide by the treaty, a certain unnamed foreign power would cooperate with great lords to bakufu detriment.[5]

The pressure from within and without was sufficient. Tokugawa leaders in Kyoto decided to get daimyo approval for the opening and armed with that to secure court consent. On 2/19 Itakura sent a formal inquiry to Shungaku and eight other major lords. He reminded them of the approaching deadline, said the treaty would be hard to change, and asked their advice on whether to obtain imperial approval of the Hyōgo opening. He urged some of the lords to come to Kyoto, but insisted only that they give a written reply within a month.

Almost at once that plan of action was disrupted—primarily, it appears, by Satsuma men who first manipulated Parkes and then the court. On about 2/24 Yoshinobu came under renewed pressure from Parkes. Reportedly egged on by Satsuma men, Parkes urged the shogun to move promptly on the port-city matter, and he may have threatened again to proceed to Kyoto and negotiate directly with the court if no action were taken.[6] In the face of added pressure, Yoshinobu concluded he could not wait for the daimyo replies. Accordingly even before he had their opinions to buttress his own, on 3/5 he wrote the court. He acknowledged that despite court instructions of 65/10, he had not informed the foreigners that Hyōgo was to remain closed, and now they were demanding that it be opened. Therefore he was asking the court to permit it so as to avoid calamity.[7] At court the issue led to severe disputes. Anti-bakufu nobles, who were prodded by Satsuma men, worked to prevent approval, and no reply was made for a fortnight. Then the emperor was simply caused to observe on 3/19 that the request had been rejected in 1865 and, it being a difficult matter, Yoshinobu was to consult the daimyo promptly and reflect deeply on it.[8]

Meanwhile Yoshinobu had instructed Itakura and Inaba Masakuni to assure Parkes the opening would be on schedule. Despite that assurance, on 3/16 Parkes wrote Itakura from Osaka reiterating his demand for the port-city opening. Four days later both he and the American minister Van Valkenburgh, who had just arrived for the formal shogunal reception, urged bakufu leaders to take action. Fearful perhaps that the issue might ruin the reception and thereby complicate their quest for international recognition, leaders agreed on the twenty-first to the foreign demand for a public announcement of the opening. Parkes immediately notified the foreign community of that acquiescence. Driven thus into an untenable position, on the following day Yoshinobu again requested imperial agreement, that time in a decidedly more impatient notice. He then departed abruptly for Osaka in order to receive the diplomats as earlier promised.[9]

Court officials continued to object. They complained that back in 1865 Yoshinobu had indicated Hyōgo would not be opened and the court had approved the treaties with that understanding. On 3/24 the court dispatched to twenty-five major lords instructions either to present their opinions or come to discuss the matter by 67/4. That was necessary, they were told, because in 65/10 the court had indicated Hyōgo was not to be opened but the matter had come up again.

While those instructions were traveling to the *han* in late 67/3, Yoshinobu was at Osaka greeting the diplomats. Earlier on 3/15 he had had Sadaaki state very clearly at court that the formal diplomatic reception did not signify agreement to open Hyōgo, but court suspicions were not so easily allayed. Nor did his acerbic note of the twenty-second or his abrupt departure for Osaka improve the mood. Doubtless the court had also learned of his agreement to announce publicly the coming opening, and on the twenty-ninth it sharply forbade him to open Hyōgo until the emperor permitted it. The court also instructed the bakufu to acknowledge promptly receipt of the prohibitory notice, and on the next day Itakura, Inaba, and Ogasawara dutifully did so.[10]

On 3/29 the court also pardoned those nobles who earlier had been punished for staging an anti-Yoshinobu protest at court late in 66/8. Coming together with the prohibitory notice about Hyōgo, it indicated how badly Yoshinobu's rapport at court had eroded and how valuable the diplomatic issue was proving to Satsuma, its allies, and sympathizers in the struggle for symbolic power.

The administrators who actually had to arrange the opening of ports and cities found the delays intolerable. On 4/1, even as senior councillors were acknowledging the court's prohibitory order, the several foreign magistrates then assembled in the Kinai, including Tsukahara, Shibata, Kurimoto Kon, Hirayama Keichū, and Kawakatsu Hiromichi, wrote their two colleagues in Edo. They reported that representatives of the four principal foreign powers had been informed the cities and ports would be opened as per treaty, and they instructed their colleagues to have representatives of the other treaty states similarly notified.[11]

The divergence between bakufu words and deeds continued to grow as administrators pressed on with their preparation. On 4/13 Itakura, In-aba, and Ogasawara presented the four ministers at Osaka with detailed plans for foreign residence in both that city and Hyōgo. The plans in-cluded not only extensive regulations for foreigners living in the cities but also carefully prepared maps indicating precisely where the foreign quar-ters would be located.[12] Clearly administrators had been at work on the matter for some time.

Despite this evidence that Yoshinobu was meeting the foreign de-mands, Parkes continued to complicate his problems at Court. On the thirteenth he asked Itakura for an escort on an overland trip to Tsuruga on the seacoast north of Lake Biwa. Although his ostensible purpose was to see if the port would make an acceptable substitute for Niigata, the trip, which a Satsuma activist may have suggested to him,[13] would take him right by Kyoto and predictably embarrass the bakufu. For good rea-sons, however, Itakura could not refuse. First, just the preceding day he reportedly had dissuaded Parkes from insisting on entering Kyoto itself, and the trip past the city may thus have represented a compromise. More-over on that day Itakura, Inaba, and Ogasawara had just written the ministers of the four major foreign powers asking for a two-year delay in the remaining Shimonoseki indemnity payments.[14] Angering Parkes would hardly help that request. But in any case Parkes had treaty authori-ty for the trip, and he had already shown his willingness to implement by threats when necessary those treaty clauses advantageous to himself.

Accordingly Itakura acquiesced, and on 4/15 Parkes and seven other foreigners and a legation guard force of thirty-six departed Osaka on the two-day trip.[15] The situation was ideally suited to inflame *sonnō jōi* sen-sibilities at the bakufu's expense. News of the foreigners' approach created a furor at court, provided a fertile ground for agitation by court radicals, generated much anger among samurai in the city, and fostered a host of rumors. The anger focused on Parkes' seemingly insolent behav-ior, the prospect of nearby Tsuruga being opened, and the bakufu's will-ingness to tolerate the venture.

In an effort to dissociate the court from the whole matter, a number of court officials resigned their positions. The court also issued orders pro-hibiting foreigners from traveling henceforth on the Fushimi highway. And in an obvious slap at bakufu, Aizu, and Kuwana, it ordered Satsu-ma, Tottori, and Okayama *han* to mount extra guard forces in the city due to rumors that some foreigners were hiding there. Late on 4/18, in a long and heated session at court, Yoshinobu, Itakura, and Sadaaki, who suspected Satsuma handiwork in the whole affair, protested both the defense orders to the three *han* and the court resignations. Their pressure led the court to cancel its defense orders and punish some courtiers. But under the strain more key court officials resigned. On the twentieth, therefore, Yoshinobu again had Itakura try to pacify the court. Instead of quieting things, however, he found himself criticized by an influential court official for being disobedient to the former emperor in his handling of both the foreign and the Chōshū matters. The charges prompted more bakufu gestures of coercive solicitude, with guards being posted at the homes of several recalcitrant nobles. That move helped stifle the unrest, but several days passed before the furor quieted down.

For a few days it had looked as though anti-bakufu elements in Kyoto might successfully use Parkes' ploy to unseat the bakufu there, but in the end the scheme backfired, and the bakufu's unusually forceful actions prevented its loss of control. Indeed the intemperate court reaction had been exploited as justification for punishing some unfriendly nobles, and in the outcome Yoshinobu recovered much of the ground recently lost over the Hyōgo issue.

At a higher level of abstraction one may even suggest that the combined affairs of Hyōgo and Tsuruga had forced Yoshinobu to abandon at last even the facade of his older strategy of trying to claim the *sonnō jōi* rhetoric for his own. Despite doing so, however, he had managed to keep control of the court. He had at last done as Hisamitsu had urged in early 1863, but he had done it in defiance of Satsuma pressure rather than in line with it. That meant the bakufu had at last ceased trying even nominally to manage the "rebels at home and aggressors abroad" by driving the latter away. Instead it had committed itself to moving Japan fully and permanently into the current stream of global history. For the bakufu the diplomatic revolution had been completed.

2. *The Four Lords Play Symbolic Politics*

While the Tsuruga tempest was blowing itself out, the key lords were reaching Kyoto. On 4/12 Hisamitsu and his son the Satsuma daimyo reached the city, reportedly with a force of several thousand troops. Three days later Munenari of Uwajima arrived, having come by Satsuma warship, and the next day Shungaku arrived. A fortnight later on 5/1 Yōdō of Tosa entered town. The other daimyo mostly begged off, alleging illness. They did express opinions on Hyōgo, however, the majority arguing that opening it was unavoidable.

On 4/20 Yoshinobu summoned Shungaku, Munenari, Hisamitsu, and his son to a meeting, but only Shungaku and Munenari went. The following day the lords, disgruntled that Yoshinobu had not even waited for their opinions before approaching the court, criticized the shogun for actually agreeing to open Hyōgo without imperial permission. Since none of the lords in fact opposed its opening, they clearly were using the issue as a stick to beat the bakufu. But it was much more than a mere device for scoring political points. It was also a crucial test in the struggle over symbols. It was an issue on which Yoshinobu could demonstrate with great clarity either that he was prepared to sacrifice Tokugawa claims to national authority, as they wished, or that he was not prepared to do so, as they feared.

In succeeding days the genteel war of nerves was waged fiercely by the lords, their advisors, bakufu leaders, and court nobles.[16] The bakufu tried to get formal court approval of the port-city openings and was unable to do so. The lords procrastinated on the Hyōgo matter, refused to meet Yoshinobu, and tried to break the stalemate by getting more supporters into influential posts at court. The bakufu resisted, and the lords found their efforts achieving nothing.

In the process of surviving the Tsuruga affair, Yoshinobu had strengthened his position at court sufficiently to thwart Satsuma's strategy of verbal *jōi*. In consequence the four lords were forced to work out a new plan of attack, and they did so by about 5/10. The device they chose was to connect the diplomatic issue to that of Chōshū. Having settled upon that familiar strategy, they were ready to confront Yoshinobu and on 5/12 so informed him, apparently in a trade-off for token changes in court personnel.

Two days later, when the four met him, the shogun explained at length how one thing had led to another to cause delay in getting daimyo and imperial approval on Hyōgo. After some discussion Hisamitsu suggested briefly that the Chōshū matter should be settled before that of Hyōgo. It was a skillful argument, lifted directly from Yoshinobu's own mouth. In equally skillful response the shogun suggested that since the war in fact had long since ended, Hisamitsu's proposal would make a minor matter take precedence over a critical one. Hisamitsu argued its advisability nonetheless.

In succeeding days this question of sequence remained the focus of debate. On 5/19 and 21 Shungaku, Munenari, and Hisamitsu (but not Yōdō, who was ill) met Itakura and Inaba and advised the bakufu first to settle the Chōshū matter leniently and then get court approval on Hyōgo.[17] The lords were not precise about the content of leniency, but on the twenty-second a Satsuma man indicated it would mean repudiating all prior punitive orders. Despite the vagueness of phrasing, it appears Satsuma's intent was to have the bakufu admit it was wrong in attacking Chōshū, and Satsuma and other *han* right in opposing the policy. Such an acknowledgment would demonstrate Yoshinobu's ''change of heart''—that is, his admission of harm done by the expedition.[18] More practically it would enable the lords' allies at court to claim the former emperor had been wrongly maneuvered into ordering Chōshū's punishment. That would then justify a sweeping change of court officials and break Yoshinobu's control of the imperial symbol.

The lords wished also to make changes among bakufu officials. Perhaps their ultimate goal was to discredit architects of the Keiō reform, but their targets as of 5/17 were the more visible exponents of a punitive Chōshū policy and a strong shogun, specifically Ogasawara Nagamichi and Yoshinobu's long-time vassal Hara Ichinoshin. In the end, however, the lords' energies were devoted so fully to the issue of sequence that they never got around to pursuing the matter of Hara and Ogasawara.

At Yoshinobu's request the court at last confronted the joined issues of Hyōgo and Chōshū. On 5/23 it held a great conference attended not only by court officials but also by Yoshinobu, Sadaaki, Itakura, Inaba, junior councillor Ōkōchi Masatada, other bakufu officials, and after a while Shungaku and Munenari. Yōdō stayed away, and Hisamitsu also did not go despite repeated urging. Probably he refused to attend because he had failed to get prior bakufu agreement on the matter of sequence and was reluctant to argue his case in a formal situation where his low status (he was not even a daimyo or ex-daimyo) would be pitted against the high status of the shogun and elegant men of court.

At court the verbal struggle over both sequence and Hyōgo wore on all night and into the next day. Finally the exhausted participants reached a decision acceptable to the shogun: the court (and bakufu) would be lenient toward Chōshū, and as shogun and daimyo had advised, the court would revoke its prior prohibition on opening Hyōgo.[19]

The outcome of the 5/23–24 conference amounted to a bakufu triumph. Leaders had received what they needed—namely, court acquiescence on Hyōgo. In return they had agreed only to an unspecific statement about leniency toward Chōshū, although it doubtless was understood that all prior punitive orders were nullified. Yoshinobu had preserved his claim to a national leadership role and had reaffirmed his abandonment of the old verbal *jōi* strategy.

3. Yoshinobu Triumphs in Symbolic Politics

The bakufu moved quickly to implement the court's decision and thereby consolidate its triumph.[20] On 5/25 leaders indicated they would invite Chōshū to apologize; when that had been done, they would be lenient. Then, probably to ensure that the matter would not be undone, Itakura instructed Hiroshima to deliver the notice to Chōshū promptly, and the bakufu posted widely public announcements that the court and four lords had approved its policy of leniency. The second Chōshū expedition was not about to be repudiated.

The hard line toward Chōshū was easier adopted than implemented, however. The notice was held up by the opposition of Hiroshima and others, and by mid-67/6 leaders had agreed to delete the egregious demand for an apology. Due largely to Hiroshima's continuing refusal to cooperate, however, action was stalled for more than a month after that. Finally the bakufu instructed Hiroshima simply to have a Chōshū delegate come to Osaka by late 67/9 to discuss the leniency order. That notice was delivered, and at the last moment on 9/29 Hiroshima reported that Chōshū was sending an official to Osaka, ostensibly to arrange the lenient settlement.

The actions relative to Hyōgo were much more substantial. On 5/28 officials were appointed to new positions necessitated by the port opening, and in succeeding days they and others continued the procedural preparations. On 6/6 the bakufu publicly announced that Hyōgo, Osaka, and Edo would be opened on 12/7 and that foreigners could then reside and freely pursue their commercial activities therein. Subsequently preparations went ahead. Although other serious diplomatic problems arose, as summer passed and chilly autumn nights were again settling on the land, it seemed the new stage of trade relations might be established with unprecedented tranquillity at higher political levels.

The great lords had been roundly outmaneuvered, and despite differences among themselves, they knew it. On 5/26 the four jointly denounced as a betrayal of their views the court decision of two days before. In following days that blunt statement combined with other matters to sustain heated discussions. The court's decision was not changed, however, and subsequently the lords failed to mount any effective joint efforts in the sphere of symbolic politics. Even before the showdown on 5/23 they had been bedeviled by their habitual inability to sustain cooperation, and during much of the struggle the views of Shungaku and Yōdō had not fitted at all well the considerably more militant views of Munenari and Hisamitsu. Those differences led to damaging misunderstandings that helped prompt Yōdō to ask court permission to go home on 5/21. Six days later he left. The others continued to talk and maneuver but to no avail. From 6/15 Shungaku also began asking permission to leave, but his requests were refused, and during the next two months he reluctantly stayed on at Kyoto. Hisamitsu and Munenari also stayed, perhaps because they knew bakufu leaders hoped they would go home. Despite their presence, however, they and the few other lords in town had only fitful contact with either court or bakufu. And that contact, handled mostly by vassals, achieved nothing, except to reaffirm the estrangement of bakufu and great *han*.

During the weeks of Yoshinobu's triumph there were of course continuing grounds for concern. Most visibly, existing lines of dispute among the related daimyo were reconfirmed. To elaborate, on 6/17 representatives of Fukui, Mito, Kii, and Aizu met in Kyoto. In their meeting the Aizu men denounced the great daimyo statement of 5/26, objecting particularly to criticism of the second Chōshū expedition. Kii men supported the Aizu view, and Fukui came under attack for participating in the statement. Mito men tried to quiet the quarrel, but the meeting only reaffirmed the division between Fukui on one hand and Aizu and Kii on the other. Then later, on about 7/10, an important official of Owari *han* reached Kyoto and displayed an uncooperative attitude toward the bakufu. Shortly he too came under attack by Aizu men who charged that as a related house Owari should be actively supporting Tokugawa leaders.[21] That attack too did no good, only demonstrating the distance between the two.

Aizu was thus preserving its role as forceful defender of Tokugawa interests, but, as we noted earlier, Aizu men also continued trying to get Katamori out of politics and back to Wakamatsu. Partly, no doubt, those efforts were designed to keep Yoshinobu on a firm course, but surely they also betrayed Aizu's feeling of isolation and terrible vulnerability.

The quarrels among related *han* could only have reminded bakufu leaders that they were not likely to have solid related daimyo support in a showdown: to pacify Fukui they must lose Aizu and vice versa. During those weeks, too, Kyoto leaders heard rumors of plots, and they worried about the mysterious activities of *rōnin* and of Satsuma and Tosa men. In response to those worries they increased their military presence in Kyoto and tried to strengthen friendly daimyo control in nearby provinces.[22]

During 67/7–9, however, those concerns were overshadowed by the evidence of Yoshinobu's symbolic triumph. On 8/4 the court finally responded to the four lords' formal protest of 5/26. It claimed the court's order had been in accord with the views expressed on 5/23–24, but that anyway the lords should speak to the bakufu, not the court, concerning the intent of the order. The response prompted another protest by Hisamitsu and Munenari on 8/6, but that was rejected a few days later. Shungaku did not join the two in that protest; rather he departed for home at high noon that day, having finally obtained Yoshinobu and the court's permission to do so.[23] A few days later Munenari asked permission to go home and Hisamitsu requested permission to go to Osaka to recover from illness. On the thirteenth the court approved both requests, and a few days later the two men left.

Yoshinobu's repudiation of the old verbal *jōi* policy had reduced appreciably the difficulty of managing the confrontation of western imperialism and Japanese ethnicity. Then the defeat of the four lords temporarily eased the danger of the domestic court-daimyo-*shishi* coalition's reviving. The rumors of plots and mysterious activities suggested, however, that the reprieve might not last long, and so the shogun took what measures he could to prevent the coalition's reviving. Probably in hopes of denying daimyo and *shishi* any symbols of national authority, he worked hard to salvage the *sonnō* part of his old *sonnō jōi* stance.

There were several aspects to Yoshinobu's wooing of the court. During 67/6 he urged the reappointment to court office of some friendly nobles who had left their posts during the Tsuruga tempest. More strikingly, during the next two months he granted the court substantial estates. Back in 67/2 he had ordered that no men of samurai status take the honorary title *Yamashiro no kami* (governor of Yamashiro province), the province surrounding Kyoto. Then in 67/7 he wrote the court that although Iemochi had promised it grants of 150,000 *koku*, due to fiscal difficulties the grants had not been made. Therefore, he stated, he was canceling the promise and instead assigning the court all the tax income of Yamashiro province except that of temples, shrines, and highway stations. Then on 8/5 the bakufu ordered the several daimyo and 204 liege vassals with lands in that province to return them to the bakufu in exchange for other holdings because the income from them was to go to the court.[24]

One other major expression of the growing court-bakufu intimacy was a new marriage alliance between the shogunal and imperial families. On 9/14 the court officially approved a plan for an imperial prince whose family had earlier marriage ties to the Tokugawa house to marry a younger sister of Yoshiatsu (and a half sister of Yoshinobu) whom the shogun had adopted as a daughter. Then on 9/21 Yoshinobu received more high titles—being designated *naidaijin*, *ukonoe taishō*, and *kubōsama*, and his wife, *midaidokoro*—and he moved at last into Nijō castle, a shogun in every nuance of every formal sense of the word.[25] If the symbol were the substance, Yoshinobu had every reason to anticipate a very good winter. In the course of a year he and the bakufu seemed to have moved from the brink of disaster to the brink of triumph.

THE IMPERIALIST MENACE

The behavior of Yoshinobu and the four lords in mid-1867 demonstrated how fully the Hyōgo issue had become a stick to beat the bakufu. Yet one should not conclude therefrom that the imperialist menace had somehow ceased to be a threat to Japan or a direct cause of bakufu difficulty. To the contrary, during the year several aspects of the imperialist intrusion reached new levels in Japan. Most obvious was the opening of more ports and cities on terms favoring the imperialists. That development, moreover, was accompanied by a number of notable ancillary problems and trends, some with immediate political impact, others with long-range implications. In addition, developments in the Anglo-French rivalry took turns the worse for the bakufu and potentially for Japan. But perhaps the most threatening new development was the reappearance during 1867 of the classic problem of subversive foreign missionary involvement in society. And finally there was ominous evidence that Japanese leaders were learning very fast the ways of enlightened states: they showed a growing willingness to abandon the diplomatic tradition of nearly three centuries and fight fire with fire—to assure Japanese sovereignty by applying nascent imperialist tactics in Korea.

1. Treaty Port Annoyances

Previously we noted that in 1865 the territorial threat to Japan escalated sharply with the Russian migratory advance into Karafuto. In early 1867 a bakufu mission to Russia negotiated a temporary arrangement there. As the year advanced, however, the other form of territorial threat, treaty ports and their ancillary privileges, again came to the forefront of politics.

One of the most troublesome ancillary matters was a substantial increase in inland travel by foreigners. The travel had begun with diplomats and expanded as movement between Yokohama and diplomatic residences in Edo increased. There was yet more inland travel after the bakufu allowed French technicians to move about in search of coal and other resources. Then in 1867 the opening of Hyōgo and Osaka led to a rapid expansion of such travel. During the first half of the year the bakufu issued a series of notices allowing foreigners to travel more widely: to visit the Tokugawa mausolea (Tōshōgū) at Ueno in Edo, to visit the great Buddha statue (daibutsu) of the Tōdaiji in Nara, and to enter theaters and restaurants in Edo and Osaka. And during 67/8 the Dutch minister Van Polsbroek climbed Mt. Fuji, surely the ultimate travel privilege.[26]

These several actions were taken despite the court's furor over Parkes' trip to Tsuruga and despite a court order countermanding the notice about Ueno. They were taken, too, despite evidence the populace did not welcome foreigners. On occasion commoners pelted them with stones and weighty epithets, a habit that prompted the bakufu in 67/2 to admonish the good folk to forbear. They did not, however, and later in the year the bakufu again warned people to do nothing illegal to foreigners traveling about the cities.[27]

What all this suggests is that despite court opposition and public displeasure, the bakufu had resigned itself to an open country fully accessible to foreigners. It was another expression of the diplomatic revolution. Bakufu acceptance of foreigners was not matched by public acceptance, however, and the court's indignation and people's sticks and stones proved to be the least troublesome of resulting complications. As the foreigners' presence increased, so too did their exposure to samurai anger. During 1867 there was a recrudescence of attacks on foreigners, some of them serious incidents reminiscent of the early 1860s. During 67/4 an imperial delegation to Nikkō was returning from a commemorative service for Ieyasu and passing through Kakegawa *han* in Tōtōmi. There it encountered the British diplomatic functionary Ernest Satow traveling eastward from Osaka with a British newspaperman. Some attendants of the imperial delegate chose to attack the Englishmen at night, but fortunately for the latter they were guarded by a detachment of legation guards *(bette gumi)*, which successfully fended off the assailants. No harm was done the foreigners, but as soon as Parkes learned of the incident, he seized upon it to harass the bakufu. He demanded that the assailants be brought promptly to Edo for severe punishment on the usual ground that it would deter future attackers.[28]

While the Kakegawa matter was hanging fire, another more serious incident occurred.[29] On the night of 7/6 two British sailors, who were in the licensed quarter of Nagasaki for their own purposes, were attacked and killed. The two city magistrates, upon learning of the murders, immediately ordered the assailants arrested, but their identity being unknown, none was apprehended. On 7/15 Parkes reached the city. Having convinced himself that the culprits were Tosa men who had left the city by ship just a few hours after the murders, he denounced the magistrate Tokunaga Masachika for failing to apprehend them. He then steamed up to Osaka where he berated Itakura and put pressure on Yoshinobu for a settlement satisfactory to himself. During succeeding weeks the issue waxed hot, with Parkes demanding various things, among them that the bakufu seize the murderers. The bakufu tried to pacify him by deploying more troops to Nagasaki to protect foreigners. Also bakufu leaders at Kyoto tried to deal with Tosa, hoping to reach a peaceful settlement. English officials tried too for their own reasons, but Tosa leaders stoutly and rightly protested the *han*'s innocence, and the culprits were never caught.

In the meantime other assaults were occurring. Earlier in the year an American merchant seaman had been killed in Nagasaki, and three foreign-employed Chinese had been attacked there. On 7/15 two Prussian diplomats traveling in Edo were attacked, and they countered with pistols, wounding a bystander in the process. The next day they demanded the capture of their would-be killer, a Numata *han* vassal, and the latter was jailed. Later in the month a *rōnin* in Osaka attacked a minor English naval advisor, and on 8/2 in Hyōgo the same man assaulted a Frenchman. Those attacks also prompted Parkes to demand that the bakufu punish the would-be killer.[30] Parkes took that occasion, in line with Satow's opinion, to assert to the senior councillors that their regime was really not legitimate and authority properly resided with the emperor. They denied the charge, but not to Parkes' satisfaction.[31]

By the end of 67/9 with the Kakegawa and Nagasaki incidents still unsettled, it was clear enough that opening the new ports and cities would only complicate affairs at the public level. The imperialist-ethnic confrontation was not creating the political turmoil within the bakufu that it had during the early 1860s, but it certainly had not disappeared. It likely would eventuate in more indemnity demands and other diplomatic complications, but the bakufu pressed on, convinced evidently that the domestic turmoil was less damaging than would be further resistance to foreign demands.

2. *The Changing Impact of Anglo-French Rivalry*

As 1867 progressed, both bakufu and great lords found their politics becoming more and more deeply enmeshed in the machinations of English and French representatives in Japan and the policies of the two governments in Europe.

Looking first at the Franco-bakufu aspect, the Keiō reform, as we note in the next chapter, was intensifying the bakufu's dependence upon France. Moreover, Roches was continuing to advance his interests by playing upon bakufu fears of daimyo-British cooperation. Thus when he met Yoshinobu at Osaka on 2/6 and 7, he explained that the great western *han*, especially Satsuma, Chōshū, and Tosa, were working with Parkes against bakufu interests. To deal with that menace, he urged extensive social change that would make Japan a more perfect replica of France, which country, he assured the shogun, was firmly supporting the bakufu.

Then on 4/13 Roches again stimulated bakufu fear of Anglo-daimyo cooperation by sending leaders a copy of a French newspaper article reporting the views of Satsuma men in Europe.[32] The article spoke of the displeasure of Shimazu and other daimyo because authority properly lay with the emperor, the shogun merely being a usurper who should be eliminated. At present, the report went on, the shogun was professing friendship abroad, borrowing monies, employing military advisors, and buying warships. His intention was to strengthen himself, boost his own interests, crush court and *han*, and then drive out the foreigners. The Satsuma source of the article reported that he himself was seeking foreign help to restore the emperor's authority and prevent the shogunal scheme from succeeding. To deal with that Satsuma maneuver, Roches suggested that Yoshinobu send to Europe a formal shogunal statement justifying bakufu rule. And by way of turning bakufu worry to French profit, in the same communication he reiterated an older proposal that the bakufu open Kagoshima and Shimonoseki to trade and arrange loans with France and Britain by giving gold and silver mines in Ezo as security.

Looking at the British-daimyo side of the coin, there is, as we have seen, the considerable evidence of Parkes' willingness to embarrass the regime and his eventual open assertion in 67/8 that the bakufu was not a legitimate government. Meanwhile Satow was pursuing an energetic effort to poison great *han* attitudes toward both bakufu and France. In mid-1867 he gave substance to Parkes' rhetorical stance by offering Satsuma and Chōshū British assistance in overthrowing the bakufu.[33]

The British-daimyo connection was also evident in Europe. There Satsuma men, with the support of some Europeans, most notably Englishmen, helped persuade the French government to repudiate Roches's policy and throttle rather than encourage loan arrangements that bakufu negotiators were then seeking. And while bakufu funding was growing ever more tenuous, Satsuma was reportedly securing foreign aid. One report spoke of speculative merchants advancing 400,000 francs (about $73,000) of credit in France for Satsuma's military strengthening. Another spoke of credits for a $200,000 warship and six thousand rifles for Satsuma and Chōshū.[34] How much of that was supposedly English in origin is not clear.

Inevitably the real and imagined foreign involvement of both domestic protagonists generated an ever higher level of mutual distrust and worry.[35] Thus on 6/1 during the hot debate over Chōshū, Hara Ichinoshin bitterly denounced Satsuma for allying with foreigners in a movement to destroy the bakufu. Then on 7/4 Shungaku wrote Ōkubo Toshimichi of Satsuma, replying to a letter in which Ōkubo expressed belief that England should be relied upon. Shungaku said that a great disaster was befalling the country. By way of explanation he reported, in apparent reference to the Ezo mines scheme, that at Yokohama a French loan was being arranged. Funds would be loaned for a fixed time, and if not repaid when due, land would be given instead. That, he argued, was essentially how the British loaned money to Indians and got control of their land, thus acquiring territory without war, and he warned against Satsuma and Uwajima associating thus with England. In one other instance, six days later when Yoshinobu was urging Shungaku to stay in Kyoto, one argument he used was that rumors indicated Satsuma was encouraging Englishmen to come to Kyoto in the near future, and in such an event he wished Shungaku to be in town.

By the latter part of 1867, even as the bakufu was learning that its French connection was of no real value, the daimyo were finding their British connection of increasing utility. The shifting balance of advantage was ominous for Edo. And more broadly, the foreign contacts of both sides were contributing to the mutual suspicions that shortly would culminate in open warfare, thereby creating a situation that could very easily precipitate significant new imperialist inroads into Japan.

3. The Missionary Problem

During 1867 bakufu leaders revealed a much greater willingness to accept the ramifications of renewed foreign contact. They were not, however, ready to accept one expression of the foreign intrusion that appeared during the year. That was the reestablishment of a direct link between domestic Christians, foreign missionaries, and foreign governments.

To summarize briefly the background of the problem, in treaty negotiations of the 1850s the bakufu had repeatedly shown concern about Christianity being brought again into Japan. In late 1856 a number of active Christians at Nagasaki were jailed, but after foreign diplomats protested, they were released. The next year the bakufu agreed of necessity to let foreigners practice their own religion in the treaty ports, but the prohibition on Christianity for Japanese was not changed. Missionaries nonetheless began to arrive. Secret proselytizing went on, and in 1861 it led to a minor problem when a Frenchman at Yokohama started Japanese-language instruction about Christianity. By early 1862 his activities had precipitated a dispute with the Kanagawa magistrate, and the Japanese-language teaching, whose purpose was obviously not sanctioned by treaty clauses, was stopped.[36] Two years later an attempt by that same missionary to obtain French government support for his enterprise came to nought. The next year, however, French missionaries opened a church in Nagasaki, and in 65/8 the bakufu received reports of indeterminate validity linking Christians with the gun smuggling between Chōshū and foreign traders in that city.[37] These first renewed signs that the foreign religion and foreign state power still were not easily separable constituted grist for the mill of fear, and in succeeding years Nagasaki became the focus of concern.

During 1866 some two hundred local Japanese Christians secretly began going to services in the new church at Nagasaki. The missionaries condoned that illegal activity and also reportedly went out into the local long-hidden Christian community in Uragami village to carry on their religious business. Being far from the political center but near the turmoil of the Summer War, that activity did not elicit a quick bakufu response. In 1867, however, more missionaries arrived. By then reports said some seven hundred converts were openly practicing the religion and another two thousand were responding to the propaganda. With missionary support, believers apparently began to oust nonbelievers from local office and promote vigorous proselytizing campaigns in the nearby daimyo domains of Ōmura, Shimabara, and Karatsu and in bakufu lands in the Amakusa islands. The missionaries actively visited villages, stayed in homes of the faithful, and collected money tithes to build churches in the area. They promised believers protection from ''the Japanese government,'' and their self-confidence was greatly heightened in 67/4 when Roches visited them at Nagasaki and expressed support for their venture.[38]

The accelerating missionary activity around Nagasaki angered the lords of Ōmura and Shimabara, as well as *rōnin* and *han* vassals in Nagasaki who demanded that matters be brought under control. The Nagasaki magistrates, however, were fearful of French displeasure and took no action. As the situation deteriorated, magistrate Tokunaga Masachika grew frantic. On 5/8, just after Roches's departure,[39] he wrote a lengthy report to Itakura warning that conditions were growing more and more lawless. He said the numbers of *rōnin* and commoner believers were rapidly increasing and stressed that delay would only compound the difficulty. He argued that either a firm policy of enforcement should be pursued or ''the old laws'' should be changed.[40]

At Kyoto, however, leaders were engrossed in other matters, notably the struggle over Chōshū and Hyōgo, and no decision on Tokunaga's problem was forthcoming. The situation at Nagasaki consequently worsened, with officials there unable to decide which they feared more—to act and bring foreign wrath down upon their heads or do nothing and let a Shimabara-type insurrection erupt.

Renewed pleas for guidance from Kyoto went unanswered. Finally in a desperate attempt to prevent crisis and force leaders to move, on the night of 6/13 Tokunaga acted on his own. He sent a force of about 170 men, some with firearms, to round up believers, and 68 were arrested. Then he fired off a notice reporting his unauthorized actions, which, he charged, had been necessitated by bakufu failure to address the problem.

The next morning some five hundred Christians assembled and asked him to release the captives. Then on 6/15 and 16 respectively the local French and Portuguese consuls also protested and demanded "freedom of religion" for the Japanese. When Tokunaga did not yield, the missionaries and consuls sought support from their governments' ministers in Yokohama.[41]

Thus the political problem of a militant, foreign government-supported religion—the problem that more than anything else had originally led to the full-blown policy of isolation—had again come to the surface, and it pitted the bakufu against its sometime ally, France. At both Kyoto and Edo high officials discussed the crisis. On 7/7 Ogasawara Nagamichi wrote Roches protesting the illegal French missionary activities at Nagasaki: their preaching in villages, staying in people's homes, collecting gold and silver, traveling in neighboring daimyo areas, and encouraging people to refuse burial according to law. He insisted those activities had to be stopped because they were contrary to treaty, undermined the law, and caused unrest. He asked Roches to explain the Japanese situation to his government, and he proposed that if the missionaries were required to abide by the treaty and stop their proselytizing, the captives at Nagasaki would be released as soon as they displayed penitence.[42] It was the start of a search for a compromise settlement.

On 7/21 the American Van Valkenburgh added his voice to the foreign clamor, protesting the arrests of people who had done nothing wrong, calling for their release, arguing that old laws should be changed, and warning that the alternative was to lose foreign goodwill.[43]

Even without Van Valkenburgh's barely concealed threat, bakufu leaders knew the issue could lead to a disastrous quarrel with France, and they strove to avoid that. On the twenty-fifth Itakura and junior councillor Ōkōchi Masatada met Roches at Osaka, and he told them the law should be changed. Officials countered that the best policy would be to pardon and send home the captives and forbid the missionaries' activities. Yoshinobu took the same position in his discussions with Roches. Perhaps with Chōshū in mind, he also argued that as lawbreakers the believers could not be let off completely lest others too be encouraged to defy the law. It was a line the foreigners had been using for years, and Roches responded favorably, at least agreeing to instruct missionaries not to encourage Japanese to break the law. On 7/29 he wrote them that the bakufu had agreed to be lenient and that henceforth they were to cease their propagandizing and stay out of the villages.[44]

Those Kyushu daimyo and samurai who had demanded a halt in the missionary activity had learned meanwhile of the bakufu proposal to release the captives in return for cessation of missionary activity. Displeased with such leniency, they began to discuss more carefully plans for direct action—namely, burning churches and killing missionaries. Tokunaga reported their activity to bakufu leaders. His report together with the problem of the British sailor murders in Nagasaki apparently prompted them to delay implementing the 7/25 proposal and to move instead to a somewhat more rigorous position. At Yoshinobu's order Itakura went again to Osaka on 8/5 to call on Roches. His task was to explain that due to the situation in Kyushu it would be dangerous to pardon the Christians and release them right away. Therefore the bakufu wished to hold them in detention until they recanted or until the situation had quieted down. Roches, however, refused to agree, insisting that the 7/25 proposal be implemented. The next day Itakura reported that to Yoshinobu, and it was decided *faute de mieux* to proceed as earlier proposed.

On the following day Yoshinobu wrote directly to Napoleon III explaining that conditions in Japan made it impossible at that time to permit the religious practices of "enlightened countries" and reminding him that missionaries were forbidden to practice their trade in Japan. He wrote Roches similarly, as did Itakura, and Ogasawara wrote bakufu diplomats in France, instructing them to discuss the matter with the French government so as to avoid misunderstanding. Bakufu leaders suggested that at some future unspecified date, when affairs were less disturbed, they would permit the foreign creed, but for the time being it could not be allowed.[45]

As decided after Itakura's return from Osaka, the bakufu on 8/10 ordered the Nagasaki magistrate simply to have the Christians released from jail and returned to their own villages and not dispersed, as in past practice. On the next day Roches was informed of the order.

Meanwhile at Nagasaki foreign magistrate Hirayama Keichū, who was there dealing with the English sailor problem, had already arranged with Tokunaga simply to release all who would formally recant, hoping thus to avoid more foreign trouble. Twenty-eight of the arrested went home in that way before the order of 8/10 was received. When it arrived, Tokunaga informed the local French consul of its contents and reiterated that missionaries must be kept out of villages. The French consul accepted the arrangement and, as his part of the settlement, ordered the missionaries to stop their illegal activities. Those believers remaining in detention were pardoned; only one, who had earlier refused to recant, reportedly was placed in village custody.

The missionaries, however, were enraged at the arrangement, and shortly afterward the French consul and Tokunaga collided over charges that believers were being tortured before being released. That quarrel led Roches to protest on 9/21, and the ensuing embarrassment contributed to dismissal of both Tokunaga and his fellow magistrate on 67/12/12. Locally also the problem had repercussions, leading to renewed conflicts within villages, conflicts which were eventually passed on to the central government. By then, however, it was no longer the Tokugawa bakufu, and someone else had to handle that aspect of the ethnic-imperialist confrontation.

4. The Korean Problem

Accompanying bakufu acceptance of an open country was evidence that the foreign intrusion was prompting Japanese leaders to address territorial matters beyond both Japan proper and such marginal areas as the Ogasawara islands and Karafuto. During 1867 the ''Korean problem''[46] came to life.

As a topic of discussion within the bakufu the Korean question dated from the Tsushima crisis of 1862, in which bakufu complaints and British military pressure dislodged a Russian naval group that had tried to establish an outpost on the island. From the start the advocates of a forceful Japanese role in Korea were the ''progressive'' voices in the bakufu, notably Katsu Kaishū and Itakura Katsukiyo.[47] However, during the years of conservative reaffirmation their schemes were repeatedly confounded by rivals and events. Then during 1865 Edo heard rumors of Russian designs on Korea and of growing British and French interest in the peninsula. Moreover rumors of 65/8 said Chōshū planned to establish ties with Korea. The rumors failed to provoke any clear response, however. Rather, it was imperialist intrusions precipitated by missionary activity in Korea in 1866 that finally revived the matter, and it was the discrediting of conservative leaders at home that at last made action possible.[48]

To elaborate, in the spring of 1866 a few French missionaries who had entered Korea without permission were executed by the government in Seoul. France sent a reprisal squadron of seven ships in 66/10, and it presented demands for compensation. It then launched an assault, was repulsed, and upon withdrawal threatened to return the following spring for more satisfaction. Just previously in 66/7 an American ship had reached Korea, and its disorderly crew had gotten into trouble. By year's end two foreign powers thus had diplomatic matters to settle with the Korean government.

Well aware of his domain's vulnerability in the event of imperialist enterprises in Korea, the daimyo of Tsushima urged the bakufu to mediate the French-Korean issue. Accordingly in 67/2 Yoshinobu discussed the matter with Roches and instructed Hirayama Keichū and an inspector to go to Tsushima and, if the situation developed favorably, to go on to Korea ''to work for peace.'' Hirayama proposed to take a warship and two battalions of troops for use in settling the matter. As planning went ahead, on 4/7 Itakura, Inaba, and Ogasawara at Kyoto wrote Van Valkenburgh that the bakufu was willing to mediate the quarrels between the Koreans on the one hand and the French and Americans on the other and was dispatching Hirayama to Korea for that purpose. During that month, however, Hirayama's procedures were modified, and it was decided to use not bakufu forces but Tsushima troops whom Hirayama would train in the use of firearms.[49] It doubtless occurred to bakufu leaders that Tsushima might thus also serve as a threat to the Chōshū rear.

By that time, however, this Japanese diplomatic tentative was already in trouble. The Korean government had heard via a Canton newspaper report of 66/12 of a Japanese intent to combine the forces of court, bakufu, and all 250 daimyo so as to send against Korea an armada of eighty ships and an army of young soldiers from age twelve to twenty-two trained by the British.[50] That bizarre report, which reflected contemporary military reforms in Japan and evoked recollections of Hideyoshi, reached Korea in the spring. A statement of concern about it was sent from Seoul to Tsushima in 67/4, and on 5/15 the daimyo sent a report of the Korean concern on to leaders at Edo. A fortnight later senior councillors Matsui and Inoue received it and sent it on to Itakura, Inaba, and Ogasawara, who were all presumed to be at Kyoto.

By the time the notice reached Kyoto, Ogasawara and Inaba had left. Accordingly on 6/5 Itakura sent a reply of his own, presumably after consulting Yoshinobu. He instructed a Tsushima vassal to have his lord convey the following information to the Korean government. The report that Korea had received was absurd and was merely the opinion of an uninformed vagrant. Since the new shogun's accession, it was to be reported, great efforts had been made to carry out reform. Matters were progressing, national strength was gaining, and ships and weapons were being purchased from abroad. It was those developments which probably had given rise to the lunatic report. The Korean government was to be assured, however, that Japan had no intention of using such force against Korea. Rather, the two countries being intimately connected, the bakufu wished to see Korea prosper. To that end it was instructing emissaries to proceed to the Korean capital to report on the world situation and suggest desirable policies. The mission had already been prepared, and shortly the emissary would arrive to explain the bakufu's position in detail. The government's concern, it was said in closing, was the eternal well-being of both countries.[51]

For some time after that bakufu leaders were bogged down by other domestic and diplomatic affairs, but on 9/28 they returned to their planned Korean venture. Despite continuing Korean distrust and protests, the bakufu notified Tsushima that Hirayama would proceed there from Nagasaki during 67/11. He was to discuss matters with *han* officials and then go on to the peninsula kingdom. Having been burned, however, the leaders instructed Hirayama to be extremely careful and examine the situation thoroughly before proceeding to Korea.[52] Subsequently the venture was again interrupted and then abandoned due to domestic developments at year's end. But though it was never implemented, it demonstrated clearly enough that the bakufu, for better or worse, was moving Japan into a new era of foreign affairs.

1867: POLITICS AND DIPLOMACY IN RETROSPECT

Looking back on the months of symbolic warfare that eventuated in Yoshinobu's lonely triumph, one is struck by his success in manipulating the court and its stark contrast with the appalling failure of bakufu leaders in the four years before the Summer War.

How does one explain the contrast? One could point to Yoshinobu's stubbornness and abrasive intolerance of disagreement, but then Matsumae Takahiro comes to mind as a similar personality who fared quite otherwise in his efforts at court. Yoshinobu had strong connections in Kyoto, but so did Shungaku, and he had fared poorly in 1862–1863. Doubtless Yoshinobu's friends and his willingness to insist were important, but that was far from sufficient to carry the day. In addition he had the advantage of speaking for a cohesive, united, and purposeful leadership. Steadied by Itakura and stiffened by Hara Ichinoshin and others, he was able to adhere to the main purpose. Moreover, he was the unchallengeable spokesman for the bakufu. Unlike Matsumae or any other senior councillor, no one with equal authority could cancel out his voice, and it was the voice of one whose rank compelled respect at Kyoto. In the small universe of the court he was the great central star of a major political constellation, and the great daimyo were every one a lesser star in a lesser constellation. Only the highest court officials and nobles could purport to be his peers, and so, unlike a mere senior councillor, he was powerfully armed for battle in a contest of pomp and prestige.

One must note another aspect of this symbolic warfare. It seems to have lost much of the terror it had held for participants in the early

1860s. The bakufu no longer agonized over the problem of reconciling the ethnic purism of *sonnō jōi* and the reality of irresistible foreign demands. Yoshinobu abandoned his old verbal *jōi* position in blatant defiance of the court and did so to his own immediate advantage. Moreover the bakufu in preparing to open Hyōgo showed a striking unconcern for imperial sensibilities, speaking with perfect aplomb from both sides of its institutional mouth. Similarly in late 1866 daimyo and their advisors had shown they no longer were awed by the imperial symbol. And in 1867 they were able to use the Hyōgo issue with such callous contempt for its intrinsic meaning precisely because they no longer were in thrall to the imperial myth. It was not that their attitude toward the treaties was significantly changed from the early 1860s; it was not. They had been just about as resigned to the treaties then as in 1867. Rather, it was their attitude toward court, bakufu, and other verities of the *bakuhan* order that had changed. As suggested before, the *bakuhan* system no longer existed after the Summer War. And as a part of that system, the court's prestige had suffered badly with its passing. It was merely a tool to be used.

The diminished aura of the court is of interest in two contexts. The first relates to assessing the political value to the bakufu of Yoshinobu's pragmatic cultivation of imperial ties. One might argue that by engaging the lords in symbolic politics, he diverted them, unwittingly perhaps, from the real issue of military power and bought time for the Keiō reformers to strengthen their regime. The argument probably has merit: as we see later, the bakufu did make great strides in military strengthening during 1867, probably much greater than did any single *han*, many of which made a sudden rush for modern weapons at the last minute in 67/11-12.

One might also argue that Yoshinobu's triumph in Kyoto helped delay the recoalescence of court, great lords, and *shishi* by again depriving the alliance of its centerpiece. This second proposition is more difficult to sustain, however. For one thing, the decline in court prestige meant it was of much less value than before as either stimulus or deterrent to political action by others. For another thing, Yoshinobu's abandonment of *jōi* and retention of the court meant he could no longer present the court as the fount of ethnic purism. And that gave others, even in defiance of the court, opportunity to exploit the *sonnō jōi* spirit that still struck fire among many *shishi* and a fair number of *han* leaders. These observations suggest that Yoshinobu's control of the court was of considerably diminished value as a means of managing either lords or *shishi*.

What most diminished the value of Yoshinobu's court triumph was the

changed character of the daimyo-*shishi* relationship. In earlier years the
court had been the vehicle that brought the two elements together in actions directed against the bakufu. In response, bakufu moves to claim the
sonnō jōi rhetoric for Edo and displace the *kōbugattai* of court-daimyo
unity with the *kōbugattai* of court-bakufu unity had served repeatedly to
break up the triangular coalition. Then in 1864–1865 the *han* had suppressed independent *shishi* radicalism except in Chōshū. There radicals
triumphed in civil war and made the *han* their vehicle of political action.
Elsewhere *shishi* had to bide their time until new opportunities arose. In
subsequent years those opportunities did arise because the political process so poisoned bakufu-*han* relations that radicalism gradually found a
new voice in *han* policy. It was manifested in defiance of both court and
bakufu, in *han* internal reform, and in changing concepts of acceptable
political structure and appropriate political action at the national level.
Consequently by mid-1867 the court was no longer necessary to the
forging of an anti-bakufu *shishi*-daimyo alliance; it had been achieved
within the institution of the *han*. In this new situation the court was
merely a device of potential diplomatic utility to leaders of insurgent *han*
for purposes of securing the goodwill of other *han*, *rōnin*, and other unat-
tached elements and to appease and thereby constrain foreigners. It was a
role the shrunken imperial institution of 1867 could still perform.

In short, then, in terms of value to the bakufu of Yoshinobu's triumph
at court, one may say that it bought time but was of little value in preventing the reemergence of a court-daimyo-*shishi* coalition because of the
changed internal character of such an alignment.

The diminished aura of the court is also of interest in the context of
long-range developments. The political process of the months after the
Summer War seems to suggest that after a decade of crucial significance,
in 1866–1867 the imperial institution plummeted to a nadir of historical
importance—a position in which its abolition would have made little difference to the power struggle going on. The collapse of the *bakuhan*
system had led to a collapse of imperial prestige, and that freed men to
act in a consistent manner. But it also stripped them of a generally acceptable excuse for acting. That may help explain why Yoshinobu cultivated
the court so assiduously; and, more provocatively, it may help explain
why Meiji leaders went to such extremes to restore the honor of an archaic institution; its irrelevance had become apparent, but that in turn exposed the nakedness of the power struggle convulsing the elite. To conceal that nakedness and secure a base of legitimacy, the new leaders had
to bend every effort to restoring the debauched honor of the court, to
give it a new institutional legitimacy independent of the defunct *bakuhan*
system.

The diplomatic problems of the year also deserve some comment. The evidence suggests that by late 1867 Japanese contestants on both sides of the power struggle had gotten themselves so deeply entangled with foreigners that they would gladly have become more entangled had the foreigners been prepared to cooperate. As matters worked out, at year's end the foreign diplomats held aloof, too uncertain of the future and too far or too alienated from their home governments to take an active role either way. In consequence the foreign involvement in the civil war of the restoration was almost completely a mercenary one of gunrunning. That activity reached immense proportions and must have been of vast profit to the runners, mostly British and American. But direct foreign participation in the civil war was negligible.

In that outcome Japan was extremely fortunate, but it came perilously close to stumbling into the colonial slough. Nor can the outcome be satisfactorily explained as simply a reflection of an exceptionally strong and conscious determination on the part of the contestants to stay out of the slough. Of course they opposed reducing Japan to a condition of colonial servitude, but the contest for power grew so heated that circumstances willy-nilly drew them into positions they readily denounced in their opponents. The victors, like the vanquished, played a risky game, and the later glorification of the imperial institution and denunciation of bakufu leaders for their association with France may in some part have been a device of the Meiji leaders to conceal the embarrassment of their own dangerous association with foreigners.

Japan's escape from colonial disaster must be explained in more complex terms than simple patriotism and farsighted wisdom. It was due in part to the brevity of the civil war, which limited the opportunities for foreign intervention. Additionally, even before the war began, the leaders of all major contestant groups were aware that isolation was in fact no longer a real choice, so no real attempt was made to achieve it. Instead efforts were made to avoid extraneous foreign complications as the war progressed. Moreover Paris's repudiation of Roches in 1867 deprived him of the means to intervene on behalf of his beleaguered friends. The fact that the British backed the winners and so had no cause to try to change the outcome was likely a very important consideration: had the bakufu prevailed, one can well imagine the British, who had the capacity to do so, trying to prop up their friends as a means of advancing British interests in Japan. And finally there were such matters of chance as the contemporary eclipse of French global activity and the recent American involvement in its own civil strife, which helped remove those two threats from the Japanese scene.

It is also worth noting in passing that Japanese involvement in Korea was neither a virginal invention of Meiji leaders nor an expression of an atavistic Hideyoshi mentality. It was a venture forged in response to the imperialist onslaught in the 1860s and was a reflection of a progressive, not a conservative, orientation. It was but a step beyond the measures taken to secure the Ogasawara islands and the Ezo-Karafuto northern frontier. And it reflected the extent to which the foreign encroachment weakened any inclination to respect the national autonomy of others even as it fostered national self-consciousness among those under assault.

And that brings us finally to the question of what the foreigners' performance in 1867 signifies. It indicates that the escalating imperialist intrusion was much more than merely a stick to beat the bakufu. Rather it was developing dangerous new dimensions that drew the foreigners as religious propagandists, entrepreneurs, and political adventurers deeper and deeper into Japan. Had the domestic political stalemate dragged on much longer, that imperialist intrusion would most likely have escalated even further, quite quickly taking on the character it acquired in China or perhaps south and southeast Asia. As it worked out, the Meiji restoration saved Japanese and foreigners alike from many later regrets.

The Keiō Reform
1867

CIVIL REFORM

MILITARY REFORM

RAMIFICATIONS AND COMPLICATIONS

THE KEIŌ REFORM IN RETROSPECT

During the first nine months of 1867 Yoshinobu succeeded in protecting the Tokugawa claim to hegemonial authority, and he and others dealt more or less successfully with the diplomatic problems they faced. During those same months the bakufu also pressed on with the Keiō reform. Much of the reform had been foreshadowed in rhetoric and in actions of previous years, but both the content and the implications of reform moved to a much advanced stage in 1867. During the postwar months reform had been almost entirely military, but during 1867 it broadened to embrace basic reforms of the civil administrative structure as well as the military system. And as the year progressed, its ramifications and difficulties became more and more apparent. Gradually the reform acquired a revolutionary antifeudal character that was bound to lead, if the reform were to succeed, to unification and transformation of the Japanese polity and society.

CIVIL REFORM

During 1867 the Keiō reform began to modify the fundamental structure of the Tokugawa house—both its leadership organization and the political, fiscal, and military relationships of its several parts. In terms of civil reform, one area of great change was the central administrative structure. Another area of less extensive change was the system of land administration. The reforms themselves were carried out by bakufu officials, but they were in part a reflection of the influence of Léon Roches, whose role in affairs had grown steadily over the course of two years.

1. The Role of Léon Roches

To recapitulate briefly matters already dealt with at length, for two or three years a very few bakufu officials had been urging replacement of the *bakuhan* system with a fully centralized polity. That view had been opposed, however, by the conservative daimyo leaders of the periodic *kōbugattai* efforts, whose private interests were directly threatened by the scheme, and by those shaping the conservative reaffirmation of 1863–1864. The latter permitted the military reforms of 1862 to wither away, but then difficulty with Kantō insurgents and Chōshū helped vindicate those arguing for real military reform. During 1865 army modernization was restarted. During that year, moreover, Léon Roches began to explain to officials such as Kurimoto Kon, Yamaguchi Naoki, and Oguri Tadamasa his ideas about a bakufu-led unification of Japan and the merit of relying on French aid in the venture. In the deteriorating political context of 1865 the ideas found fertile soil. Through the efforts of Shibata Masanaka and Oguri in particular, the bakufu gradually developed the skeleton of an extensive association with France. Then during the Summer War the association was carried considerably further, most notably when the $6 million foreign loan was seemingly arranged.

By the time Yoshinobu assumed leadership of the bakufu, key officials had thus already accepted a strongly preferential attitude toward France and were attempting to turn it to Tokugawa advantage. Moreover, from his early days as Tokugawa leader, Yoshinobu too cultivated Roches's support. Thus on 66/8/2, as the loan negotiations were nearing completion, he wrote Roches, explaining that he was going to head the revitalized Chōshū expedition and asking for assistance—specifically steamships, cannon, and rifles.[1] Shortly after that he abandoned his war plan, but on 8/27, after becoming *uesama*, he again wrote Roches. He reported on recent developments, including his decision to halt the war, and said the administration was to be reformed and the military strengthened. He thanked the Frenchman for helping obtain military equipment and expressed hope he would assist in locating military advisors for infantry, artillery, and cavalry and in supplying weapons, warships, and other matériel.[2]

In line with that sentiment, on 9/2 Inoue Masanao, Matsui Yasunao, and Ogyū Noritaka, the senior councillors at Edo, asked Roches to help them purchase two warships from the French navy and arrange payment by A. M. Coullet.[3] At Yokohama, meanwhile, Roches continued to discuss matters with Oguri and others, and late in 66/9 Oguri went to Kyoto. There he obtained Yoshinobu's approval of various contracts for military purchases and reportedly gave him information on the partially negotiated Franco-bakufu trading company.[4]

Then in 66/11 Roches met Hirayama Keichū at Atami. They discussed a range of subjects: warship purchases, matters related to the opening of Hyōgo, military reform and training, the Paris Exposition, and the Yokohama foundry.[5] After Hirayama reached Kyoto on 11/20, he informed Itakura and Ogyū of the conversation and allegedly gave Yoshinobu a sealed letter whose contents evidently revealed Roches's goodwill and "pleased Yoshinobu greatly."[6] Hirayama was ordered back to Edo eight days later and there met Roches again. He reported on his conversations in Kyoto, perhaps gave him a memo from Yoshinobu proposing a meeting of the two, and continued discussing reform plans with him.[7] It was agreed to have the two meet in conjunction with a formal shogunal reception of all the diplomats in Osaka, and on 67/1/28 Roches reached the city for those purposes. In the course of somewhat over two years Léon Roches had thus successfully maneuvered into a unique position of intimacy with the highest leaders of the bakufu.

On 67/2/6–7 Roches and Yoshinobu met at Osaka and talked at length about a number of matters. Mostly they discussed diplomatic issues, but they also touched on domestic Japanese politics, reforms of bakufu administration, and problems of military, fiscal, and commercial development. On the following day, as the shogun wished, Roches also talked with Itakura and Ogyū about a variety of topics, most notably financial. They included the French trading company, the burden of liege vassal stipends, the dismissal of incompetent vassals, the development of mines, and the taxing of vassal daimyo, merchants, and religious establishments. He also spoke about the newly arrived French military mission, problems and procedures of military training and organization, and matters of general civil administration.[8] Directly afterward Ogyū returned to Edo, where he doubtless discussed these matters with other officials.

No notable reform activities followed the talks, perhaps because during the next three months leaders at Kyoto were busy obtaining imperial consent to the opening of Hyōgo. By early 67/5, however, following the skirmish over Parkes' trip to Tsuruga, Yoshinobu and Itakura seem to have concluded that consent would shortly be forthcoming. At any rate they started sending more top officials east to pursue more extensive reforms. On the eleventh Itakura gave Inaba Masakuni formal orders to return to Edo, setting his departure date at 5/18. And on the nineteenth, as planned for a fortnight at least, Ogasawara Nagamichi was also given orders to return east. The severe dispute that engulfed bakufu leaders and the four great daimyo at that time delayed the two men's departure,[9] but it did not deter their thinking about reform. Thus on the twentieth Inaba submitted to Yoshinobu a long list of specific issues on which he sought the shogun's opinion. Among the matters under consideration were reform of tribunal (hyōjōsho) regulations, reform of the death penalty and other aspects of criminal law, abolition of the tsukiban or monthly duty system among senior councillors, changes in night duty of junior and senior councillors, simplification of certain travel expense procedures, suggested changes in the sankin kōtai system, and some proposed appointments, including that of Akitsuki Taneki.[10]

By month's end the four great lords had been bested, and the two senior councillors were able to leave the Kinai. They went by ship, Ogasawara reaching Edo on 6/3 and Inaba two days later. With their return almost the entire bakufu leadership was at Edo. Only Yoshinobu, Itakura, the deputy Matsudaira Sadaaki, junior councillor Nagai Naomune, Kyoto city magistrate Ōkubo Tadayuki, and a few other subordinate officials remained at Kyoto.

The consolidation of leadership at Edo was soon followed by a spate of reforms, some of which reflected Roches's advice to Yoshinobu, some of which did not. Again Roches talked at length with both senior and subordinate officials. On 6/24, for example, as the leadership structure was being reorganized, junior councillors Kyōgoku Takatomi, Kawakatsu Kōun, and Hirayama Keichū, inspector general Takikawa Tomoshige, foreign magistrate Kawakatsu Hiromichi, and two other officials spoke with him. Their talk ranged over the western cabinet system, its divisions, the role of a prime minister, organization of ministries, promotion procedures, police and judicial matters, and ways of modifying bakufu organization to fit those patterns. They also discussed again the problems of liege vassal costs, the taxation of those men and of commercial production, and the means of administering such a tax system.[11]

What all this contact between Roches and officialdom meant in terms of the Keiō reform is not entirely clear. It must be kept in mind that there were a number of men in Edo, such as Shibata and Ikeda Chōhatsu, whose thoughts on reform and unification were similar to those of Roches but had developed more or less independently of him. And they participated in various steps of planning and implementation. It appears from the sequence of actions that many discussions and written exchanges with Roches were undertaken by officials seeking a clearer understanding of how to implement measures previously discussed or even decided upon. Some of the measures originated with ideas earlier advanced by Roches; others seem to have arisen among officials themselves. Certainly officials recognized what their problems were. And they also developed themselves the main lines of the preferred overall strategy of exclusivistic unification. They needed military advisors, equipment, and financial aid and found Roches eager to help them—for a handsome price. In the specific content of reform plans, especially where they involved practices found in Europe, officials sought and obtained details from Roches, and that part of his contribution may have been the most important. But in the end it was they who effected the changes and they who decided precisely what their content would be. They were selective in accepting Roches's advice, and of the ideas adopted, not all survived the test of application. On the other hand, just as the Meiji reformers found in Europe models of possible total political systems, so Roches furnished the Keiō reformers with the vision of a total system. In their picking and choosing, they were able to proceed in a relatively purposeful manner in great part perhaps because they could repeatedly measure their actions against the model of a larger system that seemed to work.

2. Administrative Reform

The administrative reform of 1867 had several aspects. It involved a basic reorganization of top levels of the bureaucracy, replacing the old councillor-magistrate system with an embryonic cabinet organization. It introduced freer personnel promotion in new ministerial hierarchies under the several cabinet ministers. And it introduced a graduated, simplified, and fully monetized salary system for officials in those hierarchies.

The most visible aspect of administrative reform was the gradual modification of top levels of bakufu organization. For years the senior council's procedures had been badly disrupted. Having councillors in Kyoto and Edo, and later in Kyoto, Osaka, and Edo, meant that decision-making was haphazard and at times very poorly coordinated. Of necessity men were assigned particular areas of responsibility. Such assignments were not new; traditionally a rather large number of routine marginal duties had been assigned to individual councillors. Also special ongoing authority for fiscal matters had customarily been held by one of their number, usually the chief councillor *(rōjū shuseki)*, who was entitled *katte gakari*. Then with the opening of ports, one or two councillors had been assigned particular authority for diplomatic matters as *gaikoku gakari*. And during the 1860s as military reforms were undertaken and major expeditions launched, one or two councillors or other major figures received special temporary military responsibilities signified by various titles such as *kairikugun gakari* or *sōsai*. These special diplomatic and military assignments tended to be fluid, however, and were shifted about as men came and left office or gained or lost influence or effectiveness. Then in late 1866, when major military reform was initiated, the earlier precedents of special temporary military authority were reapplied in a putatively permanent manner in the designation of acting senior councillor Ogyū Noritaka as *rikugun sōsai* or army minister and his colleague Inaba Masami as *kaigun sōsai* or navy minister.

Under the influence of Léon Roches, this slowly emerging concept of individual responsibility for specified sectors of ongoing administrative authority was developed much further during 1867. On 5/6, a few days before being ordered east from Kyoto, Inaba Masakuni was given the new title of *kokunai jimu sōsai* or home minister and told he would be released from diplomatic duties as soon as Ogasawara returned to Edo. Then at Edo on the twelfth, evidently after learning of Inaba's appointment, Matsui Yasunao was similarly relieved of diplomatic and military tasks and designated *kaikei sōsai* or finance minister. Then on 6/4, after his arrival at Edo, Ogasawara was officially relieved of fiscal duties and designated *gaikoku jimu sōsai* or foreign minister. Related changes were made among the junior councillors, creating a number of vice-ministerial positions. On 6/29 the bakufu formally stated that the titles of those officials were henceforth to be as assigned, such and such *sōsai*, with the councillor title secondary. At the same time the council's vestigial monthly duty *(tsukiban)* practice was discontinued.[12]

By these changes the bakufu nominally created a cabinet with Itakura as de facto prime minister superior to the five other ministers. Roches had suggested six, one a minister of justice, but the reformers put the home minister in charge of judicial matters. Under those men were subordinate vice-ministers and lesser officials of liege vassal status who in time could presumably rise to ministerial rank.

Elaborate descriptions of the authority of ministers and their subordinates were drawn up. Their relationship to the existing structure was specified, and procedures and policy regulations were articulated at considerable length. One form of the plan spelled out in detail the cabinet structure that administrative reform was intended to create. It described organization and procedures of the several ministries and dwelt at length on taxation. It indicated that the annual tax yield of all Japan was to be determined and to serve as the basis for making allocations to the several ministries. The outline continued at length on various matters of state, administration, commerce, and foreign affairs, and it summed up other reform proposals prepared by officials at Edo. Among other things it envisaged de facto abolition of hereditary vassal status by requiring all unfit liege vassals to surrender their shogunal stipends or lands and return to farming. And it proposed establishment of a university *(daigakkō)* that would train able samurai and commoners from all over the country in a curriculum embracing agriculture, commerce, and industry. [13]

Whether this ambitious administrative reorganization would eventually have worked as theory intended is unknown, but during its few difficult months of existence it altered very little of established working procedure. The new titles tended to be treated like former particular titles such as *gaikoku gakari*. Thus in 67/10 when crisis engulfed Kyoto leaders and Ogyū and Inaba Masami were hurriedly ordered west, their army and navy ministerial titles were temporarily reassigned to other councillors. Moreover the Edo-Kyoto split still was a key determinant of actual duties. Councillors and others in Edo dealt with matters there: notably Mito, Kantō administration, structural reform, the city, and Yokohama. As the leading official at Edo, Inaba Masakuni's name appeared on all sorts of orders pertaining to civil, fiscal, and military matters, regardless of the limits implied by his title of home minister. At Kyoto Yoshinobu and Itakura, who nominally oversaw the whole operation, actually devoted most of their energy to crises involving court, great daimyo, and foreigners.

Nor did the new titles really replace the title of senior councillor. At the time of formal reorganization, Inoue Masanao, who was reputed to be a genial man, found himself a supernumerary councillor, and he was allowed to resign. But at Kyoto deputy Matsudaira Sadaaki retained the designation ''acting senior councillor while in Kyoto'' that he had received in 67/4. And other men were named senior councillor as the bakufu in crisis scrambled to mobilize support. Specifically Hisamatsu Sadaaki, newly appointed daimyo of Matsuyama and son of the lord of Tsu, was so named on 9/23 and then allowed to resign a month later because his vassals feared trouble arising from his involvement in the accelerating national power struggle.[14] Also junior councillor Ōkōchi Masatada was promoted to acting senior councillor on 12/15, and Sakai Tadatō of Himeji was appointed fifteen days later, both being released from service in 68/2.

In the few months the titles were stable, they thus did not really function as Roches had envisaged. And certainly they did not become a vehicle for drawing great lords and other outsiders into the government as he had advised in 67/2. Rather, they suggested quite clearly that a reordered political system would be dominated, initially at least, by able men selected from among vassal daimyo and talented men raised from regular liege vassal ranks.

The possibility of liege vassals rising to positions of leadership through the new ministries emerged when specific appointments opened high office to lesser men. The first of these occurred in 67/4 with the promotions at Kyoto of Asano Ujisuke and Hirayama Keichū to the title of acting junior councillor *(wakadoshiyori nami)* with specific orders that they be treated exactly like regular junior councillors. There were precedents for promoting liege vassals to vassal daimyo office, but what was unprecedented in this instance was that Asano and Hirayama were not given fief land supplements raising them to daimyo status. Rather they were authorized office supplements giving them a total of 7000 *koku* income during their tenure in office.[15] In future either they would have those supplements increased and converted into hereditary family lands, or the principle would be established that high-level office was open to lesser men. The latter was clearly the reformers' goal.

Following the promotions of Asano and Hirayama, others active in the reform movement were also promoted. In the next few months Kawakatsu Kōun, Takenaka Shigemoto, and Tsukahara Masayoshi were all promoted to acting junior councillor *(nami)* and Mukōyama Eigorō to acting junior councillor *(kaku)*. During the same months six men of modest daimyo rank, including Akitsuki Taneki, Nagai Naokoto, and Hori Naotora, were also appointed regular junior councillor. And men from both groups were given specific ministerial titles as vice-ministers of foreign affairs, home affairs, finances, army, and navy. Thus a bridge from liege vassal to vassal daimyo posts was established and connected to the new ministerial system.

The reformers also pushed ahead with fundamental reorganization of the payroll system. Their main fiscal objective seems to have been to get more output per unit by eliminating a host of perquisites and by replacing expensive payment in kind with cheapened money stipends. On 9/26, after the high-level ministerial reorganization had been implemented, reformers issued an extraordinarily long and sweeping set of instructions that changed thoroughly the bakufu's salary system.[16] All officials from senior councillor down who had court rank (*hoi ijō*: roughly speaking all officials of vassal daimyo and *hatamoto* rank) were stripped of their several forms of income—office stipend, supplement, expense account, and staff allowance (*tashidaka, yakuchi, yakuryō, yakufuchi*)—and granted instead a single monetary office salary. Lower-ranking men were told they would still receive their complex supplemental incomes, but they were assured that eventually they too would be put on standardized salaries. Retirement salaries and several other fiscal matters were also changed. The reorganization simplified matters immensely and shifted the bakufu to an almost fully monetized fiscal system. Even more notably the designation of salaries for senior and junior councillors, hitherto normatively unsalaried positions, meant that henceforth the possession of a fief was not assumed to be a prerequisite for office-holding. It was a major step in the process of erecting an institutional foundation for an open promotion system and ultimately for the abolition of the *han* themselves.

3. Consolidating the Kantō

While high-level administrative reforms were preparing the way for other major changes in future, considerably less visible reforms, moves to strengthen bakufu control of the Kantō, also seemed to be leading in the same direction. The series of actions taken vis-à-vis the Kantō during 1867 reflected a long-standing desire to expand production and improve control of the entire Kantō economy. It was a desire whose antecedents reached well back into the eighteenth century. In 1867, however, the actions were taken within the larger context of fundamental reform, and thus they were part of a much more ambitious centralizing enterprise than had been the earlier efforts.

The Keiō attempt to improve bakufu control of the Kantō had begun in late 1866, as we noted before, and was pursued through 1867. On 67/1/26 the post of Kantō *gundai*, recently created in the wake of the Kanto insurrection, was abolished. Kimura Katsunori and one other occupant of the post were each retitled acting superintendent of finance (*kanjō bugyō nami*) and concurrently overseer of the Kantō hinterland (Kantō *zaikata gakari*). Then they were ordered to administer affairs from an intendancy *(jin'ya)* at Iwabana in Kōzuke.[17] The move was apparently intended to give the two men high enough positions to facilitate extending bakufu control into privately held estates, mostly those of liege vassals and vassal daimyo.

An order of 3/18 revealed one reason for the move.[18] On that day the bakufu reported hearing that in recent years *rōnin* in the countryside had been training peasants and others in military skills and that groups of like-minded peasants had been assembling and drilling together. Then it went on to warn that no one was to devise any scheme that might hinder agricultural production, that anyone who forgot his proper station and acted arrogantly was to cease forthwith, and that no one was to go and stay in any village for the purpose of giving inhabitants thereof unauthorized military instruction. Turning to a different aspect of popular restlessness, the order referred to reports of peasants purporting to be firemen, going to fight fires, and taking the opportunity to smash houses of wealthy people whom they resented. Some men were even calling themselves leaders of groups, and they were reportedly engaging in quarrels and argumentation. These matters were all thoroughly unwarranted, and people were admonished to behave themselves. They were to abide by an ordinance of 1839 forbidding improper military training by peasants and unauthorized residence in villages. And finally the order specified that any daimyo wishing to form and drill peasant units *(nōhei)* was to arrange it through the acting superintendent newly stationed at Iwabana.

It is clear from both the order's phrasing and the bakufu's own recruiting practices that the government did not object to peasant soldiers per se. What it objected to was peasant forces it did not control. To prevent their creation, whether by commoners, *rōnin*, or daimyo, the bakufu was making tactical use of classic status arguments of the Great Peace and a district office specifically authorized to regulate peasant militia matters even in daimyo domains.

One concern of bakufu leaders was thus the danger of unrest in the Kantō, which reduced agricultural production and directly threatened the regime's stability. More about bakufu objectives was revealed in a notice of 4/8 distributed to all liege vassal fief holders in Kōzuke and much of Musashi province.[19] The notice stated that frequently there were no vassal administrators resident on small and scattered parcels of liege vassal lands and consequently they were not well supervised. It observed that the acting superintendent at Iwabana already had authority to handle such parcels and that the records and information necessary to that duty were supposed to be sent to his office. In many instances, however, it had not been done. Therefore, to improve land supervision, holders of large fiefs were to send vassals out to manage them, and men with minor holdings were to let the Iwabana office handle all police and legal problems on them.

Besides keeping the peace, another objective in reorganizing Kantō administration was to maximize the regime's tax income by assuring complete records of current production and capacity to develop new production. That objective was revealed in an order of 6/29.[20] On that day the new Iwabana office was ordered to open a second office at Fusa village in Shimōsa province northeast of Edo. The office was to assist any who wished to open more lands or start raising cattle. Records of Maebashi *han* indicate that the Fusa office was supposed to improve official ties to village leaders, secure information on village production, improve management of mountains, fields, rivers, and shores, and facilitate opening new lands and reporting such lands to the authorities.

During autumn the bakufu continued to deepen control of the Kantō. To eliminate some scattered parcels of private land and thereby facilitate their supervision, on 8/3 it ordered nine vassal lords and some thirty landholding liege vassals to surrender small plots they held in Musashi province. In return they were to receive not other lands, as in the past, but cash payments equal to five years of tax income from the lands returned.[21] It was a formula that could conceivably be applied to entire daimyo domains.

Then on 10/11, even before the Fusa office was in operation, home minister Inaba announced that another intendant's office was being opened at Machiba village in Musashi province. That office was to take over in specified adjacent districts the aspects of fief administration hitherto held by Kimura's office at Iwabana. In those areas of Kōzuke, Shimozuke, and Musashi provinces under its jurisdiction, the new office would handle judicial and travel matters and supervise other affairs as per bakufu instructions. Two months later, on 12/4, the bakufu ordered Oguri Tadamasa at the finance office to take charge of the rest of Musashi and all of Sagami province, handling matters in accord with the regulations guiding Kimura at Machiba.[22]

Between Kimura's offices at Machiba and Iwabana and Oguri at the finance office, the bakufu had units prepared to control all the western Kantō. At the end of the month, 12/29, another order indicated that Okada Tadayoshi, an older man whose bakufu service dated back to Abe Masahiro's day, was established at his office at Fusa. He would handle, as Kimura was doing in his jurisdiction, judicial and travel matters of fief holders in the eastern Kantō, specifically Awa, Kazusa, Shimōsa, and Hitachi. Reflecting the escalating level of activist unrest in the Kantō, the order also said fief holders were to obey any orders Okada might issue for deployment of troops, either from Edo or from their castles.[23]

These several measures largely completed the basic administrative reorganization of the Kantō. By themselves they were not notably radical, but other things being equal, they could have led eventually to a basic reconstruction of the Kantō and a substantial increase in its fiscal value to the regime. They were thus the foundation blocks of a consolidated Kantō from which one day might have stemmed a Tokugawa conquest of the rest of the country. The hour was late, however, and other things did not prove equal.

MILITARY REFORM

Any Tokugawa conquest of the great domains ultimately would require maintenance of a formidable military force, whether for actual use or simply for intimidation by threat. The military reform of 1867 was intended to create that force, and in it three major projects were pursued simultaneously. One was creation of a cadre of French-trained officers and men, which was the central element in the broader foreign-related military effort. Another was continued elimination of obsolete forces and transfer of men to modernized units, which resulted in formation of a very large army. The third was establishment of a more satisfactory manpower-fiscal basis for the armed forces, which constituted a defeudalization of the system.

1. Foreign-related Army Reforms

During 66/12 the French military mission requested back in 1865 finally reached the partially prepared barracks and training facilities at Yokohama. By the end of 67/2 it had begun giving drill there to some 230 men.[24] Two months later, however, the reformers decided to transfer the new training program to Edo, as Roches and Charles Chanoine, the mission leader, advised. It took some time to get the new areas set up, but by the start of 67/6 housing for the French advisors was ready near the Hitotsubashi gate and training areas were prepared for the infantry at Kanda and for the cavalry and artillery at Komabano on the southwest edge of the city.[25] Public notices announced that the troops would enter the city with weapons unsheathed, rather than wrapped as in the past, and barrier and gate guards were instructed to let them pass. On 6/9–10 the trainees, all nattily dressed in their new uniforms, marched up to Edo. There were some two to three hundred cavalry, a few cannon, and some infantry who eventually would carry the Chassepot breechloaders then under order from France.[26]

While relocating the training program, the bakufu launched a recruiting campaign. On the tenth a notice announced that young men aged fourteen to nineteen and interested in military instruction should apply at the training center for modern forces in the army institute (*rikugunsho*, formerly *kōbusho*).[27] By the end of 67/10 the program appears to have created a drilled cavalry force of more than five hundred horse.[28] Its infantry and artillery output is not clear.

Perhaps because the men recruited in 67/6 were completing their training that month, on 10/6 Inaba Masakuni issued orders that liege vassals and their sons or younger brothers aged fifteen to thirty-five should apply to the army institute if interested in French military training. Whether the orders were poorly received, or whether the year-end crisis simply made army expansion imperative, is unclear, but on 11/1 the bakufu issued new recruitment orders. Those said French training was henceforth compulsory for all unemployed 15 to 35-year-old liege vassals, sons, and younger brothers, regardless of their preference. They were to register for drill and instruction within eight days. Again the response seems to have been inadequate, and on 12/25, as crisis rushed toward climax, Inaba issued yet another training order. Lesser men (*gokenin*), their younger brothers, and dependents if in good health and over fifteen years of age (and apparently even if over thirty-five) were to report for training in the new-style army. A deadline of 1/7 was set for enlistment.[29] By then it was too late, and the experience seemed mainly to reinforce the proposition that as things stood liege vassals were not eager to become cannon fodder.

The attempt to create a French-trained force encountered a variety of other obstacles. It cost a great deal, of course, but there were also problems in finding training areas due to local opposition and shortage of space. In a revealing incident of 11/13, French instructors and a training force went to practice on land the bakufu had recently taken over at Tokumaruhara. When they arrived, however, they were met by a large assemblage of local farmers armed with bamboo spears and other weapons and determined to keep the troops off their farmland. When the Frenchmen and their foreign-dressed troops arrived, the farmers attacked at the sound of the conch, indicating they had leaders and organization. Their assault sent the foreigners and most troops fleeing. A few were captured, however, and became bargaining pawns for the irate farmers. In subsequent discussions the latter threatened to wreak more havoc, and officials decided to abandon plans to train there.[30]

From beginning to end petty obstacles of that sort plagued the training effort. The French mission itself delayed training in some ways too. It was very slow in getting to Japan, and then the transfer to Edo held matters up for yet another two or three months. In a different kind of problem, men who had trained previously at the army institute had received certificates permitting them in turn to instruct later cycles of troops, but in 67/2 Roches argued that they were not properly trained for such duty. Bakufu military leaders accepted his verdict, and the men were not allowed to train others. More months were lost and, moreover, men who seemed ready to support the regime found themselves swept aside unless they were willing to serve in other less prestigious ways.[31]

Even if training had gone smoothly, that alone would not have sufficed. The men also needed adequate arms. The bakufu had been interested in modern arms for years, and during 1867 reformers tried to get the most up-to-date weaponry. As noted previously, they had been informed in 66/9 of various types of breechloaders and repeaters. By 67/5 they had outstanding orders for forty thousand French Chassepot breechloaders and some thousand other pieces, of which three hundred were field cannon. Although the evidence is inconclusive, it appears that at least 775 and perhaps as many as 3000 Chassepot were at Edo by year's end.[32] They apparently were not used in fighting, however, perhaps because proper ammunition was not available or because there had not been time to issue the pieces and instruct men in their use.

Bakufu cannon purchases and use during the years 1865–1868 revealed its possession of the whole range of artillery types. In terms of bore, it had pieces ranging from small guns of perhaps an inch or two to large pieces of several inches that could fire 20- and even 40-pound shot. In terms of range, it had mortars to lob large rounds short distances; howitzers to fire further in a lower arc; and higher-velocity rifle cannon firing at longer range in a low arc. The shot they fired included solid shot, chain shot, and explosive shrapnel shells. In terms of weapon weight, it had light metal-framed boat cannon, portable mountain guns, portable and heavier wooden-carriaged fieldpieces, and large siege artillery and coastal defense cannon for permanent emplacement. In this complex of artillery pieces, however, it also had a great variety of quality. Some pieces were very up to date, with explosive shells and rifled barrels. But many more were the less effective pieces cast by Egawa Tarōzaemon and other domestic gunsmiths of both bakufu and daimyo employ. And some were ancient guns dating from much earlier years or older weapons purchased from abroad. The great variety and inconsistency of bores made it difficult to use the pieces efficiently in combat, and inadequacies of artillery were considered a serious problem for the bakufu in the military showdown.

While securing weapons from abroad, Oguri and others continued long-range technical reform projects. For example, an effort to import and erect a modern gunpowder factory had begun in 1864 and had never been abandoned. But it had repeatedly stalled because of fiscal and political problems. In 67/5 a new Dutch gunpowder-making machine was finally received at Yokohama, but its installation—and other aspects of the renewed technical effort in 1867—were ultimately unsuccessful, foundering on technical and then political obstacles.[33] Like the Yokosuka shipyard project, it was inherited half-built by the Meiji regime. On balance foreign-related army reforms consumed much energy and even more wealth, but in their brief lifetime they were of little real benefit to the bakufu.

2. Reform and Expansion of Combat Forces

While foreign-related reforms were pursued, officials also continued reorganizing liege vassal forces and expanding the conscript infantry. In both endeavors they made substantial progress, much more than in the foreign-related efforts. But in both they also encountered serious difficulties.

Looking first at liege vassal reform, military leaders continued abolishing obsolete units and transferring their men to new ones. Ever since the first changes had begun during autumn of 1866, there had been a steady trickle of men into them. Hardly a day passed without one or two men being admitted to *sappei, jūtai, yūgekitai,* or *okuzume jūtai,* and periodically large groups of men, tens, scores, or even a hundred or more, would be enrolled.[34] That pattern continued through 1867. In addition, particularly during 67/5, more old-style units were eliminated, their men reassigned, and their guard functions taken over by new units.[35]

In the reassigning process reformers continued to respect status distinctions. For example, the Osaka *jōban* (permanent guard) was abolished on 5/21 and its personnel reassigned. Its sixty hereditary *yoriki* were assigned to the Osaka city magistrate's office and three temporary *yoriki* were transferred to the *sappei* at their existing stipends. Two hundred hereditary *dōshin* were assigned to the *sappei* at 30 *hyō* and two-man *fuchi* levels and eight temporary *dōshin* at their existing stipends.[36]

These status considerations hindered reform by lowering the quality of some forces. Only low-ranking liege vassals were admitted to *sappei* units, for example, which appear to have functioned primarily as guard, supply, and labor troops for artillery batteries *(hōhei).* Commanders of artillery became convinced, however, that those heavy duties required especially healthy and strong men whom they were unable to get because status restrictions limited their freedom of choice. Accordingly in 67/6 they petitioned for several changes, most notably a change of title for such troops from *sappei* to *hōhei* and revised recruiting criteria allowing them to recruit freely and offer salaries of 30 *ryō* per year. The request led to a restudy of artillery organization, its personnel regulations, and funding. And the following month leaders approved both the change of title and the open recruiting. They also established a salary scale that averaged 30 *ryō* but actually started at a basic 18 *ryō* and then carried supplements in proportion to rank and seniority.[37] It is not entirely clear what changes flowed from that decision, although it may have given rise to the two battalions of artillery guards *(taihōtai shōjūtai)* distinct from *sappei* that were in existence by 9/15.

The persistence of status distinctions in the new forces also exacerbated interforce competition for funds. According to a report probably dated 67/8 or later, *sappei* consisted of some 5000 men. But of them some 700 to 800 were too old or too young for effective service, another 1250 or so were otherwise unfit, and so only about 3000 really counted. The report estimated that *sappei* were costing about 300,000 *ryō* per year to maintain and urged that regular infantry *(hohei)* be trimmed by about a thousand men so that *sappei* could be paid more and their quality improved.[38] It is not clear whether that was an artilleryman's brief at the expense of infantry or an effort by someone to aid liege vassals at the expense of commoners in the infantry. In any case there is no indication of regular infantry being trimmed to help artillery, and problems of liege vassal hardship and artillery inadequacy remained to the end.

In several ways, then, bakufu reformers encountered persistent difficulties in forging an efficient army out of liege vassals. They were reluctant to undergo training, insisted on status distinctions, and tried to keep their higher salaries. And being of hereditary status, they were not selected on any really rigorous basis of competence. All these liabilities worked to sustain an enduring bakufu interest in recruiting peasants from the domain to form regular infantry battalions. That force expanded significantly during 1867, and both its quality and its size were of concern to military leaders.

As leaders expanded their infantry force, they strove to maintain its quality. Thus in a memorial of 67/2 infantry commanders expressed concern because large numbers of men would shortly be completing their five-year period of service, having been recruited initially in 1862. Their loss would be serious because they had seen combat in both the Kantō insurrection and the Aki campaign, and that made them invaluable in training new recruits. The writers hoped pay raises would be granted to induce the men to reenlist so they could assist in weeding out unfit recruits and help assure an effective army.[39] The arguments evidently proved persuasive because the proposal was approved and elaborate regulations for service increments and retirement benefits were spelled out. The desire to retain experienced men seems also to have been reflected in an infantry recruiting notice of 7/17 that was restricted to men earlier recruited by liege vassals in fulfillment of military obligations.[40]

Army commanders indicated the size of their infantry forces during the first half of 1867 in this manner:[41]

1st Infantry Regiment: 1000 men
4th Infantry Regiment: 1000 men
5th Infantry Regiment: 800 men
6th Infantry Regiment: 600 men
7th Infantry Regiment: 800 men
8th Infantry Regiment: 800 men
11th Infantry Regiment: 900 men
1st Training Battalion: 800 men
2nd Training Battalion: 600 men
Mess personnel: 400 men

The force totaled 7700 men plus a senior officer corps of 60. Back in late 1865, by comparison, the regime appears to have had only some 5400 infantrymen.

This regular infantry was the core of the Tokugawa army, but it was nonetheless only a portion of the total. By 67/9 the year of reform had given the bakufu an army of great size. Although there are inconsistencies among the various relevant documents, an exceptionally complete summary dated 9/15 gives this breakdown:[42]

1. Units composed of liege vassals assigned modern arms since the start of reform in 66/8:
     Four battalions of *okuzume jūtai*
     One battalion of *yūgekitai*
     Two battalions of artillery guards *(taihōtai shōjūtai)*
     Seven and a half battalions of *sappei*
     Four and a half battalions of cavalry
     Two and a half battalions of *kachi jūtai*
     Fifteen battalions of *kumiai jūtai*
     Unspecified numbers of men designated Kanagawa *jūtai*—men who apparently refused to abandon their swords even when bearing firearms
2. Other forces:
     Infantry *(hohei)* formed before and during the Summer War
     Militia composed of peasants *(nōheitai)*
     Militia composed of Edo city commoners *(machihei jūtai)*
     Forces that had received French training at Yokohama and Edo

This army reportedly totaled some 24,000 troops, equivalent to forty-eight battalions of about 500 men apiece. The bakufu was making substantial progress in modernizing and expanding its military system. Indeed, it had been so successful it had formed a larger army than it could support. Accordingly the reformers tried to improve it by eliminating some of the least effective and most expensive units.

The units chosen for elimination were *kumiai jūtai*, the army's most feudal element. They were formed late in 66/8 and initially were composed, as noted before, of recruits or retainers of high-ranking liege vassals commanded by their lords. They gradually had been combined and expanded to battalion size and by mid-67 were said to number in aggregate over seven thousand men, a figure that may be inflated. On 67/9/26, thirteen months to the day from original creation, they were abolished. Thirty-seven commanders and vice-commanders, all liege vassals with fiefs ranging from 3000 to 8000 *koku*, were notified that their units were dissolved. Units in Edo were abolished immediately; those stationed in the Kinai would be disbanded after their return to Edo. Of the several thousand men immediately affected, only five hundred were directly transferred to other units.[43] The others were dropped from bakufu manpower rolls.

This scrapping of *kumiai jūtai* was the reformers' last real attempt to improve the quality of their new army. In the crisis of the next three months their concern with quality was completely overshadowed by a concern to increase as quickly as possible the army's size. During 67/10 news from Kyoto indicated it was an inauspicious time to reduce the standing army. Consequently on the twenty-second, Edo leaders decided to recruit another six thousand regular infantry *(hohei)*. In succeeding weeks they admitted men from defunct *kumiai jūtai* and took several other steps to obtain infantrymen. On 11/24 they reduced and reorganized a number of minor servant and attendant positions to form more flexible military-size groups. And they abolished more offices and in following days enrolled the unemployed in rifle units. During 67/12 they tried to shift yet more men from surviving *kumiai jūtai* into *hohei* units. Those *kumiai jūtai* stationed in the Kinai seem to have begun returning east then, and orders from Inaba on the eighteenth informed the men they would be admitted to *hohei* units even without a test of skills.[44] In short, Edo leaders might be getting the desired numbers of men, but in the disintegrating year-end situation the process did not assure them competent fighters. It was a chaotic last chapter to a year-long effort at military strengthening whose achievements were really quite striking.

3. Defeudalizing the Military System

Besides French training, technical modernization, and overall force expansion and reorganization, the bakufu in 1867 addressed itself to more difficult problems lying at the very base of its military, indeed its whole political, system. The bakufu's solution to those problems appeared most clearly in the reform measures of 67/9/26. The crucial reforms of that day were four in number:

1. Introduction of a rationalized salary system in which all supplementary forms of office salary for higher officeholders were abolished and replaced with a single, fully monetized salary scale.
2. Replacement of all military service obligations of fief-holding liege vassals with money taxes paid at the rate of 50 percent of their average real land-tax income.
3. Abolition of *kumiai jūtai*.
4. Warning to lesser liege vassals that they would ultimately have to accept the same salary and tax arrangements as higher vassals.

As a whole the changes were potentially revolutionary. When fully implemented they would convert the bakufu's internal structure from that of an essentially feudal order to that of an essentially modern bureaucratic order. Had the bakufu rather than great *han* won the civil war of 1868, the date 67/9/26 (October 28, 1867) might have become known as an important date in Japanese history, the day the modern polity began.

The drastic reforms of 9/26 did not emerge easily. They were the result of a long and frustrating attempt by bakufu leaders to make the immense resources of the Tokugawa domain and vassal bands again serve efficiently the interests of the Tokugawa ruling institution. As we noted in earlier chapters, the bakufu's army depended on liege vassals for both manpower and money, obtaining them at rates based on hereditary family incomes. The arrangement was not very satisfactory, however, and reformers repeatedly tried to improve it. During the Keiō reform they first tried to extract more from the existing system, but even then it was inadequate. Finally they junked the whole military levy technique, replacing it in the orders of 9/26 with a completely new system of taxation. The administrative struggle that preceded the orders of that day were long and difficult. Examination of it will help illuminate the process that converted a former bastion of conservatism into an instrument of revolution and will also suggest why the instrument failed of its task.

The manpower schedules issued after the Summer War in 66/8 had proved very hard to enforce and unsatisfactory in yield. In succeeding months reformers tried to improve their operation,[45] but problems persisted. Too often liege vassals simply did not honor their obligations; and when they did, the manpower levies worked hardship on their villages. And in any case, the regime needed money even more than it needed manpower. In consequence, by the end of 1866 the regime was modifying its levies in hopes of solving those problems.

Thus on 66/12/19 the bakufu informed liege vassals that military training was to begin on 67/1/11 and the men required by levy must be present on that day for the start of their training cycle. They were told, however, that those who wished would be permitted to make annual payments of 50 *ryō* in place of each man not supplied. Any who chose to do so were to make necessary arrangements at army headquarters within ten days. Evidently the response was unsatisfactory, so the bakufu tried again. On 1/4 it observed that in the previous year's reform liege vassals had been ordered to make military contributions, but there had been reports of fief holders making excessive demands upon their villagers and causing distress here and there. Accordingly such men were permitted "for the moment" to meet their obligations by paying money at the reduced conversion rate of 20 *ryō* per man. Those receiving warehouse rice were to continue paying at the rate of 10 percent of their combined rank and office stipends *(kuramai* and *tashidaka)*.[46] Even the reduced rates failed to secure cooperation of landed vassals. On 4/16 leaders in Kyoto complained that despite the prior notice some were indifferent and did not pay. They warned that in future such people would be dealt with strictly, so men should take care to obey the regulation.[47]

Some liege vassals had legitimate grievances of course. Many were serving as officials, and in preceding months they had lost a number of office perquisites and were understandably reluctant to contribute to the military levy as fully as those having no other obligations. To accommodate those men, on 7/17 the bakufu specified a long list of officials serving outside Edo who were excused from military levies. Their subordinates were only required to pay at half-rates.[48] By listing the exceptions, leaders probably hoped to reduce the grounds for quibbling avoidance by others.

All these attempts to improve the established military foundation were inadequate, however. The foundation had two basic flaws: it was technically obsolete and fiscally inefficient. The bakufu's acceptance of a western military system meant it needed large numbers of healthy young men chosen on the basis of serviceability rather than rank. Moreover, those men needed to be trained, controlled, and maintained not as individualistic samurai but as faceless integers in large military units. The units had to be commanded by career professionals organized in a sharply delineated hierarchy and subject to full central control. The existing system failed to meet those needs in several ways. High-ranking liege vassals furnished recruits whom they themselves commanded in *kumiai jūtai* regardless of their own command ability. Lesser vassals themselves served regardless of their ability. The recruits furnished by vassals were not carefully selected and not necessarily very competent. And a pervasive concern for status considerations made some units very costly, stymied attempts to train men, and undercut the effectiveness of the army as a whole.

Furthermore the system was fiscally inefficient. It failed to identify all taxable resources of liege vassals and hence failed to make them available to the regime. It was based directly or indirectly on the 66/8 schedule, and that in turn was based upon official records of liege vassal income. Those records were only partial estimates of actual income, however. The official productivity estimates of landholders *(chigyōtori)* were less than the actual production of their domains, though how much less is unclear. Moreover, despite the economizing efforts of 1866 stipended vassals *(kuramaitori)* still received substantial income in forms other than basic family stipend. Even when income calculations included office supplements *(tashidaka)*, they still missed important parts of vassal income. Finally, the system still furnished too much manpower and too little money. The orders of early 1867 betrayed the wish for more money, but they were ineffective. Perhaps liege vassals generally found it easier to compel their villagers to furnish men than money. Or perhaps they could use their tax income to hire recruits at rates lower than those stipulated by Edo, pocketing the difference themselves. In any case, the regime was not getting what it wanted.

The reformers early on realized the inadequacy of their system but only gradually devised an alternative. One rather lengthy analysis, probably of late 1866, suggested the direction of their thinking. It started out by estimating that the manpower schedule of the Bunkyū reform as revised in 62/11 would have yielded only 3500 men and that the schedule of 66/8 would have yielded some 13,500. Then it outlined a new and even higher estimate of liege vassal manpower potential. In that estimate, in addition to the basic family stipend *(chigyō* or *kuramai)* used in calculating earlier force figures, supplementary stipends *(tashidaka)* paid in connection with official duties were also included. All liege vassals between 10,000 and 500 *koku* basic stipend were then judged to have a total income of 2,740,055 *koku*, which would yield either 781,313 *ryō* or, at 50 *ryō* per man, 15,626 men in military obligations.[49]

This report not only implied that liege vassals were not currently furnishing sufficient aid to the bakufu but also that their obligations could be calculated in money as easily as in men. It was, however, still based upon the highly unrealistic official records of liege vassal incomes. Then early in 67/1 the finance office completed a study of estimated actual income of liege vassals. It concluded that if fief holders paid a standardized money tax on actual income at a rate of 50 percent, the yield would be about 4 million *ryō* annually, sufficient to meet the costs of infantrymen, sailors, and their military paraphernalia. And liege vassals paid in warehouse rice, it was calculated, could furnish 961,260 *ryō* if their total income were taxed at a rate of 50 percent. This latter sum, finance officials figured, would nearly cover annual costs of other army, navy, legation guard, and military administrative personnel.[50] If men were excused from all other military obligations, it was reasoned, they could justifiably be taxed at that rate, much to bakufu advantage.

The study seemed to offer solutions to both the problems of technical obsolescence and fiscal inefficiency. It seemed to uncover funds sufficient for the new army and navy. And it would enable the regime to abandon entirely its reliance on liege vassal manpower, permitting it to recruit freely and on the basis of competence among the considerably less expensive and less status-conscious commoners, who could, after all, march, shoot, and die in service of the state just as well as their more literate betters.

To effect the plan would require adequate income statistics on each liege vassal. It would be rather easy to calculate incomes of men paid from the warehouse, but to get adequate figures on fief holders would be more difficult.[51] In 67/4, as the regime was gearing up for a second spurt of reform, the latter task was undertaken. On the twenty-third the bakufu ordered all landholders to forward to the finance office records of their actual land-tax receipts for the ten years 1857–1866. Predictably landed vassals did not cooperate. Therefore on 7/22 home minister Inaba again ordered them to provide the records and set a compliance deadline of 8/15. Coming as it did amid plans to reorganize the entire liege vassal salary and stipend system, this pressure evoked varied responses. Six days later, for example, the extraordinary number of ninety-seven liege vassals retired and had their sons succeed as heads of their houses with family incomes unchanged. Their probable intent was to secure official statements assuring their sons full incomes and they themselves customary retirement benefits.

Some men no doubt did provide the required records, but the response was still unsatisfactory, most likely because liege vassals wished to conceal the extent of their unreported tax income. Accordingly on 9/6 Inaba issued a third notice, that time with a nine-day deadline and with a special exemption only for those serving at distant posts and unable to respond on time. Again, however, the response appears to have been poor.

Liege vassals probably had good enough grounds for their continuing resistance to the tax survey. Fully satisfactory statements about their finances are hard to make because their basic fiscal situation is unclear. Furthermore the economic disorders of the 1860s complicate analysis because they worked both for and against the vassals. One recent attempt to assess their condition is Kozo Yamamura's study of samurai income, in the course of which he has worked out a table of *hatamoto* income indices, the relevant part of which is reproduced here.[52]

Year	Nominal Income	Real Income I	Real Income II
1800–1857		145.4*	
1802–1857			124.8*
1862	307.0	161.6	160.3
1863	316.9	162.9	126.7
1864	384.7	172.2	96.5
1865	765.8	247.3	184.0
1866	2120.2	533.0	272.3
1867	1957.0	423.6	263.4

*Mean.

The figures suggest that because inflation of rice prices was greater than that of other commodities, these vassals were then better off than earlier in the century and that the last two years of the regime were their best years. These conclusions assume that the bakufu was still paying stipendiaries in rice at regular rates and that fief holders were still collecting their own tax income in rice as in prior years. It seems quite likely, however, that by the mid-1860s an unprecedented proportion of both groups' income had been monetized, probably at rates disadvantageous to themselves as a result of actions by bakufu above and taxpayers below. Moreover the considerable military duties and other special costs imposed on them during the sixties constituted a severe new burden. On the other hand the reluctance of fief holders to provide tax-income records on request suggests their actual income for prior years may have been appreciably higher than formal bakufu records indicated.[53] Moreover much of their income was committed to fixed expenses, including the maintenance of retainers, fief administrators, and a substantial debt service, and many of those costs may have been reduced by inflation. The net effect of these several trends is not certain. But it does seem that in 1867 fief holders were trying to conceal from the bakufu tax resources they expected it to commandeer.

Whatever the real condition of fief-holding liege vassals, bakufu reformers evidently chose to assume they had gained by inflation, could tighten their belts, and would dismiss retainers no longer needed because of military reform. For liege vassals, however, neither form of economizing was desirable. Hence they resented and resisted attempts to extract more income from them.[54]

After the deadline of 9/15 passed, the reformers apparently concluded that they had reached the point of diminishing return. On 9/26 Inaba issued through the inspectorate new military regulations in which fief holders were notified that because of their difficulties in providing troops in accord with earlier levies, they would henceforth pay a money levy instead. It would be set at 50 percent of their fief-tax income averaged over ten years. The concurrent dissolution of *kumiai jūtai* was a major corollary of the larger reform. As in the case of salary reform, the changes applying to lesser vassals were less radical. Stipended vassals were not switched to the 50 percent rate but were simply notified during 67/9 that the 66/12 regulations permitting payment of 50 *ryō* in lieu of each conscript would apply to them.[55] Since these latter vassals actually provided few troops, however, the order affecting landholders constituted the decisive step toward converting all liege vassals to tax-paying landlords or stipendiaries who would henceforth have no other necessary connection to the bakufu military system.

In succeeding weeks work continued on the new tax system. On 10/3 Edo leaders notified vassals that payments of the coming year's tax would be in four installments in mid-67/11 and 68/2, 5, and 8. They still had not obtained all necessary fief-income records, however, and so on the twenty-fifth Inaba again instructed fief holders to furnish the ten-year tax receipts previously ordered. Even then obstructionism apparently continued, probably in the form of delinquency in payment of 67/11 installments. On 12/10, after again indicating which officials were exempt from the order, leaders warned men that half their fief-tax income was to be paid as military tax and they had better make the payments as ordered.[56] Other notices pertaining to the reform were also issued. However, the fact that nearly a year was spent trying to get the change effected suggests the monumental difficulty reformers were having converting vested interests of liege vassals into productive resources for the regime.[57] Peaceful defeudalization was not a simple matter.

RAMIFICATIONS AND COMPLICATIONS

In all aspects of their venture the Keiō reformers encountered problems or created them. Yet they continued to press ahead in their attempt to rejuvenate the regime and transform Japan. Inevitably the main efforts had a host of subsidiary ramifications, many minor in themselves but cumulatively pregnant with implications of future change. Even as hints of a new age were proliferating, however, late in the year the Keiō reformers experienced great disappointment in major attempts to finance their venture. And they watched in dismay as their demoralized new army erupted in explosive rioting.

1. Ramifications of Reform

Technologically, bakufu military reform was designed in the main to replace obsolete seventeenth-century weaponry with the most up-to-date instruments of carnage available anywhere. However, the rapidity of change in western weaponry forced reformers to abandon new ways as even newer ways became available. Moreover they kept discovering that one change led to another, so that the introduction of new military technology had a host of nonmilitary ramifications.

We noted how, in terms of shoulder arms, the bakufu proceeded through two generations of weaponry in five years. It settled upon Mini-style muzzleloaders as the best weapon in 1862 but moved on to Chassepot breechloaders in 1867. A similar but far more expensive case of technological obsolescence occurred in coastal defense. There the bakufu moved from an 1850s policy of defense based on coastal artillery to an 1860s policy based primarily on warships. This study has deliberately avoided the complex but well-documented and accessible story of bakufu naval development. It must suffice here to state that attempts to form a modern navy and train naval personnel were slow and difficult, plagued by much the same sorts of problems as army reform.[58]

Delays in naval development notwithstanding, the program was expensive. And just as requirements of army reform eventually drove the bakufu to scrap its old feudal levy system, so requirements of naval development were goading it to extend its fiscal authority into daimyo domains. In early 67/2 Katsu Kaishū noted that Oguri Tadamasa had outlined a plan to levy a regularized tax on all daimyo of under 100,000 *koku* as a means of supporting the navy. The plan was not implemented, but the idea that daimyo should support the navy was revealed in another proposal of uncertain date. That one recommended steady naval expansion, regular commercial runs to Hong Kong and Shanghai by three or four vessels, dispatch of more students abroad for naval training, and, most notably for our purposes, imposition of levies on vassal daimyo to support these measures.[59] Thus fiscal demands created by naval expansion were prompting the bakufu to contemplate taxing the daimyo. But that would have required destroying the feudal system itself, replacing it with a unified political order capable of carrying out such taxation.

In other ways, too, naval reform was undermining the old order. The decision of 1864 to build a major shipyard at Yokosuka quickly generated a host of secondary activities. It led to creation of a French-language school in Yokohama, then to recruitment of some fifty-odd students, and later to expansion of the school.[60] It also gave rise to extensive exploration for iron and coal resources. Some Frenchmen were hired to survey Kazusa, and by 67/1 they had reported their findings. Three months later the bakufu loaned M. Verny, supervisor of the Yokosuka works, a ship with which to travel to Izu and Musashi provinces in search of coal, lumber, and other resources. Then at the end of 67/6 it announced that some Frenchmen were going into Shimozuke to look for coal.[61] To the extent the prospectors were successful, they would set in motion profound changes in the Kantō economy.

Quite apart from changes precipitated by naval development, the Keiō reformers initiated a variety of other technical changes. Most notable, perhaps, were changes in transportation. In 66/10 bakufu leaders in Kyoto ended the classic prohibition on horse-drawn wheeled vehicles, permitting their use for freight cartage on the five major highways and in Edo.[62] On the seas the bakufu and *han* had for some time used their new steamers for fast travel between Osaka and other points, and during 1867 the practice began to be standardized. In early 67/3 bakufu leaders at Kyoto ordered one ship from the navy to carry goods between Edo and Osaka. According to the notice, the service was being started to relieve impoverished and overburdened highway stations, and merchants were invited to inquire at the naval institute *(kaigunsho)* concerning freight charges. Six months later the freight service was regularized, and the steamer was assigned to carry goods and passengers between the two cities on a fixed sailing schedule.[63]

During the year bakufu officials in Europe investigated the importation of telegraph equipment to Japan.[64] And at home on 67/2/1 a certain Carle L. Westwood asked permission to build a railroad between Edo and Yokohama. He argued it would profit both government and people. In their reply a few days later the foreign magistrates explained that matters were so unstable just then it would be difficult to build a railroad.[65] By year's end, however, with Edo opened to foreigners, officials had changed their minds and agreed to its construction. On 12/23, even as

Edo leaders were preparing military action against Satsuma, foreign minister Ogasawara dispatched to the American minister A. L. C. Portman a license and detailed set of regulations permitting an American entrepreneur to construct within three years a railroad between Edo and Yokohama. The regulations spelled out details of foreign financing and a series of restraints to prevent undue construction abuse. The bakufu secured special rights for Japanese officials and guarantees that the Japanese public could use the line. It set limits on the authority of foreigners and retained for the Japanese government future rights of purchase.[66] The agreement was never implemented, but it did indicate that in their last major move to usher the new age into Japan, bakufu negotiators understood the importance of safeguarding national sovereignty.

During its last year the bakufu also pursued a much broader effort at learning about the west. During 66/9–10 a group of a dozen or more scholars was dispatched to Europe, and the following month more liege vassals were invited to apply for study abroad. At the same time the English-French language school at Yokohama was being greatly expanded, and more students were being recruited for it. At the new year the school was opened with an expanded curriculum that included geography, logic, military science, and history, as well as language study. As the year progressed, the bakufu pushed on with its foreign study program, tried to expand English-language training, and also proposed to send more students abroad.[67]

This accelerating study of things alien reflected a significant change in bakufu leadership. By 1867 a number of the most important officials were men who had been abroad or who had actively studied western languages and matters civil and military in Japan. They included Shibata Masanaka, Ikeda Chōhatsu, Mukōyama Eigorō, Oguri Tadamasa, Kurimoto Kon, Hirayama Keichū, Asano Ujisuke, Kawakatsu Kōun, Ogyū Noritaka, and probably several others. Politically less important men with foreign knowledge included Katsu Kaishū, Enomoto Takeaki, Nishi Amane, and Tsuda Mamichi. Having some knowledge of varied facets of contemporary European society, they were able to accept a host of changes in Japan that their predecessors could not. This capacity to accept the foreign proved valuable in 1867, for during the year Japan encountered a number of rather more exotic aspects of the foreign intrusion.

For example, the bakufu was learning, of necessity, how to live with an uncontrolled and hostile press. For some time the English-language press at Yokohama had been critical of the Tokugawa, and that posture was particularly pronounced during 1866–1867 when the Satow orientation was most in favor. During those months the bakufu endured several thorny essays appearing there. Then on 67/9/13 the *Japan*

Times of Yokohama stated that Yoshinobu intended to resign as shogun. Foreign minister Ogasawara denied the report, which no doubt was planted by someone familiar with the maneuvering of anti-bakufu elements. The bakufu then instructed the Kanagawa magistrate to negotiate with the English consul for retraction of the story, but to no avail.[68] And so the regime let the matter pass.

In other matters,[69] during 67/5 at the request of Portman the bakufu agreed to forbid reproduction by any Japanese of the forthcoming Hepburn English-Japanese dictionary then being printed at Yokohama. During the same month the bakufu announced that foreigners could enter restaurants in or near Edo and Osaka, and two months later an enterprising restaurateur moved from Yokohama to Kanda in Edo, opening there the city's first western-style restaurant. The following month, aware perhaps of a growing culinary demand by foreigners, bakufu leaders in Kyoto encouraged villagers in Tajima province west of the city to purchase and graze cattle. To expedite the venture, they appointed a vassal of Tsu *han* to take charge of developing the cattle industry. They gave him the title *bokugyū gakari*, or overseer of animal husbandry, and instructions to travel through the villages of Tajima, teaching men how to obtain and care for livestock. Buddhists might object, but butter and beef would have their day. During 67/7 leaders were presented by the Kanagawa magistrate with another perplexing and equally emotion-laden problem. They dealt with it by informing him that marriages between Japanese and foreigners might be freely made. Then on 9/14 the bakufu bade farewell to the architectural style of centuries, permitting the construction of three-story buildings in cities. The order, issued in Kyoto, said such buildings were permitted because of the crowded condition of cities. A series of construction stipulations was inserted to minimize fire hazards and assure privacy of toilet facilities.

In many ways, then, the first year of Yoshinobu's rule had seen the bakufu again seizing the lead. It was propelling Japan into the future, into an alien world at a rate that outstripped the vision of those dissidents who in secret were scheming to topple the regime even in these months of its apparent triumph.

2. The Bitter Fruits of Reform

A new age was upon Japan, perhaps, but for the bakufu it seemed to constitute an endless series of problems and precious little reward. In military modernization the problems had been confronted, and a foreign-guided program of army training had at last begun to function. A naval program was limping into operation. Critical technological purchases and developments were being made. The regular army had been greatly expanded, and with the dissolution of *kumiai jūtai* one of its greatest, most archaic, and most costly elements had been abolished. Contemporary moves to eliminate liege vassals as the primary source of manpower opened the way for gradual elimination of other unsatisfactory units and even of the whole debilitating concern for hereditary status distinctions.

Such profound changes obviously must have had a traumatic impact on the people whose whole way of life and base of security were being sledgehammered to pieces. Indeed, well before the changes of 9/26 occurred, the reform process was generating bitterness and unrest. We noted previously Ōkubo Ichiō's explanation of how military reform was dismaying liege vassals in Edo in late 1866. Then in 67/3 several Shinsengumi troops absconded from Kyoto because of their resentment at orders to adopt firearms. Three days later a serious confrontation occurred in the city between about two hundred pike-carrying city patrols *(mimawari)* and perhaps a battalion of infantry *(hohei)* armed with rifles. After several hours of tension the deployed forces were quieted and no serious damage was done, but the presence of severe hostilities had been made apparent.[70] The Shinsengumi was one of the most vigorously loyal patrol groups in Kyoto, and its men were fiercely proud of their function and capacity. The city patrols were similarly proud of their peacekeeping roles in the imperial capital. The two incidents occurred during the dispute over opening Hyōgo, and they may suggest how high-level wrangles over foreign policy could bring to the surface ethnic sensibilities implicit in both the rhetoric of *sonnō jōi* and opposition to western weaponry. More certainly they betrayed patterns of intraforce frustration and interforce hostility related in some degree to weapon type and associated considerations of status and self-respect.

Some liege vassals expressed their bitterness about developments in ethical terms, protesting that although their families had been loyal for generations, they nonetheless were being ill-used.[71] For others it was simply the brute economics of reform that embittered, but doubtless for most men the crisis of the age was both material and moral. The conjunction of issues of principle and interest easily led to violence, not only by those opposed to bakufu leaders such as Ii Naosuke or to the bakufu itself, but also by those supporting the regime. Materials relating to one incident—the murder of Hara Ichinoshin—suggest the character of the problem.

These materials pertain to the men who murdered Hara on 67/8/14.[72] The main source is testimony furnished bakufu investigators by Yoda Sasuke, guardian of Yoda Yūtarō, one of the three men involved.

Hara, it will be recalled, was originally from Mito and became a Hitotsubashi vassal. He was a close and effective advisor to Yoshinobu, and after the latter's succession to the Tokugawa headship, he became an inspector and a successful politician in Kyoto. He labored mightily to preserve the authority of Yoshinobu and the bakufu, and yet in the weeks of Yoshinobu's triumph he was slain by men who sought the same goals as he.

Sasuke wrote in his deposition that he was fifty-three years old, a resident of Koishikawa, and holder of a 100-*hyō* stipend. He had no duty at the moment and was responsible to the office of the army commander *(rikugun bugyō)*. His father had been a *yoriki*, and he in turn at age eighteen in 1835 had become an apprentice *yoriki*. In 1849 he succeeded to his father's post when the latter sickened, retired, and died. Thereafter he served as a *sakite yoriki* until 66/11, when his position was abolished. Then he was reassigned to a 100-*hyō* unemployed position as *kobushin* under authority of the army commander. The bakufu's postwar military reform, in other words, had thrown him out of a job.

After thus identifying himself, Sasuke wrote that Yūtarō, the 25-year-old charged with Hara's murder, had grown up in his care and had entered the military institute *(kōbusho)* for training. When Yoshinobu went to guard Kyoto in 62/12, Yūtarō went too as member of a guard unit. But in 63/3 he was sent back to Edo to help manage *rōnin* in the Kantō. A month later his unit (probably the Shinchōgumi) was abolished and he had to return to live with his guardian. The latter, who was then standing guard at the shogun's summer residence (Hamagoten, then a coastal defense post), arranged to have Yūtarō assist him there. Later the young man found temporary duty in a *sakite* unit, but the reform of 66/8 ended most such temporary *yoriki* posts, and he again lost employment. Thus reform deprived both men of the kind of work they expected for a career and left them to their own alternative devices.

Sasuke then seemed to imply that despite his family's loyal efforts these developments had created family financial difficulties. At least he reported that his own sixteen-year-old son was in rifle training and mentioned that he had three living daughters to support and that another who had been unhealthy had died. Referring to Yūtarō's character, he said that from youth the young man had had a strong will to win and at times had protested matters, that he was of somewhat violent disposition and tended to be strongly opinionated, but that he had not been troublesome to his guardian.

Having furnished this background information on Yūtarō and his family, Sasuke then proceeded to report developments prior to the incident. He wrote that in 65/5 he himself had been reassigned from duty at the summer residence to his original *sakite* unit and had gone to Osaka with the shogun, returning to Edo in 66/11 after his *yoriki* position was abolished. Yūtarō had remained in Edo. During his guardian's eighteen-month absence he began studying and traveling together with the Suzuki brothers, Tsunetarō and Toyojirō, age thirty and twenty-four. Then on 67/7/11 Yūtarō left home, leaving only a message saying he was off to serve a great purpose with a few like-minded men who were jointly resolved to repay their ancestral obligations.[73] And that, evidently, was the last Sasuke heard of Yūtarō until he learned of Hara's death.

As it turned out, the great purpose that led the three, like so many *shishi*, to journey secretly to Kyoto was murder. After practicing their swordsmanship for a few days, they slipped out of Edo on 7/23 and made their way westward past highway barriers and inquisitive people. They did so by saying they were on a pilgrimage to Ise shrine and wished to sightsee at Kyoto. Making travel arrangements with acquaintances en route, they arrived in the city on 8/11. There they managed to conceal their purpose long enough to implement at least part of their scheme, and three days later Hara lay dead.

The three left as explanation of their deed a statement pointing out that Hara (and Umezawa Ryō, whom they also presumably intended to kill) was from Mito, home of the great *sonnō* principles of Nariaki. And yet he had, by wrongly influencing "our young lord," helped to arrange the opening of Hyōgo contrary to the former emperor's wishes. Thus he was wrecking the national polity *(kokutai)*. In the rhetoric of ethnicity and unity these men, like so many others, thus found a satisfactory justification for political assassination.

The three were not, however, simply passive traditionalists angry at changes necessitated by the foreign intrusion. All three were activists but of dissimilar sorts. Yūtarō had served for a while as a supervisor of the Shinchōgumi in 1863, but despite his service he had twice been thrown out of his job. By contrast the Suzuki brothers were enrolled in the western studies center *(kaiseijo)* and Tsunetarō may have been in a western-style legation guard unit *(bette gumi)*. The three may have had more in common in spirited personalities. Sasuke's testimony suggests that Yūtarō was a person who could have been moved to murder by his convictions. And the Suzuki brothers were reported to be sufficiently upset to risk their lives by admonishing the bakufu in those perilous times. The three were said to be dismayed at the decline of bakufu power and desirous of stopping it. And like so many others, they evidently saw the regime's capitulation to foreign demands as a major expression of that decline.

Caught in the throes of changes they could not control, facing severe moral contradictions and unprecedented uncertainty, they, like so many *shishi*, had constructed their own personalized explanation of why the times were out of joint and proceeded on that basis to set matters right. And in the background, Sasuke's testimony suggests, was the disturbing experience of having family life interrupted and career prospects damaged and confused by the changing times. Murdering Hara did nothing to solve the crisis of their age, but it did reveal the magnitude of tensions people were experiencing.

The Suzuki brothers and Yoda Yūtarō were hardly alone in their dissatisfaction. Incidents involving bakufu vassals and troops litter the pages of 1860s history. Some, such as Hara's murder, were overtly political incidents. Others were equally products of the times but were more private in nature. Most evident of these were soldierly discontents expressed in rowdyism, interforce conflict, and explosions arising from the tension, frustration, and economic stringency of barracks life.

Over the years military commanders expended considerable energy establishing elaborate rules of conduct, enforcing controls on the issue and accounting of weapons and ammunition, and maintaining city patrols and other security measures. Much of the infantry force was rough, young country men, however, of whom many doubtless were not really there by choice, anyway. And all were poorly paid and exposed to samurai and urban snobbery. Despite the bakufu's efforts, trouble erupted from time to time.

The rapid growth of armed forces in Edo during 1867 only exacerbated the problem. Accordingly in 67/8 army commanders (*rikugun bugyō nami*) Takenaka Shigemoto, Komai Chōon, and colleagues and their subordinate infantry commanders drew up and promulgated a long set of regulations on military justice, presumably in accord with French statutes. The severity of stipulated punishments suggests how serious they considered the problems of discipline and the risk of an outbreak.[74] Thus some typical crimes and punishments were these:

Article 10: neglect of duty when at post—eight days in jail

Article 18: pawning a government-issue rifle—banishment; selling one—death

Article 20: drunk and disorderly conduct in billets:—a regular beating and four days and nights in jail

Article 22: acting unlawfully toward civilians or being rowdy in town —a severe beating and fifteen days in jail

Article 23: forming a gang and extorting: if a leader—death; if a follower—banishment

Article 27: theft of over 10 *ryō*—death

Article 28: murder—death

Article 29: refusal to obey an order—death or banishment

Article 34: inducing another to steal—death

These stern punishments doubtless helped keep men under control, but they proved insufficient in the face of the extreme difficulties troops experienced late in 1867.

It was the reform orders of 9/26 that precipitated serious trouble among the troops. Everything about the orders of that day antagonized men. The tax levies generated widespread bitterness among the liege vassals, adding to discontent caused by mass dismissal from office, slashing of salaries, and abolition of treasured posts and perquisites. Nor were the dispossessed pleased to see the handsome salaries reformers gave themselves on the same day.[75] To help the cause, senior councillors advocated cooperation in a strong appeal to the mens' sense of loyalty,[76] but it proved of little value. Even some officials themselves were remiss in enforcing the reforms among their subordinates, some of whom said the 50 percent tax would impoverish themselves or their retainers and turn the latter into *rōnin*.

Liege vassals were hurt, but they were not ruined by the orders of that day. Despite all the change with its demeaning impact and economic ramifications, they still had, for the moment anyway, their hereditary fiefs or stipends, and they were mostly content to grumble and try to sabotage matters by noncooperation. Lesser people were far more grievously wounded. Rear vassals and commoner recruits who lost their positions might end up with nothing at all thanks to the reform. Hence it was the abolition of *kumiai jūtai*, the mass dismissal of thousands of rear vassals and commoners, that precipitated the overt large-scale trouble.

In previous months *kumiai jūtai* troops seem not to have been very rowdy, perhaps because they were commanded by their own lords and therefore were treated better, felt less vulnerable, or were constrained. Whatever the cause, the situation changed dramatically on 9/26.[77] Within hours of learning the news, men in groups of up to three hundred began to assemble at various spots in Edo and run amok. There was a great deal of argumentation, agitation, and verbal protest, and groups began milling about the city. Hours turned into days; conduct got uglier. On the twenty-ninth, home minister Inaba Masakuni tried to quiet the men by instructing them to go to infantry headquarters and apply for admission and training in the regular infantry *(hohei)*. The men, however, did not wish to abandon their former units, and unrest continued. By 10/3 one group estimated at three hundred had gone to Shinagawa, then billeted at the Ikegami Honmonji south of there, and then wandered into the countryside in Kawasaki, probably plundering as they went, until assembled peasant militia *(nōhei)* turned them back. Then they wandered northeast to Meguro on the south edge of Edo, again staying at a temple where they were fed, and in the evening they went northeast to Shiba. There they were joined by a motley, rather unsavory crowd of local folk: people in rags, men with no swords, and others with short swords. Worried shopkeepers quickly began handing out money and closing their shops in hopes of avoiding a riot. That group was relatively peaceable, but elsewhere in the city in the early days of 67/10 impoverished ex-soldiers were not so quiet. Other groups cruised about extorting monies from shopkeepers, ransacking, and smashing. In response a curfew was imposed, some streets were closed at dusk, and on the fourth more notices informed men that if they were accepted for infantry training, they would immediately be paid 1 *ryō* apiece.

Likely some men enlisted and probably others went home, for in following days the situation appears to have quieted down. Then later in the month men suddenly found their services as infantrymen warmly welcomed by the regime. However, even inclusion in the infantry was not really a satisfactory solution because infantrymen were not being paid their full salaries. Their pathetic condition was revealed a month later.[78]

On the night of 11/12 a few infantrymen were murdered near Yoshiwara. The next day several hundred of their comrades from barracks all around the castle poured out in response, rifles and sabers in hand. Some rampaged through the city and out to the licensed quarter, while others sacked some warehouses containing money. Reinforced city patrols were unable to contain the eruption, and for the next five days the Asakusa-Yoshiwara area was subjected to looting, fighting, extorting, and general turmoil as hundreds of troops in both conventional and western uniforms vented their fury on the vulnerable, immediate sources of their frustration.

Subsequent investigation revealed clearly how the regime's new army was being ravaged by the government's fiscal crisis. Each infantryman was to receive 15 *ryō* per year, of which 1 *ryō* was paid each month and the balance saved until his five-year term of service was over. In addition, every month he was authorized one day off for relaxation and on that day was given 2 *monme* of silver for recreation expenses. Due to the fiscal crisis, however, men were reportedly receiving neither monthly *ryō* nor recreation silver. Consequently many had piled up debts, and some had begun eating and drinking and then refusing to pay. Thus a situation of conflict had built up that pitted the troops against operators of restaurants, sake shops, whorehouses, and the like. The outcome was the eruption of mid-67/11.

The implications of the soldierly turmoil were ominous. The *kumiai jūtai* eruption revealed clearly how slender was the line between inertia and upheaval that reformers must walk. And the infantry outburst revealed that in its bankrupt condition the regime was rapidly losing its last real line of defense, the young conscripts in its new army.

3. Fiscal Policies and Problems

The Keiō reform's reorganization of civil structure and Kantō administration constituted undertakings of long-range significance, but they had little short-run impact because they did not address directly any immediately critical problems. They encountered relatively modest complications and displayed a certain structural grandeur. Military reform had at least an equal grandeur, but it did address critical problems and encountered massive difficulties. Finance was an area of intense immediate concern, and in 1867 as in prior years bakufu fiscal policies were more marked by pragmatism and pervasiveness than by architectonic elegance. Within the continuing mad scramble for funds, however, were two sets of policies of impressively ambitious magnitude. One set was aimed at raising money abroad; the other, at raising it from merchant sources at home.

The basic goals of fiscal policy as a whole were unchanged from prior years: to cut costs and raise funds. To cut costs the bakufu abolished more obsolete military units and abolished or consolidated a variety of civil offices and ceremonial positions. It simplified clothing requirements, abolished a number of once-important procedures, and further reduced travel allowances and travelers' retinues. It attacked such old and honored fiscal abuses as liege vassals refusing to repay loans, securing unauthorized supplemental income, and concealing family deaths so as to keep drawing retirement benefits.[79]

To raise funds, the regime continued to utilize its whole range of techniques. It again tried to obtain more bullion by reiterating an earlier order forbidding commercial use of certain old coins and offering to accept them at rates advantageous to itself. It revived plans to establish various commercial and land taxes following Roches's advice to that effect, but the venture never got beyond the planning stage. It also tried without great success to increase its tax lands. In the most notable cases the regime reiterated during 67/6 punitive claims first made in 1862 to lands of Ii,

Andō, Kuze, and others. The efforts seem to have been more nominal than real and no more successful than before; at least no positive response is recorded.[80]

These several gestures amounted to very little: the regime's major efforts lay elsewhere. As noted earlier, the agreement of 66/8 for a $6 million foreign loan had been delayed by the unwillingness of the Oriental Bank's Yokohama branch to underwrite more than a million of it. Subsequently at Osaka on 67/2/8 Roches reportedly proposed to Itakura and Hirayama that they try to obtain the $5 million balance from Britain and France by giving as surety authority for foreigners to open mines in Ezo.[81] From Roches's viewpoint that was a skillful proposal. Not only would it permit a vast new stage of profitable imperialist intrusion into Japan's economy, but it also would pit British against Russians along the northern rim of Japan, prompting Britain to support Japanese claims in the area, and so perhaps in effect propping up the bakufu. Roches assured Itakura that the proposal would be attractive to France since the money would return there anyway (in the form of military purchases and then repayment at interest) and France would have mine rights in the interim.

Bakufu leaders were interested in opening mines to obtain resources for the Yokosuka foundry and shipyard, and accordingly they decided to pursue at least part of the scheme. On 2/28 senior councillors Inoue, Matsui, and Ogasawara at Edo wrote Parkes proposing to employ a certain Erasmus Gower to open coal mines in Ezo. On 3/1 Parkes replied, approving the request and saying he considered the undertaking basic to naval development and defense and settlement of Ezo. Gower was given a three-year contract, and details of the project were then worked out.[82] No loan negotiations flowed from the agreement, however.

Meanwhile the bakufu was also approaching the loan from another angle. The mission that left for France in 67/1 had been instructed to seek a loan through M. Coullet. However, the negotiating team was headed by Mukōyama Eigorō, who had been to England with Shibata in 1862, and he allegedly preferred Britain to France as an ally. For that reason he may not have pursued the matter very vigorously. At least Fleury-Herard, who was having trouble getting Frenchmen to risk capital in the trading company, reported in 67/7 that the bakufu had given up attempts to secure a loan there, in favor of England and the United States. And Kurimoto Kon later denounced Mukōyama's handling of the matter.[83] Even if Mukōyama did try, however, changes in French foreign policy had resulted by 67/4 in a decision at Paris to repudiate Roches's policy, and with that decision French governmental support for the loan scheme rapidly evaporated. On 7/27, after some bad disagreements with Fleury-Herard and others, Mukōyama wrote Edo that the attempt to secure a loan of $6 million from the French trading company had completely collapsed. Indeed, he reported, he had even encountered opposition to a simple $100,000 loan.[84]

It is not clear when that bad news reached Edo, but on 6/17 or thereabouts Oguri received an earlier letter indicating that the negotiations in Paris might well be failing. Almost surely Mukōyama's letter of 7/27 reached Edo by 9/1, because on that day Oguri learned that the mission to Europe needed funds, and that was information contained in his letter.[85] Probably awareness of the loan scheme's failure was one factor prodding reformers to issue the edicts of 9/26, which, as we have seen, attempted to trim costs and raise new income by drastic domestic action.

The foreign loan plan thus never materialized. According to an unsympathetic English report, however, the French furnished 3 million francs (about $545,000) worth of military supplies during the development of the Franco-bakufu connection. It was a considerable quantity, but most of it apparently did not reach Japan until after the bakufu had fallen.[86]

While the French loan was being pursued, the regime was also trying to obtain substantial funds domestically. One major effort was made in the Kinai; two were made in the Kantō. The former related to the opening of Hyōgo; one of the latter related to the opening of Edo; the other was a form of forced loan.

The rationale behind the plan for Hyōgo was spelled out in 67/4 by Tsukahara Masayoshi, Oguri Tadamasa, and two other superintendents of finance.[87] While preparing to open the port, they drew up, apparently for submission to higher officials, a long statement recommending formation of a trading company with authority to print money and manage the Hyōgo trade. They identified the immediate problem as expenses involved in opening the port. They said that opening Nagasaki and Yokohama had cost the government a great deal, and they estimated that setting up foreign residence areas and constructing a customs office, guard, port, and municipal service facilities in Hyōgo, along with an adequate highway from there to Nishinomiya, would consume about 900,000 *ryō* during the current year. They pointed out that such sums were not available and obtaining them from customs receipts would require years. Consequently they proposed a trading company that could pool resources sufficient to underwrite a note issue covering opening costs. They recommended that about twenty major Osaka merchants be incorporated as founders of the organization and other merchants be encouraged to invest in the venture.

They also defended the proposal by asserting that it would help solve a long-range problem. They argued that whereas western societies were profiting from foreign trade, Japan was not because Japanese merchant organization was so weak that traders could only pursue short-run individual gain at one another's expense. Creation of a trading company would enable merchants to avoid the internal competition that hitherto had permitted foreigners to reap all the profit. The existing situation, they warned, threatened to reduce Japan to a mere area of exploitation for westerners.

To cope with these problems, they suggested the company issue about 1 million *ryō* of notes. The figure was not excessive, they argued, because so many merchants would be involved and experience at Yokohama indicated that in about three years' time tariff receipts would be sufficient to cover the merchants' investment.

The proposal was accepted. On 6/5 the bakufu formally instructed a group of some twenty Osaka merchants headed by three of their number to form the company by investing sums ranging from 89,000 to 22,000 *ryō* apiece. The men given these orders were rewarded for their ''service to the country.'' The three greatest contributors received 100 *koku* of land apiece and permission to wear swords; the others were given, in proportion to their contributions, 50 *koku*, lesser sums, or simply permission to use surnames.[88]

In succeeding days the group organized itself and set up a company headquarters in the city. On 8/19 the company was instructed to invite the participation of investors and those with goods to trade. To facilitate trade, it was instructed to print money in denominations of 100, 50, 10, and 1 *ryō* and 2 and 1 *bu*. The paper was to circulate freely in the Osaka-Kyoto region and be honored as gold or silver in all commercial transactions and all tax payments except regular agricultural taxes. And eventually it was to be exchangeable for gold at no discount.[89] The company did print some 100,000 *ryō* of notes, about one-tenth of the planned issue, and put it into circulation in 67/11. It informed the public that the paper was sponsored by trading-company merchants, would circulate for three years, and could then be exchanged at face value for gold or silver. By then, however, the general situation had changed drastically. No one had confidence in the notes, and the company was unable to get them into circulation. It also failed to attract investors, even when the city magistrate put pressure on people to participate.[90]

Paralleling the attempt at a note issue in Osaka were two major attempts to print paper money in the Kantō.[91] Both issues were to be printed in the Ginza, where the big merchant house of Mitsui was to handle their circulation. From 67/5 money to facilitate foreign trade at Edo was discussed, and planning envisaged putting some 100,000 *ryō* of silver certificates into circulation over a period of months. During 67/11, as the opening date neared, foreigners were notified of the impending issue. Then, however, the matter was lost in the political turmoil of year's end.

The other attempt to print notes at Edo was a more naked move to secure money in a hurry. It proceeded further than the other Ginza venture, but in the end had little more success. From 67/9, probably after hearing of the failure in Paris, the bakufu began notifying merchants in Edo that paper certificates would shortly be issued for domestic use. The total intended is not clear, but during 67/11 Katsu reported an intended *goyōkin* levy in Edo of 800,000 *ryō*.[92] That is probably the general magnitude of the planned issue because a *goyōkin* levy was apparently to be the vehicle for getting it into circulation. Specifically on 10/20 home minister Inaba instructed city magistrates to notify ward officials *(machi toshiyori)* in Edo and district administrators throughout the Kantō that those being called upon to provide *goyōkin* would be issued paper certificates covering the levy. Until 69/3 the certificates would not be discounted and could be used in Edo and the Kantō in all transactions except regular agricultural tax payments. After that date the notes could be redeemed for metal at Mitsui's at full face value. In following weeks the notes were prepared in 25, 50, 100, and 200-*ryō* denominations, and during the last days of 67/11 and early 67/12 specific levels of merchant obligation were indicated, commonly 1000 or 2000 *ryō* per house. The levy on several wholesalers *(ton'ya)* called for a *goyōkin* exchange of 277,000 *ryō*. Almost at once, however, merchants begged off and people began to protest that notes were not being accepted in transactions. During 67/12 and 68/1 Edo officials kept trying to get the paper into circulation, but the repetitive nature of their action suggests they failed.

With the failure of the foreign loan scheme and the trading-company and note-issue ventures, the great fiscal hopes of the regime collapsed. Just where that left a government that had been more or less bankrupt for a year and a half is not clear, but some aspects of the situation are suggested by two entries in Katsu Kaishū's diary.[93] On 67/9/11 Katsu reported that bakufu receipts (for some unspecified period, but probably a year) were these: 40,000 *koku* of rice; 1 million *ryō* of gold; 80,000 *ryō* of tariff income *(unjō)*; 400,000 *ryō* of military levy *(gun'yaku)*. At the same time military costs were these: 450,000 *ryō* per year for foundry and shipyard; 50,000 *ryō* per month for the army; 130,000 to 140,000 *ryō* per year for army training. Thus monies received were

1,480,000 *ryō* plus rice that was, by my calculation, worth in that time of inflation some 360,000 *ryō*, or a total of some 1,840,000 *ryō*. Military expenses for a year were about 1,200,000 *ryō*. Unpaid for in that accounting were costs of the shogunal household, the civil bureaucracy, overhead of equipment such as castle buildings, domestic debt service, foreign debts and indemnities, plus the costs of the navy, its training, and its fleet.

Apart from suggesting the regime's bankruptcy, the income figures of Katsu, notably the small amount of rice, also seem to imply certain other very significant considerations. With the crop failure of 1866 the bakufu, it appears, had lost most of its rice tax-in-kind. What that suggests is that either there was simply too little rice to collect or, more likely, farmers were shrewdly selling their rice at the immensely inflated prices of the day and paying their taxes in money at standing conversion rates of pre-inflation years. The latter was an old dodge, but if it underlay the lack of rice tax income, it was being used to great new advantage by farmers. That explanation of the low rice receipts seems to fit other aspects of the situation very well. It helps explain the quietude and good humor of the general populace during 1867, even to year's end. It also helps explain the bakufu's attention to riparian repair and strengthening of Kantō administration. And it may help explain the bakufu's rapid shift to a fully monetized salary system: the regime had no rice with which to pay rice stipends and did not wish to buy it in the open market.

Then on 11/12 Katsu reported that even as the bakufu was deploying troops westward, it owed them back pay of nearly 150,000 *ryō*. It was a situation unlikely to stimulate fanatic military commitment. Katsu added, in a somewhat garbled reference to the 9/26 reforms defeudalizing the military levy system, that while the order to lesser liege vassals (*gokenin*) to contribute half their stipends to the regime was theoretically supposed to yield receipts of up to 3 million *ryō*, in fact it had unearthed only 50,000 *ryō*. Even acknowledging that Katsu was neither fully informed nor particularly sympathetic to the Keiō reform, still and all, his figures are doubtless a fair indicator that the bakufu was going into a major confrontation in deplorable financial shape.

As early as 8/7 a pessimistic Katsu had written Shungaku confessing boredom with his job (as *kaigun bugyō* or naval magistrate), displeasure with developments, and disbelief about what he heard. He said that at Edo both money and grain were growing short and rulers and ruled were hard pressed. Reform was difficult, plans nonexistent, the ruler's authority gone. There was, he asserted, need for ''a great change''—the universal term for a restoration of imperial rule—because even if warehouses had been filled, the popular heart was alienated. As for the navy, nothing had changed. There were no plans. Officials were petty. And none was thinking about the post-*sakoku* world.[94]

Katsu's assessment was hardly a balanced one, but it fairly reflected the malaise that beset the regime and the capitulationist tendencies that lay close to the surface of at least one man even during the months of the Keiō reform's success.

THE KEIŌ REFORM IN RETROSPECT

I suggested earlier that the Summer War marked the end of the old era and start of the new. In the fifteen-odd months following that war, many aspects of the new era were revealed in the initiatives of rejuvenated ba-kufu leadership. By the latter part of 1867 it was beyond question that Japan was fully in the stream of contemporary world history and the na-tion's leaders and would-be leaders were determined to guide society's movements along that stream.

While Yoshinobu's maneuvering at Kyoto preserved and even extend-ed Tokugawa pretensions to national authority and perhaps bought time, most of the substantive changes of the Keiō reform occurred at Edo. To say they occurred at Edo is not to say that leaders at Kyoto were not cen-trally involved in them. The evidence indicates quite strongly that many crucial initiatives flowed from those at Kyoto, perhaps from Yoshinobu himself. And at critical junctures careful effort was made, as in late 1866, to be certain that men in the two cities coordinated their actions. The Keiō reform was truly a bakufu effort in a way that no undertaking of the preceding decade had been.

It may be useful to sum up the range and content of the reform. At the center it moved to rationalize the bureaucracy from top to bottom in terms of recruitment, promotion, organization, and reward. It formed an administrative organization that could, when the time came, move to assume direct control of the whole country, and it began to lay the foun-dations for that unification. Steps were taken to strengthen control of existing land and manpower; plans and propositions were developed for extending the Tokugawa writ into the private lands of liege vassals and vassal daimyo. Vast effort was directed toward creating the modern mili-tary forces necessary to the later task of absorbing great daimyo domains. Major enterprises were undertaken to secure the monies necessary to see the program of unification through to completion. And the leaders of the Keiō reform showed a striking readiness to accept and even foster radical new departures in terms of foreign relations, industry, transportation, and matters of culture and social organization. In its entirety the Keiō reform was a revolutionary venture that promised to transform Japan.

As we have seen, however, from first to last the effort encountered an endless stream of obstacles, great and small, that slowed progress severely. In the conclusion to this study, where I assess the reform more fully, I suggest that the effort was quite unlikely to have succeeded even if the great lords had not chosen to rebel at year's end.

Here I would like to return to a tangential point—to argue that the Keiō reform, like the collapse of imperial prestige, contributed to the extreme emphasis Meiji leaders later gave to restoring imperial honor. The severity of the obstacles Edo was encountering in its reform was not fully apparent to the regime's enemies. Rather, they saw it as very successful and as an ominous threat to their own ambitions. Accordingly the Keiō reform presented them with this dilemma: if the rejuvenated bakufu, after all, were going to unify and strengthen Japan, then how could a true national patriot refuse to cooperate with bakufu leaders in their great enterprise? If one opposed them, he could be accused of being moved only by provincial loyalty to his *han*, which was by definition not sufficient to the day, or by personal ambition in disregard of the need for national solidarity, which was by definition an overweening and unworthy posture. To avoid such criticism one had to argue, as Satsuma men argued in Europe, that the bakufu's goal was a selfish one that endangered the dignity of the court, whereas one's own efforts were selflessly devoted to enhancing that imperial dignity. Within months, however, the same men were embarked on policies of radical change very similar to those of the Keiō reform. To avoid being tarred with the same brush of selfishness they had used against the Tokugawa, they had to put maximum ethical distance between themselves and the Keiō reformers. To that end they continued cultivating the imperial myth—thus protesting the generosity of their own motives in contrast to the base designs of the vanquished. To say that their argument was utilitarian is not to say it was insincere; it is more fruitfully seen as a happy convergence of principle and interest.

Part FIVE

THE COLLAPSE

CHAPTER 12

The Crisis
of Late 1867
1867/10-12

THE PUBLIC CONDITION

THE RESTORATION OF 67/10

1. *The Tosa Proposal*
2. *Why Yoshinobu Accepted the Tosa Proposal*
3. *The Restoration Process: 10/12-27*
4. *Tokugawa Resistance to Restoration*
5. *The Outcome of the Tosa Effort: 10/28-11/29*

THE CRISIS OF 67/12

1. *The Kinai I: Retreat to Osaka, 12/1-12*
2. *The Kinai II: Stalemate, 12/13-30*
3. *Edo under Stress*

From its beginning the year 1867 had been a highly unusual one for Japan. The bakufu, the central institution of the old order, had abandoned its classic role as defender of the status quo and become the principal vehicle of that order's destruction. The enterprise was marked by difficulties commensurate with its magnitude, and yet leaders plodded on with their task. The high point of their venture was the reform measures initiated on 67/9/26. Within hours, however, those measures precipitated massive internal resistance and within days they were followed by a major external challenge: the Tosa proposal for an imperial restoration.

That proposal changed completely the tenor of affairs, initiating a new period of political crisis that culminated in destruction of the bakufu and its Keiō reform.

During its months of success the Keiō reform had been facilitated by a degree of social tranquillity unknown in Japan for several years, and that tranquillity persisted right through the reform's final months. During those last hectic months of 1867 the backdrop of popular goodwill contrasted strikingly with the agony convulsing the elite. That tranquillity was of some consequence in the early phase of civil war in 1868 because it helped limit the scope of domestic turmoil and enabled the victors to restore order in central Japan with relative speed and facility. For the bakufu there was not much to choose between the fire of public anger and the ice of public disdain, but for Japan the difference may have been crucial. In the absence of relative public tranquillity the victors might have been quite unable to restore order, and in that case the subsequent history of Japan might have been very different.

THE PUBLIC CONDITION

The latter half of 1866, as we noted before, had been a hectic time for Japan with the man-made disaster of war and heaven-sent disasters of nature joining to wreak havoc upon the land. By the first months of 1867, however, the worst was past, and through most of the year the country was remarkably quiet at all social levels. Reports of daimyo hardship dropped off sharply. The most notable problems afflicted Kaharu (formerly Kokura) *han*, due to defeat in the Summer War, and Kubota in the northeast, which suffered badly from the 1866 crop failure. Some placarding by dissidents continued, but prior to 67/10 the only *rōnin* incidents seem to have been the attacks on foreigners earlier noted and a report in late 67/8 of *rōnin* assembling west of Kyoto. Edo was generally quiet again, except for soldiers' riots after 9/26, and the country at large was almost entirely free of popular disturbances. The highway system was still overburdened, and the bakufu's transportation changes did not solve the problem,[1] but perhaps because armies were back at home where they could keep the peace, the country lay quiet.

The quiet did not deceive bakufu leaders. They knew well enough that the margin to disaster was slender. Indeed, it had been touch and go ever since winter. Thus on 3/20 the finance office ordered twelve vassal *han* in the Kantō to bring over 500 *koku* of rice to Edo, saying it was needed for the city populace. The next month Edo officials tried to ease public discontent by modifying a number of commodity tax rates. In explaining the changes, they observed that although sake production had been slashed by 75 percent, prices had been going up for months and people were impoverished. They referred to the recent unrest of winter, specifically house smashings and robberies in Kōzuke and Shimosuke, and expressed their concern about keeping the peace.[2]

The bakufu's concern to keep the fragile public peace was a factor in the previously mentioned changes in Kantō administration, and it was reflected in further actions taken during 67/9. Specifically, as the new rice crop came in, the regime ordered again a two-thirds reduction in rice allocated for sake production in the Kantō. It canceled, in the name of general hardship, the circuit inspection tour *(junkenshi)* that was supposed to get underway following Yoshinobu's accession as shogun. And it ordered daimyo in central Japan to pay an added tax for further riparian repairs in the region.[3] With good fortune and that sort of attention to matters, the respite of 1867 might be sustained long enough to save the regime from disaster.

During the next three months, 67/10–12, the political struggle between bakufu and great *han* progressed in a highly unusual social environment. The bakufu received almost no reports of popular upheaval or suffering,[4] and the probable reason is not hard to find. For the first time in three years the entire country had a bountiful harvest. Typhoons did not come; the soil was not parched; the earth did not tremble or erupt; frost did not strike. It was as though the gods had tired at last of tormenting the archipelago. Moreover armies were mostly at home where they consumed fewer goods and could keep the peace. Only a few *han* were moving large numbers of troops about, and those movements involved little hardship for the general public. Much travel was by ship. Troops stayed in cities, not in the countryside. And they were supported by their *han*, not by the local populace.

What news the regime did receive of the public condition was a large number of reports of peculiar celebrations in much of central Japan. The reports did not strike the rulers as cause for deep worry but elicited, rather, occasional cautionary admonitions and comments on similar experiences years before.[5]

The first reports were dated late 67/8 and indicated that in Owari *han* religious amulets had suddenly begun to appear. Who was producing or distributing them or why was not clear, but mostly they were slips of paper decorated with Buddhist or assorted godly images or talismanic phrases. Many were associated with the Ise shrine while many others were issued, it appears, by a large number of minor shrines, mostly in Nagoya. During 67/9 and 10 the amulets continued to appear around

Nagoya and gradually spread from there to the Kyoto area and elsewhere. Other reports spoke of people gathering and dancing and traveling freely and cheerfully from village to village. Along with the travelers went a considerable store of political information, both reliable and unreliable. Some amulets celebrated the imperial house, but most were invocations of good fortune, and there was no notable anti-Tokugawa content in the amulets and rhetoric.

By late 67/9 the amulets were appearing as far east as Sumpu and by 67/10 they were turning up in Odawara, clearly moving along the Tōkaidō. During 66/11 they spread up the Tōkaidō into the Kantō as far as Yokohama and Edo. During those weeks they also made their way out from Kyoto on the Nakasendō up into Mino and Shinano provinces, appearing in Matsumoto, Suwa, and eventually Kōfu. Some amulets bore the stamp of Ise shrine; others were from other shrines and temples, sometimes shrines dedicated to deceased emperors. Wherever they appeared, they seem to have elicited rejoicing and celebrations at local shrines and temples.

In the Matsumoto region the harvest disasters of 1865–1866 had been especially cruel. According to the Matsumoto city history, during 1867 people there had been vigorously invoking cooperation of the dieties in their struggle to see the crop through to the granary. As autumn progressed and good weather held and fields ripened down and grueling days of harvest paid off in bulging warehouses and the promise of a secure winter, there seemed ample reason to rejoice and to be grateful for the amulets that had mysteriously appeared at doors throughout villages and towns in the region.[6] Perhaps they did not have anything to do with it; but then again, perhaps they did.

During 67/10 the Kinai region was inundated by amulets, and at month's end there were uproarious celebrations in Kyoto, Osaka, Fushimi, Uji, and elsewhere. Crowds shouting *eejanaika* and other slogans over and over danced and cavorted, their spirits heightened by sake that was again in full supply and distributed with largesse. The celebrations prompted the Kyoto city magistrate on 11/13 to admonish city folk not to engage in any disturbances merely because amulets continued to appear. The magistrate's notice said there were reports of people roaming about and dancing into houses without removing their shoes. That was undesirable because it was irrational and disturbed productive activities. Therefore there was to be no dancing and rambunctious conduct.[7] Frolicking continued, however, perhaps as people paid off debts and then showed the usurers the respect they were thought to deserve. At any rate on 11/16 Kyoto officials gathered again to discuss what to do about it.

There was not much authorities could do, however. The good harvest not only restored the supply of sake but by 67/12 was causing rice prices in the Kinai to fall,[8] and that extraordinary turn of events added to the popular mood. During that month the dancing continued—old and young, men and women, rejoicing in life and setting a splendid contrast to the agonies just then afflicting the ruling elite.

It is inconceivable to me that the public was entirely ignorant of the contemporary imperial restoration activity, and surely news of it contributed to the good humor, if only because it suggested that the old tax collectors and disciplinarians had lost their grip without suggesting that new ones might be worse. Yet it does not appear from the record that public behavior played any active role in the political crisis of year's end. Rather the elite was able to pursue its own quarrels relatively free of worry about mass upheaval, engaging finally in decisive battles at Fushimi-Toba in the first days of 1868. Those battles ended Tokugawa hope for supremacy and led within four months to insurgent conquest of all central Japan. During those four months some angry popular turbulence did appear again, but when it did, it was very unlike the *eejanaika* of late 1867. The revived public disorder of early 1868 thus followed, rather than preceded, the decisive events of Fushimi-Toba. It is better seen as an outgrowth of renewed civil hostilities and disruption than as a lineal extension of *eejanaika* activity, which seems best viewed as a happy celebration of good fortune real and anticipated.[9] And even the angry public turbulence of 1868 was sufficiently limited in scope that victorious insurgents were able to bring it under control with ease, thereby freeing their armies to face the continuing resistance of domains in the northeast and hence carrying their insurrection to a successful conclusion.

THE RESTORATION OF 67/10

In early autumn of 1867 the Tokugawa cause seemed by recent standards to be flourishing. The regime was enjoying the most prosperous and tranquil autumn Japan had had in years. Its leaders at Kyoto still controlled the symbols of authority they had lost temporarily during 1862–1863. Its leaders at Edo continued, despite great obstacles, to forge ahead on their projects of reform and strengthening in the Kantō, thereby laying a more solid foundation for the symbols. And in the process they continued accepting many transformational implications of the regime's fully open foreign policy. The one area of clearly perceived fundamental difficulty was in the realm of finance.

One might argue that continuing defiance by major daimyo was an impediment, but to do so may obscure the changed nature of the *bakumatsu* crisis. In former years when Edo's policy had sought to preserve the *bakuhan* system, daimyo defiance and obstructionism had been a central obstacle. But in undertaking the Keiō reform, the bakufu had committed itself to replacing that system with a centralized state. Whatever its real origins, therefore, great *han* defiance in 1867 was an inevitable by-product of the new Tokugawa venture. The problem for the regime was essentially whether it could destroy the great *han* (by cooptation and gradual undermining, frontal assault, or some combination of strategies) before some of them destroyed it.

From about 1865 some *han* activists and leaders had begun to suspect that Edo had ambitions beyond a mere defense of the status quo. At first the suspicions were not well founded, but the Keiō reform did give them validity, and Yoshinobu's symbolic triumph at Kyoto in mid-1867 turned suspicions into decisions for action. The first overt *han* attempt to contest the bakufu design for a new order was that implemented by Tosa in its 67/10 proposal for an imperial restoration (*ōsei fukkō*). In form the Tosa attempt was a continuation of the preceding months of activity, one last maneuver focusing on the symbols of authority. When it changed nothing, the issue of primacy was addressed at last in the ugly, elemental terms of military power.

1. The Tosa Proposal

From about the time the bakufu outmaneuvered the four *han* in 67/5, groups of men from Tosa and Satsuma began planning countermoves. In following weeks the Tosa plans developed greatly and won support from some leaders of a few other major *han*, notably Fukui. Basically the Tosa ideas were rather like those Shungaku had advocated the previous autumn: to restore authority to the emperor and govern Japan through a coalition of daimyo and their vassals meeting together with court nobles in an assembly functioning under imperial auspices.

During the same period Satsuma planners were developing a considerably more punitive scheme, and they too won support from key leaders in other *han*, notably Hiroshima and Chōshū. Their vision foresaw not simply a Tokugawa surrender of governing authority but also the intentional use of military force to assure that surrender and destroy the very domanial foundation of Tokugawa supremacy as well.

Tosa men explained their plan to Nagai Naomune at Kyoto, apparently during 67/6, before being distracted by the sailor murders in Nagasaki. Then during 67/9 they brought the matter to his attention again. He probably had discussed it with Itakura some weeks earlier, evidently had been advised to follow it up, and instructed the Tosa spokesman on 9/ 20 to present his ideas to Yoshinobu in writing.[10] Accordingly on 10/3 the Tosa proposal was presented to Itakura as an official statement of Yamauchi Yōdō. With it came other verbal and written statements advocating restoration for all the right reasons: reform; unity of court, samurai, and people; development of unparalleled military strength; righteous government by consultation; use of able men; encouragement of learning; protection of the court; and preservation of national independence. When bakufu leaders in Kyoto did not leap at the opportunity to surrender authority, Tosa men began to lobby among court and bakufu officials and even Aizu leaders. They also conveyed the suggestion that Tosa spurned would join hard-line anti-bakufu *han* such as Satsuma, whose concurrent plotting was carefully brought to bakufu attention.[11]

After discussing the matter with Itakura and Nagai, but before those outside Kyoto had time to make their opinions known, Yoshinobu decided to accept the Tosa proposal. Having made his decision, he assembled inspectors and other officials at Kyoto on the twelfth and explained his position in an elegant speech. He observed that the Tokugawa house and many *han* were weak in the face of the foreign menace. A more important point was that the Tokugawa had received and held authority in order to perpetuate the peace. Now he was returning it in order to unify the country and thereby sustain the peace. He observed that many were committed to preserving bakufu authority and some were advocating a forceful policy for that purpose, but the proper reason for their being in Kyoto was to keep the peace. Because some advocated bakufu supremacy, however, people were saying the bakufu was merely talking loyalty and would only pretend the return of authority. In actuality, he asserted, he had tried to surrender shogunal authority a year earlier, but had had to take it anyway. A great change was still necessary, however, and Itakura had agreed on that point. Should the shogunal office disappear, he assured his loyal followers, there would still be an emperor to serve. In closing, after talking more about Japan's changed diplomatic situation, he added, lest the point be forgotten, that there were lords who were refusing to respond to bakufu or even imperial orders. If he were to return authority, however, then they too would cooperate and national unity would be secured.[12] The Tokugawa shogun had voluntarily agreed to turn over to the emperor authority his family had held for 264 years.

2. Why Yoshinobu Accepted the Tosa Proposal

Mindful of our evidence that Edo had been making substantial progress in restoring Tokugawa power and prestige, Yoshinobu's decision of 10/12 commands attention and prompts a query: Why did he make it? The question is complex because the decision had several levels of significance. It affected Yoshinobu's personal role, the role of the Tokugawa house in the national polity, and its role as a domanial entity. The evidence suggests that Yoshinobu was concerned about all three levels of significance, but in differing ways and differing degrees.

Perhaps the whole issue is quite simple. Perhaps the immediate context of the decision was sufficient to override any other possible considerations. Massive troop movements made by Satsuma during 67/9 had been worrisome in themselves, and they appeared all the more dangerous as leaders in Kyoto learned more and more about the Satsuma scheme in early 67/10. On the sixth, moreover, Itakura received a long notice from the daimyo of Hiroshima urging that authority be returned to thc court. The following day Nagai was informed by an Okayama vassal that a Chōshū official was heading for Osaka with armed forces. His trip was explained as a response to the earlier bakufu summons, but the accompanying troops were a different matter, and the report prompted leaders to reinforce the palace guard. In this suddenly deteriorating situation Yoshinobu grew fearful of more assassination attempts. On the eighth he informed Katamori that in view of the recent murder of Hara Ichinoshin, special guards should be placed around Itakura and Nagai lest they be similarly treated.[13] It is perhaps indicative of his mood that he was concerned for the safety of those officials most inclined to conciliate the lords rather than those most committed to bakufu supremacy.

Predictably the city was alive with a host of unnerving rumors, and leaders took them seriously. As Kondō Isami reported it on the ninth, the main rumor spoke not merely of joint Satsuma-Chōshū plotting but also indicated that ''Tosa *rōnin*'' and ''Nakatsugawa *rōnin*'' were involved. Their plans reportedly envisioned armed seizure of Nijō castle, the Shinsengumi barracks, and Katamori's headquarters. The putsch was to occur on 10/15.[14]

Kondō's report clearly disturbed leaders in Kyoto. In a notice of the same day to senior councillors in Edo, Itakura and the deputy Sadaaki emphasized the critical nature of the situation and the severe risk if the Tosa plan were not utilized. As they reported it, the plotters of violence were men from powerful *han*, notably Chōshū, who intended to elicit support with *jōi* rhetoric, foster riots, and set fires in the city to create the chaos necessary for their putsch. Hence, they reported, Yoshinobu was inclined to accept the Tosa proposal, seeing it as the lesser of evils. And they indicated they shared his view.[15]

In succeeding days the rumor world grew steadily darker, with *rōnin* in huge numbers, Chōshū samurai, and others reportedly assembling and the putsch deadline of 10/15 or 16 nearing. Anti-bakufu rumors began to paint a picture of the regime becoming a French tool, with Akitake in France named an officer in the French navy and married to a daughter of Napoleon III and Roches appointed to high bakufu office. In response to the growing tension defenses at Nijō were strengthened, and Katamori ordered further defense preparations and placed more units on alert. [16]

In the face of these menacing developments and absurd reports, the bakufu, as Yoshinobu surely knew, was ill-prepared for a showdown. Its armies were in disarray, the old system having been recently disestab-lished, the new one just starting to develop and already badly scarred by troubles of its own. French army training had only just begun in earnest; the Yokosuka foundry was only partially built. Weapons were still en route, and western-style naval training had been stopped pending arrival of British advisors. The treasury was empty. Foreign loan negotiations had fallen through. The trading companies at Osaka and Edo had not yet gotten their monies into circulation. It was clearly no time for war, and the Tosa proposal, which closely paralleled Shungaku's *kōbugattai* ideas, may have appeared acceptable as a way to buy time precisely because ex-perience had shown that such a scheme would not succeed.

Thus it may well be that Yoshinobu saw himself facing an exceptional immediate problem and buying time, expecting matters later to revert to ''normal.'' Meanwhile the Keiō reform would continue forging ahead. But even if Yoshinobu hoped the Tosa venture would lead nowhere, he could not assume that outcome. In terms of the three levels of significance—pertaining to his personal role, the Tokugawa domanial role, and the Tokugawa national role—one can see enough consistency in Yoshinobu's acceptance of the Tosa proposal and his earlier and later con-duct to make the decision rationally understandable as more than just an act of panic or opportunism.

In terms of his own position, there is plenty of evidence that he was not consistently eager to govern. In the late 1850s he had waxed hot and cold on the prospect of becoming shogunal heir. After the Hyōgo crisis in 65/10 he had refused to accept any shogunal authority. From the time of Iemochi's death he had displayed great reluctance to assume responsibili-ty for affairs of state, and in the end he willingly gave up the burdens of national office.

In terms of the Tokugawa domanial position, the Tosa proposal seemed to constitute no threat. Rather, it seemed to be a way to avoid the threat stemming from the contemporary Satsuma scheme. That Yo-shinobu was concerned to preserve Tokugawa domanial strength was evident in the Keiō reform. It was demonstrated again at year's end when his refusal to surrender territory to the Satsuma insurgents forced the issue of domestic primacy onto the field of battle.

It is in explaining Yoshinobu's perception of the proper Tokugawa role in the national polity that one encounters the greatest difficulty, probably because his perception of it was vague and confused. He knew what the old role was, but not a feasible new one. Time after time he had demonstrated clearly by word and deed that he wished to keep daimyo under control and at a level inferior to the Tokugawa. His handling of the Tosa restoration proposal suggests that he believed he could do so within its framework. But just how he expected Tokugawa superiority to be preserved is not clear. Perhaps he accepted the Tosa proposal in the belief (or hope) it would assure court support for him, which would in turn guarantee Tokugawa well-being. That view implies that Yoshinobu rather naively saw the symbol as basic to the substance of power and believed Tokugawa interests depended most fundamentally on retention of close ties to the court. His conduct during the preceding years certainly supports that proposition, and in the final crisis at year's end he was to show a concern for imperial goodwill that in retrospect seems grotesquely ill-proportioned.

Perhaps, however, he saw the court-Tokugawa-daimyo relationship in more complex terms. It is surely beyond doubt that he was the classic intellectual in politics, readily seeing the present in the sweeping context of history.[17] Accordingly Yoshinobu's acceptance of the Tosa proposal may have reflected a sophisticated vision of government in which the flourishing of the Tokugawa was inextricably tied to the flourishing of the court, thence the warrior estate, and thence the whole polity and society.[18] In this grand context the apparent conflict between exclusivistic and inclusivistic strategies could easily disappear, buried in a larger unity embracing the reform visions of both men such as Ikeda Chōhatsu, Asano Ujisuke, Oguri Tadamasa, and Kurimoto Kon and men such as Matsudaira Shungaku and Katsu Kaishū. In the combined ideal the modernized Tokugawa power would join and guide *han* power to sustain formal court primacy and benefit the nation even while in fact assuring Tokugawa interests and even Tokugawa primacy. This great ideal, which found overt expression in the ''court-bakufu unity'' version of *kōbugattai*, may well have been what Yoshinobu truly sought. Certainly it was an ideal he had advocated often enough. In practice, however, the idea was almost surely unworkable. While it might have met the needs of ''Japan,'' it did not accommodate the ambitions of many politicized individuals nor the immediate needs of many interest groups. But it could still have been Yoshinobu's vision.

One can argue that his role in the Keiō reform was minor and distant and that he did not necessarily grasp the reform's real implications. One can also argue that the late 1866 and mid-1867 political outcomes in which he had triumphed at the expense of great lords were not what he really hoped for and that his eventual defiance of the court on Hyōgo was an agonizing act of necessity, not one of indifference. Then one can reasonably view his actions over the preceding year and his explanations and actions during 67/10 as an attempt to achieve that relatively conservative *kōbugattai* type of unification in which exclusive Tokugawa authority in national affairs could willingly be surrendered to the court without necessarily jeopardizing either *han* autonomy or Tokugawa preponderance.

The most substantial evidence that Yoshinobu adhered to some such larger vision is the people he chose to keep around himself. Although he employed the able and vigorous advocates of exclusivistic reform such as Kurimoto, Oguri, Asano, Ikeda, Tsukahara Masayoshi, and Kawakatsu Kōun, and gave high office to such forceful Tokugawa supporters as Ogyū Noritaka, Inaba Masami, and Ogasawara Nagamichi, he chose for close advisors those most inclined to the old Abe Masahiro inclusivistic orientation. In the decision of 67/10/12 it was their advice he had access to, and it may well be that in that instance their advice was more significant than any predisposition of Yoshinobu himself.

The most important of his advisors was Itakura, whose career had begun under Abe, who had been cashiered by Ii, who had retained the goodwill of Shungaku, and who enjoyed a reputation for probity and reasonableness that attached to few senior councillors during the 1860s. Then there was Nagai Naomune, one of the most experienced of officials, having been in responsible office almost continuously from the days of Perry. He had consistently favored an inclusivistic policy, enjoyed the high regard of Shungaku, and had even gained the respect of outside *han* vassals such as those of Tosa who confided in him during 1867. In 67/2 he had been promoted to acting junior councillor (*wakadoshiyori kaku*); by summer and autumn he was playing an important role in affairs, for example in obtaining the court's decision of 5/24.[19] Another key official was inspector general Togawa Hanzaburō. He had been with Nagai at Hiroshima during Yoshikatsu's settlement of the first Chōshū expedition, had resigned office with him in the turmoil of early 1865, and had been reappointed inspector on the same day Nagai returned to office in the personnel shake-up of 65/10. He had been promoted to inspector general just after Iemochi's death and in 66/9 had been attached to Yoshinobu's retinue and continued to work at his side thereafter. On occasion he helped in negotiating with great lords, presumably because he was relatively effective at it. It was with these three men in particular that Yoshinobu discussed affairs during 1867, especially after Ogasawara and Inaba Masakuni returned to Edo and Hara Ichinoshin was murdered.

The advocates of exclusivistic reform were noteworthy for their absence. The protector Katamori of Aizu and his brother the deputy Sadaaki of Kuwana were in Kyoto, but they apparently acquiesced, impressed with the dangers of the situation.[20] The other voices of forceful Tokugawa leadership were in Edo, too far away to influence affairs. Army minister Ogyū and navy minister Inaba Masami, foreign minister Ogasawara, home minister Inaba Masakuni, and finance minister Matsui Yasunao were all there handling one thing or another. Most of the forceful lesser officials were either there pursuing affairs or off to France, Nagasaki, or elsewhere on particular assignments.

This situation indicates the extent to which the bakufu had been quietly shifting itself back to Edo as part of the larger program of reconstruction. As a consequence of that shift, when the Tosa proposal was received it had to be handled by head of state Yoshinobu and the skeleton crew of officials with him. That crew did not include major advocates of exclusivistic renewal, and it was exposed to the concessive influences ever present in Kyoto. Officials at Edo simply were not consulted, perhaps because of the time factor, but more likely because their response was predictable. On matters of that sort the posture of Edo was always known; it had not changed a bit in years. If asked, of course Edo would have opposed the Tosa proposal.

In sum, then, given the very worrisome context, Yoshinobu's ambiguity of purpose, his ambivalence about governing, the relatively concessive orientation of those about him, the absence of forceful countervailing pressure, the limited objectives of the Tosa proposal, and the very real likelihood that it would peter out in any case as its predecessors had done —given all these considerations, Yoshinobu's decision was not so surprising after all.

3. The Restoration Process: 10/12–27

Yoshinobu's concern to escape the burdens of public office while preserving the base of Tokugawa power was apparent in his handling of the restoration.[21]

Having informed Tokugawa officials in Kyoto of his decision on 10/12, Yoshinobu had Itakura assemble men from some forty han and explain the decision to them the next day. Then on the fourteenth he submitted to the court a written request that it take back authority, and the request was delivered despite an apparent effort by a vassal of Kuwana or perhaps Kii to prevent it. On the following day his request was accepted in a formal court audience. The court stated that major matters such as foreign affairs were to be settled in deliberation with assembled daimyo, but until the new system was functioning, the Tokugawa should administer ''the domains and cities'' *(shihaichi shichū)* as in the past. [22]

On the next day, 10/16, those liege vassals in Kyoto were assembled at Nijō castle and informed of the restoration. On the same day Itakura and Sadaaki wrote the senior councillors at Edo, explaining the dire conditions that compelled the action. They instructed their colleagues to notify foreign diplomats and the bakufu delegates in France of the restoration and to postpone Tsukahara's planned mission to England and Hirayama Keichū's mission to Korea. [23]

Bakufu leaders in Kyoto sensed in the court's response of the day before a clear suggestion that after the assembly system began to function the Tokugawa house might be ordered to cease administering its domain. That was not at all what they intended by ''restoration,'' and therefore on the seventeenth Yoshinobu asked the court for clarification of some phrases. He inquired directly whether its reference to ''the domains'' meant the Tokugawa domain proper or those lands in Yamashiro and elsewhere that were assigned to the court. Much to Yoshinobu's satisfaction the court's reply two days later indicated it had only meant the imperial territories.

In his inquiry of the seventeenth Yoshinobu also warned that certain diplomatic matters could not necessarily be delayed until daimyo reached Kyoto. To handle such matters, he suggested the court simply assemble the lords and vassals in town. In its reply of 10/19 the court failed really to address the issue, simply reiterating its earlier statement that major matters await the lords' assembly—a formulation nearly identical to one made a year earlier when Shungaku's *kōbugattai* effort was also stalled awaiting daimyo cooperation. On the next day, however, the court put to some daimyo representatives in town a series of questions on implementing the restoration. After getting their responses, it instructed Yoshinobu on the twenty-second to handle matters as of old until the lords had assembled, and specifically to consult with two or three lords on foreign affairs. [24]

That order was not what Yoshinobu wanted. Indeed it was just about the worst of possibilities, leaving him to take the blame for all that might go wrong without even the implicit court commitment to bakufu decisions inherent in the earlier imperial orders of 1863, 1864, and 1865 that reaffirmed or restored authority to the shogun. Accordingly, he continued to seek imperial approval of all actions relating to foreign affairs.

Nor was foreign policy the only issue on which Yoshinobu wished to avoid political embarrassment. On the twenty-fourth he tried to avoid another pitfall by asking the court for instructions on Chōshū. He pointed out that a representative of that *han* had been summoned to the Kinai, but those instructions now seemed imappropriate since major issues were to be dealt with only after daimyo had assembled. Finally on 11/9 the court instructed him to have the Chōshū representative delay his trip to Osaka, and the bakufu promptly instructed Hiroshima to relay the order westward.²⁵ The maneuver presumably would assure that the court, not the bakufu, was the recognized fount of policy toward Chōshū and that if Chōshū men came to the Kinai, they would be doing so in defiance of a court order and not pursuant to any earlier bakufu order. It was a legal posture that might later be helpful.

By the twenty-fourth Yoshinobu was sufficiently displeased with his situation that even as he solicited guidance on the Chōshū matter, he was adopting a stronger stance. On the same day he sent Sadaaki to court with his resignation as shogun. To that the court simply replied two days later that after the lords had assembled, there would be further orders, but until then he was to handle matters as of old. That response was not satisfactory either, and Yoshinobu decided to announce his resignation publicly and formally. On the following day, 10/27, representatives of the *han* assembled at Nijō castle as previously instructed by bakufu leaders, and Togawa presented them copies of Yoshinobu's resignation statement together with the court's response.²⁶ Yoshinobu did not recant his resignation and did not formally accept the court's reply. Rather, his actions made it clear he was serving under protest. Blame for the deadlock and for anything that might go wrong would lie not with himself but with the court and uncooperative daimyo whose refusal to come to Kyoto delayed the restoration. With that action the Tosa proposal entered a state of limbo where it persisted for a full month until a new initiative displaced it.

4. Tokugawa Resistance to Restoration

The Tosa proposal had thus petered out even more quickly than the several earlier *kōbugattai* maneuvers. Despite that outcome, however, and despite the arguments Yoshinobu used in his original acceptance of it, bakufu leaders at Kyoto must have known their policy would elicit intense opposition from Tokugawa vassals. Indeed the nine-day delay between Yoshinobu's receipt of the plan and his acceptance of it may have sprung largely from concern about vassal reaction. His interest in assuring the security of Itakura and Nagai suggests that. And in his address to officials at Nijō on the twelfth he betrayed a keen awareness of potential resistance. Kyoto leaders' care to keep Edo fully informed of developments also suggests a high degree of concern about it.

To elaborate that last point, on 10/9 when Itakura and Sadaaki sent Edo a report on the Tosa plan, they took pains to stress anti-bakufu plotting and dangers in the situation. Then on the twelfth the two informed Inaba Masakuni and Masami of Yoshinobu's acceptance and of his wish that a senior councillor, one or two junior councillors, and representatives of the military and finance staffs come to Kyoto. Again they emphasized the menacing character of developments, insisted on the propriety of acceptance, and admonished their colleagues to be certain that all at Edo approved and continued serving loyally. Four days later the two wrote Edo yet again, reporting developments and again stressing the turmoil, the necessity of using the Tosa plan, and the importance of assuring that liege vassals be correctly informed about the situation.[27]

These attempts to keep Edo informed did not close the communication gap, however. The crisis was taking place in the Kinai, far enough from Edo that most officials had only a modest appreciation of its context and no satisfactory way to influence it. Uncertain of what was happening or what they should do and unable to know what the outcome would be, officials had to predicate their conduct on the assumption that the familiar world was not about to end. One consequence was that routines of government and programs of the Keiō reform continued at Edo, right through the crisis of 67/10, interregnum of 67/11, and crisis of 67/12, ending only when Edo learned of hostilities at Fushimi-Toba.

Alongside this continuing routine, however, was intense dismay and frenetic political activity. One reason for the dismay was that after a year of careful coordination between Kantō and Kinai, Yoshinobu had acted alone. And he had done so on a momentous matter. His action cracked the bakufu wide open, reviving the intense distrust and internal quarreling that had been so successfully overcome for an entire year. At Edo that process began on the evening of 10/16 with the arrival of Hirayama Keichū and an inspector, who had been ordered east on the twelfth with Itakura's second message. For the first time Edo leaders heard from authoritative sources full details of the Kinai situation.

On the next day key officials were assembled at Chiyoda castle to discuss matters. Ogyū Noritaka was reportedly ill, and he and Matsui Yasunao did not attend, but Inaba Masakuni, Ogasawara, most junior councillors, and the principal magistrates *(san bugyō)* were there.[28] According to Inaba's record of the session two general proposals were developed.[29] One identified the enemy as Satsuma, Tosa, Chōshū, Hiroshima, and any others who might be disobedient. It called for bakufu forces to go directly to Kyoto, open hostilities, drive the enemy back to their *han*, and destroy them. The other proposal called for the bakufu to acquiesce nominally in the ''impractical theory'' of *ōsei fukko*, withdraw the shogun to the east, and devote energies to pacifying the Kantō and establishing there a secure domain.

In Inaba's view both proposals were unsatisfactory. The bakufu's unprepared military forces could not achieve the former, he argued, and the latter was poor because it would invite charges of selfishness, which he felt must be avoided. Rather, he argued, the Tosa plan should be accepted and Yoshinobu should take the position of imperial regent *(sesshō* or *kanpaku)* and preside over a bicameral assembly at Kyoto. Then Edo castle would be assigned to a deputy *(jōdai)* and liege vassals would resettle in Kyoto, by their numbers establishing a preponderant role at court and thereby preventing trouble by *rōnin* or agitators from the *han*. In effect Inaba would preserve Tokugawa interests by incorporating the daimyo in a new order whose overwhelming element would be loyal Tokugawa supporters. He found distasteful the idea of a return east, but in closing he argued that if the court refused his proposal, then the shogun should request permission to return east; and if that too were refused, he should resign his national duties and return east anyway. Then, presumably, the second proposal would be implemented.

The following day Ogyū prepared a long statement that reflected his extensive involvement with military reform. He suggested reasons why an imperial restoration might have to be accepted but argued that actual government by the court was inconceivable. Rather, a political structure should be established with a bicameral assembly system, which he discussed in detail. To assure it a strong popular base, he recommended abolition of the traditional four-caste system of samurai, peasants, artisans, and merchants. He urged formation of a national military force supported by taxes drawn equitably from all domains, temples, and merchants. In this new order the head of the Tokugawa house should become head of the upper house of the national assembly and should also be commander in chief of the national military organization.[30]

These views of the two senior councillors appear to have been about the most creative and conciliatory ones expressed. Oguri Tadamasa reportedly spoke stoutly in defense of the shogun's existing authority.[31] Individual views of others are not recorded, but the policy decisions that emerged were decidedly more militant than those implied in the councillors' positions. On 10/19 Inaba Masakuni issued orders for a battalion of *sappei*, a battalion of regular infantry *(hohei)*, a large company of mixed liege vassals (*yūgekitai*), a battery of artillery, and a cavalry force to head for Kyoto at once. Other commanders were also sent west, some to Kyoto, others to Osaka. And a higher-ranking commander was instructed to assure that troops in western-style uniforms, which were anathema to Kyoto, were kept out of sight.[32] On the next day patrol forces at Edo were put on 24-hour duty, and several more units of *hohei*, *okuzume jūtai*, and *yūgekitai* were committed to patrol.[33]

In succeeding days the forces going west were mobilized and moved out, and decisions were made as to which officials would go to Kyoto. Daimyo in Edo were informed of developments, advised to make military preparations, but firmly admonished to stay in line. Officials realized that they needed vassal daimyo support, but they also knew that vassal *han* forces were not very competent. Accordingly on the twenty-second they announced that another six thousand infantrymen (*hohei*) were to be recruited. Army and navy ministers Ogyū Noritaka and Inaba Masami, together with some subordinates and part of their military force, left for the Kinai on the twenty-fourth on the warship *Jundōmaru*. Other officials left in succeeding days by sea and by land, taking more infantry, cavalry, and artillery units with them. Some angry liege vassals apparently departed of their own volition. On 10/30 Ogyū and Inaba reached Kyoto.[34]

Even before the Edo contingent arrived, the situation at Kyoto had also become tense. From the outset some officials, such as Hirayama, had been dismayed by Yoshinobu's decision. By the middle of the month pro-bakufu placards were appearing, and the city was buzzing with rumors of pro-bakufu plots. In one of these, men of Ōgaki and other *han* were reportedly plotting to burn the Satsuma mansion and whisk the imperial carriage off to Osaka castle.[35]

These tensions reflected another aspect of the Kyoto situation—namely, the split between bakufu leaders and followers. Katamori cooperated with Yoshinobu from the first, perhaps because he found the Tosa logic persuasive. It did after all accord with his own *sonnō* sentiments, and it could be said to fit his anti-Satsuma-Chōshū orientation. Or perhaps he cooperated simply because the emotional tension between himself and others earlier in the year had been unacceptably severe and so he chose docility. Whatever the case, his vassals were less cooperative. Indeed men of Aizu and Kuwana were most commonly considered the key pro-bakufu plotters, and Yoshinobu and others feared an outburst by them. Yoshinobu reportedly suggested reducing Aizu, Kuwana, and even bakufu forces in Kyoto to avoid trouble, only dropping the idea after being so advised by Itakura. The Kyoto populace was also much agitated by rumors of pro-bakufu plotting, as were some anti-bakufu activists who appreciated the damage to their cause that angry Aizu-Kuwana men could do.[36]

Thus, however well founded Yoshinobu's reasons for accepting the Tosa proposal, it was apparent even during 67/10 that Tokugawa supporters in neither city were prepared to accept the restoration gracefully. In following days Yoshinobu was able to keep officialdom under control, but not his vassal bands in general.

Looking first at officialdom, after Ogyū, Inaba, and others reached Kyoto on 10/30, they met Yoshinobu and discussed the situation. Apparently Ogyū, Inaba, and junior councillors Kawakatsu Kōun and Nagai Naokoto were relatively restrained even if openly displeased with developments. However, accompanying inspectorate officials argued vigorously that the shogun should go east.[37] Yoshinobu nonetheless defended his action. Supported by Itakura and Nagai Naomune, he stood his ground and on 11/10 ordered the four councillors to return the following day and mollify officials at Edo. He gave them a statement in which he admitted making the restoration decision arbitrarily and said he appreciated the loyal concern prompting them to urge his return east. He acknowledged also that affairs in the Kantō were very disturbed and that he should return to restore order. He insisted, however, that he was very busy with crucial tasks and argued that if the restoration effort succeeded, the country would be unified under the crown and able to withstand foreign dangers. Until his return, he said in closing, he wished his vassals to continue serving loyally on behalf of Ieyasu's memory (Tōshōgū).[38] Equipped with that message and a set of practical instructions from Itakura, the officials left as ordered and reached Edo on the seventeenth. On the next day Ogyū, who a month earlier had complained of ill health and the costs of office, and who was frustrated by the difficulty of military reform, ''became ill'' and ceased to play an active role in affairs, perhaps because he could guess what was in store.[39]

In the meantime leaders at Edo were continuing with great reluctance to act as though the restoration had indeed been achieved. From about 10/19 Ogasawara began informing foreign diplomats of the gist of developments while minimizing their seriousness.[40] Then on 11/9 councillors at Edo notified the foreigners more fully and formally of the event. They explained how bakufu authority had weakened after Perry's arrival and how in consequence it had been restored to the emperor, but they asserted that diplomatic relations would not be hurt as a result.[41] Despite that statement Edo leaders were not throwing in the towel. On 11/1, as we noted earlier, they made French military training compulsory for unemployed liege vassals and gave them only eight days in which to enroll.

Then on the third and fourth Inaba Masakuni informed assembled vassal daimyo that they must adopt western-style rifles for their *han* forces, reminding them that in both the Chōshū war and the Kantō insurrection the superiority of those arms had been demonstrated.[42] Officialdom, in short, would cooperate, but it was doing so on the assumption that Tokugawa well-being was not about to be sacrificed.

Many vassal and related daimyo and their advisors were considerably less responsive to the shogun. In 67/10 they indicated their ethical dilemma: Were they as daimyo to obey court orders, or were they as Tokugawa vassals and relatives to obey the head of their house?[43] During 67/11, as I have pointed out elsewhere, the vassal daimyo gave an answer that was both resounding and roundly at odds with Yoshinobu's overall enterprise. Singly and in groups they said they were Tokugawa vassals before they were daimyo and therefore would obey no orders except those coming directly from their lord, Yoshinobu.[44] Among related houses, Kii was the most actively opposed to the Tosa initiative. On 11/3 Mochitsugu and some of his vassals met officials of Owari, Mito, and several other *han* at his mansion in Edo. In that discussion and succeeding communications the men of Kii betrayed great frustration that their lord had no influence because of the way matters were being decided. To improve the situation, they proposed that the group work out a unified position, go with it to Kyoto, and thereby resolve the disastrous split that had developed between Kyoto and Edo leaders. Of the assembled delegates from related *han*, it was reported that only the man from Fukui disapproved the proposal.[45]

Among lesser Tokugawa vassals in Kyoto there was also evidence of a slowly crystallizing opposition to the great daimyo challenge. On 11/11 Kondō Isami wrote a friend in Edo that men there should hasten to Kyoto and, with a zealous resolve to die for their lord, smash the opposing daimyo and nobles and thereby restore Tokugawa fortunes. For such a swift action to succeed, however, it must be done within a month or so. Four days later Shibusawa Kisaku said he had been urging Owari and other related *han* to take the lead in a concerted military action designed to restore Tokugawa authority. Neither Nagai Naomune nor men of Owari accepted his view, but Aizu men reportedly favored it.[46]

Thus in 1867, as in 1866, the scheme to surrender Tokugawa prerogatives encountered opposition among the rank and file. The opposition was much more widespread in 1867 than a year earlier because the formal surrender of authority actually was made. However, whereas pro-Tokugawa opinion had played a crucial role in thwarting Shungaku's venture because it emanated from the center of officialdom, in 1867 it had little effect because Yoshinobu kept control of those who could turn opinion into policy. Rather, Tokugawa displeasure seems to have helped confound the Tosa venture only insofar as wholesale vassal daimyo defiance was part of a general daimyo resistance that wrecked the Tosa venture. However, that outcome then permitted a Satsuma initiative to come to the fore in 67/12, and in a final irony the Tokugawa sentiments that had appeared in response to the Tosa proposal eventually played a key role in shaping the outcome of the Satsuma initiative.

5. The Outcome of the Tosa Effort: 10/28–11/29

For one reason or another practically all daimyo refused to cooperate with the Tosa leaders, even though daimyo seemed to be the primary beneficiaries of their scheme. That alone was enough to wreck the project, but in addition the small group of Satsuma-led anti-bakufu plotters that had been planning armed revolt since midyear was only spurred to greater effort by the restoration maneuver. Their decision to act cut short the stalled Tosa effort in early 67/12.

During the last days of 67/10 and through the following month daimyo replies to the court's order for their assembly came in. The overwhelming majority of them—outside, related, and vassal—were regretfully ill. Even during 67/12 replies continued to arrive, and their tenor was the same. Some were ill and asked to delay their trip. Others were ill and would send a substitute. Some were too young. Some gave no reason. Perhaps the most appealing reply was that of the minor outside lord of Naeki in Mino province, who regretfully reported on 12/8 that though he had recovered from the illness he reported previously, he must again delay his trip because his mother had died a few days earlier.[47] Just as in 1866, this general daimyo skepticism was the critical factor in the *kōbugattai* failure. In the end the daimyo response was somewhat better than before, if only because so many more were invited. By mid-67/11 sixteen daimyo had come to the city, but by then the Tosa initiative had stalled.

Looking at other factors, we noted earlier that Tokugawa opposition was not an effective obstacle to the Tosa effort. Similarly tensions within the court were much less important than a year earlier. In part that was because Yoshinobu and his advisors had introduced the proposal to the court themselves and did not urge friendly courtiers to oppose it. In part too it was because the scheme had support from Tosa, Hiroshima, and those Satsuma spokesmen in Kyoto, and so anti-Yoshinobu elements also did not overtly resist it.[48]

As 67/11 passed, however, and supporters of the plan waited for daimyo to appear, other developments in the city worked to poison the atmosphere in a manner very different from the year preceding. Anti-bakufu plotting intensified the mutual suspicions. Leaders at Kyoto were aware of worrisome plots concerning Edo, and on 11/15 guardsmen of the city patrol force (*mimawari*) discovered and killed two influential Tosa men plotting with other radicals. More deadly to the tranquillity of Kyoto than rumors, reports, and incidents was the turning of the gentle old city into an armed camp of unfriendly forces assembled and ready for war.

Earlier in the year there had been some 14,000 *han* troops in the city, of whom about 3000 were from Kaga, 1400 from Satsuma, and the rest from about forty other *han*.[49] In addition various patrol forces of the bakufu were there. From 67/9 the troop figures grew rapidly. During that month Satsuma brought in about a thousand new troops. According to Kumamoto reports, they brought the total Satsuma presence in the Kinai region to 4100 men, of whom 1900 were swordsmen (*shi*) and 2200 *ashigaru* or other foot soldiers. Then during 67/10, some 436 Hiroshima troops entered the city. Over 500 Tosa men also arrived, and a large shipment of rifles, perhaps as many as a thousand, was reportedly brought in to Tosa forces in the area. Then early in 67/11 several hundred more bakufu troops reached the city, and more would have come had officials from Kyoto not met them en route and turned them back to Edo. On the third a battalion (some 500 men probably) of Kii troops entered the city, and early in the month Hirosaki sent some artillerymen and other troops totaling about 150. Ii of Hikone arrived on the eighth with a force reported, perhaps in exaggeration, at 3000 men. On the twenty-first, Itakura received from Aizu a request to borrow 500 Mini rifles, and the bakufu responded favorably. Two days later another force of 1500 Satsuma troops arrived, of whom 200 were swordsmen and 853 foot soldiers. And on the twenty-eighth the Hiroshima heir reached the city with some 300 to 400 more troops.[50]

While these forces and armaments were actually pouring into Kyoto, the world of rumor was conjuring up thousands and tens of thousands more poised for descent upon the city. By 11/29, moreover, Chōshū troops numbering about 700 in combat units plus 250 other personnel were actually on board ship offshore near Nishinomiya.[51] Their arrival unleashed another rash of unnerving rumors about impending invasion. By month's end, then, upward of 8000 to 10,000 more troops had joined the nearly 14,000 already there, and the environment had been considerably changed by introduction of all that war-making potential and the rumors that accompanied it.

Far to the west in Nagasaki there also was evidence of the extent to which leaders were anticipating a military solution to the political stalemate.[52] For years there had been a modest trade in foreign weapons

there, mostly by Glover of Jardine Matheson. During 67/10–11, however, the business turned into a boom, with Saga, Kumamoto, Uwajima,
Satsuma, Fukuoka, Hiroshima, and other *han* buying hundreds of weapons apiece as well as cannon and powder. The most popular weapons
were Enfields modified to Mini-style, both long infantry weapons and
short carbines for cavalry use. But sales were also made of other Mini
weapons and a very few breech-loading Spencer, Sharps, and Snider
rifles, the last being Enfields further modified for horizontal breech-
loading.

During 67/12 the gunrunning trade continued to flourish. Kaga
ordered or secured 1020 Enfields, about half long rifles and half carbines.
Hiroshima ordered or obtained 560 rifles, of which 500 were for infantry. Saga ordered or obtained 800, of which 500 were Enfields. Nobeoka ordered or obtained 750, mostly Enfields. Satsuma ordered 780, of
which 100 were Sniders. It was an expensive business, with prices ranging from 9 to 30 *ryō* apiece, depending upon the style. The repeaters
were by far the most expensive—Mini, 9 *ryō*; Enfield, 17; Snider, 26;
Sharps, 30. Whereas the munitions trade at Nagasaki had been worth
some $304,000 in 1866, in 1867 the figure was $1,400,000.[53] Insurrection and civil war in Japan were already bringing considerable profit to
western industry. As long as buyers took Enfields and other obsolete
weapons, moreover, peddler countries were not threatened.

In face of this warlike trend, Tosa men, Yoshinobu, and the court
pressed on with their quixotic venture. Supported by Shungaku, who had
skeptically and after much procrastination returned to the city on 11/8,
and by Yoshikatsu, who had arrived ten days earlier, Yoshinobu struggled to hold his subordinates in line, to induce vassal lords to obey the
court, and to get other daimyo to assemble. Meanwhile he and the court
continued trying to implement the venture by working out particulars of
the planned new government. By month's end, however, even Tosa proponents of the plan knew it had failed. When explaining the failure to
Shungaku, they pointed to Satsuma's refusal to cooperate.[54] It was as
good a scapegoat as any on which to blame the failure of a proposal that
probably was unworkable anyway.

THE CRISIS OF 67/12

By the end of 67/11 the political environment in the Kinai area had deteriorated sharply from what it had been earlier in the year. Stagnation of
the Tosa initiative, rumors and unrest, armed maneuvers, and continued
scheming all served to generate a state of tension and worry.

The new month of 67/12 was destined to push that tension to the breaking point, and the new stage of crisis was introduced on the first day of the month. On that day messengers headed up the Yodo river to Kyoto with news that hundreds of Chōshū troops were landing along the coast of Settsu and establishing their beachhead command post at Nishinomiya, only about 15 kilometers from the Tokugawa bastion of Osaka.

1. The Kinai I: Retreat to Osaka, 12/1–12

On 12/2 bakufu leaders at Kyoto received news of the Chōshū arrival and intention of advancing on the city.[55] In the ensuing discussion some officials such as inspector Umezawa Ryō urged a forceful response, but other participants, including Shungaku, advised restraint. It was decided simply to obtain an imperial order diverting the Chōshū men to Osaka until daimyo could assemble to discuss the matter. In the meantime Itakura instructed nearby vassal *han* to strengthen barrier guard units, keep him posted on Chōshū movements, and avoid any trouble.[56]

By obtaining a court order directing the Chōshū men to Osaka, Yoshinobu was doing two things. He was assuring that the court bear full responsibility for major decisions, even while he handled affairs as per the imperial orders of 10/22 and 26. Moreover, he was fitting the Chōshū action into the plan of 67/5 that had summoned a Chōshū delegation to Osaka at imperial behest to settle the outstanding bakufu-Chōshū dispute. On 11/9 the court had ordered the Chōshū delegation to delay its trip, and by treating the new Chōshū arrivals as such a delegation, Yoshinobu could claim that their presence in the Kinai was in defiance of a court order. The decision to send them to Osaka also constituted a simple delay in response and reflected Shungaku's intention of having daimyo finally handle affairs, as the Tosa scheme and his own earlier one had envisaged. Court nobles, fearful of another 1864-type clash in the city, quickly approved the diversionary plan, and on 12/3 Itakura relayed to the keeper of Osaka castle instructions that *han* defense forces allow the Chōshū men to proceed toward that city.

This first procrastinating decision angered some people. Men of Tsu, who manned a crucial defense point midway between Kyoto and Osaka, and who were to play a modest historic role a month later, argued that if Chōshū men insisted on passing, they should be attacked ruthlessly. Aizu-Kuwana leaders, including a newly articulate Katamori, angrily argued at court that the Chōshū force should be ordered home forthwith. To counter that pressure, on the fifth Shungaku complained to Yoshinobu about Katamori's activity and persuaded him to instruct the Aizu leader to cease his unauthorized lobbying at court and abide by its decision.

That instruction was also to be given to Sadaaki and other related daimyo.

Shungaku's voice was particularly influential that day because Yoshinobu's most trusted advisors, Itakura and Nagai, were away. On the previous day they had gone down to Osaka to talk with Harry Parkes about the city's opening, which was scheduled for the seventh. They discovered at once that they were again being trapped in intertwined domestic and foreign pressures. Parkes warned them in their first meeting that the assembling of so many daimyo troops in the Osaka area might lead to complications between Japanese troops and foreigners. Therefore, he reasoned, it was the Japanese who should be withdrawn. On the following day he talked again with Itakura and gave him a menacing letter warning that ''the Japanese government'' would be held responsible for any trouble that might arise.[57] Well aware of the British-Satsuma-Chōshū intimacy, well aware that Parkes no longer considered the bakufu a legitimate regime, and well aware that he would call it ''the Japanese government'' only for the purpose of harassing it, bakufu leaders dared not ignore his threat. On 12/6, after Yoshinobu had silenced Katamori, Itakura reached Kyoto, having left Nagai at Osaka. He explained the diplomatic problem to Yoshinobu, and the Kyoto bakufu at once asked the court's guidance in responding to Parkes' demand. The court offered no guidance, however, and instead promptly passed the buck back to the bakufu. Yoshinobu thus found himself again under threat of conjoint domestic and foreign trouble.

For all Parkes' belligerent harassment, Yoshinobu's domestic troubles were still the worse of the two. After Itakura reached Kyoto, he and his lord had a conference with Yoshikatsu of Owari in which the latter urged them to be lenient with Chōshū and avoid any ''private'' fighting in Kyoto. Also on the sixth Yoshinobu met Nakane Yukie of Fukui, who furnished details of Satsuma's restoration plan. As Yoshinobu recalled it years later, he took the bad news in stride and passed it on to Itakura, who agreed with him they must follow a conciliatory policy and keep the peace.[58]

It was in this all too familiar context of combined domestic and foreign threat and related daimyo pressure for concessions that the few bakufu leaders in Kyoto received late in the day a court inquiry. The court wished to learn bakufu sentiments toward a proposal that both Chōshū and radical courtiers be pardoned for past offenses and Chōshū men admitted again to Kyoto. Yoshinobu, Itakura, unspecified junior councillors, Katamori, and Sadaaki discussed the proposal. Katamori and Sadaaki argued with logical consistency that until daimyo were assembled, no action should be taken. Others apparently disagreed, and no final decision seems to have been made that night. However, early on the next day, the seventh, Yoshinobu sent to court his opinion on both the Chōshū and diplomatic problems. In a brief statement dated 12/6 he said the Chōshū matter should await decision by the assembled lords, though he had no objection to the proposal as set forth by the court. In a separate note he said the foreign issue too should be settled by discussion, and he wished the assembly to meet and do so quickly.[59]

In line with Yoshinobu's wish, the court decided to convene a formal assembly the next day. It would include Yoshinobu and all daimyo or their representatives in town. On the eighth the assembly convened, but Yoshinobu, Sadaaki, and Katamori all refused to go. The men who might have posed an effective block to court extremists were thus absent from the debate that day. Perhaps they stayed away in belief their boycott would prevent a formal decision, or perhaps they did so out of fear their view already had been repudiated.

After an all-day discussion the court decided by evening to ratify the proposal regarding Chōshū that had been communicated to Yoshinobu on the sixth. When informed of that, Yoshinobu again expressed no objection. That night, however, when discussion continued at court, the topic broadened to the larger question of Satsuma's restoration scheme. The participants had by then come to include directly or indirectly the key planners of the Satsuma effort and their sympathizers in Fukui and Nagoya. That enlarged body was unable to form a consensus, and the matter was put off until the next morning. Had Yoshinobu, Sadaaki, and Katamori been participating, the discussion might have gone otherwise. As it was, however, on the morning of 12/9 Iwakura Tomomi and other antibakufu nobles and their Satsuma allies obtained imperial agreement to their scheme, and the larger reassembled group acquiesced. The plan called for removing bakufu, Aizu, and Kuwana forces from Kyoto, replacing them with troops from the *han* involved in the coup, and abolishing the offices of shogun, protector, and deputy. A number of court offices also were to be abolished, thereby removing pro-bakufu officials from the court and putting it in the hands of cooperative nobles.

During the day discussion continued even as prior decisions were being implemented. Iwakura forcefully advocated court acceptance of the brutal heart issue of the Satsuma plan—namely, the order that Tokugawa domains and people be surrendered to the newly dominant forces at court. Despite the opposition of Yamauchi Yōdō, Shungaku, Yoshikatsu, and others, who were perhaps beginning to grasp the implications of Satsuma's ambitions, by evening the court had accepted Iwakura's position. In

two days of hard politicking the most implacable enemies of the Tokugawa house had gained control of the court, committed it to a frontal
assault on Tokugawa power, and still managed to retain more or less the
support of such great *han* as Tosa, Owari, and Fukui. It was a political
achievement of the first magnitude.

Yoshinobu's role in the process was remarkable for its passivity. In
face of sharply escalating danger, he continued to operate in the 67/10
kōbugattai frame of reference, handling issues in terms of ''court-bakufu-
daimyo'' cooperation. His actions revealed clearly his readiness to surrender his own power, his desire to avoid any sort of armed collision, and
even his willingness to disestablish the institutions of formal Tokugawa
hegemony. That very passivity, however, eventually involved a bakufu
refusal to participate in the critical court conference of 12/8–9. And that
refusal permitted the insurgents to escalate their demands step by step
until finally the issue of Tokugawa domain and private power, the issue
on which Yoshinobu seemed unlikely to cooperate, had been brought to
center stage. Whether or not Satsuma had overreached itself remained to
be seen.

While these dramatic developments were taking place, bakufu leaders
in Kyoto were quietly helping the insurgents secure their earlier objectives
peacefully. Both Katamori and Sadaaki were instructed by the bakufu to
resign their Kyoto duties so that Satsuma would be unable to fire them.
On the ninth Itakura informed the court that Yoshinobu had accepted Katamori's resignation ''due to illness,'' and Sadaaki informed the court of
his own resignation ''due to illness.'' Katamori then instructed the old,
the young, and the ladies at his residence to head back to Wakamatsu,
and the court assured them safe passage out of town.[60]

As the day passed, all bakufu forces in the city were called into Nijō
castle, and by evening it was jam-packed with thousands of angry
troops. The stock figures of 5000 bakufu, 3000 Aizu, and 1500 Kuwana men are of little use. Later deployment figures indicate that Kuwana
probably had about 400 troops and Aizu about 1600. Bakufu forces are
difficult to estimate but may have numbered two or three thousand.
There were also other troops in the castle: men of Ōgaki and Tsu and
probably Obama, Zeze, Matsuyama, and Mito.[61] For three hectic days
this army was confined to the little castle. Anger was openly expressed,
frustration was intense, but remarkably the men did not erupt in a mind-
less attack on either their enemies in the city or one another in the castle.

On the tenth, Yoshinobu was told that the court had decided to order
him to resign as shogun and surrender some 2 million *koku* of Tokugawa
lands. Yoshinobu asked the imperial messengers, Shungaku and Yoshika-

tsu, to tell the court he was agreeable to the resignation demand but wished to delay reply until the turmoil was past. That night or the next day Itakura formally announced Yoshinobu's resignation as shogun. The sole issue that remained was the critical one of Tokugawa lands.[62]

While that exchange between castle and palace was proceeding, intense discussions were also going on within the castle.[63] On the tenth an Aizu vassal proposed to junior councillor Ōkōchi Masatada that the best policy would be to retreat to Osaka, regroup, and launch a massive punitive expedition. Next best would be to return to Edo, gather troops, enlist daimyo support, and then commence a drive westward. The worst policy would be to throw down the gauntlet within Kyoto. It was a view that compromised Aizu concern for imperial sensibilities and Aizu conviction that decisive action must be taken. Ōkōchi, who was less troubled about imperial comfort, replied that with each step of retreat the enemy would advance a step and that a return east would wreck the morale of bakufu troops. The following day discussion resumed, the participants including Takenaka Shigemoto, other bakufu military commanders, and some Kuwana and Aizu men. The Aizu men still wished to retreat to Osaka and strike from there, and Ōkōchi reiterated his conviction that a fast assault was essential. Takenaka and others expressed concern that fighting might well involve the imperial palace, but Yoshinobu, who was present, left the issue unresolved. Later Takenaka stridently told Itakura that the Satsuma mansion must be attacked quickly, despite Yoshinobu's vacillation (and evidently despite danger to the palace), but Itakura also declined to respond.

Yoshinobu thus found himself presented in effect with two military strategies: immediate attack or regrouping in Osaka. In the course of the day he finally chose the one that showed greater solicitude for court welfare, offered greater opportunity for maneuver, and presented less risk of immediate confrontation. In line with the Aizu view he decided to withdraw to Osaka. Accordingly he proposed to Shungaku, who had come again as court delegate, that he be allowed to withdraw to avoid trouble. On the following day, the twelfth, that proposal was presented to court by Shungaku and Yoshikatsu with the argument that when the army had been quieted, Yoshinobu would return to Kyoto to complete terms of capitulation. The court agreed and so the way was clear for a peaceful Tokugawa departure from the city.

The ambiguity of purpose implicit in withdrawal to Osaka was evident in other policy decisions. On the eleventh Itakura sent a secret message to the five senior councillors in Edo. In it he said very quickly that the situation was incredible, that it was hard to tell how soon fighting would erupt, but that he wished reinforcements as quickly as possible. He asked for four battalions of infantry, two troops *(shōtai)* of cavalry, two batteries of artillery, and any available warships.[64] Also on the eleventh the court ordered Yoshinobu to send Katamori and Sadaaki back to their *han*, and on the twelfth he dutifully issued a brief order to that effect. At the same time, however, he also summoned an Aizu official, told him he had decided to go to Osaka, and said Katamori was to go too. Thus he nominally accommodated the court but retained Aizu's military presence intact. By these several measures Yoshinobu and Itakura escaped their cul de sac and kept their options open, for whatever purpose, if any, they had in mind.

After Yoshinobu spoke to the Aizu official, he had an extremely tense meeting with Katamori, Sadaaki, and several Aizu and bakufu commanders. Aizu turned out to be deeply divided on the question of withdrawal to Osaka, and so those bakufu commanders who wished immediately to counterattack found their position greatly strengthened. However, Yoshinobu argued with rare heat the importance of moving that night. After demanding obedience, he indicated somewhat obscurely that from Osaka he would deal with the insurgents.[65] Those exertions restored his control and enabled him to proceed with his planned retreat.

As the day progressed, leaders in the castle dismantled the bakufu political apparatus in Kyoto, assigning to other positions the Kyoto city magistrate, *kinrizuki*, *mimawari*, and other administrative, guard, and attendant personnel. Then they quickly designated a group of officials and troops to stay at Nijō castle. Junior councillor Nagai Naomune, who had returned from Osaka on the eighth, was left to handle political contacts. Kondō Isami, who insisted on the need to retain the castle, was left with some Shinsengumi men. A few bakufu troops may have remained, and some Mito officials with about three hundred men were left as the main guard force.

With those actions taken, the retreat began. At about 6 or 7 PM the back gate was opened and one after another military units filed out and headed away, following their leaders south through Toba, past Yodo castle, by Hashimoto, and into Osaka late the following day.[66] Yoshinobu had again gained time. What he intended to do with it was a mystery.

2. *The Kinai II: Stalemate, 12/13–30*

During the remainder of the month Kinai politics amounted to a stalemate that proved highly frustrating to both sides. Several days passed before the insurgents at Kyoto got themselves sufficiently organized to launch a new political offensive. In the interim Osaka leaders debated policy and made some modest moves that attempted to preserve flexibility but left initiative in the hands of those at Kyoto.[67]

Yoshinobu continued to worry about court sensibilities. On 12/14 a delegate from Kyoto asked him for funds because the court was bankrupt. Yoshinobu replied that he dared not give an open gift because his men were so angry, but he did agree to let the delegate obtain funds from a bakufu intendant's office. The money value of the grant is unclear, but the gesture did suggest Yoshinobu's ongoing hope that out of the disaster something could be salvaged by political maneuver.

Itakura's sense of his predicament was suggested by a letter of the fourteenth that he apparently intended for Edo but may never have sent. Reporting on Kyoto developments, he blamed Satsuma for the Tokugawa defeat. He said Aizu, Kuwana, Shinsengumi, and *yūgekitai* troops wished to launch an attack, and he said Yoshinobu was furious and nearly ready to unleash his army. He also wrote, however, that daimyo, both vassal and great lords, were not very outspoken, that Kaga, which had deployed troops, had taken them home again, and that lesser lords seemed to be following Kaga's lead. He said one reason they were hesitant was that the evil *han* had secured an imperial order to pacify the insurgent Tokugawa, and he noted it would be extremely dangerous for a *han* to be labeled an "enemy of the court."[68] Daimyo had earlier shown a considerable disregard for court wishes, but Itakura's letter suggests their (and his) keen awareness that an insurgent force as powerful as Satsuma could use imperial authority to justify wreaking havoc on any who stood in its way.

On the same day Itakura did send a series of short letters to Edo. Perhaps he sent several instead of one because he wrote them during spare moments in a hectic schedule. Or perhaps he did so to increase the chance of their reaching Edo and reduce the incriminating nature of any that fell into enemy hands. In one of the shorter letters he reported abolition of the Kyoto office structure. In another he reported the move to Osaka. In another he halted action on the still-pending imperial-Tokugawa marriage and asked for more inspectors (who could serve as messengers in peace or army coordinators in war). In another he asked Ogyū and Inaba Masami to send more military forces and half the French advisors. He also inquired if the newly purchased warship en route from the United States (meaning the armored *Stonewall*) had arrived, stating that if it had, he wished it sent to Osaka at once with its American crew intact. On the following day he and Ōkōchi wrote Ogyū and foreign minister Ogasawara about Yoshinobu's resignation, advising them not to give foreign diplomats too many details on the titular changes. And he also advised them to have Charles Chanoine, the French military mission leader, help them select four or five French advisors to send to Osaka.[69] These several letters suggest that Itakura was doing his best to assure Yoshinobu's capacity to fight if necessary and to claim authority as head of state if things worked out favorably.

While Itakura worked to preserve flexibility of policy and Yoshinobu continued to cultivate the court, several other bakufu officials apparently lobbied vigorously during the first days at Osaka to move Yoshinobu to a firmer line. There were several facets to their proposals: use of foreign assistance, forceful denunciation of the Satsuma insurgents, expansion of Tokugawa military forces, and deployment of those forces for action.

Léon Roches, whose prestige was by then bound to Tokugawa well-being, apparently advised bakufu officials upon their arrival that the moment had come to utilize foreign support. And as Yoshinobu recalled it forty years later, Ōkōchi Masatada (who was promoted to acting senior councillor on the fifteenth) argued, along with others, that use of foreign assistance was essential if disaster were to be avoided. Roches arranged for a meeting with Yoshinobu on the fourteenth, and Parkes was scheduled to meet him the following day. When Parkes learned of Roches's appointment, however, he hurried to the castle and demanded to be present at the session, presumably to assure that Roches would not arrange enough new foreign support to outweigh the weapons and assistance the insurgents already had obtained from foreigners. One can only speculate on what might have transpired had Roches been able to deal secretly with Yoshinobu. As it turned out, the latter asked for no foreign support, and two days later when he formally met the several diplomats at Osaka, he simply informed them at some length of the restoration and then correctly expressed his hope for continued amicable Japanese-foreign relations.[70] One aspect of the Tokugawa activist enterprise was thwarted. And one more step toward colonial status was avoided. The foreigners then adopted an overall policy of neutrality and subsequently played no significant role in shaping the outcome. Their contribution had already been made.

In other ways the advocates of a forceful strategy were more successful. The agitation for expansion of forces was partly accommodated by Itakura's letters to Edo. The agitation for deployment of forces got results after Osaka leaders learned of a new threat to their flank. At Mt. Kōya 50 kilometers southeast of Osaka an anti-bakufu restorationist agitation erupted. Undertaken by a small group of *rōnin* and nobles after 12/8, it began active recruiting on the fourteenth and grew rapidly thereafter. In swift response on the fifteenth Osaka leaders ordered *han* in that area to quiet the unrest and also began deploying forces to defense positions. Hikone troops were ordered to guard ammunition depots in Osaka while Himeji, Kameyama, Obama, Tsu, and other *han* forces were assigned specific guard duties on the Nara highway, on the highway to Nishinomiya, on the roads to Kyoto, and at a host of points around the city.[71]

For all its worrisomeness, the activity at Mt.Kōya was not Osaka's primary concern. Kyoto filled that position. While bakufu leaders deployed *han* forces to face Mt. Kōya, their own armies were deployed with the threat from Kyoto uppermost in mind. Most bakufu battalions were stationed here and there in Osaka, but a few were placed to the north where they erected modest fortifications at selected points at Hirakata, Yamazaki, Yahata, Yodo, and at the Fushimi magistrate's compound. The forces stationed from Hirakata northward probably totaled about 2500 to 3000 men. Aizu and Kuwana forces were at that time mostly in or very near Osaka, but as the month passed, units gradually moved up the Yodo river to selected defense points.[72]

The Tokugawa deployment was essentially defensive and indicates that Osaka leaders were more concerned to avoid surprise attack or serious infiltration than to launch a venture of their own. However, the deployment had been matched by deployment of Kyoto forces, and so by late 67/12 hostile troops were facing one another across a narrow neutral area cutting through central Fushimi town and extending across the flat river plain to the area between Upper and Lower Toba villages some 3 kilometers to the west.

Those urging Yoshinobu to denounce the Satsuma insurgents won his consent soon after Osaka learned of the Mt. Kōya agitation. Hirayama Keichū, Togawa Hanzaburō, and an inspector drew up a strong statement reaffirming Tokugawa support for the earlier Tosa proposal, denouncing the "one or two *han*" that had forcibly seized the court, and contrasting their conduct with the good intentions and honorable actions of Yoshinobu. The three wished the statement sent to court and distributed to daimyo as a means of rallying them. Late on the seventeenth or on the eighteenth Yoshinobu accepted the statement, and on the latter day Togawa left for Kyoto with a copy. In Kyoto the next day Togawa's message was skillfully diverted so that the court did not formally receive it. He failed in repeated efforts to get it delivered to the throne and returned in anger to Osaka. Other copies, however, were sent to Edo and distributed to daimyo, and those, as we see later, had consequences gratifying to the Osaka activists.

News from Edo probably contributed to Yoshinobu's decision to de-

nounce Satsuma. Reports of *rōnin* activity in the Kantō were periodically
sent westward. Osaka leaders discussed the activity and its apparent connection to Satsuma groups at Edo and doubtlessly associated it with the
developments at court and near Mt. Kōya. On 12/23 Ōkōchi and Itakura notified their Edo colleagues that if it were necessary in restoring the
peace in Edo, they were to deal with the trouble ''at its source,'' presumably meaning the Satsuma mansion. On the following evening they
and Sadaaki repeated the advice, arguing that it was a necessary step to
preserve bakufu authority. And they said it was the wish of Yoshinobu.[73]
They did not know it, but the timing of their statement was exquisite.

In sum the interim actions of Osaka leaders rejected foreign collaboration, promoted expansion of military forces at Osaka, deployed them in a
set of defensive positions, denounced the insurgents, and encouraged
leaders at Edo to be firm.

While Osaka leaders were implementing these measures, Kyoto leaders were trying to decide their next steps. Finally on the twenty-second
delegates arrived at Osaka with instructions for Yoshinobu to proceed to
Kyoto for an imperial audience in which he would formally resign as shogun and surrender his lands. Osaka leaders agreed to the resignation but
rejected the land surrender, proposing instead that the court obtain lands
from all lords in proportion to their putative yield *(kokudaka)*. That skillful proposal was carried back to Kyoto where it reopened the basic split
between the extreme insurgents on the one hand and on the other the
great lords of Owari, Fukui, and Tosa and their growing body of daimyo
supporters.[74] Then during the days 12/26–29 delegates from Kyoto,
notably Shungaku, Yoshikatsu, and Nakane Yukie, again journeyed
south, talked with leaders at Osaka, narrowed the verbal differences between the two camps, and then returned to Kyoto to continue their mediation.

While this political dialogue was proceeding, Osaka leaders continued
to talk among themselves about the need to punish Satsuma, and Yoshinobu continued to worry about being labeled an ''enemy of the court.''
Even as they talked and fretted, however, key allies were beginning to
desert them. On the twenty-fifth Mochitsugu of Kii, who had recently
come up from Wakayama, and whose troops were included in Osaka military planning, decided to disengage from the whole worrisome situation
and took his troops back home. Two months earlier he had worked diligently to mobilize support for the Tokugawa house, but apparently the
monumental indecisiveness of Tokugawa leaders in the Kinai had convinced him he was backing a losing cause. At about the same time Osaka
men learned, to the anger and disgust of many, that Ii of Hikone had

declared his support for the court, apparently regardless of whose interests it served.[75]

The actions of Kii and Hikone suggested that time was not necessarily Osaka's ally. That was all the more so because large numbers of daimyo, vassal as well as outside, had small numbers of troops in Kyoto, and court leaders were rapidly putting them into service as city patrols, thus freeing more and more of the growing Satsuma-Chōshū force for offensive operations. In future that trend could only continue unless the Osaka situation improved because more and more daimyo forces would reach Kyoto where the insurgents could utilize them. One reason that would happen was that many daimyo were receiving court orders to go to Kyoto, and inevitably some would conclude that prudence at least required some gesture of cooperation with the emperor. Another reason was that back on 11/27, after being inundated by vassal daimyo refusals to accept orders from court, Yoshinobu and his assistants at Kyoto had prepared a reply instructing them to obey the court's order to proceed to Kyoto. That reply had been sent to Edo where on 12/5 Inaba Masakuni had sent it on to the daimyo.[76] Ironically, then, vassal daimyo began receiving bakufu instructions to go to Kyoto as per court order at a time when such an act would mean something very different from what Yoshinobu had intended. Prudence would still require them to respond in some degree, however, particularly when the confused situation became known to them in whatever garbled form it took. The implications for Osaka were clear enough: inaction was likely the worst of all choices.

Then, just to add grist to the mill of fear, on the night of 12/28 a fire broke out in Osaka castle. It was quickly extinguished, but its origins were not determined, and occurring against a background of fear and a legacy of suspicious castle fires at Edo, it fostered rumors, precipitated more guard duty orders, and generated more nervousness about the future.[77]

By the last few days of 67/12, then, the psychological situation at Osaka was growing very precarious. In the meantime, however, negotiations in Kyoto and between Kyoto and Osaka had by subtle rephrasing partially obscured the issue of land surrender. The extremists at court had rejected the proportional land surrender scheme but in the process had alienated some of their semicollaborators. By 12/29, moreover, Yoshinobu had indicated a willingness to go to Kyoto to resign despite the general Osaka hostility toward the whole trend of affairs. He had not agreed to surrender his lands, but he was willing to make the trip despite the objections of Katamori and Sadaaki, who understandably feared the outcome if he were permitted to bargain in Kyoto. It was in this situation of extreme tension and subtle maneuver, whose possible outcomes were several and unclear, that reports of events in Edo precipitated some decisive moves at Osaka.

3. Edo under Stress

Yoshinobu and his few accompanying officials were handling affairs in the Kinai region, but the bakufu proper was in Edo, and as so often in the past, Edo was more pro-Tokugawa than the Tokugawa spokesmen to the west. This phenomenon, so consistently evident earlier in the sixties, had been concealed during the Keiō reform because Kinai policy had then followed lines satisfying to those in charge at Edo. The Edo-Kinai split reappeared during 67/10, however, when Yoshinobu accepted the Tosa proposal. The split persisted through the next month, but during 66/12 it gradually closed as events to the west drove leaders in Osaka back to a posture closer to that of Edo. During the same period developments in the Kantō were placing severe stress on leaders there, and by year's end both wings of the old bakufu were ready to fight in defense of Tokugawa interests.

Back on 10/27 a vassal of Maebashi *han* asked to meet with the senior councillors in Edo. He had, he said, an urgent matter to report. He met Matsui three days later and presented details of an elaborate plot by Satsuma men. Their intent, he reported, was to start a rash of forty or more fires in the city during the next night, 11/1. Amid the resulting panic they would break into Chiyoda castle, seize the shogun's ladies, and spirit them out of town, either westward to Kōfu or northeast by way of Hitachi province.[78]

The senior councillors were a bit dubious about the story, but on the next day there were more reports of suspicious activity at the Satsuma mansion. Accordingly though the night passed without incident, on the following day the bakufu ordered massive additional guard forces deployed around the city and castle, calling upon seventy-three *han*, mostly those of vassal lords, to place men at a host of bridges and gates. Reluctant to reveal the cause of concern, the councillors merely referred to "the critical situation" as reason for the deployment. They also dispatched to Kyoto that day a report of the rumored plot, mentioning fifty or more planned fires. During the next few days menacing placards appeared at Nihonbashi. One put up on the second, for example, denounced the bakufu for intimacy with foreigners and abuse of the court and warned that in two or three days a force of 1800 "imperial loyalists" would burn the city and castle and slaughter officials. The placards, other reports and rumors of plots, and scattered acts of violence prompted nervous leaders to deploy yet more guard forces. And at last they explained officially that the measures were being taken ''in case of fire or trouble caused by Satsuma, Chōshū, and Tosa vassals and *rōnin* who are concealed in Kyoto, Edo, and elsewhere and whose evil intentions are unpredictable.''[79]

In succeeding days the city was quieter. There still appeared a few reports and rumors of plots, commonly blamed on *rōnin*, Satsuma men, or unspecified commoners. There were reports of brigandage and of noise associated with contemporary *eejanaika* activity, and some pundits spoke of Satsuma's rise and the Tokugawa fall. The infantry riots of midmonth temporarily upset the city, but then matters grew quiet again, although a few *rōnin* were arrested. As 67/12 began, the respite ended. City leaders began to hear about gangs of robbers, some carrying firearms, and started to receive rumors of *rōnin* plots. One rumor said some *rōnin* planned to use cannon to blast open the city magistrate's office and steal the monies reputedly stored there.[80]

Part of the unrest was, as reported, a product of plotting and organizing by Satsuma men working with ''Kantō *rōnin*.'' In late 67/11 small numbers of Satsuma vassals and affiliated *rōnin* left the city to stir up the Kantō. They gathered some followers in the hills of Shimozuke and elsewhere and on about the twenty-eighth proclaimed a rebellion, labeling themselves the Satsuma vanguard of the imperial army.[81] By 12/9 news of the insurrection reached Edo leaders, and they promptly ordered more vassal *han* forces to guard the city. The following day some 250 more troops (*yūgekitai, jūtai,* and *sappei)* were put on patrol, and four vassal lords in the vicinity of the rebels were ordered to deploy troops to quell them. They were instructed to use without hesitation such force as was necessary to crush them promptly.[82]

It was in this context of a worsening situation in the Kantō that Edo leaders received alarming reports from the Kinai.[83] On the fourteenth they received their first solid news of the Satsuma-sponsored restoration, most notably Itakura's report of the eleventh from Kyoto. In it he asked for military reinforcements and instructed the messenger to provide Edo officials with full details. With the arrival of that and subsequent reports the issues of an apparently growing insurrection in the Kantō and of massive daimyo military activity, Satsuma ambitions, and chaotic developments in the Kinai became intertwined and led to a great intensification of political discussion, general anger, impatience, and military preparation.

Inaba Masakuni was the most influential official at Edo, and hence Edo's handling of the twin threats from Kantō and Kinai was essentially Inaba's work. As rapidly as he learned of developments, he took steps to inform others and start military preparations.[84] Thus on the fourteenth he, Inaba Masami, and Ogasawara promptly summoned and met vassal lords and representatives in Edo. They reported Kyoto developments, including the palace guard changes, the Chōshū pardon, and the resignations of Katamori and Sadaaki. They warned the men to be cautious but to start military preparations since it was hard to tell what might happen. In reply to Itakura's request for troops, Masakuni instructed inspectors to prepare two battalions of infantry (*hohei*) for immediate sailing on two bakufu warships. He also ordered two batteries of artillery and three troops (*shōtai*) of cavalry to prepare for deployment to the west.

Edo leaders thus tried to answer Itakura's request. Given the recent reports of Satsuma plots in the Kantō, however, they could not have believed the Kantō and Kinai problems unconnected, and hence their actions had a strong defensive character. More vassal daimyo forces were deployed in and around Chiyoda castle, and, "because the city is disturbed, evil gangs active, and the people restless," *yūgekitai* forces were increased and put on 24-hour patrol.[85] As preparation against general upheaval, vassal lords were ordered to bring every bit of rice in their castles to the city for storage in bakufu warehouses. Edo leaders also showed great concern for those shogunal ladies who had long been the alleged target of Satsuma conspirators, increasing their guard forces and moving them into the recently rebuilt second enceinte (*ninomaru*), well protected behind great walls and moats.[86]

For the next several days it was the Kantō situation that compelled attention. Developments continued to suggest that a *shishi*-led *sonnō jōi* restorationist movement like that of 1863–1864 was growing. Reports on the sixteenth spoke of activity by Chōshū men and *rōnin* in Sagami province, which was nearer to both Edo and Yokohama than the recently reported uprising in Shimozuke. Edo leaders learned that on the fifteenth a band of some thirty-six *rōnin* had attacked and plundered arms, supplies, and money from the small headquarters of Ogino Yamanaka *han* in Sagami. They promptly ordered Odawara and Takasaki *han* forces to quell the *rōnin* quickly, killing them if necessary. Soon afterward forces of the Kanagawa magistrate met and captured the troublemakers near Atsugi as they moved toward Yokohama. Then on the seventeenth someone attacked two British consular officials in Shiba. In the face of the growing turmoil, on that day and the next the bakufu deployed some legation guard (*bette gumi*) units around the castle and sent others to Yokohama to replace those sent elsewhere by the Kanagawa magistrate. It also ordered an infantry force to Totsuka to suppress *rōnin* reportedly active there, and it commanded about fifty vassal daimyo again to deploy forces night and day to pacify the city.[87]

Doubtless the deteriorating situation put men in mind of the Tsukuba phase of the Kantō insurrection. And shortly Edo heard reports of *rōnin* activity near the new Fusa intendancy not far from Tsukuba. Accordingly on the twenty-first Inaba ordered Tsuchiya of Tsuchiura *han* to deploy forces there to help quiet the area and protect the intendancy.

Even as he was dealing with rapidly spreading disorder in the Kantō, Inaba was trying to keep vassal lords and officials posted on Kinai developments. As fast as he could assemble men and bring them up to date, however, his reports were made obsolete by new information. Thus on 12/17 he instructed lords to come to the castle on the following day. When they assembled, he reported details of the imperial government reorganization of the ninth and admonished them to adhere carefully to bakufu orders. They were summoned to the castle again on the twentieth, that time to be told by Matsui and Inaba Masami that Yoshinobu had resigned as shogun and moved to Osaka. Again they were admonished to cause no trouble and keep their vassals severely under control.[88] Even as Matsui and Inaba gave the lords this latest news, however, an inspector who had left the Kinai on the thirteenth reached Edo castle and walked from office to office, giving men extensive details on the situation. He informed Inaba and the other councillors of Yoshinobu and Itakura's view that the move to Osaka was necessary. He reported that Katamori and Sadaaki disagreed and were still not reconciled even after the move. And he stressed the Kinai leaders' belief that it was important the Tokugawa side not start the war.

That report, which made clear not only what had happened but also the existence of severe disagreement among Osaka leaders, precipitated intense discussion. Army officers urged that more troops be sent westward, while members of the inspectorate and Oguri Tadamasa urged the senior councillors to send someone or some group to Osaka to investigate the situation, preferably by ship and at once. Leaders decided this newest information should be spelled out to all officials, and so on the next day, the twenty-first, representatives from every office were assembled to hear the inspector's detailed report.[89] Within twenty-four hours of that assembly a new and dramatic notice arrived from Osaka. That message prompted Edo leaders to notify the daimyo yet again that they together with high-ranking liege vassals *(kōtai yoriai* and *kōke)* and representatives from all offices were to come on the morrow to the castle to receive the notice. Something big clearly was in the wind, but even before the men could gather to learn what it was, an unnerving event at Edo compounded the crisis.

Only eight days before, the shogun's ladies had been moved for safety's sake into the newly reconstructed second enceinte, together with household officials, attendant personnel, and enlarged guard forces. There deep in the heart of the castle ground they would presumably be safe from the Satsuma plotters who supposedly were scheming to burn the town, invade the castle, and snatch the ladies away. Despite these precautions, at 5 AM on the twenty-third a fire of unexplained origin broke out in the brand-new buildings in the area of the ladies themselves. Immediately the castle was thrown into confusion. The ladies were hustled hither and thither. Officials rushed to the castle, and large numbers of people turned out to fight the fire. By about 8 AM the flames were extinguished, but the ladies' quarters had been gutted. Lest the fire be a signal for some sort of eruption, immense guard forces including artillery units were deployed at once to patrol the city and castle environs and set up defense points at crucial approaches to the castle.[90]

Then, even as the smoking remains cooled, the representatives of *han* filed together with officials through the acrid fumes of the wasted castle, past the emergency guard units, across the moat, and through the gate into the western enceinte for their 10 AM assembly. And there, in an atmosphere of anger, fear, and the deepest suspicion, they were read Yoshinobu's message of the seventeenth to the court. Yoshinobu had written:[91]

I, your servant Yoshinobu, although unworthy, have hitherto received great favor unfailingly, and my gratitude is immeasurable. I have worried and labored unceasingly to understand fully the prospects of the world, to unify the polity, and to establish the nation's prestige on a par with that of all nations. I have struggled to arrange broad discussion of matters, and my sole wish has been to secure a lasting foundation for affairs. I returned the hereditary authority of my ancestors, hoping to promote a system for unity and cooperation. I urged the many *han* to present their opinions, and I even resigned my office of shogun, but was instructed to handle matters as before until the lords had assembled at Kyoto and the conference had been arranged. I have had absolutely no desire except that the lords assemble, work together in harmony, engage in fruitful public discussion, and so establish a supremely just system of rule. My humble heart has been burdened with dedication, and day and night I have hoped and worked thus.

Now, to my amazement, although I, your servant, received no report on details of the matter and though there was no conference of assembled *han*, yet one or two *han* by use of armed troops thrust themselves into the imperial palace and brought about an unprecedented reorganization. In this effort they dismissed the regent who had been designated by the former emperor. Then without justification they ostracized princes and nobles with older attachments and abruptly selected for office nobles whom the former emperor had excluded from the court. Meanwhile vassals of these *han* loitered about close to the emperor, quite without authority, thus sullying imperial customs that are thousands of years old.

Already formal notices on matters such as these have been issued, utterly contrary to heaven and earth. It is shocking beyond words. Even if these were the result of imperial desires, I would have to make loyal remonstrance —how much more so at the present time of a child emperor. Things having come to such a pass, the realm is on the verge of upheaval and the people are in distress. Already petitions of request cannot be presented, and so the state of our immaculate imperial line is a cause of the greatest worry. I, your vassal Yoshinobu, am deeply distressed by this. In particular, matters pertaining to foreign relations affect the whole country. In the event difficulties arise, if the impulsive ideas of those disreputable men who have falsified the imperial will become policy, the credibility [of the Japanese government] will evaporate, which inescapably will in future lead to great disaster for the imperial land.

Above all, while this situation is very worrisome, until matters are settled by public debate, they should be handled as in the past, in accord with the prior and genuine imperial wish. Requesting that this humble opinion be accepted and thereby justice secured, that the *han* be assembled in council, that the righteous unite and the wicked be driven out, that the foundations of an enduring order be laid, and that the imperial desire be served above and the people be made tranquil below, I, your servant Yoshinobu, do sorely entreat you thus.

It was a handsome statement, claiming for the Tokugawa the moral high ground and offering a base for broad cooperation against Satsuma and whomever else were the implied culprits. The tone of the letter must have been satisfying to the beleaguered men gathered in the castle that grim morning. One can readily understand why Satsuma men had prevented its delivery to the court.

Moreover, the letter was sent under a cover notice by Itakura and Ōkōchi Masatada. They referred to it as a splendid statement that should be announced to all daimyo and upper liege vassals *(hatamoto)*. More importantly they ordered all available troops and mounts assembled and dispatched to Osaka at once, with as many officers and units as possible to be sent by ship.[92] At last, it appeared, Edo and Osaka were in agreement. The gap opened two months before by Yoshinobu's decision to accept the Tosa proposal had been closed. The basis of that reforged unity was brutally clear: there must be war.

Ogasawara observed to the assembled men that the Kyoto situation was truly extraordinary, that there was no hope the peace could be kept, and that therefore in this autumn of the nation each must act out of his own innermost loyalty. Realizing that Yoshinobu was making great efforts for the nation, each must be loyal and make equal effort.[93] While Ogasawara rallied the men, Inaba Masakuni gave them marching orders. Those assembled were told to send troops westward at once. Others were similarly instructed in writing, and they were ordered to furnish details of their deployment to inspectors. Those notified in writing were admonished to obey in payment of three hundred years of obligation to the Tokugawa, out of loyalty to their lord, and on behalf of the imperial country.

While Inaba thus took decisive steps to support Osaka's apparent newfound resolve, he also took steps to strengthen yet further the citadel in the east. More guard forces were deployed around the castle and much tighter controls on castle entry were established.[94] Despite the precautions, that night someone with firearms took potshots at the mansion of Shōnai *han*, which had a major role in the city guard. When Shōnai men pursued the gunmen, they chased them all the way to the Satsuma and Sadohara mansions of the Shimazu family. Whoever they were, the gunmen evidently had friends among the Shimazu.

Too many incidents had occurred. Too much suspicion, too much anger, too much desperation had developed. Several forceful officials had for some time believed the Satsuma bastion in the city needed to be eliminated. At Osaka, as we noted earlier, Itakura and Ōkōchi believed such action warranted after learning of the early 67/12 troubles in Edo and the Kantō. At Edo Oguri Tadamasa and military commanders advocated it after the castle fire. Then after the Shōnai mansion incident that same evening, Sakai Tadasumi, the Shōnai daimyo, threatened to quit his city guard duty unless action were taken to eliminate the source of trouble. On the night of 12/24 the senior councillors yielded to the accumulated arguments. In view of Osaka's new posture, it seemed the least one could do to prepare the heartland defense. A large number of vassal *han* troops plus patrol forces of Shōnai were deployed, and early the next morning the Satsuma and Sadohara mansions were overrun. A few men were killed and their heads sent westward for Satsuma's edification. The other 150 or so *rōnin* found there were arrested and put in detention in the city.[95]

Accompanying this ''surgical strike'' were a number of other preparatory measures.[96] On the twenty-fifth Inaba issued a general mobilization order to lesser liege vassals (*gokenin*) to report for military training. Another half-battalion of regular infantry (*hohei*) was put aboard ship and sent to Osaka. To get rid of another internal threat and release more troops for combat, it was decided to send westward those several hundred or more men held from the Kantō insurgency as lifetime prisoners of certain vassal *han*. The next day highway barriers around Edo that had been torn down only three months before—at Shinagawa, Naitō Shinjuku, Itabashi, Iwabuchijuku, and Senju—were ordered reestablished, and vassal *han* were ordered to man them with sizable forces of foot soldiers and some pieces of artillery. All travelers were required henceforth to have exit and entry permits. City patrols were strengthened, and in following days a host of other urban defense preparations were made, some of them justified on the ground that though the occupants of the Satsuma mansion had been captured, doubtless there were other troublemakers in the city who would be difficult to control. As never before the city was preparing for siege. For Edo nearly three hundred years of peace apparently had ended.

A report of the decision to send forces westward and an explanation of the assault on the Satsuma mansion were duly carried to Osaka by inspector general Takikawa Tomoshige and another official. They reached Osaka late on the twenty-eighth. Their reports of the rumors and actions in the Kantō, of the castle fire there, and of the Shōnai and Satsuma mansion incidents, coming as they did just when a fire erupted in Osaka castle itself, set in train an intense reconsideration of policy that led to decisive actions within two days.

Thus after two and a half months of tension, discord, and rancorous interaction, the bifurcated bakufu leadership finally encountered a situation in which actions of each half helped provoke the other half into moves that the leadership of neither part sought in the first place nor felt satisfied with when they occurred. Regardless of intention or rhetoric, the net result, as we see in the next chapter, was a decision to go to war.

CHAPTER 13
The End
1868/1–4

Yoshinobu launched the New Year with a greeting to the court. It was not the usual greeting. Rather, it was a notice proclaiming the great sins of "the Satsuma traitors" and calling for a righting of their wrongs. He wrote:[1]

With all respect to the court, I, your servant, Yoshinobu, am painfully aware that developments since the ninth of last month have not been in accord with the imperial wish. As everyone knows, those developments have transpired entirely because traitorous retainers of Shimazu Hisamitsu have engaged in plotting. Most notably there has been violence and banditry in Edo, Nagasaki, and Shimozuke and Sagami provinces, and Hisamitsu's vassals have fostered it in order to speed an alliance of east and west and confound the imperial land. Those activities are reported in the attached paper. They being activities hateful to heaven and earth, an order should be issued that the above-mentioned traitors are to be handed over. If by rare chance this request is not honored, then it is unavoidable that the death penalty be imposed on them. This is my respectful report.

The Crimes of the Satsuma Traitors

ITEM: Although much effort was expended for the great event of the restoration and an open political conference was announced, on 12/9 in the guise of a great reform they acted abruptly, showing contempt for the young emperor's actions and insisting upon their own opinions.

ITEM: Although the emperor is very young, they dismissed the regent on whom the prior emperor had relied and prevented his attending imperial conferences.

ITEM: For selfish reasons they have had princes and court nobles appointed and dismissed arbitrarily.

ITEM: In the name of guarding the nine palace gates and other points, they instigated action by men of other *han*. And using armed soldiers, they seized the imperial palace, which action was unscrupulous and constituted a major act of disrespect toward the court.

ITEM: Satsuma vassals and vagrant bands in Edo talked together, assembled in the Satsuma mansion, and pillaged and bullied about the city, firing upon the personnel and residence of Sakai [of Shōnai]. They also attacked, burned, and pillaged here and there in Shimozuke and Sagami. Of these matters there is ample proof.

Lest the notice be taken lightly, the officials who prepared it for transmittal attached a cover statement summing up the note's contents and announcing that Yoshinobu was going to proceed at once to Kyoto, accompanied by his army, to address the emperor.

Then Takikawa Tomoshige, who on 12/28 had brought news of the Edo situation to Osaka, was instructed to take the note to Kyoto. En route he was intercepted by Satsuma guardsmen, and his note did not reach the court until 1/5. By then, however, Tokugawa actions had spoken decisively, if not as Tokugawa actors had intended, and the insurgent response had proved more effective than any words.

Defeat: 68/1/3–6

The decision to advance toward Kyoto was made after Takikawa reached Osaka. He championed strongly the Edo view that Satsuma had to be dealt with sternly, and his position was supported by many of those at Osaka who had been arguing for weeks that political maneuver was an insufficient response. Yoshinobu later claimed to have been in bed with a cold at the time, and he doubtless was reluctant to fight. Itakura too was reluctant, but he apparently believed that angry subordinates would not accept further inaction. Advocates of war pointed confidently to their great, and sometimes exaggerated, numerical superiority, and in that climate it became impossible to refuse.[2]

Even when the decision to move troops was made, however, it was so handled as to avoid the charge that Osaka had precipitated civil war. Yoshinobu was merely going to Kyoto, after all. For weeks, it was reasoned, those who controlled the court had been calling upon him to do so, and thus the decision was not necessarily belligerent in content. The notice, moreover, denounced not the court but Satsuma. Indeed, it denounced not even Satsuma but only certain ''traitorous'' vassals of Hisamitsu. On the other hand the court leaders had ordered Aizu and Kuwana forces to go home, and they had not gone. Moreover court leaders intended that Yoshinobu indicate a willingness to surrender his lands before proceeding to Kyoto, and he had not done that. And Kyoto certainly did not intend that his advance be preceded by major Tokugawa military deployments.

Thus while Yoshinobu may have been able to convince himself that his decision was not really belligerent, the thin disguise of a virtuous protest to court did not conceal the basic fact that the troop deployment constituted a direct challenge to Satsuma's designs of conquest. Had Satsuma leaders permitted Yoshinobu to go to Kyoto as he proposed, it would certainly have constituted a major defeat, perhaps a final defeat, for their ambitions. They recognized that, and so they fought.

1. The Bakufu Army

The army that Satsuma and its allies faced was a large one, but only a portion was both available for and capable of effective offensive fighting. And that portion was handled poorly. At the start of 1868 the Osaka leaders had at their command the forces described in the table at the top of page 419.[3]

There were thus about thirteen thousand troops available for Yoshinobu's venture, plus a thousand or so Tsu troops on barrier guard duty at Yamazaki, and, potentially at least, other vassal *han* troops. Of this force a substantial portion was tied down on guard duty in and around Osaka, so those available for combat were fewer.

The forces considered available for offensive operations were indicated in the marching orders of 12/30. Those orders grouped units into composite regiments and identified them by their destinations. One regiment

Force	Strength
Twelve regular infantry battalions *(hohei)*	6000
Two battalions of French-trained *sappei*	900
Two battalions with miscellaneous firearms *(jūtai, okuzume jūtai)*	1000
One and a half battalions of men with mixed weapons *(yūgekitai, shin yūgekitai, mimawari,* Shinsengumi*)*	750
Two battalions of miscellaneous men at Fushimi	1000
Some artillery and cavalry	?
Vassal *han* forces	
Obama, Kameyama, Himeji	1100
Aizu	1600
Kuwana	340–400
Others	?
Total strength	12,750

was to advance to Katamori's former mansion in Kyoto; another to billeting areas in a temple in the city; another to Nijō castle; another to positions in Fushimi; and another to Toba. Other units were to take up positions at several points on the routes from Osaka—specifically Yodo, Hashimoto, Nishinomiya, Hyōgo, and Osaka itself. To indicate the character of a composite regiment, the forces headed for Katamori's mansion are described in the table below.

This regiment probably totaled about two thousand men. Similar but smaller groups of troops were being sent to the other places. Those bound for Kyoto totaled about 5500; those for Fushimi-Toba, about

Force	Strength
Two infantry battalions *(hohei)*	1000
Half a battery of cannon (four cannon)	40*
A *yūgekitai* force	130
Three cavalry units	120*
An engineer unit	40
An Aizu battalion	400
An Aizu cannon unit	40*
Forces of Matsuyama (eight *shōtai*)	160–320*

*Estimated strength.

3000; those for Yodo and south, about 4500 plus large numbers of unspecified vassal *han* forces who were expected to participate. Of the total 13,000, then, about 8500 would presumably come in contact with the enemy at Fushimi or Toba on their way north.

The deployment had certain flaws. The composite regiments mixed troops together so that the best had their capacity hobbled by association with inferior forces. Moreover the deployment involved some calculated gambles. Although most of the offensive forces actually existed (except probably for artillery), parts of the rearguard were imaginary or unreliable. In three of the most notable instances, men of Hikone were given duty guarding munitions transport, but Hikone leaders had already switched sides. Men of Kii were to patrol Osaka, but the Kii forces had already gone home. Men of Ōgaki were among those deployed to the north, but leaders of Ōgaki forces at Osaka openly stated their opposition to fighting the imperial army even as the war progressed.[4] By listing those forces in the deployment, Osaka leaders made it possible for them to return to the fold, putatively having never been absent, should developments encourage such a return. For the moment, however, their inclusion only fostered the illusion of great numbers. And a glaring problem of the Osaka force was that some middle-level and lower-ranking officers were badly overconfident because their calculations persuaded them they had the numbers necessary to steamroll right over anyone who got in their way.

The advance began on New Year's Day, and during the next two days forces headed northward toward their destinations. The advance revealed more problems. Some units went up the Yodo river piecemeal in small boats while others went by foot, and in the outcome the regiments did not cohere in their advance. Thus parts of Kuwana lead forces were several hours behind the infantry whom they were supposed to precede at Toba. And Aizu artillery at Fushimi took up advance positions but lacked adequate infantry cover. Moreover, not all the troops and commanders were really expecting to fight. Thus the bakufu infantrymen who ended up in the lead at Toba were neither deployed nor armed for combat when fighting erupted all around them. The cumulative effect of all these considerations was to vitiate the bakufu's manpower advantage even before fighting began.

2. The Battle of 1/3

On the third some units from Osaka proceeded north beyond Yodo to the vicinity of Lower Toba.[5] There they halted while Takikawa talked with Satsuma barrier guards near Upper Toba during the sunny, cold after-

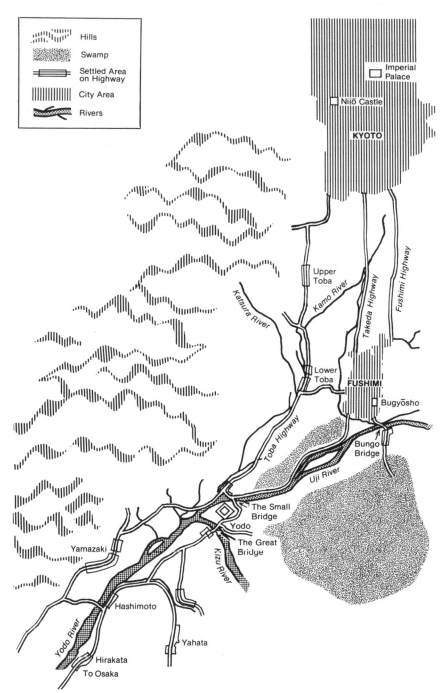

MAP 5. Fushimi-Toba. Adapted from map no. 63, *Dai Nihon dokushi chizu* by Yoshida Tōgō (Tokyo: Fuzambō, 1935).

noon. Simultaneously other units proceeded up the Uji river to the south end of Fushimi. There they rested in the lower part of town and across the river to the south pending receipt of orders from their overall commander *(rikugun bugyō)* Takenaka Shigemoto to proceed to their destination in Kyoto.

The Osaka forces at Lower Toba were under army vice-commander *(rikugun bugyō nami)* Ōkubo Tadayuki, who had been Kyoto city magistrate until 12/12, and they were heading for Nijō. In the vanguard was a group of four hundred *mimawari* (city patrol forces) armed with pikes and some firearms. Their presence in the lead suggests how little expectation of war the advancing men really had. The other major group was regimental vice-commander *(hohei bugyō nami)* Tokuyama Kōtarō's two infantry battalions stretched out in file on the narrow road, in close formation, no flankers deployed, their rifles empty. Kuwana forces consisted of eight companies and four cannon that were supposed to be with the vanguard but were actually to the south, some still in boats. A few Matsuyama, Takamatsu, and other troops apparently were there, and a few bakufu cavalry and artillery were supposed to have been there but likely were not. Against that force of some 2000 to 2500 troops were several Satsuma units, perhaps totaling about 900 men with four cannon.[6]

After Takikawa's request to advance had been rejected by the barrier guards, he returned to discuss with Ōkubo what to do. Meanwhile Satsuma forces were deployed, ambushers were sent out on the flanks, and a main assault force with cannon amassed on the highway. Carefully coordinated, the force attacked fiercely, its attack all the more unexpected because it came at dusk. At once it threw the lead elements of *mimawari* and infantry into confusion and retreat. As the dark settled, the situation remained chaotic. Infantrymen began burning houses as they retreated, but the flames only illuminated them, giving Satsuma snipers better targets. As the hours passed, however, the contest gradually stabilized in a dark, confused, indecisive firefight. The situation was very worrisome to the Satsuma men who knew Osaka still had large numbers of uncommitted troops nearby. The worries proved unnecessary, however, because the Kuwana forces for some reason responded very belatedly to orders to move to the front. They did not arrive until shortly after midnight, and by then the situation had grown quiet and remained so until dawn.

On the Fushimi front the action was more decisive. There men heard from across the fields and flood plain sounds of the Satsuma assault at Toba. That apparently prompted some Aizu men to move north and west through Fushimi toward the crossroad leading to Lower Toba. Their movement in turn prompted Satsuma men to launch an attack.

At the time firing commenced, Osaka forces in and near Fushimi seem to have consisted of nearly five hundred Aizu men with four cannon, while another four hundred were to the southwest between Yodo and Fushimi. The vanguard of the bakufu regiment was a Shinsengumi unit, probably about 150 men, together with a half-battalion of infantry, a handful of Hamada and perhaps other vassal *han* troops, and guard forces of the Fushimi magistrate's office. Just south of town were another battalion and a half of infantry under two commanders, one of them identified as Kubota Bizen no kami. There also were supposed to have been four cannon and some engineers and cavalry, but as at Toba they seem to have been absent. Against that force of about 3000 the Kyoto leaders had deployed at the north end of town perhaps 500 or more Satsuma troops, mostly with rifles and four cannon, a reported 725 Chōshū men, and about 200 Tosa troops, or a total of some 1400.

When Satsuma troops commenced firing, the aged commander of the Aizu artillery battery deployed north of the magistrate's office ordered his men to reply. Then the engagement became general, and Aizu men made a northward thrust. Like the Shinsengumi, they had more pikes than firearms, and they were repulsed. Then their artillery, which was defended by pikemen, was overrun with frightful casualties and the loss or destruction of three of their four fieldpieces. Bakufu infantry were thrown in and started driving the Satsuma-Chōshū attackers back, but by then sappers had set fire to the area around the magistrate's office, and snipers began to rake the men exposed by firelight.

As the situation in town was growing awkward for Osaka, Chōshū men secreted in a bamboo grove overlooking the east side of the magistrate's office launched a daring assault. Shooting fire arrows, bullets, and cannon shot into the compound, they made a bold frontal drive into it. There they caught forces whose arms were inadequate and who had been panicked by fire and bullets. A disorderly retreat to the south was commenced, with only the infantry holding together. They maintained a beachhead at the Bungo bridge over the Uji river, thereby enabling the others to withdraw and take their casualties with them. When more Aizu men tried to move out to the west, Tosa troops opened fire, driving them back into town and into an ambush set up by Satsuma and Chōshū forces. A few got through to the Toba battle, but the rest had to fall back to the south.

After that disastrous evening battle, units started retreating toward Yodo. Contact was broken, and the freezing night grew quieter. At daybreak senior commanders at Yodo, presumably Takenaka, Ōkubo, and perhaps Ōkōchi Masatada and Takikawa, chose to report to superiors at Osaka and Edo that the outcome was indecisive and to profess that very soon the enemy would be defeated. In line with that optimistic assessment, they proposed an immediate advance to recapture Fushimi, but unit commanders refused to obey. They insisted their bone-weary troops had to rest, and because it was they who had the troops, there was no counterattack at dawn.

On both fronts the northbound advance had been stopped. At Toba the Osaka forces had been surprised and repulsed. In the end the nocturnal contest there was indecisive, personnel and matériel losses were modest, and there was no significant territorial change. At Fushimi, however, Osaka was clearly defeated and took serious losses of manpower, matériel, and territory. Aizu was so badly mauled that by mid-twentieth-century American military standards one of its two artillery units would have been described as wiped out. The bakufu lost some able commanders killed and wounded in action. The most grievous matériel loss probably was the cannon. Fieldpieces previously ordered from Edo had not reached Osaka, and those supposedly with the advance regiments seem not to have been there. Field commanders and Osaka officials kept appealing for more artillery; to lose any of those that were available was dismaying. In terms of territory the neutral zone that previously had run east and west from the middle of Fushimi to the middle of Toba village had become a disputed no-man's land running from the swamps between Fushimi and Yodo northwest to near its original line in Toba. The beginnings of war had been inauspicious for the old bakufu.

3. The Battle of 1/4

During the morning of the fourth, Osaka forces returned to the advance on both fronts.[7] At Toba a combined Kuwana-bakufu infantry force advanced at daybreak and quickly recovered the road to Lower Toba. By then, however, the shaky Satsuma forces on that front had been bolstered by massive transfers of men from Fushimi and Kyoto and by the arrival of an imperial prince whose presence signified imperial commitment to their venture. This enlarged and newly inspired force drove the Kuwana men back, and the latter were then replaced by Aizu troops. When these latter moved up, they encountered heavy cannon and rifle fire from an enemy who by then seems to have had a slight numerical superiority on that front. In hard fighting the Aizu men ran low on ammunition. The lead infantry took punishing casualties, losing more officers and men, and by early afternoon they were driven back nearly to the Small Bridge across the Uji river just north of Yodo castle.

That severe reverse threatened the entire Osaka position at Yodo, led to the frantic commitment of other Aizu men, and elicited from them one of their best and most fearsome performances during the four-day war. Supported by Kuwana artillery, they attacked the overextended Kyoto force at about 5 PM, hitting them with pikes and swords in close-quarter combat. Apparently the Satsuma riflemen were cut off from reinforcements and unable to reload in the face of the onslaught. The Aizu pikemen scored a savage triumph, ravaging their enemy and driving the survivors back to Lower Toba. By then it was night, units were rotated, and the front stabilized. Toba remained in Satsuma hands, but the outcome was again essentially a stalemate, despite the great expansion of the Kyoto force.

Meanwhile the outcome on the Fushimi highway was similar, but more to the insurgents' advantage despite their temporarily reduced forces there. During the morning Aizu and infantry units advanced up the Uji river with the former in the lead. Some Aizu men were then recalled, however, to assist the hard-pressed forces south of Toba, and the others were repulsed by Chōshū and Tosa units, with infantrymen reportedly performing poorly in the contest. The Osaka units then withdrew and went on the defensive northeast of the castle as yet more men were hurriedly transferred to the other front during the midday crisis at the Small Bridge. The Fushimi front then grew quiet.

The size of forces committed that day is difficult to ascertain. Osaka probably deployed 3500 bakufu infantry, some cavalry who had to leave their mounts south of Yodo, and probably odds and ends of other forces. Takamatsu, Hamada, and other vassal *han* were mostly out of action due to losses the previous night. Aizu probably was still able to deploy six hundred or more men and Kuwana about three hundred. Perhaps five thousand men were available in all for fighting on 1/4.

The total Kyoto force was smaller, although enlarged from the previous day. Chōshū numbers were perhaps little changed, but Satsuma had received several hundred more men from Kyoto, and Tottori had sent some three hundred to Fushimi where they were occupied setting up camp but would have been available had the battle south of town gone poorly. Perhaps the Kyoto force totaled three thousand men or so. They had fewer available reserves than did Osaka and hence less opportunity for rest, and that limited their capacity to sustain an advance. Thus at Toba they achieved superiority of numbers only by committing nearly all available forces. Hence when they were dealt a severe setback late in the afternoon, they had no reserves to throw in to stem the reverse and were saved only by darkness and the limitations of the Osaka army. Those limitations were revealed the following day, which turned out to be the day of decision.

4. The Battle of 1/5

The decisive events of the war began at daybreak with Kyoto forces pushing on Yodo from both Toba and Fushimi.[8] On the Toba road fighting was intense and swayed back and forth as the two large and rather well-balanced armies each in turn gained the advantage and then revealed its inability to sustain momentum. The insurgents finally wore down their Aizu and bakufu opponents, however, even though the latter were aided for a while by some Ōgaki men. By early afternoon they had been driven across the Small Bridge to Yodo, where they took up defensive positions. There they were supported by some western-uniformed, French-trained units whose performance was praised and whose methodical movements were an object of admiration for Aizu personnel.[9]

On the Fushimi front insurgent leaders withdrew the four Tosa companies to guard duty in Fushimi and replaced them with two artillery pieces and crews from Tottori plus whatever Satsuma and Chōshū troops were released from guard duty by Tosa's transfer. The reorganized attack force then advanced southward and encountered Aizu-bakufu units moving up from Yodo. In the ensuing firefight Kyoto troops initially drove the Osaka force back some 300 meters. As the main force pulled back, however, Aizu pikemen deployed in the bulrushes on both sides of the road. Units of Chōshū riflemen, encouraged by their capture of two artillery pieces, incautiously moved down the road into the ambush. Pikemen sprang from cover; Aizu artillery commenced firing, bakufu infantrymen launched a frontal assault, and the Chōshū riflemen were dealt a severe reverse, much as Satsuma had been the previous day. They retreated pell-mell toward Fushimi, but the Osaka army again failed to exploit its opportunity, some units disregarding orders to advance. The routed Chōshū unit (a *chūtai*) was replaced by reserves supported by the Tottori artillery, and later attempts by Aizu men to repeat their feat were unsuccessful. After hard fighting the Osaka troops fell back to Yodo. There they fired the village north of the river, crossed the Small Bridge, and joined their fellows defending the north side of Yodo town. Insurgent units from Fushimi then linked up with those from Toba, drew their artillery into place, and began methodically pounding to pieces the hastily erected barricades in front of Yodo castle.

By early afternoon the Osaka army had thus been driven back across the Uji to Yodo, and both highways north of town had fallen to the insurgents. Other manifestations of defeat also were becoming apparent. The fighting had taken a high toll in casualties, and boatload after boatload of dead and wounded were sent down the Yodo river to Osaka hospital and morgue facilities. That not only reduced the combat force but also fostered demoralization all the way from the front to the former shogun's sickbed. By afternoon some Aizu men were sufficiently exhausted to argue with considerable justification that they should be moved to the rear and others sent in to replace them. That was done, but it meant Osaka had lost some of its most vigorous units, their place being taken by less effective ones.

Demoralization was reflected also in spreading rumors that supplies were running low and some units were destroying matériel, supposedly to keep it from enemy hands. The implication, however, was of betrayal and sabotage. Nor was the implication entirely misdirected. The daimyo of Yodo, Inaba Masakuni, was at Edo in charge of the bakufu, but his vassals holding the castle at Yodo decided on their own initiative not to cooperate with Osaka. When Osaka commanders asked to enter the castle for shelter and defense, their request was refused. When Takikawa Tomoshige insisted, the Yodo gate guards threatened to shoot him on the spot if he did not leave. In futile anger he denounced them as traitors, and furious Osaka troops set fire to houses around the castle. But for all the gestures of bitterness, the fact remained that the castle was shut. That meant Osaka troops were exposed to Kyoto cannon and rifle fire, were exposed potentially to hostile fire from the castle, and risked being trapped should the Great Bridge across the Kizu river south of town be destroyed. Indeed, rumors soon spoke of the Yodo men making a break for the south, burning the Great Bridge, and leaving Osaka troops stranded.

Osaka leaders quickly concluded that Yodo's decision made their position untenable, and during the afternoon they ordered all units withdrawn southward across the Great Bridge to previously prepared defense points at Hashimoto, Yahata, and Hirakata. That redeployment gave them control in depth of the approach to Osaka on the east side of the Yodo river. And the west bank was secured at Yamazaki by a large force of Tsu artillery and infantrymen.

The day's events had changed the war prospect drastically. On the morning of the fourth, Osaka commanders had been able to send guardedly optimistic reports to their superiors in Osaka and Edo. By night of the fifth, however, their tone was entirely changed. In a report sent hurriedly to Osaka, two battalion commanders acknowledged that though many forces had been deployed, they had been compelled to pull back to Hashimoto. Casualties being great, they asked that all available manpower, including naval personnel and civil officials, be committed to the struggle.[10] Gone was the brash assurance of two days before. It was a ragged wreck of a once-arrogant army that faced the cold dawn of the new year's sixth day.

5. The Battle of 1/6

The new day was another clear and cold one with the wind still blowing prophetically from the north.[11] As Kyoto units advanced, Tottori men found themselves unable to get their cannon across the river, and so 140 Hiroshima troops took their place. The remainder of the recognized Kyoto army consisted of Satsuma and Chōshū men, some 2500 in number according to a Satsuma source. Other reports spoke of fifteen Satsuma units of about ninety men apiece, which was slightly reduced from the *han*'s peak efforts of the fourth and fifth. Chōshū furnished four half-battalions *(chūtai)* and one company, plus three companies from Tokuyama and Iwakuni, making an alternative total of about 2340 men. And across the Yodo at Yamazaki were unrecognized members of the Kyoto army, 983 Tsu men consisting of cannoneers with several pieces of artillery, some western-style rifle units, large numbers of support personnel, and regular samurai. Adding the Tsu and Hiroshima men to those of Satsuma and Chōshū, the Kyoto army totaled about 3500.

Opposing them was an army of uncertain size, this very uncertainty itself evidence of disintegration. Much of the Aizu force had been withdrawn to Hirakata, and the Osaka force on line appears to have consisted of men of Kuwana (about 300), Miyazu (some 250), Obama (250 to 500), Aizu (about 250), and perhaps 2000 to 3000 bakufu infantry, both French-trained and regular. The force total was somewhere between 3050 and 4300 troops. In gross numbers, then, the Osaka combat force had lost almost completely its early numerical superiority. And it was weakened further by low morale, poor coordination, and loss of its most effective units.

From Yodo some Satsuma and Chōshū units moved across the Kizu river in small boats and then approached the Osaka east flank at Yahata. Others crossed the Kizu near Yodo castle and followed the east bank of the Yodo down to Osaka's west flank just above Hashimoto. Others moved down the road for a frontal assault on the defense line looping north from Yahata over to Hashimoto. Fighting was joined at about 10 AM on both the east flank around Yahata and the central front. The flank was manned by Miyazu and bakufu units, but they were short of artillery because Miyazu pieces were on loan to Obama forces posted on the west flank. Consequently attackers on the east drove the defenders back with little difficulty while indecisive fighting progressed on the central front.

Miyazu artillery had been loaned to Obama so that it could combine

with the remaining Aizu artillery on the west flank. The plan was to trap
the enemy advancing along the Yodo embankment in an artillery crossfire
provided by Miyazu-Aizu pieces in front and Tsu in the rear. But even
after the Kyoto forces commenced firing and the west flank defenders
began to reply, Tsu artillery remained silent. Then at noon it did engage,
but not as Osaka men expected. Rather, as per secret agreement made
with a Kyoto delegate the night before, the Tsu cannoneers directed their
fire at the Miyazu and Aizu men, reportedly pouring in shrapnel shot
from their small cannon. The Osaka troops hunkered down behind their
walls and *tatami* barricades and angrily debated what to do. Plans to
cross the Yodo and destroy the Tsu positions were abandoned when the
west flank came under assault from assembled insurgent infantry. The
bakufu's French-trained infantry reportedly performed well in fending off
that drive. Before long, however, they learned that forces at Yahata,
hearing of Tsu's betrayal, had panicked in fear of losing their route of retreat and had headed south for the next defense point at Hirakata. With
the collapse at Yahata, troops on the west flank found their own rear exposed and decided to retreat. By late afternoon the defeated Osaka army
had pulled back to Hirakata, and the victorious insurgents were getting
ready for the next day's advance.

In the end that proved unnecessary because that night Itakura sent
messengers up to Hirakata with orders that forces there retreat to Osaka.
For the bakufu the war in fact had ended, and with it ended the Tokugawa era.

For leaders the war may have ended, but for some of their followers
the suffering had not. Compared with the fighting of a year earlier at
Aki, it had been a larger and more sanguinary conflict in absolute terms,
if not in proportion to the numbers committed.[12] Consistent casualty
figures are hard to find. The only really satisfactory ones are those of Satsuma and Chōshū, a fact surely related to their triumph. Those figures
indicate that Satsuma lost 61 dead (those killed plus those who shortly
died from wounds) and 124 wounded. Chōshū lost 35 dead and 106
wounded. Alternative figures for those *han* are almost the same.

Aizu figures vary much more, fatality records for the four days ranging
from a low of 92 to a high of 138 and injury figures from 116 to 185.
Bakufu figures are thoroughly unreliable because records are lacking. One
estimate of 163 dead is the sum of a hard figure of 13 officers and a
guess of 150 enlisted men, a number that is plausible. The total wounded is unknown, the recorded figure of 26 wounded officers being credible, that of 24 wounded soldiers worthless. If the killed/wounded ratios

of Satsuma and Chōshū are a guide, and they likely are as close as one can get, the infantry probably had 300 to 500 enlisted wounded. Kuwana figures are not available, but one source speaks of Aizu, Kuwana, and bakufu having 280 killed in all. If the bakufu lost 163 and Aizu 92, then Kuwana fatalities would be 25, a credible figure for the Kuwana force of 400. And if 25 is a credible figure for fatalities and the Satsuma-Chōshū killed/wounded ratio is valid, then Kuwana probably had some 50 to 70 wounded.

The other marginal combatants also had losses, but they were fewer. Takamatsu, Matsuyama, and Hamada all had severe casualties the first day, and Ōgaki, Obama, and Miyazu had some losses in following days. Probably an adequate overall figure for the four days of war would be nearly 500 dead and 1000 to 1500 wounded.

6. Analysis of Fushimi-Toba

The disastrous outcome of the Tokugawa resort to war requires analysis. Was bakufu defeat a result of betrayal, inadequate arms, faulty organization, low morale, poor leadership, or some combination of factors?

Reviewing the chronology of defeat will give a clearer sense of the problem. To start at the end, the outcome of battle on the sixth was not crucial. The sharply reduced casualty figures of the day suggest that by then the Osaka will to fight had evaporated. Many battle reports also spoke of widespread defeatism among bakufu unit commanders and troops that day, even the French-trained troops.[13] With Aizu largely out of combat and bakufu forces disintegrating, the Kyoto forces' contemporary problems of extended supply lines and ammunition shortages were trivial by comparison. Tsu's betrayal merely accelerated a process of collapse that was already well advanced.

Even the result of battle on the fifth was not the crux of the issue, although fighting that morning was decisive in the sense of confirming the outcome of war. Had men of Yodo thrown their lot in with Osaka, the latter still would have been on the defensive, having lost some of their best units and commanders and having fallen back on second-rate troops. By then, moreover, the insurgents had won complete imperial commitment to their venture and were vigorously using imperial authority to order other *han* forces to cooperate in various ways. Had Yodo not switched, it would have made the insurgent triumph rather more difficult, but by noon of the fifth the chance of an Osaka triumph was already practically nonexistent.

Accordingly it is the fighting of the first forty to forty-five hours, from dusk of the third to about noon of the fifth, that commands our attention.

The outcome of that period was partly determined by what went before and partly by actions taken during the hours themselves.

One cannot but be struck by the indecisiveness of bakufu leadership in prior weeks. Even after it was apparent in the final months of 1867 that Satsuma ambitions could be contained only by military action, the highest bakufu leaders persisted in trying to succeed by manipulation and maneuver. Admittedly their situation was poor, but they hardly made the best of it, failing to give clear leadership or inspiration to either supportive *han* or their own troops. The loss of Kii and Hikone, for example, surely was not inevitable. Even when at last the decision for war was made, it was made precipitously and without resolute plans for a decisive military effort. It was political, not military, considerations that determined the composition of lead forces and the manner of their deployment. Consequently the combat initiative was left in insurgent hands, and war was waged on their terms.

Even saying that, however, does not explain why of a total force of some thirteen thousand troops only about six thousand or so were near enough the enemy to be of any use during those crucial forty hours. One answer probably was that commanders knew full well that a lot of the thirteen thousand would be more menace than help in a crisis, which is itself evidence of the inadequate purposefulness of leadership in earlier months. But a more important reason probably was that bakufu leaders had long seen a close connection between great *han* and *rōnin* activism, and they had a pervasive fear of violence erupting in their midst. The fear of a reforged court-daimyo-*shishi* coalition was certainly strengthened by the insurgency at Mt. Kōya, news from the Kantō, and the continuing possibility of more great *han* forces arriving west of Osaka. It may have been sustained also by the perplexing *eejanaika* activity. And the presence in Osaka harbor of substantial British military power also may have worried Osaka leaders. Whatever the reason, they chose to deploy the bulk of their forces in and near the city, leaving a minority force to conduct offensive operations.

That minority included their best units, but it was not good enough, given the quality of its deployment and leadership. Leadership at both strategic and tactical levels was inadequate. At the very top, throughout the war Yoshinobu was in bed with a severe chill, brought on, a cynic might suspect, by a bad case of cold feet. It was hardly a posture likely to elicit enthusiastic effort. At the next level the chain of command was formally from Ōkōchi to Takenaka to regimental commanders, but in the early hours Ōkōchi was at Yodo and Takenaka initially at Fushimi; as things developed, their ability to coordinate efforts at the front was very limited. In part that was due to the abrupt outbreak of fighting, and in part it was due to the limited obedience of subordinate commanders.

Two key instances of command breakdown can be cited. One was the delayed advance of Kuwana at Toba on the night of the third after hostilities had commenced. The delay may have been due to snarled command connections within the bakufu's regimental leadership or it may have been due to Kuwana procrastination or something else. Whatever its cause, it meant they were absent from a critical period of combat and their absence may have denied the Osaka army an opportunity to repulse the Satsuma attackers at a moment of perceived vulnerability. The second instance, on the early morning of the fourth, was the refusal of both bakufu and Aizu unit commanders to counterattack promptly at Fushimi. Had a determined effort been made there, it might have changed the shape of the outcome—so many insurgent units had been hurriedly dispatched to shore up the fragile line at Toba that the insurgents at Fushimi were temporarily much reduced and vulnerable.

Beyond the problem of insubordination was the problem of pursuing a two-front war in which defeat on either front posed an immediate threat to the rear of the other. On both fronts there were instances during those crucial hours of units withdrawing or halting their advance because of reports of trouble on the other front. It was a problem that had plagued the allied forces at Aki a year earlier. The insurgents also faced that problem initially, but Osaka forces failed to exploit the transient insurgent weakness at either Toba or Fushimi, and after midday of the fourth the two-front problem did not trouble Kyoto again.

These several problems all contributed to the early setbacks that rapidly ate away at Osaka morale. Even more than at Aki in the Summer War, the malign influence of long-range trends within the Tokugawa camp had created such a fragile state of morale that only early and exhilarating victories could have given the Osaka forces an élan sufficient to their task. Those initial victories did not occur, and the resultant decay of Osaka morale, contrasting so strongly with the growing strength and attractiveness of the insurgent position, made the events after noon of the fifth anticlimactic.

The question of weaponry also requires examination. The problem of inadequate Osaka artillery has been referred to previously. The problem is not, however, as simple as it may appear. It must be pointed out that considerable numbers of fieldpieces were placed at defense points between Yodo and Osaka; if they had adequate ammunition, then the shortage of artillery was essentially an aspect of the larger problem of conservative overall deployment. Had all the cannon emplaced at Yodo and southward been properly deployed on line and adequately supplied, manned, and commanded on the night of the third, they might well have been able to blow the insurgents out of town. It must also be observed, however, that artillery (like gunships and bombers in a later day) serve unmotivated armies as a crutch to support troops who see no good reason to take risks. A highly motivated force might have felt no shortage of artillery.

The more crucial problem is infantry weapons and ammunition, but the imprecision of battle reports conceals important differences in the quality of arms men bore. Some evaluation is possible, however, because the scattered records of weapon imports indicate the general character of arms available,[14] and battle reports suggest which units had firearms and which did not. The massive import of Mini weapons at both Nagasaki and Yokohama meant that the two sides had access to similar weapons. But whereas the Chōshū forces and the main Satsuma units all had modern rifles and only the marginal insurgent groups, for the most part, were poorly armed, the main Osaka forces carried a mixed bag of armaments. The best bakufu battalions, the *hohei* and French-trained forces, had weapons as good as those of the insurgents, but the battalions of *jūtai*, *yūgekitai*, and others, with mixed firearms or miscellaneous arms, were decidedly inferior. And other units that were in the thick of it at first, notably *mimawari*, Shinsengumi, and many Aizu men, used pikes rather than firearms. While the pikemen turned in some fine performances, as we noted, they and the swordsmen tired more easily than the riflemen for obvious reasons and hence acted as a severe drag on the capacity of the latter to sustain an attack. It appears that the insurgents were substantially more successful in having their best weapons at the right place at the right time, and that achievement contributed significantly to the initial victories which led to ultimate triumph.

Since Aizu troops and bakufu infantry were the key elements in the Osaka attack force, they merit particular attention. Records of Aizu organization at the time of the Kyoto coup back in 63/8 indicate that main Aizu battle units then consisted of about 150 men apiece, of whom 60 were *ashigaru* with old-style firearms *(teppō)* or spears, 50 were regular samurai, 20 were *yoriki*, and 18 were officers and other personnel. The total *han* force at Kyoto then was some 1500 men. In succeeding months and years Katamori advocated military reform, and he did succeed a year later in switching the firearms units to modern rifles.[15] During the final crisis, however, Aizu military organization remained essentially that of 1863. Battle units contained some 120 to 130 men apiece and consisted of both men with firearms and others with pikes and swords. These units were lumped together in makeshift battalions for the advance northward, but they lacked any effective level of integration above the large company size.

Bakufu infantry forces were much more fully modernized. They consisted of 50-man rifle companies organized in 500-man battalions that fought in alternating half-battalions (in conjunction theoretically with supporting cavalry, artillery, and engineer units). They were armed with modern rifles, drilled in unit tactics, and led by field-grade officers promoted through the ranks and trained in modern tactics at the military institute. Unfortunately the infantry either left no battle reports or they have been lost, so there is only scattered information on their actual performance in combat. When referred to, they were generally praised as disciplined, reliable forces, particularly the French-trained forces, although some comments suggest they thoroughly lacked the Aizu samurai's zeal and willingness to make an ultimate personal commitment. And their performance on the Fushimi road on the fourth was by all accounts inadequate.

Infantry commanders received a much more mixed evaluation. There were cases of great heroism and resolve, such as regimental commander (hohei bugyō) Sakuma Nobuhisa, who led his force into combat on the Fushimi road on the fourth. In the first assault his troops were repulsed, and in an effort to start a second assault, he made great effort to rally them. Exposed to enemy fire, he kept moving among his men, encouraging them to advance until the enemy finally succeeded in wounding him badly. He was carried from the field and died later after being sent to a hospital at Osaka. On the same front battalion commander (hohei gashira) Kubota Bizen no kami also led his troops that morning and was killed in action while leading an assault.[16]

More common though are reports, usually by Aizu men, complaining bitterly about cowardly or timid bakufu commanders who seemed interested only in retreat. The criticisms may have been justified or they may have been the complaints of old-fashioned samurai accustomed to individual heroics who neither understood nor appreciated the tactics of unit maneuver and command. If the latter is the case, however, one may have to conclude that such unit tactics were not a source of strength for Osaka.

To put the performance of Aizu and bakufu infantry in proper perspective, it is helpful to compare the Satsuma-Chōshū achievement. At the command level one can only look with admiration at the apparent clarity of purpose that moved the insurgent leaders despite the obfuscating maneuvers of Shungaku and other daimyo. From early in 1865 the men who led Chōshū had understood that the issue of primacy, whose solution was necessary before they could address other national issues, would ultimately be settled on the battlefield, and they had prepared single-mindedly for that day of decision. Satsuma leaders do not appear to have understood that until mid-67, but Yoshinobu's triumph at that time cleared Hisamitsu's vision, and thereafter the *han* prepared accordingly.

The different dates of *han* commitment to armed insurrection were reflected in the quality of the armies they fielded. Chōshū had a small force of the finest-quality troops. They were without peer in Japan. Organized in forty-man companies grouped into battalions of four hundred who functioned in combat as coordinated alternating half-battalions, they were totally armed with up-to-date rifles, were well drilled and well led, and fought with both zeal and discipline. They made ideal cannon fodder. Satsuma's armies were much larger and much less efficient. They were organized as ninety-man companies that had only minimal high-level coordination. Their weapons were mixed, partly modern firearms and partly pikes and swords, but they made up in judicious deployment, zeal, numbers, and leadership resolve what they lacked in quality of organization and weaponry. In terms of army organization and weaponry, then, the four main protagonists probably rank in this order: Chōshū was best; bakufu infantry was next; Satsuma was next; and Aizu and most liege vassal forces were last.

Aizu men tried to do with zeal what they could not do for lack of weapons, organization, and numbers. They were brave, and those who did not die or sustain debilitating wounds exhausted themselves in their hopeless effort.

The bakufu infantry performance was not as good as that of Satsuma despite their numbers, weapons, and high-quality organization. Their mediocre performance was in the last analysis an expression of poor leadership and the absence of a high level of troop motivation. The former, which we have dwelt on, can in the end be traced, I believe, to the very top—to the ambiguous intentions and apparent political naiveté of Yoshinobu. Only he could have made the army an effective military tool, and by his indecisiveness he squandered it and hence sabotaged the year long effort of the Keiō reform. The poor infantry motivation, which probably was reflected in the clamor for artillery, was in part a product of that inept leadership. But it also had other roots revealed in the troop unrest that rocked Edo during 67/9–11. That aspect of the motivation problem suggests that fiscal and other difficulties plaguing the Keiō military reform finally came home to roost as a significant factor in the military defeat at Fushimi-Toba. Fine weapons in the hands of unmotivated soldiers were not a great boon. It was a lesson the Meiji leaders took to heart.

CAPITULATION: 68/1–4

The defeat at Fushimi-Toba was decisive, but that became apparent only some ten days afterward. During the six days immediately following defeat, the vanquished army started heading eastward and its Osaka leaders returned to their bastion at Edo.[17] During the next five days, Tokugawa leaders were occupied with crucial political discussions and decisions in Chiyoda castle. After the decision to capitulate was made, leaders of the vanquished worked methodically to disestablish their regime and prepare for a new and smaller role as a minor polity in a corner of the conqueror's Japan. And as they did so, the victors at Kyoto equally methodically deployed their forces across the country whose governance had become their responsibility.

1. The Retreat to Edo: 1/6–12

At Osaka Yoshinobu had learned by the sixth of the army's reverses, and he prepared and sent to the front a morale-boosting statement assuring men that the effort would not be abandoned. But a few hours later, during the afternoon, news of the day's defeat at Hashimoto arrived, making it clear that his words had not stemmed the insurgent tide.[18] That news led to a major policy conference and heated disagreement. In the end Yoshinobu, with the support of newly appointed senior councillor Sakai Tadatō and junior councillors Nagai Naomune and Asano Ujisuke (the latter just arrived from Edo), insisted the fighting be halted despite the contrary arguments of those most fully involved in the war effort, particularly Ōkōchi Masatada, Takenaka Shigemoto, Tsukahara Masayoshi, Hirayama Keichū, other army officers, and men of Aizu and Kuwana.

Orders to withdraw were sent up to the front, and shortly afterward decisions were made on retreating to the east. The purpose of retreat was unstated, but it was generally presumed to involve another stand. Advocates of continued resistance, notably Ōkōchi, Takenaka, and Tsukahara, were ordered to stay at Osaka to bring the army home. The supporters of retreat, notably Itakura, Sakai, and Nagai, together with Hirayama, whose real forte was diplomacy, were ordered to accompany Yoshinobu.[19]

The latter group then secretly left the castle and in an extremely difficult night and morning managed at last to get aboard their warship despite high waves, darkness, inept boatmanship, and menacing maneuvers by British warships in the port. After a day waiting for rough seas to quiet and attending to minor matters from shipboard, the vessel steamed eastward late on the eighth despite protests of the ship's captain and crew and despite a defective engine. The half-crippled vessel was unable to make progress against the strong north wind and so worked its way directly eastward toward Hachijō island. On the tenth when the wind had abated, it turned north and on the twelfth reached Edo, docking at Hamagoten. The ill and exhausted Yoshinobu entered the western enceinte together with his officials just before noon. It was the first time since becoming Tokugawa chief that he had set foot in the great Chiyoda castle of his illustrious ancestors.

At Osaka Ōkōchi and his assistants proceeded with the bitter task of liquidating the Tokugawa position in the Kinai. Officials arranged on the seventh to transport eastward the treasury collection of 180,000 *ryō* of old gold coins, while other funds were distributed to the city populace. The disorderly and confused city guard forces were reduced, vassal daimyo being instructed to send their men home to their *han*. Along the coast near the city infantrymen boarded ship for the east, Ōkōchi taking the major units to Suruga and from there heading via the Tōkaidō to Edo. Other elements of the defeated army were ordered to retreat into Kii for transfer to the east by boat and highway. Then on the ninth, as the city began to sprout fires and violence, the conquerors from Kyoto arrived and took charge of affairs. As Kyoto forces entered the city, bakufu, Aizu, Kuwana, and other troops headed into Kii as ordered. They received a hostile reception from Tokugawa Mochitsugu's troops but managed nonetheless to hire small boats or secure passage on warships that picked men up here and there along the coast. Some got rides all the way to Yokohama; others were deposited in Mikawa, Suruga, or elsewhere on the way and walked or foraged for other rides from there. Some went the whole distance overland. Some went home instead.

By late in the month defeated troops began to reach Edo in force. Some were billeted around the castle. Many *han* vassals and liege vassals were sent on home, and many infantrymen were mustered out. The Tokugawa army had been disbanded.

2. The Decision to Capitulate: 1/12–17

By the end of 68/1 most of the defeated army had reached the Kantō, and by then the regime was well on the way to liquidating itself.

The decision to capitulate was made despite profound intentions to the contrary among leaders who had been at Edo during the Fushimi-Toba battles. During those days of disaster Edo leaders proceeded unaware of the tumultuous events occurring to the west. They attended the usual New Year greeting ceremonies, issued orders pertaining to city and Kantō

guard duty, and on the fourth and fifth issued orders of a cautionary nature because of rumors of trouble in Edo and the Kantō. On the sixth
they ordered officials in Izu to organize a peasant militia to keep the province pacified. On that day and the next they continued preparing more
routine ceremonies, and on the eighth they ordered modern military
forces in the city to drill. On yet the next day the finance office completed a long revision of regulations dealing with paying and punishing
military personnel.[20] In short, the regime died in battle before its leaders
at Edo even knew the question of life and death had at last been confronted.

On the ninth, even as Yoshinobu's vessel was struggling toward Hachijō island, Edo leaders received their first news from the west. On that
day Inaba Masakuni reported to officials news of disadvantageous fighting at Fushimi on the third and fourth. Lest disaster befall, he ordered
daimyo to make preparations at once so they could proceed to Osaka
with troops within two or three days.[21] During the next two days some
orders were issued in preparation for a westward deployment as news of
the fourth and perhaps the fifth reached Edo.[22] Then the whole world
was turned topsy-turvy with the sudden appearance of Yoshinobu, Itakura, and others on the twelfth. At once a conference of officials and important vassal lords got underway. It quickly developed into a tumult as men
learned of the Kinai disaster and debated what to do. In the outcome it
was decided to rally forces and implement a plan to march west. Specific
proposals were advanced, and disorderly preparations were begun.[23]

During the next four days that initial resolve slowly disintegrated. A
host of military orders were issued, but they were all defensive in nature.
They deployed some infantry and artillery to Sunpu, and they strengthened the vassal daimyo presence in the Kantō plain, in the process getting
those men nearer to their castles. Apparently other military preparations
also began at Edo. But in any case until the army returned from Osaka,
not much could be done by way of a march west.[24] That was so because
the bakufu had deployed almost its entire army to the west before
Fushimi-Toba. As of the ninth it had at Edo some 5750 men. Of them
2000 were tied down with city patrol and gate guard duty; 1600 had
just been conscripted; 700 were in the midst of basic training; and 600
were in miscellaneous units of doubtful value; only 850 were infantry
deemed ready for combat.[25]

Heated and indecisive discussions continued between Yoshinobu, Itakura, other junior and senior councillors, Matsudaira Naokatsu of Kawagoe, and a few other vassal daimyo. The ex-shogun also continued to
come under pressure from lesser men, including retired Mizuno Tadanori,

who urged him to implement the war policy decision of the twelfth. Officials and teachers in the western studies center *(kaiseijo)* drew up an extensive plan of military action and political reform designed to salvage the regime and presented it to him on the fourteenth. Others, such as men of Kuwana and Aizu, lobbied unsuccessfully to get him to act. Some, such as Kondō Isami of the Shinsengumi, were refused audience. And on the fifteenth the militant and highly agitated Oguri Tadamasa was fired. From about then old Ōkubo Ichiō began attending discussions and counseling a pacific settlement, advice men began to heed after Oguri's dismissal. By the sixteenth Yoshinobu had made it clear to key officials that he would not fight to preserve Tokugawa preeminence. Instead he tried to persuade the Hitotsubashi lord, Tokugawa Mochiharu (formerly Mochinori of Owari), to succeed him as head of the Tokugawa house.[26]

On the following day there was more evidence that despite continuing disagreement Yoshinobu at last had taken a stand. Junior councillor Hori Naotora, who had helped draft the militant statement of the twelfth, committed suicide in despair, reportedly in the senior council office. Moreover, Yoshinobu sent Shungaku a letter protesting his peaceful intentions and seeking Shungaku's intercession on his behalf. Furthermore Katsu Kaishū, who had had no significant role in affairs since his mission to Miyajima back in 66/9, was temporarily promoted to acting commander of the navy *(kaigun bugyō nami)*, the first step in moving him to an active political position in a shrunken Tokugawa house.[27] The evidence thus suggests that by 68/1/17 the implications of Fushimi-Toba had been confirmed in a Tokugawa political decision to abandon all pretensions to a national leadership role. The future of Japan lay in the hands of others.

3. Liquidating the Regime: 1/17 and After

After the seventeenth, Yoshinobu's program of capitulation gained momentum. When Léon Roches urged him to try again on the nineteenth, the advice was gently rejected.[28] Instead on the same day Yoshinobu explained somewhat disingenuously to assembled daimyo and high liege vassals *(kōtai yoriai)* that he had surrendered his governing authority without regret and had loyally prepared to go to Kyoto. Fighting had broken out by mistake, however, causing him to be wrongfully labeled an enemy of the court. He had been unable to get the label erased despite great efforts, and so he was asking them all to exert themselves, pleading to Kyoto on his behalf.[29] On the following day he, Itakura, Inaba Masakuni, and other officials visited Aizu and Shinsengumi wounded at their hospital quarters, consoling them and thanking them for their brave service. Militant Ōkōchi Masatada had just brought part of the army back from Osaka, and Yoshinobu got him out of town by relieving him of his army command and ordering him home to his castle at Takasaki "to prepare defenses."[30]

In succeeding days he intensified and expanded his efforts to open up channels to the court and began a complete change of officialdom. On the twenty-third Ōkubo Ichiō was called out of retirement and named finance minister *(kaikei sōsai)*. Katsu, who had begun writing on behalf of Yoshinobu and peace from the eighteenth, accepted the title of *rikugun sōsai*, head of Yoshinobu's evaporating army, but he rejected the added title of junior councillor. Then the Tokugawa lord at last met him. After Katsu suggested the possibilities and limits of a naval strategy for victory, Yoshinobu insisted he was determined to surrender. Katsu at once indicated his support for a policy of capitulation.[31]

Other promotions of the twenty-third put other liege vassals in top ministerial and vice-ministerial positions. On the next day a large number of vassal daimyo were released from office and instructed to devote attention to their own *han* affairs. In succeeding days all the senior councillors, including Itakura, Inaba Masakuni, and Ogasawara, and all those junior councillors who were daimyo thus left the Tokugawa service. Large numbers of lesser officials also were dismissed as Yoshinobu cut his government down to a size appropriate to a daimyo's *han*. Liege vassals with lands in central and western Japan were ordered to go home and accept imperial leadership. During 68/2 the policy intensified. In a steady stream of orders, more officials were dismissed and more vassal daimyo and liege vassals were relieved of duty and ordered home to obey the court.

Paralleling this liquidation of the regime was an intensifying effort to negotiate a peaceful settlement of the conflict by getting the court to modify its denunciation of Yoshinobu. In that campaign, as a gesture intended to show his submission, on 2/12 Yoshinobu turned Edo castle over to two Tokugawa relatives and moved into seclusion in a villa at Ueno.

While leaders of the defunct bakufu were thus scrambling to save themselves from the conqueror's vengeance, the troops they no longer needed were beginning to get out of hand. As the defeated army straggled into town, hospital facilities filled with wounded and sick survivors, and infantrymen and others freshly out of employment began to plunder and create trouble.[32] During 68/2 the growing chaos led caretakers of the regime to order those *han* troops guarding the city to round up any troublemakers who stayed in town. Some of those who left town continued to be a problem in the countryside, plundering for survival and in some cases trying to mobilize local resistance to the imperial advance. Later in the month *han* troops also were sent home, leaving the city in the inadequate hands of those forces still maintained by the regime. Some loyalists formed units to protect Yoshinobu, but the city in general was marked by escalating confusion and lawlessness. Many commoners fled and others ran amok. It would be in the interests of the conquerors to take control before the city lost all semblance of order.

4. The Insurgent Conquest: 68/1-4

Yoshinobu's refusal to fight and his decision to yield meant that the imperial army's task was essentially to overrun the garrisons at castle towns scattered across Japan.[33] That proved an easy task because of the character and situation of garrison forces, the actions of Yoshinobu, and the skillful strategy of the insurgents.

Castle garrison forces were very weak. In almost no cases were *han* forces all at home. Rather, most *han* had some men in Edo, Kyoto, Osaka, or at various other places on long or short-term duty, and so most garrisons were small. A few vassal daimyo were at Kyoto and many more were at Edo. The latter rapidly returned home in the last days of 68/1 and during 68/2, some arriving in time to surrender their castles to the advancing imperial army. Others did not, however, and when their garrison commanders were unable to secure guidance from their lords, they had to make whatever decisions they could on the basis of the immediate tactical situation plus their knowledge of the larger political situation.

For most of them the tactical situation was bad. Many had very good reason to expect strong nearby *han* to support, or at least accept, the insurgent conquest, and the actions of such nearby *han* tended to shape their own decisions. Moreover some garrisons were tied down quelling local peasant outbursts. Others were bothered by *rōnin* groups, and others hesitated to open hostilities lest conflict ignite local unrest. Even those garrisons with no such concerns had few men present, however, and the most they could do would be to make a sortie or two and then seal their castles and go on the defensive. And they had absolutely no good reason to expect a relieving bakufu army to appear.

Garrisons could expect no relief from Edo if they knew what was going on there. And even if they did not know that Edo leaders were quitting, still they did know the thrust of developments over the last two or three months. They did know of the 67/10 Tosa action, the 67/12 Satsuma action, and Yoshinobu's general response to both. Moreover the advancing imperial army's vanguard units doubtlessly brought garrison commanders up to date when necessary. Then the problem was much simplified during 68/2 as more and more garrisons learned that Yoshinobu expected them—as he had in 67/11—to accept imperial leadership.

Nor were the garrisons all dominated by diehards more royalist than the king. *Sonnō jōi* sentiments could be found in all camps, even among liege vassals at Edo in the days immediately following Yoshinobu's return. Some *han* vassals who found their loyalties cruelly torn sought desperately to devise rationales resolving their dilemmas, and Yoshinobu's actions helped them move into the imperial camp with a clear conscience. Among the nonideological, moreover, Yoshinobu's maneuvering and equivocation during the last months of 1867 had generated a great deal of political uncertainty and pragmatic contingency planning. Even before Osaka raised the standard of resistance at year's end, influential men in many *han* had been in contact with the court. Before 1/6 a number of crucial choices had been made, and after that date others quickly and easily followed, thanks to the prior contingency planning.

The insurgents' political strategy of conquest also encouraged capitulation by garrison forces. On 1/11 the court issued a public list of its enemies. The list included Yoshinobu, Katamori, Sadaaki, the lord of Takamatsu, ex-senior councillor Hisamatsu Sadaaki of Matsuyama, Itakura, Ōkōchi, and twenty lesser officials who had been active in advocating the war. Except for the vassal lords of Obama, Ōgaki, Miyazu, Nobeoka, and Toba, some of whose vassals had joined the Tokugawa forces at Fushimi-Toba, no other vassal daimyo were named. The list, however, could always be lengthened. That possibility doubtless gave retainers of vassal daimyo great incentive to join the insurgent armies. And as the armies advanced, garrison commanders were apprised of developments, given opportunity to pledge their loyalty, and enrolled therein or otherwise dealt with in accordance with the particular degree of reward or punishment that each *han* was judged to deserve in view of recent performance.

During 67/1–3 as the imperial armies fanned out, the cautious procedure of approach, explain, invite and receive cooperation was repeated scores and scores of times. During those weeks the imperial forces also accepted a stream of oaths of loyalty delivered by liege vassals, vassal daimyo, and their retainers heading westward from Edo. By the time the insurgent vanguard reached Edo in mid-68/3, most component parts of the Tokugawa house had moved piecemeal into the imperial camp. And the peasant militia forces that had been organized by Edo in 1867 had been ordered to submit. Well before Edo castle itself fell, the Tokugawa had ceased to be a national political entity.

In great part the evaporation of Tokugawa power could be seen as a product of the capitulationist policy Yoshinobu was pursuing at Edo even as the imperial armies advanced. Perhaps because the victors saw it in that way, or perhaps in order to restore order in Edo quickly, by 68/3 they were willing to accommodate the numerous requests for leniency for Yoshinobu and to spare the Tokugawa house utter destruction. Katsu Kaishū handled the final stages of negotiation, and on 4/4 the vanguard of the imperial army entered Chiyoda castle peacefully. Daimyo in northeast Japan put up a fierce resistance to the conquest for several months thereafter, but their struggle was not a defense of the Tokugawa bakufu. With the defeat at Fushimi-Toba the regime had failed. With the decision to capitulate, its pretensions to leadership had been abandoned. With the surrender of Edo castle the last dead symbol of Tokugawa hegemony had fallen. The Great Peace had become history.

Recapitulation and Analysis

A Chronological Evaluation: 1862–1868
1. *The Bunkyū Reform*
2. *Conservative Reaffirmation*
3. *The Summer War*
4. *The Keiō Reform*

Why the Bakufu Fell As It Did When It Did
1. *The Role of Commoners*
2. *The Imperialist Intrusion*
3. *Foundations of the Ad Hoc Coalition*
4. *The Elements of Bakufu Weakness*

Last Reflections

The Great Peace had ended. The Tokugawa hegemony was gone. Its passing was of consequence not only to Japan but to all future generations of humankind because it marked the end of that long era in which Japanese activities were of only minor and occasional consequence to the external world and set the stage for later active and influential Japanese dealings with that world. Having completed the narrative study of bakufu collapse, I now wish to make explicit and concise some answers to the questions posed in the introduction. Then I shall undertake to elaborate my initial explanation of why the regime fell as it did when it did and in closing reconsider the Tokugawa collapse in more general terms of political failure.

A Chronological Evaluation: 1862–1868

The questions posed in the introduction were these: What was the Bunkyū reform all about and why did it work out as it did? What did the conservative reaffirmation achieve, and why did it fail? Why was the Summer War so traumatic for the bakufu? And finally, what did the Keiō reform attempt to do, what did it accomplish, and why ultimately did it fail?

1. The Bunkyū Reform

During 1862 the bakufu's hegemonial position was challenged when three segments of society that normally were excluded from any active role in national politics began participating concurrently in those politics. Several great lords (those of Satsuma, Chōshū, Fukui, Owari, Aizu, Tosa, and Tottori most notably), vigorous members of the imperial court, and politicized lesser samurai or *shishi* all became active at that time for two principal reasons. First the salutary fears that Ii Naosuke had instilled in them had worn off by 1862, and aggrieved parties felt the chance had come to right past wrongs. Second the growing foreign presence, with its intrinsic threat to ethnic sensibilities, and foreign trade, with the economic imbalances and inflation that were attributed to it, generated anger and a desire to set things right. That was especially so among Edo and Kyoto residents, including samurai and nobles, who were most exposed to the foreign presence or affected by the economic dislocation.

This ad hoc coalition of court, daimyo, and *shishi* made its power felt during the first half of the year in many ways: in the assault on Andō Nobuyuki, the threats to other officials, the attacks on foreigners, and the political and military maneuvers of Shimazu Hisamitsu, Chōshū leaders, Matsudaira Shungaku, other daimyo, and the nobles of the Ōhara mission. The midyear turnover of personnel and changes in policy at Edo revealed that established bakufu leaders were utterly unable to cope with the combined assault. Instead they allowed Shungaku, Tokugawa Yoshinobu, and others into office and then agreed to undertake that wide-ranging series of changes I have labeled the Bunkyū reform.

To explain what the Bunkyū reform was all about is rather difficult because its character was highly ambiguous. At inception it was a Fukui venture of quite clear purpose. For Shungaku and such supporters as Komai Chōon, Ōkubo Ichiō, Okabe Nagatsune, and Asano Ujisuke the reform was an attempt to revive and develop to a higher level the inclusivistic general strategy earlier pursued by Abe Masahiro. In 1862 it constituted a *kōbugattai* strategy which assumed that institutionally autonomous great daimyo could work together effectively as participating elements in a national coalition regime functioning under imperial auspices and using a modified bakufu as its administrative structure.

From the first, however, this improbable venture encountered difficulties. Externally the rivalries and disputes among the intruders, between Shungaku and Yoshinobu and between Satsuma and Chōshū most notably, tangled matters badly. Moreover Hisamitsu's shortsighted handling of the Namamugi incident precipitated a diplomatic crisis that thoroughly confounded affairs by early 1863. Internally Shungaku's policy stretched the inclusivistic ideal so far as to make it as much threat as promise to the bakufu, and consequently it could not be a wholehearted bakufu venture. Officialdom in general, and vassal daimyo officials in particular, were opposed to surrendering bakufu authority and their own political prerogatives, and the pressure necessary to overcome their opposition only exacerbated tensions within the bakufu. With one thing and another, the inclusivistic vision of the Bunkyū reform aborted, and five years later the bitter lesson of 1862 probably was a factor in making Komai and Asano active participants in the exclusivistic unification strategy of the Keiō reform.

That alternative vision of exclusivistic reform was under a cloud during the first months of the Bunkyū reform, having been badly tarnished by Ii Naosuke's Ansei purge. For most of 1862 those officials who saw Shungaku's strategy as an attack on bakufu supremacy and established privilege did little more than protest and obstruct his policies. The administrators who pursued constructive military reforms from about midyear were doubtless attempting to preserve bakufu supremacy, however, and by 62/11, when the Fukui venture was beginning to founder badly, the Bunkyū reform's internal character began to change, becoming more exclusivistic. It appears that Ogasawara Nagamichi and others, probably including Itakura Katsukiyo and even Yoshinobu, began subtly to alter the purpose of the reform, and most particularly the aim of the scheduled shogunal trip to Kyoto. They intended to use it as a means of reasserting Tokugawa leadership rather than as further evidence of Tokugawa subordination to the court.

By year's end the Bunkyū reform had become a political vehicle driven for contradictory purposes. For some it remained a means of reducing the bakufu's role in a restructured polity; for others it had become a means of revitalizing that role. In the end, however, the reform was a success from no viewpoint, leaving the polity in a shambles awaiting the appearance of some group capable of putting it back together again.

The failure of the Bunkyū reform can be explained in part by its internal contradictions. But that leads one to ask why regular bakufu leaders were unable to prevent either Shungaku's initial intrusion into their ranks or the adoption later of reform proposals they could not really approve.

There were several reasons why senior councillors Kuze Hirochika, Wakizaka Yasuori, Itakura Katsukiyo, and others could stop neither the

midyear tide from without nor the erosion of control that continued nearly to year's end. For one thing bakufu leaders were committed to the
principles of hierarchy and status respect. When nobles and others speaking in the name of the emperor demanded that the court be respected and
foreigners expelled, those leaders felt obligated to listen respectfully,
argue discreetly, and yield when reason and genteel coercion could not
prevail, even though that yielding created rancor within the bakufu itself.
Bakufu leaders were by custom predisposed to govern by consensus and
conciliation, yielding to pressure when necessary in order to find mutually
tolerable middle ground. When nobles and daimyo argued their positions
forcefully, bakufu leaders tried to compromise in 1862 as they had most
of the time before and would do repeatedly in later years, even though
the outcome was a constant shifting of policy content that also generated
quarrels among officials themselves.

Moreover, in terms of foreign policy, which eventually became the
crux of the struggle, bakufu leaders were not in any case satisfied with
opening the country, seeing in it far more potential for harm than good.
Consequently they were rather willing to try something else and predisposed to find other proposals convincing, even when their own second
thoughts or the arguments of colleagues told them the proposals were ill-
advised. Furthermore the men who controlled the bakufu did not want to
die. The recent rash of murders and attempted murders, the direct
threats, and the constant rumors of plots and schemes served to intimidate those who most vigorously opposed the assault on bakufu leadership.

Finally in the background was the fact of a decidedly uncertain military
capability and a correspondingly profound reluctance to submit any issue
to arbitration by sword. Doubtless a man of Ii Naosuke's forcefulness
could have held the dam a while longer, but the limited promise of his
technique was amply demonstrated in the outcome of his own rule.

Besides these characteristics reducing the forcefulness of regular bakufu
leadership, one characteristic of its opposition was of critical importance.
That was its character as an ad hoc coalition. The bakufu's political resources were sufficiently varied that it could almost certainly have withstood an assault from just some great lords, or just an ambitious court, or
just angry samurai. But when the pressure from these several sources
came conjointly, as in 62/6 or 10, it was able to overwhelm even the
most adamant official resistance. And when that pressure coincided with
foreign pressure, as in 62/8, it was sufficient to wreak even more havoc.

By year's end the consequences of this multiheaded assault were fully
visible. The shogun was bound for Kyoto despite the nearly universal opposition of officialdom. Officialdom itself was in a state of profound

shock and disarray. The institutional key to Tokugawa supremacy at home, the *sankin kōtai* system, had been emasculated. The symbolic relationship of shogun and emperor had been profoundly altered. And a program of administrative and military reform that was intended to strengthen the regime was becoming bogged down, its harmful consequences largely realized, its promise largely stillborn.

When at year's end nobles and samurai activists demanded the restoration of imperial rule, there was almost no opposition from the paralyzed, demoralized members of the bakufu—either the many who had opposed the Bunkyū reform or the few who had supported it. The only reason the restoration did not occur in early 1863 was that the groups who had joined, however awkwardly, in assault upon the bakufu fell to quarreling among themselves. And significantly, just as the foreign issue had been central to their coalescence in the first place, it was the impossible choices of foreign policy more than anything else that broke up the coalition and confounded the proponents of restoration. In 63/3 Shungaku fled in disgrace to his castle after it had become apparent how complete was his failure to reorganize and revitalize the polity. At about the same time the external challengers in their disarray abandoned the restoration project before its completion. They had failed to create a new central regime, but they had destroyed the old one, such as it was. The bakufu thereafter was only a regional polity but still formally saddled with the burden of conducting foreign affairs.

2. Conservative Reaffirmation

As it turned out, then, in early 1863 the restorationist movement had fallen apart because of its internal divisions, and the Bunkyū reform had sputtered out because of its internal contradictions and external complications. Before their passing the undertakings made a shambles of the bakufu, but in the end the bakufu's disarray was not as great as that of the court-daimyo-*shishi* coalition. The bakufu, which had been something to begin with, had not quite been reduced to nothing. The coalition, which had risen abruptly from nothing, returned to nothing. Consequently bakufu officials were able to use their surviving institutional advantages to pull their regime back together and begin a long, tortuous attempt to reconstruct the old order.

Most of the bakufu's energies during the years until the Summer War of 1866 were consumed by immediate crises. Some were produced by court conniving, some by daimyo *démarches*, some by *shishi* initiatives, and some by foreign demands; but as in 1862, time after time it was the conjunction of these external pressures that proved Edo's undoing. The bakufu did survive those crises, however, and as we noted in summing up Chapter 4, it also made modest progress in the larger venture of reconstructing the old order. Still, the progress did not necessarily demonstrate bakufu effectiveness, and it was trivial compared to the considerable evidence that the years 1863–1866 were cumulatively very damaging to the regime. Perhaps most importantly those three years drove Edo to the edge of fiscal ruin as income grew ever more unreliable, as self-destructive fiscal practices became prevalent, as expenditures skyrocketed, and as inflation undermined the currency. It was apparent that the *han* also were approaching fiscal catastrophe and, more ominously, that economic disruption was beginning to affect the elemental well-being of large numbers of common people.

In terms of diplomatic relations, too, those three years carried ominous implications. It was then that foreigners began to choose sides in Japanese domestic affairs. The bakufu started developing ties with France that exacerbated daimyo distrust of Edo just as severely as the growing British association with Satsuma and Chōshū fed Edo's suspicions of the great *han*. The foreign trade itself also began to have deleterious ramifications. As bakufu finances grew more strained and the regime became ever more needful of tariff income, it became more and more interested in controlling all foreign trade itself. The great *han* also wished to profit from that trade, however, and so the trade question, which previously had been basically a foreign demand upon reluctant Japanese, was transformed into another issue that pitted bakufu against *han*.

At many levels, then, the years of conservative reaffirmation were more harmful than helpful to Tokugawa interests, and the political gains that were scored were of very dubious value. The effort must be judged on balance another bakufu failure. While admitting that the plague of disruptive issues was a severe complicating factor, the root reason for failure of conservative reaffirmation was the fundamental inadequacy of its informing vision. The bakufu lacked the power necessary to drive the foreigners away, to manage them so as to make their presence palatable to the politicized public, to control that public, or to change its attitude. It also was unable to compel the great lords to return to Edo and could offer them no good reason to return voluntarily. It made no sense, from a great daimyo vantage point, to return to the old pre-1862 order, and as conflicts of interest fed misunderstanding, distrust grew like topsy, and more and more lords and *han* vassals became convinced that bakufu orders were misguided and could safely be ignored. Having chosen to pursue an anachronistic vision, bakufu leaders squandered ever more political goodwill, and the price was fully paid in the Summer War of 1866.

3. The Summer War

The Summer War was the final overwhelming blow that destroyed the conservative orientation of bakufu policy. In part the events of the war were crucial in themselves. But to a certain extent the war was crucial only as the last in a cumulative string of events that discredited the strategy of forcing Chōshū to submit.

The regime's attempts to force the men of Mōri back into line were disastrous in several ways. They underlay much of the regime's demoralization and domestic isolation. They were a key factor in its fiscal crisis. They contributed to the broader economic dislocation and public disorder that culminated in the upheavals of 1866. The failure to subdue Chōshū by either diplomacy or war in turn undermined the more general conservative strategy for forcing all great *han* and other recalcitrants back into line. With the failure of that venture, the bakufu was forced to adopt a radical new strategy for survival. Hence, insofar as it was Chōshū's deportment that forced the main element in the old order to abandon its defense of that order, one can say the dispute that culminated in the Summer War destroyed the *bakuhan* system well over a year before the Meiji restoration took place.

Furthermore it was primarily the bakufu-Chōshū quarrel that drew the imperialist powers into Japanese domestic politics by prompting Satsuma and Chōshū to develop their ties with British merchants and officials while the bakufu actively cultivated its French connection. Well before the fighting began, that process had assured that any group aspiring to a leading role in Japanese politics must establish foreign ties sufficient to offset those which Kagoshima, Hagi, and Edo had developed. Unless a conservative bakufu leadership could crush Chōshū and then undo its own ties to France, there was no way the old order could avoid further drift into the colonial slough. But the bakufu was defeated on the field and a political stalemate ensued. Edo refused to capitulate and Chōshū could not complete its destruction. Attempts at peaceful reconciliation failed, and so the contest for supremacy was unresolved. In consequence increased foreign ties were unavoidable as the rivals prepared for further struggle. In that sense, too, the process that culminated in the Summer War destroyed the old order by reducing Japan's choices to those of radical reform, chaos, or colonialism.

In the war itself the fortuitous fact of Iemochi's death was surely of consequence in the bakufu's abrupt change of direction because it created an extraordinary opportunity to change personnel close to the shogun. It enabled proponents of a new strategy to dislodge traditionalists close to

Iemochi and put more progressive figures in their place. That was particularly important because the man who became shogun, Yoshinobu, was prone to abrupt changes of opinion despite, or more likely due to, his elemental commitment to both national unification and Tokugawa well-being. Such constancy as he showed in his support for Tokugawa leadership in the new strategy was likely due in great part to the sustained influence of those about him.

In the fighting, notably that at the Aki front where the bakufu was most directly involved, there were lessons whose implications could not be mistaken. It was the quality of weapons, training, and combat organization that was most demonstrably crucial to the outcome. Whereas the Mini-armed and company-battalion structured forces of bakufu infantry, Shingu, and then Kii proved effective if unexciting, the old-style forces of Takata and Hikone proved a disaster. The unmistakable nature of those lessons was quickly reflected in the radical military reorganization that was undertaken even as the war ground on. By the nature of that reform, however, once it was really begun, it created its own new demands for reorganization of command structure, revision of recruitment criteria, and then fundamental reform of the military's money-manpower base. Those latter changes in turn compelled reexamination of the very structural foundation of the entire old order. In that way, too, the Summer War helped destroy the *bakuhan* system.

The Summer War of 1866 was thus an event of profound importance in Japanese history, marking the end of the old order and reducing the central historical issues to this two-tier question: Who would build the new order; or if no one, was Japan to slide into chaos, colonial subordination, or both? The elemental questions that had been latent from the day Commodore Perry's cannon faced Edo had come to the fore, and the Keiō reform was the Tokugawa attempt to answer them.

4. The Keiō Reform

Concerning the Keiō reform our questions are three: What was it supposed to achieve; what did it accomplish; why did it fail? The purpose of the Keiō reform probably changed as time passed, growing as the confidence of its leaders grew. In the aftermath of defeat in 1866 bakufu leaders simply tried to survive, disengaging from a lost war, hurriedly throwing together an army sufficient to hold off any other attackers, and cutting expenses enough to avoid fiscal disaster. The regime's shattered leadership was consolidated, basic policy choices were sorted out, claims to national authority were judiciously insisted on, and efforts were made to reconstruct some degree of mutual goodwill between the bakufu and the court, related lords, and vassal daimyo. By year's end the worst aftereffects of war had been surmounted and bakufu leaders began to develop long-range programs of military, fiscal, and administrative reform while maintaining a political front of conciliation and maneuver.

During 1867 the reform progressed; and as it did, its leaders, such as Itakura Katsukiyo, Inaba Masakuni, Ogyū Noritaka, Asano Ujisuke, Hirayama Keichū, Oguri Tadamasa, Takenaka Shigemoto, and Tsukahara Masayoshi, formulated and implemented more extensive schemes. They were driven in part by intention and in part by the force of events and the logic of steps previously taken. By midyear, as we have seen, they were working on a program of national unification and modernization that puts one very much in mind of what the Meiji leaders actually were to do.

One cannot find the reformers' objectives fully spelled out anywhere, as far as I know. Like the Meiji leaders, they did not really know where they were headed; much was a matter of seeing what developed and then improvising. But also, their strategy severely limited their freedom of expression. A bit earlier, in 1864–1866, a few bakufu officials and leaders had discussed the necessity of abolishing daimyo domains and establishing a unified state organized in prefectures and districts *(gun* and *ken)*. News of their ideas had leaked out, and they had been sharply denounced by friends of Shungaku and men of Satsuma and others who opposed any threat to daimyo autonomy. By 1867 officials knew they dared not write about any such plans, even when they had them. Rather, bakufu leaders pursued a quiet strategy of building from the bottom, attacking first the most vulnerable vested interests, reorganizing them to form a more solid power base, and then attacking more powerful interests piecemeal, until in the end, they hoped, they would be strong enough to take on the great daimyo and forge a truly unified order.

The reformers' strategy for their eventual attack on daimyo autonomy is not known, but it was probably foreshadowed in their policy toward landholding liege vassals, whose military levies were replaced by a heavy money tax. As discussions relating to naval development suggested, reformers probably intended later to impose similar money taxes on the daimyo. Those by their magnitude would pressure the lords, where pressure was necessary, into abolishing the expensive private armies that no longer were justified by bakufu order. Then as those private armies shrank, the central regime's army grew, and the balance of power shifted more and more in Edo's favor, bakufu leaders would be better able to introduce administrative reforms leading to gradual unification of the country. This latter aspect of the overall strategy seems to have been prefigured in the 1867 reorganization of Kantō administration and acquisition of private lands by purchase. Those policies were intended to improve bakufu control of the Kantō estates of landholding liege vassals and minor daimyo. Later, presumably, administrative tentacles of that sort could eventually penetrate even the great *han* of the southwest.

The Keiō reformers probably intended eventually to end not only daimyo autonomy but also the hereditary character of daimyo status. That aim was suggested by the discussions about abolishing hereditary liege vassal status in order to replace unfit men with competent personnel recruited and trained from the populace at large. Probably because of liege vassal opposition, the proposal was not implemented in 1867; but had it finally been applied to them, it likely would at a later date have been applied to the daimyo as well. Such an intention was also expressed by senior councillor Ogyū Noritaka in his reform proposal of 67/10, which called, among other things, for abolition of the four-class system. His proposal, as we noted, was a response to the Tosa restoration activity, but the latter carried no such egalitarian message, and it seems almost certain that Ogyū, long active in forming the bakufu's new mass army, was giving expression to an idea then circulating within the bakufu.

The overarching goal of the Keiō reformers eluded them in the end, but they did make remarkable progress nonetheless. At the highest political level they did retain Tokugawa shogunal authority despite military defeat in 1866. They retained court support and successfully turned back the great daimyo political assault of 67/4–5. They obtained the foreign diplomats' recognition of their claim to national leadership and in the process asserted an unprecedented degree of national sovereign authority. They also successfully coped with a number of thorny diplomatic questions that arose during the year. Finally they established the most stable, cohesive, competent, and progressive leadership group that Edo had enjoyed since at least the days of Abe Masahiro.

In terms of structural reform, they carried out a military reorganization whose implications were nothing less than revolutionary. That undertaking not only involved the adoption of modern weapons, drill, and organization, but more basically the end of the feudal system of vassal levies and the formation of a mass army of commoners, an embryo national conscript force. Their administrative reform was equally radical in its implications. It created the skeleton of a western-type ministerial organization utilizing greatly expanded criteria of merit selection and promotion in which the old vassal daimyo and liege vassal domination of affairs was abandoned in principle and denied its base in a restrictive salary system. In practice the administrative reform did not during its brief lifetime approach its potential for change in either the way matters were handled or the way men were selected for office. But just as the Meiji leaders eventually found that the structure they created undermined the Sat-Chō oligarchical hegemony, so the administrative changes of the Keiō reform, unless modified, eventually would have deprived vassal lords and liege vassals of their monopoly of power.

Around the edges of the Keiō reform one could also see a miscellany of minor changes that cumulatively revealed the pervasive social ramifications of the reform and individually carried the seeds of yet greater changes.

There was, however, one basic theoretical issue the reformers do not appear to have resolved: the relationship of shogun and emperor, or bakufu and court. Doubtless one problem they faced in conceptualizing the desired relationship was that they were utilizing a French model that included an active emperor as chief of state and afforded no real leading position for a redefined ex-shogun. Surely, too, the task was complicated by Yoshinobu and Itakura's long-standing commitment to court-bakufu unity. There is, to my knowledge, no statement indicating what they thought a reorganized shogun-emperor relationship might appropriately be. Back in 65/10 it had been reported that certain bakufu officials proposed to abolish the emperor's position and designate the shogun *daitō-ryō*, evidently meaning some sort of presiding executive or ''president.'' What model lay behind the title is unclear, but in any event the alleged advocates of the scheme were soon drummed from office. If the Keiō reformers entertained before 67/10 any idea of naming Yoshinobu *daitō-ryō*, they did not admit as much.

The absence of official statements seems to imply that bakufu leaders were unable to perceive, or unwilling to articulate, an acceptable theoretical relationship between shogun and emperor. When we look at what the Keiō reformers did and did not do, however, it becomes possible to infer a line of bakufu thought on the matter. In practice, as we have seen, the Keiō leadership vigorously cultivated imperial goodwill. Yoshinobu governed from Kyoto, not Edo. Moreover, he took care to assure that the court sanctioned all his major decisions, in effect making them imperial decisions. At the same time, however, the bakufu asserted a national sovereign function vis-à-vis foreigners that left little real authority with the emperor. And it set up an incipient national administrative system independent of the vestigial imperial bureaucracy in Kyoto. It appears, therefore, that a successful Keiō reform would have led to an imperial institution that was preserved as a closely integrated, legitimizing fount of government but did not purport to be the national government itself. Rather, it might have survived primarily as a monarchial household supported by its newly acquired private lands in Yamashiro province and re-sembling, in terms of political influence, the British crown or perhaps the post-1947 Japanese imperial institution.

In this scheme of things, the plausible role for Yoshinobu would be as prime minister. In this regard it is probably significant that when the new ministerial titles were announced in mid-67, Itakura was never entitled prime minister. It was the obvious position for him, but to title him thus would have foreclosed the title to Yoshinobu, branding the post one beneath the dignity of an ex-shogun. But Itakura very pointedly did not take any such title, and so a future position for Yoshinobu was preserved.

The Keiō reform was, in sum, revolutionary in implication. In practice too it achieved a great deal. Yet it failed. Why? Probably fiscal inade-quacy must be judged the Achilles heel of the reform. The demands of the 1860s had come to exceed the regime's income by so much that there was no way it could balance its books until it secured control of the entire country's taxable resources. In the meantime it could only maximize the yield from its existing tax base and borrow the difference. Attempts to do both had minimal success. This fiscal inadequacy was important because it forced the reformers to beggar their army and squeeze liege vassals to the point of defiance and demoralization. The inadequacy also may have deprived them of weapons, ammunition, and other matériel that could have been crucial to the regime's survival and success. And it clearly ate away at the morale of officialdom itself.

By 1867 the bakufu had acquired a competent leadership and had adopted a policy adequate to the day, so it is entirely conceivable that with sufficient financing it could have completed its Keiō reform and uni-fied the country much as the Meiji leaders in fact were to do. That san-guine view is far from certain, however. In the first place the goad of fis-cal need had been one important element forcing the regime to adopt its radical posture. Without that goad, conservatives might not have been overcome. But even disregarding that possibility, had the fisc been ade-quate, there still were other obstacles aplenty to the Keiō reform. Internal resistance to it was not merely opposition to increased tax levies. Men also objected for a number of nonmaterial reasons to both the military and administrative reforms and other aspects of Keiō policy. Yoda Yūtarō, a loyal Tokugawa trooper, felt strongly enough about matters to kill Yo-shinobu's advisor Hara Ichinoshin. And for every Yoda who would com-mit murder to set things right, a hundred liege vassals labored diligently to sabotage the Keiō reform in safer and subtler ways.

Just as important as this aspect of internal resistance were the external obstructions to reform. To its advantage the regime was blessed during the months of reform with benign weather, a bountiful harvest, and a quiescent general populace. Daimyo, court, *shishi*, and foreigners repeatedly disrupted bakufu leaders, however, diverting their attention and delaying their moves, thus helping to confound the reform. Moreover leaders of the great *han* sensed in the latter months of 1867 that bakufu leaders were no longer defending the old decentralized Tokugawa order. To protect their own interests and realize their own ambitions, they finally reactivated in new form the court-daimyo-*shishi* coalition, and in the outcome their actions proved far more effective than those of the bakufu. Fiscal adequacy would have done little to prevent the reactivation of that threat.

In the end, of course, the fate of the Keiō reform was settled by men tearing cruelly at one another on the field of battle. The battles at Fushimi-Toba ended in Tokugawa defeat for several reasons, as we witnessed earlier, and only some of them can be attributed to fiscal inadequacy. In contrast to the shortcomings of the bakufu war effort, the insurgents made superbly good use of their somewhat better arms and far more highly motivated personnel. And once the tide had turned in their favor, they enjoyed extraordinary success in optimizing each new favorable development as it appeared.

For the second time in eighteen months decisive defeat in battle persuaded Yoshinobu to abandon the contest, and in following weeks he supervised the disestablishment of the bakufu and finally acquiesced in nearly total surrender to the imperial insurgents. Six years after the Bunkyū reform the bakufu was no more.

Why the Bakufu Fell As It Did When It Did

Vertical or chronological analysis can thus suggest the reasons for the sequential failures of the bakufu in its final years. Horizontal or factor analysis will permit us to view the regime's collapse in other perspectives —to examine the limited and ambiguous role of commoners; the critical and complex role of foreigners; the character of the anti-bakufu coalition; and the major elements of bakufu weakness.

1. The Role of Commoners

Our evidence has indicated, to almost no one's surprise, that commoners did not play a direct role in bringing down the bakufu. Indeed, as militia, as infantrymen, as source of *goyōkin*, and as helpers in policing Edo, the commoners were of considerable assistance to the regime. On the other hand as rioters, as effective tax delinquents, as supporters of *shishi*, and as organized opponents of various bakufu commercial policies, they were distinct problems to the regime. On balance it is difficult to assert whether commoners ended doing more to help or to hurt the regime in its final agonies.

One must not confuse the question of the commoners' role in that issue with the larger question of the growth of an ''antifeudal'' impact or attitude on the part of the populace. We have seen plenty of evidence of an ''antifeudal'' mentality: merchants who refused to loan money or otherwise cooperate; producers who lobbied for preferred arrangements; urban and rural commoners who rioted and marched in protest of poor conditions; commoners and marginal people who consciously participated in national political activities; people who rejoiced not only at their own good fortune but in part at the regime's difficulties; city folk who proposed to govern and police themselves; rulers who relied on city folk to do just that; rulers who expressed quite frankly their fear of the public's revolutionary potential; and evidence that the fear played some modest part in shaping their decisions about military deployment, domanial management, and other aspects of governance and reform.

This ''antifeudal'' mentality did not become an anti-bakufu mentality, however, and the reason seems to be that the political contest of the 1860s was pitting some parts of the ruling or feudal elite against others. From a commoner's vantage point, there was little to choose between one side and the other in terms of ''feudalism.'' Insofar as a commoner had to take a stand, he had to do it on the basis of other considerations, including such ''feudal'' considerations as who among the elite he felt most affinity to. In consequence one finds commoners in all camps and on all sides of major disputes insofar as the disputes encroached on their lives. And their choice of sides and levels of involvement showed about as high a degree of rationality as one commonly encounters in human affairs.

Whether the popular political consciousness manifested during the 1860s was a product of the times, a product of long-term trends, or an intrinsic historical characteristic of Japanese society is really beyond the scope of this study. Accordingly the very limited implications in that regard of the data assembled here can be dealt with quickly. The evidence we have seen is surely enough to sustain our disbelief in notions of ''oriental passivity,''[1] but in the absence of comparative data from an earlier era, say the 1660s, it does not demonstrate whether the ruler–ruled relationship of the 1860s was in any qualitative way changed from earlier decades or centuries.

Studies by Borton, Crawcour, Dore, Hauser, Sheldon, and Smith have all demonstrated that Tokugawa Japan experienced immense social change.[2] But to establish the connection between this change and the turbulence of the 1860s is not so easy. In terms of immediate causation, the sharp increase in popular activism during the 1860s can mostly be traced directly or indirectly to the foreign intrusion. Economic dislocations stemming from the foreign-precipitated political crises of the decade were the direct cause of much of the public discontent, agitation, and violence we have noted. Foreign trade itself also created a host of problems and opportunities at the ports, in the cities, and in processing and producing areas, and those new considerations accounted for another appreciable part of commoner political activity. In other ways too it was the specific political context of the sixties that gave the commoner more opportunities to participate in political affairs and brought out so clearly the rulers' fear of an uncontrolled public. Even the great upheavals of 1866, which were to a certain extent fostered by vagaries of nature, were also instigated by the political crisis, and they surely would have been less extensive had the armies been at home consuming less and patrolling more.

It may well be, therefore, that it was the dislocations of the decade more than the changes of prior centuries that prompted commoners to participate as they did in political affairs. But, to propose a counterfactual situation, it may be, too, that had Japan of the 1660s, let us say, encountered socioeconomic dislocations comparable to those of the 1860s, the common people would not have engaged in public activism. The data presented in this study will not sustain a position one way or the other.

Despite the rulers' fears, however, in the outcome the revolutionary potential was not realized. Consequently, while the long-term changes in Tokugawa commoner society are all germane, indeed fundamental, to inquiries concerning how the regime might have fallen had the foreigners not arrived, and why the Meiji regime—and Meiji society—took the forms they did and developed as they did, these considerations do not, in the long and short of it, go very far toward explaining why the bakufu failed as it did when it did.

2. The Imperialist Intrusion

When I undertook this study, I intended to disregard diplomatic matters in the belief they had been adequately, even excessively, dealt with. But the documents would not permit that disregard. The foreigners were a continual and critical factor in the bakufu's decline and fall because they created a new situation that brought into existence and then worked to sustain a coalition of forces hostile to the bakufu and too powerful for it to overcome.

The foreigners played such a crucial role because their impact was so many faceted and hit so many critical points in the *bakuhan* system. It was not merely a matter of barbarians inciting a cry of ethnic outrage that brought down a decadent regime in a crash and a cloud of cinders. The foreigners brought into clear focus a basic ambiguity concerning the character and limits of political authority in Tokugawa Japan. It was generally acknowledged that the bakufu had authority to enforce the policy of isolation, or *sakoku* as it came to be called. But did it have the authority on its own initiative to change that policy and enforce the change in all Japan? Embedded in that particular conundrum was the general issue of whether or not the bakufu was the government of all Japan; and if it was, how its authority was to be exercised. The issue was created by the arrival of the foreigners not only because they brought new substantive political problems of national scope but also because they demanded that some entity in Japan fill a national authority role analogous to that of a monarchy or republic in Europe—and no such entity really existed in Tokugawa Japan. It was a problem that quickly came to engage the attention of court, daimyo, and *shishi* and in the process of doing so helped give rise to the hostile coalition.

This question of authority, however, was only one and the most abstract and cerebral of issues raised by the foreigners. There were other issues: the problem of assuring national adherence to an altered foreign policy; the problem of coordinating a national defense effort; the problem of paying for defense costs; problems of morale arising from necessary military reform; the problem of turning foreign trade to equitable national advantage in a structural context of baronial localism; the problem of foreigners trying to play one group of Japanese off against another for foreign gain; and finally the problem of satisfying or containing a widespread sense of outraged ethnic sensibility. These issues were all involved in the forging of the hostile coalition and weakening of the bakufu capacity to prevail.

The foreign intrusion was critical to the emergence and flourishing of the ad hoc coalition; without it, that particular coalition almost surely would not have arisen and persisted long enough to prevail. It would not have arisen because it was an awkward and politically unnatural coalition, its unnaturalness reflected in its fragility and instability. After all, great daimyo interests were not served by *shishi* insubordination, and court interests were not in the greater likelihood served by destabilizing initiatives arising among the daimyo. No domestic famine, or peasant landlord insubordination, or merchant power, or lower samurai impoverishment, or bureaucratic frustration, or daimyo hegemonial aspirations, or imperial intrigue could by itself or in most combinations have given rise to the lethal configuration of the 1860s. It was produced by the crisis of foreign affairs. And it was able to prevail because foreign complications directly and indirectly confounded bakufu attempts to suppress it and thereby gave it time to develop an effective *modus operandi.*

As we noted at the outset, this is not to imply that sans barbarian the regime would have gone blithely on its way indefinitely. All regimes have a limited tenure; eventually the bakufu would have fallen. Quite without a foreign crisis, hostile configurations of power capable of toppling the Tokugawa certainly were possible in circumstances of severe domestic deterioration. Sooner or later such a configuration would have appeared. Its formation was precluded, however, by the imperialist intrusion and the peculiar domestic coalition forged by that intrusion, and our task does not require the examination of hypothetical alternative modalities of overthrow.

In terms of intergroup dynamics the crucial consideration in the bakufu collapse lay not in the efforts per se of foreigners or court or daimyo or *shishi* but, as we observed earlier, in the repeated conjunction of their efforts. The bakufu had the resources necessary to deal with any of those groups alone, whether by suppression, manipulation, compromise, or, in the case of foreigners, tactical capitulation. The bakufu could not, however, cope with their conjoint pressure, whether that be cooperative pressure against the bakufu or conflictive pressure that caught the bakufu in the middle. It becomes necessary, therefore, to explain why the groups acted or interacted together as they did, and why that process proved more than Edo could manage.

3. Foundations of the Ad Hoc Coalition

The court's role in the coalition was, as we have seen, a very unstable one in which the emperor served primarily and very imperfectly as a focus of unity. Even to play that role, moreover, the court was dependent upon vigorous initiatives arising from the other two elements of the coalition. The weakness of its role was a product of the court's weak power base: its lack of both autonomous lands and a significant amount of manpower. It was able to play any role at all only because the Tokugawa had preserved it as a source of legitimacy for the bakufu and the larger *bakuhan* system.

These factors of elemental imperial weakness and enduring presence were, of course, characteristics basic to the *bakuhan* system, at least as true in the seventeenth century as in the nineteenth. This does not mean that the imperial role of the 1860s was inherent in the Tokugawa order, however, because in the *bakumatsu* crisis the central role of the court found expression in the rhetoric of *sonnō jōi*, a vocabulary that was not basic to the system.

A sufficient explanation of the imperial role thus requires explanation of *sonnō jōi*, its origin and key proponents. Clearly it was the hammer blows of foreigners that prompted the explosive emergence of *sonnō jōi* activism. However, studies by Earl, Harootunian, and Webb have revealed changes in samurai thought about and attitudes toward the imperial institution that were surely important in the rapidity with which that institution moved to both a central position and an active role in the emergence and fateful linkage of court, *shishi*, and daimyo.[3]

It was *shishi* who gave effective voice and real content to this *sonnō jōi* rhetoric, and so the prominence of the imperial role is primarily attributable to *shishi* success in making their views heard. They did so despite the fact that their position lacked the institutional clarity of court and daimyo positions and they were structurally the weakest of the three elements in the coalition, lacking corporate income, status, and organization. *Shishi* strength and influence derived from the readiness of individuals to risk all for the cause, whatever it might be. Consequently an explanation of their role in the coalition requires an explanation of the sources of their discontent and their readiness to act.

The question of *shishi* discontent eventually touches upon a whole range of considerations of economic and career dissatisfaction that may be subsumed under the rubric of status incongruence, meaning a *shishi*'s conviction that he was not receiving recognition and reward commensurate with his worth.[4] The institutional basis of that dissatisfaction dates from the seventeenth century and the stabilizing of the status order, but long-term trends very likely exacerbated it. The question of discontent also touches upon ideological considerations connected to established convictions of local dignity and glory, or ''*han* nationalism'' as Craig so aptly has termed it,[5] and to evolving convictions of imperial and ethnic dignity and glory. Although the convictions of local dignity can be traced to the founding of the Tokugawa order, they may actually have grown considerably in time. And the latter phenomenon of imperial and ethnic sensibility seems largely to have been a development of the later Edo period.

The *shishi* readiness to act can be related to long-term changes in samurai attitudes toward the very idea of institutional change itself, which Najita has investigated.[6] More importantly, perhaps, it can also be considered in terms of the way that imperialist inroads of the *bakumatsu* years drove elements of discontent together so that feelings of status incongruence, *han* nationalism, and ethnic awareness became not separate semidiscordant matters but mutually reinforcing considerations, whether within the mind of a given man or in terms of men acting together for what may have been basically dissimilar reasons or purposes. By the 1860s a large number of men could reasonably believe that dramatic action leading to destruction of the bakufu would simultaneously bring recognition to themselves, glory to their families, triumph to their colleagues, honor to their lord, and salvation to emperor and nation.

Turning to the third element in the coalition, great daimyo participation stemmed from the system itself insofar as they were autonomously powerful figures whose very high status was not matched by commensurate authority in national affairs. When the foreign intrusion introduced to Japan a series of self-evidently nationwide problems of immediate importance to great lords, their lack of authority to address the problems quickly proved intolerable. Moreover the bakufu's dual character as regional barony and national regime tempted it to manipulate its national role for its regional advantage at the expense of great daimyo in such sensitive matters as trade, armament imports, and education. That situation inevitably generated tensions that otherwise would have lain dormant. And when the demands of the new age finally drove the bakufu to abandon the *bakuhan* system, that development forced the great *han* to resist lest they be utterly ruined in the process.

The daimyo role in the coalition was also shaped by long-term changes in Tokugawa society. Long-range trends had routinized the political order, turned warriors into civil servants, eroded *han* fiscal strength, and undermined the effectiveness of great *han* military forces. Those developments heightened the political sensitivity of great *han* leaders and thereby fostered great-*han* political activism. But simultaneously they discouraged military activism. Thus the great lords of the ad hoc coalition readily engaged in political maneuvers during the sixties, but only two of them resorted to war and then only as last desperate measures of self-defense against a regime that seemed bent on their destruction: Chōshū in 66/6 and Satsuma in 68/1. Hence one can suggest that long-range domestic changes in bakufu–great *han* relations exacerbated the political turbulence of the sixties but reduced the magnitude of civil war when it did occur.

In sum, then, the peculiar linkage of court, *shishi*, and great *han* that was produced by the imperialist intrusion was built into the *bakuhan* system in the sense that autonomously powerful daimyo seeking a national symbol of authority always had the court to turn to and members of court could act only with some sort of outside cooperation. Long-term developments, particularly at the level of ideology, seem to have been important in helping men to perceive the court as an active institution of government rather than as a passive symbol of authority. That latter perception facilitated both the court's decision to play an active part in affairs and *shishi* readiness to act at a national level and in terms of association with the court. The court thus provided the original nexus that enabled daimyo and *shishi* actions to be more or less coordinated despite the intrinsic contradiction between daimyo well-being and *shishi* activism. That situation changed, however, when great daimyo and *shishi* developed, following the Chōshū civil war, a new and more perfect basis for cooperation in programs of antiestablishmentarian *han* policy. With that development the function of the court in the coalition was subtly but significantly changed, as I suggested in evaluating the politics of 1867. The new basis of daimyo-*shishi* cohesion gave the coalition a solidity—a unity of resources and will—that it had previously lacked. And that brought success within its grasp when the bakufu at last forced its hand and in so doing overcame its reluctance to go to war.

4. The Elements of Bakufu Weakness

The elements of bakufu weakness vis-à-vis the hostile coalition were readily apparent in this study. The bakufu was beset by an ambiguity of self-image that confused its sense of legitimate purpose and bogged it down in intramural conflict. It suffered from fiscal limitations that inhibited its capacity to act and undermined morale. Liege vassals also had fiscal problems, and those were part of broader difficulties contributing to their demoralization and undercutting the bakufu's military capacity. Moreover, putatively supportive *han* encountered various difficulties that gradually led most of them into postures of political neutrality or inaction. These several disadvantages of the regime were then complicated by the inadequacies of its leadership during the sixties. All these problems had a pre-*bakumatsu* history whose connections to the events and final outcome of crisis require examination.

The ambiguity of bakufu self-image stemmed directly from the original Tokugawa settlement which institutionalized the bakufu as both a regional barony and a national hegemon responsible for keeping emperor and nation tranquil and safe from both barbarians without and insurgents within. As noted above, the imperialist intrusion brought to the surface the question of national authority that was latent in the bakufu's dual character, and the issue at once became central to intra-bakufu disputes. It underlay the split between exclusivistic and inclusivistic approaches to governance and found enduring expression in what might be labeled the

"Kyoto" and "Edo" viewpoints within bakufu officialdom. They can be so labeled because bakufu officials in Kyoto were almost always identified with the one viewpoint while those in Edo were almost equally consistent exponents of the other. As a matter of functional politics the division was essentially a difference in priorities, but that difference led to profound differences in policy positions.

The geography of the foreign crisis was certainly basic to the Edo-Kyoto division. Officials in Edo were directly and painfully exposed to the foreign threat and saw its accommodation as the critical consideration of policy. Officials in Kyoto were primarily exposed to the outraged ethnic sensibilities embodied in the spirit and rhetoric of *sonnō jōi* and the outsiders' frustration embodied in the collaborationist rhetoric of *kōbugattai*, and they saw the accommodation of those sentiments as the overriding necessity. Officials arguing the "Kyoto" view contended that however the foreigners were handled, it must be in a manner minimizing the ire of *sonnō jōi* and *kōbugattai* advocates. And those at Edo argued that however the Kyoto crowd was dealt with, it must be in a manner that avoided a foreign war.

As these comments imply, the Kyoto-Edo division was also a division on the practical question of how best to manage the ad hoc coalition of court, daimyo, and *shishi*. One view held that Tokugawa primacy could best be secured by retaining the goodwill of the three through strategies of conciliation and compromise; the other believed that primacy required a forceful insistence upon that unquestioned bakufu leadership in decision-making that had supposedly characterized the Edo period. One view wanted a shogun, servant of the court; the other wanted a shogun, leader of armies. In terms of the limits of Tokugawa authority as a national government, the "Kyoto" view held that a national government must somehow embrace, whether structurally or sensibly, court, daimyo, and *shishi*, while the "Edo" view held that the bakufu, perhaps with some modifications, should fill the national authority role, regardless of the wishes of those outside groups.

In the Keiō reform bakufu leaders seemed to be well on the way to forming a new self-image that overcame the older ambiguity. But certainly among many followers, and likely at some level in the consciousness of many reform leaders, the older dilemma persisted and contributed to the easy collapse of Tokugawa morale in the crisis of year's end.

One can press this idea of ambiguous self-image in a tangential direction and suggest, following an interpretive line recently advanced by Najita, that the Edo-Kyoto division reflected a tension in ethical ideals. It was a tension between the ideal of practical and rational bureaucratic

handling of affairs by competent officials on the ''Edo'' side and on the
''Kyoto'' side a governance based on a more sensitive, moralistic consideration of principles of culture and virtue. This latter ideal was one that
shishi and their sympathizers, including many vassals of the bakufu itself,
felt was embedded in the spirit of *sonnō jōi*. In a sense this division was
the ethical aspect of the issue of authority whose structural expression
was conflict over the form of a national government. The fundamental inability of bakufu officialdom to forge, adhere to, and get solid Tokugawa
vassal support for a clear vision of the bakufu as a worthy national government was an important factor in the regime's demoralization and disintegration.

Ambiguity of self-image was one weakness of the regime; fiscal inadequacy was another. Clearly the bakufu's lack of monies hampered the
regime at every turn in the 1860s, and bakufu leaders doubtless longed
for the halcyon days of the founders when coffers bulged and wealth
seemed the least of worries. The apparent contrast implies that long-run
erosion of the bakufu fisc was a major cause of the regime's collapse in
1868. I would like to argue, however, that had the foreigners come in
the 1660s or even earlier, let us say, fiscal problems would have come
into being much as they did in the 1860s. It was great new fiscal demands, not long-term fiscal erosion, that lay at the heart of the dilemma.

The prodigious wealth of the early Tokugawa house is deceptive. By
the standards of the seventeenth century it was great, but by the measure
of the 1860s it was a pittance. Thus Ieyasu's successor Hidetada reportedly bequeathed to Iemitsu reserves of some 3 million *ryō* and to others
enough other gifts so that the total value of his reserves, even after an inflationary factor of about 100 percent has been taken into account, perhaps equaled 8 to 10 million early 1860s *ryō*. Yet one must ask: How
long would an extra 10 million *ryō* have lasted the bakufu in the 1860s?
By the beginning of 1866 at the latest it would surely have been gone,
probably an appreciable part of it in fatter foreign indemnities. Indeed, if
bakufu leaders of the 1850s had had access to such funds, they likely
would have spent them all on coastal defense work even before 1862,
the date at which this study begins. And the goods acquired therewith
would still have been of almost no use against domestic enemies because
they would have been deployed for coastal defense. They would have
been of little use against foreigners, either, because they would have become obsolete so soon.

The loss of these early reserves of cash was not a critical problem. The
real reserves of the early Tokugawa lay not in readily mobilizable money
but in the enduring productive capacity of the Japanese people and land.

It was the annual production of the countryside year after year that supported the immense projects of the early Tokugawa shogun, and that production was lost to the regime in stages. Part of it reached Tokugawa hands by way of daimyo contributions and *han* expenditures in Edo. Massive daimyo contributions had mostly ceased before 1700, and so that part of *han* production was long lost to the regime. Then with the de facto end of *sankin kōtai* in 1862, Edo lost access to most other *han* production. For the bakufu the most important part of production was that coming from the bakufu's own lands, and until its last few years the regime appears to have kept that fiscal base more or less intact, losing control, as we noted earlier, only as its political grip loosened after 1862.

Even if the production of daimyo domains had still been available to Edo, however, it furnished steady income, not dramatically expandable income. It was income that could not be made available faster than seasons and metabolic processes permitted. It was a type of wealth of very limited emergency value, and the foreign danger required immense sums in a short time. In terms of quickly usable money, it is entirely conceivable that because of long-range economic development, the bakufu of the 1860s had access to more, rather than less, wealth than did the early shogun. The regime tapped that wealth through its massive recoinages, its *goyōkin*, and its free use of daimyo and liege vassal manpower, which was paid for by the deferring mechanism of massive samurai and *han* indebtedness to merchants and to each other. Given the regime's abruptly escalating fiscal needs during the 1860s, it seems entirely possible that it would have become bankrupt even more quickly than it did had its fiscal situation been unchanged from that of early Tokugawa years. Its limitations were basically a product of its limited territorial and productive tax base relative to the immense new demands of the decade and the new era that decade introduced. A fiscal solution lay not in retrogressive change but in the massive expansion of Japanese productivity and its utilization for purposes of national defense by a unified regime.

For the bakufu proper, then, it seems best to argue that it was neither the original fiscal arrangement per se nor long-term financial trends that led to the fiscal crisis of the 1860s. Rather the source of that crisis was the immense new fiscal demands presented by the foreign intrusion—demands that the bakufu as it existed could not satisfy, whether or not its fiscal situation had been modified over time.

Apart from the matter of bakufu finance proper is the important and related question of liege vassal finances. Yamamura has shown in considerable detail the long-run evolution of their financial situation, arguing that their impoverishment was a product of a long-term fixed income failing to satisfy long-term growing wants.[7] In fact, given the many sources of supplementary income available to liege vassals, it is very possible that their actual condition, and that of landholders in particular, was rather less dire than their formal income records suggested. Nevertheless we have seen that in broader social terms liege vassals fared poorly during the 1860s, and an exacerbated fiscal situation was central to their difficulty. From that it seems plausible to argue that their deteriorated economic situation was central to both their low morale and their inability or unwillingness to provide the regime with manpower or matériel for its army. Hence the bakufu was unable to intimidate or defeat its enemies and so it collapsed.

On closer examination, however, it seems less easy to assert this causal connection because to do so requires some highly questionable assumptions. Can we assume that if liege vassals had had more wealth, they would have been more devoted to the regime in the meaningful sense of having been more willing and able to provide military support? Or is it more likely that with more wealth in hand they would have used it, as Yamamura's whole analysis implies, for purposes of nonmilitary consumption? And if they had done that over the years and generations, would it not have meant that as an important part of the consuming populace in Edo their actions would have raised commodity and wage rates in some degree proportional to the extent of their resources? However much more income they might have received, would they not have spent it in larger families and more comforts, reaping the benefits of their hereditary status and going into debt as far as their regime and their creditors would have permitted? When debts had to be paid, would they not have curtailed unwanted expenses in order to spend where they chose? And would that not have meant, as it did in practice, that unnecessary retainers, useless weapons, and the other accoutrements of war would have been sacrificed in order to retain the treasures and pleasures of peace and prosperity? And would the bakufu then not have found its peacetime army just as unable and unwilling to convert itself into a lean wartime army as was the case in the 1860s?

If these questions are answered in the affirmative, then the problem of lackluster vassal performance was not so much a problem of valuables as values. Rather than arguing that liege vassal actions were determined by their impoverishment, whether caused by rising expenses or declining income, and whether in absolute or relative terms, perhaps it is better to argue that they were enmeshed in a web of civilian obligations and advantages so dense that they were unwilling to pay the price in life-style necessary to become effective participants in a rigorous military regime.

What this line of argument seems to be implying is the familiar idea that liege vassals had lived too well too long and had become effete. Are we to conclude, then, that men whose ancestors had been supremely loyal to Ieyasu had become petty, self-centered timeservers? I think not. It is one thing to serve a gifted and forceful man when such service may etch one's name in a glorious history and bring riches and honor to one's family. For such a prospect one may well risk his all. It is quite another thing to serve a group of quarrelsome and querulous men of uncertain purpose who offer one nothing and yet ask one to surrender what little one has in life. Self-sacrificing loyalty, after all, has a sound foundation in perceived self-interest, and from the viewpoint of most liege vassals bakufu leaders of the 1860s were asking much and offering little.

Perhaps the problem was broader in scope. Can we argue that the bakufu fell because decadent city samurai were no match for the rugged country samurai of the great *han*? Again I think not. To argue thusly implies that urbanness and ruralness were the determinants of behavior, and it is not clear which label one applies to whom. Were the ineffective men of Takata and Hikone, the bravely unsuccessful men of Aizu, the ponderously triumphant men of Satsuma, the brilliantly successful men of Chōshū, the ponderously unsuccessful peasant conscripts of Edo, the brashly ineffective men of the Shinsengumi, the resolute men of Shingu, the constant men of Kii, and so on and so forth rural or urban?

These approaches do not help us understand the liege vassal situation. The problem of their morale did not have such simple roots and does not reduce to such easy generalities. It was hopelessly entwined in the total dynamic of the historic process as it affected individuals. In the body of this study we have noted many specific situations that dismayed and disoriented liege vassals, and we have just discussed that ambiguity of self-image which made it difficult (but certainly not impossible) for such men to reconcile their commitments to *sonnō jōi* ideals and bakufu national leadership. In many ways, however, the liege vassal situation was only an expression, possibly in extreme form, of a much wider malaise affecting the entire samurai class. That malaise related directly, but not solely, to the disjunction between the whole Tokugawa-era samurai military system and the military requirements growing out of the foreign intrusion. The *bakuhan* military system of the nineteenth century was obviously a product of both the original Tokugawa settlement and long-term changes in the samurai condition. The original balance of military power and style of samurai warfare had been more or less maintained through the centuries, but at an ever-lower level of absolute effectiveness. The foreigners' arrival presented a radical new demand for a dramatic rise in the level of that absolute effectiveness, and the entire samurai

class found that rise extremely hard to achieve because it required fundamental and humiliating changes in fighting techniques. To say it baldly,
samurai did not want to become infantrymen.

We have seen evidence of that situation in the case of the bakufu, and
such comparative data as we have encountered suggest that the situation
was nearly universal. Despite endless talk about military strengthening,
before the Summer War of 1866 no *han* seems to have made really fundamental military reforms except for Chōshū. Whether one is dealing
with Aizu, the Shinsengumi, vassal *han* in general, Mito, or great *han* in
general, one finds persistent opposition to military reform. Even Satsuma, one of the most vigorous and progressive *han*, played a successful
role in the end not because its samurai forces were notably modernized in
organization and military techniques but because they were numerous,
well supplied with good-quality arms, well motivated, well led, and fortunate. Military reform, when it did occur, was born of defeat, as in Kii
in 1866. And the reason Chōshū was able to forge an effective modern
force from samurai may have lain precisely in the fact that the political
conflicts of 1863–1865 presented Chōshū and only Chōshū with the
possibility of destruction, whether by foreign, domestic, or combined
force. Faced with that prospect, *shishi* were able to secure control of the
han, and Chōshū samurai, who were surely aware of what was at stake,
were willing to bear the psychological costs of being turned into infantrymen. And so out of the crucible of ultimate danger was born a modern
war machine.

For most other samurai, however, the threat was not so imminent and
the price not worth paying. Accordingly liege vassals, like other samurai,
were unwilling to sacrifice the symbols and substance of their superior
status and become infantrymen.

It appears, then, that the demands of the 1860s worked in several
ways to disorient and demoralize liege vassals and undermine their willingness to support fully the bakufu cause. Primarily for that reason, the
bakufu tried to forge the core of its new army out of commoner conscripts. It began doing so in 1862 and by 1867 had had considerable
success. The strengths, weaknesses, and ultimate performance of those
infantrymen, as we noted previously, were traceable mostly to factors
other than general liege vassal demoralization.

One other factor that drove the bakufu to forge an army of conscript
peasants was the ineffectiveness and uncooperativeness of putatively
sympathetic *han* forces. Our narrative has indicated how the historic process of the sixties drove most such *han* step by step into postures of isola-

tion and inaction, too poor and too peace-oriented to modernize their armed forces, too divided internally to take decisive positions, too vulnerable or unmotivated in the end to risk willful action one way or the other.

One source of their poor motivation was the lack of satisfying leadership from Edo. The ''Edo''–''Kyoto'' split in the bakufu was present among the *han* too, both in the sense of divisions among the leaders of a given *han* and in the sense that some *han* wished forceful bakufu leadership and others wished Edo to follow a concessive *kōbugattai* strategy. This meant that Edo would lose some daimyo support, whichever policy it followed. Its repeated shifting back and forth between policies was even worse, however, serving eventually to alienate supporters of both strategies. In the end almost no *han* were prepared to risk their all for the indecisive Tokugawa.

This statement implies that most daimyo failed to support the bakufu not because they were anti-bakufu but because, given Edo's handling of affairs, they were unable to perceive a fruitful way of aiding it without excessive risk to themselves. To argue that the daimyo commonly viewed as supporters of the regime, notably the vassal daimyo, were not anti-bakufu is to imply that they did not regard it as an exploitative, damaging force in their lives. In this regard certain aspects of the bakufu-*han* fiscal and political relationship that apply particularly to vassal *han* deserve closer attention.

The military weakness of the *han* was in part a product of their poverty. Sometimes it is argued that daimyo were anti-bakufu because poor and poor because the bakufu exploited them. The bakufu is routinely pictured as purposefully beggaring the domains. During the early seventeenth century it did milk them for what they were worth, but it was great *han*, not vassal *han*, that were the main targets of that policy. In later years Edo's demands were mostly customary and modest, the routine costs of *sankin kōtai* rather than other levies being the heavy burden. Discontent with *sankin kōtai* was indisputably a source of some daimyo displeasure with Edo. However, daimyo response to reform of the system in 1862 and subsequent daimyo behavior suggests that that issue was a rather minor element in their conduct, especially in the case of vassal lords.

Moreover, such levies as Edo did still make were offset to some degree by habitual forms of bakufu aid to the *han*. There is plenty of evidence that in the sixties daimyo of all sorts, and vassal lords in particular, appealed to Edo for fiscal relief during periods of acute need. They would not have done so had they assumed it would be of no use. It seems likely the bakufu had in prior centuries played a habitual role of "reserve banker" bailing out bankrupt *han* at critical moments.[8] To do so, after all, would have been in Edo's long-run interest. During the 1860s, however, as both bakufu and *han* faced fiscal problems of unprecedented severity, the bakufu was less able to play the role of short-term benefactor, and that may have denied it one of its greatest claims to *han* loyalty. Inability to obtain aid from the bakufu in the 1860s likely undercut pro-bakufu feelings and encouraged *han* leaders, including those of vassal *han*, to look elsewhere for support.

   Han inaction is sometimes explained as deriving from a wish to escape bakufu hegemony. It is difficult to see, however, how vassal lords could rationally have envisioned a more advantageous system than what they already had. They dominated top offices of the bakufu. And liege vassals —the group with which they intermarried most extensively and which included a large number of cadet branches of vassal daimyo households —dominated the rest of the bureaucracy, with landholding liege vassals commonly in the most important administrative offices. Landholding liege vassals and vassal daimyo faced essentially the same domanial fiscal and administrative problems and hence shared similar private interests vis-à-vis the bakufu. Between them they were able to shape policy so that it served their private institutional interests about as well as those interests could be served, given the technological foundations and demographic character of Tokugawa society.

   Our evidence has suggested that during the 1860s vassal lords grew cool toward Edo not because they resented its power but, contrariwise, from a growing awareness that Edo no longer could guarantee them against ambitious neighbors—an inability fully demonstrated in the Summer War of 1866. That awareness also probably helped drive many *han* leaders to seek the goodwill or assistance of more powerful and richer neighbors. In consequence patterns of regionalism began to appear. Great *han*, such as Sendai, Kaga, Fukui, Tottori, Uwajima, and Kumamoto, acquired by default regional leadership roles that undercut bakufu influence. (That trend also may have made more plausible the idea of regional allied action that Satsuma and Chōshū implemented in 1867 and that daimyo of the northeast resorted to in 1868.) A sense of vulnerability also seems to have prompted some *han* leaders, especially vassal daimyo, to rediscover their need for the old protector at Edo and may have encouraged some to want to exchange their feudal-lord roles for other more manageable ones. It led to belated *han* military reform, bilateral ties, neutralism and noninvolvement, and such statements of group solidarity with the bakufu as those made by vassal daimyo in late 1867.

On balance these several trends reduced the numbers of *han* that would support Edo, but they did not increase the numbers who would attack it on the field out of a desire to see it destroyed.

To argue, then, that long-range changes in bakufu-*han* relations undermined the bakufu and contributed to its collapse seems to miss the point. When one discusses the effect of long-range changes in the bakufu-*han* relationship on the regime's final crisis, it seems most fruitful to focus on the evolution of that relationship from an active martial lord-vassal one to a habitual and demilitarized civil administrative one. Like liege vassals, *han* leaders and samurai generally were unready to sacrifice the life-style of two centuries of guaranteed aristocratic privilege for the chancy style of lean instruments of war. In consequence the crisis of the sixties as it related to the bakufu was finally resolved by relatively small numbers of people representing relatively small segments of the Japanese polity, really little more than Satsuma and Chōshū on the one hand and Edo and Aizu on the other. To make the point in a different way, consider this counterfactual suggestion: that because of the long-range trend of demilitarization, compared to what did happen in the 1860s, had a civil war been fought in the shadow of a *bakumatsu*-type imperialist presence but in the context of the seventeenth-century bakufu-*han* relationship, it would not have been more promising for the Tokugawa. Rather, it would likely have been more violent and protracted, the damage to Japanese society that much greater, the likelihood of a stable successor regime that much less, and so the establishment of a colonial regime that much more probable. That is to say, in fine, that long-range changes in the bakufu-*han* relationship worked not to wreck the bakufu but to reduce the capacity of the samurai class to wreck Japan by engaging in violent civil strife.

The last element of bakufu weakness requiring our attention is the inadequacy of the regime's leadership. The indecisiveness of bakufu leadership during the 1860s was pervasive in its effect. It was unquestionably a factor shaping much daimyo behavior, and it also constituted a factor in the conduct of liege vassals and bakufu infantrymen.

There is not much evidence to indicate how either of those latter groups would have performed had they been given really adequate leadership because they were given it so rarely. But there are hints of what might have been. After Iemochi's death Yoshinobu reportedly elicited strong support from the men gathered at Osaka when he resolved to crush Chōshū. In 67/10 liege vassals joined the massive Tokugawa resistance to the Tosa restoration proposal. And in the regime's final hours many of them became the last loyal holdouts long after victory had become impossible and after their leader had quit. Bakufu infantrymen, despite the callous treatment they received, appear with rare exceptions to have given worthy if unexciting service in the field, being limited in their success mostly by factors external to themselves. Had they found a leader who could have made sacrifice seem worthwhile, one suspects they would have risen to the occasion.

Scattered evidence of this sort suggests that had the bakufu been led in a competent, consistent, committed manner during the 1860s, matters might have worked out quite differently. It is necessary, therefore, to examine the bakufu's leadership system to see how structural factors may have operated to deny the regime the quality of leadership it needed.

The Great Peace had been forged by willful men the likes of Nobunaga, Hideyoshi, and Ieyasu, but the mature *bakuhan* system came to idealize two quite different autocratic types. One was a ruler, whether shogun or daimyo, who embodied authority, listened sagely to his advisors, consulted them, followed their advice, or suggested if necessary how they could compromise any differences in opinion. This ideal man played essentially a legitimizing or mediating role while real leadership decisions emerged from the discussion of his subordinates. Hoshina Masayuki in the seventeenth century and Abe Masahiro in the 1850s were two who epitomized the ideal, and Itakura Katsukiyo seems to have tried to behave in accord with it. In practice this type tended to be the figurehead leader and was not likely to give dynamic creative leadership in a situation demanding bold new initiatives in the face of overt opposition.

The other autocratic ideal was a forceful leader who surrounded himself with one or more wise advisors, who sought their views, but who clearly made his own decisions—sound decisions—and then adhered to them with vigor and certitude. Several of the great *bakumatsu* figures were of this sort; Shimazu Hisamitsu was probably the soundest of the group but also Tokugawa Nariaki and Ii Naosuke. This type of leader was effective as long as he was operating within a sanctioned structure in which he was the sole locus of authority—which is to say, a shogun, or in the case of many *han*, a daimyo or his legitimate surrogate. But it was a disastrous type of leader for the *kōbugattai* situation in which a group of independent barons representing separate polities had to cooperate in an essentially unstructured context in the resolution of common but uncommonly difficult problems. And, more important for us at this point, in the absence of a ruling shogun it was an abrasive and ineffective type of leader to have in the bakufu, given the way the bakufu leadership system had evolved from the days of Ieyasu.

To elaborate that last point, in my earlier study of the bakufu I argued that during its last century or so it was controlled by a group of cooperating officials that I labeled a ''vertical clique.'' The pertinent points of the matter are two. First, at the highest level of senior councillors, a group of status equals worked in a collegial manner that required a considerable ability at cooperative give and take. Second, access to office and the duties of office were set up in such a way that this group of cooperating officials had to include below the senior councillors men in a range of offices whose occupants ran the gamut from vassal daimyo to medium-level liege vassals. In consequence such a ruling group included men whose status and connections made them responsive to the discontents of high-ranking and even relatively low-ranking bakufu retainers. That in turn meant a bakufu leader had to be sensitive to the interests of the several levels of personnel served by his followers. Under those circumstances a forceful autocratic personality who administered medicine with a firehose was poorly equipped to function as an effective clique leader as Ii Naosuke, Matsudaira Shungaku, and Matsudaira Naokatsu all demonstrated.

The political evolution that gave the bakufu this councillor-led ''vertical'' type of leadership created one other disadvantage for the Tokugawa. When one such clique lost power, its replacement was a difficult task; and until a new cohesive ruling group was thoroughly in control, the bakufu had great difficulty in formulating any consistent policy on matters of moment. Thus, as we noted in reviewing the Bunkyū reform, Shungaku failed to forge an effective ruling group. Then the years of conservative reassertion were a period in which the bakufu stumbled along with no truly cohesive leadership. In mid-1864 such a group began to coalesce, but the reverses of early 1865 disrupted it. In the next year and a half it fell apart, and not until after the Summer War was a new and cohesive group under Yoshinobu and Itakura able to grasp control of the bakufu and initiate the Keiō reform.

Prior to Iemochi's death, then, the bakufu had tried to function as it had for decades, using a pattern of collegial leadership functioning under the auspices of a passive shogun. The disadvantages of that leadership system in a situation demanding forceful, creative action were miserably evident in the bakufu's pathetic performance of 1862–1866. But after Yoshinobu and Itakura secured control, the bakufu had in effect found a leadership combination almost ideally suited to its structure. Yoshinobu provided vis-à-vis great lords and the court an autocratic leader quite appropriate to the shogunal position. And Itakura provided an administrative leader with the requisite skills for managing the ''vertical clique'' through which the Keiō reform was implemented.

In the absence of effective leadership before Iemochi's death, the regime floundered from one inadequate strategy to another. With each successive failure its problems grew worse and worse and morale dropped further and further. In consequence, when after the Summer War it did finally find both a leadership and a strategy that seemed adequate to the age, matters had deteriorated so far that the regime's rivals were able to take decisive action before the bakufu was able to gain momentum enough to prevail. One might argue, therefore, that if a really able shogun had secured control before the situation had eroded so badly, he might well have been able to pilot the bakufu successfully through the shoals of the 1860s to a central role in a nationally unified state. In that sense the gradual evolution of the bakufu leadership system and ideal had proved a major factor in the regime's failure.

In the final analysis, however, it would be unfortunate to leave—even unintentionally—the impression that the tragic flaw lay in the inadequacy of leaders. Yoshinobu's performance was not especially bad; indeed, on balance it deserved the respect it commanded at the time. And despite the bad press of his predecessors, the failures of earlier leaders during the 1860s reflected inadequacies of the system much more than flaws in the men themselves. When an institution is so burdened with structural liabilities that it can cope with its problems only by receiving exceptional leadership, I submit one should stress those liabilities of structure and the particular problems being encountered when discussing the etiology of failure. The points of weakness that have seemed to merit attention here have been the ambiguity of self-image, the limits of the Tokugawa exchequer, the orientation and attitude of liege vassals and daimyo, and the regime's leadership structure.

The foreign intrusion that gave rise to an ad hoc coalition hostile to the bakufu presented the Tokugawa regime, both directly of itself and indirectly by way of court-daimyo-*shishi* activism, with a series of challenges that the regime was incapable of handling because of those elements of weakness. The bakufu fell as it did when it did due to the sum of the effects of this interaction of structure and unprecedented situation.

LAST REFLECTIONS

It appears, then, that the Tokugawa regime failed because the imperialist intrusion introduced a set of demands, most immediately political, that the existing system was fundamentally unable to handle. The upshot was that the old order collapsed.

To show how the conjunction of situation and structure ruined the bakufu does not explain clearly, however, why the old bakufu's leaders failed to build the new order that was needed. The reasons for their failure can be summed up in the statement that in the crisis of the sixties, the advantages of their position were outweighed by the disadvantages. Their advantages and disadvantages were those common to rulers and can be identified in universal terms.

Those controlling a government have, to begin with, some degree of prestige that helps sanction their efforts and cushion their failures. Their position, moreover, may well give them better access to information about the possibilities and problems of a situation. They have access to legitimate coercive power and to the other resources of government, notably tax income and the organs and personnel of governance. To their disadvantage they are responsible for the conduct of affairs and, whether deservedly or not, most likely will bear the onus for whatever goes wrong, unless they can use organs of propaganda to put the blame on others. They are visible, which makes them a particularly available butt of abuse and object of attack. They also are saddled with the task of protecting vested interests of one sort or another, not only their own but those of their sponsors and their followers, and that task circumscribes their range of free action.

We have seen that the Tokugawa regime's residual prestige was clearly of value in a host of ways, most notably as its strongest card in the symbolic politics central to the decade. Bakufu leaders also enjoyed some measure of informational advantage: they kept reasonably good track of domestic affairs from Ezo to Uragami and were in the van of knowledge about foreign affairs and western technology. The quality of bakufu information was probably on most counts superior to that of their adversaries.

The instruments of coercion and control that bakufu leaders commanded were a very mixed blessing. In a sense their old military forces were worse than useless because they consumed wealth and resisted change. It would have been easier to build a commoner infantry force from scratch than to convert their old forces to new, and their approach to military reform repeatedly revealed their awareness of it. Indeed the bitter trouncing of 1866 proved a blessing for military reformers because it made their point so well. The other resources of exchequer and administrative structure also were a limited boon because the former was so inadequate, the latter needed so much alteration, and addressing those problems generated such resistance.

The disadvantages of responsibility were particularly apparent. The bakufu bore almost alone the blame for yielding to the barbarians, and it was never allowed to escape that stigma. Nor did it have effective propaganda organs through which to mount a rhetorical counteroffensive. Rather, the rectification of its foreign policy became a prerequisite to satisfying the elemental ethnic sensibilities that were fundamental to the restoration movement. In consequence of its inability to overcome its diplomatic humiliations, an immense burden of moral failure had to be borne by the regime's personnel. That burden eroded morale within just as surely as it aroused alarm and and indignation without.

The erosion within was especially acute because the regime was, after all, the institutional expression of a sophisticated value system.[9] Gradual recognition that the regime was failing to cope with its problems forced men to sort out principles and decide what might be sacrificed and what must not be. But that was a slow, painful, individual task for every official and Tokugawa vassal involved. It was a task necessary to the adoption of a progressive institutional posture, and the years before 1866 were in a sense years lost to the bakufu because they were consumed in the sorting-out process. Even when the regime's leadership finally settled upon radical changes in 1866–1867, moreover, much of the followership was opposed; and their opposition was a significant obstacle to bakufu success.

Externally the sense of ethnic crisis was expressed as pious indignation, and it was central to the *shishi* activism that found its most influential form in acts of assassination. The highly visible and presumably culpable leaders of the bakufu, along with equally visible foreigners, became prime targets of these acts. By contrast the assassins themselves were not visible, and the flimsy police system of the bakufu had considerable difficulty in detecting plots in embryo or locating the guilty afterward.

Finally, of course, the regime's leaders were burdened by the restraints imposed on them by vested interests, which, as we have observed, did so much to thwart the Bunkyū reform and slow the Keiō reform and which when defied reduced the leaders' base of power. Few in the bakufu had much to gain by radical change; many had a great deal to lose.

As that last comment implies, perhaps the greatest advantage of outsiders was that they had more to gain than did Edo by changing the existing order and hence could sustain a higher level of morale and a greater degree of commitment among themselves and their followers than could the bakufu. A corollary worth noting is that in the showdown in 1866 and later at Fushimi-Toba success seemed more important to the anti-bakufu forces. For them on both occasions defeat carried with it the real and perceptible possibility of devastating punishment. It seems most unlikely, however, that the bakufu rank and file in 1866 imagined that defeat in battle could really lead to loss of the Tokugawa domanial foundation. By the time of Fushimi-Toba the awareness of risk was greater, and many were already choosing to deal with it by cutting their links to the faltering regime. Many liege vassals had been alienated by the Keiō reform and many vassal and related *han* had begun hedging their bets when possible. The bakufu itself had come to rely primarily on its infantry, and their interests were not identical with those of the regime in any case. In the end those on the Osaka side who realized that they did have as much to lose as the insurgents—namely Aizu, Kuwana, and many lesser liege vassals—were no match for the Kyoto forces either qualitatively or quantitatively.

On balance, then, within the particular context of 1860s Japan, at least, the disadvantages surely outweighed the advantages of the regime's leaders as architects of a new order. Consequently they failed to build it and instead yielded power to outsiders.

Failing to build a new order, the regime's leaders could only fall from power because preservation of the status quo was impossible given the fundamental character of the crisis of the sixties. That the crisis was created by foreign intruders rather than by slowly developing internal contradictions in no way reduces its elemental nature. It was a situation that can fairly be called a ''systemic crisis.''

By systemic crisis I mean a situation in which a society's key values and key institutions are in fundamental ways inadequate to the problems that beset it. The origins of such a crisis are not of immediate concern. It may arise from cumulative change within a society. Or perhaps a society suddenly encounters important social situations that it had not in any significant sense faced before and that consequently were not accommodated in the design and development of the society's main values and institutions. The cause of the crisis is not the point, however. Rather, it is the character of the crisis that commands our attention. Systemic crisis is of course not utterly unrelated to the more usual phenomena of personal incompetence among leaders, inadequacy of particular policies, or conditions of minor structural maladjustment, temporary imbalance, or partial obsolescence that are customary to most polities much of the time. It is, however, a situation in which the inadequate elements of structure and value are so central to the entire social order and the resulting crisis so severe that leaders are forced to abandon treasured fundamental assumptions about the proper order of the universe and fashion a new order founded on assumptions adequate to the age—or else yield up their position to others who can do so more effectively. In a systemic crisis, failure to forge this new order can lead that society, depending upon the particulars of its situation, to any of several unwanted conditions: political chaos, alien control, or even biological extinction. But the status quo can no longer endure.

The fundamental nature of the *bakumatsu* crisis is apparent in hindsight. It involved an assault on basic values and structures of both the polity narrowly defined and of the society more broadly conceived. The ideals of isolation, of hereditary status stratification, of structural decentralization, of a putatively agrarian-based polity, of a Confucian-educated ruling elite, and of a ruler–ruled cleavage that was also the politically involved–uninvolved cleavage all became obsolete. And accordingly the structure that gave form to these ideals, namely the *bakuhan* system, also became obsolete. In their place Japan was being forced to formulate ideals and structures that would make the country part of an emerging global system of interacting societies, each with a unified polity, a complexly integrated, politically mobilized society, an industrialized economy, and a secular science-oriented nationalist education for all.

These demands, quite obviously, were revolutionary. Consequently in the 1860s, even before their full implications were apparent, they were creating immense stresses throughout polity and society. Within the regime demoralization, paralysis, scapegoating, peculation, unsanctioned strong-arm tactics, and wild gyrations of policy were endemic. Ineptness of the military, inadequacies of the administrative system, and failures of the police were common.

Just as apparent were the regime's persistent and rapidly worsening fiscal problems. It lacked the income to pay for programs deemed essential and was able only after much bitter dispute and delay to agree on what constituted waste that could be eliminated. Faced by built-in costs it could not eradicate and immense new costs it had to assume, the regime resorted to ever more self-hurtful financing measures. These included cheapening its money, borrowing with no real hope of repaying, extorting under various covers, letting its physical plant deteriorate, and finally offering to trade parts of its sovereign soul for alien support.

This pervasive inadequacy of the polity was only the most visible part of the problem, however. At broader social levels—the levels of daimyo domains, samurai in general, and the masses of people— the political disruption of the 1860s had far-reaching effects. It generated severe economic dislocations, particularly inflation, but also disruptions in productive activities. These were manifested in unemployment of minor servants and retainers, economic sabotage by riots and organized plots, and the diversion of productive manpower and scarce resources to military and political service duties of various sorts.

Public disillusionment at these levels was reflected in the spread of political noncooperation, the weakening of customary norms, the spread of deviant behavior, a reactionary shrill defense of customary norms by others, and growing violence and political activism. More and more of this activism operated outside of sanctioned channels. And the young, who had the greatest future at stake and the least history to lose, tended to be the most vigorous element in this unsanctioned activity. This social disorder generated more efforts by the regime to maintain social stability, and those efforts in turn generated more dissidence by the alienated.

Attempts by the rulers to stem the societal hemorrhaging ranged in effectiveness from the positively dysfunctional to the temporarily ameliorative. Ultimately they were ineffective in controlling the malaise. The reason was that the necessary transformation was so profound it could not occur without severe dislocations of the sort being experienced. In an operational sense, however, the problem was that the new situation of *bakumatsu* Japan was so unprecedented that its magnitude and true implications were not at all understood by members of that society, whether high or low. Rather, the problems were misdefined—usually underdefined, most notably in the conservative reassertion of 1863–1864—and so the rash of efforts to cope tended to be inadequate and ineffective. Because the programs were inadequate, they failed to attain their objectives and instead seemed only to make matters worse.

Nothing seemed to work, and blundering from failure to failure, Tokugawa society's state of inner tension and disorientation grew worse and worse. As the situation deteriorated, more frenetic strategies were adopted. A few people began to look elsewhere for solutions, and some formulated out of their own agony new statements of value and purpose. During 1866–1867 these crystallized in daring plans that by their nature would overturn the established order. Whether they would eventuate in an effective new order or result in chaos or colonialism remained to be seen. But in early 1868 they did eventuate in a civil war that eliminated the Tokugawa bakufu and its leaders from any significant role in the construction of a new Japan.

APPENDIX 1:
Clock Time Conversion Table*

New Style (AM or PM)	Old Style (hours)
1	9 ½
2	8
3	8 ½
4	7
5	7 ½
6	6
7	6 ½
8	5
9	5 ½
10	4
11	4 ½
12	9

*Based on Mitamura Engyo, *Edo seikatsu jiten* (Tokyo, 1960), inside front cover. For explanation, see the discussion of dating in the Bibliographical Essay.

Calendrical Time Conversion Table*

Gregorian Calendar	Bunkyū 2 1862	Bunkyū 3 1863	Genji 1 1864	Keiō 1 1865	Keiō 2 1866	Keiō 3 1867	Meiji 1 1868
Jan. 1 (31)		**11/12**	11/22	12/4	**11/15**	**11/26**	**12/7**
Feb. 1 (28)†	**1/3**	12/13	**12/24**	**1/6**	12/16	**12/27**	1/8
Mar. 1 (31)	2/1	**1/12**	1/23	2/4	**1/15**	1/25	**2/8**
Apr. 1 (30)	**3/3**	**2/14**	2/25	3/6	2/16	**2/27**	**3/9**
May 1 (31)	**4/3**	**3/14**	**3/26**	**4/7**	**3/17**	3/27	4/9
June 1 (30)	5/4	4/15	4/27	5/8	4/18	**4/29**	i4/11‡
July 1 (31)	**6/5**	**5/16**	**5/28**	i5/9‡	5/19	5/29	
Aug. 1 (31)	7/6	6/17	6/29	6/10	6/21	7/2	
Sep. 1 (30)	**8/8**	**7/19**	**8/1**	7/12	7/23	**8/4**	
Oct. 1 (31)	i8/8‡	**8/19**	9/1	8/12	8/23	9/4	
Nov. 1 (30)	**9/10**	9/20	10/2	9/13	9/24	**10/6**	
Dec. 1 (31)	10/10	**10/21**	**11/3**	**10/14**	**10/25**	**11/6**	

* Based on Paul Y. Tsuchihashi, *Japanese Chronological Tables* (Tokyo, 1952). Months in bold face type have 30 days; others have 29.

† Except leap years 1864 and 1868, which have 29 days in February.

‡ Intercalary months.

Notes

ABBREVIATIONS

DNISK   Dai Nihon ishin shiryō kōhon
ISK   Ishin shiryō kōyō
KT   Kanbu tsuki
MHS   Mito han shiryō
OIN   Ogasawara Ikinokami Nagamichi
RR   Rikugun rekishi (edited by Katsu Kaishū)
SNS   Shichinenshi (by Kitahara Masanaga)
ZSK   Zoku saimu kiji
ZTJ   Zoku Tokugawa jikki

Citations of DNISK *kan* that were unpaginated when I perused them require explanation. Each citation is accompanied by reference to the relevant entry in ISK, which is in effect a published ten-volume summary of contents of DNISK. Thus the first DNISK entry cited in note 8 of Chapter 1 is DNISK 1422 n.p. [ISK, IV:67:2:r]. That means that the cited entry in unpaginated DNISK *kan* number 1422 is (in reverse order) the eighteenth (r) source cited (*"Togawa Yasukiyo nikki"*) under the second full topic entry (*"Bakufu, rōjū Kuze Hirochika ni jōkyō o rei zu"*) on page 67 of volume 4 of ISK. Locating the same topic entry in the indicated DNISK *kan*, one can then usually locate without difficulty the selection from the source cited.

INTRODUCTION

1. Tetsuo Najita's *Japan* is a stimulating recent discussion of this matter and provides in footnote citations an excellent guide to other works.

2. I use the term "ethnic danger" in preference to "national danger" in conformity with my later use of the term "ethnicity" rather than nationalism, protonationalism, culturalism, ethnocentrism, xenophobia, antiforeignism, or other words because these latter are burdened in various ways with pejorative

or celebratory connotations or definitional ramifications that I wish to avoid. In the body of this study I use the term in reference to *jōi* ("expel the barbarian") most commonly where I speak of the bakufu as being caught in the middle in the conflict of western imperialism and Japanese ethnicity. This use of the term admittedly does not fit with complete ease even the commendably imprecise use made by Nathan Glazer and Daniel P. Moynihan in the work they recently edited, *Ethnicity, Theory and Experience*. Nonetheless, I believe it is a valid and instructive use of the term.

3. Yoshio Sakata and John W. Hall, "The Motivation of Political Leadership in the Meiji Restoration," *Journal of Asian Studies* 16:31–50 (1956). W. G. Beasley, *The Meiji Restoration*.

4. All dates in this study are those of the Japanese calendar and are given in the rational year-month-day sequence. Intercalary ("int.") months follow those regular months of the same number: for example, 1862/int. 8 follows 1862/8.

CHAPTER 1

1. The date of this meeting is given as 62/3/5 in KT (Tokyo, 1915), I, 88, and *Saimu kiji* (Tokyo, 1922), p. 17. However, KT dating is very unreliable. SNS (Tokyo, 1904), bk. 1, pt. 1, p. 17, dates it 2/5, but SNS also errs frequently in its dating. Suematsu Kenchō, *Bōchō kaitenshi* (Tokyo, 1921), III, 189 ff., discusses the dating problem and concludes that 3/15 is the proper date. ISK (Tokyo, 1965), IV, 29, uses this date. Tokutomi Iichirō, *Kinsei Nihon kokuminshi* (Tokyo, 1935), XLVII, 20–22, also discusses the matter.

2. Some information on Itakura Katsukiyo is given in Tamura Eitarō, "Bakumatsu kakurō Itakura Iga no kami," *Nihon no fūzoku* 2(11):4–29 (1939).

3. KT, I, 5–6, 238–239. *Saimu kiji*, p. 20, reports that some two hundred *rōnin* were involved in the Kyoto activity.

4. The painful memory of Hotta Masayoshi and Manabe Akikatsu's Kyoto experiences is evident in *Saimu kiji* materials on the 62/5 political discussions.

5. DNISK 1419 n.p. [ISK (Tokyo, 1965), IV:65:1:h].

6. DNISK 1421 n.p. [ISK, IV:66:4:c,k,x,y]. *Saimu kiji* is the major published source on Shungaku's activity at this time.

7. ZTJ (Tokyo, 1907), IV, 1230, 1236. DNISK 1436 n.p. [ISK, IV:84:1:d,s,v,ff.].

8. Material on Kuze's fall is in DNISK 1422 n.p. [ISK, IV:67:2:r]; 1427 n.p. [ISK, IV:75:1:b,d,e,f,g,j]. KT, I, 241–243. Rumors are reported in KT, I, 6, 12, 13.

9. KT, I, 151–152. Shibusawa Eiichi, *Tokugawa Yoshinobukō den* (Tokyo, 1918), II, 44.

10. Shibusawa, II, 51–52.

11. Tamura, p. 19. Tokutomi, XLVII, 262, 270. *Ishinshi* (Tokyo, 1941), III, 114.

12. Shibusawa, V, 259-262. DNISK 1452 n.p. [ISK, IV:101:1:a]. KT, I, 330. *Saimu kiji*, p. 133.

13. DNISK 1458, 1459 n.p. [ISK, IV:107:3:g,h,aa,ii]; 1461 n.p. [ISK, IV:109:4:c,g,i,cc]. ZTJ, IV, 1286, 1291. Shibusawa, V, 258 ff. KT, I, 331-333, 338-340.

14. Mikami Kazuo, "Bakumatsu ni okeru Fukui han no hansei kaikaku to bakusei kaikaku undō ni tsuite," *Fukui kenritsu Fuku shōkō kenkyū shūroku* 1:36-54 (1969). Shungaku's political role continues to interest scholars. Kawakita Nobuo, "Matsudaira Shungaku no shōko kaigi seijiron no saiyō," *Shigaku* 43(1-2):307-318, discusses it in terms of an attempt to modify *rōjū* domination *(yōbeya seiji)*. Yamaguchi Muneyuki, "Shōgun keishi undō no tenkai: shōgun shinsei kara kōbugattai e," *Kyushu shigaku* 40:24-34 (1967), discusses it in somewhat larger terms of redefining the authority relationship of shogun and emperor. Mikami, in the essay cited above, discusses Shungaku's role in terms of class conflict and *zettaishugi*. In a later essay, "Bunkyū ki ni okeru Echizen han no bakusei kaikaku undō ni tsuite," *Nihon rekishi* 288:99-105 (1972), Mikami deletes most of his Marxian analysis, replacing it with discussion of the interconnection of Echizen *han* reform and nationwide reform.

15. Shibusawa, II, 122; V, 265-266. *Saimu kiji*, pp. 147-148.

16. MHS (Tokyo, 1970), III, 199 ff. ZSK (Tokyo, 1921), I, 79, 84.

17. Tōyama Shigeki, "Bunkyū ninen no seiji jōsei," *Rekishigaku kenkyū* 13(9):64-84 (1943).

18. *Ii ke shiryō: bakumatsu fūbun tansakusho* (Tokyo, 1968), III, 426. DNISK 1476 n.p. [ISK, IV:127:2:1]. KT, I, 17, 20-22, 252. MHS, III, 198. Shibusawa, V, 267-268.

19. This summary of Hikone punishment is based on materials in DNISK 1488 n.p. [ISK, IV:136:6:a,b,e,f,h]; 1500 n.p. [ISK, IV:153:3:a]; 1504 n.p. [ISK, IV:157-158:4:a,c,d,f,g]; 1607 n.p. [ISK, IV:273:2:a,c,g]. KT, I, 21, 24, 299, 310-311.

20. This summary of the Aizu situation is based on DNISK 1490 n.p. [ISK, IV:140:1:c,e,f,y,bb,cc]. SNS, bk. 1, pt. 2, pp. 9-11, 21-22. *Saimu kiji*, pp. 170-172, 174-175, passim. Shibusawa, II, 106-107; VI, 263. Yamakawa Hiroshi, *Kyoto shugoshoku shimatsu* (Tokyo, 1966), I, 28-29.

21. *Saimu kiji*, pp. 195-197. Grace Fox, *Britain and Japan, 1858-1883*, pp. 97-98.

22. DNISK 1499 n.p. [ISK, IV:150:4:b,e]; 1508 n.p. [ISK, IV:163-164:6:a,c]; 1514 n.p. [ISK, IV:171:2:h]. KT, I, 350-351, 359. *Saimu kiji*, p. 185. Tamura, pp. 25-26.

23. DNISK 1501, 1502 n.p. [ISK, IV:154:2:passim] contains a wealth of data on the ramifications of *sankin kōtai* reform. Shibusawa, II, 95, reports that the office perquisites were worth some 2000 *ryō* to *rōjū* and 1000 *ryō* to *wakadoshiyori*. Events of these weeks are also discussed at some length in

Saimu kiji, pp. 203–208; ZSK, I, 3 ff.; Shibusawa, V, 284 ff.; KT, I, 332–333.

24. Tamura, pp. 23–25. This source is not entirely dispassionate.

25. This material on Ogasawara Nagamichi is from OIN (Tokyo, 1942), pp. 99–108, 120.

26. Had Nagamichi been daimyo, he reportedly would have been given full *rōjū* status; as it was, he was to be treated as a regular *rōjū* in most respects. DNISK 1511 n.p. [ISK, IV:168:1:c,d,f,k].

27. ZTJ, IV, 1230.

28. Data on this reform are in ZTJ, IV, 1190–1666 passim. KT, I, 352–373. Yoshino Naoyasu, comp., *Kaei Meiji nenkanroku* (Tokyo, 1968), II, 839 ff. DNISK 1437 n.p. [ISK, IV:85:3:a]; 1501 [cited above in note 23]; ISK, IV, 78 ff. passim.

29. DNISK 1613 n.p. [ISK, IV:280:4:b].

30. DNISK 1506 n.p. [ISK, IV:161:2:e]; 1524 n.p. [ISK, IV:182:2: passim]. KT, I, 31, 367. Shibusawa, V, 297–298. ZSK, I, 61, 71–73. Tokutomi, XLVIII, 165–166. Minami Kazuo, ''Bunkyū ki ni okeru Edo no harifuda ni tsuite,'' *Kyoto toritsu kōkū kōsen kenkyū kiyō* 8:6 (1971).

31. *Ii ke shiryō,* III, 432–433.

32. Yoshino, II, 752–753.

33. DNISK 1457 n.p. [ISK, IV:106:5:d].

34. ZSK, I, 48, 295–299.

35. Arima Nariura, ''Bakumatsu ni okeru seiyō kaki no yunyū,'' *Nihon rekishi* 120:6 (1958).

36. RR (Tokyo, 1967), II, 106–110.

37. ZTJ, IV, 1227. KT, I, 8. Tokumaruhara is near Shimoakatsukamachi in Itabashi-ku. The Shōgetsuin nearby is the site of Takashima Shūhan's earlier training center.

38. KT, I, 17.

39. RR, II, 136.

40. RR, II, 129–145, 157–174, 327. The manpower figures given here are all rounded-off versions of Katsu's precise figures. The RR materials on the 7/27 plan are not dated 1862, but internal evidence shows clearly that this document was part of that year's planning. The plan was presented, however, by a *Kii no kami* whom I have been unable to identify, unless the title refers to *rōjū* Naitō, who had left office two months previously.

41. KT, I, 371–373. ZTJ, IV, 1528–1529. Kozo Yamamura, *A Study of Samurai Income and Entrepreneurship,* p. 17, lists the *hatamoto* rear-vassal requirements of 1649.

42. RR, I, 88–89; II, 110–112.

43. Ōtsuka Takematsu, *Bakumatsu gaikōshi no kenkyū* (Tokyo, 1966), p. 346.

44. KT, I, 473–474.

45. RR, II, 162, 237–238.

CHAPTER 2

1. DNISK 1514 n.p. [ISK, IV:172:1:b]. ZSK, I, 82, 84.

2. Yamakawa, I, 28–29. W. G. Beasley, *Select Documents on Japanese Foreign Policy 1853–1868*, pp. 225–227, is a translation of Katamori's notice. The original document, without precise date, is in SNS, bk. 1, pt. 2, pp. 37–39.

3. *Ishinshi* (Tokyo, 1941), III, 286. Tokutomi, XLVIII, 175–177. Beasley, *Documents*, p. 229. ISK, IV, 173.

4. ZSK, I, 92, 98.

5. Shibusawa, V, 311.

6. ZSK, I, 121–122.

7. Tokutomi XLVIII, 214–215. Beasley, *Documents*, pp. 227–234, translates Shungaku's 10/13 explanation of his discontent. The original can be found in ZSK, I, 144–154, and Shibusawa, V, 317–326.

8. DNISK 1539 n.p. [ISK, IV:200:5:a].

9. Shibusawa, V, 332, 335–340; II, 160–161.

10. Shibusawa, V, 340 ff. ZSK, I, 172–179, 181, 184. MHS, III, 234–235. ZTJ, IV, 1475.

11. Marius Jansen, *Sakamoto Ryōma and the Meiji Restoration*, p. 123, reports that a measles epidemic hit the Kinai area during 62/8.

12. DNISK 1555 n.p. [ISK, IV:213:3:d].

13. SNS, bk. 1, pt. 2, p. 79.

14. OIN, p. 120. This material on Ogasawara's purge is based on OIN, pp. 120–138, unless otherwise noted.

15. DNISK 1546 n.p. [ISK, IV:205:3:a].

16. *Katsu Kaishū zenshū* (Tokyo, 1972), XVIII, 19.

17. DNISK 1578 n.p. [ISK, 240–241:1:d,g,gg]. The amnesty is treated extensively in standard works.

18. Shibusawa, II, 166.

19. ZSK, I, 238–239. SNS, bk. 1, pt. 2, pp. 51–55.

20. DNISK 1574 n.p. [ISK, IV:237:1:b]. MHS, III, 251–252. KT, I, 43. ZSK, I, 246.

21. ZSK, I, 249–250.

22. ZSK, I, 350–356.

23. DNISK 1637 n.p. [ISK, IV:308:3:a,c,d,e].

24. Material on this *rōnin* force is in Tokutomi, LII, 427 ff. Hirao Michio, *Shinsengumi shiroku* (Tokyo, 1967), pp. 21 ff.

25. DNISK 1640 n.p. [ISK, IV:314:5:b,f,h,i,k].

26. DNISK 1640 cited above. The quotation is from the "Nabeshima Naomasakō den."

27. KT, I, 277, 285, 287.

28. In this study monetary figures have all been converted to Mexican dollars or gold *ryō* on fixed, approximate ratios chosen for ease of calculation.

They cannot, therefore, be used for precise figuring. For further consolidation of figures, it will suffice to use a rate of $1 = 0.75 *ryō*. In about 1860 the *ryō* was worth somewhat more, but by the late sixties currency revaluation made necessary by foreign gold-silver exchange rates, rampant inflation, and changes in the foreign trade balance had reduced the value of the *ryō* well below that rate. The following dollar conversion rates are used: $1 = 5½ francs; 2½ guilders; ¼ pound.

29. *Saimu kiji*, pp. 155–162. KT, I, 276.

30. Material on this planning for the shogunal trip is in KT, I, 273–287, 560. MHS, III, 220, 252 ff. ZTJ, IV, 1596, 1621. *Katsu zenshū*, XVIII, 6, 7, 10, 25.

31. Material on Hachisuka Narihiro is in ZTJ, IV, 1126, 1327–1328, 1550, 1596–1597, 1682. KT, I, 387–400, 455–456.

32. ZTJ, IV, 1685.

33. ZSK, I, 364–366. John R. Black, *Young Japan*, I, 188–189. Tokutomi, XLIX, 289–291; L, 11–13.

34. *Ii ke shiryō*, III, 431.

35. Kyoto politics of this period are treated extensively in ZSK, I, 362–437. Shibusawa, II, 184–260; V, 416 ff. Yamakawa, I, 44 ff.

36. ZSK, I, 400, 402–403. Of course ZSK may here be making a convenient misreading of Shungaku's intent.

37. SNS, bk. 1, pt. 3, pp. 64–68. ZSK, I, 403, 407. Shibusawa, V, 467–468.

38. ZSK, I, 341.

39. This interpretation is constructed from material in ZSK, I, 411, 415. Shibusawa, V, 471–479. MHS, III, 281–295. Tokutomi, XLIX, 332, 340–344.

40. Yamakawa, I, 101–102.

41. ZTJ, IV, 1815. ZSK, I, 421 ff.

42. Conrad Totman, *Politics in the Tokugawa Bakufu, 1600–1843*, pp. 187–188, 259–260. See also my ''Political Succession in the Tokugawa Bakufu,'' *Harvard Journal of Asiatic Studies* 26:102–124 (1966).

CHAPTER 3

1. Tokutomi, L, 31 ff., follows the Namamugi negotiations in detail.

2. Material on these defense moves is taken from KT, I, 461 ff. DNISK 1671 n.p. [ISK, IV:347:1:a,c,g,q,r]; 1673 n.p. [ISK, IV:349:1:a,f,n]; 1681 n.p. [ISK, IV:356:4:a]. E. M. Satow, *A Diplomat in Japan*, pp. 73–79.

3. DNISK 1709 n.p. [ISK, IV:393:3:a,g,i].

4. The ambiguities of Nagamichi and Yoshinobu's intentions at this time are discussed in Yamakawa, I, 107; OIN, p. 164; Shibusawa, II, 313, 323. Beasley, *Documents*, p. 243, in one of his rare mistakes, attributes the date of

early May to a statement by Ogasawara that refers to the 5/10 expulsion date. The date of 5/10 was not settled upon until 4/20 (June 6). In view of OIN's frequent dating inaccuracies, probably this entry, inserted at about 3/21–23 (May 8–10) in OIN, p. 159, is better dated as 4/21–23, or just after the major decision of 4/21 at Edo. It is clearly aimed at the bakufu leaders and others in Kyoto, whose opinion Nagamichi was evidently attempting to influence.

5. DNISK 1716 n.p. [ISK, IV:403:2:a,b,c,d] [ISK, IV:403:4:a,e,k]; 1719 n.p. [ISK, IV:407:3:b,c].

6. DNISK 1718 n.p. [ISK, IV:406:3:b].

7. SNS, bk. 1, pt. 4, p. 28. ZSK, II, 5. The *rōjū* notice said, however, that they were sending the Owari lord to Kyoto posthaste to find out why the Dutch were included in the order. Tergiversation they surely had in mind.

8. MHS, III, 331, 338. KT, I, 492–493. DNISK 1720 n.p. [ISK, IV:410:2:a,c,d,h,i].

9. Tokutomi, XLIX, 512–513. Shibusawa, II, 313–316; V, 508–509. Some claim that the note was a cover and Yoshinobu's dawdling en route reflected his attempt to give Edo time to settle affairs peacefully before his return. Then he would resign to take the blame for his "failure." On 4/26 he did send to Kyoto a request to resign as guardian, and in it he reiterated his commitment to expulsion.

10. This summary of the critical days of 63/5 is derived from materials in Tokutomi, L, 87 ff. OIN, pp. 195 ff. Shibusawa, V, 523–529, 545 ff. Satow, pp. 79–81. Fox, pp. 111–112. ZSK, II, 26. MHS, III, 341–343. SNS, bk. 1, pt. 4, p. 33. ISK, IV, 420, 422. KT, I, 566. DNISK 1726 n.p. [ISK, IV:419:1:a,b,d].

11. DNISK 1742 n.p. [ISK, IV:437:2:g]. This entry, from "Ishin kaitei zasshi," reports that Ogasawara opposed payment until he reached Yokohama but then, convinced he must, did pay. In the 1890s, when *jōi* was out of favor, Yoshinobu recalled that he had authorized Ogasawara's payment. (Shibusawa, V, 525, 548–551). In the 1930s, when imperial loyalism was in high favor, Ogasawara's biographers were glad to credit Yoshinobu with that role, saying he sent *gaikoku bugyō* Inoue Kiyonao to Yokohama with those instructions. The matter is discussed in OIN, p. 198. Tokutomi, XLIX, 517–518; L, 104 ff. Shibusawa, II, 319 ff.; V, 554–556.

12. SNS, bk. 1, pt. 4, pp. 8–25, 29, 83–90. MHS, III, 300–301. Shibusawa, II, 301–304.

13. SNS, bk. 1, pt. 4, pp. 18–23, 35–38. Shibusawa, II, 328–329; V, 504. KT, I, 560–561. MHS, III, 321, 324. *Katsu zenshū*, XVIII, 46–57.

14. This summary of the maneuvering at Kyoto is based on data in DNISK 1742, pp. 2–8; 1744, pp. 92–99; 1750, pp. 2–3. SNS, bk. 1, pt. 4, pp. 38, 48–52. Yamakawa, I, 141–142.

15. The purpose and historical significance of Ogasawara's march has re-

cently been the subject of some scholarly debate. Ishii Takashi has viewed it as designed to crush the *sonnō jōi* radicals and regards it as an expression of emerging bakufu authoritarianism based on joint efforts of the new foreign affairs officials and new-style military leaders, a compradore-militarist alliance leading to *zettaishugi*. Tanaka Akira argues more modestly that Ogasawara was using military display to coerce the court on its *jōi* policy. Kamekakegawa Hiromasa in a recent and careful study argues that the new bakufu military leaders did not play a key role in the planning and purpose of the venture and that as a historical force they really did not emerge until 1867/12. Tanaka Akira, ''Bakufu no jōiha datō kūdetā keikakusetsu ni tsuite,'' *Nihon rekishi* 171:11–18 (1962). Ishii Takashi, ''Ogasawara kakurō 'soppei jōkyō' no seikaku ni tsuite,'' *Nihon rekishi* 173:2–7 (1962). Kamekakegawa Hiromasa, ''Bakumatsu bakufu rikugun no dōkō: Bunkyū sannen Ogasawara kakurō soppei jōkyō jiken o chūshin ni shite,'' *Gunji shigaku* 7(3):2–11 (1971).

16. Meron Medzini, *French Policy in Japan during the Closing Years of the Tokugawa Regime*, p. 42. Shibusawa, V, 571. MHS, III, 399–400. DNISK 1742 n.p. [ISK, IV:437:2:a,e,j,k,l,p] contains several sources offering explanations of Ogasawara's purpose or purposes.

17. KT, I, 558–559. Tanaka Akira, ''Bakumatsu no seiji jōsei,'' in *Iwanami kōza Nihon rekishi* (Kindai I) (Tokyo, 1962), XIV, 151.

18. Tanaka, ''Bakumatsu jōsei,'' and Ishii Takashi, ''Rekkyō no tai-Nichi seisaku,'' in *Iwanami*, XIV, 149, 224. Fox, p. 114.

19. Shibusawa, V, 561. DNISK 1742 n.p. cited above in note 16.

20. KT, I, 566–569, gives an orderly account of the 5–20–21 talks but does not report Ogasawara's return to Edo. DNISK 1742 n.p., cited above in note 16, is the fullest account for the last ten days of 63/5. ''Zoku tsūshin zenran'' in this entry is the ''reliable source.'' OIN, p. 223, gives the rationale of ''coastal defense.'' Sources differ on force figures, but most are of the general magnitude given here.

21. DNISK 1750 n.p. [ISK, IV:448:3:d]. SNS, bk. 1, pt. 4, pp. 57–59. KT, I, 570, indicates that many of Ogasawara's men were on board ship until 6/3 and 4.

22. DNISK 1752 n.p. [ISK, IV:452:4:d,f].

23. DNISK 1752 n.p. [ISK, IV:452:4:b,d,e]; 1757 n.p. [ISK, IV:456: 1:a,f]; 1758 n.p. [ISK, IV:457:3:a,b]. ZTJ, IV, 1862, 1863.

24. OIN, pp. 228–233. During 63/7 Ogasawara was recalled to Edo, where he remained under close house arrest.

25. The political narrative of 63/6–8 that is summed up here I originally worked out on the basis of materials in DNISK volumes 1766 n.p. [ISK, IV:470:1:b,j] [ISK, IV:471:2:a,c,e]; 1768 n.p. [ISK, IV:473:2:b]; 1795 n.p. [ISK, IV:504:1:a]; 1799 n.p. [ISK, IV:513:2:a,e]; 1801 n.p. [ISK, IV:516:3:b,f]; 1808 n.p. [ISK, IV:528:3:f,g,h]; 1809 n.p. [ISK, IV:530: 4:b,d,g]; 1812 n.p. [ISK, IV:533:1:b,c]; 1814 n.p. [ISK, IV:539:1:b,i].

The Chōshū background originally came from Tokutomi, L, 336 ff. Additional information is in Shibusawa, II, 344–367; V, 557 ff. MHS, III, 409 ff. Tokutomi, LI, 291 ff. KT, I, 488 ff. SNS, bk. 1, pts. 4 and 5 passim. ZSK, II, 96 ff., 247–250.

26. DNISK 1768 n.p. [ISK, IV:473:2:b]. Yamakawa, I, 157–158. SNS, bk. 1, pt. 4, p. 92; pt. 5, p. 26.

27. SNS, bk. 1, pt. 4, pp. 69–73; pt. 5, pp. 12–13. *Katsu zenshū*, XVIII, 90. Tokutomi, LI, 25.

28. *Katsu zenshū*, XVIII, 90.

29. The standard works used in this study have a great deal of information on the 8/18 coup. For the bakufu response to it, I have relied primarily on material in DNISK 1837 n.p. [ISK, IV:559–560:5:b,d]; 1838 n.p. [ISK, IV: 560:3:c,d,i,l,m,s,aa]; 1851 n.p. [ISK, IV:581:5:c]. Shibusawa, V, 622 ff.

30. DNISK 1838 n.p. [ISK, IV:560:3:m,w,dd]. *Katsu zenshū*, XVIII, 93.

31. SNS, bk. 1, pt. 6, pp. 1, 11, 14–16. DNISK 1854 n.p. [ISK, IV: 588:2:f,j]. MHS, III, 500–502.

32. This closing of the Edo-Kyoto breach on foreign policy is treated in SNS, bk. 1, pt. 6, pp. 11–30. Shibusawa, V, 633. MHS, III, 506. *Katsu zenshū*, XVIII, 107 ff. DNISK 1865 n.p. [ISK, IV:614:2:a,b].

33. DNISK 1910 n.p. [ISK, V:66:1:a,b].

34. Tokutomi, LI, and ZSK, II passim, have extensive information on daimyo and noble activities preparatory to this *kōbugattai* effort.

35. SNS, bk. 1, pt. 6, pp. 29–31. ZSK, II, 163. Shibusawa, V, 632.

36. DNISK 1875 n.p. [ISK, IV:631:2:a,e].

37. SNS, bk. 1, pt. 6, pp. 44–45.

38. This narrative of 63/11–12 is based on materials in ZSK, II, 189–274, 312. *Katsu zenshū*, XVIII, 93, 119–142. SNS, bk. 1, pt. 6, pp. 42, 60–64, 92. Shibusawa, II, 433–434; V, 637–638. KT, I, 168, 527. Yamakawa, I, 217–218. Tokutomi, LI, 237–241, 344–346; LII, 188–190. DNISK 1889 n.p. [ISK, V:17:3:j]; 1891 n.p. [ISK, V:27:3:f,i,o]; 1902 n.p. [ISK, V:46:5:a] [ISK, V:47:4:f]; 1909 n.p. [ISK, V:63:1:c]; 1914 n.p. [ISK, V:73:2:a,f,g].

39. ZSK, II, 247, 276.

40. This summary of the Shinchōgumi experience is based on data taken from Tokutomi, LII, 455–465. KT, I, 468, 472, 502–506, 508; II, 7–12. Hirao, 33–38. DNISK 1681 n.p. [ISK, IV:357:2:e,f,m]; 1695 n.p. [ISK, IV:375:5:a]; 1709 n.p. [ISK, IV:394:1:d]; 1727 n.p. [ISK, IV:419: 3:a,c].

41. KT, I, 478 ff., 511–513. DNISK 1855 n.p. [ISK, IV:592:5:a,b].

42. Minami, in his study of placarding in Edo during the Bunkyū years, shows clearly that 63/9–11 was a peak of activity and also that by 63/11 the

primary concern of placarders there was the domestic economic situation, notably inflation, which they blamed on foreign trade and traders and which thus justified denunciation of bakufu failure to expel the foreigners. He gives these figures as the *machi bugyō*'s report for monthly costs for a family of three or four people (of whom one or two are children) who rent on a side street:

Item	"Normal" Cost (mon)	1862 Cost (mon)
White rice*	170 (100 *mon* for 8 *gō* at retail)	300 (100 *mon* for 5 *gō* at retail)
House rent	50 (per month)	50
Other expenses	100	150

*About 2.5 liters.

43. DNISK 1882 n.p. [ISK, IV:648:4:a,b,c,d] [ISK, IV:649:2:passim]. KT, I, 514–524.

44. KT, I, 524–525. DNISK 1881 n.p. [ISK, IV:646:2:a,c].

45. This description of the Edo city situation in 63/11–12 is based on materials in DNISK 1889 n.p. [ISK, V:17:3:b,d,h,k,s]; 1891 n.p. [ISK, V:22:1:a,g]; 1892 n.p. [ISK, V:24:1:a,b,d,g,i,j,k]; 1893 n.p. [ISK, V:25:1:a,b]. SNS, bk. 1, pt. 6, pp. 60–61. ISK, V, 29, 32–33, 37, 73–74. KT, I, 527.

46. Tokutomi, KT, and SNS all deal with the Yamato and Ikuno incidents at length. The figures given here are from Tokutomi, LI, 149, and KT, II, 93–94.

47. DNISK 1839 n.p. [ISK, IV:563:3:a,c]; 1883 n.p. [ISK, V:3:2:a].

48. DNISK 1902 n.p. [ISK, V:48:6:a,d]. ISK, V, 74. Yoshino, II, 964–974. Shibusawa, V, 647–649. MHS, III, 536. *Katsu zenshū*, XVIII, 131. Three recent studies of selected elements in the late 1863 Kantō unrest show aspects of social composition and the relationship of that unrest to the upheaval of 1864: Setani Yoshihiko, "Mito han ni okeru gōkō to sonjō undō," *Ibaragi kenshi kenkyū* 12:1–15 (1968); Takagi Shunsuke, "Bakumatsu Kantō no sonnō jōi undō ni tsuite," *Ibaragi kenshi kenkyū* 19:55–61 (1971); and Takagi Shunsuke, "Sonnō jōi undō to minshū: Chibaken Kujūkuri chihō no Shinchūgumi ikken o chūshin toshite," *Rekishigaku kenkyū* 318:39–55 (1966).

49. Ozaki Yukiya, "Bakuryō ni okeru nōhei soshiki," *Shinano* 20(10): 22–32 and 20(11):42–50 (1968), is a careful study of the formation of a local militia unit in Shinano that explores local initiative in the process. Ozaki also discusses briefly the earlier book-length literature on *bakumatsu* peasant troops. Yasuzawa Hidekazu, "Bushū ikki to nōhei," *Mita gakkai zasshi* 47(3):115–119 (1954), is a brief introduction to the subject. Aoki Michio,

"Bakumatsu ni okeru nōmin tōsō to nōheisei," *Nihonshi kenkyū* 97:104–125 (1968), studies the social composition of such units in a Dewa area and the character of local resistance to their formation.

50. DNISK 1916 n.p. [ISK, V:73:4:a].

CHAPTER 4

1. I have discussed this incident in "Tokugawa Yoshinobu and *Kōbugattai: A Study of Political Inadequacy*," *Monumenta Nipponica* 30(4):393–403 (1975).

2. ZSK, III, 105.

3. DNISK 1956 n.p. [ISK, V:178:1:a]. KT, II, 199. The treatment of Arima suggests that Yoshinobu's letter of 3/20 to Hisamitsu and Munenari urging them to continue coming to the *yōbeya* was a hollow diplomatic gesture. Shibusawa, VI, 56–57, quotes the letter.

4. This summary of Katamori's situation is based upon SNS, bk. 1, pt. 7, pp. 16–55, and scattered remarks in bks. 1 and 2 on his health, rewards, and allowances.

5. DNISK 1940 n.p. [ISK, V:137:3:a,d].

6. DNISK 1949 n.p. [ISK, V:161:1:b,e,f,g].

7. These matters are reported extensively in standard sources.

8. Recently the Kantō insurrection has been a topic of interest to Japanese historians as a case study of the antifeudal energy of the populace. Takagi Shunsuke, "Mito han sonnō jōi undō no sonraku shusshin giseisha," *Ibaragi kenshi kenkyū* 13:53–78 (1969), discusses the historiography of the matter briefly. In his "Bakumatsu Kantō" article Takagi shows the breadth of the insurgents' appeal and where the insurgency fits in the larger history of *bakumatsu sonnō jōi* action.

9. This outline of the Kantō insurgency, with its emphasis on the bakufu handling of it, I first prepared from materials in many DNISK *kan* after number 1924 n.p. (specifically materials referred to in entries in ISK, V:97, 136, 162, 198, 204, 208, 220, 225, 275, 297, 300, 304, 308, 310–311, 361–362, 370, 376, 383, 415, 441–442, 483, 486, 495, 512, 570, 577, 595, 607–608, 611, 615, 634–635, 650, 660, 691–692, 704, 715–716). I obtained some supplementary data initially from Tokutomi, LIV, which relies heavily on MHS. Later I had access to MHS, III, which has considerable data, mostly on the Mito side of the disaster. There is also some material on the insurrection in Shibusawa, III; KT, II; ZSK, III; and SNS, I. The sources vary greatly in figures, but they agree on essential points.

10. Hashida Tomoharu, "Jōshū ni okeru Tengutō rōshi no gunyōkin chōtatsu," *Gunma bunka* 100:52–61 (1968), is a very interesting study of one extortion operation of 64/5 at Isezaki, Kiryū, and elsewhere. Sasaki Junnosuke, *Bakumatsu shakairon* (Tokyo, 1969), p. 79, mentions Mito *rōnin* extortions from Yokohama merchants. Kawamura Masaru, "Bakumatsu no Mito han

sōran to Shimōsa kuni no ichi dōkō,'' *Ibaragi kenshi kenkyū* 20:73–78 (1971).

11. DNISK 2015 n.p. [ISK, V:308:4:a,b,c].

12. Katsu Kaishū noted, after the Mito tragedy had run its course, that in normal times the factional strife at Mito would not have become so bloody and that it was the foreign crisis which turned it into an ideological crusade that practically precluded reconciliation. Tokutomi, LIV, 470.

13. DNISK 2016 n.p. [ISK, V:310:2:k] reports rumors. On the *fudai han*, Takasaki refused to move until Mito *han* moved. Moreover Kasama, right on Mito's border, was excused entirely from suppression duty on 6/16, and Hotta of Sakura to the south replaced him. Although Kasama and Tsuchiura, another fief on the Mito border, were both ordered to dispatch some troops, both procrastinated, holding their men at their castles instead, allegedly in anticipation of an assault by the Mito insurgents, but doubtless also in part due to disagreement among vassals or fear they might join the insurgents. DNISK 2017 n.p. [ISK, V:311: 1:a,b,h].

14. DNISK 2049 n.p. [ISK, V: an omitted entry for 64/7/16]. Sources cited: ''Bakufu satasho''; ''Jōno jiken.''

15. Ozaki, ''Bakuryō nōhei,'' I:29.

16. MHS, III, 695–696. DNISK 2073 n.p. [ISK, V:415:5:f,g].

17. This paragraph is assembled from ISK, V, 416. MHS, III, 596–597. Shibusawa, VI, 106, 115–116. Tokutomi, LIV, 18–21.

18. DNISK 2085 n.p. [ISK, V:441–442:6:a].

19. DNISK 2093 n.p. [ISK, V:461:2:a].

20. DNISK 2100 n.p. [ISK, V:483:3] contains extensive information on this historic battle.

21. Takagi, ''Mito giseisha,'' p. 54, shows that of a group of 1302 who died in the Tsukuba eruption, 716 were identified as peasants while 454 were designated samurai, the others being commoners of several sorts. Peasants were on both sides of the war, however, and played important roles in defeating the insurgents. DNISK 2101 n.p. [ISK, V:486:2:a,b] has information on this.

22. DNISK 2149 n.p. [ISK, V:577:2:c,f,g,m,n,p,q,x]. The figure of 80 bakufu dead assumes that the abnormal figure of 278 killed under Itakura's command (Fukushima, 30,000 *koku*) should read 27 or 28.

23. DNISK 2158 n.p. [ISK, V:595:1:w].

24. DNISK 2208 n.p. [ISK, V:691–692:1]; 2213 n.p. [ISK, V:704: an omitted entry for 64/12/9]; 2222 n.p. [ISK, V:715–716:5] are replete with figures on the Kinai response to the Kantō insurgents.

25. DNISK 2148 n.p. [ISK, V:576–577:5:a].

26. It is mute testimony to the magnitude of the Mito disaster that MHS can dispose of the rest of Mito's history from 1865 to 1873 in only 225 pages while it took 450 pages just to tell the tragic story of 1864.

27. DNISK 2166 n.p. [ISK, V:611:2:w].

28. RR, II, 346–347.

29. DNISK 2166 n.p. cited above in note 27.

30. DNISK 2049 n.p. cited above in note 14, ''Jōno jiken'' entry. DNISK 2175 n.p. [ISK, V:634–635:5:a,i]. *Katsu zenshū*, XVIII, 241.

31. This résumé of the 1864/6 paralysis is a summation of a narrative that I reconstructed from data found primarily in these sources: DNISK 2008 n.p. [ISK, V:292–293:3:a,b,c,d]; 2015 n.p. [ISK, V:305:2:c,d]; 2018 n.p. [ISK, V:312:3:d]; 2019 n.p. [ISK, V:315:1:d,n; 2:a; 3:a]; 2022 n.p. [ISK, V:321:3:e,j,k] [ISK, V:322:4:b,e]; 2024 n.p. [ISK, V:324:2:k]; 2030 n.p. [ISK, V:337–338:2:k]. Tokutomi, LIII and LIV. Additional data are in MHS, III, and Shibusawa, III.

32. *Katsu zenshū*, XVIII, 176. Beasley, *Documents*, p. 75.

33. ZSK, III, 170–171. MHS, III, 649.

34. Ozaki Yukiya, ''Ishin ki ni okeru Matsudaira Noritaka no dōkō,'' *Shinano* 17(9):577, quotes Ogyū's forceful *kaikoku* statement.

35. The events of this period are so complex that it is also possible to argue that in ca. 6/14–18 bakufu leaders had resolved on quelling the Mito insurgents and the dismissals of 6/17–18 were feints designed to soothe temporarily those who were soon to see their champions, notably Naokatsu and Sawa, removed from office. In that case the foreign note of 6/19 only confirmed or accelerated a policy previously settled upon. Or the 6/17–18 dismissals may have been designed primarily to get Itakura out of office and so strengthen the hand of conservative elements represented by Ōta, Ogyū, Suwa, Matsumae, and Sakai Tadamasu. However, the central role of anti-*jōi* officials with a primary concern for foreign affairs suggests most strongly that the diplomatic crisis was the primary determinant of behavior.

36. The summer events in Kyoto are reported in great detail in all standard sources. Thus Tokutomi, LIII, is devoted entirely to the Kinmon incident, as the 7/19 battle is called, and KT, II, 298–340, has a great deal of data on the battle. *Katsu zenshū*, XVIII, front plate, displays a map showing the extent of the 7/19 fire damage to Kyoto.

37. DNISK 2068 n.p. [ISK, V:405–407:2:m].

38. DNISK 2034 n.p. [ISK, V:347:2:a,d,e,h].

39. SNS, bk. 1, pt. 8, p. 95. KT, II, 343–351.

40. Bakufu policy during this period has not been carefully studied, and this narrative relies heavily on the cited DNISK entries.

41. DNISK 2069 n.p. [ISK, V:408:3:c,e,f]. SNS, bk. 1, pt. 8, pp. 90–92, quotes Katamori's letter.

42. DNISK 2080 n.p. [ISK, V:431:2:h]. KT, II, 358–359.

43. ISK, V, 432, 434, 438.

44. DNISK 2090 n.p. [ISK, V:452:2:a]. There is only one source for this statement, the ''Shimazu-ke kokuji ōshō shiryō,'' and it may be erroneously dated, but the levy does not appear to be one of those of later years that are fully documented.

45. DNISK 2091 n.p. [ISK, V:455–457:4:b,d,e,g,i,r,v]; 2096 n.p. [ISK, V:471:3:a]. SNS, bk. 1, pt. 9, pp. 46–54. OIN, pp. 274–277. KT, II, 364.

46. KT, II, 366.

47. Medzini, pp. 82–83. Fox, pp. 141–143.

48. This summary of the Abe mission is based on information in DNISK 2099 n.p. [ISK, V:481:2:j,n]; 2102 n.p. [ISK, V:488:3:a]; 2132 n.p. [ISK, V:547:4:d,e,i]; 2141 n.p. [ISK, V:563:1:a,e,l,n,o]. *Katsu zenshū*, XVIII, 194–195, 202–203, 220. ZSK, III, 311–312. Shibusawa, VI, 210. SNS, bk. 1, pt. 10, p. 1. Tokutomi, LVI, 57, treats the exchange at Kyoto as a defeat for Abe because the shogunal trip was not canceled, but Shibusawa, III, 178, sees Abe as successful.

49. The standard sources (ZSK, III; SNS, bk. 1, pts. 9–10; Shibusawa, III; KT, II; OIN; Tokutomi, LVI) have substantial detail on the politics of 64/ 10–12.

50. DNISK 2091 n.p. [ISK, V:455–457:4:r].

51. DNISK 2172 n.p. [ISK, V:626:3:a]; 2193 n.p. [ISK, V:665: 4:a,c,d]. Shibusawa, VI, 252.

52. DNISK 2019 n.p. [ISK, V:315:3:a]; 2034 n.p. [ISK, V:348:2:a].

53. DNISK 2019, 2034 n.p., cited above in note 52. DNISK 2019 n.p. [ISK, V:315:2:a].

54. DNISK 2125 n.p. [ISK, V:533:1:b]. Yamakawa, II, 113–114.

55. DNISK 2141 n.p. [ISK, V:564:2:a].

56. Shibusawa, III, 202, citing SNS and another Aizu source, reports that in 64/9 the bakufu cut off Katamori's 10,000-*ryō* monthly stipend. SNS, bk. 1, pt. 10, p. 8, mentions bakufu suspicions of Katamori, but on pt. 9, p. 62, states that on 9/10 (9/14 according to Yamakawa, II, 112, and ISK, V, 527, citing Yamakawa, SNS, and two other sources) the bakufu established a monthly stipend of 10,000 *ryō* and 2000 *hyō*. The bakufu apparently did not pay the stipend for several months, however, and this withholding of the promised funds probably was the tactic of coercion to which reference is made. Probably another expression of Edo's displeasure with its delegates in the west was the dismissal at this time (11/10) of Katsu Kaishū, who had been at Osaka or elsewhere in the west since 64/6, along with some of his followers. *Katsu zenshū*, XVIII, 229–231.

57. DNISK 2171 n.p. [ISK, V:621:2:a].

58. Shibusawa, III, 195.

59. DNISK 2176 n.p. [ISK, V:636:4:a,d,l].

60. This summary of Matsumae and Tachibana's trip is constructed from DNISK *kan* that I perused in 1972–1973 after they had been paginated. DNISK 2188, pp. 15–30; 2211, pp. 35–38; 2215, pp. 112–114; 2220, pp. 87–88; 2226, p. 83; 2229, p. 36; 2230, pp. 2, 6; 2231, pp. 32, 57, 98–101. Also Shibusawa, III, 196; VI, 218, 225, 231. Perhaps the shift in

focus was also fostered by receipt of a letter from Inaba Masakuni, dated 11/27, in which Inaba explained how advanced Yoshikatsu's negotiations were and advised against contradicting him at that stage. *Yodo Inaba ke monjo* (Tokyo, 1926), pp. 9–10.

61. Shibusawa, III, 196–197. DNISK 2215, p. 114. *Yodo*, p. 12. Tokutomi, LVII, 10, 12.

62. DNISK 1765 n.p. [ISK, IV:467:2:c,d,e,j]; 1770 n.p. [ISK, IV:477: 3:c]. KT, I, 494–495, 575–579. Just before the 6/16 order was issued, Ii of Hikone wrote Edo protesting the conflicting orders he was receiving from both bakufu and court in Kyoto (to guard Osaka) and from Edo (to go to Edo on *sankin kōtai*). KT, I, 486–487.

63. DNISK 1877, p. 30. *Katsu zenshū*, XVIII, 125–129.

64. DNISK 1887 n.p. [ISK, V:13:1:a,b,d,i]. SNS, bk. 1, pt. 6, pp. 56–57, quotes the clothing regulations without the accompanying rationale.

65. DNISK 2005 n.p. [ISK, V:280:4:b]. In my book on bakufu politics I probably erred in writing, p. 35, that *gannoma* lords were "of little political significance."

66. DNISK 2104 n.p. [ISK, V:494:3:passim]. The 9/1 order appears in the standard published sources. An orthodox essay on this topic is Hara Denzō, "Genji gannen sankin kōtai oyobi saishi zaifusei no fukkyū jijō," *Rekishi chiri* 33(2):130–135 (1919).

67. DNISK 2165 n.p. [ISK, V:610:3:a].

68. DNISK 2157 n.p. [ISK, V:593:4:a]; 2181 n.p. [ISK, V:645:1:a]; 2189 n.p. [ISK, V:657–658:6:a]; 2215 n.p. [ISK, V:704:5:a].

69. Shibusawa, III, 452, quotes the 63/10 order. DNISK 1946 n.p. [ISK, V:151:5:a]; 2040 n.p. [ISK, V:362:2:a].

70. Conrad Totman, "Fudai Daimyo and the Collapse of the Tokugawa Bakufu," *Journal of Asian Studies* 34(3):581–591 (1975).

71. For a different view see Harold Bolitho, *Treasures among Men: The Fudai Daimyo in Tokugawa Japan*.

72. ISK, VI, 15, 41, 47, 51, 132, 134, 231–232. Jansen, pp. 148–150, treats Tosa. Tokutomi, LVII, 242–245, on Zeze. DNISK 2232 n.p. [ISK, V:730:2:b] on Himeji. DNISK 2362, pp. 101–104, on Shimabara.

CHAPTER 5

1. DNISK 2240, pp. 42–48. *Katsu zenshū*, XVIII, 239.

2. This summation of the Honjō-Abe mission is based on data in DNISK 2252, pp. 5–34; 2253; pp. 8–9, 55 ff., 72 ff.; 2255, pp. 68, 70–71. Tokutomi, LVII, 27–37, 53. *Yodo*, pp. 8–12.

3. Shibusawa, VI, 274.

4. DNISK 2252, pp. 37–55. ZSK, IV, 156–157.

5. SNS, bk. 2, pt. 1, pp. 31–32, 45–46. Shibusawa, III, 206–208. ZSK, IV, 68–69.

6. SNS, bk. 2, pt. 1, pp. 12–16, 29–30, 40–42.

7. Shibusawa, VI, 275. DNISK 2265, pp. 2–7. SNS, bk. 2, pt. 1, pp. 33–38, 43–45.

8. DNISK 2271, pp. 65, 75–76, 78. Shibusawa, III, 203.

9. DNISK 2271, pp. 106–107. ZSK, IV, 89. SNS, bk. 2, pt. 1, p. 60.

10. DNISK 2288, pp. 122, 130, 140; 2289, pp. 2–3; 2294, pp. 13–23.

11. SNS, bk. 2, pt. 2, pp. 56–57, 76.

12. The politics of these summer months are treated at some length in the standard sources: Shibusawa, III, 213 ff. *Ishinshi*, IV, 404 ff. ZSK, IV, 125 ff.

13. Shibusawa, VI, 273–274.

14. DNISK 2312, pp. 2–5. An Aizu report said the *han* had run up a deficit of 37,500 *ryō* during the period 65/2–4.

15. SNS, bk. 2, pt. 1, pp. 89–90. Shibusawa, VI, 274–279.

16. DNISK 2315, pp. 118–119.

17. DNISK 2365 (pages unidentified) [ISK, VI:194:4].

18. DNISK 2362, p. 3; 2365, pp. 87–88.

19. Beasley, *Documents*, p. 291. Medzini, pp. 94–95.

20. DNISK 2357, pp. 5, 8; 2368, p. 31. ZSK, IV, 233.

21. These matters are dealt with extensively in standard sources, both English and Japanese.

22. DNISK 2365, pp. 67–69; 2367, pp. 83–89; 2368, p. 28. OIN, p. 339.

23. OIN, pp. 346–347.

24. DNISK 2367, pp. 86–87. Fox, p. 167. This Hyōgo crisis is treated extensively in all the standard sources.

25. Shibusawa, VI, 301.

26. Shibusawa, III, 266. ZSK, IV, 297.

27. Shibusawa, VI, 272.

28. Shibusawa, VI, 294.

29. OIN, pp. 362–363.

30. Beasley, *Documents*, pp. 297–299, has translations of these documents.

31. ZSK, IV, 336.

32. Beasley, *Documents*, p. 304, translates the stipulation rather obscurely: ''With regard to Hyōgo no action is to be taken.'' The imperial phrase was ''Hyōgo no gi wa yameraresōrō koto'' or ''The matter of Hyōgo is prohibited (or halted or forbidden).''

33. DNISK 2393, pp. 139–145.

34. DNISK 2407, pp. 5, 12.

35. DNISK 2407, p. 87. This summary of Honjō's effort is based on the extensive materials in DNISK 2407, pp. 5–97.

36. Tokutomi, LXI, 277–305, discusses this later treaty revision, which was completed on 66/5/13.

37. ZSK, IV and V, carry in Shungaku's correspondence constant references to Hyōgo and his concern that the bakufu get court approval of the opening before the date actually arrived and the matter precipitated another crisis like that of 65/10.

38. Handa Yoshiko, ''Dai niji seichō o meguru bakufu no dōkō: Yoshinobu seiken no seiritsu to sono seikatsu,'' *Shisō* 8:31–49 (1967), attempts to treat the whole process of leadership change within the bakufu during 1865–1866 as a contest between two groups, Tokugawa supremacists and conciliators, with the latter winning out. The problem with this view as developed by Handa is that it ascribes to Yoshinobu a constancy that he lacked, to Shungaku, Katsu, and Ōkubo Ichiō an influence that they lacked, and to the Tokugawa supremacists a cohesion and procedural consistency that they lacked. In the outcome it makes explanation of the events in the year after 66/9 very difficult. It is probably better to argue that such was the thrust of late 1865 changes, but the realities of 1866 made such a trend untenable.

39. OIN, pp. 239–245, 287–293, 306–309.

40. DNISK 2349, pp. 5, 12; 2358, pp. 7–11; 2365, p. 74. OIN, pp. 337–340.

41. *Katsu zenshū*, XVIII, 280. Information on Matsudaira Naokatsu is scattered through many entries in ISK and DNISK.

42. ZSK, IV, 357.

43. This summary of the personnel changes of 65/10–11 is based on material in the standard sources and extensive citations in ISK, VI, 220–282 passim. Passages in DNISK 2386, pp. 53–54, 58–59; 2388, pp. 90, 97; 2390, pp. 23, 35; 2403, p. 37; 2408, p. 102; 2415, p. 114; 2422, p. 92, indicate aspects of motivation and rumors.

44. Information on Yoshinobu's military force comes from Shibusawa, VI, 103, 109–110, 167–172, 209, 236–241, 265–266, 287. DNISK 2414, p. 112; 1655, p. 35.

45. Shibusawa, VI, 326 ff., has entries on Yoshinobu's situation in late 1865.

46. DNISK 2393, pp. 144–145. OIN, pp. 391–392.

47. DNISK 2421, pp. 12–16, 47–48. OIN, pp. 403–412.

48. ZSK, V, 16–20, 27. Shibusawa, VI, 349 ff. DNISK 2424, pp. 84–86, 115–116, 118.

49. ZSK, V, 15–22.

50. DNISK 2421, p. 16; 2424, pp. 85, 97. *Katsu zenshū*, XVIII, 309.

51. ZSK, V, 27–36. SNS, bk. 2, pt. 3, pp. 1–10. OIN, pp. 414–418. Shibusawa, III, 318, 322–324; VI, 351–353.

52. OIN, p. 418. OIN, pp. 424–475, and Tokutomi, LIX, 164 ff., 220 ff., 267 ff., follow Ogasawara's effort of 65/2–5 in detail.

53. DNISK 2455, p. 38; 2458, p. 56.

54. ZSK, V, 34–35, 137, 141. *Katsu zenshū*, XVIII, 305.

55. *Yodo*, pp. 93–96.

56. OIN, p. 444.

57. OIN, pp. 472–476. SNS, bk. 2, pt. 3, pp. 3–4. Tokutomi, LIX, 401–415, traces the breakoff of negotiations and declaration of war.

CHAPTER 6

1. DNISK 2102 n.p. [ISK, V:488:3:a].

2. DNISK 2068 n.p. [ISK, V:405–406:2:x].

3. DNISK 2013 n.p. [ISK, V:301:3:a,b].

4. DNISK 2176 n.p. [ISK, V:636:4:o]. KT, II, 231. *Katsu zenshū*, XVIII, 228–229. Presumably the long negotiations concerning return of Ezo land to Matsumae, the Kawagoe-Maebashi transfer, and the proposed Utsunomiya-Tanakura-Kawagoe-Shirakawa transfer, all of which are referred to in a number of DNISK entries, were part of this "corruption."

5. ZSK volumes contain many references to Katsu's writings.

6. ZSK, V, 132–133. DNISK 2597, pp. 43–44. Concerning the *gunkensei* Katsu added that Satsuma and Chōshū feared this possibility and warned that the daimyo in general would be displeased when they heard of it. He was assured by Itakura that national unification was not bakufu policy.

7. RR, I, 147–201, 308 ff., carries many documents reflecting these military concerns of 1863–1864.

8. DNISK *kan* contain an immense amount of information on this bakufu effort at naval development. See note 58 of Chapter 11.

9. RR, II, 157 ff., has extensive documentation on this reviving military effort of late 1864.

10. RR, II, 175–181. A report dated 63/12.

11. Arima, p. 3.

12. Shibusawa, VI, 53.

13. RR, I, 147 ff., 157 ff., 202, 207–211.

14. This discussion of army expansion is based on RR, II, 252–253, 348–354, 397–398, 403–406.

15. *Katsu zenshū*, XVIII, 249. Ōtsuka, pp. 260, 346–349, speaks of a British rebuff. Fox, p. 253, speaks of British negligence. Medzini, p. 127, however, reports that as of about 65/7 London showed itself agreeable to the training request and that Parkes in 65/11 urged the *rōjū* to use some British officers in Yokohama, apparently to offset French influence.

16. ISK, VI, 102, 108.

17. RR, II, 365–370, 374–380. These barracks regulations are identified only by month and day. Internal evidence indicates that 1865 is the year.

18. Ōtsuka, pp. 346–350. Ōtsuka says Asano and Ogyū had decided by late 65/10 to rely entirely on the French, but Medzini, pp. 126–127, says

that on 65/11/12 Ogyū asked Parkes' cooperation in sending a Japanese military mission to England. The implication of Ogyū's request is not clear. It may have been a tactful way of ending the British role in training at Yokohama, as note 20 below also suggests. But more likely it was part of the attempt of the same day to get British agreement to delay the next indemnity payment. These weeks were the weeks immediately after the Hyōgo crisis when heads were rolling, and it seems unlikely that any firm policy could have existed at the time in any case. What matters is that British aid did not materialize.

19. DNISK 2420, pp. 86–95. RR, II, 261, 298–301. RR, II, 381–383 contains undated documents on recruiting that most likely pertain to the latter half of 1865 or thereabouts.

20. Medzini, pp. 127–128. Ōtsuka, pp. 264–266, 350–353. Shibusawa, III, 455–456. DNISK 2423, pp. 38, 44, 53. On 12/21 Mizuno also informed Parkes that the request for British army advisors was canceled. This decision not to keep the English advisors led, it appears, to complaints by some men who wished to continue training in English cavalry style. The advisors, it should be noted, were expensive. The bakufu on 66/6/27 proposed to pay upper-rank advisors 375 *ryō* per month plus a 6000-franc initial grant. Middle-rank advisors would get 250 *ryō* and 4000 francs, and lower-rank advisors, 37 *ryō* 2 *bu* and 2000 francs.

21. RR, II, 183–184, quotes Itakura in 66/5 approving the principle of western firearms training but fretting about troop abuse of uniform regulations.

22. DNISK 2347, pp. 107, 115–116; 2349, pp. 43–45. DNISK 2401, 2463, and 2510 also have information on the training at Osaka.

23. This material on the bakufu forces is based on information in DNISK 2406, pp. 87–94. Totman, *Politics*, 276–277.

24. My basic estimates are these:

Artillery: 320 men (five batteries of eight fieldpieces manned by 8 men apiece)
Infantry: 2600 men (six and a half *hohei daitai* at 400 men per *daitai*)
Cavalry: 70 men (two *shōtai* at 35 cavalrymen per *shōtai*)
Kōbusho: 400 men (one *daitai*)
Sennin: 400 men (one *teppō daitai*) (alternative estimate: 250 men)
Artillery guards: 1500 men (six and a half battalions *(daitai)* with six *shōtai* or so per *daitai* and perhaps 40 men per *shōtai* of *mochi kotsutsu*)
Vanguard riflemen: 550 men (eleven *sakite teppō gumi* of about 50 men apiece)
Miscellaneous: 150 men (five small *kumi*)
  Subtotal: 5990 men with firearms of some sort

Ōban: 80 men (one *kumi* of elite swordsmen)
Shoinban: 400 men (five *kumi* of 80 elite swordsmen apiece)
Sennin: 200 men (two *kumi* of pikemen: *yari*)

Spearmen: 212 men (a force armed with *yari*)

Swordsmen: 239 men (a force of swordsmen: *tsurugi*); 330 men (eleven *kachi gumi* of 30 unmounted swordsmen apiece)

Kojūnin: 80 men (four *kojūnin gumi* of perhaps 20 swordsmen apiece)

Shinban: 80 men (four *shinban gumi* of perhaps 20 swordsmen apiece)

Koshōgumi: 250 men (five *koshōgumi* of perhaps 50 swordsmen apiece) (alternative estimate: 80 men)

Miscellaneous: 100 men (a mere guess)

Subtotal: 1971 men with weapons other than firearms

Total: 7961 men in shogunal forces at Osaka

25. *Katsu zenshū*, XVIII, 296.

26. DNISK 2402, pp. 31–38. KT, II, 308–310. In 1865 Ii's forces were organized in six units of 391, 173, 190, 493, 235, and 405 men apiece, or a total of 1887 fighting men. Of these, 711 were mounted samurai in troops of about 9 men apiece. Another 160 were cannoneers with sixteen fieldpieces. Another 447 were old-style (flintlock) riflemen in companies of 25 men apiece, while only 65 men were designated as carriers of ''western style'' (probably Mini-type) firearms in two companies and three small groups. Another 320 were pikemen *(teyari)* in units ranging from 9 to 15 men apiece.

27. DNISK 2406, pp. 84–94. Sakakibara did not report a unit organization but simply listed his forces as they stretched out on the route of march. Statistical analysis is therefore very difficult, but he listed mostly individual mounted samurai interspersed among companies of foot soldiers, usually with 20 men per company. He appears to have had just about 1000 fighting men, of whom about 300 to 350 had firearms, mostly reported, perhaps erroneously, as new-style. Some 260 men were reportedly armed with lances of one sort or another *(nagae, yari, teyari)*. About 50 men were with his eight cannon, which were mostly of 3 *kanme* (about 11 kilograms or 25 pounds) weight ball. The equipment of the other 400 is uncertain, although some 60 were reported to be on horse and another 50 were listed as samurai *(shi)*.

28. DNISK 2358, p. 131.

29. *Nanki Tokugawashi* (Tokyo, 1970), XIII, 68–69. Similarly Hikone with some 1800 fighting men was later reported to have a total force at Hiroshima of 3600 men. Takata, with some 1000 fighting men, had a reported total of 3400 men. But neither, to my knowledge, later sent additional line units to Hiroshima, and I assume that the extra men were noncombat support personnel. DNISK 2579, p. 84, gives the 3600 and 3400 figures.

30. DNISK 2401, pp. 103, 119, 130, 137; 1406, pp. 96–97.

31. *Katsu zenshū*, XVIII, p. 47. Katsu wrote this on 63/4/23 when the shogun was at last riding on his boat.

32. DNISK 2607, p. 52. At least Itakura reported this to Roches on 66/7/2.

33. RR, II, 183–184.

34. DNISK 2450, 2458, 2463, 2510, and 2515 all have data on the military reviews of 66/2–4.

35. Calculated from data in DNISK 2567, pp. 86–87.

36. DNISK 2365 (pages unidentified) [ISK, VI:194:4].

37. DNISK 2408, pp. 46, 49 ff.; 2545, p. 40, on stipends. Ishii Takashi, ''Keiō ninen no seiji jōsei: dai niji Chōshū seibatsu o megutte,'' *Rekishi hyōron* 34:9 (1952), on Hikone. *Yodo*, pp. 116–120, on the artillerymen.

38. DNISK 2347, p. 13; 2359, p. 100; 2423, pp. 63–72. Shibusawa, III, 318–319.

39. Shibusawa, III, 273–274, 319.

40. Peter Frost, *The Bakumatsu Currency Crisis*, p. 20.

41. SNS, bk. 1, pt. 8, p. 4. Tokutomi, LI, 303–339. KT, II, 254.

42. DNISK 2315, pp. 118–119; 2545, p. 41. The monthly costs of the trip itself were broken down in this fashion:

53,799 *ryō*: stipends for accompanying personnel

28,770 *ryō*: supplements for those with basic stipends of under 400 *hyō*

35,859 *ryō* and 2548 *koku* of rice: provisions for accompanying personnel

13,870 *ryō*: equipment maintenance, replacement, and transportation

40,000 *ryō* and 1519 *koku*: provisions for the Hiroshima forward headquarters

   Total: 174,698 *ryō* and 4367 *koku* monthly costs

The totals here are not quite the same as those given in the sources, which report 174,235 *ryō* and 4368 *koku*.

43. These figures are assembled from ISK, IV, 570, 593, 619, 627. KT, II, 219. Shibusawa, V, 630–631; VI, 82–83, 95. DNISK 1860 n.p. [ISK, IV:603:3:a]. SNS, bk. 1, pt. 4, pp. 31, 47; pt. 5, p. 108; pt. 6, pp. 26, 40; pt. 7, pp. 10, 53, 82.

44. DNISK 2252, pp. 111–114.

45. *Katsu zenshū*, XVIII, 253.

46. DNISK 2365, p. 72.

47. DNISK 2364, pp. 161–163; 2511, pp. 100 ff., 141–142. *Katsu zenshū*, XVIII, 306. These sums are considerably under the sums that Parkes said the bakufu was spending in France: $400,000 allegedly sent and another $600,000 to be sent soon. Medzini, p. 102.

48. RR, I, 326–330, 351.

49. These figures are assembled from Shibusawa, III, 41. RR, I, 219–220. ISK, V, 484. DNISK 1964 n.p. [ISK, V:191:6:a]. RR, I, 148 ff., has many figures on particular military outlays.

50. RR, II, 398–430. RR, II, 157 ff., contains numerous examples of actual expenditures. *Katsu zenshū*, XVIII, 302.

51. ISK, VI, 112, 124, 153, 171, 208, 214, 232, 240, 243–244, 250, 256, 274, 387, 477, 483, 505.

52. DNISK 2192 n.p. [ISK, V:664–665:6:a].

53. ISK, VI, 184, 226–227, 286.

54. ISK, VI, 70–71, 106, 180, 224, 443. Most notably Naokatsu of Kawagoe kept insisting that he must have 50,000 *ryō* before returning to office, and the bakufu refused to pay. Also on 66/7/3 an Aizu man was told by Shungaku that Akitsuki Taneki would likely not take bakufu office because his *han* was impoverished and he would require a lot of money to accept the job. ZSK, V, 204.

55. *Katsu zenshū.* This is a Katsu report of 65/6/1, and he gives figures of a proposed rate of 176 *ryō* of gold per 100 *hyō* of rice at a time when in the city 1 *shō* of rice was selling for 1 *shu* of money (1.588 quart for one-sixteenth of a *ryō*).

56. DNISK 2447, pp. 174–178; 2561, p. 2.

57. DNISK 1986 n.p. [ISK, V:236:2:a,c]; 2015 n.p. [ISK, V:308:4:h].

58. ZSK, V, 35, 64. DNISK 2545, p. 40.

59. Murakami Tadashi and Ōno Mizuo, ''Bakumatsu ni okeru bakufu kanjōsho shiryō,'' *Shigaku zasshi* 81(4):49–50 (1972). Totman, *Politics,* pp. 80, 287–288. Frost has produced an excellent study of the 1859–1860 currency crisis and gives insights into one important facet of the bakufu's fiscal dilemma.

60. ISK, VI, 144, 173, 191, 211, 225, 446, 451. KT, I, 491. DNISK 2529, pp. 86–92. DNISK entries contain considerable material on the Tanakura-Utsunomiya-Shirakawa-Kawagoe-Maebashi transfer negotiations that were involved in some of this land distribution.

61. DNISK 2895, p. 76. Fox, p. 322, gives these figures for Kanagawa trade:

> 1863: imports—$1,595,170; exports—$5,134,184
> 1864: imports—$5,443,594; exports—$8,997,484

The tariff value of these sums is not clear. Fox also has useful material on daimyo trade activity.

62. Sasaki, p. 74.

63. Medzini, pp. 104–109, 211.

64. Murakami and Ōno, pp. 49–50.

65. ISK, VI, 107. DNISK 2312, pp. 33, 44–45; 2315, p. 104.

66. DNISK 2315, pp. 112–117.

67. *Katsu zenshū,* XVIII, 263–264, 268.

68. DNISK 2315, pp. 134–137; 2388, pp. 131–135.

69. DNISK 2388, p. 129; 2420, pp. 3–5. *Katsu zenshū,* XVIII, p. 301.

70. DNISK 2346, p. 93. ISK, VI, 174.

71. Ōtsuka, p. 232. The bakufu delayed payment of further indemnity bills and collapsed before paying the remainder.

72. DNISK 2315, p. 149. ZSK, V, 164–165.

73. This discussion of this *goyōkin* levy is based on information in DNISK 2545, pp. 18–22, 32–35, 41–49. Shibusawa, III, 364–365. *Katsu zenshū,*

XVIII, 329, also speaks of a levy of 66/4 or 5 made on entertainment establishments in Edo.

74. Ikeda Yoshimasa, ''Bakufu no tōkai to Boshin sensō,'' in *Iwanami kōza Nihon rekishi*, XIV, 262, citing *Osakashi shi*, is apparently referring to this levy of 66/4, which, he says, yielded some 180,000 *kanme*. This, he observes, is only about a third of the initial 7 million *ryō* and so indicates to him the magnitude of the bakufu effort's failure. If the original effort was the more limited one that our evidence indicates, however, then the total receipts were quite impressive.

75. Between 65/1 and 65/7 Fukuoka, Uwajima, Satsuma, Yonezawa, Kumamoto, Hiroshima, Shinjō in Dewa, and Tottori all refused to cooperate. On the other hand Himeji, Matsuyama in Iyo, Wakayama, Takata, Hikone, Fukiage, Kokura, Toba, Sonobe, Ono, Tsuyama, Maruyama, Odawara, Kanazawa, Shinmi, Toyooka, Karatsu, Hirose, Saeki, Morioka, and Sendai did cooperate. ISK, VI, 2–169 passim.

76. These conclusions are derived from entries in ISK, VI, 127–446 passim. During 1865 cooperative responses were received from Ōgaki, Kōriyama, Obata, Kameta, Matsushiro, Kameyama in Tanba, Nagaoka, Takashima, Sakura, Matsumoto, Maruoka, Takamatsu, Matsuyama in Iyo, and Amagasaki. However, Tsu, Owari, Tokushima, Morioka, and Sendai all tried to avoid commitment. During early 1866 Saga, Satsuma, Hiroshima, Kanazawa, Owari, Echizen, Tottori, Okayama, and Tokushima all resisted or bluntly refused to accept bakufu orders.

77. DNISK 2362, pp. 94 ff.

78. ZSK, IV, 1. An Uwajima report on other *han*.

79. ISK, VI, 71–451 passim, mentions Tatsuno, Aizu, Kokura, Matsumoto, Annaka, Kakegawa, Ueda, Kawagoe, Sasayama, and Hikone. *Yodo*, p. 32, mentions Takatō.

80. ISK, VI, 176, 184, 196, 265, 342, 401.

81. In this period, especially during the early months of 1866, one or more requests for reduced duty were made by Takatō, Tanabe, Ueda, Funai, Sakura, Kakegawa, Tsuruga, Nakamura, Utsunomiya, Oka, Obama, Oshi, and Kawagoe. ISK, VI, 117, 145, 193, 267, 296, 307, 342, 344, 368, 370, 469, 477, 489. In articles about Tanoguchi *han* published in *Shinano*, Ozaki Yukiya describes the military reform efforts of Tanoguchi, which were disrupted by the political turmoil of 1863–1865 and hampered by the *han*'s financial limitations. Ozaki Yukiya, ''Ishin ki fudai kohan no gunji kaikaku: ishin ki no Tanoguchi han, 2,'' *Shinano* 18(5)13–27 (1966); ''Ishin ki fudai kohan no ryōnai shūdatsu jittai: ishin ki no Tanoguchi han, 3,'' *Shinano* 20(5):40–48; 20(6):37–49 (1968).

CHAPTER 7

1. John A. Harrison, *Japan's Northern Frontier*; George A. Lensen, *The Russian Push toward Japan*; John J. Stephan, *Sakhalin: A History*.

2. Stephan, pp. 57–59.

3. DNISK 2350, pp. 94–95. I presume that Kushun and Kusunae (my reading) are Kushunnai at the mouth of the Kushun or Kusunai river. See Lensen, p. 545.

4. DNISK 2377, pp. 101, 136–165. Shibusawa, IV, 8–13.

5. DNISK 2484, pp. 68–70. ZSK, V, 47. Shibusawa, VI, 343.

6. ISK, VI, 508. Shibusawa, IV, 13. To complete the narrative of the Karafuto matter quickly, in 66/9 this mission departed Yokohama for Russia, and pending its success, in 66/12 preparations were intensified for more careful management of the northern boundary areas of Japan. In Russia the mission secured in 67/2 a bilateral agreement for joint residence on the island. The agreement came none too soon. During 67/3 bakufu leaders learned that following the incident of early 1866 the Russians had deposited several hundred more soldiers at Kushun. There had then been some more problems in the area, and in 67/2 Sendai had sent some fifty infantry with ten officers as replacements for guard units already deployed there to meet the threat and quiet local fears. In later months of 1867 Edo received a few more worrisome reports of military jockeying in the area, but due to the bilateral agreement the danger of a major explosion was greatly eased. It was not the final solution that the Japanese negotiators had sought, with the island divided between the two powers, but for the moment it at least preserved Japanese equal rights there, and the Karafuto issue receded from the political arena. ISK, VI, 587, 649; VII, 54, 57, 60–61, 65, 88. DNISK 2834, p. 176. Shibusawa, IV, 13–14. *Yodo*, pp. 182–187.

7. ISK, VI, 44, 196, 227, 255, 262, 268–269, 293, 328, 363, 402. Ōtsuka, p. 255.

8. ISK, VI, 42, 135, 162, 177, 230, 353, 451, 455, 490.

9. ISK, VI, is replete with instances of these matters. Medzini also discusses some aspects. Ōtsuka, pp. 258–260.

10. ISK, VI, 84, 130, 151, 169, 380. Medzini, pp. 43–44.

11. Fox, p. 185.

12. Medzini is a good recent study of French policy in Japan in the 1860s, based largely on western sources. Fox, on English policy, is helpful on Anglo-daimyo ties but has to be read with great discretion because of the severe bias that stems from dependence on British diplomatic sources. Ōtsuka has produced a skillful work in Japanese. Ishii Takashi, *Meiji ishin no kokusaiteki kankyō* (Tokyo, 1960 and later), offers a more recent work. In the revised and expanded edition of 1973, entitled *Yōtei Meiji ishin no kokusaiteki kankyō*, Takashi uses some recently published material and gives fuller insights into bakufu-French relations. I did not have access to it when doing this study.

13. Medzini, p. 63.

14. Medzini, pp. 64–67, 91–93. Beasley, *Documents*, pp. 274–282. ZSK, V, 233.

15. DNISK 2365, pp. 60–69.

16. DNISK 2358, p. 9. OIN, p. 339.

17. DNISK 2298, pp. 55–56, is an example of Roches's ingratiating technique. Ōtsuka, pp. 248 ff. Not all the pro-French diplomats fell. Kurimoto in 65/10 had given helpful advice to the Osaka leaders on how to avoid another foreign crisis and was subsequently promoted to *gaikoku bugyō*. In that position he displayed considerable forcefulness and professionalism in his willingness to scold *rōjū* and foreigners alike for their failure to handle matters in accord with approved international procedures. SNS, bk. 2, pt. 2, pp. 57, 59–61.

18. Ōtsuka, pp. 258–259. ISK, VI, 38, 61, 80, 93, 128. Tokutomi, LXI, 236–247, is on Shibata's mission. Asano Ujisuke was first named mission director in 65/2, but he refused, pleading illness, and so Shibata was chosen to replace him.

19. Ōtsuka, pp. 272–273, 339. Ishii Takashi, ''Rekkyō no tai-Nichi seisaku,'' in *Iwanami kōza Nihon rekishi* (Tokyo, 1962), XIV, 232, says that Roches spoke of using silk trade to pay for the shipyard in 64/12. Medzini, pp. 107–114, on Roches's role. DNISK 2364, pp. 154–155, is the 8/21 letter.

20. DNISK 2364, pp. 159–161. Shibata Michio and Shibata Asako, ''Bakumatsu ni okeru Furansu no tai-Nichi seisaku,'' *Shigaku zasshi* 76(8):46–71 (1967), investigates the company's founding in some detail as well as the economic background of the venture in France.

21. DNISK 2511, pp. 100 ff., 140–144.

22. Fox, pp. 100–101, 106, 136, 139, shows that a representative of Jardine Matheson was pursuing trade, perhaps partially illegal, with Satsuma from ''the late summer of 1863'' and indicates British diplomatic approval of close British-daimyo connections. Fox also shows Alcock's ambitious designs in 1864.

23. Arima, pp. 7–8. Medzini, p. 99. Fox, pp. 152–154. Fox, p. 122, indicates that by mid-1863 the British government was prepared to deal directly with daimyo, as though they were in effect sovereign states. See Fox, pp. 252, 333–334, on the profitability of gunrunning.

24. DNISK 2273, pp. 42–43. *Katsu zenshū*, XVIII, 245, 254. According to Katsu the American was a certain Boruchiin or Borudein (Borodin?) in *kana* pronunciation.

25. DNISK 2314, pp. 124–127, on the Kokura inquiry. Albert M. Craig, *Chōshū in the Meiji Restoration*, p. 316, on the arms order in 65/8. Other information is in Shibusawa, III, 233–235. ZSK, V, 10, 99, 102, 109. *Katsu zenshū*, XVIII, 254–255, 260. *Yodo*, pp. 33–41. ISK, VI, 118, 125, 135, 144, 147, 155, 173, 179, 182.

26. DNISK 2321, pp. 114–119. Parkes proceeded from Shimonoseki to Yokohama, but he evidently never did submit his credentials to the shogun, which suggests perhaps his limited respect for the government to which he was accredited. Fox, p. 211.

27. This paragraph is assembled from data in the following sources: ZSK,

IV, 387; V, 10. Fox, pp. 173–176, 180–182. Medzini, p. 145. Ivan Hall, *Mori Arinori*, pp. 73–74. DNISK 2393, pp. 139–140. Shibusawa, III, 367, 370. Shibusawa dates the Satsuma-British ties from the secret dispatch in 65/3 of Satsuma students to Europe. He says the bakufu learned of this only after Shibata reached France later in the year.

28. ZSK, V, 233–237.

29. Medzini, pp. 98–100. Ōtsuka, pp. 221–228, 243, 262–263. Shibusawa, III, 250–252, 280–284. ISK, VI, 176, 197, 201, 204, 206, 210, 282.

30. Hall, *Mori*, p. 82. Ōtsuka, pp. 235, 242, 263.

31. For this point I am indebted to Thomas Huber for material in his doctoral dissertation, ''Chōshū Activists in the Meiji Restoration.''

32. KT, II, 204. DNISK 2278, p. 107.

33. DNISK 2347, p. 75. ISK, VI, 147, 165. *Katsu zenshū*, XVIII, 266–267.

34. DNISK 2419, pp. 132, 138. Hiramatsu Yoshirō, ''Bakumatsu ki ni okeru hanzai to keibatsu no jittai: Edo Kodenmachō rōya kiroku ni yoru,'' *Kokka gakkai zasshi* 71(3):76–130 (1956). This article, based on records covering 1862–1865, is a very interesting study of the Edo city penal institution for commoners that was located in Kodenma-chō.

35. *Katsu zenshū*, XVIII, 301–302.

36. Ishii, ''Keiō ninen,'' reports the mocking in Osaka. This essay is a major statement of the historical significance of the social unrest of 1866 as an antifeudal experience. Murase Masaaki, ''Dai niji Chōshū seibatsu o meguru Nishi Mikawa no shojōsei,'' *Rekishi kyōiku* 6(1):58–62 (1958), describes briefly the situation in Mikawa as it related to the shogunal trip. He also reports a very interesting case of the formation near Kariya of a local committee of safety in 1864 in response to the 64/7 Kinmon incident. It hints at the growth of self-government in the rural areas in response to the disintegration of higher-level government. His article builds on Ishii's interpretive line. On the other hand, Ozaki, ''Bakufu ryō,'' *Shinano* 20(10):29–31, shows how a peasant militia unit functioned, not too successfully, partially as a locally organized committee of safety in 1864 and partially as a tool of bakufu interest in law and order.

37. Murase, pp. 58–62.

38. ISK, VI, 196, 315, 333, 392, 430, 438, 457.

39. DNISK 2212 n.p. [ISK, V:704:2:a].

40. Shōji Kichinosuke, *Yonaoshi ikki no kenkyū* (Tokyo, 1970), pp. 54 ff.

41. On the fire, reference is to ISK, V, 23, and ZSK, II, 245, 265. William B. Hauser, *Economic Institutional Change in Tokugawa Japan: Osaka and the Kinai Cotton Trade*, offers an excellent discussion of the background of this problem. Great quantities of cotton wadding, used as filler in bedding and winter quilted clothing, probably were lost in the fire. Rapeseed oil is an important cooking oil.

42. Kobayashi Shigeru, "Keiō gannen 'kokuso' no oboegaki," *Rekishi hyōron* 91:2–18 (1957); 92:41–52; 93:60–69 (1958), examines the two disputes.

43. ISK, VI, 111. Hirasawa Kiyoto, "Keiō gannen Shinshū Shimoina chihō nishibu yamamura chitai no kome sōdō," *Shinano* 9(9):40–48 (1957), deals with the Iida incident and the subsequent *han* investigation of its causes.

44. Data for this paragraph were assembled from DNISK 2482 (page unidentified) [ISK, VI:358:2:a]. ZSK, IV, 236. *Katsu zenshū*, XVIII, 266–267, 271.

45. The three major tables of 1862–1867 price indices are from Yamamura, pp. 53, 55, 60. Yamamura explains Methods I and II on pp. 30–31.

46. The Kariya price index is from Murase. A rice price decline of 65/12 that Katsu reported in and near Kyoto apparently did not reach as far as Kariya. *Katsu zenshū*, XVIII, 296. Ishii, "Keiō ninen," has some figures on 1865–1866 inflation in Osaka, and Hirasawa has figures showing that in Shinano the rice inflation accelerated from about 65/4.

47. DNISK 2510, pp. 10–11. Apparently all of the three hundred rice stores in Kyoto were found to be breaking price ceilings, which is pretty good evidence that the price control system was useless. OIN, p. 333, credits the recoinage with fostering the inflation.

48. This summary of the Osaka area upheaval is based on data found in DNISK 2552, pp. 24–41; 2556, pp. 37–68. Takashima Ichirō, "Keiō ninen toshi kyūmin no ishiki to kōdō," *Rekishi kyōiku* 17(3):71–77 (1969), gives different damage figures, but they are of the same general magnitude. He also has figures on inflation comparable to those of Ishii, "Keiō ninen," but more complete. Takashima is arguing that the 66/5–8 Edo-Osaka unrest was not due to the revolutionary mentality of the urban populace.

49. *Katsu zenshū*, XVIII, 346. Shibusawa, III, 364. DNISK 2664, pp. 2–3.

50. This summary of the Edo upheaval is based on data found in DNISK 2565, pp. 115–161.

51. DNISK 2603, pp. 11–39.

52. This summary of the Musashi upheaval is based on data found in DNISK 2577, pp. 6–59, 112–114. The upheaval has been extensively studied. Mori Yasuhiko, " 'Bushū yonaoshi ikki' no kisoteki kōsatsu," *Shinano* 24(10):15–40 (1972), is a particularly good study and contains a good map of the movement of the Musashi turmoil. Pertinent material is also in Fukushima Masayoshi, "Bakuhansei no hōkai to Kawagoe han no nōhei hantai ikki," *Chihōshi kenkyu* 21(1):11–25 (1971) and Yasuzawa Hideichi, "Bushū ikki to nōhei," *Mita gakkai zasshi* 47(3):115–119 (1954).

53. This summary of the Mutsu upheaval is based on data found in DNISK 2602, pp. 103–128. Also Shōji, pp. 39 ff., has considerable material on this upheaval and its antecedent and following developments along with a general interpretation of its historical meaning in terms of changing class relationships.

This rural turmoil of 1866 is usually viewed in terms of the general problem of peasant upheaval and *yonaoshi* peasant reformism. A very good and recent essay on this matter, with helpful bibliography, is Irwin Scheiner, ''The Mindful Peasant: Sketches for a Study of Rebellion,'' *Journal of Asian Studies* 32(4):579–591 (1973).

54. Fukushima, pp. 15–24. He reports that the villagers were to furnish one man per 100 *koku* of putative yield. The *han* was to furnish each conscript with an annual stipend of 15 *ryō*, plus an equipment allowance of 10 *ryō* after the first year. He also reports, p. 24, that the *tenryō* conscription rate was one man per 100 persons, which was about half the Kawagoe rate of one per 100 *koku*. He says the *tenryō* conscription went smoothly. His study is a good and thoughtful one.

55. ISK, VI, 449. ZSK, V, 148, 151, 153, 185.

CHAPTER 8

1. This summary of the early phase of the war is based on materials in ISK, VI, 475–501 passim. Shibusawa, III, 345–347. SNS, bk. 2, pt. 3, pp. 45–55. ZTJ, V, 659–662. OIN, pp. 483–484. Tokutomi, LIX, 416–426, describes the Ōshima campaign.

2. ISK, VI, 412, 416, 471, 476, 478–479, 483, 486–487, 497–500, 503–505, 512–513, 516, 546.

3. This reconstruction of Honjō's effort is from reports in DNISK 2599, p. 3. *Nanki*, IV, 67–71. SNS, bk. 2, pt. 4, pp. 2–5, 10–11. ZSK, V, 213–214, 219. OIN, pp. 486–494. Suematsu, VIII, 598–600. Shibusawa, III, 348–350. ISK, VI, 515, 522, 524, 528.

4. ISK, VI, 493–535, passim. Shibusawa, III, 347.

5. DNISK 2631, pp. 47–48.

6. ISK, VI, 549, 553–554. Shibusawa, III, 350–351.

7. This summary of the Kokura situation is based on DNISK 2567, pp. 97, 108. ZSK, V, 325–328, 384–389. *Katsu zenshū*, XVIII, 344–345.

8. This reconstruction of the Kokura collapse is derived from reports in Shibusawa, III, 351–352; VI, 433. ZSK, V, 331. SNS, bk. 2, pt. 4, pp. 26, 29. OIN, p. 502. ISK, VI, 554–563 passim. ZTJ, V, 735–736. Tokutomi, LX, 130. Some sources use the date of 7/29, others 7/30, but most are in apparent agreement that Ogasawara left after the *han* forces. Shibusawa gives 7/29 as the date of Ogasawara's departure and reports that the *rōjū* summoned him. Itakura, as reported in ZSK, does not seem to have been aware of any order recalling him. OIN gives 7/29 night for Ogasawara's departure. ISK and ZTJ, whose dating is far more reliable, give 7/30 night for his departure. The first report Fukui received gives 7/29; the second, from Itakura, gives 7/30.

9. ISK, VI, 576–577, 600, 615–616, 620, 625, 641, 643, 648, 654, 661.

10. Shibusawa, III, 345–346.

11. This description of the 6/14 battle is based on these sources: DNISK

2578, pp. 81–110; 2579, pp. 6–127; 2580, pp. 18–81. Suematsu, VIII, 432, 438–453. SNS, bk. 2, pt. 3, pp. 84–86.

12. It must be kept in mind that my figures on the Summer War are only the product of selection among conflicting figures and extrapolation from fragmentary data. In the case of casualties, they may err on the low side, particularly for the allies. I was heartened some months after preparing this chapter to run across figures for Hikone casualties in the Aki campaign in Nishida Shūhei, ''Meiji ishin ni okeru Hikone han,'' *Nihon rekishi* 203:76 (1965). Nishida reports 24 dead and 41 wounded. My figures total 24 dead and 44 wounded, which is surprisingly close, given the great variation in data. Similarly my figures for Chōshū add up to a total of 36 Chōshū dead and 107 wounded on the Aki front, 6/14–8/7, but a Chōshū report says that at least 31 died and 129 were wounded in that period. DNISK 2654, p. 69. Total force figures are also educated guesses, and they are even more confusing because battalions almost never fought as whole units. Rather they fought in company segments together with units from other battalions, and often segments of a given battalion were deployed in two or more places during the course of a day's fighting—for example, the 1st, 3rd, and 5th companies of the first bakufu infantry battalion on the coast road, the 7th company on the Matsugahara road, and the other companies in reserve. And units of Kii and Hikone or other forces might be on the coast road at the same time. Systematic bakufu infantry reports do not appear to exist, which complicates matters considerably.

13. DNISK 2578, p. 91; 2579, p. 85.

14. Later Ii was loaned 10,000 *ryō* and Ōgaki 3500 *ryō*. DNISK 2592, p. 47.

15. Tottori reports of this battle are thoroughly unreliable. Their purpose may have been to assure that Tottori would remain neutral. No reports are reliable in their statements of enemy number: they all report enemy casualties inflated by one or two digits, and they often exaggerate by a factor of two or more the size of enemy forces. The battle reports, official and unofficial, are extremely confusing, spotty, and often contradictory, and the appearance of orderliness in my account is an exercise in reconstruction, guesswork, and choice, sometimes arbitrary.

16. DNISK 2578, pp. 83, 106, 108; 2579, pp. 53–55; 2586, p. 38; 2594, p. 71. Suematsu, VIII, 440.

17. Suematsu, VIII, 604. DNISK 2594, pp. 144–145; 2579, pp. 53–55; 2644, p. 74.

18. Suematsu, VIII, 446. DNISK 2578, p. 26. *Nanki*, IV, 58. ZTJ, V, 671–677.

19. DNISK 2594, p. 134, speaks of a battalion of artillery guards being transferred, but in ZTJ, V, 676, it is reported as the 2nd company of *sappei* that was deployed temporarily to Ōshima.

20. This description of the 6/19 battle is based on *Nanki*, IV, 58–60. Suematsu, VIII, 448–455. DNISK 2579, pp. 41–46, 81; 2594, pp. 11–145.

21. *Kyūbakufu* (Tokyo, 1971), bk. 5, pt. 7, p. 28 (in bound vol. 4).

22. DNISK 2595, pp. 54–109. Suematsu, VIII, 465–468.

23. DNISK 2594, p. 73.

24. This description of the 6/25 battle is based on *Nanki*, IV, 63. ZTJ, V, 682–685. Suematsu, VIII, 456–461. DNISK 2599, pp. 96–117.

25. According to one Chōshū report, forces engaged were the 1st battalion, half the 4th battalion, half of another battalion, and Iwakuni forces reported earlier to be about 200 men, 16 field cannon, and 4 mortars with crews. The two Tokuyama *shōtai*, which would be extra, were reportedly not very effective. The 2nd and 3rd battalions and half the 4th battalion apparently were in reserve. (At least, on 7/11 Yamaguchi ordered the 1st, 2nd, and 3rd battalions to return home to be replaced by the Tatetai, which suggests that the three had been at Aki. DNISK 2615, p. 72.) DNISK 2599, p. 113. Suematsu, VIII, 460.

26. DNISK 2599, p. 116.

27. Suematsu, VIII, 457, 459.

28. Suematsu, VIII, 596–606, 614. DNISK 2642, pp. 46–67.

29. DNISK 2615, pp. 98–150.

30. *Nanki*, IV, 80–81; XIII, 68. SNS, bk. 2, pt. 4, pp. 6–7.

31. Data on this redeployment are from Suematsu, VIII, 614–615. *Nanki*, IV, 81–82; XIII, 79.

32. This description of the 7/28 battle is based on Suematsu, VIII, 607, 615. *Nanki*, IV, 82–83; XIII, 84–87. ZTJ, V, 729–730. DNISK 2641, pp. 71, 127, 147–148, 161; 2642, pp. 1–2, 15, 46–49. Takeda Katsuzo, ''Dainikai Chōshū seibatsu no Geishū hanshi no jinchū nikki,'' *Shigaku* 33(1): 99–111 (1960), which I found after preparing this summary, is an interesting observer's diary of the period 7/28–8/23.

33. Suematsu, VIII, 615–616. *Nanki*, XIII, 87–88. DNISK 2644, pp. 38–59.

34. This description of the 8/2 battle is based on ZTJ, V, 737–739. *Nanki*, IV, 87–88; XIII, 93–97. Suematsu, VIII, 607–609, 616. DNISK 2652, pp. 18, 43; 2653, pp. 32–36.

35. This description of the 8/7 battle is based on Suematsu, VIII, 609–614, 616–618. ZTJ, V, 744–746. *Nanki*, IV, 88–91; XIII, 99–108. DNISK 2653, pp. 64–99; 2654, pp. 54, 69.

36. Suematsu, VIII, 609.

37. *Nanki*, XIII, 108. If this Kii report is correct, the notice from Osaka probably reflected the intention of early 66/8 to mount a major new offensive, not Yoshinobu's intention of 8/11 to end the conflict.

38. Ōtsuka, pp. 267–268. ZSK, V, 228–230. Medzini, pp. 100–101.

39. ZSK, IV, 223, 239, letters of 65/7 to Shungaku. Fox, pp. 186–187.

40. DNISK 2607, pp. 24 ff., 55. Ōtsuka, p. 269. Tokutomi, LIX, 367–385. Fox, pp. 187–189. Ishii, *Iwanami*, pp. 243–245, argues that Parkes

was neutral, not pro-*tozama*. It is important, however, to distinguish between Parkes' rhetorical posture and the substantive implications of his conduct.

41. DNISK 2604, pp. 86–90. *Katsu zenshū*, XVIII, 337, 340–342, 350.

42. Ōtsuka, pp. 267–269, 353. Medzini, p. 130.

43. DNISK 2607, pp. 24, 33, 52.

44. Ishii, *Meiji ishin* (1960 edition), pp. 546–548. Ishii, *Iwanami*, pp. 249–250. Medzini, p. 101. Medzini, p. 116, reports that Coullet arrived in May (66/3/17—4/17). Kanai Madoka, ''Oguri Tadamasa no tai-Ei Futsu shakkan ni kan suru Kishikawa-ke denrai monjo no saihyōka,'' *Kenkyū kiyō* of Tokugawa rinseishi kenkyūjo, Shōwa 45 *nendō*, 388–403 (1971), contains newly published documents pertaining to Oguri's negotiations in late 1866 and 1867. These documents show that on 8/12 the Oriental Bank in Yokohama was contacted by Oguri on the matter of the loan.

45. *Yodo*, pp. 139–141.

46. DNISK 2646, pp. 2–13; 2659, p. 2. ZSK, V, 210–212. Shibusawa, VI, 450. Before securing the French loan, bakufu officials clearly intended to cover at least part of their warship costs by recovering funds already held by Americans. Back in 1863 the bakufu had ordered three warships from the United States, but due to the outbreak of the American Civil War, the ships were not completed. The Americans refused to return the $600,000 prepayment the bakufu had made, however. Despite repeated bakufu complaints in 1865 and 1866 the matter remained unresolved and the money tied up. During 66/7 officials at Edo again tried to get back $328,900, which they said remained from the $600,000 previously paid. It was more than enough to pay for the *Don Barton*, the vessel offered by the Dutch, if the Yankee traders could be induced to part with the funds they had in hand. DNISK 2627, pp. 102–105.

47. RR, II, 146–153. Katsu had inserted this undated plan in his chronology as part of the 1862 reform, but internal evidence makes it clear that the plan was prepared and modified between 66/6/29 and 8/2, when implementation of the reform began. ISK, VI, 497, 507. RR, II, 146. *Yodo*, pp. 141–148, has a copy with annotations for official use at Edo and, while it is almost identical, it has final figures of 10,000 men in twenty-five battalions. *Yodo* dates it roughly at 66/8–10.

48. DNISK 2606, pp. 116–128. The quotation is on pp. 127–128. Fukushima, p. 24. Men aged seventeen to fifty years were invited to volunteer, and those accepted were to serve for five years, agreeing to report for all drill and to report any absences beyond ten days sick leave per year. They would receive an annual stipend of 7 *ryō* plus one-man *fuchi* (about 1.8 *koku* of rice per year), would be able to borrow up to 18 more *ryō* per year, and would receive uniforms and, when in bivouac, food.

49. *Yodo*, pp. 549–550. This entry, dated 7/8, is a cover sheet listing the

topics, probably of a memorial, submitted by someone to an official identified
only by his formal court title, probably *wakadoshiyori* Kyōgoku Takatomi,
although conceivably Kyoto *machi bugyō* Ōkubo Tadayuki, who had the same
title. The file numbers of the preceding and following entries in the book are
the same as that of the entry cited here and seem to me to establish that the
three were all written by men in Edo at the time, making Kyōgoku the more
likely addressee.

50. *Nanki*, IV, 93. DNISK 2646, p. 124. A few days later this statement
was also issued in the Kinai.

51. DNISK 2624 (page unclear) [ISK, VI, 534:2:e]. In late 66/7 Katamori had urged converting *kobushin* to firearms. DNISK 2655, p. 36.

52. Perhaps the most interesting thing about Iemochi's death is that it does
not seem to have generated nearly as many rumors of poisoning as it might
have. Certainly the timing seems to suggest poisoning, and some people were
suspicious at the time. However, there was a considerable symptomatic literature that may have satisfied those who would suspect poisoning. According to
written reports that Shungaku received during 66/7 Iemochi first reported chest
pains and heightened sensitivity in late 66/4. After improvement, he again felt
the heightened sensitivity in mid-66/5. Then in early 66/6 he had a sore
throat and stomach discomfort. Medicine was administered, but from 6/24 his
legs began to swell (*suishu:* dropsy) and he was given a diuretic. Despite the
treatment he passed very little urine and on 7/1 began to vomit painfully. By
7/2 the vomiting had passed, but he was still unable to void water. A report of
7/14, obviously by a doctor familiar with the western medicine of the time,
spoke of the shogun as having suffered from a rheumatic illness *(reumachise)*
early in the summer and said that on 6/24 his legs and groin swelled up and
that he was given boiled sarsaparilla *(sarusabururira)*. On 6/28 and 29 Osaka
experienced heavy rains and chill, and the shogun was placed under a steam
vapor canopy. His swelling increased, but in the course of a full twenty-four
hours he passed only a tenth to a twentieth of a pint of urine (2 to 3 *shaku*).
This latter report then details the shogun's painful day of 7/1, the medicine applied, the continuing problem of liquids, the modest improvement, the dietary
measures, the ill effects of the shogun's dismay on 7/9 at learning of *rōjū* Honjō Munehide's actions at Hiroshima, the renewed vomiting two days later, and
the resort then to prayers at the various shrines, and the meetings of *rōjū* and
wakadoshiyori about the crisis, and the pessimistic judgment of the doctors. In
succeeding days the pathetic young man wasted away and at long last in the
morning light of 7/20 ended his hectic journey through life. ZSK, V,
207–208, 223–225. Tokutomi, LX, 153–166, deals with Iemochi's illness.
Yoshida Tsunekichi, ''Shōgun Iemochi no shi,'' *(Shintei zōho) kokushi taikei
geppō* 65:3–6 (1967), adds some details on Iemochi's death, including reports
suggesting beriberi and heart disease, and discusses the rumors of poisoning.

53. ZSK, V, 225–260. ISK, VI, 513, 529, 536. *Katsu zenshū*, XVIII,
345 ff.

54. Shibusawa, III, 365, 393–394; VI, 374. ZSK, V, 283–298. SNS, bk. 2, pt. 4, pp. 12, 16, 19–20.

55. Shibusawa, III, 353.

56. ZSK, V, 250–251. Shibusawa, VI, 385.

57. ZSK, V, 225, 239–261. SNS, bk. 2, pt. 4, pp. 16–24, 30–32. Shibusawa, VI, pp. 443–446, quoting Yoshinobu's memoirs.

58. Shibusawa, III, 378–391. SNS, bk. 2, pt. 4, pp. 22–23, 31. ZSK, V, 208–210, 261. Tokutomi, LX, 167–210, follows the succession in detail. Both Shibusawa and Tokutomi are relying on Yoshinobu's later memoirs for the claim that he was considering ending the shogunate forthwith. I doubt it, although in the 1900s it was a happy thought to entertain.

59. Shibusawa, III, 372–396 passim; VI, 438, 440. *Yodo*, p. 138. SNS, bk. 2, pt. 4, p. 26. ZSK, V, 260–263. *Ishinshi*, IV, 520–521. Of course there was considerable anti-Yoshinobu sentiment in the bakufu, and his appointment involved considerable maneuvering. Most of the influential anti-Yoshinobu people, notably ladies in the shogunal household, were back in Edo, however, and their choice, a young son of the Tayasu lord, was never a serious contender, though he may in fact have been Iemochi's stated choice, as one lady claimed in a 66/8/10 letter to a court official. Owari and Kii allegedly did not support Yoshinobu, but they too were not in a strong position to shape the affair.

60. DNISK 2655, p. 36.

61. SNS, bk. 2, pt. 4, pp. 27, 38–39. Shibusawa, III, 392–393. ZSK, V, 298. Evidently the idea of making Mochitsugu subordinate to Yoshinobu caused some discontent at Kii.

62. ZSK, V, 281. Shibusawa, III, 392.

63. This summary of the military reorganization is based on data in these sources: DNISK 2655, pp. 4, 10, 20, 30. ZTJ, V, 741–742, 751. ZSK, V, 281. Shibusawa, III, 391, 393. *Katsu zenshū*, XVIII, 354. As an example of the salary system, *kachi* put into the new force were to be paid 27 *ryō* per month for *kachi gashira*, 5 *ryō* 3 *bu* for *kachi gumi gashira*, and 5 *ryō* 1 *bu* for *kachi* proper. They would receive no supplemental *fuchi*.

64. ZSK, V, 195–201. Shibusawa, III, 353. *Katsu zenshū*, XVIII, 355.

65. On Yoshinobu's gear, see ZSK, V, 280, 282; on bakufu goals, ZSK, V, 308, 319.

66. ISK, VI, 481, 491, 498, 501. *Katsu zenshū*, XVIII, 335, 338–339, 342, 344.

67. This recapitulation of Shungaku's activity is based on ZSK volumes III, IV, and V. Kawakita Nobuo, ''Dai ikkai seichō mondai ni kan suru Matsudaira Shungaku no iken ni tsuite,'' *Shigaku* 39(3):65–95 (1966), surveys one aspect.

68. On Shungaku's activities in 66/6–7, material is from ZSK, V, 190–225. On Katsu, see ZSK, V, 190–261, 271 ff. passim, and *Katsu zenshū*, XVIII, 341 ff. Nagai's comment, in ZSK, V, 239, suggests that when he

urged reopening the Aki front after the 8/7 defeat there, either he wished to do so for negotiating purposes or he had changed his mind following Yoshinobu's acceptance of authority and his avowal to fight on. On the hard-liners, reference is to ISK, VI, 556, 564, 577. Shibusawa, III, 390.

69. ZSK, V, 199.

70. This summary of the Fukui lobbying effort is based on information in ZSK, V, 261–323.

71. Shibusawa, III, 394, 396. ZSK, V, 303–304, 322–323. SNS, bk. 2, pt. 4, pp. 32, 34, 36.

72. SNS, bk. 2, pt. 4, p. 35. ISK, VI, 564.

73. SNS, bk. 2, pt. 4, pp. 36, 45. ZSK, V, 330–338.

74. The day's activity is recorded in SNS, bk. 2, pt. 4, pp. 37, 45–46. Shibusawa, III, 395, 397; VI, 413–414, 421, 455, 469. ZSK, V, 344, 356–357.

75. As soon as he heard of the Kokura collapse, Yoshinobu had asked Shungaku to come to discuss affairs. The latter, however, was so discontented at the recent trend of events that he refused to come, sarcastically pleading illness— hemorrhoids, he said once, and a sore foot the next time. On 8/13 Yoshinobu made it clear to Shungaku that he was ready to try a radically new course, and so Shungaku agreed to meet him on the following day. ZSK, V, 332–348. Shibusawa, VI, 415, 419–420.

76. This political maneuvering is treated extensively in the standard sources. ZSK, V, 342–353. Shibusawa, III, 397–399; VI, 420–423. SNS, bk. 2, pt. 4, pp. 43–44. ISK, VI, 577–585 passim. *Ishinshi*, IV, 521–523, 526.

CHAPTER 9

1. Inoue Isao, ''Shōgun kūi jidai no seijishi: Meiji ishin seijishi kenkyū,'' *Shigaku zasshi* 77(11):1–58 (1968), is a straightforward recent discussion of central politics of the period 66/8–67/8 using standard categories and based upon the major customary sources, and it includes much fuller consideration of daimyo maneuvers than does the summary analysis made here.

2. This Keiō reform may be viewed as the principal historical manifestation of what some Japanese scholars have in mind when they speak of Tokugawa absolutism or *zettai shugi*. For a partly dissenting example, see Inoue Kiyoshi, *Nihon gendai shi I: Meiji ishin.* (Tokyo, 1967), pp. 59 ff., who discusses the early nineteenth-century antecedents of this orientation that came to the fore in late 1866 together with some of the historiographical problems of the topic.

3. This discussion of Shungaku's effort of 66/8–9 is based primarily on the extensive material in ZSK, V and VI.

4. ZSK, V, 334–335. The statement also is reproduced in Shibusawa, VI, 416–417.

5. ZSK, V, 260, 343. In addition to ZSK, material on Katsu's effort is in *Katsu zenshū*, XVIII, 358–369.

6. ZSK, V, 259.

7. ZSK, V, 378. The Katsu statement of 8/17 is at ZSK, V, 365–366.

8. Shibusawa, III, 428; VI, 446. *Ishinshi*, IV, 545. Tokutomi, LX, 445–448, 457, stresses Hara Ichinoshin's role in these matters.

9. In addition to ZSK, this matter is treated in Shibusawa, III, 411–414; VI, 424, 430–436. *Ishinshi*, IV, 531–534.

10. The court claimed on 8/19 that it was Itakura who asked that Yoshinobu's patent of authority include the phrase ''just like the previous shogun'' *(mae shōgun dōyō).* Shibusawa, VI, 441–442. But on 8/3 and 8/8 the court said in two differing contexts that Yoshinobu was to be treated just as the shogun (Iemochi) was. SNS, bk. 2, pt. 4, pp. 32, 36. Evidently both sides wished to pass the buck to the other. On Yoshinobu's succession, in addition to ZSK there is much material in Shibusawa, III, 373 ff., 415 ff.; VI, 393–395, 441–442. Shibusawa argues that Yoshinobu refused the shogun title in order to let daimyo and court attitudes clarify.

11. ZSK, V, 340.

12. ISK, VI, 581, 617.

13. In addition to ZSK, these court politics are followed extensively in SNS, bk. 2, pt. 4, pp. 56 ff., and in Tokutomi, LX and LXI.

14. Shibusawa, VI, 460–461. Also in *Yodo*, pp. 148–149.

15. *Yodo*, pp. 486–487. This entry has an estimated date of 1867. The list of items cumulatively indicates that the list was prepared at Edo, however, and suggests very strongly the dating I have indicated.

16. ZTJ, V, 764–766, 786–795.

17. Tokutomi, LXI, 27–36.

18. Shibusawa, III, 404 ff.; VI, 476 ff. SNS, bk. 2, pt. 4, p. 82, lists the titles as *sei nii, godainagon, seiitaishōgun, Genji chōja, Junwa shōgaku ryōin bettō, ubaryō gokan.*

19. ZTJ, V, 1096 ff., 1129. SNS, bk. 2, pt. 4, pp. 81–82.

20. ISK, VI, 634, 710–711; VII, 15. Medzini, p. 143.

21. DNISK 2781, p. 79, on the 12/1 order. Shibusawa, III, 486–487. Fox, p. 194. Medzini, p. 136, proposes that the formal reception of all ministers was a front for a private meeting of Roches and Yoshinobu.

22. ISK, VI, passim, refers to many such travels of officials. Also DNISK 2722, p. 30; 2731, pp. 50, 52; 2772, pp. 53–56, and *Yodo*, pp. 172–175, have further information.

23. This summary of Ogasawara's course is based on data in DNISK 2678, pp. 65–81; 2767, pp. 148, 154–156. ZTJ, V, 887, 966. *Yodo*, p. 150. OIN, pp. 513–514. *Katsu zenshū*, XVIII, 358, reports that Ogasawara was at Hyōgo by 8/14. OIN is utterly silent about the period 8/6–8/21. Nagamichi's slow boat reportedly was delayed by the great typhoon or went by ''the south sea,'' but his whereabouts are still uncertain, and at the time provoked a rash of rumors. He was reported sighted in Kyoto, for example, on 8/17 and at Osaka three days earlier.

24. Mizuno had been dismissed and ordered confined on 6/19, perhaps be-

cause he had imprudently told a Satsuma man about bakufu plans to advance against Chōshū and this man had then told Chōshū. Or he may have been ill, suffering from beriberi or maybe arthritis or rheumatism. Or he may possibly have been fired because he had objected to recent *goyōkin* demands made on the Edo populace, whose hardship he recognized and whose well-being concerned him because he was responsible for keeping the city tranquil. DNISK 2581, p. 59; 2725, pp. 101–102, 106.

25. ISK, VI, 702; VII, 10, 30, 138. *Yodo*, pp. 168–169.

26. ZTJ, V, 778–779. RR, II, 146–147, 231–232, 237–238. Sample military obligations:

	Income Level *(koku)*			
Year	500	600	1000	3000
1862	1 man	?	3 men	10 men
1866	0	3 men	6 men	24 men

In the new scale those of over 3000 *koku* were to add one more conscript for each additional 125 *koku* of income. Men under 600 *koku*, mostly *kuramaitori*, were ordered to pay a money levy rather than furnish manpower. For them the rates were 5 *ryō* per 100 *hyō* of income for men in the 300 to 600 *hyō* range and 3 *ryō* per 100 men in the 100 to 300 *hyō* range. Men with stipends of less than 100 *hyō* had to provide no funds.

27. ZTJ, V, 850 ff. ISK, VI, 608 ff. RR, II, 185–191, contains many of these orders and regulations. Also *Yodo*, pp. 155–157.

28. This paragraph is constructed from data in ZTJ, V, 811–812, 850 ff. RR, II, 153–156, 235–237. DNISK 2606, p. 114; 2954, pp. 65–66. *Yodo*, pp. 478–483, contains one set of these reform regulations under an estimated date of 1867. The RR, II, 153–156, entries are two orders undated but evidently issued between 66/9/4 and 10/28.

29. ZTJ, V, 969–970, 1007–1008. *Okuzume jūtai*, for example, were to receive a total income of 300 *koku*. *Jūtai* were to receive 70 *hyō* plus five-man *fuchi*, and *sappei* were to receive 30 *hyō* plus two-man *fuchi*.

30. ZTJ, V, 976. The conversion rate was 200 *ryō* per 35 *koku*, but over a year earlier, when prices were much lower, rice in Edo had been selling for about 200 *ryō* per 32 *koku*.

31. ZTJ, V, 936–939, 966 ff., 980 ff., 1007–1009, 1017, 1027–1028, 1032–1035. RR, II, 234.

32. This material on uniforms and duty is derived from DNISK 2723, pp. 125–126; 2745, pp. 5–6. ZTJ, V, 876–908 passim, 940–943, 1249–1250.

33. DNISK 2709, pp. 17–25.

34. ISK, VI, 644.

35. This material on the hierarchy is derived from ZTJ, V, 909, 916–917, 920, 971. ISK, VI, 735–736.

36. Aoki, pp. 120–123. Fukushima, pp. 11–13. Ozaki, ''Bakuryō nōhei,'' *Shinano*, 20(11):42–50.

37. RR, II, 48–52.

38. DNISK 2717, pp. 1–52.

39. *Yodo*, pp. 177–182, 204–211. Shibusawa III, 404. ISK, VI, 641. The Ogasawara of Kokura had retreated inland some 25 kilometers to the south and took Kaharu town (today's Kawaramachi) as their new headquarters following the Chōshū conquest of Kokura.

40. Shibusawa, VI, 492–512.

41. Over the years rumors have suggested that Iwakura Tomomi poisoned Kōmei, presumably because of his support for the bakufu. According to reports received at Fukui, however, Kōmei became ill on about 12/12, some seven days after designating Yoshinobu shogun. He showed smallpox eruptions by 12/15 and died on 12/25. ZSK, VI, 94–95. SNS, bk. 2, pt. 4, p. 82, also reports smallpox according to a court notice of 12/16. Tokutomi, LXI, 97 ff., discusses Kōmei's death in detail, also (not surprisingly) accepting the smallpox diagnosis, and on p. 102 reports a possible source of infection.

42. Shibusawa, III, 469–470.

43. Aizu's presence, as we noted earlier, had been costly for both Edo and Aizu. On 66/2/6 *han* officials had presented the bakufu with a detailed accounting showing that its Kyoto duty had been costing the *han* some 300,000 *ryō* per year over the preceding two years. The bakufu had covered only a portion of this cost. DNISK 2460, p. 35.

44. DNISK 2688, p. 84; 2697, pp. 68–71, 77–80. ISK, VI, 565, 578, 595–596, 607, 626.

45. SNS, bk. 2, pt. 4, pp. 74–75. ISK, VI, 659–660.

46. SNS, bk. 2, pt. 5, pp. 7–10.

47. SNS, bk. 2, pt. 5, p. 11.

48. Shibusawa, III, 468–471. ISK, VII, 20, 25.

49. This matter is discussed at length in SNS, bk. 2, pt. 5, pp. 15–66, 81.

50. These generalizations about daimyo behavior are based on extensive entries in ISK, VI, 586, 604–740 passim.

51. ZSK, IV, 310.

52. ISK, VI, 702, 709, 741; VII, 20, 22, 42, 53, 57, 67, 69.

53. ISK, VI, 520–732; VII, 44–90 passim, lists some forty instances of this sort, mostly in 66/9–12.

54. This paragraph is based on extensive material, mostly in MHS, III, 1026–1052, but also scattered through ISK, VI and VII.

55. ZSK, VI, 77–79, 81–83.

56. ZSK, VI, 51–52, 63. ISK, VI, 617, 626–627, 633, 642, 718,

720. SNS, bk. 2, pt. 4, p. 67, quotes Mochitsugu's 9/14 resignation statement.

57. DNISK 2799, pp. 5–10, 27; 2821, pp. 52–60; 2822, pp. 158–159; 2873, pp. 42–50.

58. *Katsu zenshū*, XVIII, 393.

59. ISK, VI, 546, 559, 609, 724, 730, 732; VII, 43, 60, 66, 71.

60. DNISK 2749, pp. 72 ff. *Yodo*, pp. 171–172.

61. DNISK 2801, pp. 63–67. ISK, VII, 20.

62. Ishii, *Meiji ishin* (1960 edition), pp. 546–548. Kanai, pp. 391–396. Tokutomi, LX, 283–285.

63. ZTJ, V, 862–863, 978, 1003, 1105–1106.

64. DNISK 2726, pp. 5–6, on the *goyōkin*. There is only one record of this, and it may be a misdated entry. ISK, VI, 656.

65. ZTJ, V, 925–930, 944 ff., and passim.

66. ZTJ, V, 899, 976, 1014, 1018–1019, 1182–1183.

67. *Yodo*, pp. 116–123, 129–133.

68. ISK, VI, 627, 631, 636, 638. ZSK, VI, 41.

69. DNISK 2716, p. 112. Quoting U.S. diplomatic correspondence.

70. DNISK 2716, p. 114; 2725, pp. 28–40.

71. ZTJ, V, 903. DNISK 2737, p. 139. Medzini, p. 116, reports that the rice imports cost $100,000.

72. These two paragraphs are based on data in DNISK 2737, pp. 137, 144; 2769, pp. 33–34; 2780, pp. 192–196. The Inoue statement of 11/11 is on p. 33 of DNISK 2769.

73. DNISK 2742, pp. 104–109; 2770, pp. 38–43.

74. ZSK, VI, 42.

75. This summary of fires is based on data in ISK, VI, 686. DNISK 2507, pp. 33–39; 2520, p. 28: 2764, p. 73; 2768, pp. 71–98; 2769, pp. 41–43, 167–169; 2777, p. 181; 2795, pp. 145–163. ZTJ, V, 1018, 1125–1126. According to J. E. DeBecker, *The Nightless City*, p. 188, Fukagawa had traditionally served as a site for temporary brothels.

76. Much data on weather and its effect is from ISK, VI, 449, 510–511, 539, 570, 578, 597, 599, 637, 644, 665, 667, 671, 682, 689, 691, 695, 705, 721.

77. Shibusawa, III, 397; VI, 415.

78. DNISK 2661, pp. 10–86. SNS, bk. 2, pt. 3, pp. 32, 34. ZSK, VI, 102.

79. DNISK 2769, p. 94.

80. ISK, VI, 483, 642, 652. The cut in sake rice was two-thirds overall and three-fourths in the Kantō, a far greater reduction than the one-third that appears to have been customary in earlier periods of crop failure.

81. DNISK 2784, p. 88.

82. This upheaval in Tsuyama, which still echoes in folk memory, is recon-

structed from information in DNISK 2775, pp. 137–156; 2783, pp. 221–222. It is not clear to me whether this Kawahara is the one to the north of Tsuyama, some 10 kilometers south of Tottori city, or another, located southeast of Tsuyama, perhaps, in the direction of Akō.

83. This summary of the Shōdoshima trouble is based on Kawai Mutsuo, ''Keiō sannen shōgatsu Sanshū Shōdoshima seibu roku gō hyakushō ikki ni tsuite,'' *Hosei shigaku* 14:112–123 (1961), a very good and careful study of the incident.

84. ISK, VI, 717, 720, 737; VII, 29, 35, 40. During 67/2 unrest occurred in Shimozuke far to the east, and there was a brief peasant uprising in Kameyama *han* in Ise.

85. ISK, VII, 111. Shoji, pp. 53–55.

86. ISK, VII, 54. The same *kanji* is used as in Yoshinobu. The DNISK entry (probably 2835, page unclear) contains only two mentions of this, and only one of them gives a *furigana* pronunciation, that of Yoshihisa.

CHAPTER 10

1. ZSK, VI, 107–108.

2. Shibusawa, VI, 493 ff., are samples of daimyo opinion.

3. The politics of 67/1–4 are dealt with at length in the standard sources, and this summary is based largely on ZSK, VI, 99–157. SNS, bk. 2, pt. 5, pp. 4–43. Shibusawa, III, 476–502. Also ISK, VII, 1–112, has much material.

4. DNISK 2839, pp. 165–169. Fox, pp. 191–193, 198.

5. Shibusawa, VII, 3–37, is minutes of the 2/6–7 meetings. Roches's report of 3/6 to Paris, as presented by Medzini, pp. 138–140, gives a somewhat different version of this meeting, evidently in an effort to conceal his anti-British posture and to boost his own influence.

6. *Ishinshi*, IV, 629. Fox, pp. 195–196. Shibusawa, III, 488–490, presents the evidence for Satsuma prodding of Parkes.

7. Beasley, *Documents*, pp. 308–310.

8. Beasley, *Documents*, pp. 310–311.

9. Beasley, *Documents*, pp. 310–311.

10. Beasley, *Documents*, p. 311.

11. DNISK 2856, pp. 96–97.

12. DNISK 2861, pp. 113–124.

13. ZSK, VI, 138–139. At least an Aizu vassal strongly suspected that this was more Satsuma perfidy.

14. Shibusawa, III, 476–477. ZSK, VI, 134. DNISK 2861 (page unidentified) [ISK, VII:93–94:5]. The ''Zoku tsūshin zenran'' entry indicates that in asking delay the three *rōjū* explained that with the domestic situation precarious and the many expenses of late, the government was trying to avoid wasting funds and wished to use them for progressive purposes.

15. The Tsuruga flap is discussed in Shibusawa, III, 477–482. ZSK, VI, 131–157. SNS, bk. 2, pt. 5, pp. 37–43. ISK, VII, 99–108. *Yodo*, pp. 247–254.

16. This political maneuvering is followed in detail by ZSK, VI, 159 ff. Shibusawa, III, 494, 503 ff. Tokutomi, LXII, 329 ff.

17. Shibusawa, III, 515 ff., discusses different interpretations of the gist of the 5/19 session.

18. ZSK, VI, 284–285.

19. This court session has elicited much comment because it was the occasion for bitter charges of duplicity and betrayal. ZSK, VI, 290–300. Tokutomi, LXIII, 45–91. Shibusawa, III, 521–523; VII, 83, 104. *Yodo*, pp. 263–264. SNS, bk. 2, pt. 5, pp. 56–58.

20. The politics of Yoshinobu's symbolic triumph are treated in the standard sources. ZSK, VI, 301–435. *Ishinshi*, IV, 638–650. Shibusawa, III, 546–571. SNS, bk. 2, pt. 5, pp. 59–71. ISK, VII, 136 ff.

21. These *shinpan* matters are reported in ZSK, VI, 352–353, 377, 379–380.

22. DNISK 2922, pp. 66–68; 2940, pp. 48, 51.

23. On 7/18 Shungaku spoke bitterly to a Satsuma man about how uninfluential he was although he was a *shinpan* lord, and he noted that the situation was not that of *rōjū* domination as of old, but one of shogunal authoritarianism. ZSK, VI, 396.

24. Shibusawa, III, 483–485; VII, 110–114, 123, 127. SNS, bk. 2, pt. 5, pp. 62–63, 69–70.

25. Shibusawa, III, 451, 485. ISK, VII, 241, 249. *Yodo*, pp. 293–295.

26. ISK, VII, 58, 97, 122, 139, 224.

27. ISK, VII, 37, 189.

28. DNISK 2879, pp. 38–41. ISK, VII, 105–106. ZSK, VI, 131–132. Satow and friend had gone with Parkes as far as Fushimi and then headed east by land, though it would have been faster and easier to go by sea from Osaka. Their reason for going overland is not clear.

29. Material on this incident is in Shibusawa, IV, 28–32; VII, 125–126. ZSK, VI, 422–424, 438. Tokutomi, LXIII, 219–235. Jansen, pp. 304–305. Tokutomi, p. 219, reports that the sailors were in drunken sleep. Fox, p. 204, reports that "they were asleep on the porch of a tea house in the native section of Nagasaki." Jansen, p. 305, seems to imply that bakufu leaders welcomed this Tosa-British collision. That seems plausible, but appears not to have been so. The Kyoto bakufu leaders, who probably knew by 8/4 of the coming Tosa restoration proposal, evidently wished not to alienate Tosa unnecessarily and were hoping to avoid, not foster, a Tosa-British clash in which the bakufu must end up the ultimate loser whatever the outcome. Shungaku, knowing about as much of the matter as did bakufu leaders, saw no reason to deny the charge that Tosa men were the assailants. He urged Yōdō to surrender the guil-

ty if the charges be true, appealing with great vigor to all Yōdō's senses of virtue and self-interest in a letter whose phrasing is very similar to that used by
Yoshinobu. Much later it was learned that the murderer was a Fukuoka *han*
vassal who committed suicide.

30. ISK, VII, 184, 197–198. Shibusawa, IV, 28.

31. *Yodo*, pp. 291–294.

32. Shibusawa, III, 439; IV, 5–6. The newspaper article is quoted at
length in VII, 69–75. In 67/6 Yoshinobu did write an explanation of his position as Roches suggested. See VII, 116–122.

33. Fox, pp. 193 ff., 204.

34. Medzini, pp. 145–146, 158–159.

35. These instances are cited from ZSK, VI, 334, 365, 369–370, 376.

36. Shibusawa, IV, 34–37. DNISK 2928, pp. 63–64. This is part of a
''Zoku tsūshin zenran'' report. Medzini, pp. 12–18, 31, 38, 152–158, using western sources, traces briefly the French religious presence in Japan. Citing
a Protestant historian of Christianity, Medzini, p. 31, says of the 1862 incident only that the French missionary was teaching French to some Japanese.

37. Medzini, pp. 38, 152. *Yodo*, p. 38.

38. Shibusawa, IV, 37–38. DNISK 2928, pp. 64–65, 68. Fox, p. 483.
Medzini, p. 153.

39. Medzini, p. 141, says Roches was at Nagasaki for a fortnight after May
21, or from 67/4/18 to 5/2.

40. DNISK 2928, p. 66.

41. DNISK 2928, pp. 65–78, the ''Zoku tsūshin zenran'' report on this
Christian problem, is the basic source. See also Shibusawa, IV, 38–39, which
relies heavily on the same source. Medzini, in apparent error, reports that
seventy-eight were arrested. His source blames the trouble on Buddhist priests,
the standard *bête noire* of Christian missionaries.

42. DNISK 2911, pp. 88–91.

43. DNISK 2917, pp. 78–79. ISK, VII, 178, 190. Only Parkes and Van
Polsbroek seem to have been silent, although Shibusawa suggests that Parkes
may have mentioned the matter when he met Yoshinobu at Osaka to discuss
the sailor murders on 7/27. And Shibusawa quotes a British government protest of 67/9/26 that argued the Christians should be pardoned and the law
changed. Shibusawa, IV, 39–40, 44–45.

44. Shibusawa, IV, 39–40. DNISK 2928, pp. 70–72. Medzini, pp.
153–155, quotes Roches's letter to the missionaries.

45. The letters are quoted in Shibusawa, VII, 128–134. Other information
on this outcome of the Christian problem is derived from DNISK 2928, pp.
74–76. Shibusawa, IV, 40–48. ISK, VII, 205, 207–208, 210, 234. Medzini, pp. 156–157.

46. I put the term ''Korean problem'' in quotation marks here because
Korea of course was not the problem. The problem was western imperialism.

But since the bakufu could not repel the latter, it chose to "solve" the problem by redefining it into a Korean problem, as the Meiji leaders did later also. The Koreans presumably could be dealt with.

47. Shibusawa, IV, 26, lists Tokugawa-era advocates of Japanese control of Korea: Honda Toshiaki, Satō Shin'en, Hashimoto Sanai, Yoshida Shōin, Maki Izumi, and Hirano Jirō.

48. Bakufu attitudes toward Korea before late 1866 are discussed in Shibusawa, IV, 16–20, and *Katsu zenshū*, XVIII, 50–75 passim, 159, 256–257, 275, 325.

49. Shibusawa, IV, 21–23. ISK, VII, 90. In his 67/2/7 talk with Roches, Yoshinobu expressed his desire to mediate the matter. Shibusawa, VII, 32–33.

50. DNISK 2882, pp. 121–122.

51. DNISK 2882, pp. 131–133.

52. DNISK 2957, p. 54. ISK, VII, 257. Shibusawa, IV, 23–24.

CHAPTER 11

1. Shibusawa, VI, 398–399. This letter appears only in Kimura Kaishū, *Sanjūnenshi* (Tokyo, 1892), pp. 711–712, but its existence and proper dating are confirmed by a reference to it in Yoshinobu's widely recorded letter of 8/27. Shibusawa, III, 447, asserts that Yoshinobu refused to approve the French loan arrangements of 66/8, but according to a report that Katamori sent Shungaku on 7/9, Yoshinobu was apparently responsive to Roches's offers of aid. Itakura, however, pointed out the risk of popular anger if the bakufu were to accept foreign assistance against domestic enemies. ZSK, V, 217.

2. Shibusawa, VI, 449–451. Medzini, p. 135, quotes parts of the French version of Yoshinobu's 8/27 letter to Roches. He also quotes a French version of what may be the 8/2 letter, but if it is that letter, the French version must be judged a very creative translation, with passages flattering to Roches and France that do not appear to have been in the original.

3. DNISK 2696, pp. 45–47.

4. Ōtsuka, p. 274. Medzini, p. 117.

5. DNISK 2768, pp. 106–109.

6. Shibusawa, III, 437.

7. Medzini, pp. 136–138. This sequence of actions seems implied in Roches's report of 67/1/25.

8. Shibusawa, VII, 17–37. *Yodo*, pp. 214–236. Tokutomi, LXII, 144–202, also treats the 2/6–7 discussions in detail.

9. DNISK 2888, pp. 12–13, 17; 2891, pp. 83–91.

10. *Yodo*, pp. 260–262.

11. *Yodo*, pp. 265–270. DNISK 2903, pp. 20–24.

12. ZTJ, V, 1230 ff. SNS, bk. 2, pt. 5, p. 54. OIN, p. 524, says that Ogasawara was first designated *gaikoku jimu sōsai* on 5/24 while in Kyoto.

13. *Yodo*, pp. 467–478. This is an undated entry that appears from inter-

nal evidence to have been drawn up some time after 67/6/4. In DNISK 2987, pp. 59–96, the entry is logged under 67/10, but its contents suggest that it was developed prior to the unveiling of the Tosa restoration proposal.

14. Kageura Gatō, ''Meiji ishin no sai ni okeru Kōchi han to Matsuyama han,'' *Iyo shidan* 152:7 (1958).

15. DNISK 2859, pp. 27–29; 2869, pp. 10, 21. ZTJ, V, 1210, 1222–1223. The earlier promotion of Nagai Naomune (born the son of the *fudai* daimyo of Okudono, the *han* of *rōjū* Ogyū Noritaka) to *wakadoshiyori kaku* (not *nami*) in 67/2 was done in the customary manner with an increase in stipend of 7000 *koku*. In retrospect, however, Yoshinobu spoke of that promotion as the difficult one. If his recollection was correct, it suggests that some men saw it as precedent for more open promotion, although Yoshinobu does not identify the implied opponents of the appointment. Shibusawa, III, 448, citing Yoshinobu's memoirs.

16. ZTJ, V, 1391–1411. To cite a few examples of the new salaries: *rōjū* were to receive 10,000 *ryō*; *wakadoshiyori*, 4000; *ōmetsuke*, *machi bugyō*, and certain others, 2500; *hohei* and *kihei gashira*, 1500; *tsukaiban*, 500.

17. DNISK 2814, pp. 117–119.

18. ZTJ, V, 1192.

19. ZTJ, V, 1204–1205.

20. DNISK 2906, pp. 63–67. ZTJ, V, 1284. Perhaps Fusa is the present-day Fuse just northeast of Kashiwa.

21. DNISK 2923, pp. 119 ff.

22. ZTJ, V, 1424, 1488–1489. DNISK 2965, p. 26. I have been unable to locate either Iwabana or Machiba.

23. ZTJ, V, 1553.

24. Medzini, pp. 130–133, sums up French policy. Chanoine thought the Yokohama area was too small. RR, II, 264–267, quotes the contract for the military mission signed in Paris in 66/11.

25. Ōtsuka, pp. 354–355. ZTJ, V, 1258, 1260. RR, II, 302.

26. DNISK 2897, pp. 78, 82. Ōtsuka, pp. 254–255, speaks of two training battalions of 600 and 800 troops, but these appear to be regular infantry *(hohei)*, not French-trained units. See note 41 below.

27. DNISK 2897, p. 143. RR, II, 305.

28. DNISK 2980, p. 159; 2941, p. 179.

29. DNISK 2962, pp. 110, 112: 3065, p. 82. ZTJ, V, 1459.

30. DNISK 2999, pp. 18–19. DNISK 2941, pp. 175–179, presents data on a similar incident of 67/8.

31. Shibusawa, III, 456; VII, 26–27.

32. Arima, pp. 8–9.

33. RR, II, 232–234. Shibusawa, III, 460–461. ISK, VII, 123.

34. This pattern emerges from data in ZTJ, V, *passim*.

35. ZTJ, V, 1248–1255. ISK, VII, 66, 132, 142, 186.

36. DNISK 2886, pp. 136–137.

37. RR, II, 242–245. Some sources refer to *sappei* as though they were foreign-trained or in western-style uniforms, and there is some interchanging of the terms *sappei* and *sanpei*. Perhaps most French-trained troops were in the *sappei*, but probably not many *sappei* were French-trained. Whereas *bette gumi* wore western uniforms, *sappei* appear to have worn modernized Japanese uniforms, which might have looked outlandish enough to those who had never seen the really strange garb of the foreigners.

38. DNISK 3019, p. 62, and *Yodo*, pp. 377–378. This entry, which appears in *Yodo* among late 67/11 entries under the date ''late 1867,'' is attached incongruously to a report lamenting the bakufu's open-ports policy and French ties and referring to Hara Ichinoshin's murder. This attachment suggests, but does not establish definitively because of the incongruity of parts of the entry, that it was written after Hara's murder on 67/8/14.

39. RR, II, 241–242.

40. ZTJ, V, 1306. DNISK 2915, pp. 139–143.

41. RR, II, 373–374. Katsu places this entry in a location suggesting a date of 1865, but the 67/1–6 dating is suggested by the fact that this is the only period in which the three signatories, Yamaguchi Naoki, Komai Chōon, and Fujisawa Tsugikane were in a position to have proposed such a joint report. These two training battalions, incidentally, may be the ones Ōtsuka refers to as French-trained.

42. DNISK 2954, pp. 65–66.

43. DNISK 2954, pp. 30–35, 58.

44. DNISK 2980, p. 159; 3055, p. 5. ZTJ, V, 1476–1478, 1483, 1519.

45. RR, II, 232–234, 237–240.

46. ZTJ, V, 1065–1066, 1128–1129. RR, II, 240–241. On p. 240 is the notice of 12/19 without date. It is immediately preceded by a similarly undated notice specifying 30 *ryō* per conscript for men of 3000 *koku* or less income.

47. ZTJ, V, 1225.

48. ZTJ, V, 1305.

49. RR, II, 238–240. This report has no date but most likely is late 1866. The 1862 reform, as we noted earlier, envisaged a force of some thirteen thousand of whom over six thousand were to come from landholding *hatamoto*. RR, II, 129–135.

50. DNISK 2797, pp. 134–136.

51. These orders concerning tax records are cited in ZTJ, V, 1217, 1310, 1315, 1373. DNISK 2917, p. 105, and 2943, p. 110, identify Inaba as the issuing agent.

52. Yamamura, p. 35. On pp. 30–31 Yamamura explains how he arrived at these figures, which are based on the market value of rice at Edo (Nominal

Income); bean paste, salt, soy sauce, sake, and lamp oil (Real Income I); and these five commodities plus cotton cloth (Real Income II).

53. This comment may contradict Yamamura's assertion that over the long run liege vassals failed to benefit from increases in agricultural productivity. Yamamura, pp. 39–40.

54. Two studies that reveal aspects of the *hatamoto* situation are Fujii Sadayoshi, ''Hatamoto Ishimaru-ke zaisei no ittan,'' Osaka furitsu daigaku *Keizai kenkyū* 21:121–130 (1961) and Kitahara Susume, ''Bakumatsu ni okeru hatamoto shakuzai no tokushitsu,'' Risshō daigaku *Keizaigaku kihō* 14(12): 115–137 (1964).

55. ZTJ, V, 1408. RR, II, 247–248.

56. ZTJ, V, 1417, 1499–1500. DNISK 2982, p. 53.

57. Generalizing from material in Ozaki, ''Bakuryō nōhei,'' and Aoki, it may well be that a comparable defeudalizing process was going on in the bakufu's handling of peasant militia. During 1867 older regulations calling upon villages to furnish men were replaced by orders specifying levels of tax that the village would pay instead. The income would then be used to pay recruits who would train with firearms and be under the command of local bakufu officials. In this case, too, the new tax was resisted by villagers, and intendants had difficulty in the regime's last months in making the system operational. In any case, material in Ōmachi Masami, *Boshin sensō* (Tokyo, 1968), pp. 23–24, suggests that the peasant militia proved of no value to Edo in the crisis of 1868, some *nōhei* refusing to fight and others being ordered by bakufu officials to capitulate to the advancing imperial army.

58. Katsu Kaishū, *Kaigun rekishi*, recently republished by Hara Shobō in Tokyo, is the major standard source for information on naval development. I did not utilize it, however, instead gathering data mostly from DNISK and ISK entries.

59. *Katsu zenshū*, XVIII, 391. *Yodo*, pp. 489–490. This entry is dated ''about 1867.''

60. Recently Nishibori Akira has written a series of extremely well-documented articles, ''Waga kuni ni okeru Futsugo (kyōiku) shi,'' about the French language-training program, publishing them in seven issues of *Chiba shodai ronsō* between 1968 and 1972. They would provide a fine source of information for careful study of the creation, organization, function, content, and influence of this language-training program.

61. RR, I, 213–218. ISK, VI, 661; VII, 91, 166.

62. ZTJ, V, 897.

63. ZTJ, V, 1185. ISK, VII, 65–66, 240. *Katsu zenshū*, XVIII, 402, 407, 420, 422. One other reason for using the steamer may have been to prevent foreign coasting vessels from controlling the run. Another reason, it appears, was to help pay the costs of the growing navy. Shibusawa, III, 464–465.

64. ISK, VII, 259.

65. DNISK 2822, pp. 2, 4. This Westwood was perhaps the Westwood of the Oriental Bank who was involved in the big foreign loan negotiation of 1866.

66. DNISK 3063, pp. 61–65.

67. ISK, VI, 585, 710, 712; VII, 3, 93, 152, 156, 209. ZTJ, V, 1118. Medzini, p. 152.

68. ISK, VII, 243–244. Fox pp. 418–425. An earlier problem occurred on 65/10/21 when the newspaper *Nihon shinbun* (the translated edition of *Japan Times*) reported that the *rōjū* had forged imperial approval of the treaties in order to stop the foreigners from going to Kyoto. DNISK 2390, p. 2.

69. These items were gleaned from ISK, VII, 143, 199–200. ZTJ, V, 1375, 1390.

70. DNISK 2851, pp. 159–160. ISK, VII, 76.

71. DNISK 2955, pp. 77–78, 91.

72. This summary of the Hara affair is based on extensive information in DNISK 2931, pp. 6–146, notably pp. 13, 105–106, 120–123, 146. Sasuke seems to have been in error about his age in either 1835 or 1867, but which is unclear.

73. *Yodo*, p. 286. Tokutomi, LXIII, 315–322, deals with Hara's death. He quotes the report of the murder investigators, whose information on the assailants appears to be in some error.

74. RR, II, 383–388.

75. DNISK 2954, p. 63; 2955, pp. 77–78. *Yodo*, pp. 309–313.

76. RR, II, 248–249. This entry is undated, but its contents suggest it was issued in conjunction with the 9/26 order.

77. DNISK 2954, pp. 28–63, offers material on the *kumiai jūtai* situation.

78. Material on the *hohei* situation is derived from DNISK 3019, pp. 16–108, notably pp. 16–31, 91–92. Also *Yodo*, pp. 361–373. RR, II, 390–391, quotes a document of 68/1/9 dealing with troop problems. It reports that infantrymen only received between 6 and 10 *ryō* per year plus whatever they got from the men from whose land they came, and it regards the inadequacy of pay as a source of trouble.

79. Data to this effect are extensive in ISK, VII, 44 ff., and ZTJ, V, 1286 ff.

80. Shibusawa, III, 464. ZTJ, V, 1262. DNISK 2901, pp. 129 ff.

81. Ōtsuka, pp. 276–277. Tokutomi, LXII, 203–225, and Shibusawa, VII, 3–37, in reporting on Roches's activity at Osaka, do not report this loan proposal. However, Roches did definitely refer to the Ezo scheme in a letter to Yoshinobu that has been assigned the date of 67/4/13. Shibusawa, VII, 74.

82. DNISK 2838, pp. 82, 88–93.

83. Medzini, p. 150, reports Fleury-Herard's situation. Ōtsuka, pp. 276–277, reports on Mukōyama. Kurimoto Kon was sent to take charge of the mission in 67/5 after bad reports reached Japan about both Satsuma activity in

Paris and the bakufu delegation's handling of the exposition arrangements. When Kurimoto arrived in Paris in 67/8, he denounced the pro-British view of Mukōyama and one of his subordinates and took charge of the group himself.

84. DNISK 2920, pp. 58–59, 65–72. Medzini, pp. 144–163, explores in detail the factors that discredited Roches in the eyes of the French government. Shibata, pp. 63–64, discusses Fleury-Herard's failure in mid-1867 to implement the trading company funding arrangements.

85. Kanai, pp. 400–401, reports the letter Oguri received on 6/17; DNISK 2920, p. 77, is on the later letter.

86. Ōtsuka, pp. 274–275.

87. DNISK 2895, pp. 73–77, contains the letter.

88. DNISK 2895, pp. 83–85, 87–94; 2936, p. 30.

89. ZTJ, V, 1356–1367.

90. DNISK 3005, pp. 154–155, 157. ISK, VII, 149, 220. Shibusawa, III, 539–543.

91. This summary of the Kantō note issues is based mainly on data in Nihon keizaishi kenkyūjo, "Keiō sannen Edo Ginza hakkō kinsatsu shiryō," *Osaka keidai ronshū* 38:170–190 (1963). Shibusawa, III, 539–543, also discusses the paper issue related to the opening of Edo.

92. *Katsu zenshū*, XVIII, p. 433.

93. *Katsu zenshū*, XVIII, pp. 425, 434.

94. ZSK, VI, 436–437.

CHAPTER 12

1. ISK, VII, 44, 66, 70–71, 77, 90, 119, 122, 128–129, 142, 156, 160, 163, 176, 188, 202, 212, 225, 227, 240.

2. DNISK 2849, pp. 26–27; 2874, pp. 8–14.

3. ISK, VII, 238, 249, 252.

4. *Yodo*, pp. 344–346, a report dated 67/10, is one of the few notices of local popular discontent.

5. This discussion of *eejanaika* activity is based on data in DNISK 2988, pp. 1–145, and 2999, pp. 67–82. Aoki Michio and Miura Toshiaki, "Minami Kantō ni okeru 'eejanaika'," *Rekishigaku kenkyū* 385:55–57 (1972), discusses briefly *eejanaika* activity in the Edo-Yokohama area. There is, of course, other secondary literature on *eejanaika* activity, but it addresses problems of popular attitudes that do not directly affect the high-level political issues being dealt with here. They pertain, rather, to the character of long-range agrarian developments.

6. DNISK 2988, p. 135.

7. DNISK 2999, p. 27.

8. DNISK 2999, p. 82. This is a Tottori record, and it actually says "in and around Kyoto" (*rakuchū rakugai*).

9. This interpretation presents the *eejanaika* movement of late 1867 as qualitatively different from the *yonaoshi* activity of 1866, 1868, and later in

terms of the public mood as a factor in the immediate political process. It perhaps needs to be pointed out that in terms of basic societal predispositions, it is no less ''antifeudal'' when the poor show their disdain for their superiors with good humor and derision than when they show it in anger and violence. This seems to be the distinction Scheiner, p. 587, is making between *yonaoshi* and *okagemairi*.

10. Shibusawa, IV, 71. Tokutomi, LXIV, 88, speaks of contacts between Nagai and Gotō Shōjirō of Tosa in 67/6. ZSK, VI, 389, 444, indicates that Fukui knew of the Tosa plan by 7/16 and that by 8/25 Shungaku had heard from Nagai that the Tosa plan was probably acceptable. Perhaps it was prior knowledge of the Tosa plan that enabled Inaba Masakuni and Ogyū Noritaka to present such elegant schemes for political reform so quickly in 67/10 as noted further on in the chapter. Similarly it may have been knowledge of the Tosa scheme that prodded Tsuda Mamichi in 67/9 to formulate an alternative scheme of reform that sought to achieve unity without sacrificing Tokugawa primacy. Kamekakegawa Hiromasa, ''Bakufu tōkai ki ni okeru gunsei kaikaku no sho kōsō,'' *Gunji shigaku* 9:56 (1967). A reform proposal by Matsudaira Shungaku that has been dated tentatively by Osatake Takeshi and Kawakita Nobuo as ca. 1863 appears to me, from the character of Shungaku's analysis, to be more likely a product of 1867. Kawakita Nobuo, ''Matsudaira Shungaku no 'Kohyō henkaku bikō' kijutsu jiki,'' *Shigaku* 29(4):42–64 (1957).

11. Shibusawa, IV, 72–75. SNS, bk. 2, pt. 6, pp. 1–6. Tokutomi, LXIV, 117–119. Jansen, p. 327.

12. Shibusawa, IV, 81–85. This version of Yoshinobu's statement is taken from Nakane Yukie's ''Teibō nikki.'' It differs somewhat from the shorter version reported in SNS, bk. 2, pt. 6, pp. 12–15.

13. DNISK 2944, pp. 24–73; 2949, pp. 75–78; 2959, p. 54; 2963, pp. 27–31. Shibusawa, IV, 78, 97–104. SNS, bk. 2, pt. 6, pp. 6–9. ISK, VII, 261–262.

14. DNISK 2963, pp. 21–22, 27. SNS, bk. 2, pt. 6, p. 9, carries Kondō's report. The bakufu may also have heard something about the departure by ship from Kagoshima on 10/3 of some four hundred more Satsuma troops bound for Kyoto. And it knew that Satsuma forces in Kyoto had recently been augmented and probably numbered well over a thousand. Reports say news of the Satsuma move of 10/3 reached Kyoto on 10/8 to 10/12. DNISK 2962, pp. 168–194.

15. DNISK 2964, pp. 2–4. *Yodo*, pp. 313–316.

16. DNISK 2964, pp. 142–167.

17. To cite one manifestation of Yoshinobu's intellectual predilection, in 65/3 and 4 when he was actively creating a modern military force of his own, he wrote two letters to his vassals. In the first he dwelt on the classic issues of morality, frugality, samurai spirit, and the need for reform, particularly military reform and the abandonment of archaic practices. In the second he announced specifically the establishment of a study program they were to attend. Its sub-

ject was to be "on the general character of political upheavals in ancient and modern times" (Kokon chiran no taisei nado). Shibusawa, VI, 267. At the time he was kinri shuei sōtoku and knew that Chōshū dissidents were again waxing powerful. Yet he chose to conceptualize matters not in the blunt terms of Chōshū dissidents and bakufu weakness, but in the elegant terms of historical dynastic rise and fall.

18. In later years Yoshinobu of course insisted upon his sincerity and his long-standing wish to restore authority to a court properly supported by the daimyo. Shibusawa, IV, 79–80, citing his memoirs.

19. Shibusawa, VII, 103–104. ISK, VII, 62.

20. Ishinshi, IV, 748.

21. This narrative of the restoration process is based largely on Shibusawa, IV, 90–127. Many documents are in Shibusawa, VII, 150 ff.

22. SNS, bk. 2, pt. 6, pp. 16, 26–27, quotes the 10/15 court notice.

23. Yodo, pp. 331–334.

24. The 10/22 court reply also disturbed those han leaders who saw themselves being excluded from affairs in the injunction to Yoshinobu to consult with "two or three" on foreign affairs. Satsuma, Tosa, and Hiroshima, whose allies at court were waxing powerful, were seen as the two or three in the court's mind. On 10/23 vassals of some twenty-five or twenty-six han, mostly fudai and shinpan han but also Kumamoto, Saga, Fukuoka, Tottori, Tokushima, Tsu, and Sendai, debated the implications of the 10/22 notice, and on 10/25 spokesmen of twelve of them, mostly fudai, protested the court's statement. Later, on 11/5, Yoshinobu suggested that the phrase be changed to "discuss with the assembled lords," and four days later the court accepted this change. ISK, VII, 304, 332, 341. Shibusawa, IV, 126–127. SNS, bk. 2, pt. 6, pp. 37, 42–43.

25. SNS, bk. 2, pt. 6, pp. 42–43. ISK, VII, 306, 340.

26. DNISK 2983, p. 126. Ishii Takashi, "Tokugawa Yoshinobu no taisei hōkan to shōgunshoku jihyō teishutsu," (Shintei zōho) kokushi taikei geppō 65:1–3 (1967), also discusses the political maneuvering at Kyoto during 67/10/14–26, treating it in terms of bakufu–great han rivalry.

27. DNISK 2964, pp. 2–4; 2965, pp. 72 ff.; 2971, pp. 40–43. Yodo, pp. 319–322.

28. DNISK 2965, pp. 180–190; 2972, p. 94.

29. This summary of Inaba's view is from DNISK 2972, pp. 95–97. Yodo, pp. 329–331, gives the entry with an approximate date of 10/14.

30. DNISK 2972, pp. 98–107. Yodo, pp. 335–342.

31. Shibusawa, IV, 131–133. A more elegant reform scheme was that prepared by Nishi Amane in late 67/11, in which he proposed the creation of a western-style government. Kamekakegawa, "Bakufu kaikaku," pp. 54–56. Thomas R. H. Havens, Nishi Amane and Modern Japanese Thought, pp. 62–64, discusses the scheme briefly.

32. DNISK 2973, pp. 123–125.

33. DNISK 2975, pp. 92–109. ZTJ, V, 1438.

34. DNISK 2979, pp. 93–102; 2980, pp. 132–159; 2990, p. 96. ZTJ, V, 1443–1446. *Ishinshi*, V, 19. ISK, VII, 319.

35. Shibusawa, IV, 147. *Ishinshi*, V, 20–22. ISK, VII, 291.

36. SNS, bk. 2, pt. 6, pp. 5, 14–15, 17, 35. Shibusawa, IV, 142–143, 147–148. *Ishinshi*, V, 20–21. ISK, VII, 300, 313. Shibusawa is citing Yoshinobu's memoir on the matter of reducing bakufu forces in Kyoto.

37. DNISK 2986, pp. 61–65.

38. DNISK 2997, pp. 133 ff. The notice is quoted in Shibusawa, VI, 211–212, and *Yodo*, pp. 383–384.

39. DNISK 2997, pp. 117–133. *Yodo*, pp. 323–326, 356–357. Ozaki, ''Ishin Matsudaira,'' pp. 579–580, argues that Ogyū quit because he could not persuade Edo officials to accept Yoshinobu's orders, but Ozaki has no direct proof of this and nothing in Ogyū's career suggests such an attitude. Ozaki is trying to show, but without evidence, that Ogyū was not a firm bakufu supporter and that Oguri Tadamasa was the bad fellow running affairs.

40. Fox, pp. 209 ff.

41. ISK, VII, 341. Shibusawa, IV, 112–113.

42. ZTJ, V, 1459. DNISK 2991, pp. 107, 114.

43. *Yodo*, pp. 351–354. This is a vaguely identified entry dated 67/10.

44. See Totman, ''Fudai.''

45. DNISK 2992, p. 23. Shibusawa, IV, 137–138, reports Fukui opposition. SNS, bk. 2, pt. 6, pp. 39–40.

46. DNISK 2998, pp. 33–34; 3001, p. 102.

47. DNISK 3029, p. 12, gives the Naeki reply. The daimyo responses in general are mentioned in ISK, VII, 302–500 passim.

48. *Ishinshi*, IV, 759.

49. *Yodo*, pp. 500–511. This is an undated entry, estimated at 1867. The figure of 14,000 is my addition of several lesser figures.

50. These figures are assembled from several sources. DNISK 2944, pp. 66–73; 2949, pp. 75–76; 2972, p. 154; 2979, p. 117; 2991, pp. 92–93; 2995, p. 65; 3007, p. 148; 3010, pp. 50–60; 3011, pp. 73–74. ISK, VII, 236, 244, 292–293. SNS, bk. 2, pt. 5, p. 83. Shibusawa, III, 568. *Katsu zenshū*, XVIII, 432. Jansen, p. 326.

51. DNISK 3016, pp. 39–189, 226. The rumors are scattered widely through DNISK entries.

52. The data on gunrunning are from DNISK 2987, pp. 120–131; 3018, pp. 151–165; 3077, pp. 83–107. Arima pp. 7–8, 12. After discussing problems of monetary conversion, Arima suggests Mexican dollar values of Mini: $36; Enfield: $68; Snider: $104; Sharps: $120.

53. Fox, pp. 333–334.

54. *Ishinshi*, V, 35. SNS, bk. 2, pt. 6, p. 52.

55. This narrative of the Kyoto situation relies heavily on Shibusawa, IV, 160–195, and SNS, bk. 2, pt. 6, pp. 65–94.

56. DNISK 3021, pp. 22, 52–54.

57. DNISK 3024, pp. 109–112.

58. Shibusawa, IV, 176, citing *Sekimukai hikki.* DNISK 3024, pp. 156–165, is one exchange with Yoshikatsu.

59. SNS, bk. 2, pt. 6, pp. 66–67. Shibusawa, VII, 225. DNISK 3024, p. 113.

60. DNISK 3036, pp. 36–47. SNS, bk. 2, pt. 6, p. 82.

61. These estimates are based on figures for Tokugawa force movements contained in DNISK 3035, pp. 102–106, 138, 143, 157; 3041, pp. 66, 92, 107, 123, 127, 138; 3042, pp. 14, 20, 45, 99, 169; and in DNISK *kan* relating to the Fushimi-Toba battles and cited in the next chapter.

62. Shibusawa, IV, 192, reports that the announcement was made on the night of 12/10. DNISK 3039, pp. 71–94, indicates it was done on 12/11.

63. These intra-bakufu discussions are reported in SNS, bk. 2, pt. 6, pp. 87–88.

64. DNISK 3039, pp. 85–86. *Yodo,* p. 412.

65. SNS, bk. 2, pt. 6, pp. 93–94.

66. DNISK 3041, pp. 9–139, and 3042, pp. 14–178, are documents relating to the move to Osaka.

67. This narrative of affairs at Osaka is generally based on Shibusawa, IV, 205–255.

68. DNISK 3041, pp. 11–13. *Yodo,* pp. 417–420.

69. DNISK 3047, pp. 57–68; 3048, pp. 121–122.

70. Tokutomi, LXVI, 44, 48 ff. Fox, pp. 218–219. Medzini, pp. 164–165, does not report Roches's comment.

71. Shibusawa, IV, 174. ISK, VII, 442–443.

72. SNS, bk. 2, pt. 6, pp. 113, 115–116.

73. *Yodo,* pp. 434, 444.

74. Tokutomi, LXVI, 146 ff., follows the Kyoto-Osaka maneuvering carefully, but his estimate of the chance for a peaceful settlement strikes me as overly optimistic.

75. SNS, bk. 2, pt. 6, p. 151. ISK, VII, 485. Fujita Teiichirō, ''Bakumatsu ishin ki ni okeru han kokka shisō no tenkai: Wakayama han no baai,'' *Kinseishi kenkyū* 34:24–33 (1962), is a brief discussion of ''*han* nationalist'' thought in Wakayama in the 1860s that suggests the underlying intellectual factors in decision-making.

76. DNISK 3023, pp. 67–80, 125 ff. Shibusawa, IV, 163, and subsequently *Ishinshi,* V, 67, seem to have confused this command with Yoshinobu's 12/5 order to Katamori not to lobby at court about the Chōshū matter.

77. SNS, bk. 2, pt. 6, p. 153. Shibusawa, IV, 239–241. Tokutomi, LXVI, 186–191.

78. DNISK 2986, pp. 123–129, 143.

79. DNISK 2990, pp. 5–9, 42, 96, 105, 129. Quotation from p. 105, DNISK 3019, pp. 110–119.

80. DNISK 3019, pp. 18–26, 60–81; 3024, pp. 205–212; 3055, pp. 8, 12. *Yodo*, pp. 367, 374–375.

81. Shibusawa, IV, 244–245. *Ishinshi*, V, 117. Ōmachi, pp. 29 ff. *Yodo*, pp. 378–380, 393–400, 405.

82. DNISK 3036, pp. 9 ff.; 3037, p. 132. ZTJ, V, 1498.

83. *Katsu zenshū*, XVIII, 440–441. *Yodo*, pp. 403–405.

84. DNISK 3047, pp. 74–88, 135.

85. ZTJ, V, 1504.

86. ZTJ, V, 1502, 1504. DNISK 3047, p. 150.

87. DNISK 3050, pp. 2–5; 3051, pp. 14–15, 50 ff.; 3055, p. 31. ZTJ, V, 1514–1519. Kataoka Eizaemon and Ishii Tominosuke, ''Tokugawa bakufu makki no Odawara han,'' *Kanagawa shidan* 5:39–41 (1962), present data on this Sagami incident.

88. DNISK 3054, pp. 95 ff., 123; 3058, pp. 47–51.

89. DNISK 3058, pp. 72–76, 94. *Katsu zenshū*, XVIII, 443 ff., indicates that Katsu wrote Inaba on 12/18 advising that the vagaries of the situation made it unwise to send any forces westward, but when or whether Inaba received his letter is not clear to me.

90. DNISK 3063, pp. 83–116.

91. Shibusawa, VII, 251–254. The original has no paragraph breaks.

92. *Yodo*, p. 422.

93. SNS, bk. 2, pt. 6, p. 138.

94. DNISK 3062, pp. 96–97; 3063, pp. 17, 21–24. ZTJ, V, 1530–1534.

95. *Ishinshi*, V, 121–122. Shibusawa, IV, 248. Tokutomi, LXVI, 134, gives figures ranging from 100 to 500 at the Satsuma mansion.

96. ZTJ, V, 1535–1536, 1539–1550, 1554–1556. DNISK 3064, p. 125; 3070, pp. 126–129, 135–145.

CHAPTER 13

1. *Boshin nikki* (Tokyo, 1925), pp. 27–28. Shibusawa, VII, 271–272. There are minor differences in the two versions.

2. Shibusawa, IV, 255–256; VII, 275–277, citing Yoshinobu's memoirs. DNISK 3078, n.p. [ISK, VIII:1–2:3:l]. In 1973 when I was at Tōdai using DNISK, the volumes from 67/12/30 were not yet paginated.

3. These figures are a composite calculated from two standard sets of figures, one for mid-67/12 and one for about 12/30. The mid-12 figures can be found in several sources: Shibusawa, IV, 253–254; SNS, bk. 2, pt. 6, pp. 115–116; DNISK 3074, pp. 7–9, 13–16. The 12/30 figures can be found in ZTJ, V, 1577–1582; Shibusawa, IV, 261–263; DNISK 3074, pp. 41–42. DNISK also carries extensive figures on Aizu and Kuwana and a few on the Kyoto forces. By ''battalion'' I mean only to indicate general numbers. Except for the *hohei* most groups did not have battalion structure. Kojima Shigeo,

''Bakumatsu ishin ni okeru fudai han no dōkō,'' *Rekishi kyōiku* 16(12):21 (1968), reports that five hundred Oshi troops reached Osaka on 12/30 and were put on guard duty in the city.

4. Hosokawa Michio, ''Bakumatsu ishin ki ni okeru Ōgaki han no dōkō,'' *Nihon rekishi* 221:64–65 (1966).

5. This summary of the day is based on DNISK 3080–3082 n.p. [ISK, VIII:6–7:2:a,b,c,d,e,j,k,l,m,o,p,q,r,s,u]; 3082 n.p. [ISK, VIII:8:1:bb, qq,vv, others]. SNS, bk. 2, pt. 7, pp. 1–13. Suematsu, X, 5–13. *Kyūbakufu*, bk. 1, pt. 8, pp. 63–70; pt. 9, pp. 56–61; bk. 3, pt. 10, pp. 31–32. ZTJ, V, 1573–1576. As with the Summer War, this summary is constructed from reports that contain a host of contradictory statements, and choice is often arbitrary but follows the usual canons of historical judgment, doing, I hope, minimal violence to the truth. Tokutomi, LXVI and LXVII, carry extensive reports on the Fushimi-Toba battles.

6. This figure of nine hundred men assumes ninety or more men per unit. One unit personnel roster is given in a DNISK entry, and it lists ninety-two men.

7. This summary of the 1/4 battle is based primarily on data in DNISK 3086 and 3087 n.p. [ISK, VIII:15:1:records of Satsuma, Chōshū, Aizu, and Kuwana plus entries from Owari, Takamatsu, ff, gg, ii]. Also ZTJ, V, 1576. Suematsu, X, 14–18. *Kyūbakufu*, bk. 1, pt. 1, pp. 2–3. SNS, bk 2, pt. 7, p. 13. There is considerable confusion, with some sources describing as events on the Toba road what others attribute to the Fushimi front. Probably the mix-ups are due in part to the two roads converging and disorderly action reaching from one to the other on the riverbanks and swamp and village areas. In part too it may derive from later reports confusing the action of 1/4 with that of the morning of 1/5, which was quite similar.

8. This summary of the 1/5 battle is based on *Kyūbakufu*, bk. 1, pt. 1, pp. 3–4; pt. 9, pp. 62–64. SNS, bk. 2, pt. 7, p. 14. Suematsu, X, 18–22. DNISK 3090 and 3091 n.p. [ISK, VIII:19–20:4:records of Satsuma, Chō-shū, Aizu, Tottori, Tosa, Yodo, w, x, ee].

9. DNISK 3091 n.p. [ISK, VIII:19–20:4:x], which is an Aizu record of considerable value, reports that two mounted French observers were present at the south edge of town near the Great Bridge watching the progress of battle on 1/5. According to a report that Ogasawara sent Itakura on 12/30, four French advisors that Itakura had requested earlier in the month would leave Edo by ship on 68/1/2. If they did so, they could have been in Yodo by 1/5. DNISK 3077, pp. 37–38. Also an entry in RR, II, 323–324, indicates that French advisors had accompanied other units to Osaka in late 67/12.

10. ZTJ, V, 1577.

11. This summary of the 1/6 battle is based on material in DNISK 3093 n.p. [ISK, VIII:23–24:5:Satsuma, Chōshū, Miyazu, Aizu records and x, y, bb, cc, kk].

12. The casualty figures that I have assembled break down in this manner:

Date and Identity	Dead	Wounded	Alternative Data
1/3			
Satsuma	11	36 (6 die later)	
Chōshū	4	19 (2 die later)	
Aizu	26	49 (2 die later)	48 dead by name
Kuwana	8	1 (1 dies later)	
Others	Unknown		
1/4			
Satsuma	9	31 (5 die later)	
Chōshū	4	37 (6 die later)	
Aizu	2	9 (4 die later)	18 dead by name
Tosa	1	6	
Others	Unknown		
1/5			
Satsuma	15	48 (6 die later)	
Chōshū	7	40 (11 die later)	
Aizu	42	75 (11 die later)	49 dead by name
Tottori	0	4	
Others	Unknown		
1/6			
Satsuma	6	29 (3 die later)	
Chōshū	0	10 (1 dies later)	
Hiroshima	0	3	
Tsu	1	8	
Aizu	5	—	72 dead and 133 wounded on 1/5 and 1/6
Others	Unknown		

Alternative totals: bakufu officers: 13 dead, 26 wounded; bakufu men: 150 dead, 24 wounded; Aizu: 500 casualties; Aizu, Kuwana bakufu: 280 dead in four days.

13. DNISK 3093 n.p. [ISK, VIII:23–24:5:x].

14. Arima, pp. 10–11. After discussing the problems of calculating total weapon imports during the 1860s, Arima concludes that probably some 219,000 small arms were imported. Of them most were Mini-type and only

about 13 percent were breechloaders. His earlier figures make it clear that almost all of these latter came after Fushimi-Toba. Maruyama Kunio, "Ishin zengo ni okeru Tōhoku shohan no buki konyū mondai," *Rekishi chiri* 71(1):15–38 (1938), has good data on Tōhoku imports from about 68/3, included Sharps, Springfields, and Enfield rifles. It is perhaps worth noting that in the months following Fushimi-Toba the armies in Japan rapidly switched to breechloading rifles and repeaters with thousands upon thousands of Mini rifles of all sorts, Snider single shots, Sharps, Springfields, and other types of weapons and ammunition flooding the country following the collapse of all bakufu control of the situation, and as *han* armed feverishly and foreign gun-runners worked equally feverishly to profit from Japanese distress.

15. SNS, bk. 1, pt. 5, pp. 38, 44–45; pt. 9, p. 57.

16. *Kyūbakufu*, bk. 1, pt. 1, p. 2. This was a celebratory essay, needless to say.

17. This summary of the retreat east is based on entries in DNISK 3094 n.p. [ISK, VIII:25–26:4:records of Asano Ujisuke and Sawa Tarōzaemon]; 3098 n.p. [ISK, VIII:33:2:a,b,d,i]; 3108 n.p. [ISK, VIII:55–56:2:passim]. SNS, bk 2, pt. 6, pp. 16–26. Shibusawa, IV, 278–297. Tokutomi, LXVII, 89 ff., discusses Yoshinobu's decision to go east.

18. Tokutomi, LXVII, 87–88.

19. Nagai was later ordered to stay at Osaka for a while.

20. ZTJ, V, 1566–1588. RR, II, 390–393. DNISK 3088 n.p. [ISK, VIII:16:3:a,b]; 3094 n.p. [ISK, VIII:25:3:a,b].

21. DNISK 3101 n.p. [ISK, VIII:38:1:citation unclear]. *Yodo*, pp. 514–518, quotes the notices Inaba received but does not indicate when he received or passed them on.

22. ZTJ, V, 1589–1595. DNISK 3103 n.p. [ISK, VIII:44:3:b].

23. DNISK 3108 n.p. cited above in note 17. *Katsu zenshū*, XIX, 4–6, seems a bit confused on chronology. On another matter, it was perhaps at this time that Oguri Tadamasa sent a letter posthaste to a French merchant in Yoko-hama asking for a thousand Chassepot rifles and ammunition, but on 1/13 the merchant replied, refusing to sell the weapons without advance payment of $80,000. Kanai, p. 402.

24. DNISK 3108 n.p. cited above in note 17; 3109 n.p. [ISK, VIII: 59:3:b,c,d]; 3111 n.p. [ISK, VIII:62:2:a; 3:b]; 3116 n.p. [ISK, VIII:70–71:3:a].

25. RR, II, 393.

26. DNISK 3119 n.p. [ISK, VIII:76:2:a,b,c,e,k]. *Yodo*, pp. 521–530. *Boshin nikki*, pp. 91–93, 127. Tokutomi, LXVIII, p. 37. For our purposes it will suffice to say that Yoshinobu had taken his position by 1/16. He still hoped to preserve a more modest Tokugawa domain, however, and would resist imperial assault upon that. This view was modified in succeeding days, and it was not until the latter part of 68/1 or early 68/2 that he was prepared

to accept peacefully whatever the court decided upon. For historians dealing with the imperial aspect of the restoration, this is an important distinction. See, for example, Ishii Takashi, *Ishin no nairan* (Tokyo, 1968), pp. 56–61. Indeed, it is perhaps necessary to point out that the character of events from 67/11 onward is the subject of intense debate in both books and articles among such Japanese historians as Ishii, Haraguchi Kiyoshi, and Inoue Isao. Their concern, however, has to do with the way these events shaped modern Japan and hence the best use of interpretive categories in dealing with the restoration. Since this present study is focused on the fall of the old regime, it has seemed to me unnecessary to discuss the whole *zettai shugi–kōgiseitai* debate.

27. *Boshin nikki*, pp. 91, 116–117. *Katsu zenshū*, XIX, 6.

28. DNISK 3125 n.p. [ISK, VIII:91:1:b,f]. In his memoirs Yoshinobu claims that Roches urged resistance. Medzini, pp. 167–168, does not report it. Ishii, *Ishin no nairan*, pp. 57–60, cites material suggesting that in late 68/1 Yoshinobu was still prepared to discuss alternative strategies with Roches, but the purpose of such strategies is not indicated.

29. *Boshin nikki*, pp. 123–124. Shibusawa, VII, 322.

30. ISK, VIII, 97. DNISK 3130 n.p. [ISK, VIII:97:2:passim].

31. *Boshin nikki*, pp. 124 ff. Shibusawa, IV, 309–310; VII, 323 ff. Tokutomi, LXVIII, 15–25, 94–104, 125–143, deals with the maneuvering to secure the court's goodwill. He asserts, p. 74, that Katsu favored capitulation all along. He may be correct, but his source is Katsu, with no other corroborating evidence.

32. DNISK 3108 n.p. cited above in note 17. Ōmachi, pp. 48–51. Ishii, *Ishin no nairan*, pp. 79–85.

33. This summary statement is based on the numerous entries in ISK, VIII, 39–278 passim, and Ōmachi, pp. 17–52. Tokutomi, LXVIII, covers this topic in detail, but he focuses on the imperial army aspect. Facets of the *fudai han* situation are revealed in a number of monographic studies. Hosokawa, pp. 64–65, traces Ōgaki's switch, which began in late 67/12 and was complete by about 68/1/10. Kataoka and Ishii, pp. 42–46, have data on Odawara's maneuvers, mostly from about 68/1/20. Kageura, pp. 7–8, discusses Matsuyama of Iyo's shift from about 68/1/7, after caution in late 1867. Nishida, pp. 80–81, refers briefly to Hikone's switch in 67/12, acknowledges that evidence on the matter is very scarce, but associates it with *sonnō jōi* sentiment in the *han*. Kitahara describes how Takatō *han* responded to the imperial army's advance in 68/2. Kojima describes the ambiguous actions of Oshi *han* after Fushimi-Toba. Ozaki, ''Ishin Matsudaira,'' discusses briefly the actions in 68/2 of ex-*rōjū* Ogyū Noritaka, lord of Tanoguchi *han*. Mikami Akemi, ''Boshin senki ni okeru Bitchū Matsuyama han ni tsuite: ishin seifu no senryō seisaku no ichiruikei,'' *Rekishi kyōiku* 16(12):44–52 (1968), describes developments in Itakura Katsukiyo's *han*, Matsuyama in Bitchū, from the policy debates of 67/12 through the intense confusion following receipt of news of

Fushimi-Toba to the castle surrender in 68/2. Sugimoto Toshio, ''Fudai Sakura han no kaitai katei: sono haihan chiken e no dōtei,'' *Shundai shigaku* 11:82–111 (1961), discusses Sakura *han*'s actions from 2/24 on, when in response to Yoshinobu's order the daimyo dispatched a vassal force to Kyoto to lobby in the Tokugawa behalf. Okamoto Yukio, ''Bakumatsu Meiji ishin ni okeru gōshi no seijiteki undō no tenkai,'' *Ritsumeikan keizaigaku* 9(2):39–63 (1960), is an interesting study of the internal orientation of one *hatamoto* fief and the imperial army's approach to it.

Recapitulation and Analysis

1. In this regard see the very pertinent essay by David Plath, ''Japan and the Ethics of Fatalism,'' *Anthropological Quarterly* 39 (July 1966).

2. Hugh Borton, ''Peasant Uprisings in Japan of the Tokugawa Period,'' *Transactions of the Asiatic Society of Japan* (2nd series) 16:1–219 (1938). E. S. Crawcour, ''Changes in Japanese Commerce in the Tokugawa Period.'' R. P. Dore, *Education in Tokugawa Japan.* William Hauser, *Economic Institutional Change in Tokugawa Japan: Osaka and the Kinai Cotton Trade.* Charles D. Sheldon, *The Rise of the Merchant Class in Tokugawa Japan, 1600–1868.* Thomas C. Smith, *The Agrarian Origins of Modern Japan.*

3. David Magarey Earl, *Emperor and Nation in Japan.* Harry D. Harootunian, *Toward Restoration.* Herschel Webb, *The Japanese Imperial Institution in the Tokugawa Period* and ''The Development of an Orthodox Attitude toward the Imperial Institution in the Nineteenth Century.''

4. An important statement in this regard is Thomas Huber, ''Chōshū Activists in the Meiji Restoration.'' On status incongruence, see Andrzej Malewski in Reinhard Bendix and Seymour Lipset (eds.), *Class, Status, and Power.*

5. Albert M. Craig, *Chōshū in the Meiji Restoration.*

6. Tetsuo Najita, *Japan.*

7. Kozo Yamamura, *A Study of Samurai Income and Entrepreneurship*, pp. 39, 112 ff., 120 ff.

8. John Whitney Hall, *Tanuma Okitsugu (1719–1788): Forerunner of Modern Japan*, p. 81, notes this bakufu practice of ''providing [daimyo with] extra capital for emergency purposes.''

9. Herman Ooms, *Charismatic Bureaucrat: A Political Biography of Matsudaira Sadanobu, 1758–1829*, gives a sophisticated analysis of late Edo-period bakufu ideology.

Character List

Names of incidental *han*, modern cities and provinces, and most terms previously listed in the glossary of my *Politics in the Tokugawa Bakufu: 1600–1843* are omitted.

Abe Masatō 阿部正外
Akabanebashi 赤羽橋
Akasaka 赤坂
Akitsuki Taneki 秋月種樹
Andō Nobuyuki 安藤信睦
Anenokōji Kintomo 姉小路公知
Ansei 安政
Arima Michisumi 有馬道純
Asahara 淺原
Asakusa 淺草
Asano Ujisuke 淺野氏祐
Azabu 麻布
bakufu satasho 幕府沙汰書
bette gumi 別手組
bokugyū gakari 牧牛掛
boshin 戊辰
Bunkyū 文久
chūkō 中興
chūtai 中隊
daibutsu 大仏
daigakkō 大学校
Daimaru 大丸
daishō kansatsu 大小監察
daitai 大隊
daitōryo 大統領
Date Munenari 伊達宗城
eejanaika エージャナイカ
Egawa Tarōzaemon 江川太郎左衛門
Enomoto Takeaki 榎本武揚
Fujisawa Tsugikane 藤沢次謙

Fujita Koshirō 藤田小四郎
Fukagawa 深川
fukko itashi 復古致し
fukoku kyōhei 富国強兵
Fusa 布佐
Fuse 布施
gaikoku gakari 外国掛
gaikoku jimusōsai 外国事務総裁
Genji 元治
genkan 玄関
Ginza 銀座
gō 合
goji 五時
gosatasho 御沙汰書
Goten yama 御殿山
goyōtoritsugi 御用取次
gun 郡
gun bugyō 軍奉行
gundai 郡代
daishō kansatsu 大小監察
gunji sōsai 軍事総裁
gunkan 軍艦
gunken no sei 郡県ノ制
gun'yaku 軍役
Hachijō jima 八丈島
Hachisuka Narihiro 蜂須賀斉裕
Hamagoten 浜御殿
happō bijin 八方美人
Hara 原
Hara Ichinoshin 原巾之進
Hashimoto 橋本

(543)

Hashimoto Sanai 橋本左内
Hatsukaichi 廿日市
Hayashi Noboru 林昇
heisotsu 兵卒
henkaku 変革
Hennen zatsuroku 編年雑録
Hera 平良
Hiji 日出
Hino 日野
Hirakata 枚方
Hirakawa 平河
Hirayama Keichū 平山敬忠
Hisamatsu Sadaaki (Matsudaira)
　久松定和 (松平)
Hita 日田
Hitotsubashi ke nikki 一橋家日記
Hodogaya 保土ケ谷
hōhei 砲兵
hohei 歩兵
hoi ijō 布衣以上
Honda Tadamoto 本多忠民
Honganji 本願寺
Honjo 本所
Honjō Munehide (Matsudaira)
　本荘宗秀 (松平)
Hori Naotora 堀直虎
hyakushō 百姓
Hyōgo 兵庫
Ichikawa Hirosane 市川弘美
Iikura 飯倉
Ikeda Chōhatsu 池田長発
Ikeda Mochimasa 池田茂政
Ikeda Yoshinori 池田慶徳
Ikeda-ya 池田屋
Ikegami Honmonji 池上本門寺
Ikuno 生野
Imaichi 今市
Inaba Masakuni 稲葉正邦
Inaba Masami 稲葉正巳
Inari 稲荷
Inoue Kiyonao 井上清直
Inoue Masanao 井上正直
Inoue Yoshifumi 井上義斐
Itabashi 板橋
Itakura Katsukiyo 板倉勝静
itsutsu doki 五ツ時
itsutsu han doki 五ツ半時
Iwabana 岩鼻
Iwabuchi juku 岩淵宿
Jigozen 地御前
Jinbō Nagayo 神保長與
Jinbō Sōtoku 神保相徳
jōi 攘夷

Jundōmaru 順動丸
jūtai 銃隊
kachi jūtai 徒銃隊
Kaharu (Kawara) 香春
kaigun kata 海軍方
kaigunsho 海軍所
kaigun sōsai 海軍総裁
kairikugun sōbugyō 海陸軍総奉行
kaiseijo 開成所
Kaiyōmaru 開陽丸
kaku 格
Kamo 鴨
kan 巻
Kanda 神田
Kan'ei 寛永
kanme 貫目
Karafuto 樺太
Kashiwa 柏
Katsu Kaishū 勝海舟
Kawahara 河原
Kawakatsu Hiromichi 川勝広道
Kawakatsu Kōun 川勝広運
Kazunomiya 和宮
Keian 慶安
Keiō 慶応
ken 県
kiito 生糸
kikashi 旗下士
Kiku gun 企救郡
Kikuchi Takayoshi 菊池隆吉
Kimura Katsunori 木村勝教
Kino 木野
kinri shuei sōtoku 禁裏守衛総督
Kiso 木曽
Kitamon shikō 北門史綱
Kiyokawa Hachirō 清河八郎
Kizu 木津
Kizuki 杵築
kōbugattai 公武合体
kōbusho 講武所
Kogane 小金
Koishikawa 小石川
kōken 後見
kokuji gakari 国事縣(掛)
kokunai jimusōsai 国内事務総裁
kokutai 国体
Komabano 駒場野
Komai Chōon 駒井朝温
Komai Nobuoki 駒井信興
Kōmei 孝明
Kondō Isami 近藤勇
Konishi Shirō 小西四郎
Kotetsukan 小鉄艦

Kuba 玖波
kubōsama 公方様
Kubota Bizen no kami 窪田備前守
kumiai jūtai 組合銃隊
Kurimoto Kon 栗本鯤
Kusatsu 草津
Kushido 串戸
Kushima 玖島
Kushun 久春
Kushunnai 久春内
Kusunae 楠苗
Kuze Hirochika 久世広周
Kyōbashi 京橋
Kyōgoku Takaaki 京極高朗
Kyōgoku Takatomi 京極高富
Machiba 町場
machihei jūtai 町兵銃隊
mae shōgun dōyō 前将軍同様
Makino Tadayuki 牧野忠恭
Manabe Akikatsu 間部詮勝
Marunouchi 丸之内
Matsudaira Katamori 松平容保
Matsudaira Mochiaki 松平茂昭
Matsudaira Naokatsu 松平直克
Matsudaira Nobuyoshi 松平信義
Matsudaira Noriyasu 松平乗全
Matsudaira Sadaaki 松平定敬
Matsudaira Shungaku 松平春嶽
Matsudaira Yorinori 松平頼徳
Matsudaira Yoritane 松平頼胤
Matsugahara 松ケ原
Matsui Yasunao 松井康直
Matsumae Takahiro 松前崇広
Meguro 目黒
Meiji 明治
Meisankō iseki 明山公遺績
mimawari 見回り
Misoguchi Shōnyo 溝口勝如
Mitsui 三井
Miyauchi 宮内
Mizuno Tadakiyo 水野忠精
Mizuno Tadamoto 水野忠幹
Mizuno Tadanori 水野忠徳
mon 文
Monbushō 文部省
monme 匁
Mōri Sadahiro 毛利定広
Mōri Yoshichika 毛利慶親
Mori Arinori 森有礼
Mukōyama Eigorō 向山栄五郎
Nagai Naokoto 永井尚服
Nagai Naomune 永井尚志
Nagai Uta 永井雅樂

Nagano Shuzen 長野主膳
naidaijin 内大臣
Naitō Nobuchika 内藤信親
Naitō Shinjuku 内藤新宿
naiyū gaikan 内憂外患
Nakaminato 那珂湊
Nakane Yukie 中根雪江
Nakatsugawa 中津川
Nakayama 中山
Namamugi 生麦
nami 並
Nihonbashi 二本橋
ninen naku uchiharai 二念なく打挨
Nishi Amane 西周
Nishikubo 西久保
Nishimarushita 西丸下
nōhei 農兵
Ogasawara Nagamichi 小笠原長行
Ogawamachi 小川町
Oguri Masayasu 小栗政寧
Oguri Tadamasa 小栗忠順
Ogyū Noritaka (Matsudaira) 大給乗
　謨(松平)
Ōhara Shigetomi 大原重徳
Ōhira 大平
Okabe Nagatsune 岡部長常
Okada Tadayoshi 岡田忠養
Okata 小方
Ōkōchi Masatada (Matsudaira) 大河
　内正質 (松平)
Ōkubo Ichiō 大久保一翁
Ōkubo Tadanori 大久保忠宣
Ōkubo Tadayuki 大久保忠恕
Ōkubo Toshimichi 大久保利通
okumuki 奥向
okuzume jūtai 奥詰銃隊
Ōno 大野
Osegawa 小瀬川
ōsei fukko 王政復古
Ōshima 大島
Ōta Sukeharu 大田資始
Ōtake 大竹
Ōtemae 大手前
Ōzeki Masuhiro 大関増裕
ri 里
rikugun sōsai 陸軍総裁
Ryōgoku 両国
Saigō Takamori 西郷隆盛
Sakai Tadamasu 酒井忠毗
Sakai Tadashige 酒井忠績
Sakai Tadasumi 酒井忠篤
Sakai Tadatō 酒井忠惇
sake 酒

sakite 先手
sakujikata 作事方
Sakuma Nobuhisa 佐久間信久
Sakuma Shōzan 佐久間象山
Sanbanchō 三番町
sanbantō 三番頭
Sanjō Sanetomi 三條実万
sanpei 三兵
sanpei takuchiiki 三兵タクチイキ
sappei 撤兵
Sawa Kanshichirō 沢勘七郎
seichō senpō sōtoku 征長先鋒総督
seiji sōsai 政事総裁
seiken o henjō 政権を返上
Sekimukai hikki 昔夢会筆記
Sendagaya 千駄ケ谷
Senju 千住
sennin gumi 千人組
sesshō 摂政
Shiba 芝
Shibata Masanaka 柴田剛中
Shibusawa Eiichi 渋沢栄一
Shibusawa Kisaku 渋沢喜作
shihai 支配
shihaichi shichū 支配地市中
Shijūhassaka 四十八坂
Shimazu Hisamitsu 島津久光
Shinagawa 品川
Shinchōgumi 新徴組
shinpei 親兵
Shinsengumi 新選組
shin yūgekitai 新遊撃隊
shishi 志士
Shōdoshima 小豆島
shōtai 小隊
shōtai undō 小隊運動
shugoshoku 守護職
sobatōdori 側頭取
sonnō 尊王
Suwa Tadamasa 諏訪忠誠
Suzuki Toyojirō 鈴木豊次郎
Suzuki Tsunetarō 鈴木恒太郎
Tachibana Taneyuki 立花種恭
Taiheimaru 太平丸
taihōtai shōjūtai 大砲隊小銃隊
Takashima Shūhan 高島秋帆
Takasugi Shinsaku 高杉晋作
Takeda Kōunsai 武田耕雲斉
Takemoto Masaaki 竹本正明
Takenaka Shigemoto 竹中重固
Takikawa Tomoshige 滝川具挙
Tamaru Naonobu 田丸直允
Tameike 溜池

Tanashi 田無
Tanuma Okitaka 田沼意尊
teate fuchi 手当扶持
Teibō nikki 丁卯日記
Tenchūgumi 天誅組
tenka 天下
tenka shūgi 天下衆議
tenka yūshi 天下有志
teppō daitai 鉄砲大隊
Toba 鳥羽 (上と下)
Toda Tadayuki 戸田忠行
Tōdaiji 東大寺
Togawa Hanzaburō 戸川鉾三郎
Togawa Yasukiyo nikki 戸川安清日記
Toge 峠
Tokugawa Akitake 徳川昭武
Tokugawa Iemochi 徳川家茂
Tokugawa Mochiharu 徳川茂栄
Tokugawa Mochinori 徳川茂徳
Tokugawa Mochitsugu 徳川茂承
Tokugawa Yoshiatsu 徳川慶篤
Tokugawa Yoshikatsu 徳川慶勝
Tokugawa Yoshinobu 徳川慶喜
Tokugawa Yoshiyori 徳川慶頼
Tokumaruhara 徳丸原
Tokunaga Masachika 徳永昌新
Tokuyama Kōtarō 徳山鋼太郎
ton'ya 問屋
Totsuka 戸塚
Tōzenji 東禅寺
Tsuchiya Masanao 土屋正直
Tsuchiya Tomonao 土屋寅直
Tsuda 津田
Tsuda Mamichi 津田真道
Tsukahara Masayoshi 塚原昌義
tsuki karō 附家老
Tsukuba 筑波
Udono Chōei 鵜殿長鋭
Ueno 上野
uesama 上様
ukonoe taishō 右近衛大将
Umezawa Ryō 梅沢亮
unjō 運上
Uragami 浦上
Utsuki Rokunojō 宇津木六之丞
Uzen 羽前
Wagi 和木
Wakizaka Yasuaya 脇坂安斐
Wakizaka Yasuori 脇坂安宅
Yahata 八幡
yakuchi 役知
yaku fuchi 役扶持
yakuryō 役料

Yamaguchi Naoki 山口直毅
Yamashiro no kami 山城守
Yamauchi Toyonori 山内豊範
Yamauchi Yōdō 山内容堂
Yamazaki 山崎
Yoda Sasuke 依田左助
Yoda Yūtarō 依田雄太郎
Yodo 淀
Yokoi Shōnan 横井小楠
yonaoshi 世直し

Yoshinobukō gojikki 慶喜公御実記
Yoshiwara 吉原
Yotsuya 四谷
yūgekitai 遊撃隊
Yūki 結城
zaikata gakari 在方掛
zeni 銭
Zōjōji 増上寺
Zoku tsūshin zenran 続通信全覧

Bibliographical Essay

DNISK

OTHER MATERIALS USED

TWO PROBLEMS
1. *On Dating Events*
2. *The Meiji Bias*

DNISK

This study of the Tokugawa collapse has been constructed in great part from materials in DNISK, "Dai Nihon ishin shiryō kōhon" (Manuscript of historical materials on the restoration). DNISK is located at the Shiryō hensanjo or Historiographical Institute of Tokyo University. It is by far the greatest collection of historical materials relating to the Meiji restoration but has been almost unused by western scholars. Because it is one of the great historiographical triumphs of humankind, it deserves more fame than it has received.[1]

DNISK is a collection of historical materials dealing with the years 1846–1873. It was assembled during the two decades beginning in May 1911, when an imperial edict established the Ishin shiryō hensankai or Society for Compilation of Records of the Restoration under authority of the Monbushō or Ministry of Education. The society's staff initially numbered thirty-one, added eleven a year later, and eventually numbered nearly fifty. They gathered almost all available documents and documentary collections, including the great collections of the major daimyo and the bakufu's massive records of diplomatic correspondence, to form a corpus of some fifteen thousand titles. A single "title" in the corpus thus might constitute any independent item from a small diary to a multi-volume compendium of documents.

The compilers copied the documents in a careful, readable printed style, returned most originals to their home repositories, and kept the copies, which as a collection was entitled "Ishin shiryō bon."[2] From these copies they then constructed DNISK by the laborious process of re-copying all the material in day-by-day entries, grouping together all the entries of each day, and then regrouping them about specific topics of that day in an orderly and consistent manner. These ordered daily entries were then bound into volumes *(kan)* of some 100 to 150 double pages apiece. The initial task of compilation was completed in 1931, twenty years after it began, and its product was DNISK, in 4180 *kan*.

As the compilers were preparing to publish the material, they issued *Ishin shiryō kōyō* (ISK), a ten-volume table of contents. It lists all daily topics in the order in which they appear in DNISK. Following each topic entry ISK lists in order of their appearance in DNISK the sources from which entries have been taken. Thus, to give one example, on page 655 of volume V of ISK the first entry under the date 64/11/19 is this: ''The bakufu announces the departure of senior councillor Matsumae Ta-kahiro and junior councillor Tachibana Taneyuki for Chōshū.'' Appended to the entry in smaller type are the titles of thirteen historical sources: ''Bakufu satasho,'' ''Hitotsubashi ke nikki,'' ''Kitamon shikō,'' ''Hennen zatsuroku,'' and nine others. This means that entries dealing with Matsumae's trip were found in those thirteen sources and appear in DNISK in that sequence—the more pertinent, precise, and reliable records listed first, the more marginal materials last.

Publication of DNISK itself began in 1938, the bound volumes being titled *Dai Nihon ishin shiryō*. They appeared in three concurrent series, with volumes for 1846/2, 1854/1, and 1858/1 appearing first. World War II halted the work after nineteen volumes had appeared. Those nine-teen, which have some seven to eight hundred pages apiece, cover the periods 46/2–47/8, 54/1–3, and 58/1–5. The work was not restart-ed after the war, and so there exist only those few finished volumes of a projected several hundred. However, much of the material of which DNISK is composed has been published elsewhere in original or slightly modified form. Some of the published works are mentioned below in the discussion of other materials used in this study.

After the war most materials of the Ishin shiryō hensankai were trans-ferred to Tokyo University and incorporated in the Historiographical In-stitute at the Hongō campus. The institute, with newly expanded storage space, has recently been able to organize ''Ishin shiryō bon,'' and it is now available for scholarly use in the institute's new reading room. The institute has also completed pagination of DNISK, and it too is available there for perusal in accord with the institute's established procedures for use of special collections.

Recently a new *Dai Nihon ishin shiryō* series has been started. The new series has abandoned the DNISK format and instead publishes materials *in extenso*. The first major work in this series is entitled *Ii ke shiryō* and consists of newly released materials of Hikone dealing with the period 1858–1860. Those volumes, incidentally, are not the *Ii ke shiryō: bakumatsu fūbun tansakusho* volumes used in this study.

The internal order of DNISK, as one can see by perusing ISK, is straightforward. A day's topics are listed in sequence beginning with events concerning the emperor and then progressing through the court, the bakufu, the *han*, lesser samurai, commoners, and finally foreigners. Materials are ordered chronologically through the days of the month, with entries titled ''this month'' or ''recently'' at the end of a month and entries titled ''this year'' at the end of each year. For many trivial events only one or two records exist, and those are incorporated in larger topics where appropriate. For example, materials pertaining to Matsumae's visit to the court in 64/12 are assembled under four entries for 64/11/19, 12/15, 12/24, and 65/1/8. Those are the dates of his order to go west, his arrival in Kyoto, his message to the court, and his return to Edo. The 11/19 entry, mentioned above in reference to ISK, contains materials concerning development of his mission in prior days. The 12/15 entry contains mentions of his departure from Edo, his progress westward, and his activities at Kyoto. The 12/24 entry contains mentions of his message and of his plans to return east. The 1/8 entry contains material pertaining to his return, his entry into Edo, and his actions there upon return.

Inevitably there is some duplication of data, both in terms of similar information from several sources and in terms of the same entries appearing in two or more topics of the manuscript. And much stray information appears in many topics. Nonetheless, the mode of organization enables a reader to peruse most materials pertaining to a vast array of events of even minor historical significance without having to hunt through a host of scattered sources.

The very massiveness of DNISK makes its use difficult unless it is approached methodically. The strategy I used was this. After acquiring a basic familiarity with the 1860s, I went through ISK carefully, preparing on note cards an accurate, chronologically ordered collection of entries, such as those referring to Matsumae's trip, that seemed to deserve reading in DNISK. Preparing the notecard collection gave me a much more precise sense of the way the bakufu and its problems articulated with each other and with other aspects of the age. It also made apparent which historical sources most frequently contained pertinent materials. Armed thus with a few thousand specific dated entries to peruse and with a clearer sense of materials and the historical rhythm and relationships of the topic,

I turned to DNISK. It was then possible to obtain the pertinent *kan*
quickly, locate and read the material, collate it, and develop a reliable
body of basic information. The material was then available on cards identified by topic, date, and ISK and DNISK locations, and it was ready for
free reorganization, combination with data from other sources, and development into the present study.

As one works in DNISK, one realizes there are some awkwardnesses
in using it. One problem is that the daily breakdown makes it difficult to
find sequential entries from a particular source, and given the frequent
use of foreshortened names and nicknames of persons, places, and
events, some entries are difficult to decipher without antecedent information. Also at times one finds it difficult to identify the source of an entry
that may simply be called, for example, so-and-so's diary. Unless one
knows who so-and-so is, the entry's value is hard to assess. Fortunately
the institute has a full index of the sources used in DNISK that helps in
tracking down such information. Persons using DNISK will also find that
occasional entries do not appear in the manuscript in the order listed in
ISK due to a few final changes made in organizing the material for publication. For these reasons a researcher sooner or later will wish to inspect
the most valuable materials in their original form in order to see the
longer run of developments from a particular viewpoint. That can be
done by turning to the published volumes or, in the case of unpublished
sources, to the "Ishin shiryō bon."

DNISK is primarily political history, and students of other specialties,
such as local or social history, will have to supplement their study with
unpublished materials or with materials more recently assembled and
published in the many smaller compilation projects of postwar Japan. The
best point of departure for identifying published works is the several
volumes of cumulative bibliography by Honjō Eijirō, *Nihon keizaishi dai
ichi [ni, san,* and so forth] *bunken*. For recent publications the bibliographical sections of historical journals, most notably *Shigaku zasshi*, are
also extremely helpful. However, for almost any project one might
undertake dealing with Japan between 1846 and 1873, DNISK remains
a first and extremely valuable source of information organized with integrity and care.

OTHER MATERIALS USED

In preparing this study, I was unable to read in "Ishin shiryō bon"
because it was not ready for use during my first visit to the institute and
was in storage due to remodeling in progress during the second. I did,

however, use several of the published materials included in DNISK. Of those, some deserve particular comment.

The greatest collection of published sources on the 1860s is the 192-volume *Nihon shiseki kyōkai sōsho*, which consists of records, diaries, documents, and compilations of the nobility, *han*, and major political figures. The volumes deal with central political history for the most part and are now in the process of being republished. Several of the works discussed below have appeared in that series, as indicated in the bibliography.

The official records of the bakufu have been published as *Zoku Tokugawa jikki* (ZTJ). It is the continuation of *Tokugawa jikki* (Veritable records of the Tokugawa), modeled on the great official histories of Chinese dynasties. Organized, like DNISK, on a day-to-day basis, ZTJ records formal actions of the bakufu during the reigns of the five shogun from Ienari to Yoshinobu (1786–1868). Most ZTJ entries are routine notices of appointment, promotion, and dismissal of officials and records of the many ritual observances of the regime. But it also contains a few political commentaries, several battle reports, and materials on institutional reform. As noted below, its manner of dating records causes minor problems, and its failure to specify the exact source of orders is at times a serious shortcoming. Nevertheless it is an invaluable source of basic information, and cumulatively its entries do convey a sense of the ebb and flow of events.

There is a gap in ZTJ because the records of the period 64/6 to 65/6 were lost. The gap can largely be overcome, however, by reference to other basic chronological records. Two of these, *Kaei Meiji nenkanroku* and *Ryūei honin*, are both published, the latter in six volumes of *Dai Nihon kinsei shiryō*. More basic are the ''Bakufu satasho'' and ''Gosatasho'' (Official announcements of the bakufu), which are in DNISK. Or one can simply use the entries of ISK, which constitute the most accurate and complete chronological listing of all, even though ISK is not an original source, properly speaking.

The next most ''bakufu-centric'' general work is Shibusawa Eiichi's great piece of scholarship, *Tokugawa Yoshinobukō den*. Both it and Kitahara Masanaga's work on Matsudaira Katamori, *Shichinenshi*, are discussed in later portions of this essay.

Several related *han* have furnished extensive documentation on the 1860s. Most well known and most useful for general political history are the chronological narratives of Fukui *han*. The major ones are these: *Sakumu kiji*, four volumes covering the years 1853–1858; *Saimu kiji*, a slim volume covering Shungaku's activities at Edo during 62/4–8; *Zoku saimu kiji*, six volumes covering 62/8/27 to 67/10/13; *Teibō nikki*, a ninety-page diary of Nakane Yukie covering the period 67/10/13–12/28 and published in volume 4 of *Shiseki zassan* in 1912; and finally *Boshin nikki*, one volume covering the period 68/1/1–8/6. There are several other published works, such as Shungaku's reminiscences, *Itsuji shiho*, and, more important, substantial unpublished materials that have been organized and are available for study at Fukui.

Because of the excellence and detail of these records, historians have relied heavily upon them with the consequence that Fukui's role in late bakufu affairs has been rather exaggerated. Thus Shungaku is sometimes described as a major figure in the bakufu's last decade, but in fact except for a few months in the periods 62/6–63/3, 66/8–9, and 67/12–68/4 he was unable to play an effective role in affairs and instead contented himself most of the time with corresponding from afar. Ironically one upshot of Shungaku's impotence was the remarkable collection of correspondence that Fukui men have published and that has led to the exaggeration of his influence. Properly used, however, this great documentary collection can give an excellent insight into the process of Tokugawa failure and the search for a new order as seen by a concerned participant and observer.

For my purposes the next most valuable related *han* work was *Mito han shiryō* (MHS). It is a splendidly organized compilation whose strong political slant does not really damage it because the compilers' position is so overt and unequivocal. Another even greater work, but one that I used only in conjunction with the Summer War, is *Nanki Tokugawa shi*, a massive and carefully constructed compendium of records of Kii *han*.

Katsu Kaishū, like Shungaku, has furnished valuable materials. In this study I found helpful information in many entries of his diary, ''Kaishū nikki,'' which fills two volumes in the recently published *Katsu Kaishū zenshū*. But most useful was one of his later great works of compilation, *Rikugun rekishi*. It is a topically organized compendium of documents relating to bakufu military matters from the 1840s to 1868. Many of the records lack complete dates; a few of them are incorrectly located; and it is a rather difficult work to use because the topics are not as distinct as the internal organization suggests. Nevertheless it is a marvelous source of information on bakufu military policies. I did not use Katsu's two other great compilations, *Kaigun rekishi* and *Kaikoku kigen*, which like *Rikugun rekishi* have recently been republished.

Concerning bakufu foreign policy, as W. G. Beasley has pointed out in the bibliography of his splendid *Select Documents on Japanese Foreign Policy, 1853–1868*, several volumes on *bakumatsu* foreign relations have been published and continue to appear in the *Dai Nihon komonjo* subseries *Bakumatsu gaikoku kankei monjo*. Fortunately 1860s foreign relations have been carefully studied in both English and Japanese, and so I have been able to rely on works such as those of Beasley and Ōtsuka Takematsu's *Bakumatsu gaikōshi no kenkyū*, supplementing them when necessary with other source materials, usually from ''Zoku tsushin zenran'' entries in DNISK. ''Zoku tsushin zenran'' (The complete correspondence continued) is a massive manuscript in its own right. It also is located at the Shiryō hensanjo and is the basic source of documents published in *Bakumatsu gaikoku kankei monjo*.

Another primary source that proved very valuable is *Kanbu tsuki*, a skillfully organized assemblage of documents collected by a Sendai *han* vassal. It pertains to affairs, mostly at Edo, during the years 1862–1864. Yamakawa Hiroshi's *Kyoto shugoshoku shimatsu* is a collection of documents pertaining to Katamori of Aizu and connected by a running narrative. I used it only occasionally, however, relying instead on the more extensive and more precise *Shichinenshi*. A recently republished and very fascinating work is *Kyūbakufu*. It is a journal published in the 1890s by old Tokugawa survivors and is chock-full of memoirs, reminiscences, discussions of old events, customs, and regulations of the *ancien régime*.

Turning to secondary works, a useful and well-organized collection of essays on problems of restoration historiography is the six-volume *Meiji ishinshi kenkyū kōza*. It provides not only an introduction to the history proper but also a valuable guide to interpretive issues, main viewpoints, and the literature of the restoration. Early in my study I read through *Ishinshi*, the brilliant, orthodox history of the restoration produced in the 1930s by scholars of the Ishin shiryō hensankai. The work is valuable as an extremely reliable, old-fashioned political history. Moreover the index volume is the single most valuable research tool on the restoration. From beginning to end of this project it has been indispensable for the information in its appendices about officeholders and daimyo domains.

As the research progressed, I used the narrative section of Shibusawa's biography of Yoshinobu extensively. And in some portions I relied heavily on a major study that is rarely used, Tokutomi Iichirō's 100-volume *Kinsei Nihon kokumin shi*, of which volumes 46 to 70 cover the years 1862–1868. The work focuses on central politics and consists mostly of quoted documents interspersed with author's comments and connecting sections of narrative. It is a remarkable feat of organization and argument. It adheres faithfully to the Meiji bias discussed further on in this essay, and it gives a spicy narrative story of the restoration. I used Tokutomi's magnum opus extensively in preparing materials for the years 1862–1864, which chapters were initially written in the United States. As Tokutomi got nearer and nearer the Great Event, however, he focused more and more narrowly on the work of the Great Leaders, and so his study had less and less relevance for my research. Hence for the period 1865–1868, which chapters were initially written in Tokyo, I was able to dispense with Tokutomi and checked his volumes later only for stray information.

The other secondary Japanese works I found most useful were the many monographs published in various learned journals. These, which I consulted after completing the research in DNISK, shed additional light on a host of particular matters. A few longer studies, such as Ōtsuka's diplomatic history, also contained very useful material. The more well-known interpretive essays did not prove very useful for this study, however, primarily because they examine the historical character of those who overthrew the old regime and that of the new regime they constructed. These aspects of the restoration being marginal to this study, the arguments of those works tended not to be germane.

Two Problems

In doing this study, I encountered two problems with bibliographical dimensions. They are problems of precision in dating and the attitudes toward the Tokugawa collapse found in Meiji-period scholarship.

1. On Dating Events

One virtue of DNISK is that it helps solve many vexing problems of confusion in dating. Sometimes confusion arises simply due to dating errors that appear in the documents themselves or were made in logging documents or in later transcription. Many diary entries, especially by men reporting second-hand information, have dating errors. Errors in logging appear in many documentary collections. Among published works, *Shichinenshi* entries are erroneously dated so often that dates therein can be used only with the greatest care. *Ogasawara Ikinokami Nagamichi* also has frequent dating errors.

A less simple cause of confusion about dates of bakufu orders is the manner in which those orders were prepared. The process seems to have been essentially this. On a given day senior and junior councillors and other appropriate officials would reach a decision on some matter and decide to issue an order to effect the decision. On that day or the next the senior councillors would determine the specific phrasing of the order, and the councillor on duty *(tsukiban rōjū)* would then have it delivered to the proper officials, usually members of the inspectorate, for appropriate dissemination. The council order would be phrased as such and such an order by act of the council (or by wish of the shogun), delivered by the named councillor on duty, addressed to the inspectorate, and dated by date of its preparation by the councillor on duty.

The inspectors would then have the order rewritten, its body and origins essentially unchanged, but addressed to whomever it was aimed at (for example, a specific daimyo), forwarded by inspector so-and-so, and dated by the date it was rewritten and dispatched. Then that order would be delivered to its recipient, or else a representative of the recipient would be ordered to come for it. The order would then reach its destination, whether in Edo or elsewhere, and it would there be logged in the records of the recipient by date of receipt or in some instances by date of reply.

Thus, depending upon the source of the record a researcher has in hand, the bakufu order will be dated according to date of decision, date of senior council transcription, date of subordinate distribution, or date of receipt. The first three were often in succession, but the last might be as much as a month later.

The ZTJ entries for bakufu orders are quite consistently one day later than the date of initial senior council orders as shown in basic records such as ''Bakufu satasho.'' It appears that ZTJ entries are listed by the date in which copies of notices were received in the records office as a regular part of the distribution process.

This dating practice led to complications during the 1860s when the shogun and some senior councillors spent long periods of time at Kyoto and Osaka. Orders were issued from all three cities by senior councillors, but ZTJ entries (and entries in other collections such as MHS for that matter) usually do not indicate the source of such orders. Moreover ZTJ sometimes (but not always) dates orders according to date of logging at the Edo records office even though they may have been issued at Kyoto or Osaka some two weeks previously. For periods when the bakufu was split, therefore, ZTJ's failure to identify precisely the source of orders or to date them consistently creates an illusion of confusion and contradiction that is dispelled only when one separates the decisions of officials at Edo from those in the Kinai. DNISK is particularly helpful here because its entries enable one to identify reliably both the source and the date of most such orders.

A different dating problem arises from the use in some *bakumatsu* literature of two dating systems: the established Japanese style and the recently introduced western style for both days of the year and time of day. Concerning days of the year, in diplomatic correspondence one finds both systems used, and care must be taken in identifying dates correctly. A few secondary Japanese sources do not convert dates at all, and Tokutomi sometimes does not identify the dating system used in documents he quotes. In those western secondary works in which dates are all converted to the Gregorian calendar, errors of conversion sometimes appear. To check dates, by far the best and fullest sources for accurate dating are ISK and DNISK.

Concerning time of day, most documents use the older style, but during the 1860s some men had western timepieces and proudly recorded time accordingly. Usually the two can be distinguished easily enough by the way they were written. Thus the fifth hour old-style (eight o'clock) was written in *kanji* as *itsutsu doki* and the fifth and one-half hour (nine o'clock) as *itsutsuhan doki*, whereas five o'clock was most commonly written *goji*, although other practices appear in some sources.

Years and hours are occasionally also given in terms of the Chinese sexagenary calendar: *boshin* for 1868, for example. The yearly names are listed in standard encyclopedic chronologies *(nenpyō)*. Paul Y. Tsuchihashi's *Japanese Chronological Tables* explains the dating and conversion systems fully, and Mitamura Engyo's *Edo seikatsu jiten* has a good hourly diagram inside its front cover. In this study I have adhered to the Japanese day of the year but have converted time of day to the western clock. For readers' convenience simplified calendrical and hourly conversion charts have been included in the appendices.

2. The Meiji Bias

Two complementary sets of attitudes, what I call "the Meiji bias," pervade the later Meiji literature on the 1860s. In the many memoirs and commentaries of the era one repeatedly finds the former participants on all sides of *bakumatsu* politics or their apologists insisting upon the patriotic nature of their motivation. One finds, too, scornful reference to "the *fudai* daimyo," "bakufu officials," and "liege vassals." These general types are presented as the unimaginative, selfish, and unworthy forces who, through their ineptness rather than their dangerous ability, damaged the imperial house, wrecked the unity of court, bakufu, and lords, endangered Japan, and so led to the Tokugawa collapse by alienating well-intentioned patriots and forcing them to wage civil war.

Some of these comments are of 1860s origin and are the judgments one would expect of those locked in fierce political combat. But others are comments of the 1890s or later, written long after scapegoating and vindication should have ceased to be necessary. The persistence of the stereotypes and the absence of a literature in which the victors glorify themselves by lionizing those whom they defeated are probably reflections of the ideological strategy of the insurgents in 1868 and subsequently of the Meiji leaders. Examination of that strategy may give us insight into the historiography of the vanquished, most notably Yoshinobu and Katamori but also others among the losers.

The situational dynamic of the insurgents' ideological strategy seems straightforward. During the sixties, as we saw, political combat constantly circled around the rhetoric of *sonnō jōi* as politicians struggled to derive strength from the powerful forces of ethnic sensibility that the imperialist intrusion had activated. Even during 1867 after the rhetoric seemed to have lost its persuasiveness to those invoking it, it was still deemed sufficiently valuable to be used. Yoshinobu tied his midyear triumph to imperial loyalism, and at year's end he played the loyalist line out to its last measure, in the end saving his own skin by doing so. His very stance, however, forced the insurgents to claim an even more profound loyalism because the emperor was the most promising, or perhaps the only, symbol that could be invoked to win support from the large numbers of political fence-sitters, whose choice of sides would likely determine the outcome of the contest.

The loyalist strategy quickly paid off, as we have seen. But that very success soon bound the insurgent leaders to the court regardless of their own convictions because abandoning the symbol would have risked alienating the supporters. Similarly, to avoid alienating their many supporters-of-convenience, some of whom had long associations with one or another part of the vanquished, the victors avoided both lionizing and savage punishing, attempting instead to heal the wounds by reducing the visibility of the whole deplorable affair and treating it as a national triumph of imperial virtue over decadence and petty vice.

One consequence of the strategy, to note it in passing, was that it encouraged later generations of historians to minimize the violence and war of the restoration and to stress instead the relative absence of upheaval and conflict, reading into that situation various historical lessons.[3]

More germane to our task here, the victors' strategy provided quite clear guidelines for those seeking rehabilitation of themselves or their heroes. On the one hand one must dissociate himself from the unworthy vanquished, and on the other he must establish the purity of his own imperial commitment. This dual task was not of equal importance to all. Those, such as Tosa, Owari, and Fukui, who had been associated to the bitter end with court-daimyo *kōbugattai* efforts, had not been the princi-

pal losers in 1868 and had not been punished. But their political judgment had been impugned, and thus even for them there was an issue to
be set right. During the political struggles of the sixties they had frequently denounced "*fudai* daimyo," "officials," and so on, and by
1868 they had built up in *han* correspondence a considerable literature
demonstrative of their moral indignation at the bakufu. That literature
was of value in later years in helping them put the desired ethical distance
between themselves and the vanquished. Moreover it helped them to
present themselves as champions of change whose essential purpose was
the same as that of the victors. Indeed, since military triumph was not
being glorified, they were able to describe their *kōbugattai* strategy as
morally superior to the Satsuma-Chōshū strategy of armed conquest.
That posture doubtless helped them protect their interests and assure their
historic glory.

The Meiji bias appears in *Zoku saimu kiji*, the Fukui source I used
most fully. It shows up mainly in the choice of material included or omitted. The volumes quite consistently include material pejorative of senior
officials at Edo but omit materials that reveal the element of selfishness,
inconsistency, or weakness of Shungaku in particular and also of Yoshinobu. Where possible, too, they present Shungaku's actions as motivated by a desire to enhance imperial authority. It is in correspondence
published elsewhere or not published at all that one discovers the less
heroic dimensions of these figures, and DNISK helps one find these other
sources.

Apart from the daimyo of the northeast, whose conduct in 1868
makes them a special and separate problem, those associated with the
bakufu were the primary losers, and for them rehabilitation was both
more needed and harder to achieve. Their failure carried with it not only a
negative judgment on their competence but also a scathing condemnation
of their integrity. For them rehabilitation was initially a way to save their
lives and later a means to reassert their basic ethical worth. The way the
Meiji bias shaped attempts to rehabilitate those associated with the
bakufu was most evident in the cases of Matsudaira Katamori, Ogasawara Nagamichi, and Tokugawa Yoshinobu, but also, in a sense, Oguri
Tadamasa and Katsu Kaishū.

Of these five, Katamori, Ogasawara, and Oguri emerged as the great
villains most badly in need of rehabilitation. The first and most successful
effort on their behalf was that made for Katamori. During the 1860s
Aizu had actually been associated mostly with the Owari-Fukui *kōbugattai* group. But as events worked out, Katamori's long service at Kyoto
drew him so deeply into the political crisis that despite Aizu efforts to

avoid disaster, the *han* ended up the archenemy of the conquerors. In part that was perhaps because the very strength of Aizu's ethical posture constituted a major challenge to the ethical pretensions of the conquerors. Given the stance adopted by the victors, however, it followed that Aizu must have been particularly antiloyalist and pro-Tokugawa. For Aizu historians, therefore, the problem of rehabilitation was not simply to demonstrate à la Fukui the soundness of *kōbugattai* but to show that Aizu had been as loyal as the most loyal all along and as badly at odds with officialdom as the others. In his *Shichinenshi*, published in 1904, Kitahara Masanaga was remarkably successful in achieving that task.

Shichinenshi is a large two-volume record of Matsudaira Katamori's role as Kyoto *shugoshoku* or protector. It covers chronologically the years 1862–1868 and consists of a great assemblage of documents connected by narrative. Some of the documents, plus many others, can be found in the six-volume record *Aizu han chō kiroku*, which has been published by Nihon shiseki kyōkai, but which I used only as items in my DNISK reading.

Kitahara has been able to demonstrate that Katamori was one of the most consistent and sincere supporters of *sonnō jōi* among all the high-status political figures of the sixties. He could do so because much of Katamori's correspondence was with officials at Edo, whom he was trying to influence, and he constantly used arguments of imperial loyalism in pressing his opinions. In consequence those who opposed him were easily made to appear opposed to that loyalism, and so Katamori emerges in the correspondence as a valiant loyalist who failed to preserve court-bakufu unity because of Edo's intransigence. Katamori was confounded by unworthy others such as selfish officials, stubborn bureaucrats, and corrupt *fudai* daimyo. But he was also trapped by his duty to his Tokugawa lord, and Aizu's vassals in turn were trapped by duty to their lord, and so their defeat was not a result of their immorality but a fate determined by the malign conduct of others and their own devotion to principle. The whole argument is of course a self-serving one, but the evidence supporting it is impressive, and it cannot be lightly dismissed. It has as much validity as the arguments of any of the other apologia. The meaning of the record must be assessed by careful examination of the context in which Katamori was working and the character of his problems as he and his vassals perceived them.

The attempts to rehabilitate Oguri Tadamasa and Ogasawara Nagamichi were less successful because the correspondence was not as lengthy or as advantageous. For Oguri rehabilitation was attempted in two works by Ninagawa Arata. Those works, however, published in the late

1920s, are quite unlike the Meiji-era rehabilitative works: they are so emotional, so imprecise, and so bitter that I found them quite unhelpful and ended up disregarding them. I did use the volume *Ogasawara Ikinokami Nagamichi*, which was probably written in original form before 1900 as "Meisankō iseki" but not published until 1942. Consisting, like the other works of its sort, of a narrative interspersed with many documents, its tone is quite reasoned. But it is silent on some embarrassing matters and rehabilitative on others. It presents Nagamichi as a progressive farsighted man justly enraged at petty schemers who put their own advantage ahead of Japan's well-being. The line of argument was not unique, but a few roles were reversed from what one finds in works such as MHS or Suematsu Kenchō's excellent *Bōchō kaitenshi*.

Long before rehabilitation began, Oguri paid with his life for the position he had adopted. Ogasawara and Katamori paid not with their lives but with their honor, living in obscurity for more than twenty years after the restoration. For Katsu Kaishū, however, things worked out quite differently. He lived out a comfortable life after 1868 and a century after the restoration had acquired the stature of a major folk hero.

Katsu is sometimes, and without any justification, juxtaposed to Oguri as leader of one of the two putative main lines of bakufu officialdom. He was not. Whereas Oguri was a powerful man who played a continuous and constructive role in decision-making, Katsu was an outsider. He was unable to get along with others, did not know when to keep quiet, too often advocated impossible schemes, and repeatedly won censure and created enemies. Consequently, although his technical expertise was used by the bakufu for naval development, his political views were ignored. Perhaps officials should have listened to him, but they did not. To the contrary, his views were so distrusted that he was used for political purposes only on those rare occasions when his very "outsider" character was deemed useful by bakufu leaders trying to salvage something from a bad situation. That was the case during and after the Summer War and in early 1868 after Yoshinobu had decided to capitulate.

Katsu was an outsider, perhaps, but after 1868 he was still an ex-Tokugawa vassal, and so he too faced a job of rehabilitation. His prior experience helped him in the task. Because he, like Shungaku, had been unemployed frequently during the sixties, he had had a great deal of spare time during which he kept the diary mentioned earlier. Moreover, being an articulate, intelligent, and strongly opinionated man, he also wrote freely and bitingly to Shungaku and others about people and affairs. By the time of the restoration he had generated an extensive correspondence that could be used to demonstrate how un-bakufu and pro-imperial was his posture. The Meiji leaders evidently were not fully persuaded, however, or perhaps they found him no easier to work with than did the Tokugawa, for after 1868 he still had considerable time for writing. One invaluable product of that free time was the great compilations cited previously. Another was his memoirs and reminiscences, such as *Hikawa seiwa*, in which he continued to pursue the task of putting historical distance between himself and bakufu officialdom.

In terms of the Meiji bias, some of the most fascinating and important historiographical problems surround Yoshinobu. There are several sources of information on him. Basic documentary collections are the ''Hitotsubashi ke nikki'' and ''Yoshinobukō gojikki,'' both in DNISK, the latter also a part of ZTJ. There are also many letters by Yoshinobu in the records of Fukui and other *han* and many comments about him in the contemporary and later writings of other men. Finally there is *Sekimukai hikki*, a fascinating collection of Yoshinobu's own memoirs recorded in 1907–1911. They are the product of a carefully arranged program of interview-conversations, and they illustrate both the virtues and the limitations of good-quality oral history.

This material was used in Shibusawa's precedent-setting work of first-class scholarship, *Tokugawa Yoshinobukō den*, first published in 1919. The greatness of Shibusawa's work rests on the care with which it was done. The materials, which were assembled from 1893 onward, were carefully collated, their origins clearly identified, differences in content and even minor errors cited, and problems in dating confronted. Consisting of four volumes of narrative history, three volumes of chronologically ordered documents, and an index volume, the work established a precedent for reliable and carefully documented biographical scholarship. It proved of great value to the scholars who later worked on *Ishinshi* and its one-volume predecessor *Gaikan ishinshi*.

The central problem in Shibusawa's biography is that it is essentially designed to establish Yoshinobu's imperial loyalism and political honor. Like Kitahara, Shibusawa was successful in his task because so much documentation was amenable to his effort. For one thing, many of Yoshinobu's own statements in the 1860s could be cited to support the thesis. In his struggles with bakufu leaders, particularly when he was resident in the Kinai, he, like Katamori, frequently argued his position in terms of imperial respect. By a liberal citing of such sources, and by arguing that his contrary statements sprang from the pressure exerted by subordinates, Shibusawa was able to lay a firm foundation for his interpretation in solid primary sources. Then in early 1868 as men and women lobbied to salvage something for the Tokugawa by securing an imperial pardon of Yoshinobu, a vast additional volume of opinion asserting his imperial virtue was added to the existing record. And finally in *Sekimukai hikki*, as Yoshinobu recalled the past in his tranquil old age, he envisaged an era in which he struggled valiantly, and usually by himself, to drag a stubborn, selfish officialdom into the imperial camp.

Understandably all this rich body of material was used by Shibusawa to demonstrate the last shogun's political wisdom and rectitude. The bothersome questions of his character, the nettlesome issue of his abrupt shifts of policy and contrary statements, and the deeper question of how much or how little he really shaped affairs tend to be disposed of by uncritical quoting from contemporary materials, by easy quoting of later apologies and his own latter-day recollections, or by invoking the demons of incompetent, reactionary forces.

I believe that *Sekimukai hikki*, like the reminiscences of Katsu and Shungaku, cannot be considered a reliable guide to the motivations and intentions of actors in the 1860s. Too much time—half a lifetime—had passed, and too much history had vindicated the Meiji leaders to allow Yoshinobu to keep all his memories intact. How could anyone in 1910 argue publicly that the preservation and enhancement of the Tokugawa and the defeat of Satsuma and Chōshū were worthy central purposes of his effort?

If one does not accept interpretations based on this memoir, however, then Shibusawa's argument loses much of its force. One is left with evidence of the 1860s, most of which tells what was done and the rhetoric by which it was justified but does not shed real light on the questions of precisely who determined what was done or what really were the motivations involved. And so the student of Yoshinobu, in attempting to get beyond the Meiji bias in explaining motive and impact, ends up turning to speculative matters concerning Yoshinobu's origins as the favorite son of the willful Nariaki, as a young man growing up in the ideological storm center of Mito, as a would-be shogun hated and distrusted by the people he would lead, and then as a reluctant shogun of a failing regime. The speculations foster a vision of a young man of limited resources of will, overwhelmed by his situation, searching for a way out, and finally finding it in a process of unintentional squandering of his regime's resources, so that its defeat was the easier and his escape the more sure. This is not the picture Shibusawa sought to present; it may not be a correct picture; it certainly is not a picture fitting to a heroic age: and it does not accord with the Meiji bias. But it is one that may help us demythologize the restoration and see in it the complexities and failings as well as the aspirations and courage that are normative to the human condition.

NOTES

1. I am indebted to Professors Konishi Shirō and Kanai Madoka for information on the preparation of DNISK and ''Ishin shiryō bon.'' Also Ōkubo Toshiaki coordinated a panel discussion on the history of the Ishin shiryō hensankai that was published in *Nihon rekishi* in 1968 and is cited in the bibliography.

2. In World War II many original documents were destroyed by American fire bombers, but the ''Ishin shiryō bon'' copies, like DNISK, which was stored at Ueda city during the war, have survived.

3. The larger historiographical context of this tendency to stress the unviolent character of the restoration has been discussed by Peter Duus in his essay ''Whig History, Japanese Style: The Min'yūsha Historians and the Meiji Restoration,'' *Journal of Asian Studies* 33(3):415–436 (1974).

Bibliography

ENGLISH LANGUAGE WORKS

Beasley, W. G. *Select Documents on Japanese Foreign Policy 1853–1868.* London: Oxford University Press, 1955.
——. *The Meiji Restoration.* Stanford: Stanford University Press, 1972.
Bendix, Reinhard and Seymour Lipset, eds., *Class, Status, and Power.* New York: The Free Press, 1966.
Black, John R. *Young Japan.* 2 vols. London: Oxford University Press, 1968.
Bolitho, Harold. *Treasures among Men: The Fudai Daimyo in Tokugawa Japan.* New Haven: Yale University Press, 1974.
Borton, Hugh. "Peasant Uprisings in Japan of the Tokugawa Period." *Transactions of the Asiatic Society of Japan* (2nd series) 16: 1–219 (1938).
Craig, Albert M. *Chōshū in the Meiji Restoration.* Harvard Historical Monographs. Cambridge, Mass.: Harvard University Press, 1961.
Crawcour, E. S. "Changes in Japanese Commerce in the Tokugawa Period." In John W. Hall and Marius B. Jansen, eds., *Studies in the Institutional History of Early Modern Japan.* Princeton: Princeton University Press, 1968.
DeBecker, J. E. *The Nightless City.* Rutland, Vt.: Charles E. Tuttle Co., 1971.
Dore, Ronald P. *Education in Tokugawa Japan.* Berkeley: University of California Press, 1965.
Duus, Peter. "Whig History, Japanese Style: The Min'yūsha Historians and the Meiji Restoration." *Journal of Asian Studies* 33 (3): 415–436 (1974).
Earl, David Magarey. *Emperor and Nation in Japan.* Seattle: University of Washington Press, 1964.
Fox, Grace. *Britain and Japan, 1858–1883.* Oxford: Oxford University Press, 1969.
Frost, Peter. *The Bakumatsu Currency Crisis.* Harvard East Asian Monographs. Cambridge, Mass.: Harvard University Press, 1970.
Glazer, Nathan and Daniel P. Moynihan, eds. *Ethnicity, Theory and Experience.* Cambridge, Mass.: Harvard University Press, 1975.
Hall, Ivan Parker. *Mori Arinori.* Harvard East Asian Series. Cambridge, Mass.: Harvard University Press, 1973.
Hall, John Whitney. *Tanuma Okitsugu (1719–1788): Forerunner of Modern Japan.* Harvard-Yenching Institute Monograph Series 14. Cambridge, Mass.: Harvard University Press, 1955.
Harootunian, Harry D. *Toward Restoration: The Growth of Political Consciousness in Tokugawa Japan.* Berkeley: University of California Press, 1970.

Harrison, John A. *Japan's Northern Frontier*. Gainesville: University of Florida Press, 1953.

Hauser, William B. "The Diffusion of Cotton Processing and Trade in the Kinai Region in Tokugawa Japan." *Journal of Asian Studies* 33 (4): 633–649 (1974).

———. *Economic Institutional Change in Tokugawa Japan: Osaka and the Kinai Cotton Trade*. London: Cambridge University Press, 1974.

Havens, Thomas R. H. *Nishi Amane and Modern Japanese Thought*. Princeton: Princeton University Press, 1970.

Huber, Thomas. "Chōshū Activists in the Meiji Restoration." PhD dissertation, University of Chicago, 1975.

Jansen, Marius. *Sakamoto Ryōma and the Meiji Restoration*. Princeton: Princeton University Press, 1961.

Lensen, George A. *The Russian Push toward Japan*. Princeton: Princeton University Press, 1959.

Medzini, Meron. *French Policy in Japan during the Closing Years of the Tokugawa Regime*. Harvard East Asian Monographs. Cambridge, Mass.: Harvard University Press, 1971.

Najita, Tetsuo. *Japan*. Englewood Cliffs, N.J.: Prentice-Hall, 1974.

Ooms, Herman. *Charismatic Bureaucrat: A Political Biography of Matsudaira Sadanobu, 1758–1829*. Chicago and London: University of Chicago Press, 1975

Plath, David W. "Japan and the Ethics of Fatalism." *Anthropological Quarterly* 39 (July 1966). [Also in Irwin Scheiner, *Modern Japan: An Interpretive Anthology*. New York: Macmillan Publishing Co., 1974.]

Sakata, Yoshio and John W. Hall. "The Motivation of Political Leadership in the Meiji Restoration." *Journal of Asian Studies* 16: 31–50 (1956).

Satow, Sir Ernest. *A Diplomat in Japan*. London: Oxford University Press, 1968.

Scheiner, Irwin. "The Mindful Peasant: Sketches for a Study of Rebellion." *Journal of Asian Studies* 32 (4): 579–591 (1973).

Sheldon, Charles D. *The Rise of the Merchant Class in Tokugawa Japan, 1600–1968*. New York: Russell & Russell, 1973.

Smith, Thomas C. *The Agrarian Origins of Modern Japan*. Stanford: Stanford University Press, 1970.

Steele, William. "Katsu Kaishū and the Collapse of the Tokugawa Bakufu." PhD dissertation, Harvard University, 1976.

Stephan, John J. *Sakhalin: A History*. Oxford: Clarendon Press, 1971.

Totman, Conrad. "Fudai Daimyo and the Collapse of the Tokugawa Bakufu." *Journal of Asian Studies* 34 (3): 581–591 (1975).

———. "Political Reconciliation in the Tokugawa Bakufu: Abe Masahiro and Tokugawa Nariaki, 1844–1852." In Albert Craig and Donald H. Shively, eds., *Personality in Japanese History*. Berkeley: University of California Press, 1970.

———. "Political Succession in the Tokugawa Bakufu: Abe Masahiro's Rise to Power, 1843–1845." *Harvard Journal of Asiatic Studies* 26: 102–124 (1966).

———. *Politics in the Tokugawa Bakufu, 1600–1843*. Harvard East Asian Series. Cambridge, Mass.: Harvard University Press, 1967.

———. "Tokugawa Yoshinobu and *Kōbugattai*: A Study of Political Inadequacy." *Monumenta Nipponica* 30 (4): 393–403 (1975).

Tsuchihashi, Paul Yachita. *Japanese Chronological Tables*. (Bilingual.) Tokyo: Sophia University Press, 1952.

Webb, Herschel. "The Development of an Orthodox Attitude toward the Imperial Institution in the Nineteenth Century." In Marius B. Jansen, ed., *Changing Japanese Attitudes toward Modernization*. Princeton: Princeton University Press, 1965.

————. *The Japanese Imperial Institution in the Tokugawa Period.* Studies of the East Asian Institute. New York: Columbia University Press, 1968.

Yamamura, Kozo. *A Study of Samurai Income and Entrepreneurship.* Cambridge, Mass.: Harvard University Press, 1974.

JAPANESE LANGUAGE WORKS

Asterisked items are referred to in the Bibliographical Essay but were not used directly in my research except insofar as materials in DNISK were from some of those sources.

*Aizu han chō kiroku 会津藩庁記録 (Aizu *han* government records). Compiled by Nihon shiseki kyōkai 日本史籍協会. 6 vols. Tokyo: Tōkyō daigaku shuppan-kai 東京大学出版会, 1969.

Aoki Michio 青木美智男. "Bakumatsu ni okeru nōmin tōsō to nōheisei: toku ni Dewa kuni Murayama chihō no nōhei soshiki no tenkai o chūshin ni" 幕末における農民闘争と農兵制−とくに出羽国村山地方の農兵組織の展開を中心に−(Peasant struggles and peasant militia in the late Tokugawa period: specifically the development of peasant militia organization in the Murayama area of Dewa province). *Nihonshi kenkyū* 日本史研究, 97: 104–125 (1968).

Aoki Michio and Miura Toshiaki 三浦俊明. "Minami Kantō ni okeru 'eejanaika'" 南関東における「ええじゃないか」 (*Eejanaika* activity in the south Kantō). *Rekishigaku kenkyū* 歴史学研究, 385: 55–57 (1972).

Arima Nariura 有馬成甫. "Bakumatsu ni okeru seiyō kaki no yunyū" 幕末における西洋火器の輸入 (The import of firearms in the late Tokugawa period). *Nihon rekishi* 日本歴史, 120: 2–13 (1958).

————. *Takashima Shūhan* 高島秋帆. Tokyo: Yoshikawa kōbunkan 吉川弘文館, 1966.

Boshin nikki 戊辰日記 (A diary of 1868). Compiled by Iwasaki Hideshige 岩崎英重. Tokyo: Nihon shiseki kyōkai, 1925.

*Dai Nihon ishin shiryō 大日本維新史料 (Records of the restoration). Compiled by Ishin shiryō hensan jimukyoku 維新史料編纂事務局. 19 vols. Tokyo: Meiji shoin 明治書院, 1938–1943.

*Dai Nihon ishin shiryō: Ii ke shiryō 井伊家史料 (————: Records of the Ii family). Compiled by Shiryō hensanjo 史料編纂所. Volumes appearing periodically. Tokyo, Tokyo daigaku, 1959 ff.

"Dai Nihon ishin shiryō kōhon": see DNISK.

*Dai Nihon kinsei shiryō: Ryūei honin 大日本近世史料：柳営補任 (Historical materials on early modern Japan: government personnel roster). Compiled by Shiryō hensanjo. 6 vols. Tokyo: Tokyo daigaku, 1964–1965.

*Dai Nihon komonjo: Bakumatsu gaikoku kankei monjo 大日本古文書：幕末外国関係文書 (Historical manuscripts of Japan: documents on late Tokugawa foreign relations). Compiled by Shiryō hensanjo. Volumes appearing periodically. Tokyo: Tokyo daigaku, 1911 ff.

DNISK: "Dai Nihon ishin shiryō kōhon" 大日本維新史料稿本 (Manuscript of historical materials on the restoration). In archives of the Shiryō hensanjo (Historiographical Institute) of Tokyo University.

Fujii Sadayoshi 藤井定義. "Hatamoto Ishimaru-ke zaisei no ittan" 旗本石丸家財政の一端 (An aspect of the finances of the liege vassal family Ishimaru). *Keizai kenkyū* 経済研究 of Osaka furitsu daigaku 大阪府立大学, 21 : 121–130 (1961).

Fujita Teiichirō 藤田貞一郎. "Bakumatsu ishin ki ni okeru han-kokka shisō no tenkai : Wakayama han no baai" 幕末・維新期における藩＝国家思想の展開−和歌山藩の場合− (The development of *han* nationalist thought at the time of the restoration: the case of Wakayama *han*). *Kinseishi kenkyū* 近世史研究, 34: 24–33 (1962).

Fukushima Masayoshi 福島正義. "Bakuhansei no hōkai to Kawagoe han no nōhei hantai ikki" 幕藩制の崩壊と川越藩の農兵反対一揆 (The collapse of the Tokugawa system and antimilitia riots in Kawagoe *han*). *Chihōshi kenkyū* 地方史研究, 21 (1): 11–25 (1971).

Gaikan ishin shi 概観維新史 (A short history of the restoration). Compiled by Ishin shiryō hensan jimukyoku. Tokyo: Meiji shoin, 1940.

Handa Yoshiko 半田良子. "Dai niji seichō o meguru bakufu no dōkō: Yoshinobu seiken no seiritsu to sono seikaku.' 第二次征長をめぐる幕府の動向−慶喜政権の成立とその性格 (Trends of the bakufu associated with the second Chōshū expedition: the establishment and character of Yoshinobu's administration). *Shisō* 史艸, 8: 31–49 (1967).

Hara Denzō 原傳蔵. "Genji gannen sankin kōtai oyobi saishi zaifusei no fukkyū jijō" 元治元年参観交代及妻子在府制の復旧事情 (On the restoring of the *sankin kōtai* system in 1864). *Rekishi chiri* 歴史地理, 33 (2): 130–135 (1919).

Haraguchi Kiyoshi 原口清. *Boshin sensō* 戊辰戦争 (The war of 1868). Tokyo: Hanawa shobō 塙書房, 1966.

Hashida Tomoharu 橋田友治. "Jōshū ni okeru Tengutō rōshi no gun'yōkin chōtatsu" 上州における天狗党浪士の軍用金調達 (The procurement of military funds by *rōnin* of the Tengū gang in Kōzuke province). *Gunma bunka* 群馬文化, 100: 52–61 (1968).

Hattori Shisō 服部之總. *Ishinshi no hōhōron* 維新史の方法論 (The methodology of restoration history). Tokyo: Hakuyōsha 白揚社, 1938.

———. *Meiji ishinshi* 明治維新史 (History of the restoration). Reprint edition. Tokyo: Perikansha ペリカン社, 1967.

Hiramatsu Yoshirō 平松義郎. "Bakumatsu ki ni okeru hanzai to keibatsu no jittai: Edo Kodenmachō rōya kiroku ni yoru" 幕末期における犯罪と刑罰の実態−江戸小傳馬町牢屋記録による− (Crime and punishment in the late Tokugawa period: records of the prison at Kodenmachō in Edo). *Kokka gakkai zasshi* 国家学会雑誌, 71 (3): 76–130 (1956).

Hirao Michio 平尾道雄. *Shinsengumi shiroku* 新撰組史録 (Records of the Shinsengumi). Tokyo: Hakuryūsha 白竜社, 1967.

Hirasawa Kiyoto 平沢清人. "Keiō gannen Shinshū Shimoina chihō nishibu yamamura chitai no kome sōdō" 慶応元年信州下伊奈地方西部山村地帯の米騒動 (Rice riots in the mountain village region of western Shimoina area in Shinano province in 1865). *Shinano* 信濃, 9 (9): 40–48 (1957).

"Hiroshima" 広島. A map by Kokudo chiriin 国土地理院. Tokyo?: 1970.

Honjō Eijirō 本庄栄治郎. *Nihon keizaishi dai 1–bunken* 日本経済史第一−文献 (Bibliography of Japanese history, vols. 1 ff.). 5 or more vols. Kyoto: Nihon keizaishi kenkyūjo 日本経済史研究所 of Osaka keizai daigaku 大阪経済大学, 1933 ff.

Hosokawa Michio 細川道夫. "Bakumatsu ishin ki ni okeru Ōgaki han no dōkō" 幕末・維新期における大垣藩の動向 (Trends in Ōgaki *han* at the time of restoration). *Nihon rekishi*, 221: 58–69 (1966).

Ii ke shiryō: bakumatsu fūbun tansakusho 井伊家史料・幕末風聞探索書 (Historical records of the Ii house: reports and investigations of the late Tokugawa period). Compiled by Ii Masahiro 井伊正弘. 3 vols. Tokyo: Yūzankaku 雄山閣, 1968.

Ikeda Yoshimasa 池田敬正. "Bakufu no tōkai to Boshin sensō" 幕府の倒壊と戊辰戦争 (The bakufu's collapse and the war of 1868). In *Iwanami kōza Nihon rekishi (14) Kindai 1*. [see Iwanami.]

Inoue Isao 井上勲. "Shōgun kūi jidai no seijishi: Meiji ishin seijishi kenkyū" 将軍空位時代の政治史-明治維新政治史研究- (The political history of the shogunless period: a study of the political history of the restoration). *Shigaku zasshi* 史学雑誌, 77 (11): 1-58 (1968).

Inoue Kiyoshi 井上清. *Nihon gendai shi I: Meiji ishin* 日本現代史 I・明治維新 (The modern history of Japan I: the restoration). Tokyo: Tokyo daigaku, 1967.

Ishii Takashi 石井孝. "Keiō ninen no seiji jōsei: dai niji Chōshū seibatsu o megutte" 慶応二年の政治情勢-第二次長州征伐をめぐって (The political situation in 1866: concerning the second Chōshū expedition). *Rekishi hyōron* 歴史評論, 34: 1-16 (1952).

———. "Rekkyō no tai-Nichi seisaku" 列強の対日政策 (The policy of the great powers toward Japan). In *Iwanami kōza Nihon rekishi (14) Kindai 1*.

———. "Ogasawara kakurō 'soppei jōkyō' no seikaku ni tsuite: Tanaka Akira shi no hihan ni kotaeru" 小笠原閣老「率兵上京」の性格について-田中彰氏の批判に答える- (Concerning the character of senior councillor Ogasawara's armed approach to Kyoto: a reply to Tanaka Akira's criticism). *Nihon rekishi* 173: 2-7 (1962).

———. *Meiji ishin no kokusaiteki kankyō* 明治維新の国際的環境 (The international environment of the restoration). Tokyo: Yoshikawa kōbunkan, 1960. [Revised edition: *Yōtei Meiji ishin no kokusaiteki kankyō*, 1973.]

———. "Tokugawa Yoshinobu no taisei hōkan to shōgunshoku jihyō teishutsu" 徳川慶喜の大政奉還と将軍職辞表提出 (Yoshinobu's restoration of authority and presentation of shogunal resignation. (*Shintei zōho*) *kokushi taikei geppō* (新訂増補) 国史大系月報, 65: 1-3 (1967).

———. *Ishin no nairan* 維新の内乱 (Domestic turmoil in the restoration). Tokyo: Shiseidō 至誠堂, 1968.

Ishinshi 維新史 (History of the restoration). Compiled by Ishin shiryō hensan jimukyoku. 6 vols. Tokyo: Meiji shoin, 1941.

*"Ishin shiryō bon" 維新史料本 (Works on restoration history). 15,000 titles in the archives of Shiryō hensanjo, Tokyo University.

Ishin shiryō kōyō: see ISK.

ISK. *Ishin shiryō kōyō* 維新史料綱要 (A summary of historical documents of the restoration). 10 vols. Tokyo: Tokyo daigaku, 1965.

Iwanami kōza Nihon rekishi (14) Kindai 1 岩波講座日本歴史 (14) 近代 I (Iwanami's history of Japan, vol. 14, the modern era, no. 1). Tokyo: Iwanami shoten 岩波書店, 1962.

Kageura Gatō 景浦稚桃. "Meiji ishin no sai ni okeru Kōchi han to Matsuyama han" 明治維新の際における高知藩と松山藩 (Kōchi and Matsuyama domains at the time of the restoration). *Iyo shidan* 伊予史談, 152: 1-9 (1958).

Kamekakegawa Hiromasa 亀掛川博正. "Bakumatsu bakufu rikugun no dōkō: Bunkyū sannen Ogasawara kakurō soppei jōkyō jiken o chūshin to shite" 幕末幕府陸軍の動向-文久三年小笠原閣老率兵上京事件を中心として- (Role of the bakufu army in the late Edo period: the incident of senior councillor Ogasawara's armed march to Kyoto in 1863). *Gunji shigaku* 軍事史学, 7 (3): 2-11 (1971).

———. "Bakufu tōkai ki ni okeru gunsei kaikaku no sho kōsō (1, 2)" 幕府倒壊期における軍制改革の諸構想 (上, 下) (Plans for military reform at the time of the bakufu collapse). *Gunji shigaku* 9: 54-63 (1967); 10: 36-43 (1967).

Kanai Madoka 金井圓. "Oguri Tadamasa no tai-Ei Futsu shakkan ni kan suru

Kishikawa-ke denrai monjo no saihyōka" 小栗忠順の対英仏借款に関する岸
川家伝来文書の再評価 (A reappraisal of documents handed down in the
Kishikawa family that concern Oguri Tadamasa's loan arrangements with
the English and French), Tokugawa rinseishi kenkyūjo 徳川林政史研究所
(Institute for research on the history of Tokugawa forest administration).
Kenkyū kiyō 研究紀要. Shōwa 45 nendo 昭和45年度 (annual issue, 1971),
pp. 388–403 (1971).

Kanbu tsuki: see KT.

Kataoka Eizaemon 片岡永左衛門, assisted by Ishii Tominosuke 石井富之助.
"Tokugawa bakufu makki no Odawara han" 徳川幕府末期の小田原藩 (The
Odawara domain in the last years of the Tokugawa bakufu). *Kanagawa shidan*
神奈川史談, 5: 39–53 (1962).

Katsu Kaishū 勝海舟. *Rikugun rekishi*: see RR.

*————. *Hikawa seiwa* 氷川清話 (Quiet talks at the Hikawa mansion). In vol. 2 of
Bakumatsu ishin shiryō sōsho 幕末維新史料叢書 (A series of restoration records).
Tokyo: Jinbutsu ōraisha 人物往来社, 1968.

*————. *Kaigun rekishi* 海軍歴史 (A history of the navy). Tokyo: Hara shobō 原
書房, 1967.

*————. *Kaikoku kigen* 開国起原 (Origin of the opened country). 2 vols. Tokyo:
Hara shobō, 1968.

Katsu Kaishū zenshū 勝海舟全集 (The works of Katsu Kaishū). Compiled by
Katsube Mitake 勝部真長, Matsumoto Sannosuke 松本三之介, and Ōguchi
Yūjirō 大口勇次郎. 19 vols. [vols. 18–19: "Kaishū nikki" 海舟日記 (Katsu's
diary)]. Tokyo: Keisō shobō 勁草書房, 1972.

Kawai Mutsuo 川井睦夫. "Keiō sannen shōgatsu Sanshū Shōdoshima seibu roku
gō hyakushō ikki ni tsuite" 慶応三年正月讃州小豆島西部六郷百姓一揆につ
いて (Concerning peasant riots in six villages in the western part of Shōdoshima in Sanuki province in 1867). *Hosei shigaku* 法政史学, 14: 112–123
(1961).

Kawakita Nobuo 河北展生. "Matsudaira Shungaku no 'Kohyō henkaku bikō'
kijutsu jiki" 松平春嶽の「虎豹変革備考」記述時期 (On the dating of Shungaku's essay on "abrupt and savage change"). Mita shigakkai 三田史学会.
Shigaku 史学, 29 (4): 42–64 (1957).

————. "Dai ikkai seichō mondai ni kan suru Matsudaira Shungaku no iken ni
tsuite" 第一回征長問題に関する松平春嶽の意見について (Concerning Ma-
tsudaira Shungaku's view of the first expedition to suppress Chōshū). *Shigaku*
39 (3): 65–95 (1966).

————. "Matsudaira Shungaku no shokō kaigi seijiron no saiyō" 松平春嶽の諸侯
会議政治論の採用 (The adoption of Matsudaira Shungaku's thesis on an
assembly of the lords). *Shigaku* 43 (1–2): 307–318 (1970).

Kawamura Masaru 川村優. "Bakumatsu no Mito han sōran to Shimōsa kuni no
ichi dōkō" 幕末の水戸藩騒乱と下總国の一動向 (The disturbance in Mito
domain and one tendency in Shimōsa province in the last years of the
Tokugawa bakufu). *Ibaragi kenshi kenkyū* 茨城県史研究, 20: 73–78 (1971).

Kimura Kaishū 木村芥舟. *Sanjūnenshi* 三十年史 (A history of thirty years). Tokyo:
Kōjunsha 交詢社, 1892.

Kitahara Masanaga, *Shichinenshi*: see SNS.

Kitahara Susumu 北原進. "Bakumatsu ni okeru hatamoto shakuzai no tokushitsu"
幕末における旗本借財の特質 (The special character of *hatamoto* indebtedness
at the end of the Tokugawa period). Risshō daigaku *Keizaigaku kihō* 経済学
季報, 14 (12): 115–137 (1964).

Kitamura Katsuo 北村勝雄. "Takatō han no kangun ni kijun shimatsu: Kōshū guchi kangun no heishoku makanai" 高遠藩の官軍に帰順始末-甲州口官軍 の兵食賄- (Takatō domain's submission to the imperial army: provisioning the imperial army on the Kōshū route). *Inaji* 伊那路, 6(8): 30-34 (1962).

Kobayashi Shigeru 小林茂. "Keiō gannen 'kokuso' no oboegaki" 慶応元年「国訴」 の覚書 (Memoranda of legal proceedings in 1865). *Rekishi hyōron* 91: 2-18 (1957); 92: 41-52 (1958); 93: 60-69 (1958).

Kojima Shigeo 小島茂男. "Bakumatsu ishin ni okeru fudai han no dōkō" 幕末維 新における譜代藩の動向 (Tendencies among *fudai* domains at the time of the restoration). *Rekishi kyōiku* 歴史教育, 16 (12): 16-24 (1968).

KT: *Kanbu tsuki* 官武通紀 (Annal of court and bakufu). Edited by Hayakawa Junzaburō 早川純三郎. 2 vols. Tokyo: Kokusho kankōkai 図書刊行会, 1915.

Kyūbakufu 旧幕府 (The old bakufu). Reprint edition with 5 pts. bound in 4 vols. Tokyo: Nozokawa shoten 臨川書店, 1971.

Maruyama Kunio 丸山国雄. "Ishin zengo ni okeru Tōhoku shohan no buki kōnyu mondai" 維新前後における東北諸藩の武器購入問題 (The problem of weapons imports by the northeastern domains during the restoration). *Rekishi chiri* 71 (1): 15-38 (1938).

*Matsudaira Yoshinaga 松平慶永. Itsuji shiho 逸事史補 (Anecdotes on neglected matters). In vol. 4 of *Bakumatsu ishin shiryō sōsho*. Tokyo: Jinbutsu ōraisha, 1968.

Meiji ishinshi kenkyū kōza 明治維新史研究講座. (Symposium on research on the restoration). Compiled by Rekishigaku kenkyūkai 歴史学研究会. 6 vols. Tokyo: Heibonsha 平凡社, 1958-1962.

MHS: *Mito han shiryō* 水戸藩史料 (Records of the Mito domain). 5 vols. (vol. 3). Tokyo: Yoshikawa kōbunkan, 1970.

Mikami Akemi 三上昭美. "Boshin senki ni okeru Bitchū Matsuyama han ni tsuite: ishin seifu no senryō seisaku no ichiruikei" 戊辰戦期における備中松 山藩について-維新政府の占領政策の一類型- (Matsuyama domain in Bitchū province in the war of 1868: one instance of the restoration govern- ment's policy of occupation). *Rekishi kyōiku* 16 (12): 44-52 (1968).

Mikami Kazuo 三上一夫. "Bakumatsu ni okeru Fukui han no hansei kaikaku to bakusei kaikaku undō ni tsuite" 幕末における福井藩の藩政改革と幕政改革 運動について (Concerning bakufu reform and Fukui domain reform move- ments in the late Tokugawa period). *Fukui kenritsu Fukui shōko kenkyū shūroku* 福井県立福井商高研究集録, 1: 36-54 (1969).

————. "Bunkyū ki ni okeru Echizen han no bakusei kaikaku undō ni tsuite" 文 久期における越前藩の幕政改革運動について (Concerning Echizen *han*'s movement for reform of the bakufu in the early 1860s). *Nihon rekishi* 288: 99-105 (1972).

Minami Kazuo 南和男. "Bunkyū ki ni okeru Edo no harifuda ni tsuite" 文久期に おける江戸の張札について (Concerning placards in Edo in the early 1860's. *Tōkyō toritsu kōkū kōsen kenkyū kiyo* 東京都立航空高専研究紀要, 8 (1-12) (1971).

Mitamura Engyo 三田村鳶魚. *Edo seikatsu jiten* 江戸生活事典 (A dictionary of life in Edo). Tokyo: Seiabō 青蛙房, 1960.

Mito han shiryō: see MHS.

Mori Yasuhiko 森安彦. "Bushū yonaoshi ikki' no kisoteki kōsatsu" 「武州世直し 一揆」の基礎的考察 (A basic study of the "Musashi province world-renew- ing uprising"). *Shinano* 24 (10): 15-40 (1972).

Murakami Tadashi 村上真 and Ōno Mizuo 大野瑞男. "Bakumatsu ni okeru bakufu kanjōsho shiryō: Bunkyū sannen 'kingin nōfutsu gokanjōchō,' 'kome daizu nōfutsu gokanjōchō' ni tsuite" 幕末における幕府勘定所史料-文久三 年「金銀納払御勘定帳」「米大豆納払御勘定帳」について (Records of the bakufu's finance office in the final years: concerning registers of gold and silver tax payments and registers of rice and soybean payments in 1863). *Shigaku zasshi* 81 (4): 47–70 (1972).

Murase Masaaki 村瀬正章. "Dainiji Chōshū seibatsu o meguru nishi Mikawa no shojōsei" 第二次長州征伐をめぐる西三河の諸情勢 (Conditions in western Mikawa province relative to the second Chōshū expedition). *Rekishi kyōiku* 6 (1): 58–62 (1958).

*Nakane Yukie 中根雪江. *Sakumu kiji* 昨夢紀事 (An account of times past). 2 vols. Tokyo: Yao shoten 八尾書店, 1896.

Nanki Tokugawa shi 南紀徳川史 (The history of the Tokugawa of Kii). Compiled by Horiuchi Makoto 堀内信. 15 vols. (vols. 4, 13). Tokyo: Meicho shuppan 名著出版, 1970.

Naramoto Tatsuya 奈良本辰也. *Meiji ishin ron* 明治維新論 (Essays on the restoration). Tokyo: Tokuma shoten 徳間書店, 1968.

Nihon keizaishi kenkyūjo 日本経済史研究所. "Keiō sannen Edo Ginza hakkō kinsatsu shiryō" 慶応三年江戸銀座発行金札史料 (Documents on the issue of gold certificates by the Edo ginza in 1867). *Osaka keidai ronshū* 大阪経大論集, 38: 170–190 (1963).

Nihon rekishi daijiten 日本歴史大辞典 (Historical encyclopedia of Japan). Volume of maps. Tokyo: Kawade shobō shinsha 河出書房新社, 1961.

Nihon shiseki kyōkai sōsho 日本史籍協会叢書 (Library of works from the society of Japanese annals). 192 vols. Tokyo: Nihon shiseki kyōkai, 1916 ff. [Republished by Tokyo daigaku, 1969 ff.]

*Ninagawa Arata 蜷川新. *Ishin zengo no seisō to Oguri Kōzuke no shi* 維新前後の政争と小栗上野の死 (Political conflict of the restoration and the death of Oguri Tadamasa). Tokyo: Nihon shoin 日本書院, 1928.

*――――. *Zoku ishin zengo no seisō to Oguri Kōzuke* 續維新前後の政争と小栗上野 (Political conflict of the restoration and Oguri Tadamasa, continued). Tokyo: Nihon shoin, 1931.

Nishibori Akira 西堀昭. "Waga kuni ni okeru Futsugo (kyōiku) shi (I–VII)" わが国における仏語(教育)史 I–VII (The history of French language education in our country, pts. 1–7). *Chiba shōdai ronsō* 千葉商大論叢 (issues between 1968 and 1972; eight articles grouped in seven parts).

Nishida Shūhei 西田集平. "Meiji ishin ni okeru Hikone han" 明治維新における彦根藩 (Hikone domain in the restoration). *Nihon rekishi* 203: 73–82 (1965). [Also published in *Hikone gōshi shi kenkyū* 彦根郷士史研究, 10: 24–41 (1965).]

Ogasawara Ikinokami Nagamichi: see OIN,

OIN: *Ogasawara Ikinokami Nagamichi* 小笠原壹岐守長行. Edited by Ogasawara Ikinokami Nagamichi hensankai 小笠原壹岐守長行編纂会. Tokyo: 1942.

Okamoto Yukio 岡本幸雄. "Bakumatsu-Meiji ishin ni okeru gōshi no seijiteki undō no tenkai" 幕末-明治維新における郷士の政治的運動の展開 (The development of political activism among village samurai in the late Tokugawa-restoration period). *Ritsumeikan keizaigaku* 立命館経済学, 9 (2): 39–63 (1960).

Ōkubo Toshiaki 大久保利謙 (coordinator). "Ishinshi kenkyū no ayumi, dai ikkai: ishin shiryō hensankai no hatashita yakuwari" 維新史研究の歩み, 第一回維新史料編纂会の果した役割– (The course of historical research on the restoration, pt. 1: the role played by the *ishin shiryō hensankai* or society for compilation of records of the restoration). *Nihon rekishi* 246: 1–29 (1968).

――――. "Ishinshi kenkyū no ayumi, dai yonkai: Hattori-Hani shigaku no hatashita yakuwari (ichi, ni)" 維新史研究の歩み, 第四回-服部・羽仁史学の果した役割– (The course of historical research on the restoration, pt. 4: the role of Hattori and Hani, in two sections). *Nihon rekishi* 249: 106–127; 250: 110–130 (1969).

Ōmachi Masami 大町雅美. *Boshin sensō* 戊辰戦争 (The war of 1868). Tokyo: Yūzankaku, 1968.

Ōtsuka Takematsu 大塚武松. *Bakumatsu gaikōshi no kenkyū* 幕末外交史の研究 (A study of late Tokugawa foreign relations). Rev. ed. Tokyo: Hōbunkan 宝文館, 1966.

Ozaki Yukiya 尾崎行也. "Ishin ki ni okeru Matsudaira Noritaka no dōkō: ishin ki no kyū Tanoguchi han (1)" 維新期における松平乗謨の動向-維新期の旧田野口藩 (1)- (The attitude of Matsudaira Noritaka during the restoration: former Tanoguchi domain during the restoration: 1). *Shinano* 17 (9): 24–31 (1965).

———. "Ishin ki fudai kohan no gunji kaikaku: ishin ki no Tanoguchi han (2)" 維新期譜代小藩の軍事改革-維新期の田野口藩 (2)- (Military reform by a small *fudai han* at the time of the restoration: Tanoguchi domain during the restoration: 2). *Shinano* 18 (5): 13–27 (1966).

———. "Ishin ki fudai kohan no ryōnai shūdatsu jittai: ishin ki no Tanoguchi han (3)" 維新期譜代小藩の領内収奪実態-維新期の田野口藩 (3)- (Intra-domanial exactions in a small *fudai* domain at the time of the restoration: Tanoguchi domain during the restoration: 3). *Shinano* 20 (5): 40–48 (1968); 20 (6): 37–49 (1968).

———. "Bakufuryō ni okeru nōhei soshiki: Shinano kuni Saku-gun nai bakufu ryō no baai" 幕府領における農兵組織-信濃国佐久郡内幕府領の場合 (The organization of peasant militia in bakufu lands: the case of bakufu lands in Saku district of Shinano province). *Shinano* 20 (10): 22–32 (1968); 20 (11): 42–50 (1968).

RR: Katsu Kaishū 勝海舟. *Rikugun rekishi* 陸軍歴史 (A history of the army). Reprint edition, 2 vols. Tokyo: Hara shobō, 1967.

Saimu kiji 再夢紀事 (A recounting of times past). Tokyo: Nihon shiseki kyōkai, 1922.

Sasaki Junnosuke 佐々木潤之介. *Bakumatsu shakairon: "yonaoshi jōkyō" kenkyū joron* 幕末社会論「世直し状況」研究序論 (A thesis on late Tokugawa society: an introduction to research on the "world-renewal" phenomenon). Tokyo: Hanawa shobō, 1969.

Sekimukai hikki 昔夢会筆記 (Notes from a society for bygone days). Compiled by Shibusawa Eiichi 渋沢栄一; revised by Ōkubo Toshiaki. Tokyo: Heibonsha, 1968.

Setani Yoshihiko 瀬谷義彦. "Mito han ni okeru gōkō to sonjō undō" 水戸藩における郷校と尊攘運動 (Village schools and loyalist-expulsionist activity in Mito domain). *Ibaragi kenshi kenkyū* 12: 1–15 (1968).

Shibata Michio 柴田三千雄 and Shibata Asako 柴田朝子. "Bakumatsu ni okeru Furansu no tai-Nichi seisaku: 'Furansu yushutsunyū kaisha' no setsuritsu keikaku o megutte" 幕末におけるフランスの対日政策-「フランス輸出入会社」の設立計画をめぐって- (French policy toward Japan in the late Tokugawa period: on plans to establish the "French export-import company"). *Shigaku zasshi* 76 (8): 46–71 (1967).

Shibusawa Eiichi 渋沢栄一. *Tokugawa Yoshinobukō den* 徳川慶喜公傳 (Biography of Tokugawa Yoshinobu). 8 vols. Tokyo: Ryūmonsha 竜門社, 1918.

Shimoyama Saburo 下山三郎. *Meiji ishin kenkyū shiron* 明治維新研究史論 (An essay on studies of the restoration). Tokyo: Ochanomizu shobō 御茶の水書房, 1967.

Shiseki zassan 史籍雑誌 (A historical miscellany). Compiled by Hayakawa Junzaburō. 5 vols. Tokyo: Kokusho kankōkai, 1912.

Shōji Kichinosuke 庄司吉之助. *Yonaoshi ikki no kenkyū* 世直し一揆の研究 (A study of world-renewing movements). Tokyo: Kōkura shobō 校倉書房, 1970.

Shōwa Nihon chizu 昭和日本地図 (Atlas of Japan in the Shōwa period). Tokyo: Tokyo kaiseikan 東京開成館, 1941.

SNS: Kitahara Masanaga 北原雅長. *Shichinenshi* 七年史 (A history of seven years). 2 vols. with pagination by original *kan*. Tokyo: Keiseisha 啓成社, 1904.

Suematsu Kenchō 末松謙澄. *Bōchō kaitenshi* 防長回天史 (A history of Chōshū during the restoration). 7 vols. Tokyo: 1921.

Sugimoto Toshio 杉本敏夫. "Fudai Sakura han no kaitai katei: sono haihan chiken e no dōtei" 譜代佐倉藩の解体過程-その廃藩置県への道程- (The dissolution of the *fudai* domain of Sakura: the process of fief-dissolution and prefectural formation). *Shundai shigaku* 駿台史学, 11: 82–111 (1961).

Takagi Shunsuke 高木俊輔. "Sonnō jōi undō to minshū: Chibaken Kujūkuri chihō no Shinchūgumi ikken o chūshin to shite" 尊王攘夷運動と民衆-千葉県九十九里地方の真忠組一件を中心として (Loyalist-expulsionist activity and the people: focusing upon the Shinchūgumi affair in the Kujukuri area of Chiba prefecture). *Rekishigaku kenkyū* 318: 39–55 (1966).

―――. "Mito han sonnō jōi undō no sonraku shusshin giseisha" 水戸藩尊王攘夷運動の村落出身犠牲者 (Village-born victims of the loyalist-expulsionist movement in Mito domain). *Ibaragi kenshi kenkyū* 13: 53–78 (1969).

―――. "Bakumatsu Kantō no sonnō jōi undō ni tsuite" 幕末関東の尊王攘夷運動について (Concerning the late Tokugawa loyalist-expulsionist movement in the Kantō region). *Ibaragi kenshi kenkyū* 19: 55–61 (1971).

Takashima Ichirō 高島一郎. "Keiō ninen toshi kyūmin no ishiki to kōdō" 慶応二年都市窮民の意識と行動 (The consciousness and conduct of city poor in 1866). *Rekishi kyōiku* 17 (3): 71–77 (1969).

Takeda Katsuzō 武田勝蔵. "Dainikai Chōshū seibatsu no Geishū hanshi no jinchū nikki" 第二回長州征伐の芸州藩士の陣中日記 (The field diary of a Hiroshima samurai during the second Chōshū expedition). *Shigaku* 33 (1): 99–111 (1960).

Tamura Eitarō 田村栄太郎. "Bakumatsu kakurō Itakura Iga no kami" 幕末閣老板倉伊賀守 (Itakura Iga no kami, senior councillor in the last years of the shogunate). *Nihon no fūzoku* 日本の風俗, 2 (11): 4–29 (1939).

Tanaka Akira 田中彰. "Bakumatsu no seiji jōsei" 幕末の政治情勢 (The political situation at the end of the Tokugawa period). In *Iwanami kōza Nihon rekishi* (*14*) *Kindai 1.*

―――. "Bakufu no sonnōha datō kūdetā keikakusetsu ni tsuite: Ogasawara 'soppei jōkyō' o megutte" 幕府の尊王派打倒クーデター計画説について-小笠原「率兵上京」をめぐって- (Concerning the bakufu plan for a coup to overthrow the loyalist-expulsionist faction: Ogasawara's "armed march on Kyoto"). *Nihon rekishi* 171: 11–18 (1962).

*Tokugawa jikki 徳川実記 (Veritable records of the Tokugawa house). *Zoku kokushi taikei* 續国史大系, vols. 9–15. Tokyo: Keizai zasshisha 経済雑誌社, 1896 ff. [Also vols. 38–48 of *Shintei zōho kokushi taikei* 新訂増補国史大系.]

Tokutomi Iichirō 徳富猪一郎. *Kinsei Nihon kokumin shi* 近世日本国民史 (A national history of modern Japan). 100 vols. (vols. 47–68 cover the years 1862–1868). Tokyo: Meiji shoin, late 1930s.

Tōyama Shigeki 遠山茂樹. "Bunkyū ninen no seiji jōsei: harigami-tōbun o chūshin to shite" 文久二年の政治情勢-張紙・投文を中心として- (The political situation in 1862: focusing on posters and leaflets). *Rekishigaku kenkyū* 13 (9): 64–84 (1943).

―――. *Meiji ishin to gendai* 明治維新と現代 (The restoration and today). Tokyo: Iwanami shinsho 岩波新書, 1968.

Ueyama Shunpei 上山春平. *Meiji ishin no bunseki shiten* 明治維新の分析視点 (An analytical perspective on the restoration). Tokyo: Kōdansha 講談社, 1968.

Wakabayashi Yasu 若林泰. "Keiō ninen Hyōgo-tsu no uchikowashi no shin shiryō" 慶応二年兵庫津の打毀しの新史料 (New materials on the riots in Hyōgo port in 1866). *Hyōgo shigaku* 兵庫史学, 23: 67–69 (1960).

Yamaguchi Muneyuki 山口宗之. "Shōgun keishi undō no tenkai: shōgun shinsei kara kōbugattai e" 将軍継嗣運動の展開-将軍親政から公武合体へ (Evolution of the shogunal succession issue: from shogunal governance to *kōbugattai*). *Kyūshū shigaku* 九州史学, 40: 24–34 (1967).

Yamakawa Hiroshi 山川浩. *Kyōto shugoshoku shimatsu* 京都守護職始末 (The story of the Kyoto protector). Reissued by Tōyama Shigeki and Kaneko Mitsuharu 金子光晴. 2 vols. Tokyo: Heibonsha, 1966.

Yasuzawa Hideichi 安沢秀一. "Bushū ikki to nōhei" 武州一揆と農兵 (Riots in Musashi province and the peasant militia). *Mita gakkai zasshi* 三田学会雑誌, 47 (3): 115–119 (1954).

Yodo Inaba-ke monjo 淀稲葉家文書 (Documents of the Inaba family of Yodo). Edited by Hayakawa Junzaburō 早川純三郎. Tokyo: Nihon shiseki kyōkai, 1926.

Yoshida Tōgo 吉田東伍. *Dai Nihon dokushi chizu* 大日本読史地図 (Historical atlas of Japan). Tokyo: Fuzambō 冨山房, 1935.

Yoshida Tsunekichi 吉田常吉. "Shōgun Iemochi no shi" 将軍家茂の死 (The death of shogun Iemochi). *(Shintei zōho) kokushi taikei geppō* 65: 3–6 (1967).

Yoshino Naoyasu 吉野真保, Compiler. *Kaei Meiji nenkanroku* 嘉永明治年間録 (Records of the restoration years). 2 vols. Tokyo: Gannandō shoten 巖南堂書店, 1968.

Zoku saimu kiji: see ZSK.

Zoku Tokugawa jikki: see ZTJ.

ZSK: *Zoku saimu kiji* 續再夢紀事 (A further recounting of times past). 6 vols. Tokyo: Nihon shiseki kyōkai, 1921.

ZTJ: *Zoku Tokugawa jikki* 續徳川実紀 (Further veritable records of the Tokugawa house). 5 vols. Tokyo: Keizai zasshisha, 1907.

Index

Abe Masahiro: political role, xx–xxii, 170, 385, 446, 474; his governance compared, 3–4, 83, 281, 292, 454; aspects of his governance, 7, 10, 341; his military reforms, 21, 24–25, 27, 194

Abe Masatō: in **1864**, 125, 129, 131–132, 137, 140, 498n48; in **1865**, 150–156, 158–160, 165, 210; in **1867**, 281

Aizu: finances, 500n14, 521n43; in **67/10–68/1**, 392, 395, 401–405, 418–435, 437, 439. See also Matsudaira Katamori

Akitsuki Taneki, 165, 261, 334, 338

Alcock, Rutherford, 123, 130, 157, 183, 185, 210

American and Dutch involvement, 27, 87, 182, 194, 207, 317, 324, 345, 403, 515n46. See also Gunrunning; Harris, Townsend; Perry, M. C.; Portman, A. L. C.; Van Polsbroek; Van Valkenburgh

Andō Nobuyuki, xxi, xxii, 4–5, 8, 11–12, 39, 41, 281, 366, 446

Anenokōji Kintomo, 37

Anglo-French rivalry: before the Summer War, 208–214, 215; during the Summer War, 251–254; during **1867**, 316, 318–320, 366, 367, 404. See also Bakufu ties to France; Gunrunning; Hyōgo; Parkes, Harry; Roches, Léon; Satsuma

Ansei purge. See Ii Naosuke

Ansei reform. See Abe Masahiro

Arima Michisumi, 88, 92, 102–103

Asano Ujisuke: in Bunkyū reform, 10–11, 18–19, 41, 446–447; in **1863–1864**, 72, 77, 82, 181, 185; in **1866–1868**, 279, 282, 338, 357, 384–385, 436, 453

Bakufu administration: problems, 141–143, 176–180; leadership patterns, 473–475. See also Bakufu finances; Bakufu political postures; Liege vassals; *Sankin kōtai*

Bakufu collapse: interpreted, xiii–xv, xviii–xxiv, 326–330, 372, 375–376, 379–380, 476–481; after Fushimi-Toba, 436–443; a chronological assessment, 445–457; a factor analysis, 457–476. See also Bakufu political postures; *Bakuhan* system

Bakufu finances: in Bunkyū reform, 21–23, 30, 50–51; in **1863–1866**, 72, 106–107, 121–122, 129, 154–155, 162, 189–201, 505n42, after the Summer War, 293–295; in Keiō reform, 351–354, 365–371; in bakufu collapse, 466–468. See also *Goyōkin*

Bakufu military reform: Bunkyū, 23–31; in **1864–1865**, 180–186; in Summer War, 254–256, 258–259, 515n48, 517n63; in late **1866**, 282–286, 520n26,29; Keiō, 342–354, 434, 528n37, 529n57

Bakufu missions abroad: of **1862**, 366; Ikeda mission, 87–88, 128, 209, 214; Shibata mission, 211–212, 214; of **1867**, 279–280, 366–367

Bakufu political postures: ''Edo'' ex-